# Why Do You Need This New Edition?

If you're wondering why you should buy this new edition of *Public Speaking: An Audience-Centered Approach*, here are eight good reasons!

1. We've kept the best and improved the rest. The eighth edition of *Public Speaking: An Audience-Centered Approach* continues its unique focus on the importance of analyzing and **considering the audience** at every point in the speech-making process, but is now an easier-to-use and more effective learning tool than ever.
2. We've streamlined the book to **16 chapters**, so that every chapter can be covered during a standard semester. Chapter 1 now combines an introduction to public speaking with an overview of the audience-centered model. Chapter 6 now combines information on gathering supporting material with advice on how to integrate supporting material into a speech.
3. **New end-of-chapter *Study Guides*** are designed to help you retain and apply chapter concepts. Study Guides feature chapter summaries; "Using What You've Learned" questions posing realistic scenarios; "A Question of Ethics" to reinforce the importance of ethical speaking; and referrals to selected online resources that help you find resources to use in your own speeches.
4. **More tables and *Recap* boxes** summarize the content of nearly every major section in each chapter. These frequent reviews help you check understanding, study for exams, and rehearse material to aid retention.
5. The eighth edition continues our popular focus on controlling speaking anxiety, developed through **expanded and updated coverage of communication apprehension** in Chapter 1 and reinforced with tips and reminders in "Confidently Connecting with Your Audience" features in the margins of every chapter.
6. **New and expanded coverage of key communication theories and current research**, including studies of anxiety styles in Chapter 1, introductions to social judgment theory in Chapter 14, and emotional response theory in Chapter 15, help you apply recent theories and findings.
7. Every chapter of the eighth edition boasts engaging **fresh examples** to help you connect concepts to your own life and interests, including new references to contemporary technology such as social media sites in Chapter 4 and iPads in Chapter 12.
8. **New speeches**, including Barack Obama's inaugural speech, contribute to an impressive sample speech appendix that will inspire and instruct you as you work with your own material.

# Public Speaking

EDITION 8

# Public Speaking

## AN AUDIENCE-CENTERED APPROACH

**Steven A. Beebe**
Texas State University—San Marcos

**Susan J. Beebe**
Texas State University—San Marcos

**Allyn & Bacon**
Boston Columbus Indianapolis New York San Francisco Upper Saddle River
Amsterdam Cape Town Dubai London Madrid Milan Munich Paris Montreal Toronto
Delhi Mexico City São Paulo Sydney Hong Kong Seoul Singapore Taipei Tokyo

Editor-in-Chief, Communication: Karon Bowers
Development Editor: Sheralee Connors
Editorial Assistant: Megan Sweeney
Marketing Manager: Blair Tuckman
Media Producer: Megan Higginbotham
Project Manager: Anne Ricigliano
Project Coordination, Text Design, and Electronic Page Makeup: Nesbitt Graphics, Inc.
Cover Design Manager: Anne Nieglos
Cover Designer: Joseph DePinho
Cover Art: William Low
Manufacturing Buyer: Mary Ann Gloriande
Printer and Binder: Quad Graphics/Dubuque
Cover Printer: Lehigh-Phoenix Color/Hagerstown

**Library of Congress Cataloging-in-Publication Data**
Beebe, Steven A.
Public speaking : an audience-centered approach / Steven A. Beebe, Susan J. Beebe. — 8th ed.
p. cm.
Includes bibliographical references and index.
ISBN 978-0-205-78462-2 (alk. paper)
1. Public speaking. 2. Oral communication. I. Beebe, Susan J. II. Title.
PN4129.15.B43 2012
808.5'1—dc22
2010054152



1 2 3 4 5 6 7 8 9 10—QGD—14 13 12 11

**Allyn & Bacon is an imprint of**

www.pearsonhighered.com

ISBN-13: 978-0-205-78462-2
ISBN-10: 0-205-78462-3

Dedicated to our parents,
Russell and Muriel Beebe
and Herb and Jane Dye

And to our children,
Mark, Matthew, and Brittany Beebe

# Brief Contents

# Contents

# Developing Your Speech 111

# Gathering and Using Supporting Material 133

CHAPTER 7

CHAPTER 10

# Using Words Well: Speaker Language and Style 217

CHAPTER 11

# Delivering Your Speech 235

CHAPTER 14

# Preface

The eighth edition of *Public Speaking: An Audience-Centered Approach* is written to be the primary text in a course intended to help students become better public speakers. We are delighted that since the first edition of the book was published two decades ago, educators and students of public speaking have found our book a distinctively useful resource to enhance public-speaking skills. We've worked to make our latest edition a preeminent resource for helping students enhance their speaking skills by adding new features and retaining the most successful elements of previous editions.

## New to the Eighth Edition

We've refined and updated the book you are holding in your hands to create a powerful and contemporary resource for helping speakers connect to their audience. We've added several new features and revised features that both instructors and students have praised.

### Streamlined Organization

In response to suggestions from instructors who use the book, we've consolidated related topics to reduce the book to a total of 16 chapters, allowing instructors to include every chapter during a standard semester. Chapter 1 now offers a preview of the audience-centered speaking model as well as introducing students to the history and value of public speaking and starting the process of building their confidence as public speakers. Chapter 6 now not only shows students how to gather supporting material, but also immediately provides them advice and examples for effective ways to integrate their supporting materials into a speech.

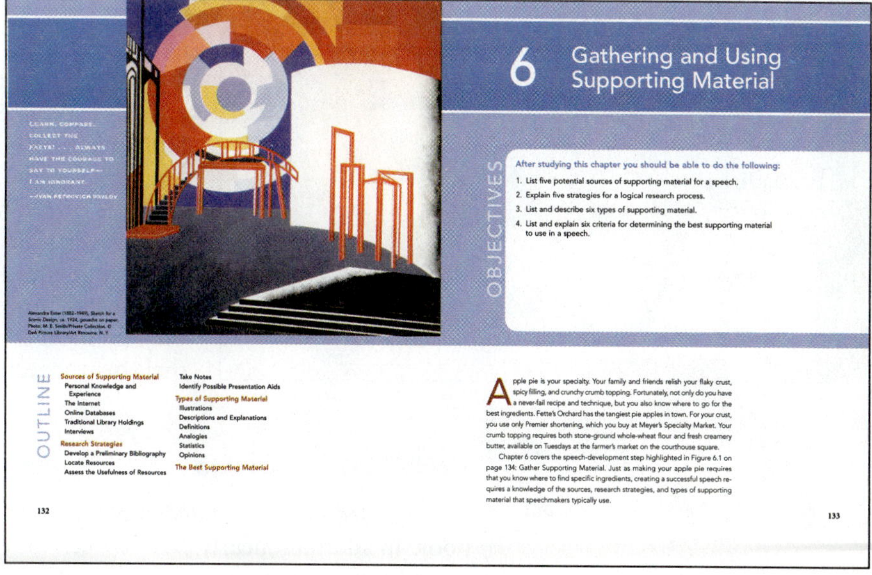

LEARN, COMPARE, COLLECT THE FACTS! . . . ALWAYS HAVE THE COURAGE TO SAY TO YOURSELF—I AM IGNORANT.
—IVAN PETROVICH PAVLOV

Alexandra Exter (1882–1949), Sketch for a Scenic Design, ca. 1924, gouache on paper. Photo: M. E. Smith/Private Collection. © DeA Picture Library/Art Resource, N.Y.

OUTLINE

**Sources of Supporting Material**
- Personal Knowledge and Experience
- The Internet
- Online Databases
- Traditional Library Holdings
- Interviews

**Research Strategies**
- Develop a Preliminary Bibliography
- Locate Resources
- Assess the Usefulness of Resources
- Take Notes
- Identify Possible Presentation Aids

**Types of Supporting Material**
- Illustrations
- Descriptions and Explanations
- Definitions
- Analogies
- Statistics
- Opinions

**The Best Supporting Material**

132

6 Gathering and Using Supporting Material

OBJECTIVES

After studying this chapter you should be able to do the following:

1. List five potential sources of supporting material for a speech.
2. Explain five strategies for a logical research process.
3. List and describe six types of supporting material.
4. List and explain six criteria for determining the best supporting material to use in a speech.

Apple pie is your specialty. Your family and friends relish your flaky crust, spicy filling, and crunchy crumb topping. Fortunately, not only do you have a never-fail recipe and technique, but you also know where to go for the best ingredients. Fette's Orchard has the tangiest pie apples in town. For your crust, you use only Premier shortening, which you buy at Meyer's Specialty Market. Your crumb topping requires both stone-ground whole-wheat flour and fresh creamery butter, available on Tuesdays at the farmer's market on the courthouse square.

Chapter 6 covers the speech-development step highlighted in Figure 6.1 on page 134: Gather Supporting Material. Just as making your apple pie requires that you know where to find specific ingredients, creating a successful speech requires a knowledge of the sources, research strategies, and types of supporting material that speechmakers typically use.

133

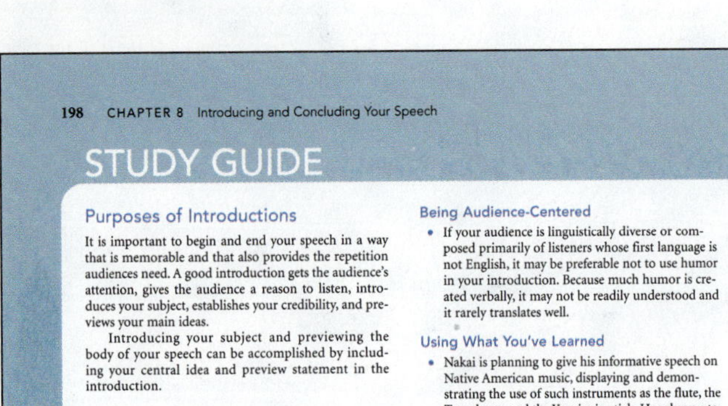

198 CHAPTER 8 Introducing and Concluding Your Speech

STUDY GUIDE

Purposes of Introductions

It is important to begin and end your speech in a way that is memorable and that also provides the repetition audiences need. A good introduction gets the audience's attention, gives the audience a reason to listen, introduces your subject, establishes your credibility, and previews your main ideas.

Introducing your subject and previewing the body of your speech can be accomplished by including your central idea and preview statement in the introduction.

Being Audience-Centered

- Introductions and conclusions provide audiences with important first and final impressions of speaker and speech.
- As a speaker, your task is to ensure that your introduction convinces your audience to listen to you.
- A credible speaker is one whom the audience judges to be a believable authority and a compe-

Being Audience-Centered

- If your audience is linguistically diverse or composed primarily of listeners whose first language is not English, it may be preferable not to use humor in your introduction. Because much humor is created verbally, it may not be readily understood and it rarely translates well.

Using What You've Learned

- Nakai is planning to give his informative speech on Native American music, displaying and demonstrating the use of such instruments as the flute, the Taos drum, and the Yaqui rain stick. He asks you to suggest a good introduction for the speech. How do you think he might best introduce his speech?

A Question of Ethics

- Marty and Shanna, who are in the same section of a public-speaking class, are discussing their upcoming speeches. Marty has discovered an illustration that she thinks will make an effective introduction. When she tells Shanna about it, Shanna is genuinely enthu-

## New End-of-Chapter Study Guides

We've provided a new, consolidated *Study Guide* at the end of each chapter. This practical feature helps students to review and check their understanding of chapter topics. The *Study Guide* summarizes the content of each major section of the chapter; restates the chapter's best ideas for being an audience-centered speaker; poses discussion-sparking scenarios that show how chapter concepts might apply in real speaking and ethical situations; and points readers in the direction of relevant online resources that they can use as speakers.

RECAP

Adapting to Your Audience

To ethically use information to help an audience understand your message, consider your:

- listeners
- speech goal
- speech content
- delivery

Avoid pandering to listeners or making up information.

## Updated Features

In the eighth edition, we have added more marginal *Recap* boxes and tables to summarize the content of nearly every major section in each chapter. Students can use the Recaps and tables to check their understanding, review for exams, and to reference key advice as they prepare their speeches.

TABLE 4.3 Adapting Your Message to Different Types of Audiences

| Type of Audience | Example | How to Be Audience-Centered |
|---|---|---|
| Interested | Mayors who attend a talk by the governor about increasing security and reducing the threat of terrorism | Acknowledge audience interest early in your speech; use the interest they have in you and your topic to gain and maintain their attention. |
| Uninterested | Junior-high students attending a lecture about retirement benefits | Make it a high priority to tell your listeners why your message should be of interest to them. Remind your listeners throughout your speech how your message relates to their lives. |
| Favorable | A religious group that meets to hear a group leader talk about the importance of their beliefs | Use audience interest to move them closer to your speaking goal; you may be more explicit in telling them in your speech conclusion what you would like them to do. |
| Unfavorable | Students who attend a lecture by the university president explaining why tuition and fees will increase 15 percent next year | Be realistic in what you expect to accomplish; acknowledge listeners' opposing point of view; consider using facts to refute misperceptions they may hold. |
| Voluntary | Parents attending a lecture by the new principal at their children's school | Anticipate why listeners are coming to hear you, and speak about the issues they want you to address. |
| Captive | Students in a public-speaking class | Find out who will be in your audience and use this knowledge to adapt your message to them. |

180 CHAPTER 7 Developing Your Speech

SPEECH WORKSHOP

Organizing Your Ideas

Use this worksheet to help you identify the overall organizational strategy for your speech.

GENERAL PURPOSE:

___ To inform

___ To persuade

___ To entertain

SPECIFIC PURPOSE:

At the end of my speech, the audience will be able to __________

We've updated the extended example that appears in *Developing Your Speech Step by Step* boxes throughout the book. We've also updated our popular *Learning from Great Speakers* features, which identify specific tips and lessons students can learn from great speakers, and our practical *Speech Workshop* worksheets, which end each chapter and guide students in implementing chapter advice. These worksheets are designed as aids to help students with what they are most concerned about: developing and delivering their own speeches with confidence.

## New Speeches

We've added new annotated student speeches and speech examples throughout the book. In addition, nearly every speech in our revised Appendix B is new, selected to provide readers with a variety of positive models of effective speeches.

## New Examples and Illustrations

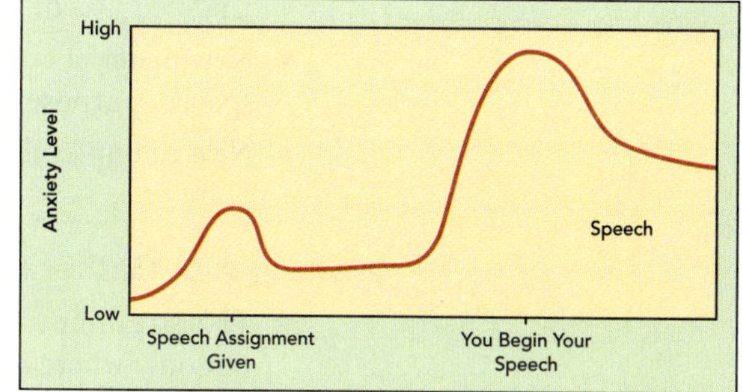


New examples and illustrations integrated in every chapter provide both classic and contemporary models to help students master the art of public speaking. As in previous editions, we draw on both student speeches and speeches delivered by well-known people.

## New Material in Every Chapter

In addition to these new and expanded features, each chapter has been revised with new examples, illustrations, and references to the latest research conclusions. Here's a summary of the changes and revisions we've made:

### Chapter 1: Speaking with Confidence

- The chapter now includes a preview of the audience-centered speaking process to offer a more complete introduction to public speaking.
- New research on biological causes and effects of speech anxiety provides advice for channeling physiological arousal in ways that help the speaker.
- A new discussion of anxiety styles helps readers choose confidence-building tips that are most effective for their style.
- A new figure and a new discussion of the timing of speech anxiety help speakers to time their use of confidence-building strategies for maximum effect.

### Chapter 2: Speaking Freely and Ethically

- A revised and updated discussion of free speech helps students understand the evolution of interpretation of the First Amendment.
- New examples throughout the chapter keep material current and relevant to readers.
- A new section, *Speaking Credibly,* reinforces the importance of ethics and remaining audience-centered and connects concepts across chapters of the book.

### Chapter 3: Listening to Speeches

- A new introduction to working memory theory helps students understand how to cope with information overload that can impede listening.
- A new summary of research on the importance of awareness of one's own listening guides students to assess how well they stay on-task as listeners.
- The chapter is streamlined by removing discussion of note-taking, a skill most students at this level have learned in other contexts.
- A new *Listening Ethically* section helps to reinforce the importance of ethics introduced in the previous chapter.

### Chapter 4: Analyzing Your Audience

- Our discussion of methods for gathering information has been updated to include use of the Internet and social media.
- New definitions of race, ethnicity, and culture help readers to clarify the importance of adapting to the audience's cultural diversity.

### Chapter 5: Developing Your Speech

- A new speech, in the *Developing Your Speech Step by Step* featured in several chapters, provides an extended example of how to implement audience-centered speechmaking concepts.

- Updated lists of potential speech topics can spark students' own topic brainstorms.
- New material helps students to clarify and distinguish among the general purpose, specific purpose, and central idea of their speeches.
- New examples throughout the chapter keep material current and relevant to readers.

### Chapter 6: Gathering and Using Supporting Material

- This streamlined chapter combines two previously separate chapters to show students not only where to find supporting material but also how to most effectively use the material they find.
- A thoroughly updated section on sources of information guides students to use Internet sources, online databases, traditional library holdings and more, without rehashing research basics students have learned in other contexts.
- The revised end-of-chapter *Speech Workshop* offers students structured guidance for planning their use of supporting materials.

### Chapter 7: Organizing Your Speech

- New examples provide clear demonstrations of how to use popular organizational patterns, establish main ideas, integrate supporting material, and signal transitions with signposts.

### Chapter 8: Introducing and Concluding Your Speech

- New examples of effective introductions and conclusions from both student and seasoned speakers show students how to implement the techniques described in the chapter.

### Chapter 9: Outlining and Revising Your Speech

- We've moved our discussion of editing to Chapter 10, where it helps students to focus on the process of rehearsing with a preparation outline as a way to guide them in revising their speeches.
- We've included a new *Sample Preparation Outline* and *Delivery Outline* to give students complete models of the best practices in organization and revision.

### Chapter 10: Using Words Well: Speaker Language and Style

- A discussion of editing your speech, formerly in Chapter 9, helps students to understand how to make their speeches more effective by keeping their words concise.
- New examples throughout the chapter clarify discussions of memorable word structures, including similes, metaphors, inversion, suspension, parallelism, antithesis, and alliteration.

### Chapter 11: Delivering Your Speech

- New information offers guidance in using eye contact effectively.
- A new table summarizes recommendations for working with a translator when speaking to audiences who do not speak English.
- We've streamlined the chapter by removing discussion of adapting speech delivery for television.
- A revised end-of-chapter *Speech Workshop* offers students structured guidance for evaluating how to improve their speech delivery.

### Chapter 12: Using Presentation Aids

- Updated information on two-dimensional presentation aids suggests more effective, economical technological alternatives when using photographs, slides, and overhead transparencies.
- We've added new information on the latest research about using PowerPoint™.
- New discussions of using video aids and audio aids include references to current storage technology, such as iPods and iPads, as well as current content sources, such as YouTube.

### Chapter 13: Speaking to Inform

- A new section shows readers how to appeal to a variety of listener learning styles when speaking to inform.
- Another new section shows the applicability of every step of the audience-centered model of public speaking to informative speeches.

### Chapter 14: Understanding Principles of Persuasive Speaking

- A clarified definition helps students to understand key elements of persuasion.
- New and expanded discussion of ELM persuasion theory and how it compares to Aristotle's classical theory focuses on how persuasive speakers can effectively apply both theories.
- A new discussion and figure on social judgment theory help students to apply theoretical concepts to their own real-life speaking situations.
- An expanded section *How to Develop Your Persuasive Speech* shows students how to apply every step of the audience-centered speaking model to their persuasive speeches.

### Chapter 15: Using Persuasive Strategies

- Our updated discussion of credibility helps students to plan how to establish and support their own credibility at various phases of their speech.
- New examples help to clarify explanations of strategies for organizing persuasive messages, including refutation, cause and effect, and the motivated sequence.
- A new *Sample Persuasive Speech* gives students a complete model of how to use the motivated sequence and other principles of persuasion.

### Chapter 16: Speaking for Special Occasions and Purposes

- New chapter opening examples reinforce the value of public speaking with dollars-and-cents evidence.
- New examples throughout the chapter demonstrate models of speeches for ceremonial occasions including award acceptances, commencement addresses, and eulogies, as well as humorous speaking.

## Successful Features Retained in This Edition

The goal of the eighth edition of *Public Speaking: An Audience-Centered Approach* remains the same as that of the previous seven editions: to be a practical and user-friendly guide to help speakers connect their hearts and minds with those of their listeners. While adding powerful new features and content to help students become skilled public speakers, we have also endeavored to keep what students and instructors liked best. Specifically, we retained five areas of focus that have proven successful in previous editions: our audience-centered approach; our focus on overcoming communication apprehension; our focus on ethics; our focus on diversity; and our focus on skill development. We also continue our partnership with instructors and students by offering a wide array of print and electronic supplements to support teaching and learning.

## Our Audience-Centered Approach

The distinguishing focus of the book is our audience-centered approach. Over 2,300 years ago, Aristotle said, "For of the three elements in speechmaking—speaker, subject, and person addressed—it is the last one, the hearer, that determines the speaker's end and object." We think Aristotle was right. A good speech centers on the needs, values, and hopes of the audience, who should be foremost in the speaker's mind during every step of the speech development and delivery process. Thus, in a very real sense, the audience writes the speech. Effective and ethical public speaking does not simply tell listeners only what they want to hear—that would be a manipulative, speaker-centered approach. Rather, the audience-centered speaker is ethically responsive to audience interests without abandoning the speaker's end and object.

It is not unusual or distinctive for a public-speaking book to discuss audience analysis. What *is* unique about our audience-centered approach is that our discussion of audience analysis and adaptation is not confined to a single chapter; rather, we emphasize the importance of considering the audience throughout our entire discussion of the speech preparation and delivery process. From the opening overview of the public-speaking process until the final chapter, we illuminate the positive power of helping students relate to their audience by keeping their listeners foremost in mind.

Preparing and delivering a speech also involves a sequence of steps. Our audience-centered model integrates the step-by-step process of speech preparation and delivery with the ongoing process of considering the audience.

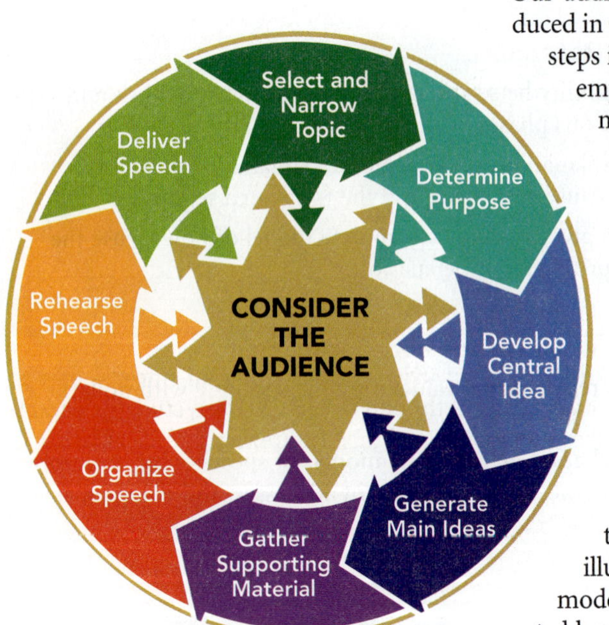


Our audience-centered model of public speaking, shown here and introduced in Chapter 1, reappears throughout the text to remind students of the steps involved in speech preparation and delivery, while simultaneously emphasizing the importance of considering the audience. Viewing the model as a clock, the speaker begins the process at the 12 o'clock position with "Select and Narrow Topic" and moves around the model clockwise to "Deliver Speech." Each step of the speech preparation and delivery process touches the center portion of the model, labeled "Consider the Audience." Arrows connecting the center with each step of the process illustrate how the audience influences each of the steps involved in designing and presenting a speech. Arrows pointing in both directions around the central process of "Consider the Audience" represent how a speaker may sometimes revise a previous step because of further information or thought about the audience. A speaker may, for example, decide after having gathered supporting material for a speech that he or she needs to go back and revise the speech purpose. Visual learners will especially appreciate the illustration of the entire public-speaking process provided by the model. The colorful, easy-to-understand synopsis will also be appreciated by people who learn best by having an overview of the entire process before beginning the first step of speech preparation.

After introducing the model in the very first chapter of the book, we continue to emphasize the centrality of considering the audience by revisiting it at appropriate points throughout the book. A highlighted version of the model appears in several chapters, as a visual reminder of the place the chapter's topic occupies in the audience-centered speechmaking process. Similarly, highlighted versions appear in *Developing Your Speech Step by Step* boxes. Another visual reminder comes in the form of a miniature version of the model, the icon shown here in the margin. *When you see this icon, it will remind you that the material presented has special significance for considering your audience.*

## Our Focus on Communication Apprehension

> **CONFIDENTLY CONNECTING WITH YOUR AUDIENCE**
>
> **Look for Positive Listener Support**
>
> Audience members want you to do well. Many if not most listeners will express their support for your ideas with eye contact, nods of the head, and supportive facial expressions. Make a point to look for these reinforcing nonverbal cues as you deliver your message. (But don't forget to maintain eye contact with all members of the audience.) Let these signs of positive support from your listeners remind you that listeners want you to succeed.

One of the biggest barriers that keeps a speaker, especially a novice public speaker, from connecting to his or her audience is apprehension. Fear of failure, forgetting, or fumbling words is a major distraction. In this edition, we help students to overcome their apprehension of speaking to others by focusing on their listeners rather than on their fear. We've updated and expanded our discussion of communication apprehension in Chapter 1, adding the most contemporary research conclusions we can find to help students overcome the anxiety that many people experience when speaking publicly. To help students integrate confidence-boosting strategies through their study of public speaking, we offer students powerful pointers for managing anxiety in the *Confidently Connecting with Your Audience* features found in the margins of each chapter. To provide yet additional help for managing apprehension, we've distilled several seminal ideas keyed to our audience-centered model on the inside back cover. So, from Chapter 1 until the literal last page in the book, we help students manage their apprehension.

## Our Focus on Ethics

Being audience-centered does not mean that a speaker tells an audience only what they want to hear; if you are not true to your own values, you will have become a manipulative, unethical communicator rather than an audience-centered one. Audience-centered speakers articulate truthful messages that give audience members free choice in responding to a message, while they also use effective means of ensuring message clarity and credibility.

From the first chapter onward, we link being an audience-centered speaker with being an ethical speaker. Our principles and strategies for being rhetorically skilled are anchored in ethical principles that assist speakers in articulating a message that connects with their audience. We not only devote an entire chapter (Chapter 2) to being an ethical speaker, but we also offer reminders, tips, and strategies for making ethical speaking and listening an integral part of human communication. As part of the *Study Guide* at the end of each chapter, students and instructors will find questions to spark discussion about and raise awareness of ethical issues in effective speechmaking.

## Our Focus on Diversity

Just as the topic of audience analysis is covered in most public-speaking textbooks, so is diversity. Sometimes diversity is discussed in a separate chapter; sometimes it is presented in "diversity boxes" sprinkled throughout a book. We choose to address diversity not as an add-on to the main discussion but rather as an integral part of being an audience-centered speaker. To be audience-centered is to acknowledge the various ethnic and cultural backgrounds, attitudes, beliefs, values, and other differences present when people assemble to hear a speech. We suggest that inherent in the process of being audience-centered is a focus on the diverse nature of listeners in contemporary audiences. The topic of adapting to diverse audiences is therefore not a boxed afterthought but is integrated into every step of our audience-centered approach.

## Our Focus on Skill Development

We are grateful for our ongoing collaboration with public-speaking teachers, many of whom have used our audience-centered approach for nearly two decades. We have retained those skill-development features of previous editions that both teachers and students have applauded. What instructors tell us most often is "You write like I teach" or "Your book echoes the same kind of advice and skill development suggestions that I give my students." We are gratified by the continued popularity of *Public Speaking: An Audience-Centered Approach.*

**Clear and Interesting Writing Style** Readers have especially valued our polished prose, concise style, and engaging, lively voice. Students tell us that reading our book is like having a conversation with their instructor.

**Outstanding Examples** Not only do students need to be *told* how to speak effectively, they need to be *shown* how to speak well. Our powerful and interesting examples, both classic and contemporary and drawn from both student speakers and famous orators, continue to resonate with student speakers.

**Built-in Learning Resources** We've retained the following built-in pedagogical features of previous editions:

- Chapter outlines
- Learning objectives
- Crisply written narrative summaries
- End-of-chapter speech workshop worksheets that students can use to apply speaking principles from the chapter to their own speeches.

In the eighth edition, we have added more *Recap* boxes and tables to summarize the content of nearly every major section in each chapter. We've also provided a new, consolidated *Study Guide* at the end of each chapter.

## Our Partnership with Instructors and Students

Public speaking students rarely learn how to be articulate speakers only from reading a book. Students learn best in partnership with an experienced instructor who can guide them through the process of being an audience-centered speaker. And experienced instructors rely on the some support from textbook publishers. To support instructors and students who use *Public Speaking: An Audience-Centered Approach*, Pearson offers various supplements, described in the following pages. For more information about all of our book- and course-specific supplements for public speaking, as well as to view samples, please visit www.mycoursetoolbox.com.

## Resources in Print and Online

| Name of Supplement | Available in Print | Available Online | Instructor or Student Supplement | Description |
|---|---|---|---|---|
| Instructor's Classroom Kits, Volumes I and II (Vol. I ISBN: 0205032524 Vol. II ISBN: 0205032451) | ✓ | ✓ | Instructor Supplement | Pearson's unparalleled Classroom Kit includes every instruction aid a public speaking professor needs to manage the classroom. Organized by chapter, each volume contains materials from the Instructor's Manual and Test Bank, as well as slides from the PowerPoint™ Presentation Package that accompanies this text.<br>The fully updated Instructor's Manual, prepared by Joy Daggs, Columbia College, offers a chapter-by-chapter guide to teaching Public Speaking, including chapter overviews, chapter summaries, learning objectives, lecture outlines, discussion questions, activities, online teaching plans, and handout masters.<br>The Test Bank, prepared by Steve P. Strickler, Southwest Oklahoma State University, contains multiple choice, true/false, completion, short answer, and essay questions. Each question has a correct answer and is referenced by page and difficulty level. Electronic copies of all of the resources are available on Pearson's Instructor's Resource Center at www.pearsonhighered.com/irc (access code required). |
| MyTest (ISBN: 0205828116) | | ✓ | Instructor Supplement | This flexible, online test generating software includes all questions found in the Test Bank section of the Classroom Kits, allowing instructors to create their own personalized exams. Instructors can also edit any of the existing test questions and even add new questions. Other special features of this program include random generation of test questions, creation of alternate versions of the same test, scrambling of question sequence, and test preview before printing. Available at www.pearsonmytest.com (access code required). |
| PowerPoint™ Presentation Package (ISBN: 0205055648) | | ✓ | Instructor Supplement | This text-specific package, prepared by Kim Higgs, University of North Dakota, provides a basis for your lecture with *visually enhanced* PowerPoint™ slides for each chapter of the book. In addition to providing key concepts and select art, these presentations bring the content to life with pedagogically valuable text animations as well as detailed instructor notes. Available at www.pearsonhighered.com/irc (access code required). |
| Pearson's ClassPrep | | ✓ | Instructor Supplement | New from Pearson, ClassPrep makes lecture preparation simpler and less time-consuming. It collects the very best class presentation resources—art and figures from our texts, videos, lecture activities, audio clips, classroom activities, and much more—in one convenient online destination. You may search through ClassPrep's extensive database of tools by content topic (arranged by standard topics within the public speaking curriculum) or by content type (video, audio, activities, etc.). You will find ClassPrep in the Instructor's section of MySpeechLab (access code required). |
| Contemporary Classic Speeches DVD (ISBN: 0205405525) | ✓ | | Instructor Supplement | This exciting supplement includes over 120 minutes of video footage in an easy-to-use DVD format. Each speech is accompanied by a biographical and historical summary that helps students understand the context and motivation behind each speech. Speakers featured include Martin Luther King Jr., John F. Kennedy, Barbara Jordan, the Dalai Lama, and Christopher Reeve. Please contact your Pearson representative for details; some restrictions apply. |
| Pearson's Public Speaking Video Library | ✓ | | Instructor Supplement | This series of videos contains a range of different types of speeches delivered on a multitude of different topics, allowing you to choose the speeches best suited for your students. Please contact your Pearson representative for details and a complete list of videos and their contents to choose which would be most useful in your class. Samples from most of our public speaking videos are available on www.mycoursetoolbox.com. Some restrictions apply. |

| Name of Supplement | Available in Print | Available Online | Instructor or Student Supplement | Description |
|---|---|---|---|---|
| *A Guide for New Public Speaking Teachers*, Fifth Edition (ISBN: 0205828108) | ✓ | ✓ | Instructor Supplement | Prepared by Jennifer L. Fairchild, Eastern Kentucky University, this guide helps new teachers prepare for and teach the introductory public speaking course effectively. It covers such topics as preparing for the term, planning and structuring your course, evaluating speeches, utilizing the textbook, integrating technology into the classroom, and much more (available for download at www.pearsonhighered.com/irc; access code required). |
| *Public Speaking in the Multicultural Environment*, Second Edition (ISBN: 0205265111) | ✓ | | Student Supplement | Prepared by Devorah A. Lieberman, Portland State University, this booklet helps students learn to analyze cultural diversity within their audiences and adapt their presentations accordingly (available for purchase). |
| *The Speech Outline* (ISBN: 032108702X) | ✓ | | Student Supplement | Prepared by Reeze L. Hanson and Sharon Condon of Haskell Indian Nations University, this workbook includes activities, exercises, and answers to help students develop and master the critical skill of outlining (available for purchase). |
| *Multicultural Activities Workbook* (ISBN: 0205546528) | ✓ | | Student Supplement | By Marlene C. Cohen and Susan L. Richardson of Prince George's Community College, this workbook is filled with hands-on activities that help broaden the content of speech classes to reflect the diverse cultural backgrounds. The checklists, surveys, and writing assignments all help students succeed in speech communication by offering experiences that address a variety of learning styles (available for purchase). |
| *Speech Preparation Workbook* (ISBN: 013559569X) | ✓ | | Student Supplement | Prepared by Jennifer Dreyer and Gregory H. Patton of San Diego State University, this workbook takes students through the stages of speech creation–from audience analysis to writing the speech–and includes guidelines, tips, and easy-to-fill-in pages (available for purchase). |
| Study Card for Public Speaking (ISBN: 0205441262) | ✓ | | Student Supplement | Colorful, affordable, and packed with useful information, the Pearson Study Cards make studying easier, more efficient, and more enjoyable. Course information is distilled down to the basics, helping students quickly master the fundamentals, review a subject for understanding, or prepare for an exam. Because they are laminated for durability, they can be kept for years to come and pulled out whenever students need a quick review (available for purchase). |
| Pearson's Public Speaking Study Site | | ✓ | Student Supplement | This open access student Web resource features practice tests, learning objectives, and Web links organized around the major topics typically covered in the Introduction to Public Speaking course. The content of this site has even been correlated to the table of contents for your book (available at www.abpublicspeaking.com). |
| VideoLab CD-ROM (ISBN: 0205561616) | ✓ | | Student Supplement | This interactive study tool for students can be used independently or in class. It provides digital video of student speeches that can be viewed in conjunction with corresponding outlines, manuscripts, note cards, and instructor critiques. Following each speech there are a series of drills to help students analyze content and delivery (available for purchase). |
| MySpeechLab | | ✓ | Instructor & Student Supplement | MySpeechLab is a state-of-the-art, interactive and instructive solution for public speaking courses. Designed to be used as a supplement to a traditional lecture course or to completely administer an online course, MySpeechLab combines a Pearson eText, MySearchLab™, MediaShare, multimedia, video clips, activities, research support, tests and quizzes to completely engage students. MySpeechLab can be packaged with your text and is available for purchase at ww.myspeechlab.com (access code required). See next page for more details. |

# Save time and improve results with PEARSON myspeechlab

Designed to amplify a traditional course in numerous ways or to administer a course online, **MySpeechLab** (www.myspeechlab.com) combines pedagogy and assessment with an array of multimedia activities—videos, speech preparation tools, assessments, research support, multiple newsfeeds—to make learning more effective for all types of students. Now featuring more resources, including a video upload tool (MediaShare), this new release of **MySpeechLab** is visually richer and even more interactive than the previous version—a leap forward in design with more tools and features to enrich learning and aid students in classroom success.

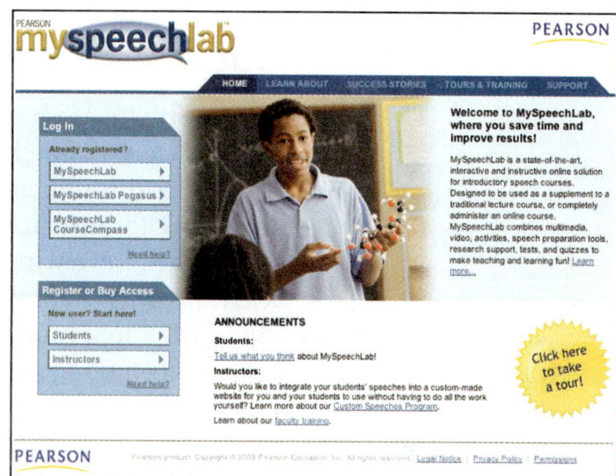


## Teaching and Learning Tools

**NEW VERSION! Pearson eText** Identical in content and design to the printed text, a Pearson eText provides students with access to their text whenever and wherever they need it. In addition to contextually placed multimedia features in every chapter, our new Pearson eText allows students to take notes and highlight, just like a traditional book. The Pearson eText of this book is also available for the iPad.

**Videos and Video Quizzes** Interactive videos provide students with the opportunity to watch and evaluate sample speeches, both student and professional. Select videos are annotated with instructor feedback or include short, assignable quizzes that report to the instructor's gradebook. Professional speeches include classic and contemporary speeches, as well as video segments from communication experts.

**MyOutline** MyOutline offers step-by-step guidance for writing an effective outline, along with tips and explanations to help students better understand the elements of an outline and how all the pieces fit together. Outlines that students create can be downloaded to their computer, emailed as an attachment, or saved in the tool for future editing. Instructors can either select from several templates based on our texts, or they can create their own outline template for students to use.

**Topic Selector** This interactive tool helps students get started generating ideas and then narrowing down topics. Our Topic Selector is question based, rather than drill-down, in order to help students really learn the process of selecting their topic. Once they have determined their topic, students are directed to credible online sources for guidance with the research process.

**Self-Assessments** Online self assessments including the PRCA-24 and the PRPSA provide students with opportunities to assess and confirm their comfort level with speaking publicly. Instructors can use these tools to show learning over the duration of the course via MyPersonalityProfile, Pearson's online self-assessment library and analysis tool. MyPersonalityProfile enables instructors to assign self-assessments, such as the PRPSA, at the beginning and end of the course so students can compare their results and see where they've improved.

**Study Plan** Pre- and Post-tests for each chapter test students on their knowledge of the material in the course. The tests generate a customized study plan for further assessment and focus students on areas in which they need to improve.

**Speech Evaluation Tools** Instructors have access to a host of Speech Evaluation Tools to use in the classroom. An additional assortment of evaluation forms and guides for students and instructors offer further options and ideas for assessing presentations.

**Building Speaking Confidence Center** In this special section of **MySpeechLab**, students will find self-assessments, strategies, video, audio, and activities that provide additional guidance and tips for overcoming their speech apprehension—all in one convenient location.

**ABC News RSS Feed** **MySpeechLab** provides online feeds from ABC news, updated hourly, to help students choose and research their speech topics.

## Cutting Edge Technology

**MediaShare** With this new video upload tool, students are able to upload their speeches for their instructor and classmates to watch (whether face-to-face or online) and provide online feedback and comments at time-stamped intervals, including the option to include an evaluation rubric for instructors and/or students to fill out. Instructors can also opt to include a final grade when reviewing a student's video. Grades can be exported from MediaShare to a SCORM-compliant.csv spreadsheet that can be imported into most learning management systems. Structured much like a social networking site, MediaShare can help promote a sense of community among students.

**AmericanRhetoric.com Partnership** This exclusive partnership with AmericanRhetoric.com, allows students to access great speeches of our time directly from **MySpeechLab** (without linking out to another site and without advertisements or commercials!). Many speeches are also accompanied by assessment questions that ask students to evaluate specific elements of those speeches.

**NEW! Audio Chapter Summaries** Every chapter includes an audio chapter summary for online streaming use, perfect for students reviewing material before a test or instructors reviewing material before class.

## Online Administration

No matter what course management system you use—or if you do not use one at all, but still wish to easily capture your students' grades and track their performance—Pearson has a **MySpeechLab** (www.myspeechlab.com) option to suit your needs. Contact one of Pearson's Technology Specialists for more information and assistance.

A **MySpeechLab** access code is provided at no additional cost when packaged with selected Pearson Communication texts or can be purchased separately. To get started, contact your local Pearson Publisher's Representative at www.pearsonhighered.com/replocator.

# Acknowledgments

Writing a book is a partnership not only with each other as co-authors, but with many people who have offered us the benefit of their experience and advice about how to make this the best possible teaching and learning resource. We appreciate all of the authors and speakers we have quoted or referenced; their words and wisdom have added resonance to our knowledge and richness to our advice. We are grateful for our students, colleagues, adopters, friends, and the skilled editorial team at Allyn & Bacon.

Many talented reviewers have helped us shape the content and features of this edition. These talented public speaking teachers have supplemented our experience to help us make decisions about how to present and organize the content of this book. We express our sincere appreciation to the following reviewers who have shared their advice, wisdom, and expertise:

**Reviewers of the eighth edition:**
John S. France, Owens State Community College; Kristina Galyen, University of Cincinnati; Tina Harris, University of Georgia; Kherstin Khan-Brockbank, Fresno City College; Christine Mixan, University of of Nebraska at Omaha; Barbara Monaghan, Berkeley College; Karen O'Donnell, Finger Lakes Community College; Jamille Watkins-Barnes, Chicago State University; Marcy Wong, Indian River State College.

**Reviewers of previous editions:**
Melanie Anson, Citrus College; Richard Armstrong, Wichita State University; Nancy Arnett, Brevard Community College; David E. Axon, Johnson County Community College; Ernest W. Bartow, Bucks County Community College; John Bee, University of Akron; Jaima L. Bennett, Golden West College; Donald S. Birns, SUNY—Albany; Tim Borchers, Moorhead State University; Barry Brummett, University of Wisconsin, Milwaukee; John Buckley, University of Tennessee; Thomas R. Burkholder, University of Nevada—Las Vegas; Judy H. Carter, Amarillo College; Mark Chase, Slippery Rock University; Marilyn J. Cristiano, Paradise Valley Community College; Dan B. Curtis, Central Missouri State University; Ann L. Darling, University of Illinois, Urbana—Champaign; Conrad E. Davidson, Minot State University; Terrence Doyle, Northern Virginia Community College; Gary W. Eckles, Thomas Nelson Community College; Thomas G. Endres, University of St. Thomas; Richard I. Falvo, El Paso Community College; Darla Germeroth, University of Scranton; Donna Goodwin, Tulsa Community College; Myra G. Gutin, Rider University; Larry Haapanen, Lewis-Clark State College; Dayle C. Hardy-Short, Northern Arizona University; Carla J. Harrell, Old Dominion University; Phyllis Heberling, Tidewater Community College; James L. Heflin, Cameron University; Susan A. Hellweg, San Diego State University; Wayne E. Hensley, Virginia Polytechnic Institute and State University; Patricia S. Hill, University of Akron; Judith S. Hoeffler, Ohio State University; Stephen K. Hunt, Illinois State University; Paul A. Hutchins, Cooke County College; Ann Marie Jablonowski, Owens Community College; Elaine B. Jenks, West Chester University; Nanette Johnson-Curiskis, Gustavus Adolphus College; Cecil V. Kramer, Jr., Liberty University; Michael W. Kramer, University of Missouri; Linda Kurz, University of Missouri, Kansas City; Ed Lamoureux, Bradley University; David Lawless, Tulsa Junior College; Robert S. Littlefield, North Dakota State University; Jeré W. Littlejohn, Mississippi State University; Harold L. Make, Millersville University of Pennsylvania; Jim Mancuso, Mesa Community College; Deborah F. Meltsner, Old Dominion University; Rebecca Mikesell, University of Scranton; Maxine Minson, Tulsa Junior College; Jay R. Moorman, Missouri Southern State University; Marjorie Keeshan Nadler, Miami University; Rhonda Parker, University of San Francisco; Roxanne Parrott, University of Georgia; Richard L. Quianthy, Broward Community College; Carol L. Radetsky, Metropolitan State College; Renton Rathbun, Owens Community College; Mary Helen Richer, University of North Dakota; K. David Roach, Texas Tech University; Kellie W. Roberts, University of Florida; Rebecca Roberts, University of Wyoming; Val Safron, Washington University; Kristi Schaller, University of Hawaii at Manoa; Cara Schollenberger, Bucks County Community College; Shane Simon, Central Texas College; Cheri

J. Simonds, Illinois State University; Glenn D. Smith, University of Central Arkansas; David R. Sprague, Liberty University; Jessica Stowell, Tulsa Junior College; Edward J. Streb, Rowan College; Aileen Sundstrom, Henry Ford Community College; Susan L. Sutton, Cloud County Community College; Tasha Van Horn, Citrus College; Jim Vickrey, Troy State University; Denise Vrchota, Iowa State University; Beth M. Waggenspack, Virginia Polytechnic Institute and State University; David E. Walker, Middle Tennessee State University; Lynn Wells, Saddleback College; Nancy R. Wernm, Glenville State College; Charles N. Wise, El Paso Community College; Argentina R. Wortham, Northeast Lakeview College; Merle Ziegler, Liberty University;

Kosta Tovstiadi is a good friend and trusted researcher who assisted with research for this edition. We are grateful that Karon Bowers, editor-in-chief Communication, continued to be a strong source of support and encouragement to us as we worked on this edition, as she was on previous editions. Sheralee Connors, our development editor, has done an exceptional job of offering skilled advice and creative suggestions to make this a better book. She helped lighten our workload with her many helpful comments and suggestions.

We have enjoyed strong support and mentorship from a number of teachers, friends, and colleagues who have influenced our work over the years. Our colleagues at Texas State University–San Marcos continue to be supportive of our efforts. Tom Willett, retired professor from William Jewell College; Dan Curtis, emeritus professor at the University of Central Missouri; John Masterson, emeritus professor at Texas Lutheran University; and Thompson Biggers, professor at Mercer University are longtime friends and exemplary teachers who continue to influence our work and our lives. Sue Hall, Department of Communication Studies senior administrative assistant at Texas State, again provided exceptional support and assistance to keep our work on schedule. Meredith Clayton, also an administrative assistant at Texas State, helped us in innumerable ways.

We view our work as authors of a textbook as primarily a teaching process. Both of us have been blessed with gifted teachers whose dedication and mentorship continues to inspire and encourage us. Mary Harper, former speech, English, and drama teacher at Steve's high school alma mater, Grain Valley High School, Grain Valley, Missouri; and Sue's speech teacher, the late Margaret Dent, who taught at Hannibal High School, Hannibal, Missouri, provided initial instruction in public speaking that remains with us today. We also value the life lessons and friendship we receive from Erma Doty, another former teacher at Grain Valley High, who continues to offer us encouragement and support not only with what she says but by how she lives her life in service for others. We appreciate the patience and encouragement we received from Robert Brewer, our first debate coach at the University of Central Missouri, where we met each other more than forty years ago and where the ideas for this book were first discussed. We both served as student teachers under the unforgettable, energetic guidance of the late Louis Banker at Fort Osage High School, near Buckner, Missouri. Likewise, we have both benefited from the skilled instruction of Mary Jeanette Smythe, now retired from the University of Missouri--Columbia. We wish to express our appreciation to Loren Reid, emeritus professor from the University of Missouri—Columbia; to us, he remains the quintessential speech teacher.

Finally, we value the patience, encouragement, proud support, and love of our sons and daughter-in-law, Mark, Matthew, and Brittany Beebe. They offer many inspiring lessons in overcoming life challenges and infusing life with music. They continue to be our most important audience.

Steven A. Beebe
Susan J. Beebe

# Public Speaking

There are two kinds of speakers: those that are nervous and those that are liars.

—Mark Twain

Arthur Segal (1875–1944), *The Speaker,* 1912. Collection of Henri Nannen, Emden, Germany. Photo: Erich Lessing/Art Resource, N.Y.

# OUTLINE

# 1 Speaking with Confidence

OBJECTIVES

**After studying this chapter you should be able to do the following:**

1. Explain why it is important to study public speaking.
2. Sketch and explain a model that illustrates the components and the process of communication.
3. Discuss in brief the history of public speaking.
4. Describe why speakers sometimes feel nervous about speaking in public.
5. Use several techniques to become a more confident speaker.
6. Explain why it is important to be audience-centered during each step of the speechmaking process.
7. Identify and describe the key steps of designing and presenting a speech.

Perhaps you think you have heard this speaker—or even taken a class from him: His eyes were buried in his script. His words in monotone emerged haltingly from behind his mustache, losing volume as they were sifted through hair. Audiences rushed to see and hear him, and after they had satisfied their eyes, they closed their ears. Ultimately, they turned to small talk among themselves while the great man droned on.[1]

The speaker described here in such an unflattering way is none other than Albert Einstein. Sadly, although the great physicist could attract an audience with his reputation, he could not sustain their attention and interest because he lacked public-speaking skills.

As you begin reading this book, chances are that you are also beginning a course in public speaking. You're in good company; nearly a half million college students each year take a public speaking class.[2] If you haven't had much previous experience speaking in public, you're also in good company. In a recent study, 66 percent of students beginning a public-speaking course reported having had little or no public-speaking experience.[3]

The good news is that this book and this course will provide you with the knowledge and experience needed to become what Einstein was not: a competent public speaker. Right now, however, gaining that experience may seem less like an opportunity and more like a daunting task. Why undertake it?

# Why Study Public Speaking?

**Public speaking** is the process of presenting a message to an audience, small or large. You hear speeches almost every day. When watching a newscast on TV or via the Internet, you get a "sound bite" of some politician delivering a speech. Each day when you attend class, an instructor lectures. When you hear a comedian delivering a monologue on a late-night talk show or the Comedy Channel, you're hearing a speech designed to entertain you. But although you've heard countless speeches during your lifetime, you may still have questions about why it's important for *you* to study public speaking. Here are two reasons: By studying public speaking you will gain long-term advantages related to *empowerment* and *employment*.

## Empowerment

You will undoubtedly be called on to speak in public at various times in your life: as a student participating in a seminar class; as a businessperson convincing your boss to let you undertake a new project; as a concerned citizen addressing the city council's zoning board. In each of these situations, the ability to speak with competence and confidence will provide **empowerment**. To be empowered is to have the resources, information, and attitudes that allow you to take action to achieve a desired goal. Being a skilled public speaker will give you an edge that other, less skilled communicators lack—even those who may have superior ideas, training, or experience. It will position you for greater things. Former presidential speechwriter James Humes, who labels public speaking "the language of leadership," says, "Every time you have to speak—whether it's in an auditorium, in a company conference room, or even at your own desk—you are auditioning for leadership."[4]

You feel truly empowered when you speak with confidence, knowing that your ideas are expressed with conviction and assurance. Yet if you're typical, you may experience fear and anxiety about speaking in public. As you start your journey of becoming an effective public speaker, you may have questions about how to bolster your confidence and manage your apprehension. Before you finish this chapter, you'll have read about more than a dozen strategies to help you feel both more empowered and more confident. Being both a confident and an empowered public speaker is within your grasp. And being an empowered speaker can open up leadership and career opportunities for you.

## Employment

It was industrialist Charles M. Schwab who said, "I'll pay more for a person's ability to speak and express himself than for any other quality he might possess."[5] If you can speak well, you possess a skill that others will value highly. Whether you're currently employed as an entry-level employee or aspire to the highest rung of the corporate leadership ladder, being able to communicate effectively with others is key to success

**public speaking**
The process of presenting a message to an audience

**empowerment**
Having resources, information, and attitudes that lead to action to achieve a desired goal

TABLE 1.1 Top Skills Valued by Employers

| Rank | Results of Survey of Personnel Directors[6] | Results of Survey of a College Career Services Department[7] | Results of Survey of Prospective Employers[8] | Survey Results from Several Research Studies[9] |
|---|---|---|---|---|
| 1 | Spoken communication skills | Communication and interpersonal skills | Communication skills | Communication skills |
| 2 | Written communication skills | Intelligence | Honesty and integrity | Analytical/research skills |
| 3 | Listening ability | Enthusiasm | Teamwork | Technical skills |
| 4 | Enthusiasm | Flexibility | Interpersonal skills | Flexibility/adaptability |
| 5 | Technical competence | Leadership | Motivation/initiative | Interpersonal skills |

in any line of work. The skills you learn in a public-speaking course, such as how to ethically adapt information to listeners, organize your ideas, persuade others, and hold listeners' attention, are among the skills most sought after by any employer. In a nationwide survey, prospective employers of college graduates said they seek candidates with "public-speaking and presentation ability."[10] Other surveys of personnel managers, both in the United States and internationally, have confirmed that they consider communication skills the top factor in helping graduating college students obtain employment (see Table 1.1).[11]

RECAP

Why Study Public Speaking

- Empowerment and confidence
- Career and leadership opportunities

## The Communication Process

Even the earliest communication theorists recognized that communication is a process. The models they formulated were linear, suggesting a simple transfer of meaning from a sender to a receiver, as shown in Figure 1.1. More recently, theorists have created models that better demonstrate the complexity of the communication process. Let's explore what some of those models can teach us about what happens when we communicate.

### Communication as Action

Although they were simplistic, the earliest linear models of communication as action identified most of the elements of the communication process. We will explain each element as it relates to public speaking.

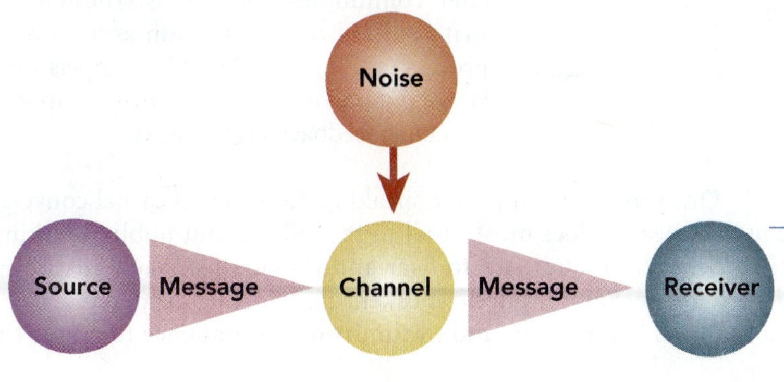


FIGURE 1.1 *The earliest models viewed communication as the action of transferring meaning from source to receiver.*

**source**
The public speaker

**encode**
To translate ideas and images into verbal or nonverbal symbols

**code**
A verbal or nonverbal symbol for an idea or image

**message**
The content of a speech and the mode of its delivery

**decode**
To translate verbal or nonverbal symbols into ideas and images

**channel**
The visual and auditory means by which a message is transmitted from sender to receiver

**receiver**
A listener or an audience member

**external noise**
Physical sounds that interfere with communication

**Source** A public speaker is a **source** of information and ideas for an audience. The job of the source or speaker is to **encode**, or translate, the ideas and images in his or her mind into verbal or nonverbal symbols (a **code**) that an audience can recognize. The speaker may encode into words (for example, "The fabric should be 2 inches square") or into gestures (showing the size with his or her hands).

**Message** The **message** in public speaking is the speech itself—both what is said and how it is said. If a speaker has trouble finding words to convey his or her ideas or sends contradictory nonverbal symbols, listeners may not be able to **decode** the speaker's verbal and nonverbal symbols back into a message.

**Channels** A message is usually transmitted from sender to receiver via two **channels:** *visual* and *auditory*. Audience members see the speaker and decode his or her nonverbal symbols—eye contact (or lack of it), facial expressions, posture, gestures, and dress. If the speaker uses any visual aids, such as graphs or models, these too are transmitted along the visual channel. The auditory channel opens as the speaker speaks. Then the audience members hear words and such vocal cues as inflection, rate, and voice quality.

**Receiver** The **receiver** of the message is the individual audience member, whose decoding of the message will depend on his or her own particular blend of past experiences, attitudes, beliefs, and values. As already emphasized, an effective public speaker should be receiver- or audience-centered.

**Noise** Anything that interferes with the communication of a message is called *noise*. Noise may be physical and **external**. If your 8 A.M. public-speaking class is frequently interrupted by the roar of a lawn mower running back and forth under the window, it may be difficult to concentrate on what your instructor is saying. A noisy air conditioner, a crying baby, or incessant coughing may make it difficult for audience members to hear or concentrate on a speech.

Noise may also be **internal**. It may stem from either *physiological* or *psychological* causes and may directly affect either the source or the receiver. A bad cold (physiological noise) may cloud a speaker's memory or subdue his or her delivery. An audience member worrying about an upcoming exam (psychological noise) is unlikely to remember much of what the speaker says. Regardless of whether it is internal or external, physiological or psychological, or whether it originates in the sender or the receiver, noise interferes with the transmission of a message.

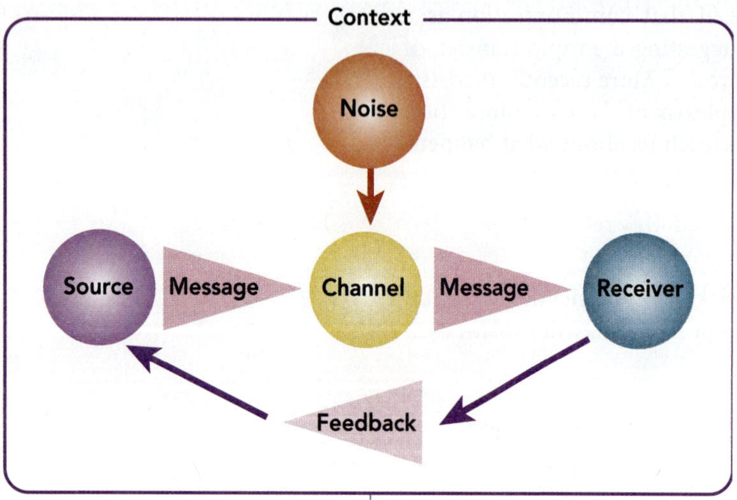

Context
Noise
Source
Message
Channel
Message
Receiver
Feedback

FIGURE 1.2 *Interactive models of communication add the element of feedback to the earlier action models. They also take into consideration the communication context.*

## Communication as Interaction

Realizing that linear models were overly simplistic, later communication theorists designed models that depicted communication as a more complex process (see Figure 1.2). These models were circular, or interactive, and added two important new elements: feedback and context.

**Feedback** One way in which public speaking differs from casual conversation is that the public speaker does most or all of the talking. But public speaking is still interactive. Without an audience to hear and provide **feedback**, public speaking serves little purpose. Skillful public speakers are audience-centered. They depend on the nods, facial expressions, and murmurs of the audience to adjust their rate of speaking, volume, vocabulary, type and amount of supporting material, and other variables to communicate their message successfully.

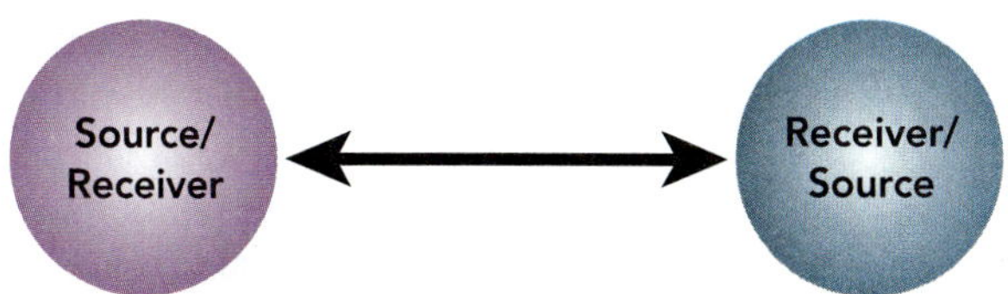


FIGURE 1.3 *A transactive model of communication focuses on the simultaneous exchanges that happen between source and receiver.*

**Context** The **context** of a public-speaking experience is the environment or situation in which the speech occurs. It includes such elements as the time, the place, and the speaker's and audience's cultural traditions and expectations. To rephrase John Donne, no *speech* is an island. No speech occurs in a vacuum. Rather, each speech is a blend of circumstances that can never be replicated exactly.

The person whose job it is to deliver an identical message to a number of different audiences at different times and in different places can attest to the uniqueness of each speaking context. If the room is hot, crowded, or poorly lit, these conditions affect both speaker and audience. The audience that hears a speaker at 10 A.M. is likely to be fresher and more receptive than a 4:30 P.M. audience. A speaker who fought rush-hour traffic for 90 minutes to arrive at his or her destination may find it difficult to muster much enthusiasm for delivering the speech.

Many of the skills that you will learn from this book relate not only to the preparation of effective speeches (messages), but also to the elements of feedback and context in the communication process. Our audience-centered approach focuses on "reading" your listeners' responses and adjusting to them as you speak.

## Communication as Transaction

The most recent communication models do not label individual components. Transactive models focus instead on communication as a simultaneous process. As the model in Figure 1.3 suggests, we send and receive messages concurrently. In a two-person communication transaction, both individuals are sending and receiving at the same time. When you are listening, you are simultaneously expressing your thoughts and feelings nonverbally.

An effective public speaker should not only be focused on the message he or she is expressing, but should also be tuned in to how the audience is responding to the message. A good public speaker shouldn't wait until the speech is over to gauge the effectiveness of a speech but rather, because of the transactive nature of communication, should be scanning the audience during the speech for nonverbal clues to assess the audience's reaction.

Although communication models have been developed only recently, the elements of these models have long been recognized as the keys to successful public speaking. As you study public speaking, you will continue a tradition that goes back to the very beginnings of Western civilization.

RECAP

### The Communication Process

Audience and speaker send messages simultaneously. Elements of the process include:

- Source
- Message
- Channel
- Receiver
- Feedback
- Context

# The Rich Heritage of Public Speaking

Long before many people could read, they listened to public speakers. **Rhetoric** is another term for the use of words and symbols to achieve a goal. Although rhetoric is often defined as the art of speaking or writing aimed at persuading others (changing or reinforcing attitudes, beliefs, values, or behavior), whether you're informing, persuading, or even entertaining listeners, you are using rhetoric because you are trying to achieve a goal.

**internal noise**
Physiological or psychological interference with communication

**feedback**
Verbal and nonverbal responses provided by an audience to a speaker

**context**
The environment or situation in which a speech occurs

**rhetoric**
The use of words and symbols to achieve a goal

The fourth century B.C.E was a golden age for rhetoric in the Greek Republic, where the philosopher Aristotle formulated guidelines for speakers that we still follow today. As politicians and poets attracted large followings in ancient Rome, Cicero and Quintilian sought to define the qualities of the "true" orator. On a lighter note, it is said that Roman orators invented the necktie. Fearing laryngitis, they wore "chin cloths" to protect their throats.[12]

In medieval Europe, the clergy were the most polished public speakers. People gathered eagerly to hear Martin Luther expound his Articles of Faith. In the eighteenth century, British subjects in the colonies listened to the town criers and impassioned patriots of what was to become the United States.

Vast nineteenth-century audiences heard speakers such as Henry Clay and Daniel Webster debate states' rights; they listened to Frederick Douglass, Angelina Grimke, and Sojourner Truth argue for the abolition of slavery, and to Lucretia Mott plead for women's suffrage; they gathered for an evening's entertainment to hear Mark Twain as he traveled the lecture circuits of the frontier.

Students of nineteenth-century public speaking spent very little time developing their own speeches. Instead, they practiced the art of **declamation**—the delivery of an already famous address. Favorite subjects for declamation included speeches by such Americans as Patrick Henry and William Jennings Bryan, and by the British orator Edmund Burke. Collections of speeches, such as Bryan's own ten-volume set of *The World's Famous Orations*, published in 1906, were extremely popular.

Hand in hand with declamation went the study and practice of **elocution**, the expression of emotion through posture, movement, gesture, facial expression, and voice. From the mid-nineteenth to the early twentieth century, elocution manuals—providing elaborate and specific prescriptions for effective delivery—were standard references not only in schools, but also in nearly every middle-class home in the United States.[13]

**declamation**
The delivery of an already famous speech

**elocution**
The expression of emotion through posture, movement, gesture, facial expression, and voice

In the first half of the twentieth century, radio made it possible for people around the world to hear Franklin Delano Roosevelt decry December 7, 1941, as "a date which will live in infamy." In the last half of the century, television provided the medium through which audiences saw and heard the most stirring speeches:

## LEARNING FROM GREAT SPEAKERS

### Martin Luther King Jr. (1920–1968)

Civil rights leader and human rights activist Dr. Martin Luther King Jr. delivered one of the great speeches of history as the keynote of the August 1963 civil rights march on Washington, D.C. Addressing an audience of some 200,000 people from the steps of the Lincoln Memorial, King used Biblical language, African American oral traditions, stirring examples, and the simple repetition of the line "I have a dream" to move both his audience and the United States Congress to action. Two months after King's speech, Congress passed a new civil rights bill.[14]

Dr. King was a master extemporaneous speaker. He planned his messages well in advance of his presentation, yet he was also skilled in observing and responding to his listeners during his speech. He used his clear objectives and well-prepared outline to create a powerful message, keenly focusing on the reactions of his audience to his prepared remarks. As you deliver your speeches, being aware of your listeners' responses to your message, especially their nonverbal responses, will help you decide what to emphasize or what to delete from your talk. You'll also find that by focusing more on connecting with your listeners than on any fear of speaking you may have, you'll give a better presentation.

[Photo: AP Wide World Photos]

- Martin Luther King Jr. proclaiming, "I have a dream"
- Ronald Reagan beseeching Mikhail Gorbachev to "tear down this wall"
- Holocaust survivor Elie Wiesel looking beyond the end of one millennium toward the next with "profound fear and extraordinary hope"
- Eleven-year-old Paris Jackson delivering her brief but heartfelt eulogy for her father, Michael, tearfully saying, "I just want to say, ever since I was born, Daddy has been the best father you could ever imagine. I just want to say I love him so much."

With the twenty-first century dawned a new era of speechmaking. It was to be an era that would draw on age-old public-speaking traditions—an era in which U.S. soldiers serving in Iraq and Afghanistan would watch their children's commencement addresses live via streaming video. And it was to be an era that would summon public speakers to meet some of the most difficult challenges in history—an era in which a U.S. president would face a nation badly shocked by the events of September 11, 2001, and assure them that "terrorist attacks can shake the foundations of our biggest buildings, but they cannot touch the foundation of America. These acts shattered steel, but they cannot dent the steel of American resolve."[15] Speakers of the future will continue to draw on a long and rich heritage, in addition to forging new frontiers in public speaking.

RECAP

### The Rich Heritage of Public Speaking

| Period | Event |
|---|---|
| Fourth century B.C.E. | Greek rhetoric flourishes—Age of Aristotle. |
| Fifteenth century | European clergy are the primary practitioners of public speaking. |
| Eighteenth century | American patriots make impassioned public pleas for independence. |
| Nineteenth century | Abolitionists and suffragists speak out for change; frontier lecture circuits flourish. |
| Twentieth century | Electronic media make possible vast audiences. |
| Twenty-first century | A new era of speechmaking uses rapidly evolving technology and media while drawing on a rich heritage. |

## Improving Your Confidence as a Speaker

Actor and celebrated emcee George Jessel once wryly observed, "The human brain starts working the moment you are born and never stops . . . until you stand up to speak in public." Perhaps public speaking is a required class for you, but, because of the anxiety you feel when you deliver a speech, you've put it off for as long as possible.

The first bit of comfort we offer is this: *It's normal* to *be nervous.* In a survey seeking to identify people's phobias, public speaking ranked as the most anxiety-producing experience most people face. Forty-one percent of all respondents reported public speaking as their most significant fear: fear of death ranked only sixth![16] Based on these statistics, comedian Jerry Seinfeld suggests, "Given a choice, at a funeral most of us would rather be the one in the coffin than the one giving the eulogy." Other studies have found that more than 80 percent of the population feel anxious when they speak to an audience.[17] Some people find that public speaking is quite frightening: studies suggest that about 20 percent of all college students are highly apprehensive about speaking in front of others.[18]

You may find comfort in knowing you are not alone in experiencing speech anxiety. Even if your anxiety is not overwhelming, you can benefit from learning some positive approaches that allow your nervousness to work *for you.*[19] First, we will help

*Physical symptoms of nervousness are signs that your body is trying to help you meet the challenge of public speaking. Labeling your body's arousal as excitement can help build your confidence as you speak, as can the other tips described in this chapter.*

[Photo: Cultura Limited/SuperStock Royalty Free]

you understand why you become nervous. Then we will offer specific strategies to help you speak with greater comfort and less anxiety.

## Understand Your Nervousness

What makes you feel nervous about speaking in public? Why do your hands sometimes shake, your knees quiver, your stomach flutter, and your voice seem to go up an octave? What is happening to you?[20]

Researchers have found that public-speaking anxiety is both a *trait* (a characteristic or general tendency that you may have) and a *state* (anxiety triggered by the specific incidence of giving a speech to an audience).[21] A study by two communication researchers found that among the causes of public-speaking anxiety were fear of humiliation, concern about not being prepared, worry about one's looks, pressure to perform, personal insecurity, concern that the audience wouldn't he interested in oneself or the speech, lack of experience, fear of making mistakes, and an overall fear of failure.[22] Another study found that men are likely to experience more anxiety than women when speaking to people from a culture different from their own.[23] As you read the list of possible speaking-anxiety causes, you'll probably find a reason that resonates with you because most people feel some nervousness when they speak before others. You're not alone if you are apprehensive about giving a speech.[24] Understanding why you and many others may experience apprehension can give you insights in how to better address your anxiety.[25]

**Your Biology Affects Your Psychology** Increasingly, researchers are concluding that communication apprehension may have a genetic or biological basis: Some people may inherit a tendency to feel anxious about speaking in public.[26] You may wonder, "So if I have a biological tendency to feel nervous, is there anything I can do to help manage my fear?" The answer is *yes*. Even if you are predisposed to feel nervous because of your genetic makeup, there are strategies you can use to help manage your apprehension.[27] A better understanding of why you feel apprehensive is a good starting point on the journey to speaking with greater confidence.[28]

Although you may have not asked your brain for help, believe it or not, your brain becomes aware of your stress when you are speaking, and it signals your body to help you with this difficult task. Sometimes, however, because your brain offers more "help" than you need, this assistance is not useful. Your biology is affecting your psychology—what you think and feel about giving a speech.

What factors trigger a specific biological brain response? Your view of the speaking assignment, your perception of your speaking skill, and your self-esteem interact to create anxiety.[29] You want to do well, but you're not sure that you can or will. Presented with this conflict, your body responds by increasing your breathing rate, pumping more adrenaline, and causing more blood to rush through your veins.[30] In short, your body summons more energy to deal with the conflict you are facing. Your brain switches to its default fight-or-flight mode: You can either fight to respond to the challenge or flee to avoid the cause of the anxiety. To put it more technically, you are experiencing physiological changes because of your psychological state, which explains why you may have a more rapid heartbeat, shaking knees and hands, a quivering voice, and increased perspiration.[31] You may also experience butterflies in your stomach because of changes in your digestive system. As a result of your physical discomfort, you may make less eye contact with your audience, use more vocalized pauses ("Um," "Ah," "You know"), and speak too rapidly. Although you see your physical responses as hindrances, your body is simply trying to help you with the task at hand.

**Your Apprehension Follows a Predictable Pattern** When are you most likely to feel nervous about giving a speech in your communication class? Research suggests there are typical times when people feel nervous. As shown in Figure 1.4, many people feel most nervous right before they give their speech. That's when the uncertainty of what will happen next is very high.[32] If you're typical, you'll feel the second-highest level of anxiety when your instructor explains the speech assignment. You'll probably feel the *least* anxiety when you're preparing your speech.

One practical application of this research is that now you can understand when you'll need the most help managing your anxiety—right before you speak. It will also help to remember that as you begin speaking, anxiety begins to decrease—often dramatically. Another application of the research is to help you realize that you'll feel less anxious about your speech when you're doing something positive to prepare for it. Don't put off working on your speech; if you start preparing well in advance, you'll not only have a better speech, you'll also feel less anxious about presenting it.

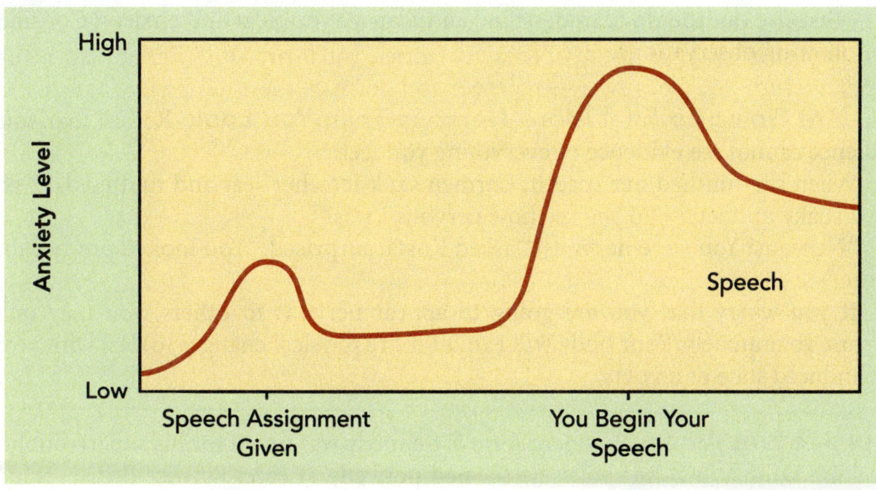


FIGURE 1.4 *Research reveals a pattern of nervousness common to many public speakers, who feel the most nervous right before their speech begins, with anxiety tapering off as the speech continues. Students may also feel a smaller peak of worry at the time their instructor assigns them to give a speech.*

To identify patterns in how people experience communication apprehension, one researcher measured speakers' heart rates when they were delivering speeches and asked them several questions about their fear of speaking.[33] After studying the results, he identified four styles of communication apprehension.

- **Average.** You have an *average style* of communication apprehension if you have a generally positive approach to communicating in public; your overall heart rate when speaking publicly is in the average range. Speakers with this style rated their own speaking performance the highest compared to those with other styles.
- **Insensitive.** The *insensitive style* is likely to be your style only if you have had previous experience in public speaking. Perhaps because of your experience, you tend to be less sensitive to apprehension when you speak; you have a lower heart rate when speaking and rate your performance as moderately successful.
- **Inflexible.** If you have the *inflexible style,* you have the highest heart rate when speaking publicly. Some people use this high and inflexible level of anxiety to enhance their performance: Their fear motivates them to prepare and be at their best. For others, the anxiety of the inflexible style creates so much tension that their speaking performance is diminished.
- **Confrontational.** You have a *confrontational style* if, like many people, you have a very high heart rate as you begin presenting a speech, and then your heart rate tapers off to more average levels. This style occurred in people who reported a strong emotional, or affective, response to speaking and was characteristic of more experienced speakers, or people with at least some public-speaking background.

What difference does it make what style of communication apprehension you have? First, it may help to know that you are not alone in how you experience apprehension and that others likely share your feelings. Although each person is unique, there are nonetheless general styles of apprehension. Second, having a general idea of your own style may give you greater insight into how to better manage your apprehension. For example, if you know that your apprehension tends to spike upward at the very beginning of speaking to an audience (the confrontational style), you will need to draw on strategies to help manage your anxiety at the outset of your talk. Finally, the research on apprehension styles lends support to the theory that communication apprehension may be a genetic trait or tendency.[34] That doesn't mean that there's nothing you can do to manage your anxiety; but it does mean that, depending on your own tendencies, you may need more information to help *you* develop constructive ways of managing the apprehension you may feel.

What else can you do to understand and manage your fear and anxiety? Consider the following observations.

**You Are Going to Feel More Nervous Than You Look** Realize that your audience cannot see evidence of everything you feel.

When she finished her speech, Carmen sank into her seat and muttered, "Ugh, was I shaky up there! Did *you* see how nervous I was?"

"Nervous? You were nervous?" asked Kosta, surprised. "You looked pretty calm to me."

If you worry that you are going to appear nervous to others, you may only *increase* your anxiety. Your body will exhibit more physical changes to deal with your self-induced state of anxiety.

**Your Are Not Alone** President John F. Kennedy was noted for his superb public-speaking skills. When he spoke, he seemed perfectly at ease. Former British prime minister Winston Churchill was also hailed as one of the twentieth century's great orators. Amazingly, both Kennedy and Churchill were extremely fearful of speaking in public. The list of famous people who admit to feeling nervous before they speak may surprise you: Katie Couric, Conan O'Brien, Jay Leno, Carly Simon, and Oprah Winfrey have all reported feeling anxious and jittery before speaking in public.[35] Almost everyone experiences some anxiety when speaking. It is unrealistic to try to eliminate speech anxiety. Instead, your goal should be to manage your nervousness so that it does not create so much internal noise that it keeps you from speaking effectively.

**You Can Use Your Anxiety** Extra adrenaline, increased blood flow, pupil dilation, increased endorphins to block pain, increased heart rate, and other physical changes caused by anxiety improve your energy level and help you function better than you might otherwise. Your heightened state of readiness can actually help you speak better, especially if you view the public-speaking event positively instead of negatively. Speakers who label their increased feelings of physiological arousal as "nervousness" are more likely to feel anxious and fearful, but the same physiological feelings could also be labeled as "enthusiasm" or "excitement." You are more likely to gain the benefits of the extra help your brain is trying to give you if you think positively rather than negatively about speaking in public. Don't let your initial anxiety convince you that you cannot speak effectively.

RECAP

**Understand Your Nervousness**

Keep in mind:

- Nervousness is your brain trying to help you.
- Nervousness is predictable.
- You'll feel more nervous than you look.
- You are not alone.
- It's normal to be nervous.
- You can relabel and use your feelings to your advantage.

## How to Build Your Confidence

"Is there anything I can do to help manage my nervousness and anxiety when I give a speech?" you may wonder. Both contemporary research and centuries of experience from seasoned public speakers suggest some practical advice.[36] We summarize their suggestions in Table 1.2 on page 14.

**Know Your Audience** Know to whom you will be speaking, and learn as much about your audience as you can. The more you can anticipate the kind of reaction your listeners will have to your speech, the more comfortable you will be in delivering your message.[37] As you are preparing your speech, periodically visualize your listeners' response to your message. Consider their needs, goals, and hopes as you prepare your message. Be audience-centered rather than speaker-centered. Don't keep telling yourself how nervous you are going to be.[38] An audience-centered speaker focuses on connecting to listeners rather than focusing on fear. Chapter 4 provides a detailed approach to analyzing and adapting to your audience.

**Don't Procrastinate** One research study confirmed what you probably already know: Speakers who are more apprehensive about speaking put off working on their speeches, in contrast to speakers who are less anxious about public speaking.[39] The lack of thorough preparation often results in a poorer speech performance, reinforcing the speaker's perception that public speaking is difficult. Realize that if you fear that you'll be nervous when speaking, you'll tend to put off working on your speech. Take charge by tackling the speech assignment early, giving yourself every chance to be successful. Don't let your fear freeze you into inaction. Prepare early.

**Select an Appropriate Topic** You will feel less nervous if you talk about something you are familiar with or have some personal experience of. Your comfort with the subject of your speech will be reflected in your delivery.

Judy Shepard, whose son Matthew Shepard was brutally murdered in 1998 for being gay, is a frequent conference speaker and ardent proponent of gay rights. Always apprehensive about giving a speech during her college years, she said "Speech class was my worst nightmare."[40] But today, because of her fervent belief in her cause,

TABLE 1.2 Tips for Building Confidence

**What to Do Before You Speak**

- Don't procrastinate; give yourself plenty of time to work on your speech.
- Learn as much as possible about your audience.
- Select a topic you are interested in or know something about.
- Be prepared and well-organized.
- Be familiar with how you will begin and end your speech.
- Rehearse aloud while standing, and try to re-create the speech environment.
- Use breathing techniques to help you relax.
- Channel nervous energy.
- Visualize being successful.
- Give yourself a mental pep talk.

**What to Do as You Speak**

- Focus on connecting your message to your audience rather than on your fear.
- Look for and respond to positive listener support for you and your message.

**What to Do After You Speak**

- Focus on your accomplishments and success rather than only reviewing what you may have done wrong.
- Seek other speaking opportunities to gain experience and confidence.

she gives hundreds of speeches. "This is my survival; this is how I deal with losing Matt," she explained to students at South Lakes High School in Reston, Virginia.[41] Talking about something you are passionate about can boost your motivation and help you manage your fear. In the chapters ahead, we offer more detailed guidance about how to select a topic.

**Prepare** One formula applies to most speaking situations you are likely to experience: The better prepared you are, the less anxiety you will experience. Being prepared means that you have researched your topic and practiced your speech several times before you deliver it. One research study found clear evidence that rehearsing your speech reduces your apprehension.[42] Being prepared also means that you have developed a logically coherent outline rather than one that is disorganized and difficult to follow. Transitional phrases and summaries can help you present a well-structured, easy-to-understand message.

**Be Organized** One of the key skills you'll learn in *Public Speaking: An Audience-Centered Approach* is the value of developing a well-organized message. For most North American listeners, speeches should have a beginning, middle, and end and should follow a logical outline pattern. Communication researcher Melanie Booth-Butterfield suggests that speakers can better manage their apprehension if they rely on the rules and structures of a speaking assignment, including following a clear outline pattern, when preparing and delivering a speech.[43] Anxiety about a speech assignment decreased and confidence increased when speakers closely followed the directions and rules for developing a speech. So, to help manage your apprehension about speaking, listen carefully to what the specific assignment is, ask for additional information if you're unclear about the task, and develop a well-organized message.

**Know Your Introduction and Your Conclusion** You are likely to feel the most anxious during the opening moments of your speech. Therefore, it is a good idea to have a clear plan for how you will start your speech. We aren't suggesting memorizing your introduction word for word, but you should have it well in mind. Being familiar with your introduction will help you feel more comfortable about the entire speech.

If you know how you will end your speech, you will have a safe harbor in case you lose your place. If you need to end your speech prematurely, a well-delivered conclusion can permit you to make a graceful exit.

**Make Practice Real** When you practice your speech, pretend that you are giving the speech to the audience you will actually address. Stand up. Imagine what the room looks like, or consider rehearsing in the room in which you will deliver your speech. What will you be wearing? Practice rising from your seat, walking to the front of the room, and beginning your speech. Practice aloud, rather than just saying the speech to yourself. A realistic rehearsal will increase your confidence when your moment to speak arrives.

**Breathe** One symptom of nervousness is a change in your breathing and heart rates. Nervous speakers tend to take short, shallow breaths. To help break the anxiety-induced breathing pattern, consider taking a few slow, deep breaths before you rise to speak. No one will detect that you are taking deep breaths if you just slowly inhale and exhale before beginning your speech. Besides breathing deeply, try to relax your entire body. Deep breathing and visualizing yourself as successful will help you relax.

**Channel Your Nervous Energy** One common symptom of being nervous is shaky hands and wobbly knees. As we noted earlier, what triggers this jiggling is the extra boost of adrenaline your body is giving you—and the resulting energy that has to go somewhere. Your muscles may move whether you intend them to or not. Take control by channeling that energy. One way to release tension is to take a leisurely walk before you arrive wherever you will be speaking. Taking a slow, relaxing walk can help calm you down and use up some of your excess energy. Once you are seated and waiting to speak, grab the edge of your chair (without calling attention to what you arc doing) and gently squeeze the chair to release tension. No one needs to know you're doing this—just unobtrusively squeeze and relax, squeeze and relax. You can also purposely tense and then release your muscles in your legs and arms while you're seated. You don't need to look like you're going into convulsions; just imperceptibly tense and relax your muscles to burn energy. One more tip: You may want to keep both feet on the floor and gently wiggle your toes rather than sit with your legs crossed. Crossing your legs can sometimes cause one leg or foot to go to sleep. Keeping your feet on the floor and slightly moving your toes can ensure that all of you will be wide awake and ready to go when it's your turn to speak.

As you wait to be introduced, focus on remaining calm. Act calm to feel calm. Give yourself a pep talk; tense and release your muscles to help you relax. Then, when your name is called, walk to the front of the room in a calm and collected manner. Before you present your opening, attention-catching sentence, take a moment to look for a friendly, supportive face. Think calm and act calm to feel calm.

**Visualize Your Success** Studies suggest that one of the best ways to control anxiety is to imagine a scene in which you exhibit skill and comfort as a public speaker.[44] As you imagine giving your speech, picture yourself walking confidently to the front and delivering your well-prepared opening remarks. Visualize yourself giving the entire speech as a controlled, confident speaker. Imagine yourself calm and in command. Positive visualization is effective because it boosts your confidence by helping you see yourself as a more confident, accomplished speaker.[45]

Research has found that it's even helpful to look at a picture of someone confidently and calmly delivering a speech while visualizing yourself giving the speech;

such positive visualization helps manage your apprehension.[46] You could even make a simple drawing of someone speaking confidently.[47] As you look at the image, imagine that it's you confidently giving the speech. It's helpful if the visual image you're looking at is a person you can identify with—someone who looks like you or someone you believe is more like you than not.[48]

**Give Yourself a Mental Pep Talk** You may think that people who talk to themselves are slightly loony. But silently giving yourself a pep talk can give you confidence and take your mind off your nervousness. There is some evidence that simply believing that a technique can reduce your apprehension may, in fact, help reduce your apprehension.[49] Giving yourself a positive message such as "I can do this" may be a productive way to manage your anxiety. Here's a sample mental speech you could deliver to yourself right before you speak: "I know this stuff better than anyone else. I've practiced it. My message is well organized. I know I can do it. I'll do a good job." Research provides evidence that people who entertain thoughts of worry and failure don't do themselves any favors.[50] When you feel yourself getting nervous, use positive messages to replace negative thoughts that may creep into your consciousness. Examples include the following:

| Negative Thought | Positive Self-Talk |
|---|---|
| I'm going to forget what I'm supposed to say. | I've practiced this speech many times. I've got notes to prompt me. If I lose my place, no one will know I'm not following my outline. |
| So many people are looking at me. | I can do this! My listeners want me to do a good job. I'll seek out friendly faces when I feel nervous. |
| People think I'm dull and boring. | I've got some good examples. I can talk to people one-on-one, and people seem to like me. |
| I just can't go through with this. | I have talked to people all my life. I've given presentations in classes for years. I can get through this because I've rehearsed and I'm prepared. |

**Focus on Your Message, Not on Your Fear** The more you think about being anxious about speaking, the more you will increase your level of anxiety. Instead, think about what you are going to say. In the few minutes before you address your listeners, mentally review your major ideas, your introduction, and your conclusion. Focus on your ideas rather than on your fear.

**Look for Positive Support** Evidence suggests that if you think you see audience members looking critical of you or your message, you may feel more apprehensive and nervous when you speak.[51] Stated more positively, when you are aware of positive audience support, you will feel more confident and less nervous. To reiterate our previous advice: It is important to be audience-centered. Although you may face some audience members who won't respond positively to you or your message, the overwhelming majority of listeners will be positive. Looking for positive, reinforcing feedback and finding it can help you feel more confident as a speaker. One study found that speakers experienced less apprehension if they had a support group or a small "learning community" that provided positive feedback and reinforcement.[52] This research finding has implications for you as a speaker and listener. When you have a speaking assignment, work with others to provide support both as you prepare and when you present your speech. When you're listening to speakers in your communication class, help them by being a positive, supportive listener: Provide eye contact and offer additional positive nonverbal support, such as nodding in agreement and maintaining a positive but sincere facial expression. You can help your fellow students feel more comfortable as speakers, and they can do the same for you; watch for their support. One study found that non-native speakers may feel anxious and nervous because English is not their native language; so providing positive supportive feedback is especially important when you know a speaker is quite nervous.[53]

**Seek Speaking Opportunities** The more experience you gain as a public speaker, the less nervous you will feel.[54] As you develop a track record of successfully delivering speeches, you will have more confidence.[55] This course in public speaking will give you opportunities to enhance both your confidence and your skill through frequent practice. Researchers have found that those speakers who were the most nervous at the beginning of a public-speaking class experienced the greatest decreases in nervousness by the end of the class.[56] Another research study found that students who took a basic public-speaking course reported having less apprehension and more satisfaction about speaking than students who had not had such a course.[57] To add to the practice you will get in this class, consider joining organizations and clubs such as Toastmasters, an organization dedicated to improving public-speaking skills by providing a supportive group of people to help you polish your speaking and overcome your anxiety.

**Focus on What You Have Accomplished, Not on Your Fear** When you conclude your speech, you may be tempted to fixate on your fear. You might amplify in your own mind the nervousness you felt and think everyone could see how nervous you looked. Resist that temptation. When you finish your speech, tell yourself something positive to celebrate your accomplishment. Say to yourself, "I did it! I spoke and people listened." Don't replay your mental image of yourself as nervous and fearful. Instead, mentally replay your success in communicating with your listeners.

Because managing communication apprehension is such an important skill for most public speakers, in each chapter of this book we'll remind you of tips to help you enhance your confidence. Look for techniques of *confidently connecting with your audience* in the margin.

### CONFIDENTLY CONNECTING WITH YOUR AUDIENCE

#### Begin with the End in Mind

One of the habits cited by Stephen Covey in his well-known book *The 7 Habits of Highly Successful People* is "Begin with the end in mind."[58] From the moment you begin thinking about preparing and presenting your speech, picture yourself being confident and successful. If you find your anxiety level rising at any point in the speech-preparation process, change your mental picture of yourself and imagine that you've completed your speech and the audience has given you a rousing round of applause. Begin imagining success rather than focusing on your fear. Using the principles, skills, and strategies we discuss in this book will help you develop the habit of speech success.

### RECAP

#### Build Confidence

- Label your physical arousal as *excitement*.
- Understand and plan for your anxiety style.
- Focus on your audience and message.
- Don't wait; prepare early.
- Follow guidelines for speech assignments carefully.
- Make practice as real as possible.
- Breathe and exercise to channel nervous energy.
- Visualize success and use mental pep talks.
- Look for support from listeners.
- Form a "support community" of classmates.
- Congratulate yourself after you speak.

# An Overview of Audience-Centered Public Speaking

Although you've been speaking to others since you were two years old, the process of preparing and presenting a speech may seem daunting and even frightening. But a better understanding of the entire process of how to design and deliver a speech can help you manage your apprehension. The skill of public speaking builds upon your normal, everyday interactions with others. But there are three key differences between conversation and public speaking:

- *Public speaking is more prepared than conversation.* Although there may be times when you are asked to speak on the spur of the moment, you will usually know in advance whether you will be expected to give a talk on a specific occasion. A public speaker may spend hours or even days planning and practicing his or her speech.
- *Public speaking is more formal than conversation.* The slang or casual language we often use in conversation is usually not appropriate for most public speaking. Audiences expect speakers to use standard English grammar and vocabulary. The nonverbal communication of public speakers is also more formal than the nonverbal behavior of ordinary conversation.
- *Public speaking involves more clearly defined roles for speaker and audience than conversation.* During a conversation, there is typically interaction between speaker and listener. But in public speaking, the roles of speaker and audience are more clearly defined and remain stable. Although in some cultures a call-and-response speaker-audience interaction occurs (such as saying "That's right" or "Amen" when responding to a preacher's sermon), audience members rarely interrupt or talk back to speakers *during* most speeches. And if there is an interruption, it's unusual and noteworthy, as when President Obama's speech to Congress on September 9, 2009, was interrupted by Florida Congressman Joe Wilson's shouting "You lie!" in response to something the President said.

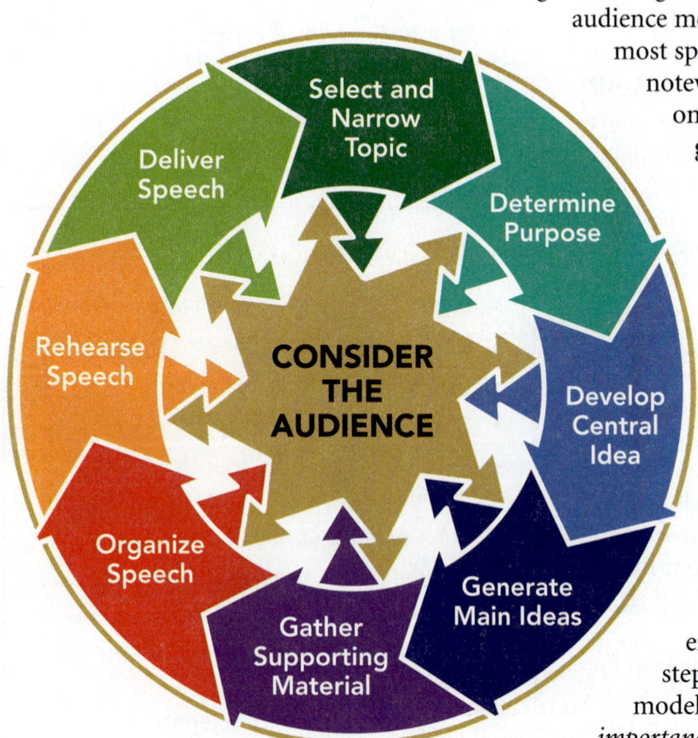


FIGURE 1.5 *The reminder to consider the audience is at the center of this model of the speechmaking process because your audience influences your work on each task involved in designing and presenting a speech. As we discuss each task in depth throughout the book, we also use a smaller image of this model to flag information and advice that remind you to consider your audience.*

As you think about preparing your first speech for your speech class, you may wonder, "What do I do first?" Your assignment may be to introduce yourself to the class. Or your assignment may be a brief informative talk—to describe something to your audience. Regardless of the specific assignment, however, you need some idea of how to begin. Instead of reading this book cover-to-cover before your first speech, you can consider this chapter's overview of the steps and skills involved in giving a speech.

To help you visualize this overview, Figure 1.5 diagrams the tasks involved in the speechmaking process, emphasizing the audience as the central concern at every step of the process. We'll refer to this audience-centered model of public speaking throughout the text. *To emphasize the importance of being audience-centered, we have placed a smaller version of this model in the margins throughout the text to draw your attention to information that discusses the importance of always being mindful of your audience.* (See the icon in the margin.) When you see the icon, it means we're discussing the central theme of this book: Always make choices in designing and delivering your speech with your audience in mind.

Audience analysis is not something you do only at the beginning of preparing your speech. It is an ongoing activity. The needs, attitudes, beliefs, values, and other characteristics of your audience influence the choices you make about your speech at every step of the speech-preparation process. That's why, in the audience-centered speech model, arrows connect the center of the diagram with each stage of designing and delivering your speech. At any point during the preparation and delivery of your message, you may need to revise your thinking or your material if you learn new information about your audience. So the model has arrows pointing both ways across the boundary between the central element and each step in the process. (Chapter 4 includes a comprehensive discussion of the principles and strategies involved in analyzing your audience.)

Our discussion of the speechmaking process begins with the central element: considering your audience. We then discuss each step of the process, starting with selecting and narrowing a topic, and moving clockwise around the model.

# Consider Your Audience

Why should the central focus of public speaking be the audience? Why is it not topic selection, outlining, or research? The simple truth is that your audience influences the topic you choose and every later step of the speechmaking process. Your selection of topic, purpose, and even major ideas should be based on a thorough understanding of your listeners. In a very real sense, your audience "writes" the speech.[59]

## Gather and Analyze Information about Your Audience

Being audience-centered means keeping your audience in mind at every step of the speechmaking process. To do that, you need to first identify and then analyze information about your listeners. For example, just by looking at your audience in your speech class, you will be able to determine such basic information as approximately how old they are and the percentage of men and women in your audience; you also know that they are all students in a public-speaking class. To determine other, less obvious information, you may need to ask them questions or design a short questionnaire.

Being audience-centered involves making decisions about the content and delivery of your speech *before* you speak, based on what you know about your audience's values, beliefs, and knowledge. It also means being aware of your audience's responses *during* the speech so that you can make appropriate adjustments.

## Consider the Culturally Diverse Backgrounds of Your Audience

You need not give speeches in foreign countries to recognize the importance of adapting to different cultural expectations of individual audience members. People in the United States are highly diverse in terms of their culture, age, ethnicity, and religious tradition. Consider the various cultural backgrounds of your classmates. How many different cultural and ethnic traditions do they represent? Several years ago, the typical college student was likely to be a recent high-school graduate between the ages of 18 and 21. Today your classmates probably reflect a much wider range of ages, backgrounds, and experiences. You will want to adjust not only your delivery style but also your topic, pattern of organization, and the examples you use, according to who your audience members are and what subject or subjects they are interested in.

Different cultures have radically different expectations about public speaking. In Russia, for example, speakers have a "no frills" approach that emphasizes content over delivery. A presentation that seems perfectly sensible and acceptable to a U.S. businessperson who is accustomed to straightforward, problem-oriented logic may seem shockingly rude to a Chinese businessperson who expects more circuitous, less overtly purposeful rhetoric. And some African American audiences "come to participate in a speech event,"[60] expecting the speaker to generate audience response through rhythmic "call response formulas"[61] from the African American oral tradition. When one of this book's authors taught public speaking for several semesters in the Bahamas, he shocked students by suggesting that they should achieve a conversational, informal delivery style. Many Bahamian audiences, he quickly discovered, expect formal oratory from their speakers, very much as U.S. audiences in the nineteenth century preferred the grandiloquence of Stephen A. Douglas to the quieter, homespun style of Abraham Lincoln. So your author had to embellish his own style when he taught the Bahamian class.

Being sensitive to your audience and adapting your message accordingly will serve you well not only when addressing listeners with different cultural backgrounds from your own, but in all types of situations. If you learn to analyze your audience and adapt to their expectations, you can apply these skills in numerous settings: at a job interview, during a business presentation or a city council election campaign—even while proposing marriage.

# Select and Narrow Your Topic

While keeping your audience foremost in mind, your next task is to determine what you will talk about and to limit your topic to fit the constraints of your speaking assignment. Pay special attention to the guidelines your instructor gives you for your assignment.

If your first speech assignment is to introduce yourself to the class, your **speech topic** has been selected for you—*you* are the topic. It is not uncommon to be asked to speak on a specific subject. Often, though, you will be asked to speak but not given a topic. The task of selecting and narrowing a topic will be yours. Choosing or finding a topic on which to speak can be frustrating. "What should I talk about?" can become a haunting question.

It's a good idea to give yourself plenty of time to select and narrow your topic. Don't wait until the last minute to ponder what you might talk about. One of the most important things you can do to be an effective speaker is to start preparing your speech well in advance of your speaking date. One research study identified some very practical advice: The amount of time you spend preparing for your speech is one of the best predictors of a good grade on your speech.[62]

Although there is no single answer to the question of what you should talk about, you may discover a topic by asking three standard questions:

1. *Who is the audience?* Your topic may grow from a basic knowledge of your audience. For example, if you know that your audience members are primarily between the ages of 25 and 40, this information should help you select a topic of interest to people who are probably working and either seeking partners or raising families.
2. *What are my interests, talents, and experiences?* Rather than racking your brain for exotic topics and outlandish ideas, examine your own background. Your choice of major in college, your job, your hobbies, and your ancestry are sources for topic ideas. What issues do you feel strongly about? Chapter 5 contains a discussion of specific tips for finding topics.
3. *What is the occasion?* Besides your audience, you should consider the occasion for the speech when choosing a topic. A speech to your speech class probably calls for a different topic, for example, than a speech to a religious group, a model railroad club, or a city council meeting. You'll also want to consider the physical setting of your speech. In Chapter 4 we'll amplify our discussion of how the occasion and the physical setting for your speech affects your topic selection.

**speech topic**
The key focus of the content of a speech

# Determine Your Purpose

You might think that once you have your topic, you are ready to start the research process. Before you do that, however, you need to decide on both a general and a specific purpose.

## Determine Your General Purpose

Your **general purpose** is the overarching goal of your speech. There are three types of general purposes for speeches: *to inform*, *to persuade*, and *to entertain*.

**Speaking to Inform** When you inform, you teach, define, illustrate, clarify, or elaborate on a topic. The primary objective of class lectures, seminars, and workshops is to inform. Chapter 15 will show you how to construct an effective speech with an informative purpose.

**Speaking to Persuade** A speech to persuade seeks to change or reinforce listeners' attitudes, beliefs, values, or behavior. Ads on TV, radio, and the Internet; sermons; political speeches; and sales presentations are examples of messages designed to persuade. To be a skilled persuader, you need to be sensitive to your audience's attitudes toward you and your topic. Chapters 14 and 15 will discuss principles and strategies for preparing persuasive speeches.

**Speaking to Entertain** To entertain listeners is the third general purpose of a speech. After-dinner speeches and comic monologues are mainly intended as entertainment. Often the key to an effective entertaining speech lies in your choice of stories, examples, and illustrations, as well as in your delivery. Appendix B includes examples of speeches designed to inform, persuade, and entertain.

## Determine Your Specific Purpose

Your **specific purpose** is a concise statement indicating what you want your listeners to be able to do, remember, or feel when your finish your speech. A specific purpose statement identifies the precise audience response you desire. Table 1.3 compares general and specific purposes.

Deciding on a specific purpose is not difficult once you have narrowed your topic: "At the end of my speech, the class will be able to identify three counseling facilities on campus and describe the best way to get help at each one." Notice that this purpose is phrased in terms of what you would like the audience to be able to *do* by

**general purpose**
The overarching goal of a speech—to inform, persuade, or entertain

**specific purpose**
A concise statement of the desired audience response, indicating what you want your listeners to remember, feel, or do when you finish speaking

TABLE 1.3 General and Specific Purposes

| General Purpose | Specific Purpose |
|---|---|
| To inform | At the end of my speech, the audience will be able to identify three counseling facilities on campus and describe the best way to get help at each one. |
| To persuade | At the end of my speech, the audience will visit the counseling facilities on campus. |
| To entertain | At the end of my speech, the audience will be amused by the series of misunderstandings I created when I began making inquiries about career advisors on campus. |

the end of the speech. Your specific purpose should be a fine-tuned, audience-centered goal. For an informative speech, you may simply want your audience to restate an idea, define new words, or identify, describe, or illustrate something. In a persuasive speech, you may try to rouse your listeners to take a class, buy something, or vote for someone.

Once you have formulated your specific purpose, write it down on a piece of paper or note card and keep it before you as you read and gather ideas for your talk. Your specific purpose should guide your research and help you choose supporting materials that are related to your audience. As you continue to work on your speech, you may even decide to modify your purpose. But if you have an objective in mind at all times as you move through the preparation stage, you will stay on track.

## Develop Your Central Idea

You should now be able to write the **central idea** of your speech. Whereas your statement of a specific purpose indicates what you want your audience to do when you have finished your speech, your central idea identifies the essence of your message. Think of it as a one-sentence summary of your speech. Here's an example:

| | |
|---|---|
| TOPIC: | The South Beach diet |
| GENERAL PURPOSE: | To inform |
| SPECIFIC PURPOSE: | At the end of my speech, the audience will be able to identify the three key elements in the South Beach diet. |
| CENTRAL IDEA: | The South Beach diet is based on reducing the amount of carbohydrates you eat, drinking more water, and increasing the amount of exercise you get. |

Here's another way to think about how to develop your central idea sentence. Imagine that you have just finished presenting your speech and you get into an elevator. Someone who missed hearing your talk says, "Oh, I'm sorry I missed your speech. What did you say?" Between the second floor and the first, you have only 15 seconds to summarize your message. You might say, "I said there are two keys to parent and child communication: First, make time for communication, and second, listen effectively." That brief recap is your central idea sentence. To clarify the difference between your purpose and the central idea sentence: Your purpose sentence is what you want the audience to be able to *do*; the central idea sentence is your speech in a nutshell—your speech in one sentence.

## Generate the Main Ideas

In the words of columnist H. V. Prochnow, "A good many people can make a speech, but saying something is more difficult." Effective speakers are good thinkers; they say something. They know how to play with words and thoughts to develop their **main ideas.** The ancient Romans called this skill **invention**—the ability to develop or discover ideas that result in new insights or new approaches to old problems. The Roman orator Cicero called this aspect of speaking the process of "finding out what [a speaker] should say."

Once you have an appropriate topic, a specific purpose, and a well-worded central idea down on paper, the next task is to identify the major divisions of your speech, or the key points that you wish to develop. To determine how to subdivide your central idea into key points, ask these three questions:

**central idea**
A one-sentence summary of the speech content

**main ideas**
The key points of a speech

**invention**
The development or discovery of ideas and insights

1. *Does the central idea have logical divisions?* If, for example, the central idea is "There are three ways to interpret the stock-market page of your local newspaper," your speech can be organized into three parts. A speech about the art of applying theatrical makeup could also be organized into three parts: eye makeup, face makeup, and hair coloring. Looking for logical divisions in your speech topic may be the simplest way to determine key points.
2. *Can you think of several reasons why the central idea is true?* If you're trying to prove a point and you have three reasons to show that your point is true, you could organize your speech around those three reasons. If you have reasons that explain that your central idea is true, you are probably presenting a persuasive speech. If your central idea is "Medicare should be expanded to include additional coverage for individuals of all ages," each point of your speech could be a reason why you think Medicare should be expanded.
3. *Can you support the central idea with a series of steps?* Speeches describing a personal experience or explaining how to build or make something can usually be organized in a step-by-step progression. Suppose your central ideas is "Running for a campus office is easy to do." Your speech could be developed around a series of steps, telling your listeners what to do first, second, and third to get elected. Your time limit, topic, and the information gleaned from your research will determine how many major ideas will be in your speech. A three-to-five minute speech might have only two major ideas. In Chapters 5 and 8 we provide more details about how to generate major ideas and organize them.

# Gather Supporting Material

With your main idea or ideas in mind, your next job is to gather material to support them—facts, examples, definitions, and quotations from others that illustrate, amplify, clarify, and provide evidence. Here, as always when preparing your speech, the importance of being an audience-centered speaker can't be overemphasized. There's an old saying that an ounce of illustration is worth a ton of talk. If a speech is boring, it is usually because the speaker has not chosen supporting material that is relevant or interesting to the audience. Don't just give people data; connect facts to their lives. As one sage quipped, "Data is not information any more than 50 tons of cement is a skyscraper."[63]

## Gather Interesting Supporting Material

Supporting material should be personal and concrete, and it should appeal to your listeners' senses.

Don Hewitt, the founding and longtime producer of TV's popular and award-winning *60 Minutes*, was repeatedly asked by young journalists, "What's the secret of your success as a communicator?" Hewitt's answer: "Tell me a story." *Everyone* likes to hear a good story. As Hewitt noted, the Bible does more than describe the nature of good and evil; it masterfully tells stories about Job, Noah, David, and others.[64]

Tell stories based on your own experiences and provide vivid descriptions of things that are tangible so that your audience can visualize what you are talking about. Besides sight, supporting material can appeal to touch, hearing, smell, and taste. The more senses you trigger with words, the more interesting your talk will be. Descriptions such as "the rough, splintery surface of weather-beaten wood" and "the sweet, cool, refreshing flavor of cherry Jell-O" evoke sensory images.

In addition, relating abstract statistics to something tangible can help communicate your ideas more clearly. For example, if you say Frito-Lay sells 2.6 billion pounds

*Good research skills are essential to the speechmaking process.*

[Photo: CREATAS/JUPITER IMAGES/Alamy Images]

of snack food each year, your listeners will have a hazy idea that 2.6 billion pounds is a lot of Fritos and potato chips; but if you add that 2.6 billion pounds is triple the weight of the Empire State Building, you've made your point more memorably.[65] Or, rather than simply saying that 4,000 teens die each year in car accidents, say this: "If 12 fully loaded jumbo jets crashed every year, something would be done about it. Every year, more than 4,000 teens die in car crashes—the equivalent of 12 large plane crashes." Relating statistics to something listeners can visualize makes the point more effectively.[66] We will discuss in Chapter 8 the variety of supporting material available to you.

How does a public speaker find interesting and relevant supporting material? By developing good research skills. President Woodrow Wilson once admitted, "I use not only all the brains I have, but all that I can borrow." Although it is important to have good ideas, it is equally important to know how to build on existing knowledge.

In addition to becoming a skilled user of electronic and library resources, you will also learn to be on the lookout as you read, surf the Internet, watch TV, and listen to the radio for ideas, examples, illustrations, and quotations that could be used in a speech. Finally, you will learn how to gather information through interviews and written requests for information on various topics. Chapter 6 will explain more thoroughly how to use all these resources.

## SAMPLE OUTLINE

### TOPIC

How to invest money

Your instructor may assign a topic, or you may select it.

### GENERAL PURPOSE

To inform

To inform, persuade, or entertain. Your instructor will probably specify your general purpose.

### SPECIFIC PURPOSE

At the end of my speech, the audience should be able to identify two principles that will help them better invest their money.

A clear statement indicating what your audience should be able to do after hearing your speech

### CENTRAL IDEA

Knowing the source of money, how to invest it, and how money grows can lead to increased income from wise investments.

A one-sentence summary of your talk

### INTRODUCTION

Imagine for a moment that it is the year 2050. You are 65 years old. You've just picked up your mail and opened an envelope that contains a check for $100,000! No, you didn't win the lottery. You smile as you realize your own modest investment strategy over the last fifty years has paid off handsomely.

Attention-catching opening line

Today I'd like to answer three questions that can help you become a better money manager: First, where does money come from? Second, where do you invest it? And third, how does a little money grow into a lot of money?

Preview major ideas.

Knowing the answers to these three questions can pay big dividends for you. With only modest investments and a well-disciplined attitude, you could easily have an annual income of $100,000 or more.

Tell your audience why they should listen to you.

## Gather Visual Supporting Material

For many people, seeing is believing. Besides searching for verbal forms of supporting material, you can also seek visual supporting material. Almost any presentation can be enhanced by reinforcing key ideas with visual aids. Often the most effective visual aids are the simplest: an object, a chart, a graph, a poster, a model, a map, or a person—perhaps you—to demonstrate a process or skill. Today there are many technologies, such as PowerPoint™, for displaying visual aids.

In Chapter 12 we discuss some basic advice about using presentation aids: Make your visual images large enough to be seen and allow plenty of time to prepare them; look at your audience, not at your presentation aid; control your audience's attention by timing your visual displays; and keep your presentation aids simple. Always concentrate on communicating effectively with your audience, not on dazzling your listeners with glitzy presentation displays.

# Organize Your Speech

A wise person once said, "If effort is organized, accomplishment follows." A clearly and logically structured speech helps your audience remember what you said. A logical structure also helps you feel more in control of your speech, and greater control helps you feel more comfortable while delivering your message.

Classical rhetoricians—early students of speech—called the process of developing an orderly speech **disposition**. Speakers need to present ideas, information, examples, illustrations, stories, and statistics in an orderly sequence so that listeners can easily follow what they are saying.

**disposition** The organization and arrangement of ideas and illustrations

### BODY

I. There are two sources of money. — *I. Major Idea*
   A. You already have some money. — *A. Supporting idea*
   B. You will earn money in the future. — *B. Supporting idea*

II. You can do three things with your money. — *II. Major Idea*
   A. You can spend it. — *A. Supporting idea*
   B. You can lend it to others. — *B. Supporting idea*
   C. You can invest it. — *C. Supporting idea*

III. Two principles can help make you rich. — *III. Major Idea*
   A. The "magic" of compound interest can transform pennies into millions. — *A. Supporting idea*
   B. Finding the best rate of return on your money can pay big dividends. — *B. Supporting idea*

### CONCLUSION

Today I've identified three key aspects of effective money management: (1) sources of money, (2) what you can do with money, and (3) money-management principles that can make you rich. Now, let's go "back to the future"! Remember the good feeling you had when you received your check for $100,000? Recall that feeling again when you are depositing your first paycheck. Remember this simple secret for accumulating wealth: Part of all I earn is mine to keep. It is within your power to "go for the gold."

*Summarize main ideas and restate central idea.*

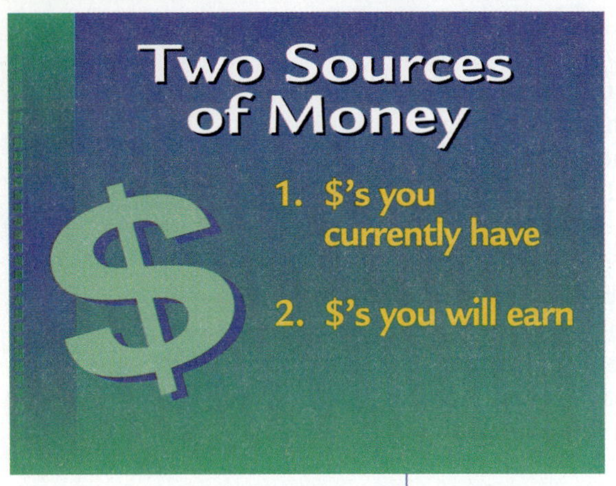


FIGURE 1.6 *Presentation graphic for the first major idea in your speech.*

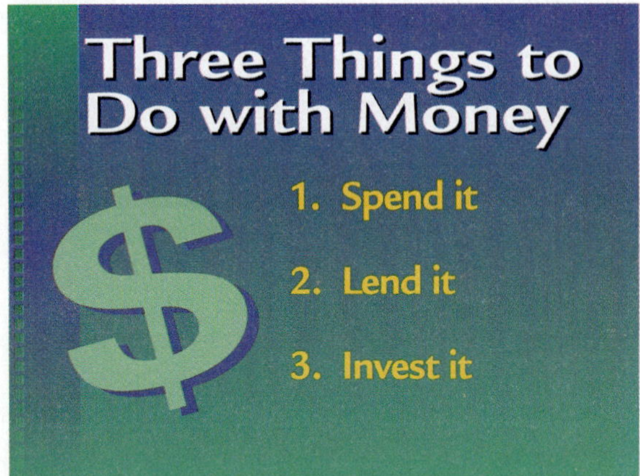


FIGURE 1.7 *Presentation graphic for the second major idea in your speech.*

FIGURE 1.8 *Presentation graphic for the third major idea in your speech.*

Every well-prepared speech has three major divisions: the introduction, the body, and the conclusion. The introduction helps capture attention, serves as an overview of the speech, and provides your audience with reasons to listen to you. The body presents the main content of your speech. The conclusion summarizes your key ideas. You may have heard this advice on how to organize a speech: "Tell them what you're going to tell them (the introduction), tell them (the body of the speech), and tell them what you told them (the conclusion)."

As a student of public speaking, you will study and learn to apply variations of this basic pattern of organization (chronological, topical, cause–effect, problem–solution) that will help your audience understand your meaning. You will learn about previewing and summarizing—methods of oral organization that will help your audience retain your main ideas. In the sample speech outline on page 25,[67] notice how the introduction catches the listener's attention, the body of the speech identifies the main ideas, and the conclusion summarizes the key ideas.

Because your introduction previews your speech and your conclusion summarizes it, most public-speaking teachers recommend that you prepare your introduction and conclusion *after* you have carefully organized the body of your talk. If you have already generated your major ideas by divisions, reasons, or steps, you are well on your way to developing an outline. Indicate your major ideas by Roman numerals. Use capital letters for your supporting points. Use Arabic numerals if you need to subdivide your ideas further. Do *not* write your speech word for word. If you do, you will sound stilted and unnatural. It may be useful, however, to use brief notes—written cues on note cards—instead of a complete manuscript.

You may want to look in Chapters 7 and 9 for approaches to organizing a message and sample outlines. Chapter 9 provides more detailed suggestions for beginning and ending your speech. Some public-speaking teachers may require a slightly different outline format. For example, your teacher may want you to outline your speech using a Roman numeral I for the introduction, II for the body, and III for your conclusion. Make sure you follow the precise guidelines your instructor provides for outlining your speech. For your first speech, you may want to adapt the sample outline format shown on pages 24–25. Your instructor may want you to add more detailed information about your supporting material in outlines you submit in class.

In addition to developing a written outline to use as you speak, consider using presentation aids to add structure and clarity to your major ideas. Simple visual reinforcers of your key ideas can help your audience retain essential points.

In Chapter 12 we offer tips for designing computer graphics using software such as PowerPoint. For example, the first major idea in the sample outline on page 25 could be summarized in a visual aid such as the one in Figure 1.6. The second major idea in our speech example could be emphasized with a visual like the one in Figure 1.7. The third major idea could be reinforced with a visual such as the one in Figure 1.8.

For all the steps we have discussed so far, your success as a speaker will ultimately be determined by your audience. That is why throughout the text we refer you to the audience-centered speechmaking model presented in this chapter.

Once you are comfortable with the structure of your talk and you have developed your visual aids, you are ready to rehearse.

## Rehearse Your Speech

Remember this joke? One man asks another, "How do you get to Carnegie Hall?" The answer: "Practice, practice, practice." The joke may be older than Carnegie Hall itself, but it is still good advice to all beginners, including novice speakers. A speech is a performance. As with any stage performance, be it music, dance, or theater, you need to rehearse. Experienced carpenters know to "measure twice, saw once." Rehearsing your speech is a way to measure your message so that you get it right when you present it to your audience.

The best way to practice is to rehearse your speech aloud, standing just as you will when you deliver it to your audience. As you rehearse, try to find a comfortable way to phrase your ideas, but don't try to memorize your talk. In fact, if you have rehearsed your speech so many times that you are using exactly the same words every time, you have rehearsed long enough. Rehearse just enough so that you can discuss your ideas and supporting material without leaving out major parts of your speech. It is all right to use notes, but most public-speaking instructors limit the number of notes you may use.

As you rehearse, practice making eye contact with your imaginary audience as often as you can. Also, be certain to speak loudly enough for all in the room to hear. If you are not sure what to do with your hands when you rehearse, just keep them at your side. Focus on your message, rather than worrying about how to gesture. Avoid jingling change with your hand in your pocket or using other gestures that could distract your audience. If you practice your speech as if you were actually delivering it, you will be a more effective speaker when you talk to the audience. And there is evidence that, like preparing early for your speech, spending time rehearsing your delivery will enhance the overall quality of your speech.[68]

Besides rehearsing your physical delivery, you will also make decisions about the style of your speech. "Style," said novelist Jonathan Swift, "is proper words in proper places." The words you choose and your arrangement of those words make up the style of your speech. Some audiences respond to a style that is simple and informal; others prefer a grand and highly poetic style. To be a good speaker, you must become familiar with the language your listeners are used to hearing, and you must know how to select the right word or phrase to communicate an idea. Work to develop an ear for how words will sound to your audience.

**RECAP**

### Steps in Audience-Centered Speechmaking

Considering your audience will affect the way you

- Select and narrow your topic.
- Determine your general and specific purposes.
- Develop your central and main ideas.
- Choose supporting material.
- Organize your speech.
- Rehearse and deliver your speech.

## Deliver Your Speech

The time has come, and you're ready to present your speech to your audience. Delivery is the final step in the process. Before you walk to the front of the room, look at your listeners to see if the audience assembled is what you were expecting. Are the people out there of the age, race, and gender that you had predicted? Or do you need to make last-minute changes in your message to adjust to a different mix of audience members?

When you are introduced, walk calmly and confidently to the front of the room, establish eye contact with your audience, smile naturally, and deliver your attention-catching opening sentence. Concentrate on your message and your audience. Deliver your speech in a conversational style, and try to establish rapport with your listeners. Deliver your speech just as you rehearsed it before your imaginary audience: Maintain eye contact, speak loudly enough to be heard, and use some natural variation in pitch. Finally, remember the advice of columnist Ann Landers: "Be sincere, be brief, and be seated."

Table 1.4 summarizes this chapter's introduction to the audience-centered speaking process and refers you to later chapters for in-depth information about each step. For a model of many of the attributes of a well-crafted message speech that we have discussed, read the speech by student Pao Yang Lee on page 29.

## TABLE 1.4 An Overview of the Public-Speaking Process

| Public-Speaking Step | What to Do | Where to Find More Information in this Book |
|---|---|---|
| 1. Consider the Audience | Gather information about your audience.<br>Analyze the information to help you make choices about every aspect of preparing and presenting your speech. | Chapter 4: "Analyzing Your Audience" |
| 2. Select and Narrow Your Topic | To select a good speech topic, consider<br>• Your audience<br>• Your own interests<br>• The specific occasion when you will be speaking | Chapter 5: "Developing Your Speech" |
| 3. Determine Your Purpose | Determine whether your general purpose is to inform, to persuade, or to entertain.<br>Decide on your specific purpose—a statement of what you want your audience to be able to do when you finish your speech. | Chapter 5: "Developing Your Speech"<br>Chapter 13: "Speaking to Inform"<br>Chapter 14: "Understanding Principles of Persuasion"<br>Chapter 15: "Using Persuasive Strategies"<br>Chapter 16: "Speaking for Special Occasions and Purposes" |
| 4. Develop Your Central Idea | Develop a one-sentence summary of your speech. | Chapter 5: "Developing Your Speech" |
| 5. Generate Your Main Ideas | Identify your major ideas by determining whether your central idea has logical divisions, reasons it is true, or steps. | Chapter 5: "Developing Your Speech" |
| 6. Gather Supporting Material | Conduct research to identify useful and interesting stories, descriptions, definitions, statistics, analogies, and opinions that support your major ideas. | Chapter 6: "Gathering and Using Supporting Material" |
| 7. Organize Your Speech | Develop your introduction, body, and conclusion.<br>Use signposts and transitions to clarify your organization. | Chapter 7: "Organizing Your Speech"<br>Chapter 8: "Introducing and Concluding Your Speech"<br>Chapter 9: "Outlining and Editing Your Speech" |
| 8. Rehearse Your Speech | Prepare your speaking notes and practice using them well in advance of your speaking date.<br>Practice your speech out loud, standing as you would stand while delivering your speech.<br>Develop appropriate and useful presentation aids. | Chapter 10: "Using Words Well: Speaker Language and Style"<br>Chapter 11: "Delivering Your Speech"<br>Chapter 12: "Using Presentation Aids" |
| 9. Deliver Your Speech | Present your speech, using<br>• Good eye contact<br>• Appropriate gestures and posture<br>• Appropriate vocal volume and variation | Chapter 11: "Delivering Your Speech" |

## SAMPLE SPEECH

### OUR IMMIGRATION STORY

*By Pao Yang Lee*

Each one of us has our own story, a history of our lives that helps explain who we are and what motivates us to be the best we can be. My story starts with my parents. Most of our parents worked hard to raise us and get us an education. Today, I'm going to share with you a part of my story. I will tell you about my parents' struggle to leave Laos and a refugee camp in Thailand, and about our new life in America.

Pao captures his listeners' attention by telling them about his parents' struggle to leave Laos.

I will start my story with my parents' struggle to leave Laos to make their way to Thailand. As most of you know, many Hmong people had escaped Laos because they were being persecuted by the Communists and had to escape for their lives and freedom. My parents, who hadn't met yet, each took their journey across the Mekong River on a bamboo raft. My parents were lucky. They made it across to Thailand. According to my Dad, about 1000 Hmong people died making that exact journey. My parents' story merged at a refugee camp in Thailand. In Thailand, although they had escaped with their lives, their lives did not improve much because the camp that the Hmong people were put in when they came to Thailand was in very poor condition. My parents met at the refugee camp in Bon Vinai a couple months later when they arrived in Thailand. My Dad asked for my Mom's hand in marriage. At that time, my parents were very young. They didn't have any support from anybody. I was born in the refugee camp in Bon Vinai, February 18, 1980. Six months after I was born, we were sponsored by an American family, which allowed us to come to the United States.

He sets the scene and provides a preview of what will be presented; audience members know that more details about the journey will be forthcoming, so they tune in to listen.

The speech is organized chronologically. Pao uses a step-by-step arrangement to describe the events that occurred.

The next chapter in our story continues in America, where each of us has had our own challenge. My Dad had the most responsibility when it came to supporting our family. He knew it was important to get an education, so he started attending college. However, shortly after our arrival, my sisters were born. To make ends meet, my Dad had to drop out of college and work full time to support us all. My Mom also struggled with all the new aspects of her life. For example, in Laos, where she used to live, there wasn't any machine that would wash your clothes. However, in the United States, there are machines that will wash clothes for you. Another thing that she struggled with was using other appliances as well. Being able to operate the machine and use it properly was the hardest thing for my Mom because she wasn't able to read the directions. Probably the biggest struggle for my Mom was learning how to speak English and understand the language. It is interesting that when people can't understand you, they think you're stupid. But we are the people who speak the second language.

Note how Pao signals a new idea by using the transition phrase "The next chapter in our story . . . ."

Revealing personal details and information adds interest to a story and holds listeners' attention.

Like my Mother and Father, I had my own challenge. I had to live in both cultures at the same time. At school, I was trying to fit in by learning the rules about how to act. While at home, I was trying to be respectful to the Hmong custom and language. This is a very difficult thing to do. It was also difficult for me to be a translator for my parents. I was just a little kid and was expected to translate an adult conversation. I was also expected to be there for my parents whenever they needed me.

Now I'm able to see my life as a part of a bigger picture—a bigger story. I have learned that you have to work hard to succeed in life. Coming from a first-generation family in the United States, I have lived through and seen the struggle that my parents went through to raise my siblings and me.

As Pao concludes his speech, he summarizes by noting the "bigger story," or the implications of what he has learned. Speeches based on personal experiences are enhanced when the speaker can draw some concluding point or idea from the story.

Well, today I told you a little bit about my story, a part of my ancestry that has helped make me who I am. It is a story that has been repeated by 90,000 Hmong people in the United States. As you have taken the journey with my parents from Laos, to Thailand, and to America, I hope you will be able to think of your own stories and how they have brought us to this present place and time, to learn and grow together.

The speech ends with a concise summary of the major idea of the speech. Pao also invites the audience to relate his story to their own lives.

# STUDY GUIDE

## Why Study Public Speaking?

Since you are likely to be called on to speak in public at various times throughout your life, skill in public speaking can empower you. It can also help you secure employment or advance your career.

### Being Audience-Centered

- As a public speaker, you will learn to adapt to your audience based on who your listeners are, their expectations for your speech, and their reactions to what you are saying.

### Critical Thinking

- How do you think this course in public speaking can help you with your career goals? With your personal life?

### Speaker's Homepage: The Power of the Internet

The Allyn & Bacon Public Speaking Web Site provides a wealth of ideas and Internet links to help you throughout your course in public speaking.

- wps.ablongman.com/ab_public_speaking_2/

## The Communication Process

Like other forms of communication, public speaking is a process. Different theorists have explained the communication process as: (1) an action, by which a source transmits a message through a channel to a receiver; (2) an interaction, in which the receiver's feedback and the context of the communication add to the action; and (3) a transaction, in which source and receiver simultaneously send messages to build a shared meaning.

### Being Audience-Centered

- The audience is the most important component in the communication process.
- The decoding of a speaker's message depends on the receiver's, or listener's, particular blend of past experiences, attitudes, beliefs, and values.
- An audience member experiencing either external or internal noise is unlikely to hear or remember much of what a speaker says.
- Skilled speakers depend on feedback from the nods, facial expressions, and murmurings of the audience to adjust their rate of speaking, volume, vocabulary, type and amount of supporting material, and other variables in order to communicate their message successfully.

### Critical Thinking

- Give an example of internal noise that is affecting you as you read this question.

## The Rich Heritage of Public Speaking

As you develop your own public-speaking skills, your study will be guided by experience and knowledge gained over centuries of making and studying speeches.

### Being Audience-Centered

- Throughout history, speechmakers have acknowledged that the audience is the most important element in the communication process.

### A Question of Ethics

- *Declamation* is defined in this chapter as "the delivery of an already famous address." Is it ethical to deliver a speech written and/or delivered by someone else? Explain your answer.

## Improving Your Confidence as a Speaker

Some beginning public speakers feel nervous at even the thought of giving a speech. Don't be surprised if you feel more nervous than you look to others. Remember that almost every speaker experiences some nervousness and that some anxiety can be useful. Specific suggestions to help you manage your apprehension include being prepared and knowing your audience, imagining the speech environment when you rehearse, and using relaxation techniques such as visualization, deep breathing, and focusing thoughts away from your fears.

### Being Audience-Centered

- Focus on connecting your message to your audience rather than dwelling on your fear and anxiety about public speaking; being audience-centered can help you manage your apprehension.

### Critical Thinking

- Mike Roberts, president of his fraternity, is preparing to address the university academic council in an effort to persuade council members to support establishment of a Greek housing zone on campus. This is his first major task as president, and he is understandably nervous about his responsibility. What advice would you give to help him manage his nervousness?

### Speaker's Homepage: Managing Your Nervousness

Take a quiz to measure how nervous different communication situations make you. Then visit just two of the many useful Web sites that offer other strategies for managing your nervousness.

- Assessing Your Communication Apprehension www.jamescmccroskey.com/measures/prca24.htm
- Overcoming the Fear of Speaking to Groups www.school-for-champions.com/speaking/fear.htm
- Speech Anxiety: Overcoming the Fear of Public Speaking http://www.speechcoachforexecutives.com/speech_anxiety.html

## An Overview of Audience-Centered Public Speaking

Being audience-centered means considering the background and interests of your listeners at each step in developing and presenting your speech. Based on information about your listeners, you select and narrow your topic, determine your purpose, develop your central idea, and generate the main ideas. These speech-preparation steps are followed by gathering and organizing your supporting material, including visual aids. You are then ready to rehearse and deliver your speech.

### Being Audience-Centered

- The cultural background of your audience will have a major effect on your listeners' expectations as to how you should organize, support, and present your speech.
- Focusing on and considering the audience helps a speaker understand, affirm, and adapt to even those audiences whose expectations for appropriate and effective speech topics, argument structure, language style, and delivery may differ from those of the speaker.
- Adapt your language and choice of words to the education level of your listeners; be mindful of your listeners' backgrounds so that you neither speak over their heads nor use simplistic words and phrases that insult their intelligence.
- Although audience members rarely interrupt or talk to speakers, some cultures and contexts invite more speaker-audience interaction than do others.

### Critical Thinking

- Jason Reed has just received his assignment for his first speech in his public-speaking class. What key skills does he need to master to become a competent public speaker?
- Shara Yobonski is preparing to address the city council in an effort to tell them about the Food for Friendship program she has organized in her neighborhood. What steps should she follow to prepare and deliver an effective speech?

### A Question of Ethics

- One of your friends took a public-speaking course last year and still has a file of speech outlines. Since you will give the speech yourself, is it ethical to use one of her outlines as a basis for your speech? Explain.

- Your first assignment is to give a speech about something interesting that has happened to you. You have decided to talk about the joys and hassles of a train trip you took last year. Your sister recently returned from a cross-country train trip and had several interesting tales to tell. Would it be ethical to tell one of her experiences as if it had happened to you? Why or why not?
- You read an article in *Reader's Digest* that could serve as the basis for a great speech about the ravages of AIDS. Would it be ethical to paraphrase the article, using most of the same examples and the overall outline as the basis for your speech, if you *told* your listeners that your speech was based on the article?

# SPEECH WORKSHOP

## Improving Your Confidence as a Public Speaker

The following list identifies behaviors that will make your nervousness *worse*. Place a 1 in front of the behavior that you do most often when preparing or presenting a speech. Continue to rank the behaviors by placing a 2 beside the practice you do the next most often, a 3 by the third most common behavior, and so on, until you've ranked the top five behaviors that *increase* your anxiety.

______ **1.** I usually procrastinate and often wait until the last minute to prepare my speech.

______ **2.** I typically don't learn much information about my audience or think about my audience.

______ **3.** I often select a topic that I don't know much about.

______ **4.** My outline of my speech is often poor or disorganized.

______ **5.** I often don't have a clear notion of how I will begin my speech.

______ **6.** I often haven't carefully thought out how I will end my speech.

______ **7.** I don't rehearse aloud while standing up; I just think about my speech rather than practice it.

______ **8.** I usually don't use deep breathing techniques to help me relax.

______ **9.** I usually don't channel my nervous energy.

______ **10.** I rarely visualize myself confidently giving my speech before I present it.

______ **11.** I usually don't give myself a pep talk to boost my confidence.

______ **12.** When I get nervous, I often focus on my nervousness rather than thinking about connecting my message with my audience.

______ **13.** I usually don't try to find friendly faces in the audience while I'm speaking; I just focus on my notes and try to get through the speech.

______ **14.** I avoid every speaking opportunity that comes my way because I'm so nervous.

______ **15.** When I'm finished with a speech, I focus on what I did wrong rather than congratulating myself on what I did well.

After you've identified the top five things you usually do to make your nervousness worse, develop a specific plan to change your behavior. Based on information presented in this chapter, identify specific strategies you could implement to counteract the behaviors that increase your nervousness. Begin with the behavior that you ranked number one.

Make a point of practicing these new strategies as you prepare for and present your next speech. Even if you don't practice all of the strategies for every speech, pick a few to focus on to help boost your confidence.

FREE SPEECH NOT ONLY LIVES, IT ROCKS!

—OPRAH WINFREY

William H. Johnson (1901–1970), *Lift Up Thy Voice and Sing*. c. 1942–44. Oil on paperboard, 64.9 x 54.0 cm. Smithsonian American Art Museum, Washington, D.C./ Art Resource, N.Y.

OUTLINE

# 2 Speaking Freely and Ethically

OBJECTIVES

**After studying this chapter you should be able to do the following:**

1. Define ethics.
2. Explain the relationship between ethics and free speech.
3. List and explain five criteria for ethical public speaking.
4. Define and discuss how best to avoid plagiarism.
5. Explain the relationship between ethics and credibility.

In July 2009, a popular radio host in Austin, Texas, known for his sarcastic humor, used on the air an "insulting and highly offensive" ethnic slur.[1] Radio station KLBJ cancelled the offender's show, suspended him for two weeks without pay, and permanently removed him from the air. When a station manager announced these actions to the local newspaper, he acknowledged.

> There will be members of the community who feel we did not do enough and I think there might be members of the community who feel we did too much.

The reason for the difference in public opinion? Although the radio host exercised his right to *free speech*, he did not exercise his *ethical* responsibility.

In the United States, the right to speak freely goes hand in hand with the responsibility to speak ethically. **Ethics** are the beliefs, values, and moral principles by which we determine what is right or wrong. Some ethical values appear to be universal, or nearly so. For example, the major world religions share a remarkably similar moral code for how people should treat others.[2] For Christians, the Golden Rule—"Do unto others as you would have others do unto you"—is a fundamental value. Buddhism teaches a similar value: "One should seek for others the happiness one desires for oneself." Hinduism asks adherents to live by the precept "Do nothing to others which would cause pain if done to you." Judaism teaches, "What is hateful to you, do not do to others." And Islam declares, "No one of you is a believer until he desires for his brother that which he desires for himself."

Although the underlying ethic of how to treat others is fundamental to the world's religions, other ethical principles may reflect cultural norms, professional standards, or individual beliefs and values. Ethics serve as criteria for many of the decisions we make in our personal and professional lives, and also for our judgments of others' behavior. The student who refuses to cheat on a test, the employee who will not call in sick to gain an extra day of vacation, and the property owner who does not claim more storm damage than she actually suffered have all made choices based on ethics. We read and hear about ethical issues every day in the media. Cloning, stem-cell research, and drug testing have engendered heated ethical debates among medical professionals. Advertising by some attorneys has incensed those who believe that an overall increase in frivolous litigation is tarnishing the profession. And in the political arena, debates about reforms of social programs, fiscal responsibility, and the regulation of financial institutions all hinge on ethical issues.

Although you are undoubtedly familiar with many of these ethical issues, you may have given less thought to ethics in public speaking. They center on one main concern: In a country in which **free speech** is protected by law, the right to speak freely must be balanced by the responsibility to speak ethically. The National Communication Association's Credo for Communication Ethics emphasizes the fundamental nature and far-reaching impact of ethical communication:

> Ethical communication is fundamental to responsible thinking, decision making, and the development of relationships and communities within and across contexts, cultures, channels, and media. Moreover, ethical communication enhances human worth and dignity by fostering truthfulness, fairness, responsibility, personal integrity, and respect for self and others.[3]

Ethical considerations should guide every step of the public-speaking process. As you determine the goal of your speech, outline your arguments, and select your supporting material, think about the beliefs, values, and moral principles of your audience, as well as your own. Ethical public speaking is inherently audience-centered, always taking into account the needs and rights of the listeners.

In our discussion of speaking freely and ethically, we will turn first to free speech—both its protection and its restriction by law and public policy. Then we

**ethics**
The beliefs, values, and moral principles by which people determine what is right or wrong

**free speech**
Legally protected speech or speech acts

will discuss the ethical practice of free speech by speakers and listeners, providing guidelines to help you balance your right to free speech with your responsibilities as an audience-centered speaker. Within this framework, we will define and discuss plagiarism, one of the most troublesome violations of public-speaking ethics. And finally, we will discuss the relationship between ethics and speaker credibility.

# Speaking Freely

In April 2007, CBS radio fired controversial talk-radio host Don Imus for derogatory comments he had made on the air about members of the Rutgers University women's basketball team. In a commencement address at Queen's College two months later, author Susan Isaacs questioned the firing. "He is pretty much a pig," Isaacs agreed. "But the demands for his ouster were wrong." She went on to explain,

> If you get rid of one talk show host, next to go is an offensive comedy show such as *South Park*, shock jock Howard Stern and conservative host Rush Limbaugh. Then it's your turn (to be quieted).[4]

While critical of Imus's *ethics*, Isaacs nevertheless defended his right to *free speech*.

*Since the 1700s, court rulings and laws have continued, and will continue, to shape our interpretation of the First Amendment. The Amendment protects free speech, including the rights of protest speakers to speak out about controversial issues.*

[Photo: A. Ramey/PhotoEdit Inc.]

## Free Speech and the U.S. Constitution

In 1791, the **First Amendment** to the U.S. Constitution was written to guarantee that "Congress shall make no law . . . abridging the freedom of speech." In the more than 200 years since then, entities as varied as state legislatures, colleges and universities, the American Civil Liberties Union, and the federal courts have sought to define through both law and public policy the phrase "freedom of speech."

Only a few years after the ratification of the First Amendment, Congress passed the Sedition Act, providing punishment for those who spoke out against the government. When both Thomas Jefferson and James Madison declared this act unconstitutional, however, it was allowed to lapse.

## Free Speech in the Twentieth Century

During World War I, the U.S. Supreme Court ruled that it was lawful to restrict speech that presented "a clear and present danger" to the nation. This decision led to the founding, in 1920, of the American Civil Liberties Union, the first organization formed to protect free speech. In 1940, Congress declared it illegal to urge the violent overthrow of the federal government. However, even as they heard the hate speech employed by Hitler and the Nazis, U.S. courts and lawmakers argued that only by *protecting* free speech could the United States protect the rights of minorities and the disenfranchised. For most of the last half of the twentieth century, the Supreme Court continued to protect rather than to limit free speech, upholding it as "the core aspect of democracy."[5]

In 1964, the Supreme Court narrowed the definition of slander, or false speech that harms someone. The Court ruled that before a public official can recover

**First Amendment**
The amendment to the U.S. Constitution that guarantees free speech; the first of the ten amendments to the U.S. Constitution known collectively as the Bill of Rights

damages for slander, he or she must prove that the slanderous statement was made with "actual malice."[6] Another 1964 boost for free speech occurred not in the courts but on a university campus. In December of that year, more than 1,000 students at the University of California in Berkeley took over three floors of Sproul Hall to protest the recent arrest of outspoken student activists. The Berkeley Free Speech Movement that arose from the incident permanently changed the political climate of U.S. college campuses. In a statement on the thirty-year anniversary of the protest, Berkeley's vice chancellor Carol Christ wrote, "Today it is difficult to imagine life in a university where there are serious restrictions on the rights of political advocacy."[7]

Free speech gained protection in the last two decades of the twentieth century, when the Supreme Court found "virtually all attempts to restrain speech in advance . . . unconstitutional," regardless of how hateful or disgusting the speech may seem to some.[8] In 1989, the Supreme Court defended the burning of the U.S. flag as a "**speech act**" protected by the First Amendment. In 1997, the Court struck down the highly controversial federal Communications Decency Act of 1996, which had imposed penalties for creating, transmitting, or receiving obscene material on the Internet. The Court ruled that "the interest in encouraging freedom of expression in a democratic society outweighs any theoretical but unproven benefit of censorship."[9]

Perhaps no test of free speech received more publicity than the sensational 1998 lawsuit brought by four Texas cattlemen against popular talk-show host Oprah Winfrey. In a show on "mad cow disease," Winfrey had declared that she would never eat another hamburger. Charging that her statement caused cattle prices to plummet, the cattlemen sued for damages; however, Winfrey's attorneys successfully argued that the case was an important test of free speech. Emerging from the courtroom after the verdict in her favor, Winfrey shouted, "My reaction is that free speech not only lives, it rocks!"[10]

## Free Speech in the Twenty-first Century

No sooner had the new century begun than the right to free speech experienced one of its most historically significant challenges. One month after the September 11, 2001, terrorist attacks on the United States, the pendulum again swung toward restriction of free speech with the passage of the Patriot Act, which broadened the investigative powers of government agencies. The Patriot Act was roundly criticized by various civil-rights, free-speech, and publishing groups. One coalition of such groups described the Patriot Act as "the latest in a long line of abuses of rights in times of conflict."[11]

> It is ironic that even as Americans debate the restrictions imposed by the Patriot Act, they recognized and offered restitution for historical infringement on free speech. In May 2006, Montana Governor Brian Schweitzer formally pardoned 78 late citizens of Montana who had been imprisoned or fined under the Montana Sedition Act of 1918, convictions that "violated basic American rights of speech. . . ."[12]

The pendulum swung back in June 2010, when the exercise of free speech created controversy for and hastened the retirement of veteran White House correspondent Helen Thomas. Asked by a rabbi to comment on Israel, Thomas responded that the Israelis should get out of Palestine. Although Thomas later both apologized and resigned from the White House Press Corps, her right to free speech was upheld by former CBS News foreign correspondent Terry Phillips, who noted wryly, "Apparently, journalists are now only willing to defend free speech when it is safe."[13]

**speech act**
A behavior, such as flag burning, that is viewed by law as nonverbal communication and is subject to the same protections and limitations as verbal speech

We summarize the history of the First Amendment in Table 2.1. There can be little doubt that in the months and years to come, the United States and its citizens will

## TABLE 2.1 History of Free Speech in the United States

|  |  |
|---|---|
| 1791 | First Amendment guarantees that "Congress shall make no law . . . abridging the freedom of speech" |
| 1798 | Sedition Act is passed (expired in 1801) |
| 1919 | Supreme Court suggests that speech presenting a "clear and present danger" may be restricted |
| 1920 | American Civil Liberties Union is formed |
| 1940 | Congress declares it illegal to urge the violent overthrow of the federal government |
| 1964 | Supreme Court restricts definition of slander; Berkeley Free Speech Movement is born |
| 1989 | Supreme Court defends the burning of the U.S. flag as a "speech act" |
| 1997 | Supreme Court strikes down Communications Decency Act of 1996, in defense of free speech on the Internet |
| 1998 | Oprah Winfrey successfully defends her right to speak freely on television |
| 2001 | September 11 terrorist attacks spark passage of the Patriot Act and new debate over the balance between national security and free speech |
| 2006 | State of Montana pardons those convicted under the Montana Sedition Act of 1918 |
| 2010 | White House correspondent Helen Thomas retires amid controversy over what some saw as her exercise of free speech |

continue to debate the First Amendment as we try to achieve "balance among national security, free speech, and patriotism."[14]

# Speaking Ethically

As the boundaries of free speech expand, the importance of **ethical speech** increases. Although there is no definitive ethical creed for a public speaker, teachers and practitioners of public speaking generally agree that an ethical speaker is one who has a clear, responsible goal; uses sound evidence and reasoning; is sensitive to and tolerant of differences; is honest; and avoids plagiarism. In the discussion that follows, we offer suggestions for observing these ethical guidelines.

## Have a Clear, Responsible Goal

The goal of a public speech should be clear to the audience. For example, if you are trying to convince the audience that your beliefs on abortion are more correct than those of others, you should say so at some point in your speech. If you keep your true agenda hidden, you violate your listeners' rights. In addition, an ethical goal should be socially responsible. A socially responsible goal is one that gives the listener choices, whereas an irresponsible, unethical goal is psychologically coercive. Adolf Hitler's speeches, which incited the German people to hatred and genocide, were coercive, as were those of Chinese leader Deng Xiaoping, who tried to intimidate Chinese citizens into revealing the whereabouts of leaders of the unsuccessful 1989 student uprising in Tiananmen Square.

If your overall objective is to inform or persuade, it is probably ethical; if your goal is to coerce or manipulate, it is unethical. But lawyers and ethicists do not always agree on this distinction. As we have pointed out, Congress and the Supreme Court have at times limited speech that incites sedition, violence, and riot, but they have also protected free speech rights "for both the ideas that people cherish and the

**ethical speech**
Speech that is responsible, honest, and tolerant

## LEARNING FROM GREAT SPEAKERS

### Mohandas Gandhi (1869–1948)

The great Indian spiritual and political leader Mohandas Gandhi guided the twentieth-century campaign for Indian independence from Britain. Even as Gandhi practiced free speech in the form of nonviolent protest, he accepted the responsibilities of ethical speech. His goal was clear; he accepted the consequences of his actions by allowing himself to be jailed several times; and he insisted on the accommodation of India's Muslim citizens. This ethical position led to his assassination by a Hindu extremist.[15]

An ethical speaker is true to his or her own beliefs. Although we encourage you to adapt your message to your audience, we don't recommend that you change your fundamental ethical principles just to avoid controversy. An effective and ethical audience-centered speaker maintains his or her core ethical beliefs while also considering the best strategies to make the message clear to his or her listeners.

[Photo: AP Wide World Photos]

thoughts they hate."[16] Even those who defend a broad legal right to free speech recognize that they are defending the right to unethical, as well as ethical, speech. For example, faculty, administrators, and regents of the University of Colorado have for years debated the case of ethnic studies professor Ward Churchill, who, immediately following the 2001 terrorist attacks, compared some of those who died at the World Trade Center to Holocaust architect Adolf Eichmann. Even as the university's president and the governor of Colorado recommended Churchill's dismissal, others staunchly defended his right to speak freely.[17]

## Use Sound Evidence and Reasoning

Ethical speakers use critical-thinking skills such as analysis and evaluation to formulate arguments and draw conclusions. Unethical speakers substitute false claims and manipulation of emotion for evidence and logical arguments.

In the early 1950s, Wisconsin senator Joseph McCarthy incited national panic by charging that Communists were infiltrating every avenue of American life. Thousands of people came under suspicion, many losing jobs and careers because of the false accusations. Never able to substantiate his claims, McCarthy nevertheless succeeded in his witch hunt by exaggerating and distorting the truth. One United Press reporter noted, "The man just talked in circles. Everything was by inference, allusion, never a concrete statement of fact. Most of it didn't make sense."[18] Although today we recognize the flimsiness of McCarthy's accusations, in his time he wielded incredible power. Like Hitler, McCarthy knew how to manipulate emotions and fears to produce the results he wanted. It may sometimes be tempting to resort to false claims to gain power over others, but it is always unethical to do so.

Some speakers bypass sound evidence and reasoning in order to make their conclusions more provocative. One contemporary rhetoric scholar offers this example of such short-circuited reasoning:

> Let's say two people are observing who speaks in college classrooms and they come up with
>
> 1. Women are not as good at public speaking as men.
> 2. In college classes on coed campuses where most professors are male, women tend to talk less in class than men.[19]

The first conclusion, based on insufficient evidence, reinforces sexist stereotypes with an inflammatory overgeneralization. The second, more qualified conclusion is more ethical.

One last, but important, requirement for the ethical use of evidence and reasoning is to share with an audience all information that might help them reach a sound decision, including information that may be potentially damaging to your case. Even if you proceed to refute the opposing evidence and arguments, you have fulfilled your ethical responsibility by presenting the perspective of the other side. And you make your own arguments more convincing by anticipating and answering counterarguments and opposing evidence.

## Be Sensitive to and Tolerant of Differences

> The filmmaker who ate nothing but McDonald's meals for his Oscar-nominated movie *Super Size Me* apologized for a profanity-laced, politically incorrect speech at a suburban Philadelphia school.
>
> Among other things, Morgan Spurlock joked about the intelligence of McDonald's employees and teachers smoking pot while he was speaking at Hatboro-Horsham High School. . . .
>
> Spurlock, 35, told *The Philadelphia Inquirer* in a telephone interview that he "didn't think of the audience" and could have chosen his words better.[20]

As we noted in Chapter 1, being audience-centered requires that you become as aware as possible of others' feelings, needs, interests, and backgrounds. Spurlock violated this ethical principle in his remarks.

Sometimes called **accommodation**, sensitivity to differences does not mean that speakers must abandon their own convictions for those of their audience members. It does mean that speakers should demonstrate a willingness to listen to opposing viewpoints and learn about different beliefs and values. Such willingness not only communicates respect; it can also help a speaker to select a topic, formulate a purpose, and design strategies to motivate an audience.

Your authors are currently involved in an informal educational exchange with a professor from the St. Petersburg Cultural Institute in Russia, and we recently had a chance to visit the professor and her family in St. Petersburg. In talking with the professor's talented teenage daughter, we inquired about her plans after she finished her university education. Smiling at us in both amusement and amazement, she replied, "Americans are always planning what they are going to do several years in the future. In Russia, we do not plan beyond two or three weeks. Life is too uncertain here." Having gained this insight into Russian life, we know now that it would raise false hopes to attempt to motivate Russian audiences with promises of benefits far in the future. Our new understanding not only helps us see that speaking of immediate, deliverable rewards is a more realistic and ethical approach to communication with our Russian friends, but it has broader implications as well. DePaul University Communication Professor Kathy Fitzpatrick notes,

> Our success in public diplomacy will turn on our ability to speak in ways that recognize and appreciate how [our audiences] will interpret our messages.[21]

A speaker who is sensitive to differences also avoids language that might be interpreted as being biased or offensive. Although it may seem fairly simple and a matter of common sense to avoid overtly abusive language, it is not so easy to avoid language that discriminates more subtly. In Chapter 10, we look at specific words and phrases that can be unintentionally offensive and that ethical speakers should avoid.

## Be Honest

Knowingly offering false or misleading information to an audience is an ethical violation. In 2003, President George W. Bush and members of his staff accepted responsibility for having told the public that Iraq was getting nuclear fuel from Africa, even after intelligence reports several months earlier had discredited the

**accommodation**
Sensitivity to the feelings, needs, interests, and backgrounds of other people

claim. In 1999, Toronto Blue Jays manager Tim Johnson was fired after it was revealed that the stories he had told to his team about his combat experiences in Vietnam were false. During the war, it turned out, he had played ball while serving with the Reserves in California.[22] Perhaps most famously, in January 1998, President Bill Clinton's finger-wagging declaration that "I did not have sexual relations with that woman—Miss Lewinsky" was a serious breach of ethics that came back to haunt him. Many Americans were willing to forgive the inappropriate relationship; fewer could forgive the dishonesty.

A seeming exception to the dictum to avoid false information is the use of hypothetical illustrations—illustrations that never actually occurred but that might happen. Many speakers rely on such illustrations to clarify or enhance their speeches. As long as a speaker makes clear to the audience that the illustration is indeed hypothetical—for example, prefacing the illustration with a phrase such as "Imagine that . . ."—such use is ethical.

Honesty also requires that speakers give credit for ideas and information that are not their own. The *Publication Manual of the American Psychological Association* states that "authors do not present the work of another as if it were their own work. This can extend to ideas as well as written words."[23] Presenting the words and ideas of others without crediting them is called *plagiarism*. This ethical violation is both serious enough and widespread enough to warrant a separate discussion.

### CONFIDENTLY CONNECTING WITH YOUR AUDIENCE

#### Remember That You Will Look More Confident Than You May Feel

As you listen to other people presenting speeches, you will note that most speakers don't appear to be nervous. They are not dishonestly trying to hide their apprehension; most people simply do not appear outwardly as nervous as they may feel. This means that when you deliver your presentation, your listeners will not know that *you* feel nervous. You may feel some apprehension, but it is completely ethical to keep those feelings to yourself. Unless you tell your audience that you're nervous, it's unlikely that they will notice it.

## Don't Plagiarize

Although some cultures may view unacknowledged borrowing from sources as a sign of respect and humility and an attempt to be audience-centered, in the United States and most other Western cultures, using the words, sentence structures, and/or ideas of another person without crediting the source is a serious breach of ethics. Yet even people who would never think of stealing money or shoplifting may feel justified in **plagiarizing**—stealing words and/or ideas. One student commencement speaker who plagiarized a speech by the writer Barbara Kingsolver explained his action as resulting from the "expectation to produce something amazing."[24]

**Understand What Constitutes Plagiarism** Even if you've never plagiarized anything as public as a commencement address, perhaps you can remember copying a grade-school report directly from the encyclopedia; or maybe you've even purchased or "borrowed" a paper to submit for an assignment in high school or college. These are obvious forms of plagiarism. Less obvious forms include **plagiaphrasing**—lacing a speech with compelling phrases you find in a source; failing to give credit to a source or adequate information in a citation; or relying too heavily on the vocabulary or sentence structure of a source.

**Understand That Plagiarism May Have Significant Consequences** The Center for Academic Integrity reports that 75 percent of college students admit to having cheated at least once.[25] The Educational Testing Service has found that one Web site offering free term papers gets some 80,000 hits per day. Ironically, at least one such site claims to provide "non-plagiarized term papers"—ironic, because using any such paper is exactly what constitutes plagiarism![26] And communication researcher Todd Holm reports that more than 50 percent of 300 students surveyed reported cheating in some way in a public speaking class.[27]

**plagiarizing**
Presenting someone else's words or ideas as though they were one's own

**plagiaphrasing**
Failing to give credit for compelling phrases taken from another source

Despite the near-epidemic occurrence of plagiarism, most colleges impose stiff penalties on students who plagiarize. Plagiarists almost always fail the assignment in question, frequently fail the course, and are sometimes put on academic probation or even expelled. And the risk of being caught is much greater than you might suspect. Many colleges subscribe to a Web-based plagiarism detection company such as Turnitin; other professors routinely use free detection sites such as Grammarly or even a search engine such as Google.

A few years ago, one of your authors heard an excellent student speech on the importance of detecting cancer early. The only problem was that she heard the same speech again in the following class period! On finding the "speech"—actually a *Reader's Digest* article that was several years old—both students were certain that they had discovered a surefire shortcut to an A. Instead, they failed the assignment, ruined their course grades, and lost your author's trust. The consequences of plagiarism in other arenas can be even more dire, including the loss of a job or the end of a promising career.

**Do Your Own Work** The most flagrant cases of plagiarism result from not doing your own work. For example, while you are poking around the library for ideas to use in a speech assignment, you may discover an entire speech or perhaps an article that could easily be made into a speech. However tempting it may be to use this material, and however certain you are that no audience member could possibly have seen it, resist any urge to plagiarize. You will only be doing yourself a disservice if you do not learn how to compose a speech on your own. After all, you are in college to acquire new skills.

Another way speakers may attempt to shortcut the speech preparation task is to ask another person to edit a speech so extensively that it becomes more that other person's work than their own. This is another form of plagiarism and another way of cheating themselves out of the skills they need to develop.

**Acknowledge Your Sources** Our admonition to do your own work in no way suggests that you should not research your speeches and then share your findings with audience members. In fact, an ethical speaker is responsible for doing just that. Furthermore, some information is so widely known that you do not have to acknowledge a source for it. For example, you need not credit a source if you say that a person must be infected with the HIV virus in order to develop AIDS, or that the Treaty of Versailles was signed on June 28, 1919. This information is widely available in a variety of reference sources. However, if you decide to use any of the following in your speech, you must give credit to the source:

- Direct quotations, even if they are only brief phrases
- Opinions, assertions, or ideas of others, even if you paraphrase rather than quote them verbatim
- Statistics
- Any nonoriginal visual materials, including graphs, tables, and pictures

To be able to acknowledge your sources, you must first practice careful and systematic note-taking. Indicate with quotation marks any phrases or sentences that you photocopy or copy by hand verbatim from a source, and be sure to record the author, title, publisher or Web site, publication date, and page numbers for all sources from which you take quotations, ideas, statistics, or visual materials. Additional suggestions for systematic note-taking are offered in Chapter 6. In addition to keeping careful records of your sources, you must also know how to cite sources for your audience, both orally and in writing.

**Oral Citations.** Perhaps you have heard a speaker say "Quote" while holding up both hands with index and middle fingers curved to indicate quotation marks. This is an artificial and distracting way to cite a source; an **oral citation** can be integrated more smoothly into a speech.

**oral citation**
The oral presentation of such information about a source as the author, title, and year of publication

For example, you might use the approach illustrated in the sample oral citation above. The publication date and author of a source are usually sufficient information

## SAMPLE ORAL CITATION

On a 2010 Web page titled *Rabies*, the Centers for Disease Control and Prevention define *rabies* as

"a preventable viral disease of mammals most often transmitted through the bite of a rabid animal."

- Provide the date.
- Specify the type of resource.
- Give the title.
- Provide the author or source.
- Pause briefly to signal that you are about to begin quoting.
- Quote the source.
- Pause again to indicate that you are ending the quoted passage.

for an oral citation. In the example, the speaker also mentions the type of resource (Web page) and the title of the fact sheet (*Rabies*). Follow your instructor's preferences for the level of detail to include in your oral citations. Note that when you include an oral citation in a speech, the beginning and end of the quoted passage are indicated by pauses. The sample preparation outline in Chapter 9 gives additional examples of oral citations.

**Written Citations.** You can also provide a **written citation** for a source. In fact, your public-speaking instructor may ask you to provide a bibliography of sources along with the outline or other written materials he or she requires for each speech. Instructors who require a bibliography will usually specify the format in which they want the citations; if they do not, you can use a style guide such as that published by the MLA (Modern Language Association) or the APA (American Psychological Association), both of which are available online as well as in traditional print format. Here is an example of a written citation in MLA format for the source quoted in the sample oral citation:

**written citation**
The written presentation of such information about a source as the author, title, and year of publication, usually formatted according to a conventional style guide

*Rabies*. Centers for Disease Control and Prevention, 1 June 2010. Web. 21 June 2010.

Notice that the citation provides two dates: the date the material was posted online and the date it was accessed by the researcher. If you are unable to find the date the material was posted—or any other single element of information—proceed directly to the next item in the citation.

Additional information about citing sources and preparing a bibliography can be found in Chapter 6.

Perhaps now you are thinking, "What about those 'gray areas,' those times when I am not certain whether information or ideas I am presenting are common knowledge?" A good rule is this: When in doubt, document. You will never be guilty of plagiarism if you document something you didn't need to, but you could be committing plagiarism if you do not document something you should have documented.

**RECAP**

### The Ethical Public Speaker

- Has a clear, responsible goal
- Uses sound evidence and reasoning
- Is sensitive to and tolerant of differences
- Is honest
- Doesn't plagiarize

# Speaking Credibly

**credibility**
An audience's perception of a speaker as competent, knowledgeable, dynamic, and trustworthy

**Credibility** is a speaker's believability. A credible speaker is one whom an audience perceives to be competent, knowledgeable, dynamic, and trustworthy. The last of those four factors—trustworthiness—is dependent in large part on the speaker's known consistent adherence to ethical principles.

You trust people whom you believe to be ethical. In fact, the Greek rhetorician Aristotle used the term *ethos*—the root word of *ethic* and *ethical*—to refer to a speaker's credibility. Quintilian, a Roman teacher of public speaking, believed that an effective public speaker also should be a person of good character, a "good person speaking well."

We examine credibility in more detail in Chapter 4, where we discuss analyzing your audience's attitudes toward you; in Chapter 9, where we discuss establishing your credibility in your speech introduction; and in Chapters 14 and 15, where we discuss the role of credibility in persuading an audience.

For now, keep in mind that speaking ethically is one key to being perceived by your audience as a credible speaker.

# STUDY GUIDE

## Speaking Freely

Ethical speaking is very important in a society that protects free speech. Although Congress and the courts have occasionally limited free speech by law and policy, more often they have protected and broadened its application. The right to free speech has also been upheld by such organizations as the American Civil Liberties Union and by colleges and universities.

### Using What You've Learned

- Explain how ethical behavior serves as a balance to free speech.
- Why do you think the U.S. Supreme Court has historically considered flag burning and pornography to be "free speech acts"?

## Speaking Ethically

Speakers who exercise their right to free speech are responsible for tempering what they say by applying ethics, or moral principles and values. Although there is no definitive standard of ethics, most people agree that public speakers must be responsible, honest, and tolerant in order to be ethical.

Accommodation, or sensitivity to differences, leads speakers to demonstrate a willingness to listen to opposing viewpoints and learn about different beliefs and values. A speaker who is sensitive to differences avoids language that might be interpreted as being in any way biased or offensive.

Plagiarism is one of the most common violations of speech ethics. You can usually avoid plagiarizing by understanding what it is, doing your own work, and acknowledging—orally, in writing, or both—the sources for any quotations, ideas, statistics, or visual materials you use in a speech.

### Being Audience-Centered

- Ethical public speaking is inherently audience-centered, always taking into account the needs and rights of the listeners.
- The goal of a speech should be clear to the audience. If you keep your true agenda hidden, you violate your listeners' rights.
- A socially responsible goal for a speech is one that gives the listener choices, whereas an irresponsible, unethical goal is psychologically coercive.
- An important requirement for the ethical use of evidence and reasoning is to share with an audience all information that might help them reach a sound decision, including information that may be potentially damaging to your case.

### Using What You've Learned

- The following passage comes from the book *Abraham Lincoln, Public Speaker*, by Waldo W. Braden:

> The Second Inaugural Address, sometimes called Lincoln's Sermon on the Mount, was a concise, tightly constructed composition that did not waste words on ceremonial niceties or superficial sentiment. The shortest Presidential inaugural address up to that time, it was only 700 words long, compared to 3,700 words for the First, and required from 5 to 7 minutes to deliver [28]

Which of the following statements should be credited to Braden if you were to use them in a speech?

"Lincoln's second inaugural address is sometimes called Lincoln's Sermon on the Mount."

"Because he was elected and sworn in for two terms as president, Abraham Lincoln prepared and delivered two inaugural addresses."

"Lincoln's second inaugural address was 700 words and 5 to 7 minutes long."

### A Question of Ethics

- From at least the time of Franklin Delano Roosevelt, speechwriters have written many of the best speeches made by U.S. presidents. Is such use of speechwriters ethical? Is it ethical to give credit to the presidents for memorable lines from speeches written by professional speechwriters?

## Speaking Credibly

Speaking ethically allows your audience to trust you. Being trustworthy is an important part of being credible.

### Speaker's Homepage: Tips for Ethics and Free Speech

The following Web sites explore and debate issues of free and ethical speech:

- The Ethics Connection. Santa Clara University's Markkula Center for Applied Ethics offers you case studies in ethics, as well as advice on current and perennial ethical issues. www.scu.edu/ethics/
- The American Civil Liberties Union. Defending freedom of speech is one of the major activities of the ACLU. www.aclu.org/free-speech

# SPEECH WORKSHOP

## Avoiding Plagiarism

After you have developed your speech outline and are preparing your speaking notes, use the following questions to make certain that you are properly and ethically giving credit for the ideas, opinions, images, and words of others.

1. Am I using ideas and sources that are not my own? Specifically, am I using
   - ☐ a direct quotation?
   - ☐ someone else's idea or opinion, even if I'm paraphrasing the idea or opinion rather than directly quoting the information?
   - ☐ a statistic?
   - ☐ a nonoriginal visual aid, graph, table, or picture?
2. Have I provided the appropriate oral citation of ideas, images, and words that are not my own? A proper oral citation includes:
   - ☐ the author of the source
   - ☐ the title of the source
   - ☐ the date of the source
   - ☐ the type of source (for example, a book, an article, a Web site)
3. When quoting material from a source, am I clearly indicating with my delivery when the quotation begins and ends?
   - ☐ Pause briefly before you begin quoting.
   - ☐ Read the quotation.
   - ☐ Pause briefly at the end of the quote.

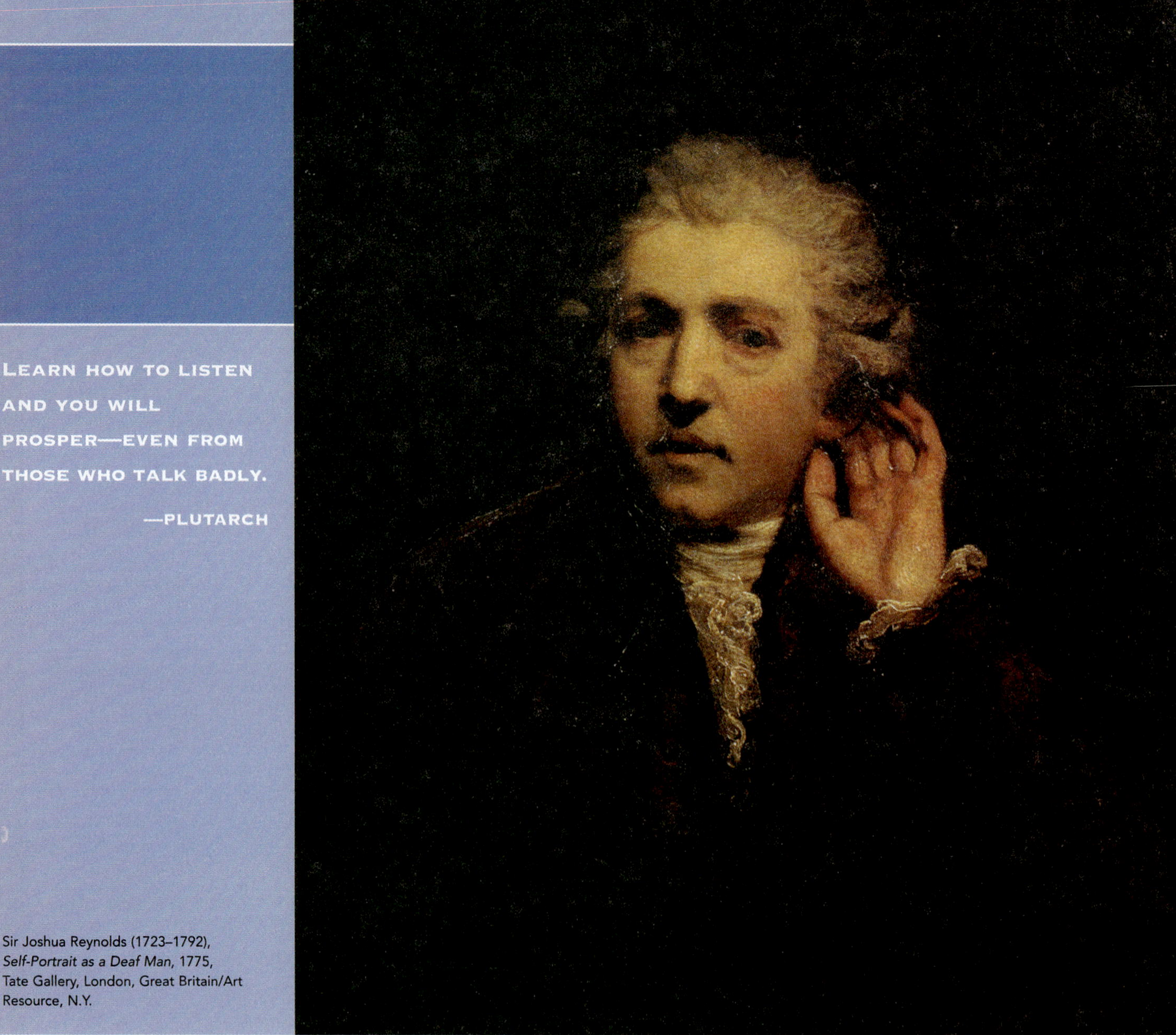

LEARN HOW TO LISTEN AND YOU WILL PROSPER—EVEN FROM THOSE WHO TALK BADLY.

—PLUTARCH

Sir Joshua Reynolds (1723–1792), *Self-Portrait as a Deaf Man*, 1775, Tate Gallery, London, Great Britain/Art Resource, N.Y.

## OUTLINE

**Overcoming Barriers to Effective Listening**
- Managing Information Overload
- Overcoming Personal Concerns
- Reducing Outside Distractions
- Overcoming Prejudice
- Using Differences between Speech Rate and Thought Rate
- Managing Receiver Apprehension

**How to Become a Better Listener**
- Listen with Your Eyes as Well as Your Ears
- Listen Mindfully
- Listen Skillfully
- Listen Ethically

**Improving Listening and Critical Thinking Skills**
- Separate Facts from Inferences
- Evaluate the Quality of Evidence
- Evaluate the Underlying Logic and Reasoning

**Analyzing and Evaluating Speeches**
- Understanding Criteria for Evaluating Speeches
- Identifying and Analyzing Rhetorical Strategies
- Giving Feedback to Others
- Giving Feedback to Yourself

# 3 Listening to Speeches

OBJECTIVES

**After studying this chapter you should be able to do the following:**

1. Identify the stages in the listening process.
2. List and describe five barriers to effective listening.
3. Discuss strategies for becoming a better listener.
4. Identify strategies for improving your note-taking skills.
5. Discuss the relationship between listening and critical thinking.
6. Use criteria for evaluating speeches.

A psychology professor had dedicated his life to teaching and worked hard to prepare interesting lectures, yet he found his students sitting through his talks with glassy-eyed expressions.[1] To find out what was on his students' minds if they were not focusing on psychology, he would, without warning, fire a blank from a gun and then ask his students to record their thoughts at the instant they heard the shot. Here is what he found:

20 percent were pursuing erotic thoughts or sexual fantasies.

20 percent were reminiscing about something (they weren't sure what they were thinking about).

20 percent were worrying about something or thinking about lunch.

8 percent were pursuing religious thoughts.

20 percent were reportedly listening.

12 percent were able to recall what the professor was talking about when the gun fired.

Like this professor, you would probably prefer that more than 12 percent of your audience could recall your messages. Understanding how listeners listen can help you improve your ability to connect with your audience. If you understand what holds listeners' attention, as well as how to navigate around the barriers to effective listening, you can make your messages stick like Velcro rather than slip off your listeners' minds like Teflon.

Considerable evidence also suggests that your own listening skills could be improved. Within twenty-four hours after listening to a lecture or speech, you will most likely recall only about 50 percent of the message. Forty-eight hours later, you are above average if you remember more than 25 percent of the message. Learning about listening can help you increase your listening skills so you can gain more benefits from the speeches your hear.

**Listening** is a complex process of selecting, attending to, creating meaning from, remembering, and responding to verbal and nonverbal messages. Understanding these components of listening can help you retain more, and it can help you be a better speaker and a better listener.

To **select** a sound, the first stage of listening, is to single out a message from several competing messages. As a public speaker, your job is to develop a presentation that motivates your listeners to focus on your message.

The sequel to selecting is attending. To **attend** to a sound is to focus on it. Most people's average attention span while listening to someone talk is about 8 seconds.[2] One of your key challenges as a public speaker is to capture and then hold the attention of your audience. Your choice of supporting material is often the key to gaining and maintaining attention.

Boiled down to its essence, communication is the process of **understanding**, or making sense of our experiences and sharing that sense with others.[3] As a speaker, your job is to facilitate listener understanding by making sure you clearly explain your ideas in terms and images to which your listeners can relate. Again, the challenge of being understood comes back to a focus on the audience.

The next stage in the listening process is *remembering*. To **remember** is to recall ideas and information. You hear more than one billion words each year, but how much information do you retain? It depends on how well you listen. Most listening experts believe that the main way to determine whether audience members have been listening is to determine what they remember. (That's the purpose of taking tests in school—to assess what you remember from what you've heard and read.)

The final stage in the listening process is **responding**. When listeners respond, they react with their behavior to what they have heard. That's why it's useful for public speakers to develop specific behavioral goals for their talks. As a speaker, you should identify what you'd like listeners to be able to *do* after you speak. It

**listening**
The process by which receivers select, attend to, create meaning from, remember, and respond to senders' messages

**select**
To single out a message from several competing messages

**attend**
To focus on incoming information for further processing

**understand**
To assign meaning to the information to which you attend

**remember**
To recall ideas and information

**respond**
to react with a change in behavior to a speaker's message

could be that you want them simply to remember and restate your key ideas. Or you may want them to vote for someone, buy something, or enroll in a course.

In this chapter we discuss how people listen, and we identify barriers and pitfalls that keep both speakers and audiences from listening effectively. Our goal is not only to help you remember what speakers say, but also to be a more thoughtful, ethical, and critical listener to the messages you hear. We'll offer tips to improve your ability to analyze and evaluate speeches, including your own.

## Overcoming Barriers to Effective Listening

Barriers are created when the listener doesn't select, attend, understand, remember, or respond to the message as planned by the speaker. The more you know about potential obstacles that keep your listeners from responding to your message the way you intend, the better able you will be to develop messages that hold their interest. Table 3.1 summarizes several barriers that keep listeners from being good listeners. We next discuss those barriers and how to deal with them.

**TABLE 3.1 Overcoming Barriers to Effective Listening**

| Barrier | Listener's Tasks | Speaker's Tasks |
|---|---|---|
| Information overload | • Concentrate harder on the message; identify the most important parts of the message. | • Develop a message that is clear and easy to understand. Use interesting supporting material. Build in redundancy. |
| Personal concerns | • Focus on the speaker's message rather than on your own self-talk | • Use attention-holding strategies and "wake-up" messages. |
| Outside distractions | • Assertively attempt to control the listening environment. | • Monitor the physical arrangements before you begin your speech. Take action by doing such things as closing the shades if there are distractions outside, or turning up the air-conditioner if it's too warm. |
| Prejudice | • Focus on the message, not on the messenger. | • Use strong opening statements that focus on listeners' interests. |
| Differences between speech rate and thought rate | • Mentally summarize the speaker's message while you listen. | • Build in redundancy. Be well organized and use strategies to maintain your listeners' attention throughout your speech. |
| Receiver apprehension | • Make an audio recording of the speaker, mentally summarize the message, and take well-organized notes. | • Provide a clear preview statement of your major ideas, use appropriate internal summaries, summarize major ideas at the end of your message, and use appropriate reinforcing presentation aids during your talk. |

## Managing Information Overload

We spend a large part of each day listening. That's good news and bad news. The good news is that because we listen a lot, we have the potential to become very effective listeners. The bad news is that instead of getting better at it, we often tune out because we hear so much information that we get tired of listening. Listening researchers have developed what they call the **working memory theory of listening,** which explains why we sometimes just don't listen well. The theory suggests that when a listener's capacity is reached (when our working memory is full), then it's harder to concentrate and remember what we hear.[4]

Although this theory may make it appear that there's nothing you can do as either a speaker or a listener to manage this problem, several strategies can both help ensure that those who listen to you continue to attend to your message and help you improve your own listening skill.

**What You Can Do as a Speaker** You can keep your audience from tuning out by making sure your speech has a balance between new information and supporting material such as stories and examples. A speech that is too dense—chock-full of facts, new definitions, and undeveloped ideas—can make listening a tedious process. On the other hand, listeners don't want to listen to a bare-bones outline of ideas; they need ideas that are fleshed out with illustrations. Pace the flow of new ideas and information. Communication expert Frank E. X. Dance recommends a 30/70 ratio: 30 percent of your speaking time should be spent presenting new ideas and information, and 70 percent of your time should be spent supporting your ideas with vivid examples and interesting stories.[5]

Another way to combat information overload as a speaker is to build redundancy into your message. If listeners miss the idea the first time you present it, perhaps they will catch it during your concluding summary. Repeating key ideas can be part of that 70 percent of your message that extends the new information you present.

**working memory theory of listening**
A theory that suggests that listeners find it difficult to concentrate and remember when their short-term working memories are full

**What You Can Do as a Listener** If you find yourself tuning a speaker out because you're just tired of listening to someone talk, make a special effort to concentrate on the information you're hearing. The key to being a good listener is to recognize when you're *not* being a good listener and then to adjust how you are listening. Making sure that you are looking at the speaker, sitting up straight, and remaining focused on the message can help perk up your listening power.

*Information overload is a barrier to effective listening for many students. You can, however, learn to overcome this and other barriers and make yourself a better listener.*

[Photo: David Butow/CORBIS SABA]

## Overcoming Personal Concerns

You are sitting in your African history class on a Friday afternoon. It's a beautiful day. You slump into your seat, open your notebook, and prepare to take notes on the lecture. As the professor talks about an upcoming assignment, you begin to think about how you are going to spend your Saturday. One thought leads to another as you mentally plan your weekend. Suddenly you hear your professor say, "For Monday's test, you will be expected to know the principles I've just reviewed." What principles? What test? You were present in class, and you did *hear* the professor's lecture, but you're not sure what was said.

Your own thoughts are among the biggest competitors for your attention when you are a member of an audience. Most of us would rather listen to our own inner speech than to the message of a public speaker. As the psychology professor with the gun found, sex, lunch, worries, and daydreams are distractions for the majority of listeners.

**What You Can Do as a Speaker** To counteract the problem of listeners' focusing on their personal concerns instead of your message, consciously work to maintain your audience's attention by using occasional wake-up messages such as "Now listen carefully because this will affect your future grade (or family, or employment)." Delivering your message effectively by using good eye contact, speaking with appropriate volume and vocal variation, and using appropriate gestures for emphasis can also help keep listeners listening.

**What You Can Do as a Listener** To stay focused, it's important that you stop the mental conversation you're having with yourself about ideas unrelated to the speaker's message. Be aware of thoughts, worries, and daydreams that are competing for your attention. Then, once you are aware that you are off task, return your attention to what the speaker is saying.

## Reducing Outside Distractions

While sitting in class, you notice that a fluorescent light is flickering overhead. Two classmates behind you are swapping stories about their favorite soap opera plots. Out the window you see a varsity football hero struggling to break into his car to retrieve the keys he left in the ignition. As your history professor drones on about the Bay of Pigs invasion, you find it difficult to focus on his lecture. Most of us don't listen well when physical distractions compete with the speaker.

**What You Can Do as a Speaker** To minimize distractions, be aware of anything that might sidetrack your listeners' attention. For example, look at the way the room is arranged. Are the chairs arranged to allow listeners a clear view of you and any presentation aids you might use? Is there distracting or irrelevant information written on a chalkboard or whiteboard? Try to empathize with listeners by imagining what they will be looking at when you speak. Check out the room ahead of time, sit where your audience will be seated, and look for possible distractions. Then reduce or eliminate distractions (such as by closing windows or lowering shades to limit visual and auditory distractions or turning off blinking fluorescent lights, if you can). Also, tactfully discourage whispering in the audience.

**What You Can Do as a Listener** When listening, you too can help manage the speaking and listening environment by being on the lookout for distractions or potential distractions. If you must, move to another seat if people near you are talking or a rude cell phone user continues a phone conversation. If the speaker has failed to monitor the listening environment, you may need to close the blinds, turn up the heat, turn off the lights, close the door, or do whatever is necessary to minimize distractions.

## Overcoming Prejudice

Your buddy is a staunch Democrat. He rarely credits a Republican with any useful ideas. So it's not surprising that when the Republican governor of your state makes a major televised speech outlining suggestions for improving the state's sagging economy, your friend finds the presentation ludicrous. As the speech is broadcast, your buddy constantly argues against each suggestion, mumbling comments about Republicans, business interests, and robbing the poor. The next day he is surprised to see editorials in the press praising the governor's speech. "Did they hear the same speech I did?" your friend wonders. Yes, they heard the same speech, but they listened differently. When you prejudge a message, your ability to understand it decreases.

Another way to prejudge a speech is to decide that the topic has little value for you before you even hear the message. Most of us at one time or another have not given our full attention to a speech because we decided beforehand that it was going to bore us.

Sometimes we make snap judgments about a speaker based on his or her appearance and then fail to listen because we have already dismissed his or her ideas as inconsequential or irrelevant. Female speakers often complain that males in the audience do not listen to them as attentively as they would to another male; members of ethnic and racial minorities may feel slighted in a similar way.

On the flip side, some people too readily accept what someone says just because they like the way the person looks, sounds, or dresses. For example, Tex believes that anyone with a Texas drawl must be an honest person. Such positive prejudices can also inhibit your ability to listen accurately to a message.

**What You Can Do as a Speaker** To keep your listeners from making snap judgments based on **prejudice**, do your best to get your audience's attention at the beginning of your message. Make sure you're not using examples, words, or phrases that could be misinterpreted. Keep your message focused on your listeners' interests, needs, hopes, and wishes.

When addressing an audience that may be critical of or hostile to your message, use detailed arguments and credible evidence. If you think audience members are likely to disagree with you, strong emotional appeals will be less successful than careful language, sound reasoning, and convincing evidence.

**What You Can Do as a Listener** One of the major problems with prejudice is being unaware of one's own preconceived notions. Guard against becoming so critical of a message that you don't listen to it or so impressed that you decide too quickly that the speaker is trustworthy without carefully examining the evidence the speaker offers. Keep your focus on the message rather than on the messenger.

## Using Differences between Speech Rate and Thought Rate

Ralph Nichols, a pioneer in listening research and training, has identified a listening problem that centers on the way you process the words you hear.[6] Most people talk at a rate of 125 words a minute. But you have the ability to listen to up to 700 words a minute, and some studies suggest that you may be able to listen to 1,200 words a minute! Regardless of the exact numbers, you have the ability to process words much faster than you generally need to. The problem is that the difference gives you time to ignore a speaker periodically. Eventually, you stop listening; the extra time allows you to daydream and drift away from the message.

Nichols suggests that the different rates of speech and thought need not be a listening liability. Instead of drifting away from the speech, you can enhance your listening effectiveness by mentally summarizing from time to time what the speaker has said.

**prejudice**
Preconceived opinions, attitudes, and beliefs about a person, place, thing, or message

**What You Can Do as a Speaker** Be aware of your listeners' tendency to stop paying attention. If they can process your message much faster than you can deliver it, you need to build in message redundancy, use clear transitions, be well organized, and make your major ideas clear. Just talking faster won't do much good. Even if you could speak as fast as 200 words a minute, your listeners would still want you to go about four times faster than that. So develop a well-structured message that uses appropriate internal summaries to help your listeners catch your message even when they've tuned out for a bit here and there.

**What You Can Do as a Listener** Because you have the ability to think much faster than people speak, you can use that dazzling mental power to stay focused on the message. Here's a powerful technique: Periodically making a mental summary of what a speaker has said can dramatically increase your ability to remember the information. The difference in speech rate and thought rate gives you time to sprinkle in several mental summaries while listening to a message.

### Managing Receiver Apprehension

You already know about speaker apprehension, or the fear of speaking to others, but did you know that some people may be fearful of *listening* to information? Researchers have discovered a listening barrier called receiver apprehension. **Receiver apprehension** is the fear of misunderstanding or misinterpreting, or of not being able to adjust psychologically to, messages spoken by others.[7] Some people are just uncomfortable or nervous about hearing new information; their major worry is that they won't be able to understand the message. If you are one of those people, you may have difficulty understanding all you hear because your anxiety about listening creates "noise" that may interfere with how much information you comprehend.

**What You Can Do as a Speaker** Be mindful that some listeners may be anxious about understanding your message. You can help people with receiver apprehension by being more redundant. Offer clear preview statements that give an overview of your main ideas. Include appropriate summaries while you're making transitions from one point to the next. Summarize major ideas at the end of your talk.[8] Using presentation aids to summarize key ideas visually—such as by listing major points on an overhead transparency, PowerPoint™ slide, chalkboard, or flipchart—can also help increase comprehension and decrease receiver apprehension.

**What You Can Do as a Listener** If you experience receiver apprehension, you will have to work harder to comprehend the information presented by others. Using a tape recorder to record a lecture may help you feel more comfortable and less anxious about trying to remember each point made by the speaker.[9] Another strategy to overcome this barrier is to summarize mentally what you hear a speaker saying during a speech. Taking accurate notes is an active strategy that can also help you feel more comfortable about being a listener.

> **RECAP**
>
> **Barriers to Effective Listening**
>
> Both speakers and listeners can use strategies to overcome these obstacles:
>
> - Information overload
> - Personal concerns
> - Outside distractions
> - Prejudice
> - Speech rate/thought rate differences
> - Receiver apprehension

## How to Become a Better Listener

Now that we have examined barriers to effective listening and suggested a few strategies to overcome those barriers and be both a better speaker and a better listener, we offer a basketful of additional strategies for improving your listening skill (summarized in

**receiver apprehension**
The fear of misunderstanding or misinterpreting the spoken messages of others

TABLE 3.2 How to Enhance Your Listening Skills

| | The Good Listener . . . | The Poor Listener . . . |
|---|---|---|
| **Listen with Your Eyes as Well as Your Ears** | • Looks for nonverbal cues to enhance understanding<br>• Adapts to the speaker's delivery | • Focuses only on the words<br>• Is easily distracted by the delivery of the speech |
| **Listen Mindfully** | • Is aware of whether or not he or she is listening<br>• Controls emotions<br>• Mentally asks, "What's in it for me?" | • Is not aware of whether he or she is on-task or off-task<br>• Erupts emotionally when listening<br>• Does not attempt to relate to the information personally |
| **Listen Skillfully** | • Identifies the listening goal<br>• Listens for major ideas<br>• Seeks opportunities to practice listening skills<br>• Understands and adapts his or her listening style to the speaker<br>• Listens actively by resorting, rephrasing, and repeating what is heard | • Does not have a listening goal in mind<br>• Listens for isolated facts<br>• Avoids listening to difficult information<br>• Is not aware of how to capitalize on his or her listening style<br>• Listens passively, making no effort to engage with the information heard |
| **Listen Ethically** | • Clearly communicates listening expectations<br>• Is sensitive to and tolerant of differences | • Makes no effort to respond appropriately to a speaker's message<br>• Expects others to have the same beliefs, values and cultural expectations he or she has |

Table 3.2). Specifically, we'll help you listen with your eyes. We'll help you be a mindful listener. And finally, we will note specific behaviors that can help you listen skillfully.

## Listen with Your Eyes as Well as Your Ears

To listen with your eyes is to be attuned to the unspoken cues of a speaker. Nonverbal cues play a major role in communicating a message. One expert has estimated that as much as 93 percent of the emotional content of a speech is conveyed by nonverbal cues.[10] Even though this statistic does not apply in every situation, emotion is primarily communicated by unspoken messages. To listen with your eyes, you need to accurately interpret what you see while ensuring that you don't allow yourself to be distracted by it, even when a speaker has poor delivery.

**Accurately Interpret Nonverbal Messages** Because the nonverbal message plays such a powerful role in affecting how you respond to a speaker, it's important to accurately interpret what a speaker is expressing nonverbally. A speaker's facial expressions will help you identify the emotions being communicated; a speaker's posture and gestures often reinforce the intensity of the specific emotion expressed.[11] If you have trouble understanding a speaker because he or she speaks too softly or speaks in an unfamiliar dialect, get close enough so that you can see the speaker's mouth. A good view can increase your level of attention and improve your understanding.

To increase your skill in accurately interpreting nonverbal messages, consider the following suggestions:

- *Consider nonverbal cues in context.* When interpreting an unspoken message, don't just focus on one nonverbal cue; consider the situation you and the speaker are in.
- *Look for clusters of cues.* Instead of focusing on just one bit of behavior, look for several nonverbal cues to increase the accuracy of your interpretation of a speaker's message.
- *Look for cues that communicate liking, power, and responsiveness.* A nonverbal cue (eye contact, facial expression, body orientation) can often express whether someone likes us. We note people's degree of power or influence over us by the way they dress, how much space they have around them, or whether they are relaxed or tense. (People who perceive themselves as having more power than those around them are usually more relaxed.) Or we can observe whether someone is interested or focused on us by eye contact, head nods, facial expressions, and tone of voice.

**Adapt to the Speaker's Delivery** Good listeners focus on a speaker's message, not on his or her delivery style. To be a good listener, you must adapt to the particular idiosyncrasies some speakers have. You may have to ignore or overlook a speaker's tendency to mumble, speak in a monotone, or fail to make eye contact. Perhaps more difficult still, you may even have to forgive a speaker's lack of clarity or coherence. Rather than mentally criticizing an unpolished speaker, you may need to be sympathetic and try harder to concentrate on the message. Good listeners focus on the message, not the messenger.

Poor speakers are not the only challenge to good listening. You also need to guard against glib, well-polished speakers. An attractive style of delivery does not necessarily mean that a speaker's message is credible. Don't let a smooth-talking salesperson convince you to buy something without carefully considering the content of his or her message.

> **RECAP**
>
> **Listen with Your Eyes as Well as Your Ears**
>
> Accurately interpret nonverbal messages:
> - Consider context.
> - Look for clusters.
> - Look for cues of liking.
>
> Adapt your listening to the speaker's delivery.

## Listen Mindfully

To be a mindful listener is to be aware of what you are doing when listening to others. The unmindful listener is not conscious of whether he or she is paying attention or daydreaming. Skilled listeners are mentally focused on the listening task. How do you do that? Here are specific strategies to help you be a mindful listener.

**Be Aware of Whether You Are Listening or Not** Listening boils down to this: You are either on-task or off-task. You are either selecting and attending to a message, or you're not mentally engaged with what you are hearing. What's vital, yet simple, is that you be *aware* of whether you are on- or off-task when listening to someone. Two listening researchers found that good listeners do the following:[12]

- Put their own thoughts aside
- Are present mentally as well as physically
- Make a conscious, mindful effort to listen
- Invest time in listening, patiently letting the speaker make his or her point
- Are open-minded

Bad listeners do just the opposite; they are distracted by their own thoughts, are mentally absent, are impatient, and are less open to what they hear.

It's important that you recognize when you are off-task. If you become aware that you're not listening, research has found that you can increase your motivation to stay on-task by reminding yourself why listening is important.[13] Periodically engage in "self-talk" to tell yourself why the message you're hearing can be helpful or useful to you.

**Monitor Your Emotional Reaction to a Message** Heightened emotions can affect your ability to understand a message. If you become angry at a word or phrase a speaker uses, your listening comprehension decreases. Depending on their cultural backgrounds, religious convictions, and political views, listeners may become emotionally aroused by certain words. For most listeners, words that connote negative opinions about their ethnic origin, nationality, or religious views can trigger strong emotions. Cursing and obscene language are red flags for other listeners.

Yin Ping is an Asian American who has distinguished himself as a champion debater on the college debate team. One sly member of an opposing team sought to distract him by quoting a bigoted statement that disparaged Asian Americans for "taking over the country." It was tempting for Yin Ping to respond emotionally to the insult, but he kept his wits, refuted the argument, and went on to win the debate. When someone uses a word or phrase you find offensive, it's important to overcome your repugnance and continue to listen. Don't let a speaker's language close down your mind.

How can you keep your emotions in check when you hear something that sets you off? First, recognize when your emotional state is affecting your rational thought. Second, use the skill of self-talk to calm yourself down. Say to yourself, "I'm not going to let this anger get in the way of listening and understanding." You can also focus for a moment on your breathing to calm down.

**Be a Selfish Listener** Although it may sound crass, being a selfish listener can help you maintain your powers of concentration. If you find your attention waning, ask yourself questions such as "What's in it for me?" and "How can I use information

## LEARNING FROM GREAT SPEAKERS

### César Chávez (1927–1993)

As a young man, American labor leader César Chávez experienced the hard work and harsh working conditions of the migrant farm worker. Listening both to his fellow farm workers and to representatives of a self-help group called the Community Service Organization, Chávez became acutely aware of the way the workers were exploited. He became a part-time organizer for the Community Service Organization, registering farm workers to vote. By the early 1950s Chávez assumed a leadership role in informing field workers of their rights. One source notes,

> He worried because he felt he wasn't a good speaker. So at first, he did more listening than speaking. In time, he grew more confident and found that people listened to him and liked his message.[14]

César Chávez found that listening to others helped him learn to motivate others to listen to him. The union he founded, the United Farm Workers of America, continues to listen to the concerns of field workers.

Effective speakers not only listen to audience-member ideas before giving a presentation but are also sensitive to listener messages, both spoken ones and especially unspoken ones, while giving a speech. Skilled speakers also listen to audience reactions after the speech because those reactions will help them in preparing for the next speech.

[Photo: Adele Starr/AP Wide World Photos]

from this talk?" Granted, you will find more useful information in some presentations than in others—but be alert to the possibility in all speeches. Find ways to benefit from the information you are receiving, and try to connect it with your own experiences and needs.

> **RECAP**
>
> **Listen Mindfully**
>
> - Be aware of whether you are listening or not.
> - Monitor and control your emotional reactions.
> - Be a selfish listener.

## Listen Skillfully

Besides being aware of nonverbal messages and being mindful listeners, good listeners practice behaviors that help them stay focused and remember what they've heard. They identify their listening goal, listen for major ideas, practice good listening methods, adapt their listening style as necessary, and are active listeners.

**Identify Your Listening Goal** As Figure 3.1 shows, you invest a lot of your communication time in listening. If you are a typical student, you spend over 80 percent of your day involved in communication-related activities.[15] You listen a lot; your challenge is to stay on course and keep your listening focused.

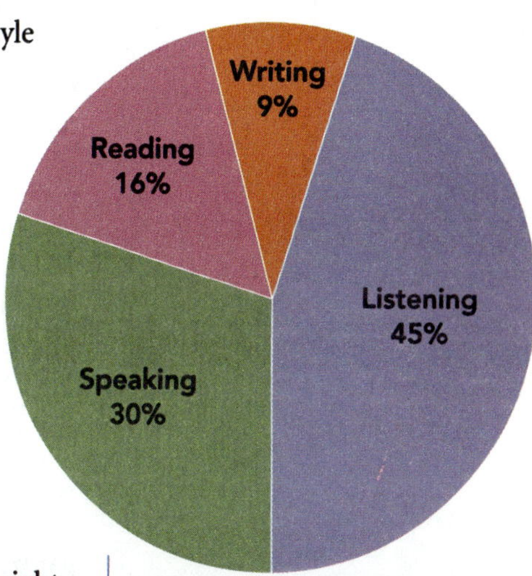


FIGURE 3.1 *You listen a lot: A typical student spends about 9% of his or her communication time writing, 16% reading, 30% speaking, and at least 45% listening.*

One way to stay focused is to determine your listening purpose. There are at least four major listening goals: for pleasure, to empathize, to evaluate, and to gain information. Being conscious of your listening goal can help you listen more effectively. If, for example, your listening goal is simply to enjoy what you hear, you need not listen with the same intensity as when you want to remember what you hear.

**Listening for Pleasure** You listen to some things just for the fun of it. You might watch TV, listen to music, go to a movie, or chat with a friend. You won't be tested on *Friends* reruns. Nor will you be asked to remember every joke in David Letterman's monologue. So, when listening for pleasure, just enjoy what you hear. You can, however, observe how effective speakers or entertainers gain and maintain your attention and keep you interested in their messages.

**Listening to Empathize** To have empathy means to feel what the speaker is feeling. Usually, empathic listening occurs in one-on-one listening situations between friends. Sometimes, in your job, you may need to listen empathically to a client, customer, or coworker. Listening with empathy requires these essential steps:

1. **Stop.** Stop what you are doing and give your complete attention to the speaker.
2. **Look.** Make eye contact and pay attention to nonverbal cues that reveal emotions.
3. **Listen.** Pay attention to both the details of the message and the major ideas.
4. **Imagine.** Visualize how you would feel if you had experienced what the speaker experienced.
5. **Check.** Check your understanding of the message by asking questions to clarify what you heard and by summarizing what you think you heard.

**Listening to Evaluate** When you evaluate a message, you are making a judgment about its content. You are interested in whether the information is reliable, true, or useful. When evaluating what you hear, the challenge is not to become so critical of the message that you miss a key point the speaker is making. That is, when listening, you must juggle two difficult tasks: You must make judgments as well as understand and recall the information you are hearing. Our point is this: When you are listening to a message and also evaluating it, you have to work harder than at other times to understand the speaker's message. Your biases and judgments act as noise that can cause you to misunderstand the intended meaning of the message.

**Listening for Information** Since elementary school, you have been in listening situations in which someone wanted you to learn something. Keys to listening for information are listening for the details of a message and making certain you link the details to major ideas. As we will describe, poor listeners either listen only for facts and pieces of a message or are interested only in the bottom line. By concentrating on both facts and major ideas, while at the same time mentally summarizing the information you hear, you can dramatically increase your ability to remember messages. Also, remember to compare unfamiliar information to ideas and concepts with which you are familiar.

**Listen for Major Ideas** In a classic study, Ralph Nichols asked both good and poor listeners what their listening strategies were.[16] The poor listeners indicated that they listened for facts, such as names and dates. The good listeners reported that they listened for major ideas and principles. Facts are useful only when you can connect them to a principle or concept. In speeches, facts as well as examples are used primarily to support major ideas. Try to summarize in your mind the major ideas that the specific facts support.

If you heard President Barack Obama deliver his Inaugural Address in Washington, D.C., on the cold morning of January 20, 2009, you heard him introduce his key idea about two minutes into his speech: "On this day, we gather because we have chosen hope over fear, unity of purpose over conflict and discord." A good listener would recognize this statement immediately as the core idea of the speech.

How can you tell what the major ideas in a speech are? A speaker who is well organized or familiar with good speaking techniques will offer a preview of the major ideas early in the speech. If no preview is provided, listen for the speaker to enumerate major points: "My first point is that the history of Jackson County is evident in its various styles of architecture." Transitional phrases and a speaker's internal summaries are other clues that can help you identify the major points. If your speaker provides few overt indicators, you may have to discover them on your own. In that event, mentally summarize the ideas that are most useful to you. Be a selfish listener: Treat a disorganized speech as a river with gold in the sands, and take your mental mining pan and search for the nuggets of meaning.

**Practice Listening** Because you spend at least 45 percent of your day listening, you may wonder why we suggest that you practice listening. The reason is that listening skills do not develop automatically. You learn to swim by getting proper instruction; you're unlikely to develop good aquatic skills just by jumping in the water and flailing around. Similarly, you will learn to listen by practicing the methods we recommend. Researchers believe that poor listeners avoid challenge. For example, they listen to and watch TV situation comedies rather than documentaries or other informative programs. Your listening skill develops as you listen to speeches, music, and programs with demanding content.

**Understand Your Listening Style** New research suggests that not everyone listens to information in the same way. There are at least four different **listening styles**—preferred ways of making sense out of spoken messages. Listening researchers Kitty Watson, Larry Barker, and James Weaver discovered that listeners tend to be either people-oriented, action-oriented, content-oriented, or time-oriented.[17] Understanding your listening style can help you become a better and more flexible listener.[18]

**listening styles**
Preferred ways of making sense out of spoken messages

About 40 percent of listeners have one primary listening style; another 40 percent use more than one style; and about 20 percent don't have a listening style preference. As you read the descriptions of the four listening styles, see if you can determine whether you are part of the 40 percent of the population who have one predominant listening style, the 40 percent who have a couple of styles, or the 20 percent who have no style preference.[19] The best listeners are flexible listeners who can adapt their style to fit the occasion and the person speaking.[20]

**People-Oriented Listeners** You're a **people-oriented listener** if you are comfortable listening to people express feelings and emotions. It's likely that you are highly empathic and that you seek common ground with the person you are listening to. You are easily moved by poignant illustrations and anecdotes.

**Action-Oriented Listeners** If you like information that is well organized, brief, and precise, but you don't like long stories or digressions from the main ideas, you're likely to be an **action-oriented listener**. The action-oriented listener wants people to get to the point and listens for actions that need to be taken. Action-oriented listeners also seem to be more skeptical than people with other listening styles. They prefer to be given evidence to support the recommendations for action.

**Content-Oriented Listeners** **Content-oriented listeners** prefer to listen to complex information that is laced with facts and details. You're a content-oriented listener if you reject messages because they don't have adequate support. Content-oriented listeners make good judges or lawyers because they enjoy listening to debates and hearing arguments for and against ideas.[21]

**Time-Oriented Listeners** You're a **time-oriented listener** if you like your messages delivered succinctly. Time is important to you; you want the information you hear to be presented concisely because you are busy. Time-oriented listeners don't like rambling, long-winded messages with lots of filler. Like action-oriented listeners, they want the speaker to come to the point, and they are even more interested in saving time and getting the essential ideas in sound bites.

Knowing your listening style can help you better adapt to a speaker whose style is not your style. For example, if you are a time-oriented listener and a speaker is telling long stories and meandering through the material, you'll have to tell yourself to concentrate harder on the message. If you are a people-oriented listener and you're listening to a message that's primarily facts, principles, and ideas, you will be a better listener if you understand why the message may not be holding your attention and work to focus on the message. We've emphasized the importance of being an audience-centered speaker, but the opposite is true as well: As a listener you can increase your concentration if you adjust and adapt your listening style to the speaking styles of the speakers you hear. As we note in Chapter 2, the key, whether you are a speaker or a listener, is to ethically adapt and adjust to enhance the quality of communication.

**Become an Active Listener** An active listener is one who remains alert and mentally re-sorts, rephrases, and repeats key information while listening to a speech. Because you can listen to words much faster than a speaker can speak them, it's natural for your mind to wander. But you can use the extra time to focus on interpreting what the speaker says.

**1. Re-sort.** Use your listening time to re-sort disorganized or disjointed ideas. If the speaker is rambling, seek ways to rearrange his or her ideas into a new, more logical pattern. For example, re-sort the ideas into a chronological pattern: What happened first, second, and so on? If the speaker hasn't chunked the ideas into a logical framework, see if you can find a structure to help you reorganize the information. Yes, it would be useful if the speaker had done that. But when the speaker isn't organized, you'll benefit if you can turn a jumbled mass of information into a structure that makes sense to you. For example, a speaker says, "There are three key dates to remember: 1776, 1492, and 1861." You re-sort: 1491, 1776, 1861.

**people-oriented listener**
Someone who is comfortable listening to others express feelings and emotions

**action-oriented listener**
Someone who prefers information that is well organized, brief, and precise

**content-oriented listener**
Someone who prefers messages that are supported with facts and details

**time-oriented listener**
Someone who likes succinct messages

RECAP

### Listen Skillfully

Identify your listening goal:

- For pleasure
- To empathize
- To evaluate
- For information

Listen for major ideas.
Practice listening.
Understand your listening style:

- People-oriented
- Action-oriented
- Content-oriented
- Time-oriented

Become an active listener:

- Re-sort
- Rephrase
- Repeat

**2. Rephrase.** Mentally summarize the key points or information that you want to remember. Listen for the main ideas and then paraphrase them in your own words. You are more likely to remember your mental paraphrase of the information than the exact words of the speaker. If you can, try to summarize what the speaker is saying in a phrase that might fit on a bumper sticker. Listening for "information handles" provided by the speaker in the form of previews, transitions, signposts, and summary statements can also help you remain actively involved as a listener. A speaker says, "If we don't stop the destructive overspending of the defense budget, our nation will very quickly find itself much deeper in debt and unable to meet the many needs of its citizens." You rephrase: "We should spend less on defense, or we will have more problems."

**3. Repeat.** Finally, do more than just rephrase the information as you listen to it. Periodically *repeat* key points you want to remember. Go back to essential ideas and restate them to yourself every five minutes or so. If you follow these steps for active listening, you will find yourself feeling stimulated and engaged instead of tired and bored as you listen to even the dullest of speakers.

## Listen Ethically

An effective listener does more than just gain an accurate understanding of a speaker's message; effective listeners are also ethical listeners. An ethical listener participates in a communication event by honestly communicating his or her expectations, providing helpful feedback, and being sensitive to and tolerating differences when listening to others. In the fourth century B.C.E., Aristotle warned, "Let men be on their guard against those who flatter and mislead the multitude." And contemporary rhetorician Harold Barrett has said that the audience is the "necessary source of correction" for the behavior of a speaker.[22] The following guidelines for ethical listening incorporate what Barrett calls "attributes of the good audience."

**Communicate Your Expectations and Feedback** As an audience member, you have the right—even the responsibility—to enter a communication situation with expectations about both the message and how the speaker will deliver it. Know what information and ideas you want to get out of the communication transaction. Expect a coherent, organized, and competently delivered presentation. Communicate your objectives and react to the speaker's message and delivery through appropriate nonverbal and verbal feedback. For example, maintain eye contact with the speaker. Nod in agreement when you support something the speaker says. There is evidence that by being a supportive listener (by having eye contact with the speaker, signaling agreement, and being attentive) you help the speaker feel more comfortable and less nervous.[23] We're not suggesting, however, that you fake your support for a speaker. If you show, with an honest quizzical look, that you do not understand a speaker's point, you can help an attentive, audience-centered speaker rephrase the message for better listener comprehension. Turn your head to one side and tilt it slightly forward to communicate that you are having trouble hearing. If a question-and-answer period follows the speech, ask questions you may still have about the speaker's topic or point of view.

**Be Sensitive to and Tolerant of Differences** As an ethical listener, remember that your preferred approach to speaking and listening may differ from the approach a speaker is using. But your preference doesn't make the speaker's approach a wrong one. For example, suppose you were to attend a high-school baccalaureate ceremony at which the speaker was a dynamic African American minister who used a duet-style, call-and-response type of speaking, in which the audience periodically responds verbally to the speaker. If you were to disregard the minister's delivery for being too flamboyant, you might miss out on a powerful message. Different cultures have different styles of speaking.

Diverse cultural norms can sometimes pose a complex ethical-listening challenge. For example, political leader and civil rights advocate Jesse Jackson has been accused of making dishonest claims in some speeches about his background and behavior. He has said that he left the University of Illinois because racism on the football team caused him to be passed over for starting quarterback—yet former teammates insist that he did not become starting quarterback simply because he was not the strongest player. Jackson has also overstated the poverty he experienced as a child, when in fact he grew up in a fairly comfortable middle-class home. Although many have criticized exaggeration of this kind, at least one communication researcher has defended Jackson, arguing that although his "tall tales" are not necessarily "the truth" in a strictly objective sense, they are part of a valid African American oral tradition that focuses on the "symbolic import of the story" and in which speakers traditionally exaggerate to enhance the impact of their illustrations.[24] When you consider the cultural expectations and backgrounds of both the speaker and the listeners, you will be in a better position to interpret what is being expressed.

Be attentive and courteous. Consider cultural norms and audience expectations as part of the context within which you listen to and evaluate a speaker. Making an effort to understand the needs, goals, and interests of both the speaker and other audience members can help you judge how to react appropriately and ethically as a listener.

RECAP

### Listen Ethically

- Communicate your expectations and feedback.
- Be sensitive to and tolerant of cultural and individual differences.

# Improving Listening and Critical Thinking Skills

Effective listening requires the ability to listen critically. Listening critically and thinking critically both involve a variety of skills we reexamine throughout this text. **Critical listening** is the process of listening to evaluate the quality, appropriateness, value, or importance of the information you hear. Related to being a critical listener is being a critical thinker. **Critical thinking** is the process of making judgments about the conclusions presented in what you see, hear, and read. The goal of a critical listener or a critical thinker is to evaluate information in order to make a choice. Whether you are listening to a political candidate giving a persuasive presentation to get your vote, a radio announcer extolling the virtues of a new herbal weight-loss pill, or someone asking you to invest in a new technology company, your goal as a critical listener is to assess the quality of the information and the validity of the conclusions presented.

We should emphasize that being a critical listener does not mean you're looking only for what the speaker says that is wrong; we're not suggesting that you listen to a speaker just to pounce on the message and the messenger at the conclusion of the speech. Listen to identify what the speaker does that is effective as well as to identify what conclusions don't hold up. How does a critical listener do this? Consider the following skills.

**critical listening**
Evaluating the quality of information, ideas, and arguments presented by a speaker

**critical thinking**
Making judgments about the conclusions presented in what you see, hear, and read

## Separate Facts from Inferences

The ability to separate facts from inferences is a basic critical-thinking and listening skill. **Facts** are information that has been proven true by direct observation. For

**fact**
Something that has been proven to be true by direct observation

*Critical listeners must pay close attention and keep an open mind in order to separate facts from inferences and to evaluate the quality of evidence, logic, reasoning, and the use of rhetorical strategies.*

[Photo:Loungepark/Getty Images Inc. RF]

example, it has been directly observed that water boils at 212 degrees Fahrenheit, that the direction of the magnetic north pole can be found by consulting a compass, and that U.S. presidents have been inaugurated on January 20 every four years since 1937. An **inference** is a conclusion based on partial information, or an evaluation that has not been directly observed. You infer that your favorite sports team will win the championship or that it will rain tomorrow. You can also infer, if more Republicans than Democrats are elected to Congress, that the next president might be a Republican. But you can only know this for a *fact* after the presidential election. Facts are in the realm of certainty; inferences are in the realm of probability and opinion—where most arguments advanced by public speakers reside. A critical listener knows that when a politician running for office claims, "It's a fact that my opponent is not qualified to be elected," this statement is *not* a fact, but an inference.

## Evaluate the Quality of Evidence

**Evidence** consists of the facts, examples, opinions, and statistics that a speaker uses to support a conclusion. Researchers have documented that the key element in swaying a jury is the quality and quantity of the evidence presented to support a case.[25] Without credible supporting evidence, it would not be wise to agree with a speaker's conclusion.

What should you listen for when trying to decide whether evidence is credible? When, for example, a radio announcer says "it is a fact that this herbal weight-loss pill helps people lose weight," your job as a listener is to determine whether that statement is, in fact, credible. Has it been proven by direct observation to be true? The speaker has an obligation to provide evidence to support the statement asserted.

Some speakers will support a conclusion with examples. But if the examples aren't typical, or only one or two examples are offered, or other examples are known to differ from the one the speaker is using, then you should question the conclusion.

Another form of evidence a speaker might use to convince you is an opinion. Simply stated, an opinion is a quoted comment from someone. The best opinions come from reliable, credible sources. What makes a source credible? A credible source

**inference**
A conclusion based on partial information, or an evaluation that has not been directly observed

**evidence**
The facts, examples, opinions, and statistics that a speaker uses to support a conclusion

is someone who has the credentials, experience, and skill to make an observation about the topic at hand. Listen for whom a speaker cites when quoting an expert on a subject.

A fourth kind of evidence often used, especially with a skeptical listener, is statistics. A statistic is a number that summarizes a collection of examples. Some of the same questions that should be asked about other forms of evidence should be asked about statistics: Are the statistics reliable, unbiased, recent, representative, and valid?

Here we've introduced you to the importance of *listening for* good evidence. Because evidence is an important element of public speaking, we'll provide more information about how to *use* evidence when we discuss using supporting material, in Chapter 6, and using evidence to persuade, in Chapter 15.

## Evaluate the Underlying Logic and Reasoning

An effective critical listener listens not only for evidence, but also for the overall structure of the logic, or argument, the speaker uses to reach a conclusion. **Logic** is a formal system of rules applied to reach a conclusion. A speaker is logical when he or she offers appropriate evidence to reach a valid, well-reasoned conclusion. For example, Angela tried to convince her listeners to take Slimlean as a weight-loss herb by pointing out that many stores sell this diet product, but that is not a logical framework for her conclusion. Just because Slimlean is readily available does not mean that it's effective and safe.

**Reasoning** is the process of drawing a conclusion from evidence within the logical framework of an argument. Can we reasonably conclude that anyone can lose weight by taking Slimlean simply because it's available in many stores? That kind of evidence does not support this conclusion. When a speaker seeks to change your behavior, listen carefully to the logic or structure of the arguments presented. Is the speaker trying to convince you to do something by offering one or two specific examples? Is the speaker reaching a conclusion based on a fundamental principle such as "All herbal diet supplements will cause you to lose weight"? The critical listener appropriately reviews the logic and reasoning used to reach a conclusion. When we discuss reasoning fallacies in Chapter 15, we will elaborate on the types of reasoning and we'll identify the ways speakers misuse logic, reasoning, and evidence.

You might reasonably suspect that a primary goal of a public-speaking class would be to enhance your speaking skill, and you'd be right. But in addition to becoming a better speaker, a study of communication principles and skills should help you to become a better *consumer* of messages. Becoming a critical listener and thinker is an important benefit of learning how messages are constructed. Researchers have found that a student who has completed any communication course—debate, argumentation, or public speaking—is likely to show improved critical-thinking ability. This introduction to critical listening and thinking skills is reinforced throughout the rest of the book by discussions of how to become an audience-centered public speaker.

RECAP

### Improving Listening and Critical Thinking Skills

Separate facts from inferences:

- Facts can be proven.
- Inferences are based on partial or unobserved evidence.

Evaluate evidence:

- Facts
- Examples
- Opinions
- Statistics

Evaluate the logic and reasoning of conclusions.

# Analyzing and Evaluating Speeches

Your critical thinking and listening skills will help you evaluate not only the speeches of others, but also your own speeches. When you evaluate something, you judge its worth and appropriateness. To make a judgment about the value of something, it's important

**logic**
A formal system of rules used to reach a conclusion

**reasoning**
The process of drawing a conclusion from evidence

to use relevant criteria. **Rhetorical criticism** is the process of using a method or standards to evaluate the effectiveness and appropriateness of messages.

To better understand the concept of rhetorical criticism, it's important to understand the meaning of the words *rhetoric* and *criticism*. The term *rhetoric* is both classical and contemporary.[26] The ancient Greek scholar Aristotle defined rhetoric as the faculty of discovering in any given case the available means of persuasion.[27] Another ancient Greek scholar, Isocrates, believed that effective rhetoric should have the "qualities of fitness for the occasion, propriety of style and originality of treatment."[28] A more contemporary rhetorical scholar, Kenneth Burke, said that rhetoric is a "symbolic means of inducing cooperation."[29] In summary, **rhetoric** is the process of using symbols to create meaning to achieve a goal. As a public speaker, you are a rhetorician in that you're using symbols (words, images, nonverbal cues) to create meaning in the minds of your listeners in order to achieve a goal (to inform, to persuade, to entertain).

To be a rhetorical critic is to evaluate the effectiveness and appropriateness of the message and the delivery of a presentation. Rhetorical critics often point to educator and philosopher John Dewey's description of criticism:

> Criticism . . . is not fault-finding. It is not pointing out evils to be reformed. It is judgment engaged in discriminating among values. It is talking through as to what is better and worse . . . with some consciousness of why the worse is worse.[30]

A critic not only evaluates a message but also helps *illuminate* it.[31] To illuminate is to shine a metaphorical light on a message to help others make better sense of that message.

One important goal of studying public speaking is to be a better rhetorical critic of the many messages you hear every day. In our discussion of how to analyze and evaluate speeches, we'll suggest criteria for evaluating messages and then offer specific strategies for sharing your evaluations with others.

## Understanding Criteria for Evaluating Speeches

What makes a speech good? For more than two thousand years, rhetorical scholars have been debating this question. Our purpose here is not to take you through the centuries of dialogue and debate about this issue but to offer practical ways to evaluate your own messages as well as the messages of others.

Your public-speaking teacher will probably have you use an evaluation form that lists the precise criteria for evaluating your speeches. Figure 3.2 lists the key questions to use in evaluating any speech. The questions reflect the audience-centered model of public speaking that we presented in Chapter 1.

Underlying any list of what a good speaker should do are two fundamental goals: *Any speech should be both effective and ethical.* The mission of the National Communication Association mirrors the same two goals—to promote effective and ethical communication. These two requirements can translate into general criteria for evaluating speeches you give as well as those you hear.

**The Message Should Be Effective** To be effective, the message of a speech should be understandable to listeners and should achieve its intended purpose.[32] Public speaking is sometimes called *public communication*. A goal of any communication effort is to create a common understanding of the message on the part of both the sender and the receiver. The words *common* and *communication* resemble each other. When listeners fail to comprehend the speaker's ideas, the speech fails. Even more difficult than saying something is saying something a listener will understand. In this course, you'll learn an array of principles and strategies to help

**rhetorical criticism**
The process of using a method or standards to evaluate the effectiveness and appropriateness of messages

**rhetoric**
The use of symbols to create meaning to achieve a goal

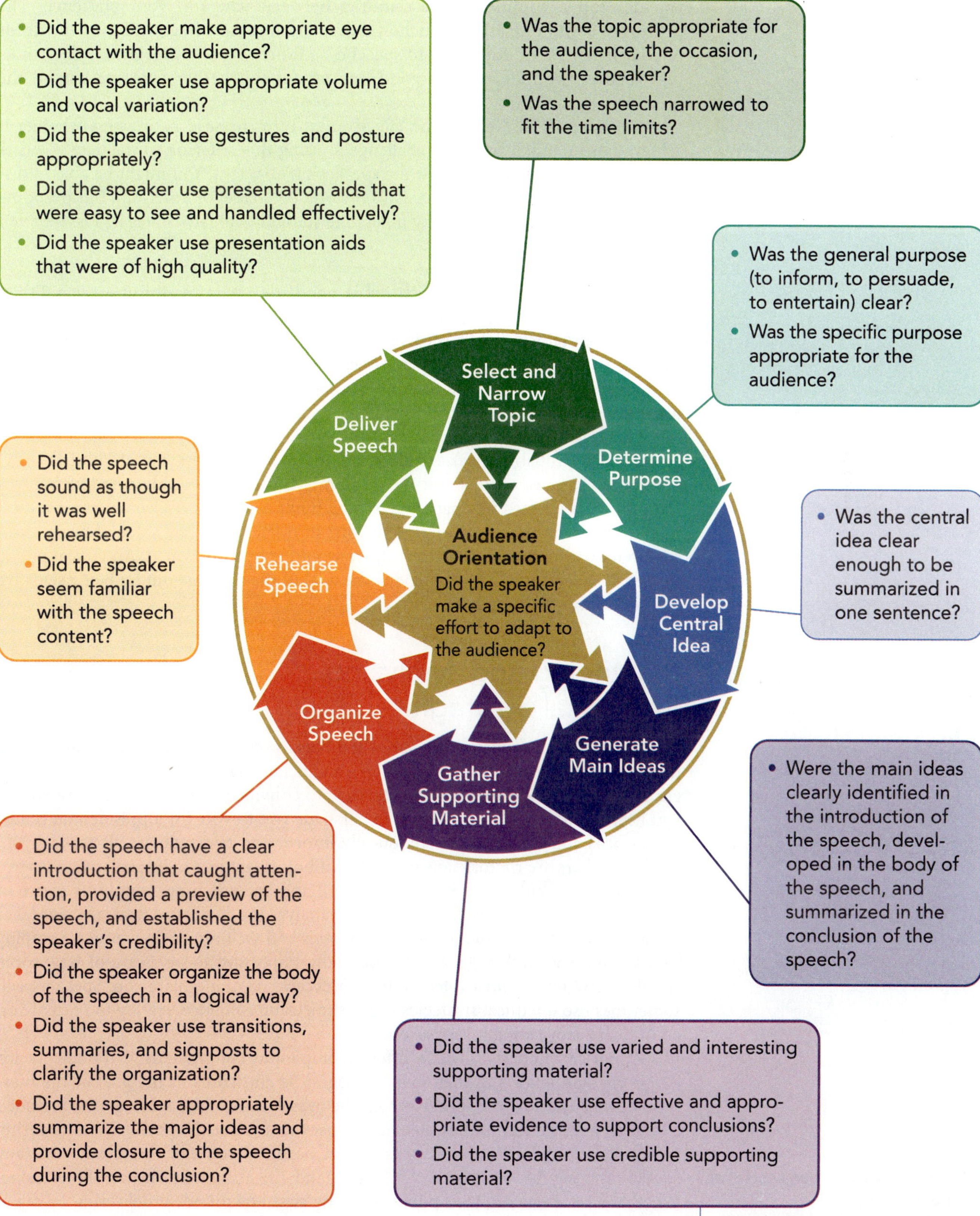


FIGURE 3.2 *Asking yourself these questions will help you evaluate any speech.*

you develop a common understanding between you and your audience. The process of communicating is anchored first and foremost in considering the needs of your listeners. As you listen to speeches, a fundamental criterion for determining whether the message is a good one or not is whether you understand the message.

Another way to evaluate the effectiveness of a message is to assess whether it achieved its intended goal. The challenge in using this criterion to evaluate speeches is that you may not always know the speaker's true intent. You might be able to discern whether the *general purpose* is to inform, persuade, or entertain, but decoding the *specific purpose* may be tricky unless the speaker explicitly states it. The best you can do is to be a careful listener.

**The Message Should Be Ethical** A good speaker is an ethical speaker. Ethics are the beliefs, values, and moral principles by which people determine what is right or wrong. An ethical public speaker tells the truth, gives credit for ideas and words where credit is due, and doesn't plagiarize. If a speaker's message is clearly understood by the audience and gets the reaction the speaker desired, but the speaker has used unethical means to achieve the goal, the message may be an *effective* message, but it is not an *appropriate* message.

You will probably speak to audiences that have a wide array of cultural backgrounds. Regardless of their cultural tradition, your listeners hold an underlying ethical code. As we noted in Chapter 2, although not every culture has the same ethical rules, many cultures adhere to precepts that in essence state the value of being audience-centered by considering how others would like to be treated. An ethical public speaker focuses not only on achieving the goal of the message but on being sensitive and responsive to listeners.

## Identifying and Analyzing Rhetorical Strategies

As we have noted, *rhetoric* is the use of symbols to achieve goals. **Symbols** are words, images (a flag, a cross, a six-pointed star), and behaviors that create meaning for others. Whether you use them in an interview to convince an employer to hire you or you hear them in a TV commercial to persuade you to vote for a presidential candidate, words and images that symbolically inform and persuade are all around you. Public speakers are rhetoricians who use symbols to achieve their goals.

One way to enhance your listening skill and become more mindfully aware of how messages influence your behavior is to analyze the rhetorical strategies a speaker is using. **Rhetorical strategies** are the methods and techniques that speakers employ to achieve their speaking goals. It's especially important to be aware of how some speakers may use rhetorical techniques to deceive or manipulate you. Speakers will sometimes use unethical strategies such as misusing evidence, relying too heavily on emotion, or fabricating information.

Rhetorican Robert Rowland offers a simple but comprehensive framework for describing and analyzing rhetorical messages: Be conscious of the goal of the message, its organization, the speaker's role, the overall tone of the message, the intended audience, and the techniques the speaker uses to achieve the goal.[33] By considering the questions in the Speech Workshop on page 74, you can figure out what any speaker is really saying and better understand the techniques he or she is using. Whether it's a speaker in your public-speaking class, the president delivering a State of the Union address, a member of the clergy delivering a sermon, or a parent addressing the school board, each speaker uses rhetorical strategies to achieve a goal. The more clearly you can identify and analyze the speaker's methods, the more effectively you can assess whether the message and the messenger are worthy of your support—and you become a more discerning rhetorical critic.

**symbols**
Words, images, and behaviors that create meaning

**rhetorical strategies**
Methods and techniques that speakers use to achieve their speaking goals

## Giving Feedback to Others

As you enhance your skills of listening to messages and identifying rhetorical strategies, you may be asked to evaluate the speeches of others and provide feedback to them. Both the speech evaluation questions in Figure 3.2 and the framework for analyzing rhetorical effectiveness in the Speech Workshop can serve you well as you evaluate others' messages. Your instructor may also provide you with a speech evaluation form that will help you focus on the essential elements of public speechmaking.

When you're invited to critique your classmates, your feedback will be more effective if you keep some general principles in mind. Because the word *criticism* means "to judge or discuss," to criticize a speech is to discuss the speech—identifying both its strengths and those aspects that could be improved. Effective criticism stems from developing a genuine interest in the speaker, not from seeking to find fault.

When given the opportunity to critique your classmates, use the following guidelines to provide feedback in a meaningful and helpful manner.

1. **Be Descriptive.** In a neutral way, describe what you saw the speaker doing. Act as a mirror for the speaker to help him or her become aware of gestures and other nonverbal signals of which he or she may not be aware. (If you and the speaker are watching a videotape of the speech together, you can point out behaviors.) Avoid providing only a list of your likes and dislikes; describe what you observe.

| | |
|---|---|
| Effective: | Stan, I noticed that about 50 percent of the time you had direct eye contact with your listeners. |
| Less Effective: | Your eye contact was lousy. |

2. **Be Specific.** When you describe what you see a speaker doing, make sure your descriptions are precise enough to give the speaker a clear image of your perceptions. Saying that a speaker had "poor delivery" doesn't give him or her much information—it's only a general evaluative comment. Be as specific and thoughtful as you can.

| | |
|---|---|
| Effective: | Dawn, your use of color on your PowerPoint slide helped to keep my attention. |
| Less Effective: | I liked your visuals. |

3. **Be Positive.** Begin and end your feedback with positive comments. Beginning with a negative comment immediately puts the speaker on the defensive and can create so much internal noise that he or she stops listening. Starting and ending with positive comments engenders less defensiveness. Some teachers call this approach the feedback sandwich. First, tell the speaker something he or she did well. This will let the speaker know you're not an enemy who's trying to shoot holes in his or her performance. Then share a suggestion or two that may help the speaker improve the presentation. End your evaluation with another positive comment or restate what you liked best about the presentation.

| | |
|---|---|
| Effective: | Gabe, I thought your opening statistic was very effective in catching my attention. You also maintained direct eye contact when you delivered it. Your overall organizational pattern would have been clearer to me if you had used more signposts and transition statements. Or perhaps you could use a visual aid to summarize the main points. You did a good job of summarizing your three points in your conclusion. I also liked the way you ended your speech by making a reference to your opening statistics. |
| Less Effective: | I got lost in the body of your speech. I couldn't figure out what your major ideas were. I also didn't know when you made the transition between the introduction and the body of your speech. Your intro and conclusion were good, but the organization of the speech was weak. |

**4. Be Constructive.** Give the speaker suggestions or alternatives for improvement. It's not especially helpful to rattle off a list of things you don't like without offering some ideas for improvement. As a student of public speaking, your comments should reflect your growing skill and sophistication in the speechmaking process.

| | |
|---|---|
| Effective: | Jerry, I thought your speech had several good statistics and examples that suggest you spent a lot of time in the library researching your topic. I think you could add credibility to your message if you shared your sources with the listener. Your vocal quality was effective, and you had considerable variation in your pitch and tone, but at times the speech rate was a little fast for me. A slower rate would help me catch some of the details of your message. |
| Less Effective: | You spoke too fast. I had no idea whom you were quoting. |

**5. Be Sensitive.** "Own" your feedback by using I-statements rather than you-statements. An *I-statement* is a way of phrasing your feedback so that it is clear that your comments reflect your personal point of view. "I found my attention drifting during the body of your speech" is an example of an I-statement. A *you-statement* is a less sensitive way of describing someone's behavior by implying that the other person did something wrong. "You didn't summarize very well in your conclusion" is an example of a you-statement. A better way to make the same point is to say, "I wasn't sure I understood the key ideas you mentioned in your conclusion." Here's another example:

| | |
|---|---|
| Effective: | Mark, I found myself so distracted by your gestures that I had trouble focusing on the message. |
| Less Effective: | Your gestures were distracting and awkward. |

**6. Be Realistic.** Provide usable information. Offer feedback about aspects of the presentation that the speaker can improve rather than about those things he or she cannot control. Maybe you have heard this advice: "Never try to teach a pig to sing. It wastes your time. It doesn't sound pretty. And it annoys the pig." Saying "You're too short to be seen over the lectern," "Your lisp doesn't lend itself to public speaking," or "You looked nervous" is not constructive. Comments of this kind will only annoy or frustrate the speaker because they refer to things the speaker can't do much to change. Concentrate on behaviors over which the speaker has control.

| | |
|---|---|
| Effective: | Taka, I thought your closing quote was effective in summarizing your key ideas, but it didn't end your speech on an uplifting note. Another quote from Khalil Gibran that I'll share with you after class would also summarize your key points and provide a positive affirmation of your message. You may want to try it if you give this speech again. |
| Less Effective: | Your voice isn't well suited to public speaking. |

As you provide feedback, whether in your public-speaking class or to a friend who asks you for a reaction to his or her speech, remember that the goal of feedback is to offer descriptive and specific information that will help a speaker build confidence and skill.

## Giving Feedback to Yourself

While you are collecting feedback from your instructor, classmates, family, and friends, keep in mind that *you* are the most important critic of your speeches. The goal of public-speaking instruction is to learn principles and skills that enable *you* to be your own best critic. As you rehearse your speech, use self-talk to comment about the choices you make as a speaker. After your speech, take time to reflect on both the speech's virtues and the areas for improvement in your speechmaking skill. As an audience-centered speaker, you must learn to recognize when to make changes on your feet, in the middle of a speech. For example, if you find that your audience just isn't interested in the facts and statistics you are sharing, you may decide to support your points with a couple of stories instead. We encourage you to consider the following principles to enhance your own self-critiquing skills.

**Look for and Reinforce Your Skills and Speaking Abilities** Try to recognize your strengths and skills as a public speaker. Note how your audience analysis, organization, and delivery were effective in achieving your objectives. Such positive reflection can reinforce the many skills you learn in this course. Resist the temptation to be too harsh or overly critical of your speaking skill.

**Evaluate Your Effectiveness Based on a Specific Speaking Situation and Audience** Throughout the book we offer many suggestions and tips for improving your speaking skill. We also stress that these prescriptions should be considered in light of your specific audience. Don't be a slave to rules. If you are giving a pep talk to the Little League team you are coaching, you might not have to construct an attention-getting opening statement. Be flexible. Public speaking is an art as well as a science. Give yourself permission to adapt principles and practices to specific speech situations.

**Identify One or Two Areas for Improvement** After each speaking opportunity, identify what you did right and then give yourself a suggestion or two for ways to improve. You may be tempted to overwhelm yourself with a long list of things you need to do as a speaker. Rather than try to work on a dozen goals, concentrate on two or three, or maybe even just one key skill you would like to develop. To help you decide which skill to focus on, keep in mind the audience-centered model of public speaking we introduced in Chapter 2.

Ultimately, the goal of this course is to teach you how to listen to your own commentary and become expert in shaping and polishing your speaking style.

## CONFIDENTLY CONNECTING WITH YOUR AUDIENCE

### Look for Positive Listener Support

Audience members want you to do well. Many if not most listeners will express their support for your ideas with eye contact, nods of the head, and supportive facial expressions. Make a point to look for these reinforcing nonverbal cues as you deliver your message. (But don't forget to maintain eye contact with all members of the audience.) Let these signs of positive support from your listeners remind you that listeners want you to succeed.

## RECAP

### Analyzing and Evaluating Speeches

Use standards to judge whether a message is effective and ethical:

- Understandable to listeners
- Achieves its purpose (inform, persuade, entertain)
- Appropriate, sensitive, and responsive to listeners

Identify and analyze rhetorical strategies:

- Speech goal
- Speech organization
- Speaker role
- Speaker tone
- Speaker techniques
- Audience

Give feedback that is:

- Descriptive
- Specific
- Positive
- Constructive
- Sensitive
- Realistic

# STUDY GUIDE

## Overcoming Barriers to Effective Listening

Listening is a process that involves selecting, attending to, understanding, and remembering. Some of the barriers that keep people from listening at peak efficiency include information overload, personal concerns, outside distractions, and prejudice.

### Being Audience-Centered

- The cultural background of your audience will affect how they listen to your message; people from some cultures prefer stories and narratives rather than a message chock-full of statistics and data.
- Some people are more apprehensive than others about listening to a message. Use clear preview statements, adequate internal summaries, and appropriate visual aids to help anxious listeners feel more comfortable when listening to your message.

### Critical Thinking

- For some reason, when Alberto hears the president speak, he just tunes out. What are some of the barriers that may keep Alberto from focusing on the message he is hearing?

### A Question of Ethics

- Chester was planning to attend a charity event at which a congressional candidate would be speaking. Chester decided he would bring a book to read during the speech because the speaker was from a different political party than Chester's. Was Chester being fair to the speaker?

## How to Become a Better Listener

Overcome barriers to effective listening by practicing listening and working to become an active listener. "Listen" with your eyes as well as your ears to accurately interpret nonverbal messages and adapt to the speaker's delivery. Understand your listening style. Listen mindfully, monitoring your emotional reactions to messages, and avoid jumping to conclusions. Identify your listening goal and listen for major ideas. Re-sort, restate, or repeat key messages. Be an ethical listener who communicates expectations and feedback. Remain sensitive to and tolerant of differences between you and the speaker.

### Being Audience-Centered

- Find out what your listeners' objectives are; do your best to adjust and adapt to achieve your listeners' goals.

### Critical Thinking

- One of your professors does nothing during lectures but read in a monotone from old notes. What strategies can you use to increase your listening effectiveness in this challenging situation?

### A Question of Ethics

- Margo bought a classmate's notes from the previous semester of her world history course. The notes allowed Margo to pass the exams without attending class. Is this kind of "listening" behavior ethical? Why or why not?

### Speaker's Homepage: Developing Your Listening Skills

Two Web sites offer many classic and contemporary speeches on which you can practice the listening and analysis skills we've emphasized in this chapter. Use the questions from the Speech Workshop at the end of this chapter to help you describe and analyze what you hear.

To hear the speeches on these Web sites, you will need software such as RealAudio, which can be downloaded from www.real.com/.

- Famous Speeches in History Archives www.history.com/speeches
- American Rhetoric www.americanrhetoric.com

## Improving Listening and Critical Thinking Skills

Evaluate the speaker's use of facts, examples, opinions, and statistics as evidence. Listen critically to separate facts, which can be proven, from inferences, which are conclusions based on partial or unobserved evidence. Examine the logic and reasoning leading to the speaker's conclusions

### Being Audience-Centered

- When speaking to an audience that may be hostile to or critical of your message, take care to use credible arguments and evidence rather than rely on emotional appeals.

## Analyzing and Evaluating Speeches

An effective speech should be understood by the audience and should achieve the intended goal. A good speech is also ethical. When offering feedback, be descriptive, specific, positive, constructive, sensitive, and realistic. Use feedback to learn your own speaking strengths, evaluate the effectiveness of specific speeches, and identify areas for improvement.

### Being Audience-Centered

- Feedback you give to a speaker should provide information and suggestions the speaker can use.

### A Question of Ethics

- Janice was assigned the task of critiquing one of her classmate's speeches. Although she thought the speech was pretty good, she gave the speaker low marks because she strongly disagreed with what the speaker was saying. Was this an appropriate evaluation? Why or why not?

# SPEECH WORKSHOP

## Evaluating a Speaker's Rhetorical Effectiveness

When listening to a speech—either a classmate's presentation or a speech you hear on TV or find on the Web—take notes in response to the following questions to help you evaluate the rhetorical effectiveness and appropriateness of the speaker and the message.

1. Speech Goal
   - What is the general purpose of the speech? (inform, entertain, persuade) ________________
   - What is the specific purpose; what does the speaker want the listener to do? ________________
   - What are the main points or themes of the message? ________________
2. Speech Organization
   - What is the overall organizational structure of the message? ________________
   - How does the conclusion summarize the message and point listeners to what the speaker wants to happen next? ________________
   - How does the body of the speech support the general and specific purposes? ________________
3. Speaker's Role
   - What kind of relationship has the speaker established with the audience? ________________
   - Does the speaker assume an explicit or implied position of power, as an authority figure or an expert on the topic addressed? or speak as an equal to the audience? ________________
   - How does the role established by the speaker influence the speech's effectiveness? ________________

**4.** Speaker's Tone

- What is the overall tone, or "feel," of the message? ______
- How does the introduction set the tone for the message? ______
- How does the speaker use supporting materials and delivery cues to establish an overall tone of the speech? ______

**5.** Speaker's Techniques

- What does the speaker do to establish credibility? ______
- Does the speaker use logical arguments, tell effective and interesting stories, use emotional appeals, and use interesting and precise language? ______

**6.** Audience

- Who is the intended audience? Is the message aimed at anyone who is not present? ______
- Who is present to hear the message? Is the message aimed at others who are not present? Is the message aimed at anyone who is not present? ______
- How effectively and appropriately does the speaker connect to the interests, needs, and background of the audience? ______
- How does the speaker make the connection with the audience? ______

For of the three elements in speechmaking—speaker, subject, and person addressed—it is the last one, the hearer, that determines the speech's end and object.

—Aristotle

Louis Leopold Boilly (1761–1845), *Theatre Box, on the Day of a Free Performance*, 1830. Oil on canvas, 32.5 X 41.7 cm. Inv. 87.7.1. Photo: Phillip Bernard/Réunion des Musée Nationaux/Art Resource, N.Y.

## OUTLINE

# 4 Analyzing Your Audience

OBJECTIVES

**After studying this chapter you should be able to do the following:**

1. Discuss the importance of audience analysis.
2. Describe informal and formal methods of analyzing your audience.
3. Explain how to gather demographic, psychological, and situational information about your audience and the speaking occasion.
4. Identify methods of assessing and adapting to your audience's reactions while your speech is in progress.
5. Identify methods of assessing audience reactions after you have concluded your speech.

It seemed harmless enough. Charles Williams was asked to speak to the Cub Scout pack about his experiences as a young cowboy in Texas. The boys were learning to tie knots, and Williams, a retired rancher, could tell them how to make a lariat and how to tie and use other knots.

His speech started out well. He seemed to be adapting to his young audience. However, for some reason Williams thought the boys might also enjoy learning how to exterminate the screwworm, a pesky parasite of cattle. In the middle of his talk about roping cattle, he launched into a description of the techniques for sterilizing male screwworms. The parents in the audience fidgeted in their seats. The 7- and 8-year-olds didn't have the foggiest idea what a screwworm was, what sterilization was, or how male and female screwworms mate.

It got worse; his audience analysis skills deteriorated even further as Williams next talked about castrating cattle. Twenty-five minutes later, he finally finished the screwworm–castration speech. The parents were relieved. Fortunately, the boys hadn't understood it.

Williams's downfall resulted from his failure to analyze his audience. He may have had a clear objective in mind, but he hadn't considered the background or knowledge of his listeners. Audience analysis is essential for the success of any speech.

Chapter 1 identified the key elements in communication: source, receiver, message, channel. All four elements are important, but perhaps the most important is the receiver. In public speaking, the receiver is the audience, and the audience is the reason for a speech. We also presented a model that provides an overview of the entire process of speech preparation and delivery; the model is shown again in Figure 4.1. We stressed in Chapter 1 and reemphasize here the concept of public speaking as an audience-centered activity.

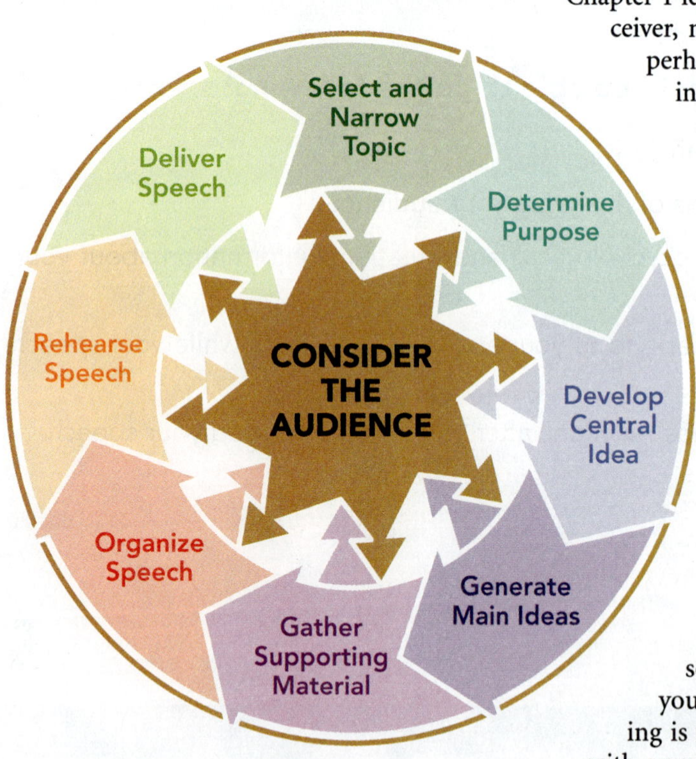


FIGURE 4.1 *Audience analysis is central to the speechmaking process.*

At each stage in crafting your speech, you must be mindful of your audience. The audience-analysis skills and techniques that we present in this chapter will help you throughout the public-speaking process. Consciousness of your audience will be important as you select a topic, determine the purpose of your speech, develop your central idea, generate main ideas, gather supporting material, firm up your organization, and rehearse and deliver your speech.

When you think of your audience, don't imagine some undifferentiated mass of people waiting to hear your message. Instead, think of individuals. Public speaking is the process of speaking to a group of individuals, each with a unique point of view. Your challenge as an audience-centered public speaker is to find out as much as you can about these individuals. From your knowledge of the individuals, you can then develop a general profile of your listeners.

How do you become an audience-centered speaker? There are three steps. First, gather information about your audience. You can gather information informally just by observing your listeners or asking general questions about them. Or you can take a more formal approach and administer a survey to obtain specific information about them.

Second, analyze the information you have gathered. Categorize and evaluate that information to determine your listeners' psychological profile, as well as to consider the occasion at which you are speaking.

Finally, once you have gathered and analyzed information about your audience, use the information to adapt ethically to your listeners. As our audience-centered model illustrates, each decision you make when designing and delivering your message should consider the needs and backgrounds of your audience. In this chapter, we'll talk about these three steps and discuss the process of analyzing your audience before, during, and after your speech.

# Gathering Information about Your Audience

As an audience-centered speaker, you should try to find out as much as you can about your audience before planning your speech. You may wonder, "How do I go about gathering information about my audience?" There are two approaches you can take: an informal one and a formal one.

**Gathering Information Informally** The simplest way to gather information about your audience informally is to observe them and ask questions before you speak. Informal observations can be especially important in helping you assess obvious demographic characteristics. **Demographics** are statistical information on population characteristics such as age, race, gender, sexual orientation, educational level, and ideological or religious views. For example, you can observe how many members of your audience are male or female, and you can make inferences from their appearance about their ethnic or cultural traits and approximate age.

If, for example, you were planning to address your local PTA about a new store you were opening to help students and parents develop science projects, you could attend a meeting before your speaking date. You might note the general percentage of men and women in the audience and the ages of the parents who attended. You could also ask whether most parents who show up for PTA meetings are parents of elementary, middle-school, or high-school students. Knowing these key pieces of information would help you tailor your speech to address your listeners' interests.

You could also talk with people who know something about the audience you will be addressing. If you are invited to speak to a group you have not spoken to before, ask the person who invited you about the audience members: What is their average age? What are their political affiliations? What are their religious beliefs? What are their attitudes toward your topic? Try to get as much information as possible about your audience before you give your speech.

**Gathering Information Formally** Rather than rely only on inferences drawn from casual observation and conversations with others, you may, if time and resources permit, want to conduct a more formal survey of your listeners. A survey allows you to gather both demographic information and information about what audience members like or dislike, believe to be true or false, or think is good or bad about the topic or issues you will discuss. To gather information formally requires that you develop a carefully written survey or questionnaire.

How do you develop a formal survey? First, decide what you want to know about your audience that you don't already know. Let your topic and the speaking occasion help you determine the kinds of questions you should pose. Once you have an idea of what you would like to know, you can ask your potential audience straightforward questions about such demographic information as age, sex, occupation, and their membership in professional organizations. Figure 4.2 shows a sample questionnaire.

You can modify the questionnaire in Figure 4.2 according to your audience and topic. If your topic is the best approach to finding a rental apartment and you are speaking in a suburban area, find out how many members of your audience own a home and how many are presently living in an apartment. You may also want to ask how they found their current apartment, how many are now searching for an apartment, and how many anticipate looking for one. Answers to these questions can give you useful information about your audience and may provide you with examples to use in your presentation.

Although knowing your audience's demographics can be helpful, you should be aware that inferences based on generalized information may lead you to make faulty conclusions. For example, it might seem reasonable to infer that if your audience

**demographics**
Statistical information about the age, race, gender, sexual orientation, educational level, and religious views of an audience

FIGURE 4.2 *You can use a questionnaire like this to gather demographic information about the people in your audience.*

**Demographic Audience-Analysis Questionnaire**

1. Name (optional): ______
2. Sex: Male ☐ Female ☐
3. Occupation: ______
4. Religious affiliation: ______
5. Marital status: Married ☐ Single ☐ Divorced ☐
6. Years of schooling beyond high school: ______
7. Major in college: ______
8. Annual income: ______
9. Age: ______
10. Ethnic background: ______
11. Hometown and state: ______
12. Political affiliation: Republican ☐ Democrat ☐ Other ☐ None ☐
13. Membership in professional or fraternal organizations: ______

RECAP

**Gathering Information to Adapt Your Message to Your Audience**

Gather demographic information informally.
Formally survey demographics and attitudes:

- Closed-ended questions
- Open-ended questions

Ethically adapt your message:

- Topic
- Objectives
- Content
- Delivery

consists mainly of 18- to 22-year-olds, they will not be deeply interested in retirement programs. But unless you have talked to them about this topic, your inference may be incorrect. Whenever possible, ask specific questions about audience members' attitudes.

To gather useful information about audience members' attitudes, beliefs, and values, you can ask two types of questions. **Open-ended questions** allow for unrestricted answers, without limitation to choices or alternatives. Use open-ended questions when you want detailed information from your audience. Essay questions, for example, are open-ended. **Closed-ended questions** offer alternatives from which to choose. Multiple-choice, true/false, and agree/disagree questions are examples of closed-ended questions.

After you develop the questions, it is wise to test them on a small group of people to make sure they are clear and will encourage meaningful answers. Suppose you plan to address an audience about in-school health clinics that dispense birth-control pills to high school students. The sample questions in Figure 4.3 are open and closed questions that might yield useful audience information on this subject.

Instead of, or in addition to, distributing a paper-and-pencil survey, you have the option of distributing your survey to your audience by means of technology. You could use e-mail, send text messages, or invite audience members to click on a Web site or a Facebook page that you've designed to identify audience-member demographics and assess their attitudes and opinions.

**open-ended questions**
Questions that allow for unrestricted answers by not limiting answers to choices or alternatives

**closed-ended questions**
Questions that offer alternatives from which to choose, such as true/false, agree/disagree, or multiple-choice questions

**audience analysis**
The process of examining information about those who are expected to listen to a speech

## Analyzing Information about Your Audience

**Audience analysis** is the process of examining information about the listeners who will hear your speech. That analysis helps you adapt your message so that your listeners will respond as you wish. You analyze audiences every day as you speak to others

FIGURE 4.3 *Samples of open-ended and closed-ended questions.*

## Open-Ended Questions

1. What are your feelings about having high-school health clinics dispense birth-control pills?
2. What are your reactions to the current rate of teenage pregnancy?
3. What would you do if you discovered your daughter was receiving birth-control pills from her high-school health clinic?

## Closed-Ended Questions

1. Are you in favor of school-based health clinics dispensing birth-control pills to high-school students?
   Yes ☐ No ☐
2. Birth-control pills should be given to high-school students who ask for them in school-based health clinics. (Circle the statement that best describes your feeling.)
   Agree strongly Agree Undecided Disagree Disagree strongly
3. Check the statement that most closely reflects your feelings about school-based health clinics and birth-control pills.
   ☐ Students should receive birth-control pills in school-based health clinics whenever they want them, without their parents' knowledge.
   ☐ Students should receive birth-control pills in school-based health clinics whenever they want them, as long as they have their parents' permission.
   ☐ I am not certain whether students should receive birth-control pills in school-based health clinics.
   ☐ Students should not receive birth-control pills in school-based health clinics.
4. Rank the following statements from most desirable (1) to least desirable (5).
   ___ Birth-control pills should be available to all high-school students in school-based health clinics, whenever students want them, and even if their parents are not aware that their daughters are taking the pills.
   ___ Birth-control pills should be available to all high-school students in school-based health clinics, but only if their parents have given their permission.
   ___ Birth-control pills should be available to high-school students without their parents' knowledge, but not in school-based health clinics.
   ___ Birth-control pills should be available to high-school students, but not in school-based health clinics, and only with their parents' permission.
   ___ Birth-control pills should not be available to high-school students.

or join in group conversations. For example, most of us do not deliberately make offensive comments to family members or friends. Rather, we analyze our audience (often very quickly) and then adapt our messages to the individuals with whom we are speaking. Public speaking involves the same sort of process.

Precisely what do you look for when analyzing the information that you have gathered about your audience? Ask yourself the following questions:

1. How are audience members similar to one another?
2. How are audience members different from one another?
3. Based on their similarities and differences, how can I establish common ground with the audience?

## Look for Audience Member Similarities

Knowing what several members of your audience have in common can help you craft a message that resonates with them. For example, if your audience members are approximately the same age, you will have some basis for selecting examples and illustrations that your listeners will understand.

When looking for similarities, consider the following questions: What ethnic and cultural characteristics do audience members have in common? Are they all from the same geographic region? Do they (or did they) attend the same college or university? Do they have similar levels of education? Do they all like the same kinds of things? Answering these and other questions will help you develop your own ideas and relate your message to your listeners.

RECAP

**Analyzing Information about Your Audience**

Look for:

- Similarities among listeners
- Differences among listeners
- Common ground with listeners

## Look for Audience Member Differences

Besides noting similarities, you should note differences among your audience members. It is unlikely that audience members for the speeches you give in class will have similar backgrounds. The range of cultural backgrounds, ethnicities, and religious traditions among students at most colleges and universities is rapidly expanding. You can also note the range of differences in age and gender, as well as the variations in perspectives about your topic.

## Establish Common Ground with Your Audience

When you know what your audience members have in common as well as how they differ, both in terms of demographic information (such as age or education level) and in terms of attitudes and beliefs they may have about you or your topic, then you can seek to establish common ground with your audience. To establish **common ground** with your audience is to identify ways in which you and your listeners are alike. The more your listeners identify with you and the goals of your message, the more likely they are to respond positively. Keep in mind that although each audience member is unique, with his or her own characteristics and preferences, when you analyze your audience, you are looking for general ways in which they are alike or different. Sometimes the only common ground you may find is that both you and your listeners believe that the issue you are addressing is a serious problem; you may have different views about the best solution. If, for example, you were addressing a group of people who were mostly against increasing taxes to pay teachers higher salaries, but you were in favor of a tax increase, you could establish common ground by noting that both you and your listeners value education and want high-quality teachers in the classroom.

When you meet someone for the first time, you may spend time identifying people whom you both know or places you've both visited; in this way you begin to establish a relationship. A **relationship** is an ongoing connection you have with another person. A public speaker seeks to establish a relationship with his or her audience by identifying what the speaker has in common with the listeners. Use the information from your audience analysis to establish a relationship with your listeners; build bridges between you and your audience.

**common ground**
Similarities between a speaker and audience members in attitudes, values, beliefs, or behaviors

**relationship**
An ongoing connection you have with another person

**audience adaptation**
The process of ethically using information about an audience in order to adapt one's message so that it is clear and achieves the speaking objective

# Adapting to Your Audience

**Audience adaptation** is the process of ethically using information you've gathered when analyzing your audience to help your audience clearly understand your message and to achieve your speaking objective. To adapt is to modify your message to enhance its clarity and to increase the likelihood that you will ethically achieve your goal. If you analyze your audience but don't use the information to customize your message, the information you've gathered will be of little value. Using your skill both to learn about

## LEARNING FROM GREAT SPEAKERS

### Winston Churchill (1874–1965)

The great British prime minister Winston Churchill was noted for his ability to connect with his listeners. He spoke to audiences as diverse as groups of school children; the citizens of Britain; academics at Westminster College in Fulton, Missouri, who first heard Churchhill use the phrase "iron curtain"; and the United States Congress. When awarding Churchill the Nobel Prize in Literature in 1953, the Nobel Committee praised his "brilliant oratory in defending exalted human values."[1]

Because Churchill was a master at empathizing with his audience's emotions, he knew how to motivate them to endure and persevere in the face of adversity. Like Churchill, you will want to be mindful of audience members' attitudes, beliefs, values, backgrounds, and emotions. An audience-centered speaker is skilled at speaking both to listeners' minds and to listeners' hearts.

[Photo: AP Wide World Photos]

your listeners and to adapt to them can help you maintain your listeners' attention and make them more receptive to your ideas.

Here's an example of how analyzing and adapting to others works: Mike spent a glorious spring break at Daytona Beach. He and three friends piled in a car and headed for a week of adventure. When he returned from the beach, sunburned and fatigued from merrymaking, people asked how his break had been. He described his escapades to his best friend, his mother, and his communication professor.

To his best friend, he bragged, "We partied all night and slept on the beach all day. It was great!" He informed his mother, "It was good to relax after the hectic pace of college." And he told his professor, "It was mentally invigorating to have time to think things out." It was the same vacation—but how different the messages were! Mike adapted his message to the people he addressed; he had analyzed his audiences.

When you speak in public, you should follow the same process. The principle is simple yet powerful: An effective public speaker is audience-centered. These key questions can help you formulate an effective approach to your audience:

## CONFIDENTLY CONNECTING WITH YOUR AUDIENCE

### Learn as Much as You Can about Your Audience

By learning about your audience's interests, attitudes, and beliefs as well as their demographic details, you'll be better able to customize a message for your listeners. The more you tailor your message directly to your audience, the more you'll be able to confidently connect to them. Because you have customized your message, they will want to hear it, and you'll be speaking directly to their interests and needs. Also, by focusing on your audience instead of on your nervousness about speaking, you will enhance your confidence. Because you're not dwelling on your own anxieties, you'll be focused on communicating your audience-centered message.

Consider Your Audience

- To whom am I speaking?
- What topic would be most suitable for my audience?

Consider Your Speech Goal

- What is my general objective (to inform, persuade, or entertain)?
- What is my specific objective (precisely what do I want the audience to do)?

Consider Your Speech Content

- What kind of information should I share with my audience?
- How should I present the information to them?
- How can I gain and hold their attention?
- What kind of examples would work best?
- What method of organizing information will be most effective?

Consider Your Delivery

- What language differences and expectations do audience members have?
- What style of delivery will my audience members expect?

*Being audience-centered does not mean you should tell your listeners only what they want to hear, or that you should fabricate information simply to please your audience or achieve your goal.* If you adapt to your audience by abandoning your own values and sense of truth, then you will become an unethical speaker rather than an audience-centered one. It was President Truman who pondered, "I wonder how far Moses would have gone if he'd taken a poll in Egypt?"[2] The audience-centered speaker adjusts his or her topic, purpose, central idea, main ideas, supporting material, organization, and even delivery so as to encourage the audience to listen to his or her ideas. The goal is to make the audience come away from the speaking situation, if not persuaded, then at least feeling thoughtful rather than offended or hostile.

In our overview of how to become an audience-centered speaker, we've pointed out the importance of gathering information, analyzing it to establish common ground, and then using the information to ethically adapt to your listeners. Now we'll discuss these ideas in more detail. You'll want to gather and analyze information and use it to adapt to your listeners at three stages of the speechmaking process: before you speak, as you speak, and after you speak.

RECAP

### Adapting to Your Audience

To ethically use information to help an audience understand your message, consider your:

- listeners
- speech goal
- speech content
- delivery

Avoid pandering to listeners or making up information.

# Analyzing Your Audience before You Speak

Learning about your audience members' backgrounds and attitudes can help you select a topic, define a purpose, develop an outline, and carry out virtually all other speech-related activities. You can gather and analyze three primary types of information:

1. Demographic
2. Psychological
3. Situational

## Demographic Audience Analysis

As we noted earlier, *demographics* are statistics about such audience characteristics as age, gender, sexual orientation, race and culture, group membership, and socioeconomic status. Now let's consider how demographic information, or **demographic audience analysis**, can help you better understand and adapt to your audience.

**Age** Although you must use caution in generalizing from only one factor such as age, that information can suggest the kinds of examples, humor, illustrations, and other types of supporting material to use in your speech. Many students in your public-speaking class will probably be in their late teens or early twenties; some may be older. The younger students may know the latest hip-hop performers or musicians, for example, but the older ones may not be familiar with Wyclef Jean, Lil Wayne, or Monica. If you are going to give a talk on music, you will have to explain who the performers are and describe or demonstrate their style if you want all the members of your class to understand what you are talking about.

**demographic audience analysis** Examining demographic information about an audience so as to develop a clear and effective message

**TABLE 4.1 Summary of Generational Characteristics**

| Generation Name | Birth Years | Typical Values and Characteristics |
|---|---|---|
| Matures | 1925–1942 | • Duty<br>• Sacrifice<br>• A sense of what is right<br>• Work hard<br>• Work fast |
| Baby Boomers | 1943–1960 | • Personal fulfillment and optimism<br>• Crusading causes<br>• Buy now/pay later<br>• Everybody's rights<br>• Work efficiently |
| Generation X | 1961–1981 | • Live with uncertainty<br>• Balance is important<br>• Live for today<br>• Save<br>• Every job is a contract |
| Millennials | 1982–2002 | • Close to parents<br>• Feel "special"<br>• Goal-oriented<br>• Team-oriented<br>• Focus on achievement |

For centuries, adults have lamented that younger generations don't seem to share the values of the older generation. The ancient Greek philosopher Socrates is reported to have complained, over two thousand years ago, "The children now love luxury; they show disrespect for elders and love chatter in place of exercise. . . . They contradict their parents, chatter before company, gobble up dainties at the table, cross their legs, and tyrannize over their teachers."[3] Two researchers who have studied generational differences have found that different generations do have distinctive values and hold differing assumptions about work, duty, and certain values. Table 4.1 summarizes the values and generational characteristics of four generations—matures, baby boomers, generation X, and millennials.[4]

What do these generational differences have to do with public speaking? Aristotle noted that a good speaker knows how to adapt to audiences of different age levels. Your credibility as a speaker—how positively you are perceived by your audience—is dependent on your sensitivity to the values and assumptions of your listeners. Of course, the broad generalizations that we've summarized here don't apply across the board, but it's wise to consider how generational differences may affect how your message is interpreted.

**Gender** Josh began his speech by thanking his predominantly female audience for taking time from their busy schedules to attend his presentation on managing personal finances. Not a bad way to begin a talk. He continued, however, by noting that their job of raising children, keeping their homes clean, and feeding their families was among the most important jobs there were. Josh thought he was paying his audience a compliment. He did not consider that most women today work outside the home as well as in it. Many of his listeners were insulted. Many of his listeners stopped listening.

A key question to ask when considering your audience is "What is the ratio of males to females?" No matter what the mix, you don't want to make judgments based on gender stereotypes. A person's **sex** is determined by biology, as reflected in his or her anatomy and reproductive system; someone is born either male or female. **Gender** is the culturally constructed and psychologically based perception of one's self as feminine or masculine. One's gender-role identity, which falls somewhere on the continuum from masculine to feminine, is learned or socially reinforced by others as well as by one's own personality and life experiences; genetics also plays a part in shaping gender-role identity. Try to ensure that your remarks reflect a sensitivity to the diversity in your listeners' points of view.

One goal of an audience-centered speaker is to avoid sexist language or remarks. A sexist perspective stereotypes or prejudges how someone will react based on his or her sex. Take time to educate yourself about what words, phrases, or perspectives are likely to offend or create psychological noise for your listeners. Think carefully about the implications of words and phrases you take for granted. For example, many people still use the words *ladies* and *matrons* without thinking about their connotations in U.S. culture. Be especially wary about jokes; many are derogatory to one sex or the other. Avoid stereotypes in your stories and examples as well.

In addition, make your language and your message as inclusive as possible. If you are speaking to a mixed audience, be sure your speech relates to all your listeners, not just to one gender. If, for example, you decide to discuss breast cancer, you could note that men, too, can be victims of breast cancer and that the lives of husbands, fathers, and brothers of female victims are also affected by the disease.

Finally, be cautious about assuming that men and women will respond differently to your message. Early social science research found some evidence that females were more susceptible to efforts to persuade them than were males.[5] For many years textbooks and communication teachers presented this conclusion to students. More contemporary research, however, suggests there is no major difference between men and women in their susceptibility to persuasive messages.[6]

Moreover, although some research suggests that women are socialized to be more emotional and empathic than men, other evidence suggests that men can be equally sensitive.[7] It is clear there are learned sex differences in language usage and nonverbal behavior, but we caution against making sweeping gender-based assumptions about your audience.

**sex**
A person's biological status as male or female, as reflected in his or her anatomy and reproductive system

**gender**
The culturally constructed and psychologically based perception of one's self as feminine or masculine

**culture**
A learned system of knowledge, behavior, attitudes, beliefs, values, and norms that is shared by a group of people

**ethnicity**
The portion of a person's cultural background that includes such factors as nationality, religion, language, and ancestral heritage, which are shared by a group of people who also share a common geographic origin

**Sexual Orientation** An audience-centered speaker is sensitive to issues and attitudes about sexual orientation in contemporary society. The audience-centered speaker's goal is to enhance understanding rather than create noise that may distract an audience from listening, regardless of the attitudes or beliefs audience members may hold about sexual orientation. Stories, illustrations, and humor whose point or punch line rely on ridiculing a person because of his or her sexual orientation may lower perceptions of your credibility not only among gay and lesbian members of your audience, but also among audience members who disdain bias against gays and lesbians.

People evaluate credibility by behavior, not by intentions. Sometimes we unintentionally offend someone by our subtle misuse of language. For example, gay men and lesbian women typically prefer to be referred to as "gay" or "lesbian" rather than as "homosexual." Further, it is not appropriate to single out gays and lesbians as separate categories of people who are assumed to hold political, ideological, or religious views consistently different from those of straight people. Monitor your language choice and use of illustrations and humor so you don't alienate members of your audience.[8]

**Culture, Ethnicity, and Race** **Culture** is a learned system of knowledge, behavior, attitudes, beliefs, values, and norms shared by a group of people. **Ethnicity** is that portion of a person's cultural background that includes such factors as nationality, religion, language, and ancestral heritage, which are shared by a group of people who also share a common geographic origin. A person's **race** is his or her biological heritage—for example, Caucasian or Hispanic. One geneticist, however, has concluded that there is much more genetic variation *within* any given racial category than *between* one race and another.[9] There really aren't vast genetic differences among people who have been assigned to different racial categories. So the term *race* is less accurate in attempting to describe a group of people than the term *ethnicity*, which, as we noted, is based on more factors than biological heritage or genetics alone. The cultural, ethnic, or racial background of your audience influences the way they perceive your message. An effective speaker adapts to differences in culture, race, and ethnicity.

As you approach any public-speaking situation, avoid an ethnocentric mindset. **Ethnocentrism** is the assumption that your own cultural approaches are superior to those of other cultures. The audience-centered speaker is sensitive to cultural differences and avoids saying anything that would disparage the cultural background of the audience.

You need not have international students in your class to have a culturally diverse audience. Different ethnic and cultural traditions thrive among people who have lived in the United States all their lives. Students from a Polish family in Chicago, a German family in Texas, or a Haitian family in Brooklyn may be native U.S. citizens and still have cultural traditions different from your own. Effective public speakers seek to learn as much as possible about the cultural values and knowledge of their audience so that they can understand the best way to deliver their message.

Researchers classify or describe cultural differences along several lines.[10] We summarize ten categories of differences in Table 4.2 and discuss them below. Understanding these classifications may provide clues to help you adapt your message when you speak before diverse audiences.

- **Individualistic and collectivistic cultures.** Some cultures place greater emphasis on individual achievement; others place more value on group or collective achievement. Among the countries that tend to value individual accomplishment are Australia, Great Britain, the United States, Canada, Belgium, and Denmark. By contrast, Japan, Thailand, Colombia, Taiwan, and Venezuela are among countries that have more collectivistic cultures.

  *How to adapt to listeners from individualistic and collectivistic cultures.* Audience members from individualistic cultures, such as the majority of people in the United States, value and respond positively to appeals that encourage personal accomplishment and recognize individual achievement. People from individualistic cultures are expected to speak up to champion individual rights.

  Audience members from collectivistic cultures, such as people who were raised in an Asian culture, may be more likely to value group or team recognition. Community is an important value for those from collectivistic cultures. They don't like to be singled out for individual accomplishments. And they value making sure that others are perceived in a positive way; it's important for them and others to be seen as valued persons.

- **High-context and low-context cultures.** The terms *high-context* and *low-context* refer to the importance of unspoken or nonverbal messages. In high-context cultures, people place considerable importance on such contextual factors as tone of voice, gestures, facial expression, movement, and other nonverbal aspects of communication. People from low-context traditions place greater emphasis on the words themselves; the surrounding context has a relatively low impact on the meaning of the message. The Arab culture is a high-context culture, as are the cultures of Japan, Asia, and southern Europe. Low-context cultures, which place a higher value on words, include those of Switzerland, Germany, the United States, and Australia.

**race**
A person's biological heritage

**ethnocentrism**
The assumption that one's own cultural perspectives and methods are superior to those of other cultures

## TABLE 4.2 Describing and Adapting to Cultural Differences

| Cultural Value | Cultural Characteristic | How to Adapt to Cultural Characteristic |
|---|---|---|
| Individualistic Culture | Individual achievement is emphasized more than group achievement. | • Stress the importance of individual rewards and recognition.<br>• Identify how audience members will benefit from your ideas or proposal. |
| Collectivistic Culture | Group or team achievement is emphasized more than individual achievement. | • Stress the importance of community values.<br>• Help audience members save face and be perceived in a positive way. |
| High-Context Culture | The context of a message—including nonverbal cues, tone of voice, posture, and facial expression—is often valued more than the words. | • Don't boast about your specific accomplishments.<br>• Use a more subtle, less dramatic delivery style. |
| Low-Context Culture | The words in a message are valued more than the surrounding context. | • Be sure to make your ideas and recommendations explicit.<br>• Although delivery cues are important, listeners will expect your message to be clear. |
| Tolerance for Uncertainty | People can accept ambiguity and are not bothered when they do not know all the details. | • It is not as important to develop a specific solution to a problem you may present in your speech.<br>• The purpose of the speech need not be clearly explicated. |
| Need for Certainty | People want specifics and dislike ambiguity. | • Provide an explicit overview of what you will present in your speech.<br>• Create a logical and clear organizational pattern for your speech. |
| High-Power Culture | Status and power differences are emphasized; roles and chains of command are clearly defined. | • Remember that listeners perceive people in leadership positions as powerful and credible.<br>• Develop messages that acknowledge differences in status among people |
| Low-Power Culture | Status and power differences receive less emphasis; people strive for equality rather than exalting those in positions of leadership. | • Discuss shared approaches to governance and leadership.<br>• Develop solutions that involve others in reaching consensus. |
| Long-Term Time Orientation | Time is abundant, and accomplishing goals may take considerable time. | • Appeal to listeners' persistence, patience, and delayed gratification.<br>• Emphasize how ideas and suggestions will benefit future generations. |
| Short-Term Time Orientation | Time is an important resource. | • Identify how the ideas and proposals you discuss will have an immediate impact on listeners.<br>• Note how actions will have a direct impact on achieving results. |

*How to adapt to listeners from high-context and low-context cultures.* Listeners from low-context cultures will need and expect more detailed and explicit information from you as a speaker. Subtle and indirect messages are less likely to be effective.

People from high-context cultures will pay particular attention to your delivery and to the communication environment when they try to interpret your meaning. These people will be less impressed by a speaker who boasts about his or her own accomplishments; such an audience will expect and value more indirect ways of establishing credibility. A listener from a high-context culture will also expect a less dramatic and dynamic style of delivery.

- **Tolerance of uncertainty and need for certainty.** Some cultures are more comfortable with ambiguity and uncertainty than others. Those cultures in which people need to have details nailed down tend to develop very specific regulations and rules. People from cultures with a greater tolerance of uncertainty are more comfortable with vagueness and are not upset when all the details aren't spelled out. Cultures with a high need for certainty include those of Russia, Japan, France, and Costa Rica. Cultures that have a higher tolerance for uncertainty include those of Great Britain and Indonesia.

*How to adapt to listeners from cultures that tolerate or avoid uncertainty.* If you are speaking to an audience of people who have a high need for certainty, make sure you provide concrete details when you present your message; they will also want and expect to know what action steps they can take. People who value certainty will respond well if you provide a clear and explicit preview of your message in your introduction; they also seem to prefer a clear, logical, and linear step-by-step organizational pattern.

People from cultures that are more comfortable with uncertainty do not necessarily need to have the explicit purpose of the message spelled out for them. In addition, they are generally less likely to need specific prescriptions to solve problems, compared to listeners who want to avoid uncertainty.

- **High-power and low-power cultures.** Power is the ability to influence or control others. Some cultures prefer clearly defined lines of authority and responsibility; these are said to be high-power cultures. People in low-power cultures are more comfortable with blurred lines of authority and less formal titles. Austria, Israel, Denmark, Norway, Switzerland, and Great Britain typically have an equitable approach to power distribution. Cultures that are high on the power dimension include those of the Philippines, Mexico, Venezuela, India, Brazil, and France.

*How to adapt to listeners from high-power and low-power cultures.* People from high-power cultures are more likely to perceive people in leadership roles—including speakers—as credible. They will also be more comfortable with solutions that identify or acknowledge differences in social class.

Those from low-power cultures often favor more shared approaches to leadership and governance. They will expect a more democratic collaborative approach to solving problems and will value the extra time it may take for many people to be consulted in order to reach consensus on an issue.

- **Long-term and short-term orientation to time.** Some cultures take the view that it may take a long time to accomplish certain goals. People from Asian cultures, for example, and from some South American cultures such as that of Brazil often value patience, persistence, and deferred gratification more than do people from cultures with a short-term orientation to time. People with a short-term time orientation, which is often a characteristic of industrialized Western cultures such as those of Canada and the United States, are very attuned to time and time management. Short-term cultures also value quick responses to problems.

*How to adapt to listeners from cultures with long-term and short-term time orientations.* When speaking to people who take a long-term orientation to time, you should to stress how issues and problems affect not only the present but also the future, especially future generations. It's not that people with a long-term orientation don't value efficiency and effectiveness; they simply accept that things don't always happen quickly.

People with a short-term orientation to time will want to know what immediate action steps can be taken to solve a problem. They are also results-oriented and expect that individual or group effort should result in a some specific positive outcome.

**Group Membership** It's said we are all members of a gang—it's just that some gangs are more socially acceptable than others. We are social creatures; we congregate in groups to gain an identity, to help accomplish projects we support, and to have fun. So it's reasonable to assume that many of your listeners belong to groups, clubs, or organizations. One way to gather information about a specific group you are going to speak to is to see if the group or organization has a Web site or Facebook page. Knowing something about the history, purpose, values, and accomplishments of a group can help you customize your message.

- **Religious groups.** Marsha is a follower of Scientology, and she believes that the philosophy outlined in *Dianetics* (the book that is the basis of Scientology) is as important as the religious precepts in the Bible. Planning to speak before a Bible-belt college audience, many of whose members view Scientology as a cult, Marsha would be wise to consider how her listeners will respond to her message. This is not to suggest that she should refuse the speaking invitation. She should, however, be aware of her audience's religious beliefs as she prepares and presents her speech.

  When touching on religious beliefs or an audience's values, use great care in what you say and how you say it. Remind yourself that some members of your audience will undoubtedly not share your beliefs, and that few beliefs are held as intensely as religious ones. If you do not wish to offend your listeners, plan and deliver your speech with much thought and sensitivity.

- **Political groups.** Are members of your audience active in politics? Knowing whether your listeners are active in such groups as Young Republicans or Young Democrats can help you address political topics. Members of environmental groups may also hold strong ecological opinions on issues and political candidates.

- **Work groups.** Most professions give rise to professional organizations or associations to which people can belong. If you are speaking to an audience of professionals, it's important to be aware of professional organizations they may belong to (there may be several) and to know, for example, whether those organizations have taken formal stands that may influence audience members' views on certain issues. Work groups may also have abbreviations or acronyms that may be useful to know. Your communication instructor, for example, may be a member of the National Communication Association (NCA) and may belong to a specific division of the NCA, such as the IDD (Instructional Development Division).

- **Social groups.** Some groups exist just so that people can get together and enjoy a common activity. Book clubs, film clubs, cycling clubs, cooking groups, dancing groups, and bowling teams exist to bring people with similar ideas of fun together to enjoy the activity. Knowing whether members of your audience belong to such groups may help you adapt your topic to them or, if you are involved in similar groups, establish common ground with them.

- **Service groups.** Many people are actively involved in groups that emphasize community service as their primary mission. If you are speaking to a service group such as the Lions Club or the Kiwanis Club, you can reasonably assume that your listeners value community service and will be interested in how to make their community a better place.

**Socioeconomic Status** **Socioeconomic status** is a person's perceived importance and influence based on such factors as income, occupation, and education level. In Europe, Asia, the Middle East, and other parts of the world, centuries-old traditions of acknowledging status differences still exist today. Status differences exist in the United States but are often more subtle. A general estimate of your audience members' incomes, occupations, and education levels can be helpful as you develop a message that connects with listeners.

- **Income.** Having some general idea of the income level of your listeners can be of great value to you as a speaker. For example, if you know that most audience members are struggling to meet weekly expenses, it will be unwise to talk about how to see the cultural riches of Europe by traveling first class. But talking about how to get paid to travel to Europe by serving as a courier may hold considerable interest.

- **Occupation.** Knowing what people do for a living can give you useful information about how to adapt your message to them. Speaking to teachers, you will want to use different examples and illustrations than if you were speaking to lawyers, ministers, or automobile assembly-line workers. Many college-age students may hold jobs but not yet the jobs they aspire to after they graduate. Knowing their future career plans can help you adjust your topic and supporting material to your listeners' professional goals.

- **Education.** About one-third of U.S. high school graduates obtain a college diploma. Less than 10 percent of the population earn graduate degrees. The educational background of your listeners is yet another component of socioeconomic status that can help you plan your message. For example, you have a good idea that your classmates in your college-level public-speaking class value education because they are striving, often at great sacrifice, to advance their education. Knowing the educational background of your audience can help you make decisions about your choice of vocabulary, your language style, and your use of examples and illustrations.

**Adapting to Diverse Listeners** The most recent U.S. Census figures document what you already know from your own life experiences: We all live in an age of diversity. For example:

- Two-thirds of emigrants worldwide come to the United States.[11]
- It is estimated that more than 40 million U.S. residents speak something other than English as their first language, including 18 million people whose first language is Spanish.[12]

**socioeconomic status**
A person's perceived importance and influence based on income, occupation, and education level

*Focus on a target audience, but use strategies to accommodate a diverse audience, too. Use a variety of supporting materials, tell stories, balance logical and emotional support, and appeal to commonly held values. You can also use visual materials to reinforce your message and help overcome any language barriers.*
[Photo: Getty Images/Digital Vision]

- Whites are the minority ethnic group in nearly half of the largest cities in the United States.[13]
- People who have traditionally been called minorities are now in the majority in four states: Hawaii (75 percent), New Mexico (57 percent), California (57 percent), and Texas (52 percent).[14]
- During the past decade in the United States, the combined population of African Americans, Native Americans, Asians, Pacific Islanders, and Hispanics grew thirteen times faster than the non-Hispanic White population.[15]

Virtually every state in the United States has experienced a dramatic increase in foreign-born residents. If trends continue as they have during the past quarter-century, cultural and ethnic diversity will continue to grow during your lifetime. This swell of immigrants translates to increased diversity in all aspects of society, including in most audiences you'll face—whether in business, at school-board meetings, or in your college classes.

Audience diversity, however, involves factors beyond ethnic and cultural differences. Central to our point about considering your audience is examining the full spectrum of audience diversity, not just cultural differences. Each topic we've reviewed when discussing demographic and psychological aspects of an audience contributes to overall audience diversity. Diversity simply means differences. Audience members are diverse. The question and challenge for a public speaker is, "How do I adapt to listeners with such different backgrounds and experiences?" We offer several general strategies. You could decide to focus on a target audience, consciously use a variety of methods of adapting to listeners, seek common ground, or consider using powerful visual images to present your key points.

- **Focus on a target audience.** A **target audience** is a specific segment of your audience that you most want to address or influence. You've undoubtedly been a target of skilled communicators and may not have been aware that messages had been tailored just for you. For example, most colleges and universities spend a considerable amount of time and money encouraging students to apply for admission. You probably received recruitment literature in the mail during your high school years. But not every student in the United States receives brochures from the same college. Colleges and universities targeted you based on your test scores, your interests, where you live, and your involvement in school-sponsored or extracurricular activities. Likewise, as a public speaker, you may want to think about the portion of your audience you most want to understand your message or to be convinced.

  The challenge when consciously focusing on a target audience is not to lose or alienate the rest of your listeners—to keep the entire audience in mind while simultaneously making a specific attempt to hit your target segment. For example, Sasha was trying to convince his listeners to invest in the stock market instead of relying only on Social Security. He wisely decided to focus on the younger listeners; those approaching retirement age have already made their major investment decisions. Although he focused on the younger members of his audience, however, Sasha didn't forget the mature listeners. He suggested that older listeners encourage their children or grandchildren to consider his proposal. He focused on a target audience, but he didn't ignore others.

- **Use diverse strategies for a diverse audience.** Another approach you can adopt, either separately or in combination with a target audience focus, is to use a variety of strategies to reflect the diversity of your audience. Based on your efforts to gather information about your audience, you should know the various constituencies that will likely be present for your talk. Consider using several methods of reaching the different listeners in your audience. For example, review the following strategies:

**target audience**
A specific segment of an audience that you most want to influence

- Use a variety of supporting materials (illustrations, examples, statistics, opinions).
- Remember the power of stories. People from most cultures appreciate a good story. And some people, such as those from Asian and Middle Eastern cultures, prefer hearing stories and parables used to make a point or support an argument, rather than facts and statistics.
- If you're very uncertain about cultural preferences, use a balance of both logical support (statistics, facts, specific examples) and emotional support (stories and illustrations).
- Consider showing the audience an outline of your key ideas using PowerPoint™. If there is a language barrier between you and your audience, being able to read portions of your speech as they hear you speaking may improve audience members' comprehension. If an interpreter is translating your message, an outline can also help ensure that your interpreter will communicate your message accurately.

• **Identify common values.** People have long debated whether there are universal human values. Several scholars have made strong arguments that common human values do exist. Communication researcher David Kale suggests that all people can identify with the individual struggle to enhance one's own dignity and worth, although different cultures express that in different ways.[16] A second common value is the search for a world at peace. Underlying that quest is a fundamental desire for equilibrium, balance, and stability. Although there may always be a small but corrosive minority of people whose actions do not support the universal value of peace, the prevailing human values in most cultures ultimately do support peace.

Cultural anthropologists specialize in the study of behavior that is common to all humans. Cultural anthropologist Donald Brown has compiled a list of hundreds of "surface" universals of beliefs, emotions, or behavior.[17] According to Brown, people in all cultures

- Have beliefs about death
- Have a childhood fear of strangers
- Have a division of labor by sex
- Experience certain emotions and feelings, such as envy, pain, jealousy, shame, and pride
- Use facial expressions to express emotions
- Have rules for etiquette
- Experience empathy
- Value some degree of collaboration or cooperation
- Experience conflict and seek to manage or mediate conflict

Of course, not all cultures have the same beliefs about death or the same way of dividing up labor—but people in all cultures address these issues.

Intercultural communication scholars Larry Samovar and Richard Porter suggest other commonalities that people from all cultures share. They propose that all humans seek physical pleasure as well as emotional and psychological pleasure and confirmation and seek to avoid personal harm.[18] Although each culture defines what constitutes pleasure and pain, it may be useful to interpret human behavior with these general assumptions in mind. People also realize that their biological lives will end, that to some degree each person is isolated from all other human beings, that we each make choices, and that each person seeks to give life meaning. These similarities offer some basis for developing common messages with universal meaning.

Identifying common cultural issues and similarities can help you establish common ground with your audience. If you are speaking about an issue on which you and your audience have widely different views, identifying a larger common value that is relevant to your topic (such as the importance of peace, prosperity, or family) can help you find a foothold so that your listeners will at least listen to your ideas.

- **Rely on visual materials that transcend language differences.** Pictures and other images can communicate universal messages—especially emotional ones. Although there is no universal language, most listeners, regardless of culture and language, can comprehend visible expressions of pain, joy, sorrow, and happiness. An image of a mother holding the frail, malnourished body of her dying child communicates the ravages of famine without elaborate verbal explanations. The more varied your listeners' cultural experiences, the more effective it can be to use visual materials to illustrate your ideas.

RECAP

### Adapting to Diverse Listeners

- Focus on a target audience.
- Use diverse supporting materials.
- Balance logic and emotion in supporting materials.
- Use visual aids.
- Appeal to such common values as peace, prosperity, and family.

## Psychological Audience Analysis

Demographic information lets you make useful inferences about your audience and predict likely responses. Learning how the members of your audience feel about your topic and purpose may provide specific clues about possible reactions. A **psychological audience analysis** explores an audience's attitudes toward a topic, purpose, and speaker while probing the underlying beliefs and values that might affect these attitudes.

It is important for a speaker to distinguish among *attitudes*, *beliefs*, and *values*. The attitudes, beliefs, and values of an audience may greatly influence a speaker's selection of a topic and specific purpose, as well as other aspects of speech preparation and delivery.

An **attitude** reflects likes or dislikes. Do you like health food? Are you for or against capital punishment? Should movies be censored? What are your views on nuclear energy? Your answers to these widely varied questions reflect your attitudes.

A **belief** is what you hold to be true or false. If you think the sun will rise in the east in the morning, you hold a belief about the sun based on what you perceive to be true or false.

A **value** is an enduring concept of good and bad, right and wrong. More deeply ingrained than either attitudes or beliefs, values are therefore more resistant to change. Values support both attitudes and beliefs. For example, you like health food because you believe that natural products are more healthful. And you *value* good health. You are against capital punishment because you believe that it is wrong to kill people. You *value* human life. As with beliefs, a speaker who has some understanding of an audience's values is better able to adapt a speech to them.

**psychological audience analysis**
Examining the attitudes, beliefs, values, and other psychological information about an audience in order to develop a clear and effective message

**attitude**
An individual's likes or dislikes

**belief**
An individual's perception of what is true or false

**value**
Enduring concept of good and bad, right and wrong

**Analyzing Attitudes toward the Topic** The topic of a speech provides one focus for an audience's attitudes, beliefs, and values. It is useful to know how members of an audience feel about your topic. Are they interested or apathetic? How much do they already know about the topic? If the topic is controversial, are they for or against it? Knowing the answers to these questions from the outset lets you adjust your message accordingly. For example, if you plan to talk about increasing taxes to improve education in your state, you probably want to know how your listeners feel about taxes and education.

When you are analyzing your audience, it may help to categorize the group along three dimensions: interested–uninterested, favorable–unfavorable, and captive–voluntary. These dimensions are summarized in Table 4.3. With an *interested* audience, your task is simply to hold and amplify their interest throughout the speech. If your

TABLE 4.3 Adapting Your Message to Different Types of Audiences

| Type of Audience | Example | How to Be Audience-Centered |
|---|---|---|
| Interested | Mayors who attend a talk by the governor about increasing security and reducing the threat of terrorism | Acknowledge audience interest early in your speech; use the interest they have in you and your topic to gain and maintain their attention. |
| Uninterested | Junior-high students attending a lecture about retirement benefits | Make it a high priority to tell your listeners why your message should be of interest to them. Remind your listeners throughout your speech how your message relates to their lives. |
| Favorable | A religious group that meets to hear a group leader talk about the importance of their beliefs | Use audience interest to move them closer to your speaking goal; you may be more explicit in telling them in your speech conclusion what you would like them to do. |
| Unfavorable | Students who attend a lecture by the university president explaining why tuition and fees will increase 15 percent next year | Be realistic in what you expect to accomplish; acknowledge listeners' opposing point of view; consider using facts to refute misperceptions they may hold. |
| Voluntary | Parents attending a lecture by the new principal at their children's school | Anticipate why listeners are coming to hear you, and speak about the issues they want you to address. |
| Captive | Students in a public-speaking class | Find out who will be in your audience and use this knowledge to adapt your message to them. |

audience is *uninterested*, you need to find ways to hook the members. In Chapter 14, we describe ways to motivate an audience by addressing issues related to their needs and interests. Given our visually oriented culture, consider using visual aids to gain and maintain the attention of apathetic listeners.

You may also want to gauge how *favorable* or *unfavorable* your audience may feel toward you and your message before you begin to speak. Some audiences, of course, are neutral, apathetic, or simply uninformed about what you plan to say. We provide explicit suggestions for approaching favorable, neutral, and unfavorable audiences in Chapter 15 when we discuss persuasive speaking. But even if your objective is simply to inform, it is useful to know whether your audience is predisposed to respond positively or negatively toward you or your message. Giving an informative talk about classical music would be quite challenging, for example, if you were addressing an audience of die-hard punk-rock fans. You might decide to show the connections between classical music and punk in order to arouse their interest.

**Your Speech Class as Audience** You may think that your public-speaking class is not a typical audience because class members are required to attend: Your speech class is a *captive* audience rather than a *voluntary* one. A captive audience has externally imposed reasons for being there (such as a requirement to attend class). Because class members must show up to earn credit for class, you need not worry that they will get up and leave during your speech. However, your classroom speeches are still *real* speeches. Your class members are certainly real people with likes, dislikes, beliefs, and values.

Your classroom speeches should connect with your listeners so that they forget they are required to be your audience. Class members will listen if your message gives them new, useful information; touches them emotionally; or persuades them to change their opinion or behavior in support of your position.

You will undoubtedly give other speeches to other captive audiences. Audiences at work or at professional meetings are often captive in the sense that they may be required to attend lectures or presentations to receive continuing-education credit or as part of their job duties. Your goal with a captive audience is the same as with other types of audiences. You should make your speech just as interesting and effective as one designed for a voluntary audience. You still have an obligation to address your listeners' needs and interests and to keep them engaged in what you have to say.

**Analyzing Attitudes toward You, the Speaker** Audience members' attitudes toward you in your role as speaker is another factor that can influence their reaction to your speech. Regardless of how they feel about your topic or purpose, if members of an audience regard you as credible, they will be much more likely to be interested in, and supportive of, what you have to say.

Your credibility—others' perception of you as trustworthy, knowledgeable, and interesting—is one of the main factors that will shape your audience's attitude toward you. If you establish your credibility before you begin to discuss your topic, your listeners will be more likely to believe what you say and to think that you are knowledgeable, interesting, and dynamic.

For example, when a high-school health teacher asks a former drug addict to speak to a class about the dangers of cocaine addiction, the teacher recognizes that the speaker's experiences make him credible and that his message will be far more convincing than a teacher's lecture on the perils of cocaine use.

An audience's positive attitude toward a speaker can overcome negative or apathetic attitudes they may have toward the speaker's topic or purpose. If your analysis reveals that your audience does not recognize you as an authority on your subject, you will need to build your credibility into the speech. If you have had personal experience with your topic, be sure to let the audience know. You will gain credibility instantly. We will provide additional strategies for enhancing your credibility in Chapters 8 and 15.

## Situational Audience Analysis

So far we have concentrated on the people who will be your listeners, as the primary focus of being an audience-centered speaker. You should also consider your speaking situation. **Situational audience analysis** includes an examination of the time and place of your speech, the size of your audience, and the speaking occasion. Although these elements are not technically characteristics of the *audience*, they can have a major effect on how your listeners respond to you.

**Time** You may have no control over when you will be speaking, but when designing and delivering a talk, a skilled public speaker considers the time of day as well as audience expectations about the speech length. If you are speaking to a group of exhausted parents during a midweek evening meeting of the band-boosters club, you can bet they will appreciate a direct, to-the-point presentation more than a long oration. If you are on a program with other speakers, speaking first or last on the program carries a slight edge because people tend to remember what comes first or last. Speaking early in the morning when people may not be quite awake, after lunch when they may feel a bit drowsy, or late in the afternoon when they are tired may mean

**situational audience analysis**
Examining of the time and place of a speech, the audience size, and the speaking occasion in order to develop a clear and effective message

you'll have to strive consciously for a more energetic delivery to keep your listeners' attention.

Another aspect of time: Be mindful of your time limits. If your audience expects you to speak for 20 minutes, it is usually better to end either right at 20 minutes or a little earlier; most North Americans don't appreciate being kept overtime for a speech. In your public-speaking class you will be given time limits, and you may wonder whether such strict time-limit expectations occur outside public-speaking class. The answer is a most definite yes. Whether it's a business presentation or a speech to the city council or school board, time limits are often strictly enforced.

**Size of Audience** The size of your audience directly affects speaking style and audience expectations about delivery. As a general rule, the larger the audience, the more likely they are to expect a more formal style. With an audience of ten or fewer, you can punctuate a very conversational style by taking questions from your listeners. If you and your listeners are so few that you can be seated around a table, they may expect you to stay seated for your presentation. Many business "speeches" are given around a conference table.

A group of twenty to thirty people—the size of most public-speaking classes—will expect more formality than the audience of a dozen or fewer. Your speaking style can still be conversational in character, but your speech should be appropriately structured and well organized; your delivery may include more expansive gestures than you would display during a one-on-one chat with a friend or colleague.

Audiences that fill a lecture hall will still appreciate a direct, conversational style, but your gestures may increase in size, and, if your voice will not be amplified, you will be expected to speak with enough volume and intensity so that people in the last row will hear you.

**Location** In your speech class, you have the advantage of knowing what the room looks like, but in a new speaking situation, you may not have that advantage. If at all possible, visit the place where you will speak to examine the physical setting and find out, for example, how far the audience will be from the lectern. Physical conditions such as room temperature and lighting can affect your performance, the audience response, and the overall success of the speech.

Room arrangement and decor may affect the way an audience responds. Be aware of the arrangement and appearance of the room in which you will speak. If your speaking environment is less than ideal, you may need to work especially hard to hold your audience's attention. Although you probably won't be able to make major changes in the speaking environment, it is ultimately up to you to obtain the best speaking environment you can. The arrangement of chairs, placement of audiovisual materials, and opening or closing of drapes should all be in your control.

**Occasion** Another important way to gain clues about your listeners is to consider the reason why they are here. What occasion brings this audience together? The mindset of people gathered for a funeral will obviously be different from that of people who've asked you to say a few words after a banquet. Knowing the occasion helps you predict both the demographic characteristics of the audience and the members' state of mind.

If you're presenting a speech at an annual or monthly meeting, you have the advantage of being able to ask those who've attended previous presentations what kind of audience typically gathers for the occasion. Your best source of information may be either the person who invited you to speak or someone who has attended similar events. Knowing when you will speak on the program or whether a meal will be served before or after you talk will help you gauge what your audience expects from you.

## TABLE 4.4 Analyzing and Adapting to the Speaking Situation

| Questions to Ask | Adaptation Strategies |
|---|---|
| **Time** | |
| What time of the day will I be speaking? | If your audience may be tired or not yet fully awake, consider increasing the energy level of your delivery. |
| Where will I appear on the program? | Audiences are more likely to get the strongest impressions from those who speak first or last. If you are in the middle of the line-up, you will need to be very dynamic in your delivery and build repetition into your speech, to aid your audience's memories. |
| What are the time limits for the speech? | Most listeners do not appreciate speakers who exceed their time limit. Unless you are a spellbinding speaker, don't speak longer than your listeners expect you to. |
| **Size** | |
| How many people will be in the audience? | Smaller audiences usually expect a more conversational, informal delivery; larger audiences usually expect a more formal presentation. |
| Will the audience be so large I'll need a microphone? | Make sure you understand the mechanics of the microphone system before you rise to speak. |
| **Location** | |
| How will the room be arranged? | If you want a more informal speaking atmosphere, consider arranging the chairs in a circle. In a large room, consider inviting people in the back of the room to move closer to the front if necessary. |
| What is the room lighting like? | If an audience is in the dark, it's more difficult to gauge their nonverbal responses. If you need to use presentation aids, make sure the room lighting is easy to adjust so people can see your images clearly, but you can also see your listeners. |
| Will there be noise or distractions outside the room? | Before the speech begins, consider strategies to minimize outside noise, such as closing windows and doors, adjusting window blinds or shades, or politely asking that people in nearby rooms be mindful of your presentation. |
| **Occasion** | |
| What occasion brings the audience together? | Make sure you understand what your listeners expect, and strive to meet those expectations. |
| Is the speech an annual or monthly event? Has a similar speaking occasion occurred with this audience before? | Learn how other speakers have adapted to the audience. Ask for examples of what successful speakers have done to succeed with this audience. Or ask whether certain issues or topics may offend your audience. |

Advance preparation will help you avoid last-minute surprises about the speaking environment and the physical arrangements for your speech. Table 4.4 provides a list of essential questions you should ask when preparing for a speaking assignment, as well as several suggestions for adapting to your speaking situation. A well-prepared speaker adapts his or her message not only to the audience but also to the speaking environment.

Also keep in mind that when you arrive to give your speech, you can make changes in the previous speaker's room arrangements. For example, the purpose of the speaker immediately before Yue Hong was to generate interest in a memorial for

Asian Americans who fought in Vietnam. Because that speaker wanted to make sure the audience felt free to ask questions, the chairs were arranged in a semicircle and the lights were turned on. But Yue Hong was giving a more formal presentation on the future of the Vietnamese population, which included a brief slide show. So when the preceding speaker had finished, Yue Hong rearranged the chairs and darkened the room.

RECAP

### Elements of Audience Analysis

Demographic Characteristics

- Age
- Gender
- Sexual orientation
- Cultural, ethnic, or racial background
- Group membership
- Socioeconomic status

Psychological Characteristics

- Attitudes: Likes and dislikes
- Beliefs: What is perceived to be true or false
- Values: What is perceived to be good or bad

Situational Characteristics

- Time
- Audience size
- Location
- Occasion

# Adapting to Your Audience as You Speak

So far, we have focused on discovering as much as possible about an audience before the speaking event. Prespeech analyses help with each step of the public-speaking process: selecting a topic, formulating a specific purpose, gathering supporting material, identifying major ideas, organizing the speech, and planning its delivery. Each of these components depends on your understanding your audience. But audience analysis and adaptation do not end when you have crafted your speech. They continue as you deliver your speech.

Generally, a public speaker does not have an exchange with the audience unless the speech is part of a question-and-answer or discussion format. Once the speech is in progress, the speaker must rely on nonverbal cues from the audience to judge how people are responding to the message.

## DEVELOPING YOUR SPEECH STEP BY STEP

### Consider Your Audience

A Chinese proverb says that a journey of a thousand miles begins with a single step. Developing and delivering a speech may seem like a daunting journey. But we believe that if you take it one step at a time and keep your focus on your audience, you'll be rewarded with a well-crafted and well-delivered message.

To help you see how the audience-centered public speaking process unfolds step by step, we will explore each step of the speechmaking process by showing how one student prepared and delivered a successful speech. In 2009, Karen Summerson participated in the Interstate Oratorical Association's 138th annual contest. Her persuasive speech, "There's a Lot Riding on Your Tires," is adapted for the preparation and delivery outlines in Chapter 9.[19] In the chapters ahead, we will walk you through the process Karen followed to develop her speech.

Even before she selected her topic, Karen thought about her audience. Realizing that her listeners would include both university students and faculty, she began to think about topics that would be relevant to both groups. And she knew that she would be able to discuss complex issues, using a fairly advanced vocabulary, for this educated audience.

The *Developing Your Speech Step by Step* feature in the chapters ahead will provide a window through which you can watch Karen at work on each step of the audience-centered public speaking process.

## Identifying Nonverbal Audience Cues

Once, when speaking in India, Mark Twain was denied eye contact with his listeners by a curtain separating him from his audience. Mark Twain's daughter, Clara, recalled this experience:

> One of Father's first lectures was before a Purdah audience; in other words, the women all sat behind a curtain through which they could peek at Mark Twain without being seen by him . . . a deadly affair for the poor humorist, who had not even the pleasure of scanning the faces of his mute audience.[20]

Mark Twain missed learning how well his speech was being received as he was speaking. You could experience the same disadvantage if you fail to look at your listeners while you speak.

Many beginning public speakers may find it challenging at first not only to have the responsibility of presenting a speech they have rehearsed, but also to have to change or modify that speech on the spot. We assure you that with experience you can develop the sensitivity to adapt to your listeners, much as a jazz musician adapts to the other musicians in the ensemble. But it will take practice. Although it's not possible to read your listeners' minds, it is important to analyze and adapt to cues that can enhance the effectiveness of your message. The first step in developing this skill is to be aware of the often unspoken cues that let you know whether your audience either is hanging on every word or is bored. After learning to "read" your audience, you then need to consider developing a repertoire of behaviors to help you better connect with your listeners.

**Eye Contact** Perhaps the best way to determine whether your listeners are maintaining interest in your speech is to note the amount of eye contact they have with you. The more contact they have, the more likely it is that they are listening to your message. If you find them repeatedly looking at their watches, looking down at the program (or, worse yet, closing their eyes), you can reasonably guess that they have lost interest in what you're talking about.

**Facial Expression** Another clue to whether an audience is with you is facial expression. Members of an attentive audience not only make direct eye contact but also have attentive facial expressions. Beware of a frozen, unresponsive face; we call this sort of expression the "listener-stupor" look. The classic listener-stupor expression consists of a slightly tilted head, a faint, frozen smile, and often a hand holding up the chin. This expression may give the appearance of interest, but more often it means that the person is daydreaming or thinking of something other than your topic.

**Movement** An attentive audience doesn't move much. An early sign of inattentiveness is fidgeting fingers, which may escalate to pencil wagging, leg jiggling, and arm wiggling. Seat squirming, feet shuffling, and general body movement often indicate that members of the audience have lost interest in your message.

**Nonverbal Responsiveness** Interested audience members respond verbally and nonverbally when encouraged or invited to do so by the speaker. When you ask for a show of hands and audience members sheepishly look at one another and eventually raise a finger or two, you can reasonably infer lack of interest and enthusiasm. Frequent applause and nods of agreement with your message are indicators of interest and support.

**Verbal Responsiveness** Not only will audiences indicate agreement nonverbally, some will also indicate their interests verbally. Audience members may shout out a response or more quietly express agreement or disagreement to people seated next to them. A sensitive public speaker is constantly listening for verbal reinforcement or disagreement.

## Responding to Nonverbal Cues

The value in recognizing nonverbal cues from your listeners is that you can respond to them appropriately. If your audience seems interested, supportive, and attentive, your prespeech analysis has clearly guided you to make proper choices in preparing and delivering your speech.

When your audience becomes inattentive, however, you may need to make some changes while delivering your message. If you think audience members are drifting off into their own thoughts or disagreeing with what you say, or if you suspect that they don't understand what you are saying, then a few spontaneous adjustments may help. It takes experience and skill to make on-the-spot changes in your speech. Consider the tips from seasoned public speakers for adapting to your listeners listed in Table 4.5 on page 102.[21]

Remember, it is not enough to note your listeners' characteristics and attitudes. You must also *respond* to the information you gather by adapting your speech to retain their interest and attention. Moreover, you have a responsibility to ensure that your audience understands your message. If your approach to the content of your speech is not working, alter it and note whether your audience's responses change. If all else fails, you may need to abandon a formal speaker-listener relationship with your audience and open up your topic for discussion. In your speech class your instructor may expect you to keep going, to fulfill the requirements for your assignment. With other audiences, however, you may want to consider switching to a more interactive question-and-answer session to ensure that you are communicating clearly. Later chapters on supporting material, speech organization, and speech delivery will discuss other techniques for adjusting your style while delivering your message.

RECAP

### Reading Audience Cues

Identify and respond to nonverbal cues that your audience is bored, doesn't understand, or disagrees:

- Lack of eye contact
- "Listener-stupor" expression
- Physical restlessness
- No response to humor, speaker invitations
- Talking to other listeners

## Strategies for Customizing Your Message to Your Audience

Many people value having something prepared especially for them. Perhaps you've bought a computer that you ordered to your exact specifications. In a restaurant you order food prepared to your specific taste. Audiences, too, prefer messages that are adapted just to them; they don't like hearing a canned message. As a speaker, you may have worked hard to adapt your message to your audience, but your audience won't give you credit for it unless you let them know that you've done so. What are some ways to communicate to your listeners that your message is designed specifically for them? Here are a few suggestions:

- **Appropriately use audience members' names.** Consider using audience members' names in your talk to relate specific information to individual people. Obviously, you don't want to embarrass people by using them in an example that would make them feel uncomfortable. But you can selectively mention people you know who are in the audience. It's become a standard technique in many State of the Union speeches for the president to have someone sitting in the balcony who can be mentioned in his talk. That person becomes a living visual aid to provide focus on an idea or a point made in the address. If you are uncertain whether you should mention someone by name, before you speak, ask the person for permission to use his or her name in your talk.

- **Refer to the town, city, or community.** Make a specific reference to the place where you are speaking. If you are speaking to a college audience, relate your message and illustrations to the school where you are speaking. Many politicians use this technique: They have a standard stump speech to tout their credentials but

## TABLE 4.5 Responding to Nonverbal Cues

| | |
|---|---|
| **If your audience seems inattentive or bored . . .** | • Tell a story.<br>• Use an example to which the audience can relate.<br>• Use a personal example.<br>• Remind your listeners why your message should be of interest to them.<br>• Eliminate some abstract facts and statistics.<br>• Use appropriate humor. If listeners do not respond to your humor, use more stories or personal illustrations.<br>• Consider making direct references to listeners, using audience members' names or mentioning something about them.<br>• Ask the audience to participate by asking questions or asking them for an example.<br>• Ask for a direct response, such as a show of hands, to see whether they agree or disagree with you.<br>• Pick up the pace of your delivery.<br>• Increase your speaking energy.<br>• Pause for dramatic effect and to gain attention. |
| **If your audience seems confused or doesn't seem to understand your point . . .** | • Be more redundant.<br>• Try phrasing your information in another way.<br>• Use more concrete examples to illustrate your point.<br>• Use a visual such as a chalkboard or flip chart to clarify your point.<br>• If you have been speaking rapidly, slow your speaking rate.<br>• Clarify the overall organization of your message to your listeners.<br>• Ask audience members whether they understand your message.<br>• Ask for feedback from an audience member to help you discover what is unclear.<br>• Ask someone in the audience to summarize the key point you are making. |
| **If your audience seems to be disagreeing with your message . . .** | • Provide additional data and evidence to support your point.<br>• Remind your listeners of your credibility, credentials, or background.<br>• Rely less on anecdotes and more on facts to present your case.<br>• Write facts and data on a chalkboard, whiteboard, or flip chart if one is handy.<br>• If you don't have the answer and data you need, tell listeners you will provide more information by mail, telephone, or e-mail (and make sure you get back in touch with them). |

adapt the opening part of their message to the specific city or community in which they are speaking.

- **Refer to a significant event that happened on the date of your speech.** Most libraries have books (such as the *Speaker's Lifetime Library*) that identify significant events in world or national history.[22] An even easier way to find out what happened on any given day in history is to go to www.history.com and click on the link called "This Day in History." Type in date and you'll quickly discover any number of events that occurred on that day. For example, on the day this paragraph was written, Julius Caesar was assassinated in 44 B.C.E. It's also known as the Ides of March—a day Caesar was warned about in Shakespeare's famous play. If you were giving a speech on this day, a reference to the Ides of March might be especially apropos if your goal was to encourage your audience to beware of whatever issue or topic you were discussing.

  Many newspapers keep records of local historical events and list what happened 10, 25, or 50 years ago on a certain date. Relating your talk to a historical event that occurred on the same date as your talk can give your message a feeling of immediacy. It tells your audience that you have thought about this specific speaking event.

- **Refer to a recent news event.** Always read the local paper to see whether there is a news story that you can connect to the central idea of your talk. Or, perhaps you can use a headline from your university newspaper or a recent story that appeared on your university Web site. If there is a newspaper headline that connects with your talk, consider holding up the paper as you refer to it—not so that people will be able to read the headline, but to emphasize the immediacy of your message.

- **Refer to a group or organization.** If you're speaking to an audience of service, religious, political, or work group members, by all means make specific positive references to the group. But be honest—don't offer false praise; audiences can sniff out phony flattery. A sincere compliment about the group will be appreciated, especially if you can link the goals of the group to the goal of your talk.

- **Relate information directly to your listeners.** Find ways to apply facts, statistics, and examples to the people in your audience. If, for example, you know that four out of ten women are likely to experience gender discrimination, customize that statistic by saying, "Forty percent of women listening to me now are likely to experience gender discrimination. That means that of the twenty women in this audience, eight of you are likely to be discriminated against." Or, if you live in a city of 50,000 people, you can cite the statistic that 50,000 people on our nation's highways become victims of drunk driving each year—and then point out that that number is equivalent to killing every man, woman, and child in your city. Relating abstract statistics and examples to your listeners communicates that you have them in mind as you develop your message.

## Analyzing Your Audience after You Speak

After you have given your speech, you're not finished analyzing your audience. It is important to evaluate your audience's positive or negative response to your message. Why? Because this evaluation can help you prepare your next speech. Postspeech analysis helps you polish your speaking skill, regardless of whether you will face the same audience again. From that analysis you can learn whether your examples were clear and your message was accepted by your listeners. Let's look at specific methods for assessing your audience's response to your speech.

*Your audience's nonverbal response, as well as their words and actions, will help you evaluate their reaction to your message. This audience's smiles and applause suggest that the person shaking the speaker's hand is offering sincere congratulations.*
[Photo: David De Lossy/Getty Images Inc. RF]

## Nonverbal Responses

The most obvious nonverbal response is applause. Is the audience simply clapping politely, or is the applause robust and enthusiastic, indicating pleasure and acceptance? Responsive facial expressions, smiles, and nods are other nonverbal signs that the speech has been well received.

Realize, however, that audience members from different cultures respond to speeches in different ways. Japanese audience members, for example, are likely to be restrained in their response to a speech and to show little expression. Some Eastern European listeners may not maintain eye contact with you; they may look down at the floor when listening. In some contexts, African American listeners may enthusiastically voice their agreement or disagreement with something you say during your presentation.[23]

Nonverbal responses at the end of the speech may convey some general feeling of the audience, but they are not much help in identifying which strategies were the most effective. Also consider what the members of the audience say, both to you and to others, after your speech.

## Verbal Responses

What might members of the audience say to you about your speech? General comments, such as "I enjoyed your talk" and "Great speech," are good for the ego—which is important—but are not of much analytic help. Specific comments can indicate where you succeeded and where you failed. If you have the chance, ask audience members how they responded to the speech in general as well as to points you are particularly interested in.

## Survey Responses

You are already aware of the value of conducting audience surveys before speaking publicly. You may also want to survey your audience after you speak. You can then assess how well you accomplished your objective. Use the same survey techniques discussed earlier. Develop survey questions that will help you determine the general reactions to you and your speech, as well as specific responses to your ideas and supporting materials.

Professional speakers and public officials often conduct such surveys. Postspeech surveys are especially useful when you are trying to persuade an audience. Comparing prespeech and postspeech attitudes can give you a clear idea of your effectiveness. A significant portion of most political campaign budgets goes toward evaluating how a candidate is received by his or her constituents. Politicians want to know what portions of their messages are acceptable to their audiences so they can use this information in the future.

If your objective was to teach your audience about some new idea, a posttest can assess whether you expressed your ideas clearly. In fact, classroom exams are posttests that determine whether your instructor presented information clearly.

## Behavioral Responses

If the purpose of your speech was to persuade your listeners to do something, you will want to learn whether they ultimately behave as you intended. If you wanted them to vote in an upcoming election, you might survey your listeners to find out how many did vote. If you wanted to win support for a particular cause or organization, you might ask them to sign a petition after your speech. The number of signatures would be a clear measure of your speech's success. Some religious speakers judge the success of their ministry by the amount of contributions they receive. Your listeners' actions are the best indicators of your speaking success.

RECAP

### Ways to Analyze Your Audience after Speaking

- Quality of applause and other nonverbal responses
- Content and tone of specific verbal responses
- Formal survey responses
- Behavioral responses

# STUDY GUIDE

## Gathering Information about Your Audience

You can gather information about your audience by informally observing their demographics. Formal surveys, with either open-ended or closed-ended questions, can add more specific information about their opinions.

### Being Audience-Centered

- Gather such demographic information about your listeners as their age, race, gender, socioeconomic status, and religious views.
- Consider the proportion of males and females in your audience to help you appropriately adapt your message to them; avoid sexist language and make sure your message addresses the needs and interests of both men and women in your audience.

### Using What You've Learned

- Phil Owens is running for a seat on the school board. He has agreed to speak to the chamber of commerce about his views, but he wants to know what his audience believes about a number of issues. How can he gather this information?

## Analyzing Information about Your Audience

Your audience analysis involves looking at the information you've gathered to find (1) similarities among audience members, (2) differences among audience members, and (3) ways to establish a relationship, or common ground, with listeners.

### A Question of Ethics

- Do most politicians place too much emphasis on the results of political-opinion polls to shape their stands on political issues? Explain your position.

## Adapting to Your Audience

Ethical speakers use their audience analysis to adapt their message so that audience members will listen.

### A Question of Ethics

- Maria strongly believes the drinking age in her state should be increased to 22. Yet when she surveyed her classmates, the overwhelming majority thought the drinking age should be lowered to 18. Should Maria change her speech topic and her purpose to avoid facing a hostile audience? Why or why not?

## Analyzing Your Audience before You Speak

Before your speech, you can perform three kinds of analysis: demographic, psychological, and situational. Demographic analysis assesses audience diversity. Psychological audience analysis helps you gauge the interests, attitudes, beliefs, and values of listeners. Situational audience analysis includes examining the time and place of your speech, the size of your audience, and the speaking occasion.

### Being Audience-Centered

- Strategies for adapting to a diverse audience include (1) focusing on a target audience, (2) using diverse strategies (3) using common audience perspectives, and (4) relying on visual materials that transcend language differences.

### Using What You've Learned

- Dr. Ruiz thought the audience for her speech on birth control would be women of childbearing age. After writing her speech, however, she found out that all the women to whom she will be speaking are at least twenty years older than she expected. What changes, if any, should she make?

### A Question of Ethics

- Dan knows that most of the women in his audience will be startled and probably offended if he begins his speech by saying, "Most of you broads are too sensitive about sexist language." But this is how Dan really feels. Should he alter his language just to appease his audience? Explain.

### Speaker's Homepage: Gathering Information about Your Audience

The following Web sites provide information that may help you better understand your listeners' backgrounds and interests.

- U.S. Bureau of Labor Statistics

  This is a great source for socioeconomic data.

  www.bls.gov

- Gallup Poll

  This provides selected results from the vast resources of the Gallup polling organization.

  www.gallup.com
- U.S. Census Bureau

  This is a valuable source that includes reports on demographics.

  www.census.gov/

## Analyzing Your Audience as You Speak

While speaking, look for feedback from your listeners. Audience eye contact, facial expression, movement, and general verbal and nonverbal responsiveness provide clues to how well you are doing.

### Being Audience-Centered

- Listeners' nonverbal reactions may indicate that you need to change or adjust your message to maintain interest and achieve your speaking objective.

### Using What You've Learned

- You are in the middle of your presentation, trying to persuade a group of investors to build a new shopping mall in your community. You notice a few of the audience members losing eye contact with you, shifting in their seats, and glancing at their phones. What do you do to regain their attention?

## Analyzing Your Audience after You Speak

Evaluate audience reaction after your speech. Again, nonverbal cues as well as verbal ones will help you judge your speaking skill. The best indicator of your speaking success is whether your audience is able or willing to follow your advice or remembers what you have told them.

# SPEECH WORKSHOP

## Developing Communication Strategies to Adapt to Your Audience

Use this worksheet to analyze your audience and adapt your message to them.

| Audience Characteristics | What strategies will you use to adapt your message to your audience? |
|---|---|
| **Demographic Characteristics** | |
| Age range: | |
| Average age: | |
| Percentage of women: | |
| Percentage of men: | |
| Predominant ethnicity: | |
| Educational backgrounds: | |
| Group memberships: | |
| Socioeconomic status: | |

| Audience Characteristics | What strategies will you use to adapt your message to your audience? |
|---|---|
| **Psychological Characteristics** | |
| Attitudes toward my topic: | |
| Beliefs about my topic: | |
| Common audience values: | |
| **Situational Analysis** | |
| Time speech will be delivered: | |
| Size of audience: | |
| Location of speech: | |
| Occasion or reason for speech: | |

IN ALL MATTERS, BEFORE BEGINNING, A DILIGENT PREPARATION SHOULD BE MADE.

—CICERO

Jacob Lawrence (1917–2000), *Builders in the City,* 1993. Gouache on paper, 19 x 28 1/2". Courtesy of SBC Communications, Inc. Private Collection. Photo: the Jacob and Gwendolyn Lawrence Foundation/Art Resource, N.Y.

OUTLINE

# 5 Developing Your Speech

OBJECTIVES

**After studying this chapter you should be able to do the following:**

1. Select a topic for a classroom speech that is appropriate to the audience, the occasion, and yourself.
2. Narrow a topic so that it can be thoroughly discussed within the time limits allotted for a specific assignment.
3. Write an audience-centered specific-purpose statement for an assigned topic.
4. Explain three ways of generating main ideas from a central idea.
5. Develop a blueprint for a speech by combining the central idea and a preview of the main ideas.
6. Apply to a speaking assignment the four steps for getting from a blank sheet of paper to a plan for the speech.

Ed Garcia has arranged the books and papers on his desk into neat, even piles. He has sharpened his pencils and laid them out parallel to one another. He has even dusted his desktop and cleaned the computer monitor's screen. Ed can think of no other way to delay writing his speech. He opens a new word-processing document, carefully centers the words "Informative Speech" at the top of the first page, and then slouches in his chair, staring glumly at the blank expanse that threatens his well-being. Finally, he types the words "College Football" under the words "Informative Speech." Another long pause. Hesitantly, he begins his first sentence: "Today I want to talk to you about college football." Rereading his first ten words, Ed decides that they sound moronic. He deletes the sentence and tries again. This time the screen looks even blanker than before. He writes—deletes—writes—deletes. Half an hour later, Ed is exhausted and still mocked by a blank screen. And he is frantic—this speech *has* to be ready by 9 in the morning.

Getting from a blank screen or sheet of paper to a speech outline is often the biggest hurdle you will face as a public speaker. Fortunately, however, it is one that you can learn to clear. If your earlier efforts at speech writing have been like Ed Garcia's, take heart. Just as you learned to read, do long division, drive a car, and get through college registration, so too can you learn to prepare a speech.

The first steps in preparing a speech are:

1. Select and narrow your topic.
2. Determine your purpose.
3. Develop your central idea.
4. Generate your main ideas.

At the end of step 4, you will have a plan for the speech, and you will be ready to develop and polish your main ideas further. For most brief classroom speeches (under 10 minutes), you should allow at least one week between selecting a topic and delivering your speech. A week gives you enough time to develop and research your speech. Many habitual procrastinators like Ed Garcia, who grudgingly decide to begin an assignment a week in advance, learn to their surprise that the whole process is far easier than it would be if they put off working until the night before they are supposed to deliver their speech.

As we observed in Chapter 4, audience-centered speakers consider the needs, interests, and expectations of their audience during the entire speech-preparation process—needs, interests, and expectations that will be as diverse as the audiences themselves. As you move from topic selection to speech plan, remember that you are preparing a message for your listeners. Always keep the audience as your central focus.

# Select and Narrow Your Topic

Your first task, as illustrated in Figure 5.1, is to choose a topic on which to speak. You will then need to narrow this topic to fit your time limit. Sometimes you can eliminate one or both of these steps because the topic has been chosen and properly defined for you. For example, knowing that you visited England's Lake District on your tour of Great Britain last summer, your English literature teacher asks you to speak about the mountains and lakes of that region before your class studies the poetry of Wordsworth and Coleridge. Or, knowing that you chair the local drug-abuse task force, the Lions Club asks you to speak at its weekly meeting about the work of your group. In both cases, your topic and its scope have been decided for you.

In other instances, the choice of topic may be left entirely to you. In your public-speaking class, your instructor may specify a time limit and the type of speech (informative, persuasive, or entertaining) but allow you to choose your topic. In this event, you should realize that the success of your speech may rest on your decision.

But how do you go about choosing an appropriate, interesting topic?

## Guidelines for Selecting a Topic

The late NBC political analyst and author Tim Russert, a popular speaker on college campuses, delivered much the same speech more than once. Finally, during a presentation at Harvard, students called his bluff:

> Equipped with cards listing pat phrases from past speeches, set out in a bingo-like format, they ticked off the passages as Mr. Russert spoke and then, having completed a row, shouted out "Bingo!"[1]

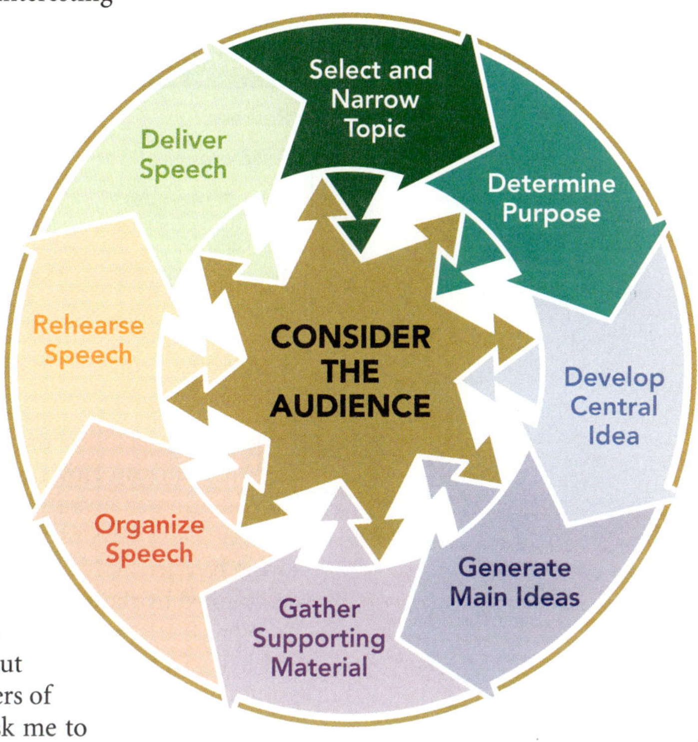


FIGURE 5.1 *Selecting and narrowing the topic and determining the general and specific purposes of the speech are early speechmaking tasks.*

**Consider the Audience** Russert's mistake was to rely on a standard spiel, rather than tailor his speeches to each specific audience. In Chapter 4 we discussed the reasons and methods for finding out about your audience. "What interests and needs do the members of this audience have in common?" and "Why did they ask me to speak?" are important questions to ask yourself as you search for potential speech topics. Keep in mind each audience's interests and expectations. For example, a university president invited to speak to a civic organization should talk about some new university program or recent accomplishment; a police officer speaking to an elementary school's PTA should address the audience's concern for the safety of young children.

Not only should a speaker's choice of topic be relevant to the *interests* and *expectations* of his or her listeners, it should also take into account the *knowledge* listeners already have about the subject. For example, the need for a campuswide office of disability services would not be a good topic to discuss in a speech to a group of students with disabilities, who would already be well aware of such a need. The speech would offer them no new information.

Finally, speakers should choose topics that are *important*—topics that matter to their listeners as well as to themselves. Student speaker Roger Fringer explains the stakes for students in a public-speaking class:

> We work hard for our tuition, so we should spend it wisely. Spending it wisely means . . . we don't waste our classmates' time who have to listen to our speeches.[2]

Several years ago communication scholar and then-president of the National Communication Association Bruce Gronbeck reminded an audience of communication instructors that students should be giving "the important kinds of . . . speeches that show . . . people how to confront the issues that divide them. . . ."[3] Table 5.1 on page 114 offers examples of topics appropriate for the interests, expectations, knowledge, and concerns of given audiences.

**Consider the Occasion** On December 17, 1877, Mark Twain was invited to be one of the after-dinner speakers at American poet John Greenleaf Whittier's seventieth-birthday celebration.[4]

### CONFIDENTLY CONNECTING WITH YOUR AUDIENCE

#### Select an Interesting Topic

The more confident you are about the topic you have selected, the more confident you will be in speaking to your listeners. Your own interest in and passion about a topic can replace some of the anxiety you may feel about speaking to others. Instead of focusing on your fear, you will more naturally express your interest to your audience, who in turn will find your topic more interesting because you do. Selecting an interesting topic will help you speak with confidence.

**TABLE 5.1** Sample Audience-Centered Topics

| Audience | Topic |
|---|---|
| Retirees | Prescription drug benefits |
| Civic organization | The Special Olympics |
| Church members | Starting a community food bank |
| First graders | What to do in case of a fire at home |
| Teachers | Building children's self-esteem |
| College fraternity | Campus service opportunities |

The guest list included the dignitaries Oliver Wendell Holmes, Ralph Waldo Emerson, William Dean Howells, and Henry Wadsworth Longfellow.

When it was Twain's turn to speak, he began with a burlesque in the style of *Saturday Night Live*, featuring Longfellow, Emerson, and Holmes as drunken card-playing travelers in Nevada. Used to laughter and applause from his audiences, Twain was stunned by the silence that descended and seemed to grow as he continued.

What had gone wrong? Was Mark Twain's topic of *interest* to his listeners? Undoubtedly. Did they *expect* to hear someone talk about the distinguished guests? Yes. Could Twain *add to their knowledge* of the subject? Probably. Was his topic *appropriate to the occasion*? Definitely not!

Although after-dinner speeches are usually humorous, Twain's irreverence was inappropriate to the dignity of the birthday observance. Even though he had considered his audience, he had not considered carefully enough the demands of the occasion. Twain's irreverent talk aroused quite a commotion at the time and is said to have embarrassed him for years afterward. To be successful, a topic must be appropriate to both audience and occasion.

**Consider Yourself** What do you talk about with your friends? You probably discuss school, mutual friends, political or social issues, hobbies or leisure activities, or whatever other topics are of interest and importance to you. Like most people's, your liveliest, most animated conversations revolve around topics of personal concern that arouse your deepest convictions.

*As you search for a topic, think about your own experiences.*
[Photo: Roca/Shutterstock]

The best public-speaking topics are also those that reflect your personal experience or especially interest you. Where have you lived? Where have you traveled? Describe your family or your ancestors. Have you held a part-time job? Describe your first days at college. What are your favorite classes? What are your hobbies or interests? What is your favorite sport? What social issues especially concern you? Here is one list of topics that was generated by such questions:

Blues music

"Yankee, go home": the American tourist in France

Why most diets fail

Behind the counter at McDonald's

My first day at college

Maintaining family ties while living a long distance from home

Getting involved in political campaigns

## LEARNING FROM GREAT SPEAKERS

### Frederick Douglass (1817–1895)

Born a slave in Maryland in 1817, Frederick Douglass became the first African American to serve in a major government position (Ambassador to Haiti) and is widely credited with convincing Abraham Lincoln to sign the Emancipation Proclamation. But Douglass was perhaps best known by his contemporaries as a great orator. He felt passionate about his topics—abolition, the rights of all people—and discovered his main ideas in his own experiences. Charles W. Chesnutt would later write about Douglass's speeches that

> *One can easily imagine their effect upon a sympathetic or receptive audience, when delivered with flashing eye and deep-toned resonant voice by a man whose complexion and past history gave him the highest right to describe and denounce the iniquities of slavery and contend for the rights of a race.*[5]

By speaking on topics about which he was passionate, Frederick Douglass was able to draw on strong personal convictions to persuade his listeners. As you select topics for speeches, consider issues and ideas about which you feel strongly. Speaking about such subjects will boost your energy and augment your power to share your ideas with your listeners.

[Photo: AP Wide World Photos]

An alternative to selecting a topic with which you are already familiar is to select one you would like to know more about. Your interest will motivate both your research and your delivery of the speech.

## Strategies for Selecting a Topic

All successful topics reflect audience, occasion, and speaker. But just contemplating those guidelines does not automatically yield a good topic. Sooner or later, we all find ourselves unable to think of a good speech topic, whether for the first speech of the semester, for that all-important final speech, or for a speaking engagement long after our school years are over. Nothing is so frustrating to a public speaker as floundering for something to talk about!

Fortunately, there are strategies that can help generate speech topics. They are somewhat more artificial than considering audience, occasion, and yourself to produce a "natural" topic choice. Nevertheless, they can yield good topics.

**Brainstorming** A problem-solving technique widely used in such diverse fields as business, advertising, writing, and science, **brainstorming** can easily be used to generate ideas for speech topics as well.[6] To brainstorm a list of potential topics, get a sheet of paper and a pencil or pen. Set a minimum time limit of, say, 3 to 5 minutes. Write down the first topic that comes to mind. Do not allow yourself to evaluate it. Just write it down in a word or a phrase, whether it's a vague idea or a well-focused one. Now jot down a second idea—again, anything that comes to mind. The first topic may remind you of a second possibility. Such "piggybacking" of ideas is perfectly okay. Continue without any restraints until your time is up. At this stage, anything goes. Your goal is quantity—as long a list as you can think up in the time you have.

The following list of 21 possible topics came from a brainstorming session of about 3 minutes:

| | |
|---|---|
| Music | Censorship of music |
| Reggae | Movie themes |
| Bob Marley | Oscar-winning movies of the 1950s |

**brainstorming**
A creative problem-solving technique used to generate many ideas

Sound-recording technology
Retro music
Buddy Holly
The Beatles
John Lennon
Alternative music
Popular rock bands
MTV
Great epic movies
*Titanic* (the movie)
Salvaging the *Titanic* (the ship)
Treasure hunting
Key West, Florida
Ernest Hemingway
Polydactyl cats

If your brainstorming yields several good topics, so much the better. Set aside a page or two in your class notebook for topic ideas, and list the topics you don't end up choosing. You can reconsider them when you get your next assignment.

RECAP

### How to Brainstorm for a Topic

- Start with a blank sheet of paper.
- Set a time limit for brainstorming.
- Begin writing as many possible topics for a speech as you can.
- Do not stop to evaluate your topics; just write them down.
- Let one idea lead to another—free-associate; piggyback off your own ideas.
- Keep writing until your time is up.

**Listening and Reading for Topic Ideas** Very often something you see, hear, or read triggers an idea for a speech. A story on the evening news or in your local paper may suggest a topic. The following list of topics was brought to mind by recent headline stories in a large daily newspaper:

Deep-water oil drilling
Hate crimes
Federal benefits for same-sex couples
Coal mine safety
Mexican drug wars
Predicting volcanic activity
"Food fraud" and the FDA

In addition to discovering topics in news stories, you might find them in an interesting segment of *20/20, Dateline*, or even a daytime talk show. Chances are that a topic covered in one medium has been covered in another as well, allowing extended research on the topic. For example, Oprah's interview of the parents of a child suffering from a genetic disease may be paralleled by *Newsweek*'s report on stem-cell research.

You may also find speech topics in one of your other classes. A lecture in an economics or political-science class may arouse your interest and provide a good topic for your next speech. The instructor of that class could probably suggest additional references on the subject.

Sometimes even a subject you discuss casually with friends can be developed into a good speech topic. You have probably talked with classmates about such campus issues as dormitory regulations, inadequate parking, or your frustration with registration and advisers. Campuswide concerns would be relevant to the student audience in your speech class, as would such matters as how to find a good summer job and the pros and cons of living on or off campus.

Just as you jotted down possible topics generated by brainstorming sessions, remember to write down topic ideas you get from media, class lectures, or informal conversations. If you rely on memory alone, what seems like a great topic today may be only a frustrating blank tomorrow.

**Scanning Web Directories** By now you probably have a list of topics from which to choose. But if all your efforts have failed to produce an idea that satisfies you, try the following strategy.

Access a Web directory such as Yahoo! and select a category at random. Click on it, and look through the subcategories that come up. Click on one of them. Continue to follow the chain of categories until you see a topic that piques your interest—or until you reach a dead end, in which case you can return to the Yahoo! homepage and try again.

A recent random directory search yielded the following categories, listed from general to specific:

Lifestyles
Green living
Carbon footprint calculator

This search took only a few minutes (as will yours, as long as you resist the temptation to begin surfing the Web) and yielded at least one possible topic: calculating your carbon footprint. An additional advantage of this strategy is that you begin to develop your preliminary bibliography while you are searching for a topic.

RECAP

### Selecting a Topic

| **Strategies** | **Guidelines** |
|---|---|
| Brainstorm. | Consider the audience. |
| Listen and read. | Consider the occasion. |
| Scan Web directories. | Consider yourself. |

## Narrowing the Topic

After brainstorming, reading the newspaper, surfing the Web, and talking to friends, you have come up with a topic. For some students, the toughest part of the assignment is over at this point. But others soon experience additional frustration because their topic is so broad that they find themselves overwhelmed with information. How can you cover all aspects of a topic as large as "television" in 3 to 5 minutes? Even if you trained yourself to speak as rapidly as an auctioneer, it would take days to get it all in!

The solution is to narrow your topic so that it fits within the time limits set by your assignment. The challenge lies in *how* to do this. If you have a broad, unmanageable topic, you might first try narrowing it by constructing categories similar to those created by Web directories. Write your general topic at the top of a list, and make each succeeding word in the list a more specific or concrete topic. Megan uses categories to help her narrow her general topic, music. She writes "Music" at the top of a sheet of paper and constructs a categorical hierarchy:

Music
Folk music
Irish folk music
The popularity of Irish folk music in the United States

## DEVELOPING YOUR SPEECH STEP BY STEP

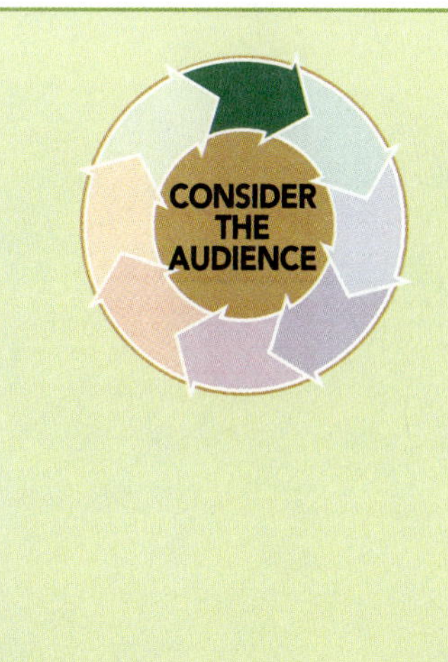


### Select and Narrow Your Topic

While watching *Good Morning America* one Wednesday morning, Karen finds herself caught up in a report on the dangers of driving on tires with unknown expiration dates. She is surprised by the opinions of several experts about the danger of driving on tires that appear stable but are more than six years old. As the feature comes to an end, Karen begins to think that perhaps tires would make a good topic for her speech. After all, most people either drive or ride on a near-daily basis.

As she thinks further and does some preliminary research, Karen realizes that her topic is too broad. To include every factor of tire safety—quality, proper inflation, regular rotation, and balance and alignment—would overwhelm one speech. So she narrows her topic to the issue that prompted it: the lack of clear expiration dates on tires.

Megan soon discovers that her topic is still too broad. She simply cannot cover all the forms of Irish folk music popular in the United States in a talk of no more than 5 minutes. So she chooses one form of music—dance—and decides to talk about the kind of Irish hard-shoe dance music featured in *Riverdance.*

Be careful not to narrow your topic so much that you cannot find enough information for even a 3-minute talk. If you do, just go back a step. In our example, Megan could return to the broader topic of the popularity of Irish folk music in the United States.

# Determine Your Purpose

Now that you have selected and narrowed your topic, you need to decide on a purpose (the next step in Figure 5.1). If you do not know what you want your speech to achieve, chances are your audience won't either. Ask yourself "What is really important for the audience to hear?" and "How do I want the audience to respond?" Clarifying your objectives at this stage will ensure a more interesting speech and a more successful outcome.

## General Purpose

The *general purpose* of virtually any speech is either to inform, to persuade, or to entertain. The speeches you give in class will generally be either informative or persuasive. It is important that you fully understand what constitutes each type of speech so you do not confuse them and fail to fulfill an assignment. You certainly do not want to deliver a first-rate persuasive speech when an informative one was assigned! Although Chapters 13 through 16 discuss the three general purposes at length, we summarize them here so that you can understand the basic principles of each.

**Speaking to Inform** An informative speaker is a teacher. Informative speakers give listeners information. They define, describe, or explain a thing, person, place, concept, process, or function. In this excerpt from a student's informative speech on anorexia nervosa, the student describes the disorder for her audience:

> Anorexia nervosa is an eating disorder that affects 1 out of every 200 American women. It is a self-induced starvation that can waste its victims to the point that they resemble victims of Nazi concentration camps.
>
> Who gets anorexia nervosa? Ninety-five percent of its victims are females between the ages of 12 and 18. Men are only rarely afflicted with the disease. Anorexia nervosa patients are usually profiled as "good" or "model" children who have not caused their parents any undue concern or grief over other behavior problems. Anorexia nervosa is perhaps a desperate bid for attention by these young women.[7]

Most lectures you hear in college are informative. The university president's annual "state of the university" speech is also informative, as is the colonial Williamsburg tour guide's talk. Such speakers are all trying to increase the knowledge of their listeners. Although they may use an occasional bit of humor in their presentations, their main objective is not to entertain. And although they may provoke an audience's interest in the topic, their main objective is not to persuade. Chapter 13 provides specific suggestions for preparing an informative speech.

**Speaking to Persuade** Persuasive speakers may offer information, but they use the information to try to change or reinforce an audience's convictions and often to urge some sort of action. For example, Brian offered compelling statistics to help persuade his audience to take steps to prevent and alleviate chronic pain:

> A hundred million Americans, nearly a third of the population, [suffer] from chronic pain due to everything from accidents to the simple daily stresses on our bodies.[8]

The representative from Mothers Against Drunk Driving (MADD) who spoke at your high-school assembly urged you not to drink and drive and urged you to help others realize the inherent dangers of the practice. The fraternity president talking to your group of rushees tried to convince you to join his fraternity. Appearing on television during the last election, the candidates for president of the United States asked for your vote. All these speakers gave you information, but they used that information to try to get you to believe or do something. Chapters 14 and 15 focus on persuasive speaking.

**Speaking to Entertain** The entertaining speaker tries to get the members of an audience to relax, smile, perhaps laugh, and generally enjoy themselves. Storyteller Garrison Keillor spins tales of the town and residents of Lake Wobegon, Minnesota, to amuse his listeners. Comedian Dane Cook delivers comic patter to make his audience laugh. Most after-dinner speakers talk to entertain the banquet guests. Like persuasive speakers, entertaining speakers may inform their listeners, but providing knowledge is not their main goal. Rather, their objective is to produce at least a smile and at best a belly laugh.

Early on, you need to decide which of the three general purposes your speech is to have. This decision keeps you on track throughout the development of your speech. The way you organize, support, and deliver your speech depends, in part, on your general purpose.

RECAP

### General Purposes for Speeches

**To inform** To share information with listeners by defining, describing, or explaining a thing, person, place, concept, process, or function
**To persuade** To change or reinforce a listener's attitude, belief, value, or behavior
**To entertain** To help listeners have a good time by getting them to relax, smile, and laugh

## Specific Purpose

Now that you have a topic and you know generally whether your speech should inform, persuade, or entertain, it is time you decided on its *specific purpose*. Unlike the general purpose, which can be assigned by your instructor, you alone must decide on the specific purpose of your speech because it depends directly on the topic you choose.

To arrive at a specific purpose for your speech, think in precise terms of what you want your audience to be able to *do* at the end of your speech. This kind of goal or purpose is called a **behavioral objective** because you specify the behavior you seek from the audience.

For a speech on how television comedy represents the modern family, you might write, "At the end of my speech, the audience will be able to explain how comedy portrays American family life today." The specific-purpose statement for a how-to speech using visual aids might read, "At the end of my speech, the audience will be able to use the principles of feng shui to select wall colors." For a persuasive speech on universal health care, your specific-purpose statement could say, "At the end of my speech, the audience will be able to explain why the United States should ban cell phone use by drivers of moving vehicles." A speech to entertain has a specific purpose, too. A stand-up comic may have a simple specific purpose: "At the end of my speech, the audience will laugh and applaud." An after-dinner speaker whose entertaining message has more informative value than that of the stand-up comic may say, "At the end of my speech, the audience will list four characteristics that distinguish journalists from the rest of the human species."

**Formulating the Specific Purpose** Note that almost all of the specific-purpose statements in the preceding paragraph begin with the same twelve words: "At the end of my speech, the audience will be able to. . . ." The next word should be a verb that names an observable, measurable action that the audience should be able to take

**behavioral objective**
Wording of a specific purpose in terms of desired audience behavior

*The specific purpose of a speaker whose general purpose is to entertain is often simply to help the audience laugh and smile about his or her topic. Entertainer Mississippi Slim (Walter Horn) also hopes these students will be able to recall and use information about the blues tradition in music.*

[Photo: *Delta Democrat Times*. Bill Johnson/AP Wide World Photos]

by the end of the speech. Use verbs such as *list*, *explain*, *describe*, or *write*. Do not use words such as *know*, *understand*, or *believe*. You can discover what your listeners know, understand, or believe only by having them show their increased capability in some measurable way.

A statement of purpose does not tell what you, the *speaker*, will do. To say, "In my speech, I will talk about the benefits of studying classical dance" emphasizes your performance as a speaker. The goal of the speech is centered on you, rather than on the audience. Other than restating your topic, this statement of purpose provides little direction for the speech. But to say, "At the end of my speech, the audience will be able to list three ways in which studying classical dance can benefit them" places the audience and their behavior at the center of your concern. This latter statement provides a tangible goal that can guide your preparation and by which you can measure the success of your speech.

The following guidelines will help you prepare your statement of purpose.

- **Use words that refer to observable or measurable behavior.**

  Not Observable: At the end of my speech, the audience will know some things about Hannibal, Missouri.

  Observable: At the end of my speech, the audience will be able to list five points of interest in the town of Hannibal, Missouri.

- **Limit the specific purpose to a single idea.** If your statement of purpose has more than one idea, you will have trouble covering the extra ideas in your speech. You will also run the risk of having your speech come apart at the seams. Both unity of ideas and coherence of expression will suffer.

  Two Ideas: At the end of my speech, the audience will be able to write a simple computer program in Just BASIC and play the video game God of War III.

  One Idea: At the end of my speech, the audience will be able to write a simple computer program in Just BASIC.

- **Make sure your specific purpose reflects the interests, expectations, and knowledge level of your audience.** Also be sure that your specific purpose is important. Earlier in this chapter we discussed these criteria as guidelines for selecting a speech topic. Consider them again as you word your specific-purpose statement.

Behavioral statements of purpose help remind you that the aim of public speaking is to win a response from the audience. In addition, using a specific purpose to guide

## DEVELOPING YOUR SPEECH STEP BY STEP

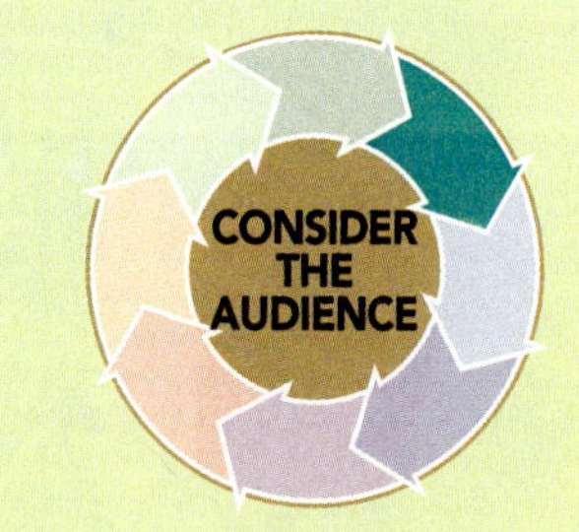


### Determine Your Purpose

Because Karen's assignment is a persuasive speech, she knows that her general purpose is to persuade. She will have to try to change or reinforce her listeners' attitudes and beliefs about the safety of outdated tires and perhaps also get them to take some sort of action.

Karen also knows that her specific purpose must begin with the phrase "At the end of my speech, the audience will be able to. . . ." So she jots down,

> At the end of my speech, the audience will be able to know about tire expiration dates.

As Karen thinks about this draft specific purpose, she sees problems with it. What specifically does she want her audience to know? How will she determine whether or not they know it? She edits the statement to read,

> At the end of my speech, the audience will be able to find the expiration date on a tire.

This version is more measurable, but perhaps it is more appropriate for an informative speech than a persuasive one. Maybe a better persuasive purpose statement would be:

> At the end of my speech, the audience will be able to take steps to ensure that they and their loved ones are driving on tires less than six years old.

Karen is pleased with her third version. It reflects a persuasive general purpose and includes a measurable behavioral objective. She is ready to move on to the next step of the process.

the development of your speech helps you focus on the audience during the entire preparation process.

**Using the Specific Purpose** Everything you do while preparing and delivering the speech should contribute to your specific purpose. The specific purpose can help you assess the information you are gathering for your speech. For example, you may find that an interesting statistic, although related to your topic, does not help achieve your specific purpose. In that case, you can substitute material that directly advances your purpose.

As soon as you have decided on it, write the specific purpose on a 3-by-5-inch note card. That way you can refer to it as often as necessary while developing your speech.

### Specific Purposes for Speeches

RECAP

Your specific purpose should . . .
- Use words that refer to observable or measurable behavior
- Be limited to a single idea
- Reflect the needs, interests, expectations, and level of knowledge of your audience

# Develop Your Central Idea

Having stated the specific purpose of your speech, you are ready to develop your *central idea*, the first step highlighted in Figure 5.2 on page 122. The central idea (sometimes called the *thesis*) is a one-sentence summary of your speech. As Table 5.2 on page 122

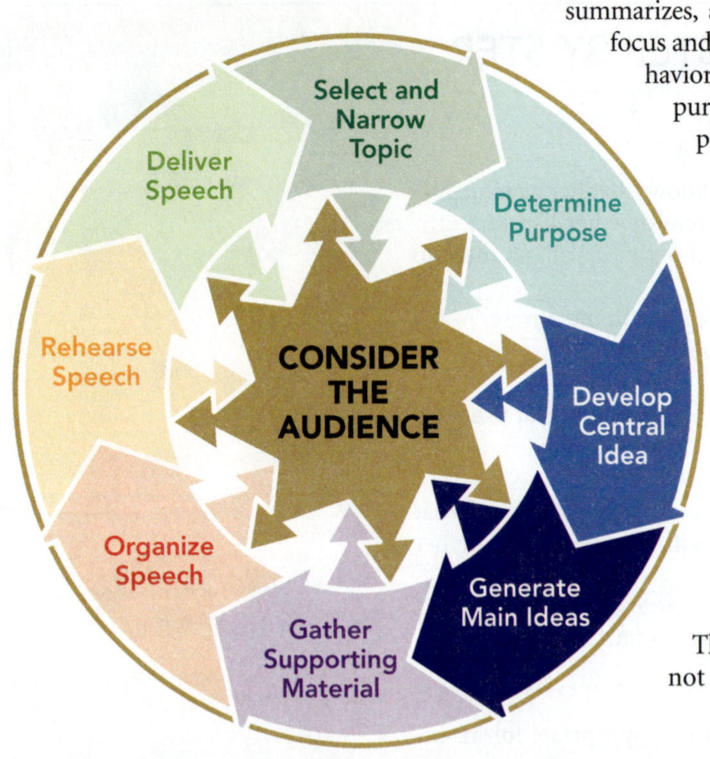


FIGURE 5.2 *State your central idea as a one-sentence summary of your speech, and then generate main ideas by looking for natural divisions, reasons, or steps to support your central idea.*

summarizes, a central idea differs from a purpose statement in both focus and application. A purpose statement focuses on audience behavior; the central idea focuses on the content of the speech. A purpose statement guides your decisions and choices as you prepare your speech; the central idea becomes part of your final speech.

Professional speech coach Judith Humphrey explains the importance of a central idea:

> Ask yourself before writing a speech . . . "What's my point?" Be able to state that message in a single clear sentence. Everything else you say will support that single argument.[9]

The following guidelines can help you put your central idea into words.

## A Complete Declarative Sentence

The central idea should be a complete declarative sentence—not a phrase or clause, and not a question.

Phrase: Car maintenance

Question: Is regular car maintenance important?

Complete Declarative Sentence: Maintaining your car regularly can ensure that it provides reliable transportation.

The phrase "car maintenance" is really a topic, not a central idea. It does not say anything about car maintenance. The question "Is regular car maintenance important?" is more complete but does not reveal whether the speaker is going to support the affirmative or the negative answer. By the time you word your central idea, you should be ready to summarize your stand on your topic in a complete declarative sentence.

## Direct, Specific Language

The central idea should be stated in direct, specific language rather than qualifiers and vague generalities.

### TABLE 5.2 Purpose Statement versus Central Idea

| The Purpose Statement | The Central Idea |
|---|---|
| Indicates what the audience should know or be able to do by the end of the speech | Summarizes the speech in one sentence |
| Guides the speaker's decisions and choices throughout the preparation of the speech | Is stated in the speech |
| | **The Central Idea Should . . .** |
| | Be a complete declarative sentence |
| | Use direct, specific language |
| | Be a single idea |
| | Be an audience-centered idea |

## DEVELOPING YOUR SPEECH STEP BY STEP

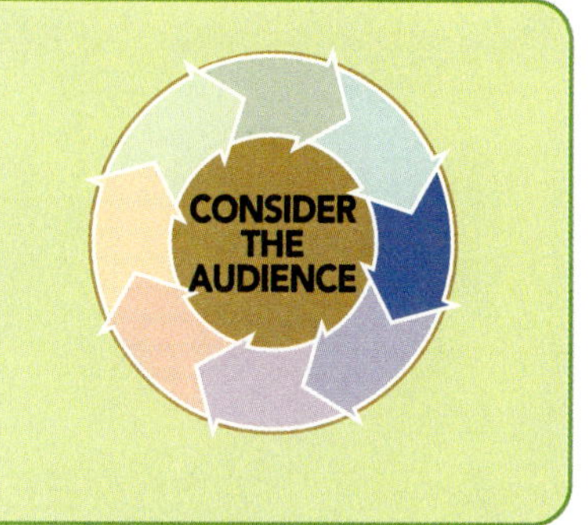


### Develop Your Central Idea

Karen knows from having read this chapter that her central idea should be a complete declarative statement of a single audience-centered idea. She writes,

It is important to ensure that we are driving on tires less than six years old.

| | |
|---|---|
| Qualified Language: | In my opinion, censorship of school textbooks threatens the rights of schoolchildren. |
| Direct Language: | Censorship of school textbooks threatens the rights of schoolchildren. |
| Vague: | A January 2010 earthquake affected Haiti. |
| Specific: | When a magnitude 7.0 earthquake occurred near Port-au-Prince, Haiti, and killed some 230,000 people on January 12, 2010, it changed forever the lives of those who survived. |

## A Single Idea

The central idea should be a single idea.

| | |
|---|---|
| Two Ideas: | Deforestation by lumber interests and toxic-waste dumping are major environmental problems in the United States today. |
| One Idea: | Toxic-waste dumping is a major environmental problem in the United States today. |

More than one central idea, like more than one idea in a purpose statement, only leads to confusion and lack of coherence in a speech.

## An Audience-Centered Idea

The central idea should reflect consideration of the audience. You considered your audience when selecting and narrowing your topic and when composing your purpose statement. In the same way, you should consider your audience's needs, interests, expectations, and knowledge when stating your central idea. If you do not consider your listeners, you run the risk of losing their attention before you even begin developing the speech. If your audience consists mainly of college juniors and seniors, the second of the following central ideas would be better suited to your listeners than the first.

| | |
|---|---|
| Inappropriate: | Scholarships from a variety of sources are readily available to first-year college students. |
| Appropriate: | Although you may think of scholarships as a source of money for freshmen, a number of scholarships are available only to students who have completed their first year of college. |

# Generate and Preview Your Main Ideas

Next to selecting a topic, probably the most common stumbling block in developing speeches is coming up with a speech plan. Trying to decide how to subdivide your central idea into two, three, or four *main ideas* can make you chew your pencil, scratch your head, and end up as you began, with a blank sheet of paper. The task will be much easier if you use the following strategy.

## Generating Your Main Ideas

Write the central idea at the top of a clean sheet of paper. Then ask these three questions:

- Does the central idea have *logical divisions*? (They may be indicated by such phrases as "three types" or "four means.")
- Can you think of several *reasons* the central idea is true?
- Can you support your central idea with a series of *steps* or a chronological progression?

You should be able to answer yes to one or more of these questions. With your answer in mind, write down the divisions, reasons, or steps you thought of. Let's see this technique at work with several central idea statements.

**Finding Logical Divisions** Suppose your central idea is "A liberal arts education benefits the student in three ways." You now turn to the three questions. But for this example, you needn't go beyond the first one. Does the central idea have logical divisions? The phrase "three ways" indicates that it does. You can logically divide your speech into ways in which the student benefits:

1. Job opportunities
2. Appreciation of culture
3. Concern for humankind

A brief brainstorming session at this point could help you come up with more specific examples of ways in which a liberal arts education might benefit students. At this stage, you needn't worry about Roman numerals, parallel form, or even the order in which the main ideas are listed. We will discuss these and the other features of outlining in Chapter 9. Your goal now is simply to generate ideas. Moreover, just because you write them down, don't think that the ideas you come up with now are engraved in stone. They can—and probably will—change. After all, this is a *preliminary* plan. It may undergo many revisions before you actually deliver your speech. In our example, three points may well prove to be too many to develop in the brief time allowed for most classroom speeches. But because it is much easier to eliminate ideas than to invent them, list them all for now.

*To choose the main points you will enumerate in your speech, look for logical divisions in your central idea, reasons that support the central idea, or steps related to the central idea.*

[Photo: © GOGO Images/SuperStock]

**Establishing Reasons** Suppose your central idea is "Upholstered-furniture fires are a life-threatening hazard."[10] Asking yourself whether this idea has logical divisions is no help at all. There are no key phrases indicating logical divisions—no "ways," "means," "types," or "methods" appear in the wording. The second question, however, is more productive: Having done some initial reading on the topic, you can think of *reasons* this central idea is true. Asking yourself "Why?" after the statement yields three answers:

1. Standards to reduce fires caused by smoldering cigarettes have lulled furniture makers into a false sense of security.
2. Government officials refuse to force the furniture industry to reexamine its standards.
3. Consumers are largely ignorant of the risks.

Notice that these main ideas are expressed in complete sentences, whereas the ones in the preceding example were in phrases. At this stage, it doesn't matter. What does matter is getting your ideas down on paper; you can rewrite and reorganize them later.

**Tracing Specific Steps** "NASA's space shuttle program has known both great achievement and tragic failure." You stare glumly at the central idea you so carefully formulated yesterday. Now what? You know a lot about the subject; your aerospace science professor has covered it thoroughly this semester. But how can you organize all the information you have? Again, you turn to the three-question method.

Does the main idea have logical divisions? You scan the sentence hopefully, but you can find no key phrases suggesting logical divisions.

Can you think of several reasons why the central idea is true? You read the central idea again and ask "Why?" Answering that question may indeed produce a plan for a speech, one in which you would talk about the reasons for the achievements and failures. But your purpose statement reads, "At the end of my speech, the audience will be able to trace the history of the space shuttle." Giving reasons for the space shuttle program's achievements and failures would not directly contribute to your purpose. So you turn to the third question.

Can you support your central idea with a series of steps? Almost any historical topic, or any topic requiring a chronological progression (for example, topics of how-to speeches), can be subdivided by answering the third question. You therefore decide that your main ideas will be a chronology of important space shuttle flights:[11]

1. April 1981: Test flight of the space shuttle.
2. January 1986: Shuttle *Challenger* explodes on launch.
3. April 1990: Hubble space telescope deployed.
4. October–November 1998: Flight of John Glenn, age 77, who had been the first American in orbit in 1962.
5. May–June 1999: Shuttle *Discovery* docks with the International Space Station.
6. February 2003: Shuttle *Columbia* disintegrates on re-entry.
7. February 2011: Shuttle *Endeavour* scheduled for fleet's final launch.

You know that you can add to, eliminate, or reorganize these ideas later. But you have a start.

Notice that for this last example, you consulted your purpose statement as you generated your main ideas. If these main ideas do not help achieve your purpose, you need to rethink your speech. You may finally change either your purpose or your main ideas; but whichever you do, you need to synchronize them. Remember, it is much easier to make changes at this point than after you have done your research and produced a detailed outline.

RECAP

**Generating Main Ideas**

Ask whether your central idea . . .

Has *logical divisions*
Is true for a number of *reasons*
Can be supported with *steps*

## Previewing Your Main Ideas

Once you have generated your main ideas, you can add a preview of those main ideas to your central idea to produce a **blueprint** for your speech. Preview the ideas in the same order you plan to discuss them in the speech. In Chapter 7, we discuss how to organize your speech.

Some speakers, like Nicole, integrate their central idea and preview into one blueprint sentence:

> Obsolete computers are straining landfills because they contain hazardous materials and take a distinctively long time to decay.[12]

In this example, Nicole started with a central idea: "Obsolete computers are straining landfills." Asking herself "Why?" yielded two reasons, which became her two main

**blueprint**
The central idea of a speech plus a preview of the main ideas

points: "They contain hazardous materials" and "They take a distinctively long time to decay." Combining these reasons with her central idea produced a blueprint.

Other speakers, like Erin, state their blueprint in several sentences:

> Today I would like to expose the myth that owning a gun guarantees your personal safety. First, I will discuss the fact that guns are rarely reached in time of need. Then I will address the risk of accidental shootings and how this is greatly increased by people's failure to receive proper gun-handling training. And finally, I will propose an alternative solution, self-defense.[13]

Erin also started with a central idea: "Owning a gun does not guarantee your personal safety." Like Nicole, she generated reasons for her central idea, which in this case were that "guns are rarely reached in time of need" and that "the risk of accidental shootings is increased." She decided also to discuss martial-arts self-defense as a solution to the problem. Thinking that a single sentence might become unwieldy, Erin decided to use four shorter sentences for her blueprint.

## Meanwhile, Back at the Computer . . .

It's been a while since we abandoned Ed Garcia, the student in the opening paragraphs of this chapter who was struggling to write a speech on college football. Even though he has procrastinated, if he follows the steps we have discussed, he should still be able to plan a successful informative speech.

Ed has already chosen his topic. His audience is likely to be interested in his subject. Because Ed is a varsity defensive tackle, the audience will probably expect him to talk about college football. And he himself is passionately interested in and knowledgeable about the subject. It meets all the requirements of a successful topic.

But "college football" is too broad a subject for a 3- to 5-minute talk. Ed needs to narrow his topic to a manageable size. He goes online to Yahoo! and clicks on the category Sports. This search yields a fairly long list of subcategories. He is just about to select College and University when another category catches his eye: Medicine. Sports medicine? Hmmmm. . . . Ed has suffered several injuries and feels qualified to talk about this aspect of football. Ed doesn't need to go further. He has his topic: "Injuries in college football."

Now that he has narrowed the topic, Ed needs a purpose statement. He decides that his audience may know something about how players are injured, but they probably do not know how these injuries are treated. He types, "The audience will be able to explain how the three most common injuries suffered by college football players are treated."

A few minutes later, Ed derives his central idea from his purpose: "Sports medicine specialists have developed specific courses of treatment for the three most common kinds of injuries suffered by college football players."

Generating main ideas is also fairly easy now. Because his central idea mentions three kinds of injuries, he can plan his speech around those three ideas (logical divisions). Under the central idea, Ed lists three injuries:

1. Bruises
2. Broken bones
3. Ligament and cartilage damage

Now Ed has a plan and is well on his way to developing a successful 3- to 5-minute informative speech.

## DEVELOPING YOUR SPEECH STEP BY STEP

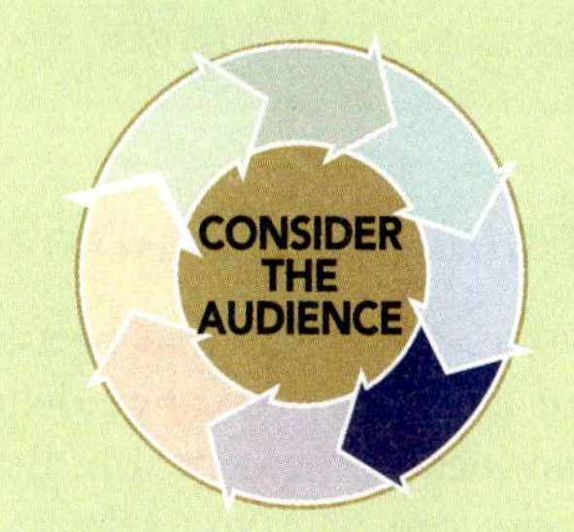


### Generate Your Main Ideas

With her central idea in hand, Karen knows that she next needs to generate her main ideas. She asks three questions:

- Does my central idea have *logical divisions*?
- Can I establish several *reasons* my central idea is true?
- Can I support my central idea by tracing specific *steps*?

Karen's central idea does not seem to have logical divisions, but she can certainly think of reasons why it is true. She jots down her central idea and writes *because* at the end of it:

It is important to ensure that we are driving on tires less than six years old because

And she quickly adds

1. We are driving on expired tires.
2. Tire companies are not taking research about tire degradation seriously.

Now Karen has two possible main ideas—a good start. But she looks back at her specific purpose statement and remembers that she also wants her listeners to take steps to solve the problem. So she adds a third main idea:

3. We must take steps that include checking the date code on our tires, questioning our mechanics, and talking with our friends and family about tire safety.

Now Karen has main ideas that both support her central idea and fulfill her specific purpose.

# STUDY GUIDE

## Select and Narrow Your Topic

As a speaker, you may be asked to address a specific topic or given only broad guidelines, such as a time limit and an idea of the occasion. Being aware of several boundaries can help you select an appropriate speech topic. Keep in mind the interests, expectations, and knowledge levels of the audience. Choose an important topic. Consider the special demands of the occasion. Be sure to take into account your own interests, abilities, and experiences. If you are still undecided, brainstorming strategies, such as consulting the media or scanning Web directories for potential topics, may give you topic ideas. After choosing a broad topic area, narrow the topic so that it fits within the time limits that have been set.

### Being Audience-Centered

- "What interests and needs do the members of this audience have in common?" and "Why did they ask me to speak?" are important questions to ponder as you search for potential speech topics.
- Another important question is "What do audience members already know about this topic?"

### Using What You've Learned

- A candidate for governor visits your public-speaking class and talks for 30 minutes on the topic "Why the state should increase funding of public transportation." Analyze the candidate's choice of topic according to the guidelines presented in this chapter.

### A Question of Ethics

- Like the late Tim Russert, many speakers prepare a stock speech and deliver it to a variety of audiences and on a variety of occasions. Is this practice ethical? Explain your answer.
- At lunch, you overhear a stranger at the next table mention a book that she used as a key reference for a political science paper she wrote. Would it be ethical for you to borrow her topic and consult the book she mentioned to prepare a speech for a public-speaking course assignment?

### Speaker's Homepage: Speech Topic Help

If you've scanned news headlines and Web directories but still can't settle on a topic, consider a visit to Speech Topic Help, Advice, and Ideas (www.speech-topics-help.com), a site that claims to suggest over 7,500 topics. The random "topic generators" built into the site are amusing and may spark an original idea of your own.

## Determine Your Purpose

After choosing a topic, decide on your general and specific purposes. Your general purpose for speaking will be to inform, to persuade, or to entertain your listeners. Your specific purpose should state what your audience will be able to *do* at the end of the speech. Specifying target behaviors in your specific-purpose statement provides a yardstick for you to measure the relevance of your ideas and supporting materials as you develop your speech.

### Being Audience-Centered

- Using a specific purpose to guide the development of your speech helps you focus on the audience during the entire preparation process.
- As you determine your purpose for speaking, ask yourself "What is really important for the audience to hear?" and "How do I want the audience to respond?"

### Using What You've Learned

Consider the following specific-purpose statements. Analyze each according to the criteria presented in this chapter. Rewrite the statements to correct any problems.

- At the end of my speech, the audience will know more about the Mexican Free-Tailed Bat.
- I will explain some differences in nonverbal communication between Asian and Western cultures.
- At the end of my speech, the audience will be able to list some reasons for xeriscaping one's yard.
- To describe the reasons I enjoy spelunking as a hobby.
- At the end of my speech, the audience will be able to prepare a realistic monthly budget.
- The advantages and disadvantages of living in a college dormitory.

## Develop Your Central Idea

Specific-purpose statements indicate what speakers hope to accomplish; they tell what the speaker wants the *audience* to be able to do. Your central idea, in contrast, summarizes what *you*, the speaker, will say. The central idea should be a single idea, stated in a complete declarative sentence. Be direct and specific, without using qualifiers.

### Being Audience-Centered

- Be sure your specific purpose and your central idea address the interests, expectations, and level of knowledge of your audience.

## Generate and Preview Your Main Ideas

After formulating your central idea, use it to generate main ideas. Determine whether the central idea (1) has logical divisions, (2) can be supported by several reasons, or (3) can be traced through a series of steps. These divisions, reasons, or steps become the blueprint, or plan, of your speech. You will preview them in your introduction and summarize them in your conclusion.

### Being Audience-Centered

- Check your main ideas against your specific-purpose statement. If an idea does not contribute to what you want the audience to do at the end of your speech, reconsider whether or not it should be in your speech.

### Using What You've Learned

Below are the topic, general purpose, and specific purpose Marylin has chosen for her persuasive speech. Write an appropriate central idea and main ideas for the speech. Be prepared to explain how you derived the main points from the central idea.

- Topic: America's crumbling roads and bridges
- General Purpose: To persuade
- Specific Purpose: At the end of my speech, the audience will be able to list and explain three reasons America should invest in its roads and bridges.

# SPEECH WORKSHOP

## Strategies for Selecting a Speech Topic

Use the following questions to identify and narrow a topic for a speech:

**Step One:** Determine the purpose of your speech.

- What is the general purpose of your speech (to inform, to persuade, or to entertain)? ____________________
- What are the time limits for your speech? ____________________

**Step Two:** Determine your audience's interests.

**Factors to consider:**

- What common interests or experiences have brought the members of your audience together? ____________________
- What are the educational, career, or other goals of your audience? ____________________
- What are the general demographic characteristics of your audience? ____________________

**Step Three:** Identify your own interests.

**You might ask yourself:**

- What do I like to do for fun?
- Where have I traveled?
- What social or political issues concern me?
- What books, magazines, Web sites, or blogs do I read?
- What movies, TV programs, or videos do I watch?
- What problems have I or someone close to me experienced that would be a good topic (e.g., serious illness or accident)?
- What world, national, or local problems do I consider interesting and important?
- What behaviors would I like people to have or not have (e.g., exercise more, eat more healthful foods)?

**Step Four:** Review newspapers, magazines, TV programs, and Web sites to identify stories and topics that are of interest to you and your audience.

**List some topics here:**

**Step Five:** Brainstorm a list of topics that relate to your own interests. Then review the list to identify those topics that would also be of interest to your listeners.

**List and review your ideas here:**

**Step Six:** Narrow the topic to fit the time limits. Identify subdivisions or elements of your topic that could fit within the scope of your speech assignment.

**Narrow your topics here:**

LEARN, COMPARE, COLLECT THE FACTS! . . . ALWAYS HAVE THE COURAGE TO SAY TO YOURSELF—I AM IGNORANT.

—IVAN PETROVICH PAVLOV

Alexandra Exter (1882–1949), *Sketch for a Scenic Design*, ca. 1924, gouache on paper. Photo: M. E. Smith/Private Collection. © DeA Picture Library/Art Resource, N. Y.

## OUTLINE

# 6 Gathering and Using Supporting Material

OBJECTIVES

**After studying this chapter you should be able to do the following:**

1. List five potential sources of supporting material for a speech.
2. Explain five strategies for a logical research process.
3. List and describe six types of supporting material.
4. List and explain six criteria for determining the best supporting material to use in a speech.

Apple pie is your specialty. Your family and friends relish your flaky crust, spicy filling, and crunchy crumb topping. Fortunately, not only do you have a never-fail recipe and technique, but you also know where to go for the best ingredients. Fette's Orchard has the tangiest pie apples in town. For your crust, you use only Premier shortening, which you buy at Meyer's Specialty Market. Your crumb topping requires both stone-ground whole-wheat flour and fresh creamery butter, available on Tuesdays at the farmer's market on the courthouse square.

Chapter 6 covers the speech-development step highlighted in Figure 6.1 on page 134: Gather Supporting Material. Just as making your apple pie requires that you know where to find specific ingredients, creating a successful speech requires a knowledge of the sources, research strategies, and types of supporting material that speechmakers typically use.

# Sources of Supporting Material

## Personal Knowledge and Experience

Because you will probably give speeches on topics you are particularly interested in, you may find that *you* are your own best source. Your speech may be on a skill or activity in which you are expert, such as keeping tropical fish, stenciling, or stamp collecting. Or you may talk on a subject with which you have had some personal experience, such as buying a used car, joining a service organization, or seeking assisted living for an elderly relative. It is true that most well-researched speeches include some objective material gathered from outside sources. But you may also be able to provide an effective illustration, explanation, definition, or other type of support from your own knowledge and experience. As an audience-centered speaker, you should realize, too, that personal knowledge often has the additional advantage of heightening your credibility in the minds of your listeners. They will accord you more respect as an authority when they realize that you have firsthand knowledge of a topic.

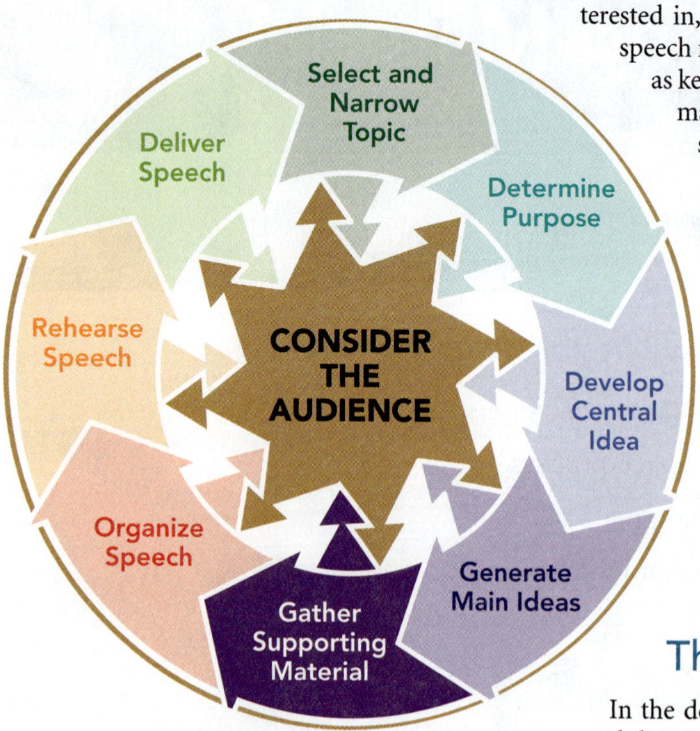

Select and Narrow Topic
Determine Purpose
Develop Central Idea
Generate Main Ideas
Gather Supporting Material
Organize Speech
Rehearse Speech
Deliver Speech
CONSIDER THE AUDIENCE

FIGURE 6.1 *Finding, identifying, and effectively using supporting material are activities essential to the speech-preparation process.*

## The Internet

In the decades since its inception, the **Internet** has gone from a novel, last-resort resource to the first place most people turn when faced with a research task. Understanding the Internet's primary information-delivery system—**World Wide Web**—the tools for accessing it, and some of the amazing types of information available on it can help make your search for supporting material more productive.

**Locating Internet Resources** You have probably accessed material on the Web by using Google or Yahoo!. If you feel overwhelmed by the number of sites these general search tools yield, a specialized **vertical search engine** can help you narrow your search. For example, Google Scholar indexes academic sources, and Indeed indexes job Web sites.

Another strategy that can help you narrow your search is a **Boolean search**, which allows you to enclose phrases in quotation marks or parentheses so that a search yields only those sites on which all words of the phrase appear in that order, rather than sites that contain the words at random. Boolean searches also permit you to insert "AND" or "+" between words and phrases to indicate that you wish to see results that contain both phrases, and, similarly, they let you exclude certain words and phrases from your search. They also let you restrict the dates of your hits, so that you see only documents posted within a specified time frame. These relatively simple strategies can help you narrow a list of hits from, in some cases, millions of sites to a more workable number.

**Internet**
A vast collection of computers accessible to millions of people all over the world

**World Wide Web**
The primary information-delivery system of the Internet

**vertical search engine**
A Web site that indexes World Wide Web information in a specific field.

**Boolean search**
An advanced Web-searching technique that allows a user to narrow a subject or key word search by adding various requirements

**Exploring Internet Resources** As you go to the Web sites you have located, you will probably find a wide variety—from sites that try to sell you something, to the official sites of government agencies and news organizations. One clue to the type of site you have found is the *domain*, indicated by the last three letters of the site's URL (for example, .com or .org).

Although sites can be classified in a number of different ways, most Web sites fall into one of the following six categories.[1]

- **Advocacy site.** Nonprofit organizations sponsor Web sites to influence public opinion and/or promote their causes. They often use the domain *.org*.
- **Commercial site.** Today almost all companies in business to promote or sell a product have a Web site; some sell exclusively online. They usually use the domain *.com* or, less often, *.net*.
- **Entertainment site.** Sites intended primarily to entertain are often interactive and sometimes require you to download specialized audio, video, and/or gaming software. Like commercial sites, entertainment sites usually use the domain *.com*.
- **Information site.** These sites usually present facts and statistics on academic, scientific, or social scientific topics. Reflecting their sponsorship by educational institutions, government entities, or the military, information sites usually use the domains *.edu*, *.gov*, and *.mil*.
- **News site.** News sites are often online versions of newspapers or news reports delivered via other media, but they have the advantage of being able to provide up-to-the-minute information. News sites usually use the domain *.com*.
- **Personal site.** Personal sites are usually pages posted to other sites, such as Facebook or popular blog sites. They may include chat rooms or discussion forums. Their domain will reflect the site to which they are posted.

**Evaluating Internet Resources** Although the Web is a great victory for those who support free speech, the lack of legal, financial, or editorial restriction on what is published on the Web presents both a logistical and an ethical challenge to researchers.

As you begin to explore the sites you discover, you will need to evaluate them according to a consistent standard. The six criteria in Table 6.1 can serve as such a standard.[2] The first four of the criteria can serve as guides to evaluating any resource, regardless of whether it is a Web site, a print document, or even information you obtain in an interview. Later in this chapter we provide additional criteria to help you make your final selection of supporting material from both electronic and print resources.

RECAP

**Finding Supporting Material on the Web**

1. Use a directory or a search engine to find relevant Internet sites.
2. Evaluate sites according to these six criteria: accountability, accuracy, objectivity, date, usability, and diversity.

## Online Databases

**Online databases** provide access to bibliographic information, abstracts, and full texts for a variety of resources, including periodicals, newspapers, government documents, and even books. Like Web sites, online databases are reached via a networked computer. Unlike Web sites, however, most databases are restricted to the patrons of libraries that subscribe to them.

**Locating and Searching Databases** To use a database to which your library subscribes, you will probably first have to go to your library's homepage and log in with your username and password. You can then find the names of the available databases, usually listed according to type and/or subjects, as well as alphabetically.

Searching a database is relatively simple. Each database opens with a search box, into which you type relevant information such as keywords and date ranges. Most also allow Boolean and other types of advanced searches.

In some cases you may be able to search more than one database at a time by searching providers that offer access to multiple databases. ProQuest, for example, provides databases of alternative newspapers, criminal justice periodicals, doctoral dissertations, and education journals as well as its popular *ABI/INFORM Global* database of business and finance publications.

**online database**
A subscription-based electronic resource that may offer access to abstracts and/or the full texts of entries, in addition to bibliographic data

## TABLE 6.1 Six Criteria for Evaluating Internet Resources

| Criterion | Applying the Criterion | Drawing Conclusions |
|---|---|---|
| **Accountability:** Who is responsible for the site? | • Check "Sponsored Links" (Google) or "Sponsor Results" (Yahoo!) to determine the individual or organization responsible for the site.<br>• Look to see whether or not the site is signed.<br>• Follow hyperlinks or search the author's name to determine the author's expertise and authority.<br>• If the site is unsigned, search for a sponsoring organization. Follow hyperlinks, search the organization's name, or consider the domain to determine reputability. | If you cannot identify or verify an author or sponsor, be wary of the site. |
| **Accuracy:** Is the information correct? | • Consider whether or not the author or sponsor is a credible authority.<br>• Assess the care with which the site has been written.<br>• Conduct additional research into the information on the site. | • If the author or sponsor is a credible authority, the information is more likely to be accurate.<br>• A site should be relatively free of writing errors.<br>• You may be able to verify or refute the information by consulting another resource. |
| **Objectivity:** Is the site free of bias? | • Consider the interests, philosophical or political biases, and source of financial support of the author and/or sponsor of the site.<br>• Does the site include advertisements that might influence its content? | • The more objective the author and sponsor of the site are, the more credible their information may be. |
| **Timeliness:** Is the site current? | • Look at the bottom of the site for a statement telling when the site was posted and when it was last updated.<br>• If you cannot find a date on the site, click on Page Info (from the View menu at the top of your browser screen) to find a "Last Modified" date.<br>• Enter the title of the site in a search engine. The resulting information should include a date. | • In general, when you are concerned with factual data, the more recent it is, the better. |
| **Usability:** Do the layout and design of the site facilitate its use? | • Does the site load fairly quickly?<br>• Is a fee required to gain access to any of the information on the site? | • Balance graphics and any fees against practical efficiency. |
| **Diversity:** Is the site inclusive? | • Do language and graphics reflect and respect differences in gender, ethnicity, race, and sexual preference?<br>• Do interactive forums invite divergent perspectives?<br>• Is the site friendly to people with disabilities (e.g., does it offer a large-print or video option)? | • A site should be free of bias, representative of diverse perspectives, and accessible by people with disabilities. |

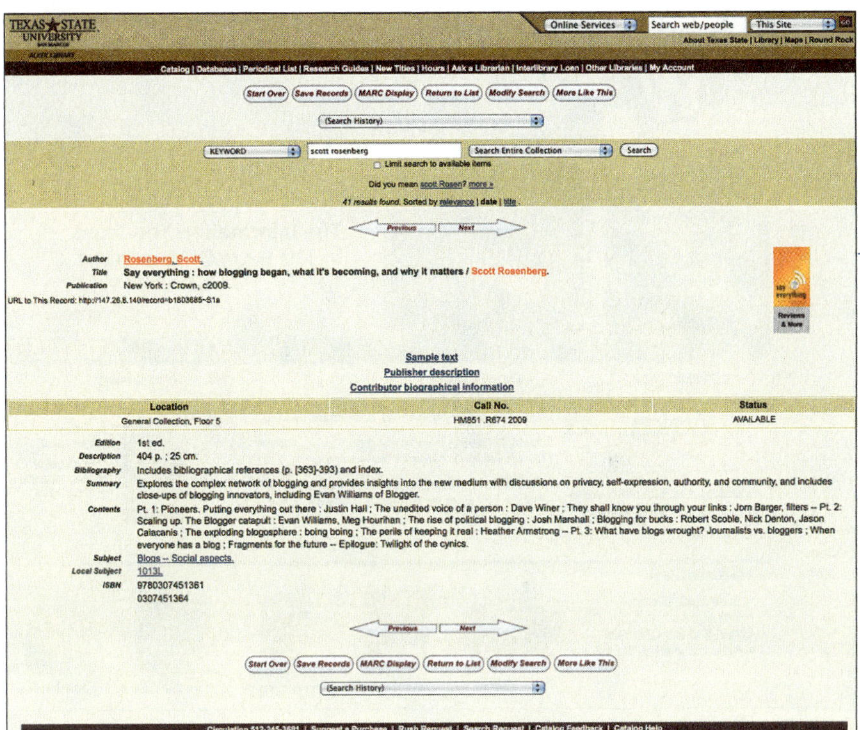


FIGURE 6.2 *An entry from a computerized card catalog. The same entry will appear on the screen regardless of whether the work is accessed using title, author, or subject.*

Source: Courtesy of Albert B. Alkek Library, Texas State University, San Marcos

**Exploring Database Resources** Many online databases that began as computerized indexes now provide access to full texts of the resources themselves. Your library may subscribe to several or all of the following popular full-text databases:

- **ABI/Inform Global.** This resource offers many full-text articles in business and trade publications from 1971 to the present.
- **Academic Search Complete.** This popular database offers many full-text articles from 1865 to the present, covering a wide variety of subjects.
- **JSTOR.** This is a multi-subject, full-text database of journal articles from the first volume to the present.
- **LexisNexis Academic.** Focusing on business, industry, and law, this database provides many full-text articles from newspapers, magazines, journals, newsletters, and wire services. Dates of coverage vary.

## Traditional Library Holdings

Despite the rapid development of Internet and database resources, the more traditional holdings of libraries, both paper and electronic, remain rich sources of supporting material.

**Locating Traditional Library Holdings** Spend some time becoming familiar with your library's services and layout so that you know how to access books, periodicals, newspapers, and reference materials.

- **Locating books through the card catalog.** You can probably access your library's computerized **card catalog** from your own computer before you ever enter the library. As shown in the example in Figure 6.2, the catalog will supply each book's *call number*, which you will need in order to find the book.
- **Locating periodicals through periodical indexes.** The term *periodical* refers to both general-interest magazines, such as *Newsweek* and *Consumer Reports*, and academic and professional journals, such as *Communication Monographs* and *American Psychologist*. Just as a card catalog can help you find

**card catalog**
A file of information about the books in a library;

FIGURE 6.3 *A typical subject entry from the* Readers' Guide.

Source: Reproduced with the permission of the W. H. Wilson Company, www.hwwilson.com

books, a **periodical index** can help you locate articles that might be useful. Formatted as large bound volumes for many years, most periodical indexes today are provided via databases. Some of the best-known include the *Readers' Guide* (see Figure 6.3) and the *Public Affairs Information Service.*

- **Locating newspapers through newspaper indexes.** Newspaper databases such as *Newspaper Source* not only index, but also provide full texts of, selected articles from newspapers and transcripts from news organizations. As with periodicals, you can use keyword searches to locate newspaper articles. If you know the date on which an event occurred, however, you can simply locate a newspaper from that or the following day and probably find a news story on the event.
- **Locating reference resources online and through the card catalog.** Many encyclopedias, dictionaries, directories, atlases, almanacs, yearbooks, books of quotations, and biographical dictionaries are now available on the Internet. But if you are not able to find a specific reference resource online, you may be able to locate a print version by using your library's card catalog.

  No discussion of encyclopedias would be complete without mentioning *Wikipedia*, the resource that often comes up as the first hit on a Web search. *Wikipedia* can be useful, especially for general information about current events and new technology that may not find its way into print encyclopedias for years. But users need to keep in mind that anyone, regardless of expertise, can add to or change the content of any entry, thereby limiting *Wikipedia*'s reliability and its appropriateness for academic use.

**Exploring Traditional Library Holdings** Although a wealth of supporting material is available online, you may still need to go to the library to find books and some articles and reference resources. It is a good idea to become familiar with your library's layout before you have to do research under the pressure of a deadline.

**periodical index**
A listing of bibliographical data for articles published in a group of magazines and/or journals during a given time period

**stacks**
The collection of books in a library

- **Books.** Libraries' collections of books are called the **stacks**. The stacks are organized by call numbers, which are available on card-catalog entries. Many libraries offer a location guide or map to guide you to the floor or section of the stacks that houses the books with the call numbers in which you are interested.

- **Periodicals.** Although full texts of many magazine and journal articles are provided by databases, publishers may not make their most recent issues available online. So finding a current article may require a trip to the library. Most periodicals are housed in a section of the library dedicated to periodicals, where bound volumes of past issues and single copies of current issues are arranged by call number. Some may be available on microfilm. Don't let microfilm intimidate you. Microfilm readers are easy to use, and most librarians or aides will be glad to show you how to set up the reader with the film you need.
- **Newspapers.** Like periodicals, most newspapers are available on databases, but the library may be the only place you can find local papers, yesterday's or today's papers, or very old editions (if you are looking for articles about a historical event). Most of a library's back newspaper holdings will likely be on microfilm.
- **Reference resources.** Printed reference resources are indexed in a library's card catalog. Their call numbers will have the prefix *ref*, indicating that they are housed in the reference section of the library. Like periodicals, newspapers, and microfilm, print reference resources are usually available only for in-house research and cannot be checked out.

Reference librarians are specialists in the field of information science. They are often able to suggest print or electronic resources that you might otherwise overlook. If you plan to use the reference section, visit the library during daytime working hours. A full-time reference librarian is more likely to be on hand and available to help you at that time than in the evenings or on weekends.

RECAP

### Supporting Material Available in the Library

Library resources may include . . .

- Books
- Periodicals
- Newspapers
- Reference resources

## Interviews

When you don't know the answers to important questions raised by your speech topic, but you can think of someone who might, consider interviewing that person to get material for your speech. For example, if you want to discuss the pros and cons of building a new prison in an urban area, you might interview an official of the correctional service, a representative of the city administration, and a resident of the area. Or if you want to explain why Al Gore lost the 2000 presidential election even though he won the popular vote, you might consult your professor of political science or American history.

Before you decide that an interview is necessary, be sure that your questions cannot be answered easily by looking at a Web site or reading a newspaper article or a book. If you decide that only an interview can give you the material you need, you should prepare for it in advance.

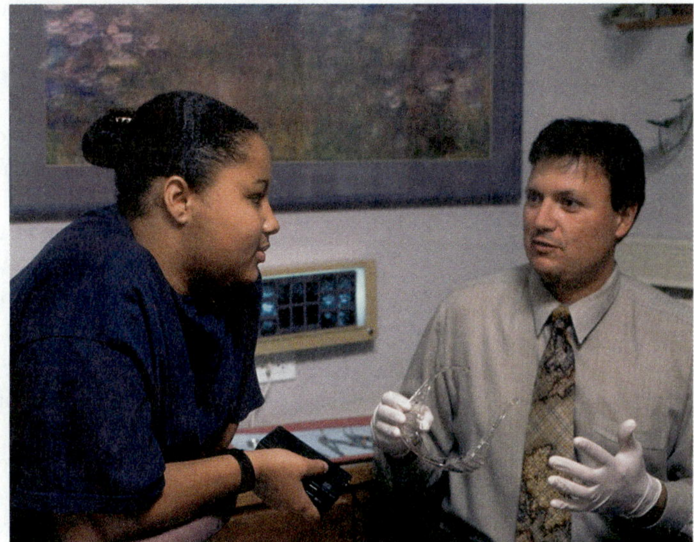

*If both parties are comfortable recording the interview, doing so can free the interviewer and the interviewee from the need to concentrate on careful note taking.*

[Photo: Bonnie Kamin/PhotoEdit Inc.]

### Preparing for the Interview

- **Determine your purpose.** The first step in preparing for an interview is to establish a purpose or objective for it. Specifically, what do you need to find out? Do you need hard facts that you cannot obtain from other sources? Do you need the interviewee's expert testimony on your subject? Or do you need an explanation of some of the information you have found in print sources?
- **Schedule the interview.** Once you have a specific purpose for the interview and have decided whom you need to speak with, arrange a meeting.

Telephone the person, explain briefly who you are and why you are calling, and ask for an appointment. Most people are flattered to have their authority and knowledge recognized and willingly grant interviews to serious students if their schedules permit.

If you are considering recording the interview on audio- or videotape, ask for the interviewee's okay during this initial contact. If the person does not grant permission, be prepared to gather your information without electronic assistance.

- **Plan your questions.** Before your interview, find out as much as you can about both your subject and the person you are interviewing. Prepare questions that take full advantage of the interviewee's specific knowledge of your subject. You can do this only if *you* already know a good deal about your subject.

  It is also helpful to think about how you should combine the two basic types of interview questions: closed-ended and open-ended. Open-ended questions often follow closed-ended questions: When the person you are interviewing answers a closed-ended question with a simple yes or no, you may wish to follow up by asking "Why?"

### Conducting the Interview

- **On your mark . . .** Dress appropriately for the interview. For most interviews, conservative, businesslike clothes show that you are serious about the interview and that you respect the norms of your interviewee's world.

  Take paper and pen or pencil for note-taking. Even if you are planning to record the interview, you may want to turn the recorder off at some point during the interview, so you'll need an alternative. Or Murphy's Law may break your recorder. Ensure that the interview can continue, in spite of any mishap.
- **Get set . . .** Arrive for the interview a few minutes ahead of schedule. Be prepared, however, to wait patiently if necessary.

  Once you are settled with the person you will interview, remind him or her of your purpose. If you are familiar with and admire the work the interviewee has done or published, don't hesitate to say so. Sincere flattery can help set a positive tone for the exchange. If you have decided to use a recorder, set it up. You may keep it out of sight once the interviewee has seen it, but never try to hide a recorder at the outset—such a ploy is unethical. If you are going to take written notes, get out your paper and pen. Now you are ready to begin asking your prepared questions.
- **Go!** As you conduct the interview, use the questions you have prepared as a guide but not a rigid schedule. If the person you are interviewing mentions an interesting angle you hadn't thought of, don't be afraid to pursue the point. Listen carefully to the person's answers, and ask for clarification of any ideas you don't understand.

  Do not prolong the interview beyond the time limits of your appointment. The person you are interviewing is probably very busy and has been courteous enough to fit you into a tight schedule. Ending the interview on time is simply returning the courtesy. Thank your interviewee for his or her contribution, and leave.

**Following Up the Interview** As soon as possible after the interview, read through your notes carefully and rewrite any portion that may be illegible. If you recorded the interview, label the recording with the date and the interviewee's name.

You will soon want to transfer significant facts, opinions, or anecdotes from either notes or recording to index cards or to a word-processing file.

# Research Strategies

You have Internet access. You know the kinds of materials and services your library offers and how to use them. In short, you're ready to begin researching your speech. But unless you approach this next phase of speech preparation systematically, you may find yourself wasting a good deal of time and energy retracing steps to find bits of information you remember seeing but forgot to bookmark, print out, or write down the first time.

Well-organized research strategies will make your efforts easier and more efficient. You need to develop a preliminary bibliography, locate potential resources, evaluate their usefulness, take notes, and identify possible visual aids.

## Develop a Preliminary Bibliography

Creating a **preliminary bibliography**, or list of promising resources, should be your first research goal. You will probably discover more resources than you actually look at or refer to in your speech; at this stage, the bibliography simply serves as a menu of possibilities. How many resources should you list in a preliminary bibliography for, say, a 10-minute speech? A reasonable number might be 10 or 12. If you have more than that, you may feel overwhelmed; if you have fewer, you may find too little information.

You will need to develop a system for keeping track of your resources. Web browsers let you bookmark pages for future reference and ready access; your bookmarks can serve as one part of your preliminary bibliography. If you are searching an online database, you may be able to print out the references you discover. These printouts can be a second part of your preliminary bibliography. If you are using more traditional catalogs and indexes, you will need to copy down the necessary bibliographical information, a process we will discuss in more detail shortly. Using 3-by 5-inch note cards will give you the greatest flexibility. Later you can omit some of the cards, add others, write comments on them, or alphabetize them much more easily than if you had made a list on a sheet of paper.

The key to developing a useful bibliography is to establish a consistent format so that you can easily find and cite the page number, title, publisher, or other vital fact about a publication. As noted in Chapter 2, the two most common formats, or documentation styles, are those developed by the MLA (Modern Language Association) and the APA (American Psychological Association). MLA style is usually used in the humanities, APA style in the natural and social sciences. Check with your instructor about which format he or she prefers.

For a book, you should record the author's name, title of the book, publisher and date of publication, and the library's call number. Figure 6.4 illustrates how to transfer information from an electronic catalog entry to a bibliography card using text style. For an article in a periodical or newspaper, you should document the author's name, title of the article, title of the periodical, date of publication, and inclusive page numbers of the article. Figure 6.5 illustrates a bibliography entry in APA style for a newspaper article.

For other print resources, as long as you record the title, author, publisher, date, and page number, you will probably have at hand the information you need. Documentation formats for electronic resources are similar to the formats for other kinds of material.

**preliminary bibliography**
A list of potential resources to be used in the preparation of a speech

FIGURE 6.4 *Transferring information from an electronic catalog entry to a bibliography card.*

| | |
|---|---|
| Author: | Jordan, Barbara, 1936-1996. |
| Title: | Barbara Jordan : speaking the truth with eloquent thunder / edited by Max Sherman. |
| Publication Info: | Austin : University of Texas Press, 2007. |
| Edition: | 1st ed. |
| URL to This Record: | *http://catalog.library.txstate.edu:80/record=b1640634a* |

| Location | Call No. | Status |
|---|---|---|
| Southwestern Writers Collection, Floor 7 | E838.5 .J6735 2007 | ROOM USE ONLY |

E838.5
.J6735
2007

Jordan. Barbara (2007). Barbara Jordan: Speaking the Truth with Eloquent Thunder. (M. Sherman, Ed.). Austin, TX: University of Texas Press.

FIGURE 6.5 *A bibliography entry in APA style for an article in* The New York Times.

Liptak, A. (2010, June 28). Study finds questioning of nominees to be useful. *The New York Times.* Retrieved from http://www.nytimes.com/

Detailed instructions for formatting bibliography citations can be found in the style guides published by the MLA and APA and on Purdue University's On-Line Writing Lab (OWL) at <http://owl.english.purdue.edu>.

## Locate Resources

You should have no trouble obtaining the actual texts of resources from the Web and online databases. For all the other items in your preliminary bibliography, you will need to locate the resources yourself. See the discussion earlier in this chapter on exploring traditional library holdings.

## Assess the Usefulness of Resources

It makes sense to gauge the potential usefulness of your resources before you begin to read closely and take notes. Think critically about how the various resources you have found are likely to help you achieve your purpose and about how effective they are likely to be with your audience. Glance over the tables of contents of books, and flip quickly through the texts to note any charts, graphs, or other visual materials that might be used as visual aids. Skim a key chapter or two. Skim articles and Web sites as well.

## Take Notes

Once you have located and assessed the usefulness of your resources, you are ready to begin your careful reading and note-taking.

- Beginning with the resources that you think have the greatest potential, record any examples, statistics, opinions, or other supporting material that might be useful to your speech. You can copy them by hand, photocopy them, download them into a computer file, or print them out.
- Even if you plan to photocopy or enter most of your notes into a word-processing file, carry a few note cards with you whenever you are working on a speech. You can use one to jot down a fact that you discover in a magazine article or hear on the evening news. An advantage of using note cards is that you can later arrange them in the order of your speech outline, simplifying the integration of supporting material into your speech.
- If you copy a phrase, sentence, or paragraph verbatim from a source, be sure to put quotation marks around it. You may need to know later whether it is a direct quote or a paraphrase. (This information will be obvious, of course, on printouts or photocopies.) Figure 6.6 illustrates two note cards—one with a paraphrased note and one with a direct quotation.
- Record the source of the supporting material. In Chapter 2, we discuss the ethical importance of crediting all sources of ideas and information. If you consistently record your sources as you take notes, you will avoid the possibility of committing unintentional plagiarism.
- Leave enough space at the top of each note card or page for a heading that summarizes the content. Such headings make it easier to find a specific note later.

## DEVELOPING YOUR SPEECH STEP BY STEP

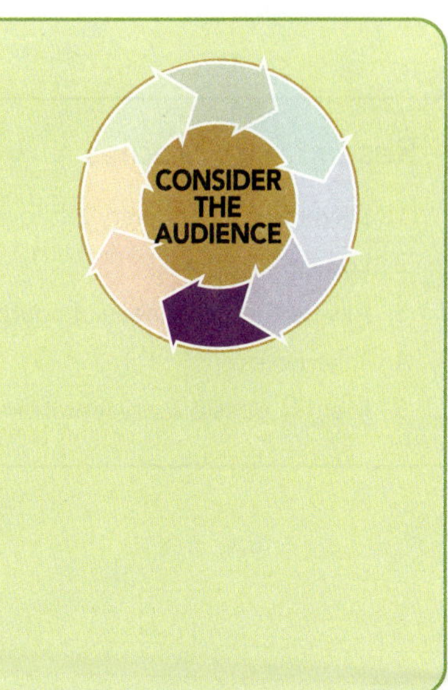


### Gather Supporting Material

With her purpose statement, central idea, and main ideas in hand, Karen begins to research tire safety.

Seeking sources that meet the criteria of accountability, accuracy, timeliness, usability, and diversity, Karen goes to her university library's databases. There she accesses the database Newspaper Source, where she discovers full texts of relevant recent articles from *The New York Times* and transcripts from CNN and CBS News. She prints out several.

Karen next checks out MSNBC on the Web. Her search yields additional useful material, and she bookmarks the site.

With her sources in hand, Karen begins to read and take notes. She is careful to copy verbatim material accurately and to put quotation marks around it.

FIGURE 6.6 *Sample note cards*

**Paraphrased Note**

Crossburning as Free Speech

Russomanno, J. (2002). Speaking our minds: Conversations with the people behind landmark first amendment cases. (p. 45). Mahwah, NJ: Lawrence Erlbaum.

R.A.V. v. city of St. Paul, MN, a case that involved a crossburning, resulted in a Supreme Court decision declaring unconstitutional a St. Paul ordinance limiting free speech acts.

**Direct Quotation**

Government Backlash against Internet Free Speech

Godwin, M. (2003). Cyber rights: Defending free speech in the digital age. (p.22). Cambridge, MA: MIT Press.

"Here in the United States, the government has frequently used the fear of Net crimes and Net criminals as justification for imposing greater control on the Net as a whole."

## Identify Possible Presentation Aids

In addition to discovering verbal supporting material in your sources, you may also find charts, graphs, photographs, or other potentially valuable visual material. You may think you will be able to remember what visuals were in which sources. But many speakers have experienced frustrating searches for that "perfect" presentation aid they remember seeing somewhere while they were taking notes for their speech. Even if you are not certain at this point that you will use presentation aids in your speech, it can't hurt to print out, photocopy, or sketch on a note card any good possibilities, recording those sources of information just as you did for your written materials. Then, when the time comes to consider whether and where presentation aids might enhance the speech, you will have some readily at hand. In Chapter 12 we discuss types of presentation aids and provide guidelines for their use.

**RECAP**

**Research Strategies**

1. Develop a preliminary bibliography.
2. Locate sources.
3. Assess the usefulness of sources.
4. Take notes.
5. Identify possible presentation aids.

# Types of Supporting Material

Once you have discovered likely sources, developed a preliminary bibliography of those sources, read them, assessed their usefulness, taken notes, and identified possible presentation aids, you are ready to make decisions about how to use your information to best advantage. You will need to look at your speech from your listeners' perspective and decide where an explanation might help them understand a point, where statistics might convince them of the significance of a problem, and where an illustration might stir their emotions. Next we will discuss these and other types of supporting material and present guidelines for using them effectively.

## Illustrations

Novelist Michael Cunningham often reads to standing-room-only crowds. He explains the appeal of live readings in this way:

> It's very much about storytelling. . . . you're all gathered around the campfire—"I'm going to tell you about these people, and what happened then."[3]

Cunningham is right. A story or anecdote—an **illustration**—almost always guarantees audience interest by appealing to their emotions. "Stories get you out of your head and into your gut" is how one professional speech coach explains the universal appeal of illustrations.[4]

Let's look more closely at three kinds of illustrations and examine some guidelines for using them.

### Brief Illustrations

A **brief illustration** is often no longer than a sentence or two. In a speech to the United Nations, Secretary of State Hillary Rodham Clinton offered three brief illustrations of women making a difference:

> In South Africa, women living in shantytowns came together to build a housing development outside Cape Town all on their own, brick by brick. And today, their community has grown to more than 50,000 homes for low income families, most of them female-headed.
>
> In Liberia, a group of church women began a prayer movement to stop their country's brutal civil war. It grew to include thousands of women who helped force the two sides to negotiate a peace agreement. And then, those women helped elect Ellen Johnson Sirleaf president, the first woman to lead an African nation.
>
> In the United States, a young woman had an idea for a Web site where anyone could help a small business on the other side of the world get off the ground. And today, the organization she co-founded, Kiva, has given more than $120 million in microloans to entrepreneurs in developing countries, 80 percent of them women.[5]

Why use multiple brief illustrations? Sometimes a series of brief illustrations can have more impact than either a single brief illustration or a more detailed, extended illustration. In addition, although an audience could dismiss a single illustration as an exception, two or more strongly suggest a trend or norm.

### Extended Illustrations

Longer and more detailed than the brief illustration, the **extended illustration** resembles a story. It is more vividly descriptive than a brief illustration, and it has a plot—an opening, complications, a climax, and a resolution.

Australian Prime Minister Kevin Rudd told this moving story of two British sisters who were forcibly taken to Australia under a Child Migrants Program in the 1950s:

> Judy remembers the day they were first taken to the home and her sister Robyn bolted from the gate and ran away.
>
> They later found her and dragged her back.

**illustration**
A story or anecdote that provides an example of an idea, issue, or problem a speaker is discussing

**brief illustration**
An unelaborated example, often only a sentence or two long

**extended illustration**
A detailed example

> Robyn and Judy remember that they kept waiting and waiting for just someone, someone to come and pick them up—but no-one, no-one ever came.
> They recall being hit with belt buckles and bamboo.
> They said the place they grew up in was utterly, utterly loveless.[6]

To use an extended illustration takes more time than to cite a brief example, but longer stories can be more dramatic and emotionally compelling. As we discuss in Chapter 8, extended illustrations can work well as speech introductions. And Chapter 13 considers the use of extended illustrations in informative speeches.

**Hypothetical Illustrations** **Hypothetical illustrations** describe situations or events that have not actually occurred. Rather, they are scenarios that *might* happen. Plausible hypothetical illustrations enable your listeners to imagine themselves or another person in a particular situation. The following hypothetical illustration comes from a speech on how cell phone technology can change communication in developing countries:

> Imagine someone in China or Africa who is gaining access to e-mail for the first time, how it will improve [his or her] efficiency and ability to connect with others.[7]

Notice the word *imagine* in this illustration. The purpose of a hypothetical illustration is not to trick your listeners into believing a bogus story. They should be aware from the beginning that the illustration is hypothetical.

**hypothetical illustration**
An example that might happen but that has not actually occurred

**Using Illustrations Effectively** Illustrations are almost guaranteed attention getters, as well as a way to support your statements. The following suggestions can help you use illustrations more effectively in your speeches.

- **Be certain that your illustrations are directly relevant to the idea or point they are supposed to support.**
- **Choose illustrations that represent a trend.** It is not ethical to find one or two isolated illustrations and use them as though they were typical. If your illustrations are rare instances, you owe it to your listeners to tell them so.
- **Make your illustrations vivid and specific.** Some years ago, a speech professor was fascinated to discover that one of his students had been on the last voyage of the ill-fated Italian ship *Andrea Doria*. Early in the semester, he

## LEARNING FROM GREAT SPEAKERS

### Eleanor Roosevelt (1884–1962)

First lady of the United States, delegate to the United Nations, and social activist Eleanor Roosevelt found supporting material for her speeches in a variety of sources. She saw poverty and racism firsthand as she traveled across the nation. She interviewed such authorities as the presidents of historically black colleges and universities. And she received thousands of letters detailing lives plagued by hardship and pleading for assistance. Eleanor Roosevelt used this material to support her tireless campaigns for civil rights, quality education, and world peace.[8]

As you seek supporting material for your speeches, draw on stories, examples, and illustrations from your own life. Anecdotes from your family, your travels, and even your everyday activities can help you support your ideas and add interest as well. In addition to your own experiences, consider interviewing persons who are experts on your topic so that you can personalize your message with comments from others.

[Photo: AP Wide World Photos]

urged the young man to relate his experience as part of an informative speech on how humans respond to danger. The professor expected a speech with great dramatic impact. Instead, much to his surprise, the student's narrative went something like this: "Well, there was a loud noise and then the sirens went off and we all got in lifeboats and the ship sank."[9] Hardly the stuff great drama is made of! If you have chosen to tell a poignant story, give it enough detail to make it come alive in the minds of your listeners.

- **Use illustrations with which your listeners can identify.** The best illustrations are those that your listeners can imagine experiencing themselves. Other compelling stories, like the sinking of the *Andrea Doria*, can illustrate such great human drama that everyone listening will be immediately interested and attentive.
- **Remember that the best illustrations are personal ones.** Speakers gain conviction and enthusiasm when they talk about their personal experiences. If you have had personal experience with the subject on which you are speaking, be sure to describe that experience to the audience.

## Descriptions and Explanations

Probably the most commonly used forms of support are descriptions and explanations. A **description** provides the details that allow audience members to develop mental pictures of what a speaker is talking about. An **explanation** is a statement that makes clear how something is done or why it exists in its present form or existed in its past form.

### Describing

> Write for the eye, the ear, the nose, and all the senses. In other words, be as vivid as you possibly can.[10]

This advice from a professional speechwriter acknowledges that effective description creates images that make people, places, and events come alive for the audience. More specific instructions for constructing word pictures are given in Chapter 13.

Description may be used in a brief example, an extended illustration, a hypothetical instance, or by itself. One speaker briefly but vividly described to his audience the iconic moon photograph taken by the Apollo 8 astronauts:

> The photograph—dubbed Earthrise—shows our small, blue planet rising above a desolate lunar landscape.[11]

**Explaining How** In a speech to the United Nations General Assembly in the fall of 2009, President Barack Obama explained *how* the United Nations works for the good of people everywhere:

> The United Nations does extraordinary good around the world—feeding the hungry, caring for the sick, mending places that have been broken.[12]

Speakers who discuss or demonstrate processes of any kind rely at least in part on explanations of how those processes work.

**Explaining Why** Explaining why involves giving reasons for or the consequences of a policy, principle, or event. The president and founder of Study Abroad Alumni International explained to a Study Abroad conference *why* global awareness is important:

> Why is global awareness so important? . . . Every six seconds a child dies of hunger. I think we all need to be aware of this . . . and we need to do something about it.[13]

**description**
A word picture of something

**explanation**
A statement that makes clear how something is done or why it exists in its present form or existed in its past form

*As a speaker, you can use words to paint pictures for your listeners. This speaker uses sensory descriptions of sight, sound, smell, taste, and touch to help her audience feel as though they are sharing her experiences as a war refugee.*

[Photo: © Ton Koene/Picture Contact BV/Alamy]

**Using Descriptions and Explanations Effectively** When large sections of a speech contain long, nonspecific explanations, audience eyelids are apt to fall. The following suggestions can help you use descriptions and explanations effectively in your speeches.

- **Keep your descriptions and explanations brief.** Too many unnecessary details may make your listeners say your speech was "everything I *never* wanted to know about the subject."
- **Use language that is as specific and concrete as possible.** Vivid and specific language helps you hold the audience's attention and paint in your listeners' minds the image you are trying to communicate. Chapter 12 provides more tips for making your language specific.
- **Avoid too much description and explanation.** You can hold your audience's attention more effectively if you alternate explanations and descriptions with other types of supporting material, such as brief examples or statistics.

## Definitions

**Definitions** have two justifiable uses in speeches. First, a speaker should be sure to define any and all specialized, technical, or little-known terms in his or her speech. Such definitions are usually achieved by *classification*, the kind of definition you would find in a dictionary. Alternatively, a speaker may define a term by showing how it works or how it is applied in a specific instance—what is known as an *operational definition.*

**definition**
A statement about what a term means or how it is applied in a specific instance

**definition by classification**
A "dictionary definition," constructed by both placing a term in the general class to which it belongs and differentiating it from all other members of that class

**Definitions by Classification** A **definition by classification** both places a term in the general class, group, or family to which it belongs and differentiates it from all the other members of that class. The president of the American Association of Retired Persons defined the term "medical error" for her audience in this way:

> A simple definition of a medical error is a preventable adverse effect of some form of medical care.[14]

**Operational Definitions** Sometimes a word or phrase may be familiar to an audience, but as a speaker you may be applying it in a specific way that needs to be clarified. In such cases you might provide an **operational definition**, explaining how something works or what it does.

Shortly after the launch of Microsoft Windows 7, Microsoft CEO Steve Ballmer operationally defined the new operating system for an audience:

> What is Windows 7 at the end of the day? What were we really most trying to do? We were trying to make the everyday usage of the PC better in the ways our customers wanted: Simpler, faster, more responsive.[15]

**Using Definitions Effectively** The following suggestions can help you use definitions more effectively in your speeches.

- **Use a definition only when needed.** Novice speakers too often use a definition as an easy introduction or a time-filler. Resist the temptation to provide a definition unless you are using a relatively obscure term or one with several definitions.
- **Be certain that your definition is understandable.** Give your listeners definitions that are immediately and easily understandable—or you will have wasted your time and perhaps even lost your audience.
- **Be certain that your definition and your use of a term are consistent throughout a speech.** Even seemingly simple words can create confusion if not defined and used consistently. For example, Roy opened his speech on the potential hazards of abusing nonprescription painkillers by defining *drugs* as nonprescription painkillers. A few minutes later, he confused his audience by using the word *drug* to refer to cocaine. Once he had defined the term, he should have used it only in that context throughout the speech.

## Analogies

An **analogy** is a comparison. Like a definition, it increases understanding; unlike a definition, it deals with relationships and comparisons –between the new and the old, the unknown and the known, or any other pair of ideas or things. Analogies can help your listeners understand unfamiliar ideas, things, and situations by showing how these matters are similar to something they already know.

There are two types of analogies. A *literal* analogy compares things that are actually similar (two sports, two cities, two events). A *figurative* analogy may take the form of a simile or a metaphor.

**Literal Analogies** Student speaker James compared insects with ocean crustaceans when he advocated utilizing insects for food:

> Crustaceans are literally the insects of the sea: They're both arthropods. But where crustaceans feed on trash, insects feed on nature's salad bar.[16]

James's comparison is a **literal analogy**—a comparison between two similar things. If your listeners are from a culture or group other than your own or the one from which the speech derives, literal analogies that draw on the listeners' culture or group may help them understand more readily the less familiar places, things, and situations you are discussing. Literal analogies are often employed by people who want to influence public policy. For example, proponents of trade restrictions argue that because Japan maintains its trade balance through stringent import controls, so should the United States. The more similarities a policymaker can show between the policies or situations being compared, the better his or her chances of being persuasive.

**operational definition**
A statement that shows how something works or what it does

**literal analogy**
A comparison between two similar things

**Figurative Analogies** On a warm July afternoon in 1848, feminist Elizabeth Cady Stanton delivered the keynote address to the first women's rights convention in Seneca Falls, New York. Near the end of her speech, she offered this impassioned analogy:

> Voices were the visitors and advisers of Joan of Arc. Do not "voices" come to us daily from the haunts of poverty, sorrow, degradation, and despair, already too long unheeded? Now is the time for the women of this country, if they would save our free institutions, to defend the right, to buckle on the armor that can best resist the keenest weapons of the enemy—contempt and ridicule.[17]

A literal analogy might have compared the status of women in medieval France to that of women in nineteenth-century America. But the **figurative analogy** Stanton employed compared the voices that moved Joan of Arc to the social inequalities facing nineteenth-century women.

Because it relies not on facts or statistics, but rather on imaginative insights, the figurative analogy is not considered hard evidence. But because it is creative, it is inherently interesting and should help grab an audience's attention. In a speech titled "Short-Term Demands Vs. Long-Term Responsibilities," PepsiCo CEO Indra Nooyi used this figurative analogy:

> Like the characters in the Hindu epic, the Ramayana, capitalism has the ability to assume different forms for different times and different nations.[18]

### Using Analogies Effectively

These suggestions can help you to use literal and figurative analogies more effectively.

- **Be sure that the two things you compare in a literal analogy are very similar.** The more alike the two things being compared, the more likely it is that the analogy will stand up under attack.
- **Be sure that the essential similarity between the two objects of a figurative analogy is readily apparent.** When you use a figurative analogy, it is crucial to make clear the similarity on which the analogy is based. If you do not, your audience will end up wondering what in the world you are talking about.

## Statistics

Many of us live in awe of numbers, or **statistics**. Perhaps nowhere is our respect for statistics so evident—and so exploited—as in advertising. If three out of four doctors surveyed recommend Pain Away aspirin, it must be the best. If Sudsy Soap is 99.9 percent pure (whatever that means), surely it will help our complexions. And if nine out of ten people like Sloppy Catsup in the taste test, we will certainly buy it for this weekend's barbecue. How can the statistics be wrong?

The truth about statistics lies somewhere between an unconditional faith in numbers and the wry observation that "There are three kinds of lies: lies, damned lies, and statistics."

**Using Statistics as Support** Statistics can be expressed as either counts or percentages. Verizon CEO Ivan Seidenberg used a count and a percentage in the same sentence in his speech to a communications conference:

> Using smart grids and mobile technologies to manage electric power could create 280,000 new jobs and cut carbon emissions by more than 20 percent by 2020.[19]

**figurative analogy**
A comparison between two essentially dissimilar things that share some common feature on which the comparison depends

**statistics**
Numerical data that summarize facts or samples

**Using Statistics Effectively** The following guidelines can help you analyze and use statistics effectively and correctly.

- **Use reliable sources.** It has been said that figures don't lie, but liars figure! And indeed, statistics can be produced to support almost any conclusion desired. Your goal is to cite *authoritative* and *unbiased* sources.
- **Use authoritative sources.** No source is an authority on everything and thus cannot be credible on all subjects. The most authoritative source is the **primary source**—the original collector and interpreter of the data. If you find an interesting statistic in a newspaper or magazine article, look closely to see whether a source is cited. If it is, try to find that source and the original reporting of the statistic. Do not assume that the secondhand account, or **secondary source**, has reported the statistic accurately and fairly. As often as possible, go to the primary source.
- **Use unbiased sources.** As well as being authoritative, sources should be as unbiased as possible. We usually extend to government research and various independent sources of statistics the courtesy of thinking them unbiased. Because they are, for the most part, supposed to be unaffiliated with any special interest, their statistics are presumed to be less biased than those coming from such organizations as the American Tobacco Institute, the AFL-CIO, or Microsoft. All three organizations have some special interest at stake, and data they gather are more likely to reflect their biases.

  As you evaluate your sources, try to find out how the statistics were gathered. For example, if a statistic relies on a sample, how was the sample taken? A Thursday afternoon telephone poll of 20 registered voters in Brooklyn is not an adequate sample of New York City voters. The sample is too small and too geographically limited. In addition, it excludes anyone without a telephone or anyone unlikely to be at home when the survey was conducted. Sample sizes and survey methods do vary widely, but most legitimate polls involve samples of 500 to 2,000 people, selected at random from a larger population. Of course, finding out about the statistical methodology may be more difficult than discovering the source of the statistic, but if you can find it, the information will help you to analyze the value of the statistic.
- **Interpret statistics accurately.** People are often swayed by statistics that sound good but have in fact been wrongly calculated or misinterpreted. In an interview for *The New York Times*, Joel Best, author of *Damned Lies and Statistics: Untangling Numbers from the Media, Politicians, and Activists*, offered his favorite "bad statistic":

  > A student of mine quoted an article that contained the sentence, "Every year since 1950, the number of American children gunned down has doubled." This is [a] mutant statistic. If one child were gunned down in 1950, and two in 1951, then by 1995 . . . there would have been 35 trillion children gunned down, more than the total number of people who ever lived.[20]

  Both as a user of statistics in your own speeches and as a consumer of statistics in articles, books, and speeches, be constantly alert to what the statistics actually mean.
- **Make your statistics understandable and memorable.** You can make your statistics easier to understand and more memorable in several ways. First, you can *compact* a statistic, or express it in units that are more meaningful or more easily understandable to your audience. A fairly common way to compact a statistic is to express a staggering amount of money in terms of cents, as PBS President and CEO Paula Kerger did in this example:

  > The United States will spend about $165 million on the arts this year. This equates to 54 cents per citizen.[21]

**primary source**
The original collector and interpreter of information or data

**secondary source**
An individual, organization, or publication that reports information or data gathered by another entity

You might also make your statistics more memorable by *exploding* them. Exploded statistics are created by adding or multiplying related numbers—for example, cost per unit times number of units. Because it is larger, the exploded statistic seems more significant than the original figures from which it was derived. Student speaker Tasha Carlson used the "exploding" strategy to emphasize the impact a single advocate can have on organ donation:

> I printed off donor cards from *organdonor.gov* and sat outside of my college cafeteria. After a mere two hours, I had persuaded seventeen nondonors to sign donor cards. Because the Transplant Society declares on their Web site that the organs donated from one individual can save up to eight lives, in reality my efforts could potentially save 136 people.[22]

Finally, you can *compare* your statistic with another that heightens its impact. After Hurricane Ike came ashore in Texas in 2008, then-mayor of Houston Bill White compared the amount of debris left behind to 390 football fields 6 feet high.[23]

- **Round off numbers.** It is much easier to grasp and remember "2 million" than 2,223,147. Percentages, too, are more easily remembered when they are rounded off. And most people seem to remember percentages even better when they are expressed as fractions.
- **Use visual aids to present your statistics.** Most audience members have difficulty remembering a barrage of numbers thrown at them during a speech. But if the numbers are displayed in a table or graph in front of your listeners, they can more easily grasp the statistics. Figure 6.7 illustrates how a speaker could lay out a table of statistics on how private health insurance coverage in the United States is distributed among various age groups. Using such a table, you would still need to explain what the numbers mean, but you wouldn't have to recite them. We discuss visual aids in Chapter 12.

## Opinions

**opinion**
A statement expressing an individual's attitudes, beliefs, or values

Three types of **opinions** may be used as supporting material in speeches: the testimonies of expert authorities, the testimonies of ordinary (lay) people with firsthand or eyewitness experience, and quotations from literary works.

**Percentage of People with Private Health Insurance Coverage in the United States by Age**

| Age | Percentage Insured |
|---|---|
| Under 18 years | 90% |
| 18 to 24 years | 71% |
| 25 to 34 years | 73% |
| 35 to 44 years | 81% |
| 45 to 64 years | 86% |
| 65 years and over | 98% |

FIGURE 6.7 *Example of a table of statistics*

Source: Data from U.S. Census Bureau, "People Without Health Insurance Coverage by Selected Characteristics: 2007 and 2008." 28 June 2010 <http://www.census.gov/hhles/www.hlthins/data/incpovhlth/2008/tables/html>.

**Expert Testimony** Having already offered statistics on the number of cigars Americans consume annually, Dena emphasized the danger to both smokers and recipients of secondhand smoke by providing **expert testimony** from a National Cancer Institute adviser:

> James Repace, an adviser to the National Cancer Institute, states, "If you have to breathe secondhand smoke, cigar smoke is a lot worse than cigarette smoke."[24]

The testimony of a recognized authority can add a great deal of weight to your arguments. Or, if your topic requires that you make predictions—statements that can be supported in only a marginal way by statistics or examples—the statements of expert authorities may prove to be your most convincing support.

**Lay Testimony** You are watching the nightly news. Newscasters reporting on the forest fires that continue to rage in California explain how these fires started. They provide statistics on how many thousands of acres have burned and how many hundreds of homes have been destroyed. They describe the intense heat and smoke at the scene of one of the fires, and they ask an expert—a veteran firefighter—to predict the likelihood that the fires will be brought under control soon. But the most poignant moment of this story is an interview with a woman who has just returned to her home and has found it in smoldering ashes. She is a layperson—not a firefighter or an expert on forest fires, but someone who has experienced the tragedy firsthand.

Like illustrations, **lay testimony** can stir an audience's emotions. And, although neither as authoritative nor as unbiased as expert testimony, lay testimony is often more memorable.

**expert testimony**
An opinion offered by someone who is an authority on a subject

**lay testimony**
An opinion or description offered by a nonexpert who has firsthand experience

**literary quotation**
An opinion or description by a writer who speaks in a memorable and often poetic way

**Literary Quotations** Another way to make a point memorable is to include a **literary quotation** in your speech. Speaking on changes essential to the survival of the automotive industry, Chrysler Corporation CEO Sergio Marchionne drew on the words of philosopher Friedrich Nietzsche:

> The philosopher Friedrich Nietzsche once said that "what really arouses indignation against suffering is not suffering as such but the senselessness of suffering. . . ." And a crisis that does not result in enduring changes, in fundamental changes, will have been very senseless indeed.[25]

Note that the Nietzsche quotation is short. Brief, pointed quotations usually have greater audience impact than longer, more rambling ones. As Shakespeare said, "Brevity is the soul of wit" (*Hamlet*, II.2).

Literary quotations have the additional advantage of being easily accessible. You'll find any number of quotation dictionaries on the Web and in the reference sections of most libraries. Arranged alphabetically by subject, these compilations are easy to use.

**Using Opinions Effectively** Here are a few suggestions for using opinions effectively in your speeches.

- **Be certain that any authority you cite is an expert on the subject you are discussing.** Advertisers ignore this advice when they have well-known athletes endorse such items as flashlight batteries, breakfast cereals, and cars. Athletes may indeed be experts on athletic shoes, tennis rackets, or stopwatches, but they lack any specific qualifications to talk about most of the products they endorse.

## CONFIDENTLY CONNECTING WITH YOUR AUDIENCE

### Prepare Early

Gathering relevant and credible supporting material for your speech takes time. So it's a good idea to give yourself plenty of time to gather examples, stories, statistics, opinions, quotations, and other supporting material. By starting your speech preparation early, you'll get a bonus: Research suggests that people who prepare early rather than waiting until the last minute experience less apprehension about speaking in public.[26] So preparing early will give you time to find good supporting material *and* help you manage your anxiety.

- **Identify your sources.** If a student quotes the director of the Harry Ransom Humanities Research Center at the University of Texas but identifies that person only as Tom Staley, few listeners will recognize the name, let alone acknowledge his authority.

In Chapter 2, we discussed the importance of citing your sources orally. In the course of doing so, you can provide additional information about the qualifications of those sources. Note how the student speakers in the following examples use a variety of phrases and sentence structures to help them identify their sources for their audiences in a fluent way:

> *MyFairCredit.com*, last accessed April 20, 2009, explains that the CRAs [credit reporting agencies] gather their information differently and independently from one another. . . .[27]

> The president [of the American Society of Civil Engineers] Wayne Klotz told *The New York Times*, January 28, 2009, "If our country and its leaders are looking for solutions to the economic crisis, investing in our infrastructure could help to create 2.6 million jobs in construction, consulting, manufacturing, public relations, research, and government positions."[28]

- **Cite unbiased authorities.** Just as the most reliable sources of statistics are unbiased, so too are the most reliable sources of opinion. The chairman of General Motors may offer an expert opinion that the Chevy Cruze is the best compact car on the market today. His expertise is unquestionable, but his bias is obvious and makes him a less than trustworthy source of opinion on the subject. A better source would be the *Consumer Reports* analyses of the reliability and repair records of compact cars.
- **Cite opinions that are representative of prevailing opinion.** Unless most of the experts in the field share an opinion, its value is limited. Citing such opinion only leaves your conclusions open to easy rebuttal.
- **Quote your sources accurately.** If you quote or paraphrase either an expert or a layperson, be certain that your quote or paraphrase is accurate and within the context in which the remarks were originally made.
- **Use literary quotations sparingly.** Be sure that you have a valid reason for citing a literary quotation, and then use only one or two at most in a speech.

RECAP

### Types of Supporting Material

| | |
|---|---|
| Illustrations | Relevant stories |
| Explanations | Statements that make clear how something is done or why it exists in its present form or existed in a past form |
| Descriptions | Word pictures |
| Definitions | Concise explanations of a word or concept |
| Analogies | Comparisons between two things |
| Statistics | Numbers that summarize data or examples |
| Opinions | Testimony or quotations from someone else |

## The Best Supporting Material

In this chapter, we discussed six criteria for evaluating Web sites: accountability, accuracy, objectivity, timeliness, usability, and diversity. We also presented guidelines for using each of the six types of supporting material effectively. However, even after you have applied these criteria and guidelines, you may still have more supporting material than you can possibly use for a short speech. How do you decide what to use and what to eliminate? The following considerations can help you make that final cut.

- **Magnitude.** Bigger is better. The larger the numbers, the more convincing your statistics. The more experts who support your point of view, the more your expert testimony will command your audience's attention.
- **Proximity.** The best supporting material is whatever is the most relevant to your listeners, or the closest to home. If you can demonstrate how an

incident could affect audience members themselves, that illustration will have far greater impact than a more remote one.

- **Concreteness.** If you need to discuss abstract ideas, explain them with concrete examples and specific statistics.
- **Variety.** A mix of illustrations, opinions, definitions, and statistics is much more interesting and convincing than the exclusive use of any one type of supporting material.
- **Humor.** Audiences usually appreciate a touch of humor in an example or opinion. Only if your audience is unlikely to understand the humor or if your speech is on a *very* somber and serious topic is humor not appropriate.
- **Suitability.** Your final decision about whether to use a certain piece of supporting material will depend on its suitability to you, your speech, the occasion, and—as we continue to stress throughout the book—your audience. For example, you would probably use more statistics in a speech to a group of scientists than in an after-luncheon talk to the local Rotary Club.

# STUDY GUIDE

## Sources of Supporting Material

Five sources of supporting material are personal knowledge and experience, the Internet, online databases, traditional library holdings, and interviews.

You may be able to draw on your own knowledge and experience for some supporting material for your speech.

Internet resources are accessible through Web directories and search engines, but you must evaluate who is accountable for the sources you find and whether the sources are accurate, objective, current, usable, and sensitive to diversity.

Online databases, accessed via a networked computer, provide access to bibliographic information, abstracts, and full texts for a variety of resources, including periodicals, newspapers, government documents, and even books.

Traditional library holdings include books, periodicals, full-text databases, newspapers, and reference resources.

When conducting an interview, take written notes or record the interview. Later, transcribe your information onto note cards.

### Being Audience-Centered

- Your audience will accord you more respect as an authority when they realize that you have firsthand knowledge of a topic.

### Using What You've Learned

- Explain how you might use each of the five key sources of supporting material to help you develop an informative speech on how to buy a new computer.

### A Question of Ethics

- Under what conditions, if any, is it ethical to use in your speech graphs, pictures, and other visual aids you find through the Internet?
- Electronic and print indexes and databases sometimes include abstracts of books and articles rather than full texts. If you have read only the abstract of a source, is it ethical to include that source on your speech bibliography?

### Speaker's Homepage: Evaluating Web Sites

The following three sites provide criteria, resources, and tips for evaluating Web sites:

- www.library.cornell.edu/olinuris/ref/research/webeval.html
- www.lib.berkeley.edu/TeachingLib/Guides/Internet/Evaluate.html
- Lib.nmsu.edu/instruction/evalcrit.html

## Research Strategies

After you discover possible sources, the next steps in the research process are to develop a preliminary bibliography of those sources, read them, assess their potential usefulness, take notes, and identify possible presentation aids.

### A Question of Ethics

- You neglected to record bibliographic information for one of your best information sources, a magazine article you found in the library. You discover your omission the night before you must deliver your speech, and you have no time to return to the library. How can you solve your problem in an ethical way?

## Ways to Use Supporting Material

You can choose from various types of supporting material, including illustrations, descriptions and explanations, definitions, analogies, statistics, and opinions. A mix of supporting material is much more interesting and convincing than the exclusive use of any one type.

### Being Audience-Centered

- An illustration almost always ensures audience interest.
- Abstract assertions and explanations by themselves will bore an audience. Use concrete examples and specific statistics.
- Vivid and specific language in any description or explanation helps you hold the audience's attention and paint in your listeners' minds the image you are trying to communicate.
- If your listeners are from a culture or group other than your own or the one from which the speech derives, literal analogies that draw on the listeners' culture or group may help them understand more readily the less familiar places, things, and situations you are discussing.

### A Question of Ethics

- Go back through the chapter and reread the guidelines for each type of supporting material. Which of these guidelines for the *effective* use of supporting material might also be considered a guideline for the *ethical* use of supporting material? Explain your choices.

- Is it ever ethical to invent supporting material if you have been unable to find what you need for your speech? Explain.

### Speaker's Homepage: Using the Internet to Find Interesting Supporting Material

These Web sites might help you in your quest to find that perfect story, riveting illustration, recent statistic, or well-worded definition.

- **Quick Reference Desk of Purdue University.** This powerful site provides links to some of the most common reference material found in most libraries. www.lib.purdue.edu/eresources/readyref/
- **Biography.com.** Use this site to find information on more than 20,000 famous people. Anecdotes about them can serve as illustrations for a speech. www.biography.com
- **Federal Government Statistics.** U.S. Bureau of the Census. www.census.gov/main/www/cen2000.html Federal Citizen Information Center: www.info.gov/

## Selecting the Best Supporting Material

Once you have gathered a variety of supporting material, look at your speech from your audience's perspective and decide where an explanation might help listeners understand a point, where statistics might convince them of the significance of a problem, and where an illustration might stir their emotions. Six criteria—magnitude, proximity, concreteness, variety, humor, and suitability—can help you choose the most effective support for your speech.

### Being Audience-Centered

- Your final decision about whether to use a certain piece of supporting material will depend on its suitability for your audience. The best supporting material is whatever is the most relevant to your listeners, or closest to home.

# SPEECH WORKSHOP

## Identifying a Variety of Supporting Material for Your Speech

A good speech includes several different types of supporting material. As you prepare your speech, use this worksheet to categorize the types of supporting material you have found. If you realize you have only one or two types of supporting material, you may need to use your research skills to find additional types in order to enhance both the clarity and the interest of your message.

| Type of Supporting Material | Material You Plan to Use |
|---|---|
| **Illustration:** A story that provides an example of an idea, issue, or problem. The illustration could be short or long, real or hypothetical (see pages 145–147). | |
| **Description or Explanation:** Words that clarify a person, place, thing, idea, or process (see pages 147–149). | |
| **Definition:** A statement about what a term means or how it is applied in a specific instance (see page 149). | |

| Type of Supporting Material | Material You Plan to Use |
|---|---|
| **Analogy:** A comparison between two things. The analogy could compare two similar things (a literal analogy) or two dissimilar things that share some common feature (a figurative analogy) (see pages 149–150). | |
| **Statistics:** Numerical data that summarize facts and examples (see pages 151–152). | |
| **Opinion:** A statement expressing a person's attitudes, beliefs, or values (see pages 152–155). | |

Organized thought is the basis of organized action.

—Alfred North Whitehead

Luigi Russolo (1885–1947), © Copyright *Music*, 1911. Photo: M. E. Smith/Private Collection. © DeA Picture Library/Art Resource N.Y.

OUTLINE

# 7 Organizing Your Speech

OBJECTIVES

**After studying this chapter you should be able to do the following:**

1. List and describe five patterns for organizing the main ideas of a speech.
2. List five patterns of organization applicable to subpoints.
3. Describe how to integrate supporting material into a speech.
4. Explain how verbal and nonverbal signposts can communicate the relationships between parts of a speech.

Maria went into the lecture hall feeling exhilarated. After all, Dr. Anderson was a Nobel laureate in literature. He would be teaching and lecturing on campus for at least a year. What an opportunity! Maria took a seat in the middle of the fourth row, where she had a clear view of the podium. She opened the notebook she had bought just for this lecture series, took out one of the three pens she had brought with her, and waited impatiently for Dr. Anderson's appearance. She didn't have to wait long. Dr. Anderson was greeted by thunderous applause when he walked onto the stage. Maria was aware of an almost electric sense of expectation among the audience members. Pen poised, she awaited his first words.

Five minutes later, Maria still had her pen poised. He had gotten off to a slow start. Ten minutes later, she laid her pen down and decided to concentrate just on listening. Twenty minutes later, she still had no idea what point Dr. Anderson was trying to make. And by the time the lecture was over, Maria was practically asleep. Disappointed, she gathered her pens and her notebook (which now contained one page of lazy doodles) and promised herself she would skip the remaining lectures in the series.

Dr. Anderson was not a dynamic speaker. But his motivated audience of young would-be authors and admirers might have forgiven that shortcoming. What they were unable to do was to unravel his hour's worth of seemingly pointless rambling—to get some sense of direction or some pattern of ideas from his talk. Dr. Anderson had simply failed to organize his thoughts.

The scenario described above actually happened. Dr. Anderson (not his real name) disappointed many who had looked forward to his lectures. His inability to organize his ideas made him an ineffectual speaker. You, too, may have had an experience with a teacher who possessed expertise in his or her field but could not organize his or her thoughts well enough to lecture effectively. No matter how knowledgeable speakers may be, they must organize their ideas in logical patterns to ensure that their audience can follow, understand, and remember what is said. Our model of audience-centered communication emphasizes that speeches are organized *for* audiences, with decisions about organization being based in large part on an analysis of the audience.

In the first six chapters of this book, you learned how to plan and research a speech based on audience needs, interests, and expectations. The planning and research process has taken you through five stages of speech preparation:

- Selecting and narrowing a topic
- Determining your purpose
- Developing your central idea
- Generating main ideas
- Gathering supporting material

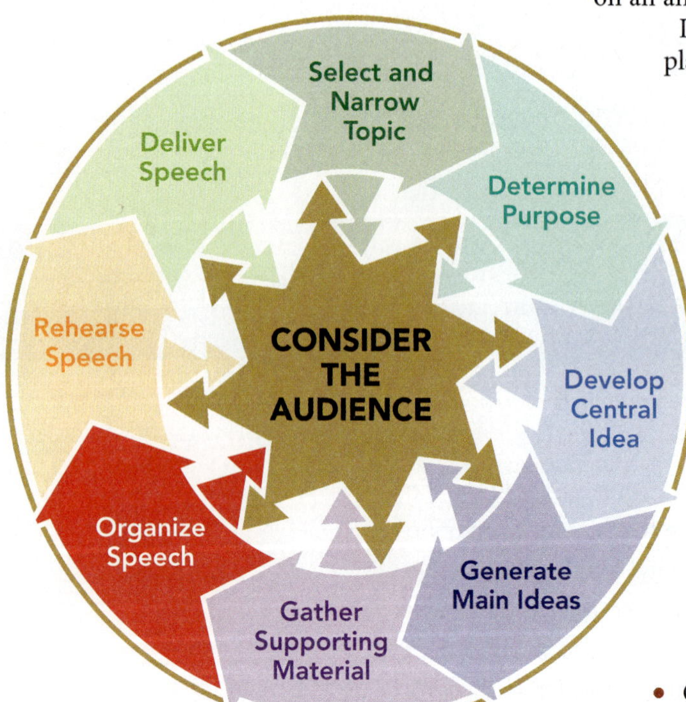


FIGURE 7.1 *Organize your speech to help your audience remember your key ideas and to give your speech clarity and structure.*

As the arrows in the model in Figure 7.1 suggest, you may have moved *recursively* through these first five stages, returning at times to earlier stages to make changes and revisions based on your consideration of the audience. Now, with the results of your audience-centered planning and research in hand, it is time to move to the next stage in the audience-centered public-speaking process:

- Organizing your speech

In this chapter, we will discuss the patterns of organization commonly used to arrange the main ideas of a speech. Then we will discuss how to organize subpoints and supporting materials. Finally, we will talk about transitions, previews, and summaries. Chapter 8 discusses introductions and conclusions, and Chapter 9 deals with outlining, the final two components of the organizational stage of the preparation process.

# Organizing Your Main Ideas

In Chapter 5, we discussed how to generate a preliminary plan for your speech by determining whether your central idea had logical divisions, could be supported by several reasons, or could be explained by identifying specific steps. These divisions, reasons, or steps became the main ideas of the body of your speech and the basis for the organization task highlighted in Figure 7.1.

Now you are ready to decide which of your main ideas to discuss first, which one second, and so on. As summarized in Table 7.1 on page 169, you can choose from among five organizational patterns: (1) topical, (2) chronological, (3) spatial, (4) causal, and (5) problem and solution. Or you can combine several of these patterns. One additional variation of the problem and solution pattern is the motivated sequence. Because it is used almost exclusively in persuasive speeches, the motivated sequence is discussed in Chapter 15.

## CONFIDENTLY CONNECTING WITH YOUR AUDIENCE

### Organize Your Message

Taking the time to plan a well-organized message can boost your confidence. A jumble of ideas and information without a logical structure is more difficult to remember and present than a well-organized speech. Researchers have discovered that the less organized you are, the more apprehensive you may feel.[1] A logically organized speech can help you feel more confident about the content you're presenting.

## Organizing Ideas Topically

If your central idea has natural divisions, you can often organize your speech topically. Speeches on such diverse topics as factors to consider when selecting a mountain bike, types of infertility treatments, and the various classes of ham-radio licenses could all reflect **topical organization**.

Natural divisions are often essentially equal in importance. It may not matter which point you discuss first, second, or third. You can simply arrange your main ideas as a matter of personal preference. At other times, you may organize your main points based on one of three principles: primacy, recency, or complexity.

**Primacy** The principle of **primacy** suggests that you discuss your most important or convincing point *first* in your speech. The beginning of your speech can be the most important position if your listeners are either unfamiliar with your topic or hostile toward your central idea.

When your listeners are uninformed, your first point must introduce them to the topic and define unfamiliar terms integral to its discussion. What you say early in your speech will affect your listeners' understanding of the rest of your speech. If your listeners are likely to be hostile toward your central idea, putting your most important or convincing point first will lessen the possibility that you might lose or alienate them before you reach the end of your speech. In addition, your strongest idea may so influence your listeners' attitudes that they will be more receptive to your central idea.

Recognizing the controversial nature of stem-cell research, the speaker in the following example arranges the three main points of the speech according to primacy, advancing the most persuasive argument first.

PURPOSE STATEMENT: At the end of my speech, the audience will be able to explain the applications of stem-cell research.

CENTRAL IDEA: Stem-cell research has three important applications.

MAIN IDEAS:

I. At the most fundamental level, understanding stem cells can help us to understand better the process of human development.

II. Stem-cell research can streamline the way we develop and test drugs.

III. Stem-cell research can generate cells and tissue that could be used for "cell therapies."[2]

**topical organization**
Organization of the natural divisions in a central idea according to recency, primacy, complexity, or the speaker's discretion

**primacy**
Arrangement of ideas from the most to the least important

**Recency** According to the principle of **recency**, the point discussed *last* is the one audiences will remember best. If your audience is at least somewhat knowledgeable about and generally favorable toward your topic and central idea, you should probably organize your main points according to recency.

For example, if your speech is on the various living arrangements available to college students, and you want your audience of fellow students to consider living at home because of the savings involved, you would probably discuss that possibility as the fourth and last option. Your speech might have the following structure:

PURPOSE STATEMENT: At the end of my speech, the audience will be able to discuss the pros and cons of four living arrangements for college students.

CENTRAL IDEA: College students have at least four living arrangements available to them.

MAIN IDEAS:

I. Living in a dormitory
II. Renting an apartment
III. Joining a fraternity or sorority
IV. Living at home

**Complexity** One other set of circumstances may dictate a particular order of the main ideas in your speech. If your main ideas range from simple to complicated, it makes sense to arrange them in order of **complexity**, progressing from the simple to the more complex. If, for example, you were to explain to your audience how to compile a family health profile and history, you might begin with the most easily accessible source and proceed to the more involved.

PURPOSE STATEMENT: At the end of my speech, the audience will be able to compile a family health profile and history.

CENTRAL IDEA: Compiling a family health profile and history can be accomplished with the help of three sources.

MAIN IDEAS:

I. Elderly relatives
II. Old hospital records and death certificates
III. National health registries[3]

Teachers, from those in the very early elementary grades on up, use order of complexity to organize their courses and lessons. The kindergartner is taught to trace circles before learning to print a lowercase *a*. The young piano student practices scales and arpeggios before playing Beethoven sonatas. The college freshman practices writing 500-word essays before attempting a major research paper. You have learned most of your skills in order of complexity.

RECAP

**Primacy, Recency, and Complexity**

- Primacy—most important point first
- Recency—most important point last
- Complexity—simplest point first, most complex point last

## Ordering Ideas Chronologically

If you decide that your central idea could be explained best by a number of steps, you will probably organize those steps chronologically. **Chronological organization** is organization by time or sequence; that is, your steps are ordered according to when each step occurred or should occur. Historical speeches and how-to speeches are the two kinds of speeches usually organized chronologically.

Examples of topics for historical speeches might include the history of the women's movement in the United States, the sequence of events that led to the 1974 resignation of President Richard Nixon, or the development of the modern Olympic Games. You can choose to organize your main points either from earliest to most recent (forward in time) or from recent events back into history (backward in time). The progression you choose depends on your personal preference and on whether you want to emphasize the

**recency**
Arrangement of ideas from the least to the most important

**complexity**
Arrangement of ideas from the simple to the more complex

**chronological organization**
Organization by time or sequence

beginning or the end of the sequence. As we observed earlier, according to the principle of recency, audiences tend to remember best what they hear last.

In the following outline for a speech on the development of the Apple iPad, the speaker moves forward in time, making his last point the one that remains fresh in the minds of his audience at the end of his speech.

PURPOSE STATEMENT: At the end of my speech, the audience will be able to trace the major events in the development of the iPad.

CENTRAL IDEA: Drawing on the technology and market success of earlier devices, the Apple iPad has quickly become a bestseller.

MAIN IDEAS:

I. 1993: Newton Message Pad marketed by Apple
II. 2001: iPod introduced
III. 2007: iPhone debuted
IV. 2010: iPad unveiled[4]

How-to explanations are also likely to follow a sequence or series of steps arranged from beginning to end, from the first step to the last—forward in time. A speech explaining how to strip painted furniture might be organized as follows:

PURPOSE STATEMENT: At the end of my speech, the audience will be able to list the four steps involved in stripping old paint from furniture.

CENTRAL IDEA: Stripping old paint from furniture requires four steps.

MAIN IDEAS:

I. Prepare work area and gather materials.
II. Apply chemical stripper.
III. Remove stripper with scrapers and steel wool.
IV. Clean and sand stripped surfaces.

In another chronologically organized speech, this one discussing the development of *YouTube*, the speaker wants to emphasize the inauspicious origins of the popular video site. Thus, she organizes the speech backward in time:

PURPOSE STATEMENT: At the end of my speech, the audience will be able to describe *YouTube*'s rapid rise from humble beginnings.

CENTRAL IDEA: The popular video site *YouTube* grew rapidly from humble beginnings.

MAIN IDEAS:

I. May 2010: *YouTube* exceeds more than two billion viewers a day, nearly double the prime-time audiences of all three major U.S. television networks combined.
II. November 2006: *YouTube* acquired by Google
III. December 2005: *YouTube* site publicly launched
IV. February 2005: *YouTube* founded in a garage in Menlo Park, California[5]

Chronological organization, then, involves either forward or backward progression, depending on which end of a set of events the speaker intends to emphasize. The element common to both organization schemes is that dates and events are discussed in sequence rather than in random order.

## Arranging Ideas Spatially

When you say, "As you enter the room, the table is to your right, the easy chair to your left, and the kitchen door straight ahead," you are using **spatial organization**: arranging ideas—usually natural divisions of the central idea—according to their location or direction. It does not usually matter whether you progress up or down, east or west, forward or back, as long as you follow a logical progression. If you skip up, down, over, and back, you will confuse your listeners rather than paint a distinct word picture.

Speeches on such diverse subjects as the National Museum of the American Indian, the travels of Robert Louis Stevenson, and the structure of an atom can all be organized spatially. Here is a sample outline for the first of those topics:

PURPOSE STATEMENT: At the end of my speech, the audience will be able to list and describe the four habitats recreated on the grounds of the National Museum of the American Indian in Washington, D.C.

CENTRAL IDEA: The grounds of the National Museum of the American Indian in Washington, D.C., are divided into four traditional American Indian habitats.

MAIN IDEAS:

I. Upland hardwood forest
II. Lowland freshwater wetlands
III. Eastern meadowlands
IV. Traditional croplands[6]

The organization of this outline is spatial, progressing through the grounds of the museum.

**spatial organization** Organization based on location or direction

**cause-and-effect organization** Organization that focuses on a situation and its causes or a situation and its effects

## Organizing Ideas to Show Cause and Effect

If your central idea can be developed by discussing either steps or reasons, you might consider organizing your main ideas by **cause and effect**. A speech organized to show cause and effect may first identify a situation and then discuss the effects that result

### LEARNING FROM GREAT SPEAKERS

#### Desmond Tutu (1931– )

When Archbishop Desmond Tutu won the Nobel Peace Prize in 1984 for his leadership in the struggle against apartheid policies in South Africa, he delivered an impassioned Nobel lecture. In that speech, Tutu combined cause-and-effect and problem-and-solution patterns of organization. He first described a cause—apartheid—and its effects: hunger, the dissolution of families, a segregated education system, legal injustice, and violence. He went on to offer a solution to the problem of apartheid: the guarantee of human rights for all.[7] Tutu continues to be a widely sought-after speaker, relaying his message of peace and equality to audiences throughout the world.

Tutu's messages have a clear, logical structure. He also masterfully uses illustrations to support his major ideas. As you organize your message, plan the structure so that it will be clear to your listeners. Then integrate the illustrations, statistics, and other materials you have chosen to support your points. Placing interesting and well-told stories and illustrations on a solid organizational scaffolding will help make your speech both easy to follow and interesting to hear.

[Photo: Alan Mothner/AP Wide World Photos]

from it (cause→effect). Or the speech may present a situation and then seek its causes (effect→cause). As the recency principle would suggest, the cause-effect pattern emphasizes the effects; the effect-cause pattern emphasizes the causes.

In the following example, Vonda organizes her speech according to cause-effect, discussing the cause (widespread adult illiteracy) as her first main idea, and its effects (poverty and social costs) as her second and third main ideas:

PURPOSE STATEMENT: At the end of my speech, the audience will be able to identify two effects of adult illiteracy.

CENTRAL IDEA: Adult illiteracy affects everyone.

MAIN IDEAS:

I. (*Cause*): Adult illiteracy is widespread in America today.

II. (*Effect*): Adult illiterates often live in poverty.

III. (*Effect*): Adult illiteracy is costly to society.[8]

In contrast, Brittany organizes her speech on hurricanes according to an effect-cause pattern, discussing the effect (hurricanes' becoming increasingly destructive) as her first main idea and its causes (the buildup of coastal communities, the warming of the ocean surface, and natural cycles) as her second, third, and fourth main ideas:

PURPOSE STATEMENT: At the end of my speech, the audience will be able to explain why hurricanes are likely to become increasingly destructive to the United States.

CENTRAL IDEA: Hurricanes are likely to become increasingly destructive to the United States for three reasons.

MAIN IDEAS:

I. (*Effect*): Hurricanes are likely to become increasingly destructive to the United States.

II. (*Cause*): The buildup of coastal communities in recent decades has put more people in harm's way.

III. (*Cause*): The warming of the ocean surface provides more energy to fuel hurricanes.

IV. (*Cause*): Natural cycles are changing in favor of hurricane formation.[9]

In both of the preceding examples, the speakers may decide in what order they will discuss the main ideas that follow the first main idea by considering the principles of recency, primacy, or complexity.

## Organizing Ideas by Problem-Solution

If you want to discuss why a problem exists or what its effects are, you will probably organize your speech according to cause and effect, as discussed in the previous section. However, if you want to emphasize how best to *solve* the problem, you will probably use a **problem-solution** pattern of organization.

Like causes and effects, problems and solutions can be discussed in either order. If you speak to an audience that is already fairly aware of a problem but uncertain how to solve it, you will probably discuss the problem first and then the solution(s), as in this example:

PURPOSE STATEMENT: At the end of my speech, the audience will be able to list and explain three ways in which crimes on university campuses can be reduced.

CENTRAL IDEA: Crimes on university campuses can be reduced by implementing three safety measures.

**problem-solution organization**
Organization focused on a problem and its various solutions or on a solution and the problems it would solve

*If your speech is about the problem of oil spills from deep water drilling operations, you could organize your main ideas in a problem-solution pattern, with a description of the problem as your first main point and potential solutions in your later points.*
[Photo: Cheryl Casey/Shutterstock]

MAIN IDEAS:

I. (*Problem*): Crimes against both persons and property have increased dramatically on college campuses over the last few years.

II. (*Solution*): Crimes could be reduced by stricter enforcement of the Student Right to Know and Campus Security Acts.

III. (*Solution*): Crimes could be reduced by assigning student identification numbers that are different from students' Social Security numbers.

IV. (*Solution*): Crimes could be reduced by converting campus buildings to an integrated security system requiring key cards for admittance.[10]

If your audience knows about an action or program that has been implemented but does not know the reasons for its implementation, you might select instead a solution-problem pattern of organization. In the following example, the speaker knows that her listeners are already aware of a new business-school partnership program in their community but believes that they may be unclear about why it has been established:

PURPOSE STATEMENT: At the end of my speech, the audience will be able to explain how business-school partnership programs can help solve two of the major problems facing our public schools today.

CENTRAL IDEA: Business-school partnership programs can help alleviate at least two of the problems faced by public schools today.

## TABLE 7.1 Organizing Your Main Points

| Pattern | Description |
|---|---|
| Topical | Organization according to primacy, recency, or complexity |
| Chronological | Organization by time or sequence |
| Spatial | Organization based on location or direction |
| Cause and effect | Organization that focuses on a situation and its causes or a situation and its effects |
| Problem-solution | Organization that focuses on a problem and then solutions to it or on a solution and then the problems it would solve |

MAIN IDEAS:

I. (*Solution*): In a business-school partnership, local businesses provide volunteers, financial support, and in-kind contributions to public schools.

II. (*Problem*): Many public schools can no longer afford special programs and fine-arts programs.

III. (*Problem*): Many public schools have no resources to fund enrichment materials and opportunities.

Note that in both of the preceding examples, the main ideas are natural divisions of the central idea.

## Acknowledging Cultural Differences in Organization

Although the five patterns just discussed are typical of the way speakers in the United States are expected to organize and process information, they are not necessarily typical of all cultures.[11] In fact, each culture teaches its members patterns of thought and organization that are considered appropriate for various occasions and audiences. On the whole, U.S. speakers tend to be more linear and direct than speakers from Semitic, Asian, Romance, or Russian cultures. Semitic speakers support their main points by pursuing tangents that might seem "off topic" to many U.S. speakers. Asians may only allude to a main point through a circuitous route of illustration and parable. And speakers from Romance and Russian cultures tend to begin with a basic principle and then move to facts and illustrations that they only gradually connect to a main point. The models in Figure 7.2 illustrate these culturally diverse patterns of organization.

Of course, these are very broad generalizations. But as an audience member who recognizes the existence of cultural differences, you can better appreciate and understand the organization of a speaker from a culture other than your own. He or she

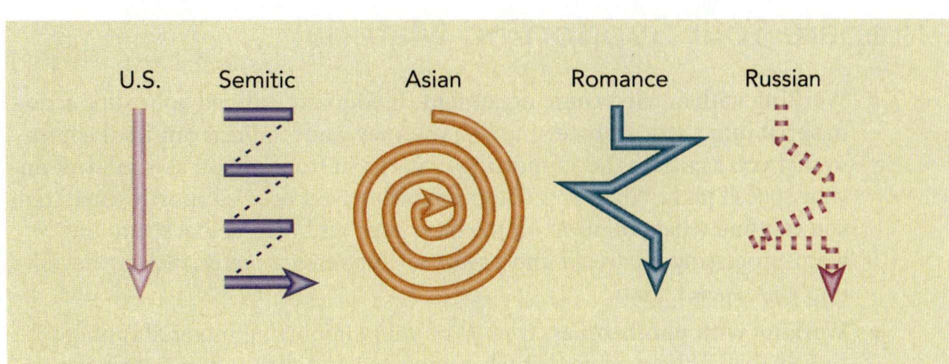


FIGURE 7.2 *Organizational patterns of speaking will vary by culture.*

Source: Lieberman, *Public Speaking in the Multicultural Environment*, "Organizational patterns by culture," © 1997. Reproduced by permission of Pearson Education, Inc.

may not be disorganized, but simply using organizational strategies different from those presented in this chapter.

## Subdividing Your Main Ideas

After you have decided how to organize your main ideas, you may need to subdivide at least some of them. For example, if you give a how-to speech on dog grooming, your first main idea may be:

I. Gather your supplies.

"Supplies" indicates that you need more than one piece of equipment, so you add subpoints that describe the specific supplies needed:

I. Gather your supplies.
  A. Soft brush
  B. Firm brush
  C. Wide-toothed comb
  D. Fine-toothed comb
  E. Scissors
  F. Spray-on detangler

Note that you can arrange your main ideas according to one pattern and your subpoints according to another. For example, the organization of the main ideas of this speech on dog grooming is chronological, but the subpoints of the first main idea are arranged topically. Any of the five organizational patterns that apply to main ideas can apply to subpoints as well.

Don't worry now about outlining details such as Roman numerals, letters, and margins. We cover them in Chapter 9. Your goal at this point is to get your ideas and information on paper. Keep in mind, too, that until you've delivered your speech, none of your decisions is final. You may add, regroup, or eliminate main ideas or subpoints at any stage in the preparation process, as you consider the needs, interests, and expectations of your audience. Multiple drafts indicate that you are working and reworking ideas to improve your product and make it the best you can. They do *not* mean that you are a poor writer or speaker.

## Integrating Your Supporting Material

Once you have organized your main ideas and subpoints, you are ready to flesh out your speech with supporting material.

### Prepare Your Supporting Material

- **Working with an electronic document.** If you have entered your supporting material into a word-processing file, you may want to print out hard copies so that you can have the supporting material in front of you as you work on your speech plan. When you determine where you need supporting material, you can find what you need on the hard copy and then go back into the word-processing file to cut and paste that supporting material electronically into your speech plan.
- **Working with photocopies.** If most of your supporting material is photocopied, search these copies for what you need and then write or type the supporting material into your speech plan.

- **Working with note cards.** If you have written or pasted supporting material on note cards, write each main idea and subpoint on a separate note card of the same size as the ones on which you recorded your supporting material. Next, arrange these note card in the order in which you have organized your speech. As you decide how best to organize your supporting material, you can place each card behind the appropriate main-idea or subpoint card. You will then have on note cards a complete plan for your speech.

Regardless of which strategy or combination of strategies you use to place your supporting material in your speech, take care not to lose track of the sources of the supporting material.

## Organize Your Supporting Material

Once you have prepared your supporting material, you are ready to organize it. You may realize that in support of your second main idea you have an illustration, two statistics, and an opinion. In what order should you present these items?

You can sometimes use the five standard organizational patterns to arrange your supporting material as you do your main ideas and subpoints. Illustrations, for instance, may be organized chronologically. In the following excerpt from a speech on childhood obesity, the speaker arranges several brief examples in a chronological sequence:

> I can think of at least three moments in the past half century that dramatically shifted the course of America's medical and scientific history.
>
> The first time came [on] March 26, 1953—when Jonas Salk called a press conference to announce the discovery of a polio vaccine.
>
> The second time, amazingly, came just four weeks later, when Watson and Crick published their discovery of the double helix structure of DNA.
>
> The third time was in 1964, when U.S. Surgeon General Luther Terry courageously reported that cigarette smoking does cause cancer and other deadly diseases. . . .
>
> On March 9, 2004, the CDC Director declared that obesity is overtaking smoking and tobacco use as the number-one cause of preventable death in America.[12]

At other times, however, none of the five patterns may seem suited to the supporting materials you have. In those instances, you may need to turn to an organizational strategy more specifically adapted to your supporting materials. These strategies include (1) primacy or recency, (2) specificity, (3) complexity, and (4) "soft" to "hard" evidence.

**Primacy or Recency** We have already discussed how the principles of primacy and recency can determine whether you put material at the beginning or the end of your speech. These patterns are used so frequently to arrange supporting materials that we mention them again here.

Suppose that you have several statistics to support a main point. All are relevant and significant, but one is especially gripping. American Cancer Society CEO John Seffrin showed images of and described the following brief examples of international tobacco advertising:

> The effort to build brand loyalty begins early. Here is an example of that in Africa—a young man wearing a hat with a cigarette brand logo. . . .
>
> Look at this innocent baby wearing a giant Marlboro logo on his shirt. . . .
>
> Notice how this ad links smoking to American values that are attractive to third-world kids—wealth, sophistication, and urbanity. It also shows African Americans living the American Dream. If you're a poor kid in Africa, this image can be very powerful.
>
> And finally, this one from Bucharest, Romania, which is my favorite. When the Berlin Wall came down, no one rushed into Eastern Europe faster than the tobacco industry. Here you can see the Camel logo etched in the street lights. In my opinion, this is one of the most disturbing examples of the public sector partnering with private industry to the detriment of its citizens.[13]

## Developing Your Speech Step By Step

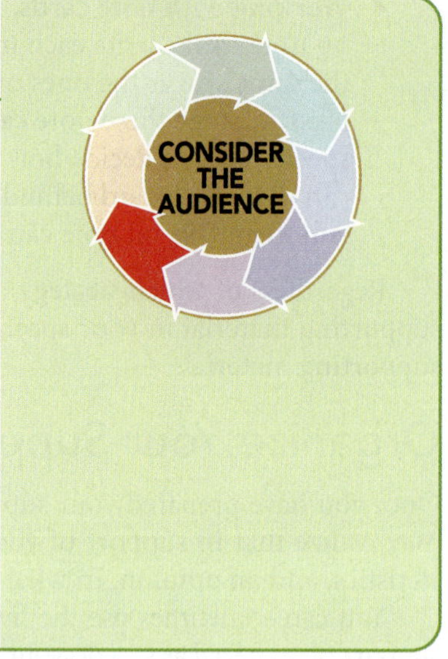


### Organize Your Speech

As she begins to organize her speech on tire safety, Karen finds that she has both *reasons* expired tires pose a problem and *solutions* for the problem. She decides to combine two organizational patterns: cause and effect, and problem and solution.

Determining that she wants to emphasize the *causes* of the safety problem posed by outdated tires, Karen applies the recency principle. She establishes first that we are indeed driving on expired tires, then turns to the causes: that tire companies are ignoring research about tire stability, and that neither the public nor our mechanics are well informed about the problem.

Karen places her *solutions* to the problem next. They include checking our tires, questioning our mechanics, keeping tire sales receipts, and sharing information with family and friends.

It is evident that Seffrin applied the principle of recency to his examples, as he identifies the final one as "my favorite" and "one of the most disturbing." The principle of primacy or recency can also be applied to groups of statistics, opinions, or any combination of supporting material.

**Specificity** Sometimes your supporting material will range from very specific examples to more general overviews of a situation. You may either offer your specific information first and end with your general statement, or make the general statement first and support it with specific evidence.

Another application of specificity might be to compact or explode statistics, as discussed in Chapter 6. In her speech on unnecessary prescription drugs, Kristin begins with a sweeping statistic and then compacts it:

> Thirty percent of Americans have asked their doctor about a medicine they saw advertised on TV. And of those, . . . 44 percent received the prescription. That translates into one in eight Americans seeing a drug on TV and later picking it up at their local pharmacy.[14]

**Complexity** We have discussed organizing subtopics by moving from the simple to the complex. The same method of organization may also determine how you order your supporting material. In many situations, it makes sense to start with the simplest ideas that are easy to understand and work up to the more complex ones. In her speech on solar radiation, Nichole first explains the most obvious effects of solar peaks—electrical blackouts and disruptions in radio broadcasts—and then goes on to the more complex effect, cosmic radiation:

> The sun produces storms on its surface in eleven-year cycles. During solar maximum, these storms will make their presence known to the land-bound public through electrical blackouts and disruptions in radio broadcasts. These storms cause the sun to throw off electrically charged ions that, combined with charged particles, enter the Earth's atmosphere from outer space. This is known collectively as cosmic radiation.[15]

**From Soft to Hard Evidence** Supporting material can also be arranged along a continuum from "soft" to "hard." **Soft evidence** rests on opinion or inference. Hypothetical illustrations, descriptions, explanations, definitions, analogies, and opinions are usually considered soft. **Hard evidence** includes factual examples and statistics.

**soft evidence**
Supporting material based mainly on opinion or inference; includes hypothetical illustrations, descriptions, explanations, definitions, and analogies

**hard evidence**
Factual examples and statistics

Soft-to-hard organization of supporting material relies chiefly on the principle of recency—that the last statement is remembered best. Note how Beth moves from an illustration to expert testimony (both soft evidence) to a statistic (hard evidence) in her speech on the danger of sand holes:

| | |
|---|---|
| Illustration (soft evidence) | An article in the *Corpus Christi Caller Times* of June 21, 2007, describes how a hidden sand hole on a beach proved fatal to 17-year-old Matthew Gauruder. Playing football on a Rhode Island beach with friends, Matthew jumped to catch a pass and came down into an 8-foot-deep hole that someone had dug on the beach earlier in the day. Almost instantly, the sand caved in around him, burying and suffocating him before rescuers could reach him. |
| Expert testimony (soft evidence) | Dr. Bradley Maron of Harvard Medical School explains that "the walls of the hole unexpectedly collapsed, leaving virtually no evidence of the hole or location of the victim." |
| Statistic (hard evidence) | Although people worry more about shark attacks, according to University of Florida statistics, 16 deaths occurred in sand holes or tunnels between 1990 and 2006, compared with 12 fatal shark attacks for that same period.[16] |

The speaker has arranged her supporting material from soft to hard.

### RECAP: Organizing Your Supporting Material

| Strategy | Description |
|---|---|
| Primacy | Most important material first |
| Recency | Most important material last |
| Specificity | From specific information to general overview or from general overview to specific information |
| Complexity | From simple to more complex material |
| Soft to hard | From opinion or hypothetical illustration to fact or statistic |

## Incorporate Your Supporting Material into Your Speech

When your supporting material has been logically placed into your plan, your next goal is to incorporate it smoothly into your speech so as to enhance the flow of ideas. The Sample Integration of Supporting Material (below) shows how one speaker skillfully met this goal while delivering a speech on modifying our approach to surviving cancer.

# Developing Signposts

Once you have organized your note cards, you have a logically ordered, fairly complete plan for your speech. But if you tried to deliver the speech at this point, you would find

## SAMPLE INTEGRATION OF SUPPORTING MATERIAL

While pink ribbons, social walks, and yellow wristbands are uplifting tokens, they reinforce the value of thinking positively at the expense of forcing us to consider the unsettling gravity of this disease. As cancer survivor Brian Wickman told *The New York Times* on June 30, 2008, when his friends placed him on a pedestal and told him how brave he was, he wasn't allowed to "be human and in pain, angry or depressed." Our awareness deprives victims of an outlet for their darker fears by deeming them weak. . . .

Source: Merry Regan, "Beyond Ribbons and Wristbands: An Honest Approach to Cancer Activism," prepared for Individual Events/Persuasive Speaking Competition, The University of Texas, Spring 2010. Reprinted by permission of Merry Regan.

State the point. The statement should be concise and clear, as it is here.

Cite the source of the supporting material: the author's name (if available) and the title and date of the publication.

Present the supporting material, here a brief illustration.

Explain how the supporting material substantiates or develops the point. Do not assume that audience members will automatically make the connection.

*Your nonverbal transition signals, as well as your verbal signposts, can help your audience follow the organization of your speech. One effective technique is to pause before moving to a new point, as this speaker is doing.*

[Photo: Kablonk!/Masterfile Stock Image Library]

yourself frequently groping for some way to get from one point to the next. Your audience might become frustrated or even confused by your hesitations and awkwardness. So your next organizational task is to develop **signposts**—words and gestures that allow you to move smoothly from one idea to the next throughout your speech, showing relationships between ideas and emphasizing important points. Three types of signposts can serve as glue to hold your speech together: transitions, previews, and summaries.

## Transitions

Transitions indicate that a speaker has finished discussing one idea and is moving to another. Transitions may be either verbal or nonverbal. Let's consider some examples of each type.

**Verbal Transitions** A speaker can sometimes make a verbal transition simply by repeating a key word from an earlier statement or by using a synonym or a pronoun that refers to an earlier key word or idea. This type of transition is often used to make one sentence flow smoothly into the next. The previous sentence itself is an example: "This type of transition" refers to the sentence that precedes it. Other verbal transitions are words or phrases that show relationships between ideas. Note the italicized transitional phrases in the following examples:

- *In addition to* transitions, previews and summaries are *also* considered to be signposts.
- *Not only* does plastic packaging use up our scarce resources, it contaminates them *as well.*
- *In other words,* as women's roles have changed, they have *also* contributed to this effect.
- *In summary,* Fanny Brice was the best-known star of Ziegfeld's Follies.
- *Therefore,* I recommend that you sign the grievance petition.

**signpost**
A verbal or nonverbal signal that a speaker is moving from one idea to the next

TABLE 7.2 Verbal Transitions

| Strategy | Example |
|---|---|
| Repeating a key word, or using a synonym or pronoun that refers to a key word | "*These problems* cannot be allowed to continue." |
| Using a transitional word or phrase | "*In addition* to the facts that I've mentioned, we need to consider one more problem." |
| Enumerating | "*Second,* there has been a rapid increase in the number of accidents reported." |
| Using internal summaries and previews | "*Now that we have discussed the problems* caused by illiteracy, *let's look at possible solutions.*" |

Simple enumeration (*first, second, third*) can also point up relationships between ideas and provide transitions.

One type of transitional signpost that can occasionally backfire and do more harm than good is one that signals the end of a speech. *Finally* and *in conclusion* give the audience implicit permission to stop listening, and they often do. If the speech has been too long or has otherwise not gone well, the audience may even express their relief audibly. Better strategies for moving into a conclusion include repeating a key word or phrase, using a synonym or pronoun that refers to a previous idea, offering a final summary, or referring to the introduction of the speech. We discuss the final summary later in this chapter. Both of the last two strategies are also covered in Chapter 8.

Internal previews and summaries, which we will discuss shortly, are yet another way to provide a verbal transition from one point to the next in your speech. They have the additional advantage of repeating your main ideas, thereby enabling audience members to understand and remember them.

A summarized in Table 7.2, repetition of key words or ideas, transitional words or phrases, enumeration, and internal previews and summaries all provide verbal transitions from one idea to the next. You may need to experiment with several alternatives before you find the smooth transition you seek in a given instance. If none of these alternatives seems to work well, consider a nonverbal transition.

**Nonverbal Transitions** Nonverbal transitions can occur in several ways, sometimes alone and sometimes in combination with verbal transitions. A change in facial expression, a pause, an altered vocal pitch or speaking rate, or a movement all may indicate a transition.

For example, a speaker talking about the value of cardiopulmonary resuscitation began his speech with a powerful anecdote about a man suffering a heart attack at a party. No one knew how to help, and the man died. The speaker then looked up from his notes and paused, while maintaining eye contact with his audience. His next words were "The real tragedy of Bill Jorgen's death was that it should not have happened." His pause, as well as the words that followed, indicated a transition into the body of the speech.

Like this speaker, most good speakers use a combination of verbal and nonverbal transitions to move from one point to another through their speeches. You will find more about nonverbal communication in Chapter 11.

## Previews

In Chapter 10, we discuss the differences between writing and speaking styles. One significant difference is that public speaking is more repetitive. Audience-centered speakers need to remember that the members of their audience, unlike readers, cannot go back to review a missed point. As its name indicates, a *preview* is a statement of what is to come. Previews help to ensure that audience members will first anticipate and later remember the important points of a speech. Like transitions, previews also help to provide coherence.

Two types of previews are usually used in speeches: the preview statement or initial preview, and the internal preview. We discussed the preview statement in Chapter 5. It is a statement of what the main ideas of the speech will be, and it is usually presented in conjunction with the central idea as a blueprint for the speech at or near the end of the introduction. Speaking on illiteracy among athletes, Melody offers the following blueprint at the end of her introduction:

> Illiteracy among athletes must be stopped. In order to fully grasp the significance of this problem, we will look at the root of it, and then move to [its] effects, and finally, we will look at the solution.[17]

In this blueprint, Melody clearly previews her main ideas and introduces them in the order in which she will discuss them in the body of the speech.

Sometimes speakers enumerate their main ideas to identify them even more clearly:

> To solve this issue, we must first examine the problem itself. Second, we'll analyze the causes of the problem, and finally we'll turn to a number of solutions to the problem of children in the diet culture.[18]

Notice that both of the preceding examples consist of two sentences. As we noted in Chapter 5, a preview statement need not necessarily be one long, rambling sentence.

In addition to using previews near the beginning of their speeches, speakers use them at various points throughout. These **internal previews** introduce and outline ideas that will be developed as the speech progresses. Internal previews also serve as transitions. One speaker, for example, had just discussed the dangers associated with organic farming. She then provided this transitional preview into her next point:

> Having seen the dangers of our anti-pesticide attitude, we can now look to some solutions to stop the trend toward organic foods.[19]

Having heard this preview, her listeners expected her next to discuss solutions to the problems associated with organic farming. Their anticipation increased the likelihood that they would later remember the information.

Sometimes speakers couch internal previews in the form of questions they plan to answer. Note how the question in this example provides an internal preview:

> Now that we know about the problem of hotel security and some of its causes and impacts, the question remains, what can we do, as potential travelers and potential victims, to protect ourselves?[20]

Just as anticipating an idea helps audience members remember it, so mentally answering a question helps them plant the answer firmly in their minds.

## Summaries

Like previews, summaries provide additional exposure to a speaker's ideas and can help ensure that audience members will grasp and remember them. Most speakers use two types of summaries: the final summary and the internal summary.

A final summary occurs just before the end of a speech, often doing double duty as a transition between the body and the conclusion.

**internal preview**
A statement in the body of a speech that introduces and outlines ideas that will be developed as the speech progresses

The final summary is the opposite of the preview statement. The preview statement gives an audience their first exposure to a speaker's main ideas; the final summary gives them their *last* exposure to those ideas. Here is an example of a final summary from a speech on the U.S. Customs:

> Today, we have focused on the failing U.S. Customs Service. We have asked several important questions, such as "Why is Customs having such a hard time doing its job?" and "What can we do to remedy this situation?" When the cause of a serious problem is unknown, the continuation of the dilemma is understandable. However, the cause for the failure of the U.S. Customs Service is known: a lack of personnel. Given that fact and our understanding that Customs is vital to America's interests, it would be foolish not to rectify this situation.[21]

This final summary leaves no doubt as to the important points of the speech. We discuss the use of final summaries in more detail in Chapter 8.

**Internal summaries**, as their name suggests, occur within and throughout a speech. They are often used after two or three points have been discussed, to keep those points fresh in the minds of the audience as the speech progresses. Susan uses this internal summary in her speech on the teacher shortage:

> So let's review for just a moment. One, we are endeavoring to implement educational reforms; but two, we are in the first years of a dramatic increase in enrollment; and three, fewer quality students are opting for education; while four, many good teachers want out of teaching; plus five, large numbers will soon be retiring.[22]

Like internal previews, internal summaries can help provide transitions. In fact, internal summaries are often used in combination with internal previews to form transitions between major points and ideas. Each of the following examples makes clear what has just been discussed in the speech as well as what will be discussed next:

> Now that we've seen how radon can get into our homes, let's take a look at some of the effects that it can have on our health once it begins to build.[23]

> So now [that] we are aware of the severity of the disease and unique reasons for college students to be concerned, we will look at some steps we need to take to combat bacterial meningitis.[24]

> It seems as though everyone is saying that something should be done about Nutra-Sweet. It should be retested. Well, now that it is here on the market, what can we do to see that it does get investigated further?[25]

RECAP

### Types of Signposts

Verbal transitions
Nonverbal transitions
Preview statements
Internal previews
Final summaries
Internal summaries

# Supplementing Signposts with Presentation Aids

Transitions, summaries, and previews are the glue that holds a speech together. Such signposts can help you achieve a coherent flow of ideas and help your audience remember those ideas. Unfortunately, however, you cannot guarantee that your audience will be attentive to your signposts. In Chapter 1, we discussed the concept of noise as it affects the public-speaking process. It is possible for your listeners to be so distracted by internal or external noise that they fail to hear or process even your most carefully planned verbal signposts.

One way you can increase the likelihood of your listeners' attending to your signposting is to prepare and use presentation aids to supplement your signposts. For example, you could display on a PowerPoint slide a bulleted or numbered outline of your main ideas as you initially preview them in your introduction, and again as you summarize them in your conclusion. Some speakers prefer to use one PowerPoint™ slide for each main point. Transitions between points are emphasized as the speaker moves to the next slide. In Chapter 12, we discuss guidelines for developing and using such presentation aids. Especially when your speech is long or its organization complex, you can help your audience remember your organization if you provide visual support for your signposts.

**internal summary**
A restatement in the body of a speech of the ideas that have been developed so far

# STUDY GUIDE

## Organizing Your Main Ideas

Organize your speech in a logical way so that audience members can follow, understand, and remember your ideas. Five common patterns of organization include topical, chronological, spatial, cause and effect, and problem-solution. These patterns are sometimes combined, and yet other organizational patterns may be dictated by culture. The principles of primacy, recency, and complexity help you decide which main idea to discuss first, next, and last.

### Being Audience-Centered

- The process of organization is by nature audience-centered. Speeches are organized for audiences, with the speaker keeping in mind at all times the unique needs, interests, and expectations of the particular audience.
- If your topic is controversial and you know or suspect that your audience will be skeptical of or hostile to your ideas, you may want to organize your main ideas according to the principle of primacy, putting the most important or convincing idea first.
- Each culture teaches its members patterns of thought and organization that are considered appropriate for various occasions and audiences. Most North Americans prefer a direct, linear organizational pattern. Semitic, Asian, Romance, and Russian speakers are more likely to prefer a less direct, less linear organizational pattern. Romance and Russian cultures tend to begin with a basic principle and then use facts and illustrations to support the main idea.

### Using What You've Learned

Here are some examples of central ideas and main ideas. Identify the organizational pattern used in each group of main ideas. If the pattern is topical, do you think the speaker also considered primacy, recency, or complexity? If so, identify which one.

**1.** PURPOSE STATEMENT: At the end of my speech, the audience will be able to explain three theories about what happened to the dinosaurs.

CENTRAL IDEA: There are at least three distinct theories about what happened to the dinosaurs.

MAIN IDEAS:
I. A large asteroid hit Earth.
II. A gradual climate shift occurred.
III. The level of oxygen in the atmosphere gradually changed.

**2.** PURPOSE STATEMENT: At the end of my speech, the audience will be able to describe the layout and features of the new university multipurpose sports center.

CENTRAL IDEA: The new university multipurpose sports center will serve the activity needs of the students.

MAIN IDEAS:
I. The south wing will house an Olympic-size pool.
II. The center of the building will be a large coliseum.
III. The north wing will include handball and indoor tennis facilities as well as rooms for weight lifting and aerobic workouts.

## Subdividing Your Main Ideas

Main ideas are often subdivided. Organize your subpoints so that audience members can readily grasp, understand, and remember them. The five patterns for organizing main ideas can apply to subpoints as well.

### Being Audience-Centered

- You may add, regroup, or eliminate main ideas or subpoints at any stage in the preparation process, as you consider the needs, interests, and expectations of your audience.

### Speaker's Homepage: Internet Resources to Help You Organize Your Speech

- The Allyn & Bacon Public Speaking Website can give you additional suggestions for organizing your speech. You can also read transcripts and listen to recordings of speeches that apply the patterns discussed: http://wps.ablongman.com/ab_public_speaking_2/0,9651,1593275-,00.html

- The Advanced Public Speaking Institute Website provides a wealth of information about speech preparation, including tips on developing and organizing ideas: http://www.public-speaking.org/public-speaking-articles.htm.

## Integrating Your Supporting Material

With points and subpoints organized, your next task is to integrate your supporting material into a speech. It may help to begin by putting all main points, subpoints, and supporting material on note cards and then arranging those cards in order. Once you have placed supporting material where it belongs in your plan, incorporate the supporting material smoothly into your speech by (1) stating the point, (2) citing the source, (3) presenting the supporting material, and (4) explaining how the supporting material substantiates or develops the point.

When you have more than one piece of supporting material for a main idea or subpoint, you can organize the supporting material according to one of the five common patterns, or according to such strategies as primacy, recency, specificity, complexity, or soft-to-hard.

### Being Audience-Centered

- Your listeners may not remember many specific facts and statistics after a speech, but they should remember the important points. Connecting ideas and supporting material make it more likely that they will.

### A Question of Ethics

- The principles of primacy and recency are referred to several times in this chapter. If a speaker has a statistic that offers overwhelming evidence of the severity of a given problem, is it ethical for the speaker to save that statistic for last, or should the speaker reveal immediately to the audience how severe the problem is? In other words, is there an ethical distinction between primacy and recency? Discuss your answer.
- In Chapter 2, we suggest that a speaker should provide the credentials of the authors of supporting material used in a speech. If a speaker is unable to discover an author's credentials, could the speaker omit the author's name altogether? If no, why not? If so, under what circumstances?

## Developing Signposts

Various types of signposts can help you communicate your organization to your audience. Signposts include verbal and nonverbal transitions, previews, and summaries.

### Being Audience-Centered

- Remember that listeners, unlike readers, cannot go back to review a missed point. Previews and summaries help to ensure that audience members will first anticipate and later remember the important points of your speech.

## Supplementing Signposts with Presentation Aids

Supplementing your words and gestures with presentation aids helps listeners notice your signposts.

# SPEECH WORKSHOP

## Organizing Your Ideas

Use this worksheet to help you identify the overall organizational strategy for your speech.

**GENERAL PURPOSE:**

____ To inform

____ To persuade

____ To entertain

**SPECIFIC PURPOSE:**

At the end of my speech, the audience will be able to ______________________________

______________________________________________________________________

______________________________________________________________________

______________________________________________________________________

______________________________________________________________________

______________________________________________________________________

**CENTRAL IDEA** (one-sentence summary of your speech):

______________________________________________________________________

______________________________________________________________________

______________________________________________________________________

______________________________________________________________________

______________________________________________________________________

**MAIN IDEAS:**

Ask yourself the following three questions to identify the organizational structure of your speech:

1. Does the central idea have logical divisions?

   ______________________________________________

   ______________________________________________

   ______________________________________________

   If the answer is yes, your speech may be organized *topically* (by natural divisions), *spatially* (by physical arrangement), by *cause and effect*, or by *problem-solution.*

2. Are there reasons that the central idea sentence is true?

   ______________________________________________

   ______________________________________________

   ______________________________________________

   If the answer is yes, then your speech is probably persuasive, and you are trying to convince the audience that your central idea sentence is true. Your reasons may be organized by *primacy* (most important reason first), *recency* (most important reason last), *complexity* (simplest reason first and most complex reason last), or *cause and effect.*

3. Does your central idea involve a series of steps?

   ______________________________________________

   ______________________________________________

   ______________________________________________

   If the answer is yes, then your speech can be organized *chronologically*. Identify the major steps involved in the process you are describing; those major steps will become your main points. Although you should have only a few main ideas, you may have several subdivisions of each one. List your main ideas here:

   ______________________________________________

   ______________________________________________

   ______________________________________________

   ______________________________________________

   ______________________________________________

   ______________________________________________

   ______________________________________________

   ______________________________________________

THE AVERAGE MAN THINKS ABOUT WHAT HE HAS SAID; THE ABOVE AVERAGE MAN ABOUT WHAT HE IS GOING TO SAY.

—ANONYMOUS

Jean Plichart (20th Century French), *Thinker of Images (Le Penseur d'Images)*, 1980. Copper engraving. SuperStock, Inc.

OUTLINE

# 8 Introducing and Concluding Your Speech

OBJECTIVES

**After studying this chapter you should be able to do the following:**

1. Discuss why introductions and conclusions are important to the overall success of a speech.
2. Explain the five purposes of the introduction to a speech.
3. List and describe ten ways to introduce a speech.
4. Explain the two purposes of the conclusion to a speech.
5. List and describe four ways to conclude a speech.

Like all teachers, public-speaking instructors have pet peeves when it comes to their students' work. Of the pet peeves identified by public-speaking teachers in a recent study, more than 25 percent relate to introductions and conclusions. They include the following:

- Beginning a speech with "OK, ah . . ."
- Apologizing or making excuses at the beginning of the speech for not being prepared
- Beginning a speech with "Hello, my speech is on . . ."
- Saying "In conclusion"
- Ending a speech with "Thank you"
- Ending a speech with "Are there any questions?"[1]

## CONFIDENTLY CONNECTING WITH YOUR AUDIENCE

### Be Familiar with Your Introduction and Conclusion

You may feel the most nervous just as you begin your speech. But if you have a well-prepared and well-rehearsed introduction, you'll be able to start with confidence. Rehearse your opening sentences enough times that you can present them while maintaining direct eye contact with your listeners. Being familiar with your conclusion can give you a safe harbor to head for as you end your message. A thoughtfully planned and well-rehearsed introduction and conclusion can help you start and end your speech with poise and assurance.

Not every public-speaking instructor considers all of the above to be pet peeves or even tactics to be avoided. But the fact that they appear on this list suggests that you will probably want to consider alternatives. After all, your introduction and conclusion provide your listeners with important first and final impressions of both you and your speech.

Like many speakers, you may think the first task in preparing a speech is to start drafting your introduction. In fact, the introduction is more often the last part of the speech you develop. A key purpose of your introduction is to provide an overview of your message. How can you do that until you know what the message is going to be? In Chapter 7, we discussed patterns and strategies for organizing the body of your speech, and we explained how to use appropriate transitions, previews, and summaries. Organizing the body of your speech should precede the crafting of both the introduction and the conclusion. In this chapter we will further explore organization by dis cussing introductions and conclusions.

# Purposes of Introductions

Within a few seconds of meeting a person, you form a first impression that is often quite lasting. So, too, do you form a first impression of a speaker and his or her message within the opening seconds of a speech. The introduction may convince you to listen carefully because this is a credible speaker presenting a well-prepared speech, or it may send the message that the speaker is ill-prepared and the message not worth your time. In a ten-minute speech, the introduction will probably last no more than a minute and a half. To say that the introduction needs to be well planned is an understatement, considering how important and yet how brief this portion of any speech is.

As a speaker, your task is to ensure that your introduction convinces your audience to listen to you. As summarized and illustrated in Table 8.1 on page 187, a good introduction must perform five important functions:

- Get the audience's attention.
- Give the audience a reason to listen.
- Introduce the subject.
- Establish your credibility.
- Preview your main ideas.

Let's examine each of these five functions in detail.

## Get the Audience's Attention

CONSIDER THE AUDIENCE

A key purpose of the introduction is to gain favorable attention for your speech. Because listeners form their first impressions of the speech quickly, if the introduction does not capture their attention and cast the speech in a favorable light, the rest of the speech may be wasted on them. The speaker who walks to the podium and drones, "Today I am going to talk to you about . . ." has probably lost most of the audience in those first few boring words. Specific ways to gain the attention of audiences will be discussed later in this chapter.

We emphasize *favorable* attention for a very good reason. It is possible to gain an audience's attention but in so doing to alienate them or disgust them so that they become irritated instead of interested in what you have to say. For example, a student began a pro-life speech with a graphic description of the abortion process. She caught her audience's attention but made them so uncomfortable that they could hardly concentrate on the rest of her speech.

Another student gave a speech on the importance of donating blood. Without a word, he began by appearing to savagely slash his wrists in front of his stunned audience. As blood spurted, audience members screamed, and one fainted. The blood was real blood, but it wasn't his. The speaker worked at a blood bank, and he was using the bank's blood. He had placed a device under each arm that allowed him to pump out the blood as if from his wrists. He certainly captured his audience's attention! But they never heard his message; the shock and disgust of seeing such a display made that impossible; he did not gain favorable attention.

The moral of our two tales: By all means, be creative in your speech introductions. But also use common sense in deciding how best to gain the favorable attention of your audience. Alienating them is even worse than boring them.

## Give the Audience a Reason to Listen

Even after you have captured your listeners' attention, you have to give them some reason to want to listen to the rest of your speech. An unmotivated listener quickly tunes out. You can help establish listening motivation by showing the members of your audience how the topic affects them directly.

In Chapter 6 we presented seven criteria for determining the effectiveness of your supporting material. One of those criteria was *proximity*, the degree to which the information affects your listeners directly. Just as proximity is important to supporting materials, it is important to speech introductions. "This concerns me" is a powerful reason to listen. Notice how Chandra involves her audience members with the Hepatitis C risk inherent in tattooing:

> If you're one of the millions wanting to show your patriotism by getting a star-spangled banner tattooed across your back, ask questions regarding its potential risks.[2]

Sheena also used proximity to motivate her audience to empathize with people who suffer from exposure to toxic mold:

> Headaches, fatigue, dizziness, and memory impairment seem like ailments that each person in this room has had at one point, right? You stay up late cramming for an exam. The next day, you are fatigued, dizzy, and cannot remember the answers.[3]

It does not matter so much *how* or *when* you demonstrate proximity. But it is essential that, like Chandra and Sheena, you *do* at some point establish that your topic is of vital personal concern to your listeners.

## Introduce the Subject

Perhaps the most obvious purpose of an introduction is to introduce the subject of a speech. Within a few seconds after you begin your speech, the audience should have a pretty good idea what you are going to talk about. Do not get so carried away with jokes or illustrations that you forget this basic purpose. Few things will frustrate your audience more than having to wait until halfway through your speech to figure out what you are talking about! The best way to ensure that your introduction does indeed introduce the subject of your speech is to include a statement of your central idea in the introduction. For example, in introducing his speech on the needs of the aged, this speaker immediately established his subject and central idea:

> If you take away just one thing from what I have to say, I hope you'll come to understand in the next few minutes that the exploding population of seniors demands a conscious, considered, and collaborative response to plan for the health, financial, and social implications of an older population.[4]

## Establish Your Credibility

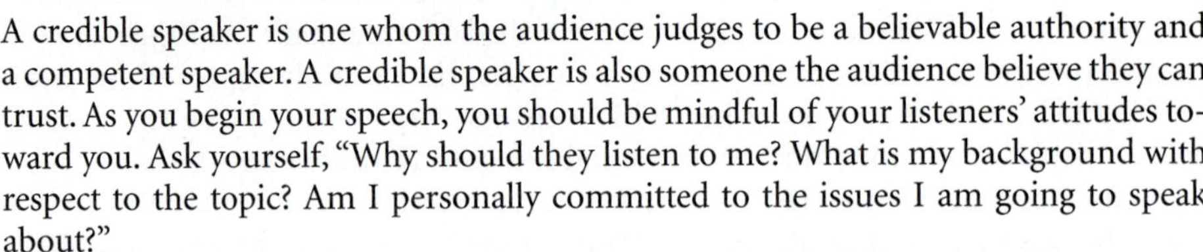

A credible speaker is one whom the audience judges to be a believable authority and a competent speaker. A credible speaker is also someone the audience believe they can trust. As you begin your speech, you should be mindful of your listeners' attitudes toward you. Ask yourself, "Why should they listen to me? What is my background with respect to the topic? Am I personally committed to the issues I am going to speak about?"

Many people have so much admiration for a political or religious figure, an athlete, or an entertainer that they sacrifice time, energy, and money to hear those celebrities speak. When Pope Benedict XVI travels abroad, people travel great distances and stand for hours in extreme heat or cold to celebrate Mass with him. But ordinary people cannot take their own credibility for granted when they speak. If you can establish your credibility early in a speech, it will help motivate your audience to listen. One way to build credibility in the introduction is to be well prepared and to appear confident. Speaking fluently while maintaining eye contact does much to convey a sense of confidence. If you seem to have confidence in yourself, your audience will have confidence in you.

A second way to establish credibility is to tell the audience of your personal experience with your topic. Instead of thinking you boastful, most audience members will listen to you with respect. In a speech to a group of women executives, the president of the St. Louis, Missouri, Board of Education offered this insight into her experience:

> If any of you have ever had the blessing of serving on a school board—and that's what I consider it to be, a blessing—you know how difficult it is. There are always too many needs to meet, never enough money to meet those needs, and a multitude of competing stakeholders who know exactly how you should allocate scarce resources: on the one thing that matters most to them, which is always different than what's important to the person standing next to them. And that's when times are good and things are going well.[5]

## Preview Your Main Ideas

A final purpose of the introduction is to preview the main ideas of your speech. As you saw in Chapter 7, the preview statement usually comes near the end of the introduction, included in or immediately following a statement of the central idea. The preview statement allows your listeners to anticipate the main ideas of your speech, which in turn helps ensure that they will remember those ideas after the speech.

As we also noted in Chapter 7, a preview statement is an organizational strategy called a *signpost*. Just as signs posted along a highway tell you what is coming up, a signpost in your speech tells the listeners what to expect by enumerating the ideas or points that you plan to present. If, for example, you were giving a speech about racial profiling, you might say,

> To end these crimes against color, we must first paint an accurate picture of the problem, then explore the causes, and finally establish solutions that will erase the practice of racial profiling.[6]

TABLE 8.1 Purposes of Your Introduction

| Purpose | Method |
|---|---|
| Get the audience's attention. | Use an illustration, a startling fact or statistic, a quotation, humor, a question, a reference to a historical event or to a recent event, a personal reference, a reference to the occasion, or a reference to a preceding speech. |
| Give the audience a reason to listen. | Tell your listeners how the topic directly affects them. |
| Introduce the subject. | Present your central idea to your audience. |
| Establish your credibility. | Offer your credentials. Tell your listeners about your commitment to your topic. |
| Preview your main ideas. | Tell your audience what you are going to tell them. |

Identifying your main ideas helps organize the message and enhances listeners' learning.

The introduction to your speech, then, should get your audience's attention, give the audience a reason to listen, introduce the subject, establish your credibility, and preview your main ideas. All this—and brevity too—may seem impossible to achieve. But it isn't!

# Effective Introductions

With a little practice, you will be able to write satisfactory central ideas and preview statements. It may be more difficult to gain your audience's attention and give them a reason to listen to you. Fortunately, there are several effective methods for developing speech introductions. Not every method is appropriate for every speech, but chances are that you can discover among these alternatives at least one type of introduction to fit the topic and purpose of your speech, whatever they might be.

We will discuss ten ways of introducing a speech:

- Illustrations or anecdotes
- Startling facts or statistics
- Quotations
- Humor
- Questions
- References to historical events
- References to recent events
- Personal references
- References to the occasion
- References to preceding speeches

## Illustrations or Anecdotes

Not surprisingly, because it is the most inherently interesting type of supporting material, an illustration or **anecdote** can provide the basis for an effective speech introduction. In fact, if you have an especially compelling illustration that you had planned to use in the body of the speech, you might do well to use it in your introduction instead. A relevant and interesting anecdote will introduce your subject and almost

**anecdote**
An illustration or story

invariably gain an audience's attention. Student speaker Matt opened his speech on the dangers associated with the chemical BPA with this extended illustration:

> Three years ago Algeta McDonald's life was taken by breast cancer. She was an absolutely amazing Italian-American woman, who was completely stubborn, but she always brought out the best in anyone she was around. Here was a woman who always ate proper foods and was conscientious of her health in general, every day of her life.
>
> Ask anyone who knew her well what their favorite memory of Algeta was, and I can almost guarantee it's of her carrying around a bright red Nalgene water bottle. This way, she could get her 64 daily ounces of water with certainty. Unfortunately, this happy memory of how she always had her water bottle might change with some information that has come to light recently.*

Matt's story effectively captured the attention of his audience and introduced the subject of his speech.

## Startling Facts or Statistics

A second method of introducing a speech is to use a startling fact or statistic. Startling an audience with the extent of a situation or problem invariably catches its members' attention, motivates them to listen further, and helps them remember afterward what you had to say. Merry's audience must have come to attention quickly when they heard the following statistics in her introduction:

> The August 28, 2008, *Globe and Mail* estimates that the United States spends three billion dollars each year on cancer research, while the *LA Times* of February 16, 2009, reports the costs of cancer care are increasing by 15% annually—nearly three times the rate of other health care.†

## Quotations

Using an appropriate quotation to introduce a speech is a common practice. Often another writer or speaker has expressed an opinion on your topic that is more authoritative, comprehensive, or memorable than what you can say. Terrika opened her speech on the importance of community with a quotation from poet Johari Kungufu:

> Sisters, Men
> What are we doin?
> What about the babies, our children?
> When we was real we never had orphans or children in joints.
> Come spirits
> drive out the nonsense from our minds and the crap from our dreams
> make us remember what we need, that children are the next life.
> bring us back to the real
> bring us back to the real
>
> "The Real." Johari Kungufu, in her poem, specifically alludes to a time in African history when children were not confused about who they were.[7]

A different kind of quotation, this one from an expert, was chosen by another speaker to introduce the topic of the disappearance of childhood in America:

> "As a distinctive childhood culture wastes away, we watch with fascination and dismay." This insight of Neil Postman, author of *Disappearance of Childhood*, raised a poignant point. Childhood in America is vanishing.[8]

* Matt Miller, "A Situational Speech: Bisphenol A," from *Winning Orations 2009*, Mankato: MN: Interstate Oratorical Association, 2009. Reprinted by permission.

† Merry Regan, "Beyond Ribbons and Wristbands: An Honest Approach to Cancer Activism," prepared for Individual Events/Persuasive Speaking Competition, University of Texas, Spring 2010. Reprinted by permission of Merry Regan.

Because the expert was not widely recognized, the speaker included a brief statement of his qualifications. This authority "said it in a nutshell"—he expressed in concise language the central idea of the speech.

Although a quote can effectively introduce a speech, do not fall into the lazy habit of turning to a collection of quotations every time you need an introduction. There are so many other interesting, and sometimes better, ways to introduce a speech that quotes should be used only if they are extremely interesting, compelling, or very much to the point.

Like the methods of organization discussed in Chapter 7, the methods of introduction are not mutually exclusive. Very often, two or three are effectively combined in a single introduction. For example, Thad combined a quotation and an illustration for this effective introduction to a speech on the funeral industry:

> "Dying is a very dull, dreary affair. And my advice to you is to have nothing whatsoever to do with it." These lingering words by British playwright Somerset Maugham were meant to draw a laugh. Yet the ironic truth to the statement has come to epitomize the grief of many, including Jan Berman of Martha's Vineyard. In a recent interview with National Public Radio, we learn that Ms. Berman desired to have a home funeral for her mother. She possessed a burial permit and was legally within her rights. But when a local funeral director found out, he lied to her, telling her that what she was doing was illegal.[9]

## Humor

Humor, handled well, can be a wonderful attention-getter. It can help relax your audience and win their goodwill for the rest of the speech. University of Texas Professor of Journalism Marvin Olasky told this humorous story to open a speech on disaster response:

> Let me begin with a Texas story about how officials do offer help. It starts with a mom on a farm looking out the window. She sees the family cow munching on grass and her daughter talking with a strange man. The mom furiously yells out the window, "Didn't I tell you not to talk to strangers? You come in this house right

*Humor can be an effective way to catch your audience's attention in your introduction. Remember, however, to use humor appropriate to the occasion and the audience.*

[Photo: Masterfile Royalty Free Division]

> now." The girl offers a protest: "But mama, this man says he's a United States senator." The wise mother replies, "In that case, come in this house right now, and bring the cow in with you."
>
> Let's talk about responses to disaster.[10]

Another speaker used humor to express appreciation for being invited to speak to a group by beginning his speech with this story:

> Three corporate executives were trying to define the word fame.
>
> One said, "Fame is getting invited to the White House to see the President."
>
> The second one said, "Fame is being invited to the White House and while you are visiting, the phone rings and he doesn't answer it."
>
> The third executive said, "You're both wrong. Fame is being invited to the White House to visit with the President when his Hot Line rings. He answers it, listens a minute, and then says, 'Here, it's for you!'"
>
> Being asked to speak today is like being in the White House and the call's for me.[11]

Humor need not always be the slapstick comedy of the Three Stooges. It does not even have to be a joke. It may take more subtle forms, such as irony or incredulity. When General Douglas MacArthur, an honor graduate of the U.S. Military Academy at West Point, returned to West Point in 1962, he delivered his now-famous "Farewell to the Cadets." He opened that speech with this humorous illustration:

> As I was leaving the hotel this morning, a doorman asked me, "Where are you bound for, General?" And when I replied, "West Point," he remarked, "Beautiful place. Have you ever been there before?"[12]

MacArthur's brief illustration caught the audience's attention and made them laugh—in short, it was an effective way to open the speech.

If your audience is linguistically diverse or composed primarily of listeners whose first language is not English, you may want to choose an introduction strategy other than humor. Because much humor is created by verbal plays on words, people who do not speak English as their native language may not perceive the humor in an anecdote or quip that you intended to be funny. And humor rarely translates well. Former President Jimmy Carter recalls speaking at a university near Kyoto, Japan, and being startled by unexpectedly hearty laughter in response to a short humorous anecdote he related. When he later asked his interpreter how he had translated the story so successfully, the interpreter finally admitted sheepishly, "I told them, 'President Carter has just told a funny story. Everyone laugh.'"[13]

Just as certain audiences may preclude your use of a humorous introduction, so may certain subjects—for example, Sudden Infant Death Syndrome and rape. Used with discretion, however, humor can provide a lively, interesting, and appropriate introduction for many speeches.

## Questions

Remember the pet peeves listed at the beginning of this chapter? Another pet peeve for some is beginning a speech with a question ("How many of you . . . ?"). The problem is not so much the strategy itself but the lack of mindfulness in the "How many of you?" phrasing. A thoughtful **rhetorical question**, on the other hand, can prompt your listeners' mental participation in your introduction, getting their attention and giving them a reason to listen. President and CEO of Coca-Cola, Muhtar Kent, began a speech to investors and financial analysts by asking,

**rhetorical question**
A question intended to provoke thought, rather than elicit an answer

> Are we ready for tomorrow, today?[14]

And Richard opened his speech on teenage suicide with this simple question:

> Have you ever been alone in the dark?[15]

To turn questions into an effective introduction, the speaker must do more than just think of good questions to ask. He or she must also deliver the questions effectively. Effective delivery includes pausing briefly after each question so that audience members have time to try to formulate a mental answer. After all, the main advantage of questions as an introductory technique is to hook the audience by getting them to engage in a mental dialogue with you. The speaker who delivers questions most effectively is also one who may look down at notes while he or she asks the question, but who then reestablishes eye contact with listeners. As we discuss in Chapter 11, eye contact signals that the communication channel is open. Establishing eye contact with your audience following a question gives them additional motivation to think of an answer.

Although it does not happen frequently, an audience member may blurt out a vocal response to a question intended to be rhetorical. If you plan to open a speech with a rhetorical question, be aware of this possibility, and plan appropriate reactions. If the topic is light, a Jay Leno–style return quip may win over the audience and turn the interruption into an asset. If the topic is more serious or the interruption is inappropriate or contrary to what you expected, you might reply with something like "Perhaps most of the rest of you were thinking . . . ," or you might answer the question yourself.

Questions are commonly combined with another method of introduction. For example, University of Akron president Luis Proenza opened a speech on new strategies for success in higher education with a question followed by a startling statistic:

> What if the airplane had advanced as far and as fast as the computer? Today's jumbo jet would carry one hundred thousand passengers, and it would fly them to the moon and back for $12.50 at 23,400 miles per hour.[16]

Either by themselves or in tandem with another method of introduction, questions can provide effective openings for speeches. Like quotations, however, questions can also be crutches for speakers who have not taken the time to explore other options. Unless you can think of a truly engaging question, work to develop one of the other introduction strategies.

## References to Historical Events

What American is not familiar with the opening line of Lincoln's classic Gettysburg Address: "Four score and seven years ago, our fathers brought forth on this continent a new nation, conceived in liberty, and dedicated to the proposition that all men are created equal"? Note that Lincoln's famous opening sentence refers to the historical context of his speech. You, too, may find a way to begin a speech by making a reference to a historic event.

Every day is the anniversary of something. Perhaps you could begin a speech by drawing a relationship between a historic event that happened on this day and your speech objective.

Executive speechwriter Cynthia Starks illustrated this strategy in a February 16, 2010, speech:

> On this date—Feb. 16, 1923—archeologist Howard Carter entered the burial chamber of King Tutankhamen. There he found a solid gold coffin, Tut's intact mummy, and priceless treasures.
>
> On Feb. 16, 1959, Fidel Castro took over the Cuban government 45 days after overthrowing Fulvencia Battista.

And America's first 9-1-1 emergency phone system went live in Haleyville, Alabama, on Feb. 16, 1968.

Today, I won't be revealing priceless treasures. I promise not to overthrow anyone, or generate any 9-1-1 calls. But I do hope to reveal a few speechwriting secrets, provide a little revolutionary thinking and a sense of urgency about the speeches you ought to be giving.**

How do you discover anniversaries of historic events? You could consult "This Day in History" online (www.history.com/this-day-in-history) or download a "This Day in History" app for the iPhone or iPad.

## References to Recent Events

If your topic is timely, a reference to a recent event can be a good way to begin your speech. An opening taken from a recent news story can take the form of an illustration, a startling statistic, or even a quotation, gaining the additional advantages discussed under each of those methods of introduction. Moreover, referring to a recent event increases your credibility by showing that you are knowledgeable about current affairs.

"Recent" does not necessarily mean a story that broke just last week or even last month. An event that occurred within the past year or so can be considered recent. Even a particularly significant event that is slightly older can qualify. The key, says one speaker,

> is to avoid being your grandfather. No more stories about walking up hill both ways to school with a musket on your back and seventeen Redcoats chasing you. Be in the now, and connect with your audience.[17]

## Personal References

A reference to yourself can take several forms. You might express appreciation or pleasure at having been asked to speak, as did this speaker:

> I would like, if I may, to start on a brief personal note. It is a great pleasure for me to be speaking in Cleveland, Ohio. This is where I grew up. Since then, I have traveled all over the world, but I have never stopped missing Ohio.[18]

Or you might share a personal experience, as did this speaker:

> Like some of you in the audience, I've held many jobs before finding my true calling, from washing cars to waiting tables and taking care of animals. . . .[19]

Although personal references take a variety of forms, what they do best, in all circumstances, is to establish a bond between you and your audience.

## References to the Occasion

References to the occasion are often made at weddings, birthday parties, dedication ceremonies, and other such events. For example, when former first lady Laura Bush spoke at a White House Salute to America's Authors, she opened her remarks this way:

> Good afternoon. Welcome to the "White House Salute to America's Authors." This program, the second in a series on American authors, celebrates one of the richest literary periods in American history, the Harlem Renaissance, and the authors whose genius brought it to life.[20]

** From "How to Write a Speech," February 16, 2010. Reprinted by permission of Cynthia J. Starks.

The reference to the occasion can also be combined with other methods of introduction, such as an illustration or a rhetorical question.

## References to Preceding Speeches

If your speech is one of several being presented on the same occasion, such as in a speech class, at a symposium, or as part of a lecture series, you will usually not know until shortly before your own speech what other speakers will say. Few experiences will make your stomach sink faster than hearing a speaker just ahead of you speak on your topic. Worse still, that speaker may even use some of the same supporting materials you had planned to use. When this happens, you must decide on the spot whether referring to one of those previous speeches will be better than using the introduction you originally prepared. It may be wise to refer to a preceding speech when another speaker has spoken on a topic so related to your own that you can draw an analogy. In a sense, your introduction then becomes a transition from that earlier speech to yours. Here is an example of an introduction delivered by a fast-thinking student speaker under those circumstances:

> When Juli talked to us about her experiences as a lifeguard, she stressed that the job was not as glamorous as many of us imagine. Today I want to tell you about another job that appears to be more glamorous than it is—a job that I have held for two years. I am a bartender at the Rathskeller.[21]

As you plan your introduction, remember that any combination of the methods just discussed is possible. With a little practice, you will become confident at choosing from several good possibilities as you prepare your introduction.

**RECAP**

**Techniques for Effective Introductions**

- Use an illustration or anecdote.
- Present startling facts or statistics.
- Share a quotation.
- Employ appropriate humor.
- Ask a rhetorical question.
- Refer to historical or recent events.
- Reveal something about yourself.
- Make note of the occasion.
- Acknowledge the speeches before yours.

# Purposes of Conclusions

Your introduction creates an important first impression; your conclusion leaves an equally important final impression. Long after you finish speaking, your audience is likely to remember the effect, if not the content, of your closing remarks.

Unfortunately, many speakers pay less attention to their conclusions than to any other part of their speeches. They believe that if they can get through the first 90 percent of a speech, they can think of some way to conclude it. Perhaps you have had the experience of listening to a speaker who failed to plan a conclusion. Awkward final seconds of stumbling for words may be followed by hesitant applause from an audience that is not even sure the speech is over. It is hardly the best way to leave people who came to listen to you.

An effective conclusion will serve two purposes: It will summarize the speech and provide closure.

Just as you learned ways to introduce a speech, you can learn how to conclude one. We will begin by considering the purposes of conclusions, and then we will explore methods to help you achieve those purposes.

## Summarize the Speech

A conclusion is a speaker's last chance to review his or her central idea and main ideas for the audience.

**Reemphasize the Central Idea in a Memorable Way** The conclusions of many famous speeches rephrase the central idea in a memorable way. For example,

General Douglas MacArthur's farewell to the nation at the end of his career concluded with these memorable words:

> "Old soldiers never die; they just fade away." And like the old soldier of that ballad, I now close my military career and just fade away—an old soldier who tried to do his duty as God gave him the light to see that duty. Good-bye.[22]

Likewise, when on July 4, 1939, New York Yankees legend Lou Gehrig addressed his fans in an emotional farewell to a baseball career cut short by a diagnosis of ALS (amyotrophic lateral sclerosis), he concluded with the memorable line,

> I may have had a tough break, but I have an awful lot to live for.[23]

But memorable endings are not the exclusive property of famous speakers. With practice, most people can prepare similarly effective conclusions. Chapter 10 offers ideas for using language to make your statements more memorable. As a preliminary example of the memorable use of language, here is how Noelle concluded her speech on phony academic institutions on the Internet:

> What we have learned from all this is that we, and only we, have the power to stop [fraudulent learning institutions]. So we don't get www.conned.[24]

This speaker's clever play on "dot.com" helped her audience remember her topic and central idea.

The end of your speech is your last chance to impress the central idea on your audience. Do it in such a way that they cannot help but remember it.

**Restate the Main Ideas** In addition to reemphasizing the central idea of the speech, the conclusion is also likely to restate the main ideas. Note how John effectively summarized the main ideas of his speech on emissions tampering, casting the summary as an expression of his fears about the problem and the actions that could ease those fears:

> I'm frightened. Frightened that nothing I could say would encourage the 25 percent of emissions-tampering Americans to change their ways and correct the factors that cause their autos to pollute disproportionately. Frightened that the American public will not respond to a crucial issue unless the harms are both immediate and observable. Frightened that the EPA will once again prove very sympathetic to industry. Three simple steps will alleviate my fear: inspection, reduction in lead content, and, most importantly, awareness.[25]

Most speakers summarize their main ideas in the first part of the conclusion or as part of the transition between the body of the speech and its conclusion.

## Provide Closure

Probably the most obvious purpose of a conclusion is to bring **closure**—to cue the audience that the speech is coming to an end by making it "sound finished."

**Use Verbal or Nonverbal Cues to Signal the End of the Speech** You can attain closure both verbally and nonverbally. Verbal techniques include using such transitional words and phrases as "finally," "for my last point," and perhaps even "in conclusion."

You may remember that "in conclusion" appears on that list of instructors' pet peeves at the beginning of the chapter. Like opening your speech by asking a rhetorical question, signaling your closing by saying "in conclusion" is not inherently wrong. It is

**closure**
The quality of a conclusion that makes a speech "sound finished"

a pet peeve of some instructors because of the carelessness with which student speakers often use it. Such a cue gives listeners unspoken permission to tune out. (Notice what students do when their professor signals the end of class: Books and notebooks slam shut, pens are stowed away, and the class generally stops listening.) A concluding transition needs to be followed quickly by the final statement of the speech.

You can also signal closure with nonverbal cues. You may want to pause between the body of your speech and its conclusion, slow your speaking rate, move out from behind a podium to make a final impassioned plea to your audience, or signal with falling vocal inflection that you are making your final statement.

*"Raise your hand if you will join me in planting the seed of hope in our youth." When you ask your audience to respond in some way to your message, you help to provide closure at the end of your speech.*

[Photo: Uppercut Images/Getty Images Inc. RF]

**Motivate the Audience to Respond** Another way to provide closure to your speech is to motivate your audience to respond in some way. If your speech is informative, you may want your audience to take some sort of appropriate action—write a letter, buy a product, make a telephone call, or get involved in a cause. In fact, an *action* step is essential to the persuasive organizational strategy called the motivated sequence, which we discuss in Chapter 15.

At the close of her speech on negligent landlords, Melanie included a simple audience response as part of her action step:

> By a show of hands, how many people in this room rely on rental housing? Look around. It's a problem that affects us all, if not directly, then through a majority of our friends. . . .[26]

Another speaker ended a speech to an audience of travel agents by recommending these specific action steps:

- Continuously develop and improve your professional and business skills.
- Embrace and utilize the new technologies. You are either riding on the new technology highway, or you are standing in the dust, left behind.
- Continuously build and strengthen your top industry organizations locally and nationally so their brands, endorsement, and influence can work powerfully on your behalf.
- Develop a passion for this business and inspire the same in your employees and co-workers.[27]

In both of the preceding examples, the speakers draw on the principle of proximity, discussed in this chapter, to motivate their audiences. When audience members feel that they are or could be personally involved or affected, they are more likely to respond to your message.

RECAP

### Purposes of Your Speech Conclusion

Summarize the Speech

- Reemphasize the central idea in a memorable way.
- Restate the main ideas.

Provide Closure

- Give verbal or nonverbal signals of the end of the speech.
- Motivate the audience to respond.

# Effective Conclusions

Effective conclusions may employ illustrations, quotations, personal references, or any of the other methods of introduction we have discussed. In addition, there are at least two other distinct ways of concluding a speech: with references to the introduction and with inspirational appeals or challenges.

## Methods Also Used for Introductions

Any of the methods of introduction discussed earlier can also help you conclude your speech. Quotations, for example, are frequently used in conclusions, as in this commencement address by U2 lead singer Bono:

> Remember what John Adams said about Ben Franklin: "He does not hesitate at our boldest measures but rather seems to think us too irresolute."
>
> Well, this is the time for bold measures. This is the country, and you are the generation.[28]

## References to the Introduction

In our discussion of closure, we mentioned referring to the introduction as a way to end a speech. Finishing a story, answering a rhetorical question, or reminding the audience of the startling fact or statistic you presented in the introduction are excellent ways to provide closure. Like bookends at either side of a group of books on your desk, a related introduction and conclusion provide unified support for the ideas in between.

Earlier in this chapter, you read the extended illustration Matt used to open his speech on the dangers associated with BPA. He concluded the speech by referring to that introduction:

> What would Algeta have said to me if I were to tell her that her healthy lifestyle would be the reason that she would die one day? Well, she was my grandmother. I knew her very well, and she was completely stubborn, so she would have called me crazy . . . but today I'm going to let you decide what her answer should have been.††

Matt's conclusion alludes to his introduction to make his speech memorable, to motivate his audience to respond, and to provide closure.

## Inspirational Appeals or Challenges

Another way to end your speech is to issue an inspirational appeal or challenge to your listeners, rousing them to an emotional pitch at the conclusion of the speech. The conclusion becomes the climax. Speechwriter and communication consultant James W. Robinson explains why such conclusions can work well:

> It's almost as if, for a few brief moments [the audience] escape from the stressful demands of our high-pressure world and welcome your gifts: insightful vision, persuasive rhetoric, a touch of philosophy, a little emotion, and yes, even a hint of corniness.[29]

One famous example of a concluding inspiration appeal comes from Martin Luther King Jr.'s "I Have a Dream" speech:

> From every mountainside, let freedom ring, and when this happens . . . when we allow freedom to ring, when we let it ring from every village and every hamlet, from every state and every city, we will be able to speed up that day when all of God's children, black men and white men, Jews and Gentiles, Protestants and Catholics, will be able to join hands and sing in the words of the old Negro spiritual, "Free at last! Thank God Almighty, we are free at last!"[30]

†† Matt Miller, "A Situational Speech: Bisphenol A" from *Winning Orations 2009*, Mankato, MN: Interstate Oratorical Association, 2009. Reprinted by permission.

## LEARNING FROM GREAT SPEAKERS

### Patrick Henry (1736–1799)

Lawyer, supporter of American independence, governor of Virginia, and staunch advocate of the Bill of Rights, Patrick Henry is today best remembered for a single line—the conclusion of a speech he delivered to the Virginia Convention on March 23, 1775. In one of the most famous inspirational appeals in history, Henry declared,

> I know not what course others may take; but as for me, give me liberty, or give me death!

As you prepare your speech introduction, consider using a powerful quotation from a great speaker to grab your listeners' attention. Or, as you conclude your talk, use a quotation to reemphasize your central idea in a memorable way.

[Image: Currier & Ives, *"Give Me Liberty, or Give Me Death!"*, 1775. Lithograph, 1876. © The Granger Collection]

That King's conclusion was both inspiring and memorable has been affirmed by the growing fame of that passage through the years since he delivered the speech.

In the conclusion of his investiture speech, Jake Schrum, president of Southwestern University in Georgetown, Texas, issued this unique and effective inspirational challenge to his listeners:

> Before I end my remarks, I invite all Southwestern alumni and all Southwestern students to stand and to remain standing for my final words.
>
> Years ago, I knew a woman named Audry Dillow who had been a school teacher all of her adult life. In her eighties when I met her, we often reflected on the attributes and beliefs of college students. Frankly, she was not as positive about the goodness of students as I was.
>
> One day, she asked me, "Jake, are there students today who truly care about someone other than themselves, who really care about the world, who are genuinely good at heart?" I said, "Yes." She said, "Who?" I said, "What do you mean, 'Who?'" She said, "Who—who are they? Give me their names."
>
> I said, "You want me to give you the actual names of people who will basically fight the world's fight?" She said, "Yes, I want names."
>
> If she were here today to ask me the same question, may I give her your name?
>
> The world is waiting for your reply.
>
> *Your answer* will *change the world.*[31]

King's and Shrum's inspiring conclusions reemphasized their central ideas in a memorable way, provided closure to their speeches, and inspired their listeners.

**RECAP**

### Techniques for Effective Conclusions

- Use any of the techniques for an effective introduction.
- Refer to the introduction of your speech.
- Issue an inspirational appeal or a challenge.

# STUDY GUIDE

## Purposes of Introductions

It is important to begin and end your speech in a way that is memorable and that also provides the repetition audiences need. A good introduction gets the audience's attention, gives the audience a reason to listen, introduces your subject, establishes your credibility, and previews your main ideas.

Introducing your subject and previewing the body of your speech can be accomplished by including your central idea and preview statement in the introduction.

### Being Audience-Centered

- Introductions and conclusions provide audiences with important first and final impressions of speaker and speech.
- As a speaker, your task is to ensure that your introduction convinces your audience to listen to you.
- A credible speaker is one whom the audience judges to be a believable authority and a competent speaker. Establishing your credibility early in a speech helps motivate your audience to listen.
- To demonstrate proximity, you must acknowledge the diverse experiences and involvement of your listeners with your topic.

### Using What You've Learned

- How could you establish a motivation for your classroom audience to listen to you on each of the following topics?

  Cholesterol

  Elvis Presley

  The history of greeting cards

  Ozone depletion

  Text messaging

  Speed traps

## Effective Introductions

You can gain favorable attention and provide a motivation for listening by using any of the following, alone or in combination: illustrations, startling facts or statistics, quotations, humor, questions, references to historical events, references to recent events, personal references, references to the occasion, or references to preceding speeches, as appropriate.

### Being Audience-Centered

- If your audience is linguistically diverse or composed primarily of listeners whose first language is not English, it may be preferable not to use humor in your introduction. Because much humor is created verbally, it may not be readily understood and it rarely translates well.

### Using What You've Learned

- Nakai is planning to give his informative speech on Native American music, displaying and demonstrating the use of such instruments as the flute, the Taos drum, and the Yaqui rain stick. He asks you to suggest a good introduction for the speech. How do you think he might best introduce his speech?

### A Question of Ethics

- Marty and Shanna, who are in the same section of a public-speaking class, are discussing their upcoming speeches. Marty has discovered an illustration that she thinks will make an effective introduction. When she tells Shanna about it, Shanna is genuinely enthusiastic. In fact, she thinks it would make a great introduction for her own speech, which is on a different topic. When the students are given schedules for their speeches, Shanna realizes that she will speak before Marty. She badly wants to use the introductory illustration that Marty has discovered. Can she ethically do so, if she cites in her speech the original source of the illustration?

### Speaker's Homepage: Using the Web to Find an Attention-Catching Introduction

Here are sites that can help in your search for the perfect, attention-catching introduction.

- **Quotations.** Don't always rely on quotations for your introduction, but when you need one, check out Bartelby, www.bartelby.com; Quote World, www.quoteworld.org; or Yahoo's directory of humorous quotation lists, http://dir.yahoo.com/reference/quotations/humorous.
- **Statistics.** Polls conducted by the Gallup organization (www.gallup.com) may provide startling statistics for your conclusions. The Cornell University Institute for Social and Economic Research offers links to other public opinion survey organizations, at http://ciser.cornell.edu/info/polls.shtml.
- **Stories From Literature.** Project Gutenberg (www.gutenberg.org) offers you the full text of thousands of books, for free.

## Purposes of Conclusions

Your speech's conclusion leaves the final impression of you in your listeners' minds. The two main purposes of the conclusion are to summarize your speech and to provide closure. Your summary should rephrase your central idea in a way that your audience will remember and repeat your main ideas to fix them in the minds of your listeners. Verbal and nonverbal clues that the speech is ending will help to provide your audience with closure. You can also use the conclusion as an opportunity to suggest an action to your audience, to motivate your audience to respond in some way to your message.

## Effective Conclusions

Conclusions may take any one of the forms used for introductions. In addition, you can refer to the introduction or make inspirational appeals or challenges.

### Using What You've Learned

- Knowing that you have recently visited the Vietnam Veterans Memorial, your American history professor asks you to make a brief presentation to the class about the Wall: its history; its symbolic meaning; and its impact on the families, comrades, and friends of those memorialized there. Write both an introduction and a conclusion for this speech.

# SPEECH WORKSHOP

## Developing the Introduction and Conclusion to Your Speech

Use this worksheet as you develop your speech introduction.

**Catch the audience's attention** using one of the following:

- Illustration
- Interesting fact or statistic
- Appropriate humor
- A quotation
- A rhetorical question
- A reference to the occasion
- A reference to an event in history

**Give the audience a reason to listen** (tell your listeners how your topic affects them). ______________

______________________________________________

______________________________________________

______________________________________________

**Introduce the subject** (state your central idea). ______________________________

______________________________________________

______________________________________________

______________________________________________

**Establish your credibility** by answering one or more of these questions:

- What are your credentials—why should audience members listen to you speak about this topic?

  ______________________________________________

  ______________________________________________

- What experience have you had with this topic? ______________________

  ______________________________________________

  ______________________________________________

- Why are you talking to this audience about this topic? ________________

  ______________________________________________

  ______________________________________________

**Preview your main ideas.**

Use these suggestions to help you develop your speech conclusion:

**Summarize your speech.**

- Reemphasize the central idea in a memorable way.
- Restate your main idea.

**Provide closure.**

- Plan verbal or nonverbal cues to signal the end of your speech.
- Motivate your audience to respond, especially if your message is persuasive.

**End with a quotation, a reference to your introduction, an answer to your opening rhetorical question, a final story or illustration, or an inspirational appeal or challenge.**

EVERY DISCOURSE OUGHT TO BE A LIVING CREATURE, HAVING A BODY OF ITS OWN AND HEAD AND FEET; THERE SHOULD BE A MIDDLE, A BEGINNING, AND END, ADAPTED TO ONE ANOTHER AND TO THE WHOLE.

—PLATO

Hopi: Native American, *Kachina Mana* (20th Century). Werner Forman/Art Resource/The New York Public Library

OUTLINE

# 9 Outlining and Revising Your Speech

OBJECTIVES

**After studying this chapter you should be able to do the following:**

1. Describe the purposes of a preparation outline and a delivery outline.
2. Prepare a preparation outline and a delivery outline for a speech you are working on.
3. Revise a speech.
4. Deliver a speech from speaking notes.

How much time do you spend preparing the speeches you give? And what percentage of your preparation time do you spend on the various individual tasks involved in the speechmaking process?

Communication researchers recently tried to determine the answers to these and related questions with a group of nearly 100 college students.[1] Students kept journals throughout the semester in their public-speaking class, using the first few minutes of each class meeting to describe in writing what they had done since the last class to prepare for their next speech and to estimate how much time they had spent on each reported activity. When the researchers examined the students' journals, they discovered that on average, students reported spending nearly half of their total preparation time outlining and revising their speeches.

If you are typical of the students in the study, then this chapter will be critical to your success as a speaker. Specifically, we will examine the purposes and requirements of three important tasks: (1) developing your preparation outline; (2) editing your speech; and (3) developing your delivery outline and speaking notes.

# Developing Your Preparation Outline

Although few speeches are written in paragraph form, most speakers develop a detailed **preparation outline** that includes main ideas, subpoints, and supporting material. It may also include the specific purpose, introduction, blueprint, conclusion, and signposts. One CEO notes,

> Unless you sit down and write out your thoughts and put them in a cogent order, you can't deliver a cogent speech. Maybe some people have mastered that art. But I have seen too many people give speeches that they really haven't thought out.[2]

## The Preparation Outline

**preparation outline**
A detailed outline of a speech that includes main ideas, subpoints, and supporting material, and that may also include specific purpose, introduction, blueprint, internal previews and summaries, transitions, and conclusion

**mapping**
Using geometric shapes to sketch how all the main ideas, subpoints, and supporting material of a speech relate to the central idea and to one another

To begin your outlining task, you might try a technique known as **mapping**, or clustering. Write on a sheet of paper all the main ideas, subpoints, and supporting material for the speech. Then use geometric shapes and arrows to indicate the logical relationships among them, as shown in Figure 9.1.

Nationwide Insurance speechwriter Charles Parnell describes yet another technique for beginning an outline:

> I often start by jotting down a few ideas on the [computer] screen, then move them around as necessary to build some sort of coherent pattern. I then fill in the details as they occur to me.
>
> What that means is that you can really start anywhere and eventually come up with an entire speech, just as you can start with any piece of a puzzle and eventually put it together.[3]

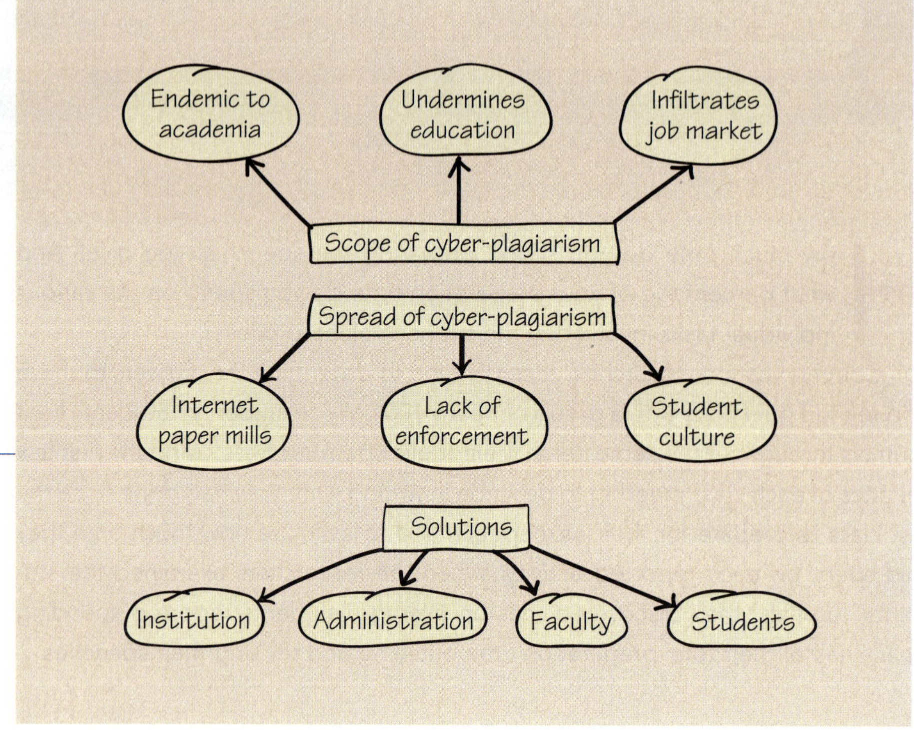


FIGURE 9.1 *A map that shows the relationships among each of a speaker's three main ideas and their subpoints. Main ideas are enclosed by rectangles; subpoints, by ovals. Supporting material could be indicated by another shape and connected to the appropriate subpoints.*

Whatever technique you choose to begin your outline, your ultimate goal is to produce a plan that lets you judge the unity and coherence of your speech, to see how well the parts fit together and how smoothly the speech flows. Your finished preparation outline will help you make sure that all main ideas and subpoints are clearly and logically related and adequately supported.

The following suggestions will help you complete your preparation outline. However, keep in mind that different instructors may have different expectations for both outline content and outline format. Be sure to understand and follow your own instructor's guidelines.

- **Write your preparation outline in complete sentences, like those you will use when delivering your speech.** Unless you write complete sentences, you will have trouble judging the coherence of the speech. Moreover, complete sentences will help during your early rehearsals. If you write cryptic phrases, you may not remember what they mean.
- **Use standard outline form.** Although you did not have to use standard outline form when you began to sketch out your ideas, you need to do so now. **Standard outline form** lets you see at a glance the exact relationships among various main ideas, subpoints, and supporting material in your speech. It is an important tool for evaluating your speech, as well as a requirement in many public-speaking courses. An instructor who requires speech outlines will generally expect standard outline form. To produce a correct outline, follow the instructions given here and summarized in Figure 9.2.
- **Use standard outline numbering.** Logical and fairly easy to learn, outline numbering follows this sequence:

I. First main idea
  A. First subpoint of I
  B. Second subpoint of I
    1. First subpoint of B
    2. Second subpoint of B
      a. First subpoint of 2
      b. Second subpoint of 2
II. Second main idea

**standard outline form**
Numbered and lettered headings and subheadings arranged hierarchically to indicate the relationships among parts of a speech

CORRECT OUTLINE FORM

| Rule | Example |
|---|---|
| 1. Use standard outline numbers and letters. | I.<br>A.<br>1.<br>a.<br>(1)<br>(a) |
| 2. Use at least two subpoints, if any, for each main idea. | I.<br>A.<br>B. |
| 3. Properly indent main ideas, subpoints, and supporting material. | I. First main idea<br>A. First subpoint of I<br>1. First subpoint of A<br>2. Second subpoint of A<br>B. Second subpoint of I<br>II. Second main idea |

FIGURE 9.2 *Use this summary as a reminder of the rules of proper outlining when you write your preparation outline.*

Although it is unlikely that you will subdivide beyond the level of lowercase letters (a, b, etc.) in most speech outlines, next would come numbers in parentheses and then lowercase letters in parentheses.

- **Use at least two subdivisions, if any, for each point.** Logic dictates that you cannot divide anything into one part. If, for example, you have only one piece of supporting material, incorporate it into the subpoint or main idea that it supports. If you have only one subpoint, incorporate it into the main idea above it. Although there is no firm limit to the number of subpoints you may have, if you have more than five, you may want to place some of them under another point. An audience will remember your ideas more easily if they are divided into blocks of no more than five.

- **Indent main ideas, points, subpoints, and supporting material properly.** Main ideas, indicated by Roman numerals, are written closest to the left margin. Notice that the periods following the Roman numerals line up, so that the first words of the main ideas also line up.

I. First main idea
II. Second main idea
III. Third main idea

Letters or numbers of subpoints and supporting material begin directly underneath the first *word* of the point above.

I. First main idea
    A. First subpoint of I

If a main idea or subpoint takes up more than one line, the second line begins under the first *word* of the preceding line:

I. Every speech has three parts.
    A. The first part, both in our discussion and in actual delivery, is the introduction.

The same rules of indentation apply at all levels of the outline.

- **Write and label your specific purpose at the top of your preparation outline.** Unless your instructor directs you to do otherwise, do not work the specific purpose into the outline itself. Instead, label it and place it at the top of the outline. Your specific purpose can serve as a yardstick by which to measure the relevance of each main idea, subpoint, and piece of supporting material. Everything in the speech should contribute to your purpose.

- **Add the blueprint, key signposts, and an introduction and conclusion to your outline.** Place the introduction after the specific purpose, the blueprint immediately following the introduction, the conclusion after the outline of the body of the speech, and other signposts within the outline. Follow your instructor's guidelines for incorporating these elements into your numbering system.

Note that if you are using a word-processing program, you may find it easier to format your outline with the Autoformat feature turned off. The program's attempt to "help" you may be more frustrating than helpful and may cause you to make more errors in your outline than you would if you formatted it yourself.

RECAP

**Preparation Outlines**

When you write your preparation outline, be sure to:

- Use complete sentences.
- Use standard outline form and numbering.
- Include your specific purpose.
- Include your full introduction and conclusion.
- Include your blueprint and key signposts.

## Sample Preparation Outline

The sample outline on pages 208–209 is for a ten-minute persuasive speech by student speaker Karen Summerson, whose speech preparation process we have been following since Chapter 4.[4] Notice that in this example, the purpose, introduction, blueprint, signposts, and conclusion are separated from the numbered points in the body of the speech. Be sure to learn and follow your own instructor's specific requirements for incorporating these elements.

Once you have completed your preparation outline, you can use it to help analyze and possibly revise the speech. The following questions can help you in this critical thinking task.

- **Does the speech as outlined fulfill the purpose you have specified?** If not, you need to revise the specific purpose or change the direction and content of the speech itself.
- **Are the main ideas logical extensions (natural divisions, reasons, or steps) of the central idea?** If not, revise either the central idea or the main ideas. Like the first question, this one relates to the unity of the speech and is critical to making certain the speech fits together as a whole.
- **Do the signposts enhance the comfortable flow of each idea into the next?** If not, change or add previews, summaries, or transitions. If signposts are not adequate, the speech will lack coherence.
- **Does each subpoint provide support for the point under which it falls?** If not, then either move or delete the subpoint.
- **Is your outline form correct?** For a quick reference, check Figure 9.2 on page 205 and the Recap on page 206.

Having considered these five questions, you are ready to rehearse your speech, using the preparation outline as your first set of notes. See Chapter 11 for additional tips on effective rehearsal.

## Revising Your Speech

Audiences will forgive a speaker many speaking errors, but one of the hardest for audiences to forgive is speaking for too long. Although you want an appreciative audience, you don't want your listeners to break into applause out of relief that you have finally finished speaking. Often when you rehearse using your preparation outline, you discover you've got too much information. You have to cut your speech. Here are a few tips to help you revise a speech that is too long.[5]

- **Review your specific purpose.** Many speeches are too long because you are trying to accomplish too much. With your audience in mind, take a hard look at your specific purpose statement. If, for example, you want your audience to be able to list and describe five advantages of staying on standard time rather than switching to daylight time, you may have to decide on a less ambitious purpose and describe only three advantages—pick your best three.
- **Consider your audience.** You may be weary of this reminder, but it is critical to consider your audience. What do audience members really need to hear? Go back over your speech outline and take a hard look at it. Which parts of your message will be most and least interesting to your listeners? Cut those portions that are of least potential interest.

- **Keep only the best supporting material.** Your stories, illustrations, quotations, and other supporting material may be soaking up your time. Of course, stories and other types of supporting material help you make your point and maintain interest. So you don't want to reduce your speech to a bare bones outline. But do you need two stories to make your point, or will one do? Is there a shorter, more pithy quotation that will add punch and power to your prose? Scan your speech for supporting material that can be cut.

## SAMPLE PREPARATION OUTLINE

### PURPOSE

At the end of my speech, the audience will be able to take steps to ensure that they and their loved ones are driving on tires less than six years old.

Placing the purpose statement at the top of the outline helps the speaker keep it in mind. But always follow your instructor's specific requirements for how to format your preparation outline.

### INTRODUCTION

An ABC report dated May 9, 2008, tells the story of 19-year-old Andy Moore, who took a graduation trip to Canada. His parents had been careful to check the van, making sure everything was secure—taking usual precautions to guarantee a safe trip. Several days after Andy left, his father received a call that Andy had been in a deadly car accident. Andy did not die from drunk driving, carelessness, or by the fault of another person. As Andy was rounding a corner, the tread on a tire split and rolled off—a tire that had passed the inspection of a professional before this trip.

Karen catches her listeners' attention by opening her presentation with an illustration. Other strategies for effectively getting audience attention were discussed in Chapter 8.

According to the August 2003 edition of *Salon*, 204 million vehicles are driven each year in the United States by 191 million drivers. This means that 816 million tires are on the road, and we assume they will keep us safe.

To increase the impact of the *Salon* statistic, Karen explodes it, multiplying the number of vehicles on U.S. roads by 4 to yield the number of tires. Chapter 6 explains in greater detail why and how a speaker might *explode* or *compact* statistics.

### CENTRAL IDEA

With safety on the line, it is important to ensure that we are driving on tires less than six years old.

### PREVIEW

We must understand the problems, effects, and solutions related to driving on tires that are past their expiration dates.

Karen writes out and labels her central idea and preview, which together form the blueprint of her speech. Again, follow your instructor's requirements for what to include in and how to label the various components of your outline.

### BODY OUTLINE

I. The problems are threefold.

The first main point of the speech, which explores the problems associated with expired tires, is indicated by the Roman numeral I. It previews the three subpoints, indicated by A, B, and C.

A. We are driving on expired tires.

Subpoints 1 and 2 provide supporting material, with oral citations, for A.

1. According to Ford, BMW, Chrysler, Toyota, VW/Audi manuals, and vehicular engineers, a tire is only safe for six years, even if it has not been driven on. According to the *Chemistry of Rubber Processing and Disposal* by Robert L. Bebb, elasticity has nothing to do with the shape or appearance of the tire, but instead is determined by the chemistry of the rubber. Just like the elasticity in a rubber band diminishes over time, so do the moisture and elasticity in tires.
2. Out of 14,000 tires recently examined by teams from the Rubber Manufacturers Association, 40% of tires being sold as new were older than four years, and .5% of these were 15 years or older. That could mean more than 70 potentially fatal accidents.
3. Compounding the problem is a lack of knowledge regarding printed birth dates on a tire. The four-digit number at the end of the sequence represent the week and year the tire was made. A tire with a code of 4202 was made in the 42nd week of 2002, making it more than six years old.

Karen *compacts* the statistic from the Rubber Manufacturers Association to yield the number of vehicles that might bear a "new" tire actually 15 years or older.

• **Look at your introduction and conclusion.** Your introduction should generally be about 10 percent of your speaking time; the same 10 percent estimate applies to your conclusion. If either your introduction or your conclusion exceeds this guideline, see if you can shorten an illustration or summarize with greater brevity.

• **Ask a listener to help you cut.** It's often easier to have someone else help you cut material. Ask a friend or roommate to listen to your speech and help you note parts that are less powerful, clear, or convincing.

B. The second problem is that tire companies are not taking research seriously. These companies believe that technologies should make tire age obsolete; yet research shows that this is incorrect.

C. Finally, we are not being well-informed.

1. Even after federal legislation—called the Transportation Recall Enhancement, Accountability, and Documentation Act, or TREAD Act—was passed in 2000, tire makers did nothing to warn the public, law enforcement, or even the automotive industry about possible harms posed by old tires.

2. On February 28, 2002, Jeffrey Runge, Administrator of the National Highway Traffic Safety Administration, or NHTSA, shared with lawmakers legislation that prohibits a tire to be sold if it is not compliant with regulations. Since this address, the only change that has been made is that a tire's code is now printed on its outside-facing wall rather than its inside-facing wall.

3. When I recently had the oil changed in my car, I asked the mechanic if he could point out the code on the tire to me and tell me how old they were. He said my tires were six years old. He read the code incorrectly. They are 16 years old.

Karen uses a personal illustration to support the point that we are not well informed about the age of our tires.

II. As well as putting the public in immediate danger, the continued use of tires beyond their expiration dates deters research into improvements in rubber technology, increasing the likelihood that the problem will persist.

*Signpost.* Now that we understand the problems and effects surrounding the issue of expired tires, it is important to better understand steps we can take to keep ourselves and those we love safe.

The signpost summarizes the problem and its effects, before Karen turns to solutions.

III. We can take at least three steps to protect ourselves and our friends and family from dangers associated with expired tires.

A. The first and most practical solution is to take responsibility and check your tires.

B. Second, question your mechanics and the companies you buy your tires from.

C. Finally, tell your friends and family this life-saving information. Remind them to change their tires every six years, rotate their tires every 8,000 miles, and regularly check their tire pressure.

### CONCLUSION

So today, we have looked at the problems, causes, and solutions surrounding tires and their lack of expiration dates. We, as forensics students, spend so much time on the road. Please check to make sure that you are safe so that you can continue doing something you love so much. By acting on this valuable information, you may prevent an accident that Andy Moore's parents could not.

In her conclusion, Karen first summarizes her main ideas, then reminds her audience why this problem concerns them. Finally, she returns to her opening illustration.

## Developing Your Delivery Outline and Speaking Notes

As you rehearse your speech, you will find that you need your preparation outline less and less. Both the structure and the content of your speech will become set in your mind. At this point, you are ready to prepare a **delivery outline.**

**delivery outline**
Condensed and abbreviated outline from which speaking notes are developed

## The Delivery Outline

A delivery outline, as the name implies, is meant to give you all you will need to present your speech in the way you have planned and rehearsed. However, it should not be so detailed that it encourages you to read it rather than speak to your audience. Here are a few tips:

- **Make the outline as brief as possible, and use single words or short phrases rather than complete sentences.** That said, make certain the information is not so abbreviated that it becomes unclear. NASA blamed the loss of the space shuttle *Columbia* in part on the fact that an outline on possible wing damage was "so crammed with nested bullet points and irregular short forms that it was nearly impossible to untangle."[6]
- **Include the introduction and conclusion in much shortened form.** As we noted in Chapter 8, you may feel more comfortable if you have the first and last sentences written in full in front of you. Writing out the first sentence eliminates any fear of a mental block at the outset of your speech. And writing a complete last sentence ensures a smooth ending to your speech and a good final impression.
- **Include supporting material and signposts.** Write out statistics, direct quotations, and key signposts. Writing key signposts in full ensures that you will

## SAMPLE DELIVERY OUTLINE

### INTRODUCTION

- ABC, May 9, 2008—19-year-old Andy Moore, graduation trip to Canada. Parents checked van, usual precautions. Several days later, father received call re: accident. Not drunk driving, carelessness, or fault of another person—tread on a tire split & rolled off—a tire that had passed the inspection of a professional before this trip.
- *Salon*, August 2003—204 million vehicles/yr. in U.S., 191 million drivers = 816 million tires. Safe?

For the delivery outline, Karen does not need to write out her purpose statement, as she will not actually say it in her speech.

Karen reformats her introduction with bullets so that she will be able to see each part at a glance.

### CENTRAL IDEA

With safety on the line, it is important to ensure that we are driving on tires less than 6 years old.

### PREVIEW

1. Problems
2. Effects
3. Solutions

} related to driving on tires that are past their expiration dates.

Karen includes and labels her initial preview and signposts throughout the outline so that she can find them quickly when she glances down while speaking.

### BODY OUTLINE

I. Problems

A. Expired tires

1. Ford, BMW, Chrysler, Toyota, VW/Audi manuals & engineers—tire safe 6 yrs., even if not driven on. *Chemistry of Rubber Processing and Disposal*, Robert L. Bebb—elasticity
   - ≠ shape or appearance of the tire, but
   - = chemistry of the rubber (rubber band)
2. 14,000 tires exam. by teams from Rubber Mfg. Assoc.—
   - 40% "new" tires > 4 yrs.
   - .5% of these > 15 yrs.
   - = > 70 fatal acc.

Although both main ideas and subpoints are shorter than in the preparation outline, source citations are still provided.

Part of the shorthand of the delivery outline includes both abbreviations (such as "yr." and "no.") and symbols such as > or < for "more than" or "less than"; @ for "at"; and w/ for "with."

not grope awkwardly for a way to move from one point to the next. In the sample delivery outline, notice the statistics and sources written out in the introduction, and the transitions written out at key junctures—between IB and II and between II and III. After you have rehearsed the speech several times, you will know where you are most likely to falter and can add or omit written transitions as needed.

- **Do not include your purpose statement in your delivery outline.**
- **Use standard outline form.** This will allow you to easily find the exact point or piece of supporting material you are seeking when you glance down at your notes.

RECAP

### Two Types of Speech Outlines

**Preparation Outline**
Allows speaker to examine speech for
- completeness
- unity
- coherence
- overall effectiveness

Serves as first rehearsal outline

**Delivery Outline**
Serves as basis for speaking notes

## Sample Delivery Outline

Note that the delivery outline (on pages 210–211) for Karen's speech on tire safety does not include a statement of the purpose and that the introduction and conclusion appear in shortened and bulleted list form.

As you rehearse your speech, you will probably continue to edit the delivery outline. You may decide to cut further or revise signposts. Your outline should provide just enough information to ensure smooth delivery. It should not burden you with unnecessary notes or compel you to look down too often during the speech.

3. Printed birth dates on tire:
   - 4-digit no. = week & yr. tire was made.
   - 4202 = 42nd week/2002; = > 6 yrs.

B. Tire cos. not taking research seriously, think tech. = tire age obsolete; not true.

C. Not well inf.

1. Transportation Recall Enhancement, Accountability, and Documentation Act (TREAD), 2000—tire makers ≠ warn public, law enf., or auto industry

~~2. Feb. 28, 2002 Jeffrey Runge, Adm., Hwy Traffic Safety Admin (NHTSA) shared wlawmakers legislation that prohibits tire not complaint with regulations. Only change code now printed on outside facing wall rather than inside facing wall~~

2. Oil change: Tires 6 yrs. old or 16?

In her revising process, Karen cut the reference to Jeffrey Runge, so she cuts it from her delivery outline as well. Her speaking notes will eliminate the reference altogether.

II. Add. effects: research deterred

*Signpost.* Now that we understand the problems & effects surrounding the issue of expired tires, it is important to better understand steps we can take to keep ourselves & those we love safe.

III. 3 steps

A. Check tires.

B. ? mechanics & tire cos.

C. Family/friends:
   - Change tires every 6 yrs.
   - Rotate every 8,000 miles.
   - Check pressure.

### CONCLUSION

- Looked @ problems, causes, & solutions
- Forensics students spend so much time on road: Check
- By acting on this valuable information, you may prevent an accident that Andy Moore's parents could not.

Karen writes out her final sentence to ensure that she can end her presentation fluently.

## CONFIDENTLY CONNECTING WITH YOUR AUDIENCE

### Use Your Well-Prepared Speaking Notes When You Rehearse

Resist the temptation to write your speech out word for word. Reading your speech will diminish your connection with your audience and may raise your anxiety. However, do use enough notes to remind you of key ideas and supporting material as you speak. And when you rehearse your speech, use the same speaking notes that you will use when you deliver your speech. Rehearsing and delivering your speech from the same notes will help enhance your confidence.

## Speaking Notes

Many speakers find paper difficult to handle quietly, so they transfer their delivery outlines to note cards. Note cards are small enough to hold in one hand, if necessary, and stiff enough not to rustle. Two or three note cards will give you enough space for a delivery outline; the exact number of cards you use will depend on the length of your speech. Type or print your outline neatly on one side, making sure that the letters and words are large enough to read easily. You may find it helpful to plan your note cards according to logical blocks of material, using one note card for the introduction, one or two for the body, and one for the conclusion. At any rate, plan so that you do not have to shuffle note cards in midsentence. Number the note cards to prevent a fiasco if your notes get out of order.

Instead of using an outline, you might use an alternative format for your speaking notes. Winston Churchill formatted the speaking notes of the message with which he rallied the British people at the outset of World War II (his "Finest Hour" speech) as blank verse. The Director of the Churchill Archives Center observed that "because it looks like poetry, it gave him, I think, the rhythm that brought life to his oratory."[7] Other formats for speaking notes include maps, like the one in Figure 9.1. Or you could use a combination of words, pictures, and symbols, as in Mark Twain's notes reproduced in Figure 9.3. Whatever form your notes take, they should make sense to *you*.

**FIGURE 9.3** *Speaking notes used by Mark Twain for a lecture titled "Roughing It," delivered in Liverpool, England, in 1874.*

Source: Milton Meltzer, *Mark Twain Himself* (New York: Wings Books, 1960) 121.

A final addition to your speaking notes will be delivery cues and reminders, such as "Louder," "Pause," and "Move in front of podium." (See Figure 9.4 below.) You could write your delivery cues in the margins by hand, or if the entire outline is handwritten, in ink of a different color. President Gerald Ford once accidentally read the delivery cue "Look into the right camera" during an address. Clearly differentiating delivery cues from speech content will help prevent such mistakes.

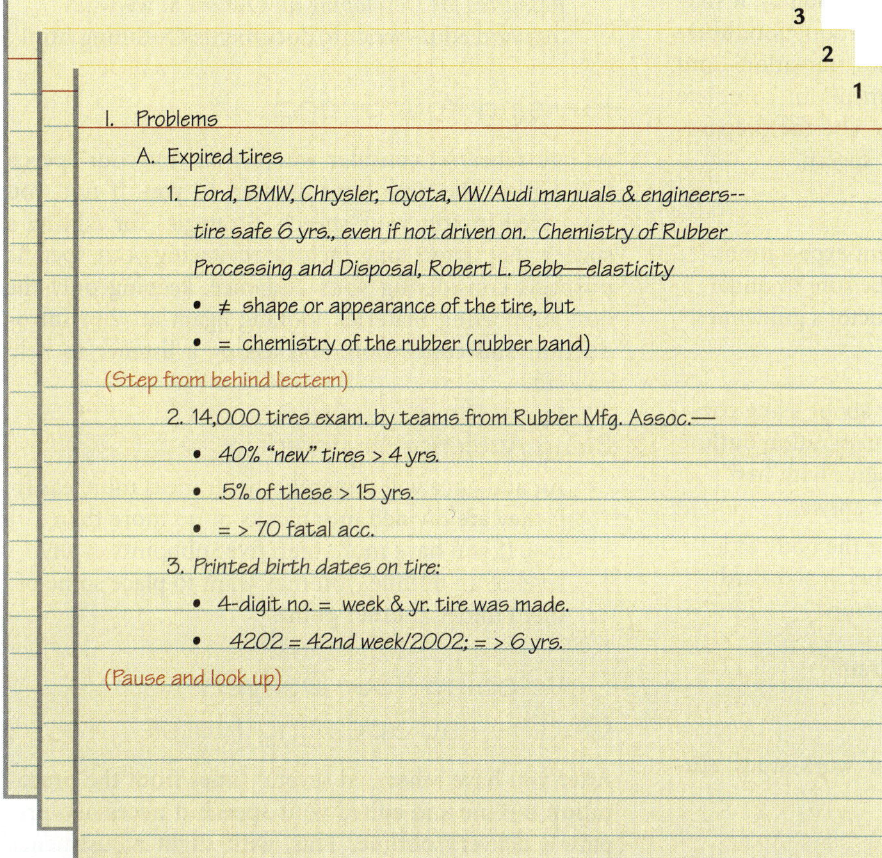


**FIGURE 9.4** *Your speaking notes can include delivery cues and reminders. Be sure to differentiate your cues from the content of your speech. One good way is to write speaking cues in a different color ink.*

## LEARNING FROM GREAT SPEAKERS

### Mark Twain (1835–1910)

American humorist Mark Twain was perhaps best known in his own time as a speaker. Years on the Redpath lecture circuit and international speaking tours, as well as innumerable after-dinner speeches, provided him with the opportunity to hone his speaking skills. Some of Twain's speaking notes survive. They combine words, pictures, and symbols in a way that may seem quite strange to most of us. What is important, though, is that they made sense to *him*.

As you prepare your speaking outline and notes, don't try to cram in so much information that it will be difficult to see at a glance the word or phrase you need to jog your memory. Make your speaking notes thorough enough that you feel secure knowing you have at hand the information you need to present your well-rehearsed talk, but not so comprehensive that you focus more on your notes than on your audience.

[Photo: North Wind Picture Archives]

# STUDY GUIDE

## Developing Your Preparation Outline

A preparation outline includes your carefully organized main ideas, subpoints, and supporting material; it may also include your specific purpose, introduction, blueprint, internal previews and summaries, transitions, and conclusion. Write each of these elements in complete sentences and standard outline form. Use the preparation outline to begin rehearsing your speech.

### Being Audience-Centered

- Different instructors have different expectations for outline content and format. Be sure to understand and follow your own instructor's guidelines.

### Using What You've Learned

- Myorka thinks it is silly to worry about using correct outline form for either her preparation outline or her delivery outline. Do you agree with her? Give at least two reasons for your answer.
- The following delivery outline for the body of a speech contains a number of errors in standard outline form. Find five of those errors.

Title: "The College Work-Study Program"

I. Program Eligibility

A. Four initial requirements for work-study students

1. Have need for employment
2. Good grades
3. Be a full-time student
4. Be a citizen or permanent resident of the United States

B. Application

1. Submit financial-form to Central State

II. Job Assignments

1. Jobs related to your major field of study
2. Jobs using your special interests and skills

### A Question of Ethics

- Can a speaker legitimately claim that a speech is extemporaneous if he or she has constructed a detailed preparation outline? Explain your answer.

### Speaker's Homepage: Internet Resources to Improve Your Outlining Skills

- Purdue University's Online Writing Lab (OWL) gives you general guidance on how to develop an outline and presents a detailed sample of an outline for a research paper: http://owl.english.purdue.edu/owl/resource/544/01/
- The Harvard College Writing Center offers *Tips and Resources for Developing an Outline* at www.fas.harvard.edu/~wricntr/documents/Outlining.html

## Revising Your Speech

As you rehearse, consider whether or not your speech falls within the time limit allotted to you. If not, you may need to edit your speech. Strategies for editing a speech that is too long include reviewing your specific purpose, considering your audience, keeping only the best supporting material, looking again at your introduction and conclusion, and asking a listener to help you cut.

### Being Audience-Centered

- An audience will remember your ideas more easily if they are divided into blocks of no more than five. If you have more than five subpoints at any level of an outline, you may want to place some of them under another point.

## Developing Your Delivery Outline and Speaking Notes

After you have rehearsed several times from the preparation outline and edited your speech if necessary, prepare a delivery outline. This, with slight adjustments, becomes your final speaking notes. You need not include the purpose statement or central idea. Note all other ideas and materials in only as much detail as you will need when delivering the speech. You may eventually transfer the delivery outline to note cards and add delivery cues.

### Being Audience-Centered

- Your delivery outline should not be so detailed that it encourages you to read it rather than speak to your audience.

### Using What You've Learned

- Geoff plans to deliver his speech using hastily scrawled notes on a sheet of paper torn from his notebook. What advice would you offer him for preparing more effective and efficient speaking notes?

# SPEECH WORKSHOP

## Outlining Your Speech

Use this worksheet to help you prepare a delivery outline for your speech. Depending on the length of your talk, you may need more or fewer main points and subpoints. Review the sample delivery outline on pages 210–211 as a model.

### Introduction

______________________________

**Blueprint** ______________________________

*Central idea* ______________________________

______________________________

*Preview* ______________________________

______________________________

### Body

**I.**

A. ______________________________

______________________________

B. ______________________________

______________________________

***Transition to next main idea***

**II.**

A. ______________________________

______________________________

B. ______________________________

______________________________

***Transition to next main idea***

**III.**

A. ______________________________

______________________________

B. ______________________________

______________________________

***Transition to conclusion***

### Conclusion

______________________________

______________________________

A SPEECH IS POETRY: CADENCE, RHYTHM, IMAGERY, SWEEP! A SPEECH REMINDS US THAT WORDS, LIKE CHILDREN, HAVE THE POWER TO MAKE DANCE THE DULLEST BEANBAG OF A HEART.

—PEGGY NOONAN

Henri Matisse (1869–1954), *Jazz* (1947), Portfolio of twenty pochoirs. Composition: various; sheet: $16^3/_4$ × $25^{11}/_{16}$". Publisher, Tériade Éditeur, Paris, Printer: Edmond Vairel and Draeger Frères, Paris, Edition: 250. The Museum of Modern Art, Gift of the artist, 1948. (291. 1948.13) © Succession H. Matisse, Paris/ARS, NY. Erich Lessing/Art Resource, N.Y.

## OUTLINE

# 10 Using Words Well: Speaker Language and Style

OBJECTIVES

**After studying this chapter you should be able to do the following:**

1. Describe three differences between oral and written language styles.
2. List and explain three ways to use words effectively.
3. Explain how to adapt your language style to diverse listeners.
4. Explain three ways to craft memorable word structures.
5. Offer tips for using memorable word structures effectively in public speeches.

Figure 10.1 shows several ads and headlines from the "Headlines" files of comedian Jay Leno.[1] As he notes, they are funny "because they were never intended to be funny in the first place. That they're checked and rechecked by a proofreader makes them funnier still." Certainly they illustrate that using language accurately, clearly, and effectively can be a challenge, even for professional writers.

For public speakers, the task is doubly challenging. One must speak clearly and communicate ideas accurately. At the same time, it is important to present those ideas in such a way that your audience will listen to, remember, and perhaps act on what you have to say.

In this chapter we will focus on the power of language. We will suggest ways to communicate your ideas and feelings to others accurately and effectively. We

FIGURE 10.1 *Sometimes our word choices are unintentionally amusing.*

**FORECLOSURE LISTINGS**
Entire state of NJ available. Deal directly with owners. 5–8 months before auction. Call 201-286-1156.

**BABYSITTER**
Looking for infant to babysit in my home. Excellent references.

**NEED** Plain Clothes Security. Must have shoplifting experience. Apply between 8 A.M.–3 P.M. Mon.–Fri., at suite 207.

Unemployment Not Working, Critics Say

**FAMILY CATCHES FIRE JUST IN TIME, CHIEF SAYS . . .**
The Richard Harder family Sunday returned home from church just in time, Lindsey Fire Chief Tom Overmyer said. The family . . . got back from church about 11:15 A.M. to find their kitchen table on fire and . . .

STORE CLERK BETTER AFTER BEING SHOT

will also discuss how the choice of words and word structures can help give your message a distinctive style.

# Differentiating Oral and Written Language Styles

Your instructor has probably told you not to write your speech out word for word. The professor has said this because there are at least three major differences between oral and written language styles.

- **Oral Style Is More Personal Than Written Style**. When speaking, you can look your listeners in the eye and talk to them directly. That personal contact affects your speech and your verbal style. As a speaker, you are likely to use more pronouns (*I*, *you*) than you would in writing. You are also more likely to address specific audience members by name.

- **Oral Style Is Less Formal Than Written Style**. Memorized speeches usually sound as if they were written because the words and phrases are longer, more complex, and more formal than those used by most speakers. Spoken communication, by contrast, is usually less formal, characterized by shorter words and phrases and less complex sentence structures. Speakers generally use many more contractions and colloquialisms than writers. Oral language is also much less varied than written language, with only fifty words accounting for almost 50 percent of what we say. Finally, spoken language is often less precise than written language. Speakers are more likely than writers to use somewhat vague quantifying terms, such as *many*, *much*, and *a lot*.

The personality of the speaker or writer, the subject of the discourse, the audience, and the occasion all affect the style of the language used. However, there are great variations within both oral and written styles. One speech may be quite personal and informal, whereas another may have characteristics more often associated with written style.

- **Oral Style Is More Repetitive Than Written Style.** When you don't understand something you are reading in a book or an article, you can stop and reread a passage, look up unfamiliar words in the dictionary, or ask someone for help. When you're listening to a speech, those opportunities usually aren't available. For this reason, an oral style is and should be more repetitive.

When you study how to organize a speech, you learn to preview main ideas in your introduction, develop your ideas in the body of the speech, and summarize these same ideas in the conclusion. You build in repetition to make sure that your listener will grasp your message. Even during the process of developing an idea, it is sometimes necessary to state it first, restate it in a different way, provide an example, and finally, summarize it.

RECAP

**Oral versus Written Style**

| | |
|---|---|
| Written style | Less personal, with no immediate interaction between writer and reader<br>More formal<br>Less repetitive |
| Oral style | More personal, facilitating interaction between speaker and audience<br>Less formal<br>More repetitive |

# Using Words Effectively

As a speaker, your goal is to use words well so that you can communicate your intended message. Ideally, language should be specific and concrete, simple, and correct. We'll discuss each of these factors.

## Use Specific, Concrete Words

If you were to describe your pet snake to an audience, you would need to do more than say it is a serpent. Instead, you would want to use the most specific term possible, describing your snake as a ball python or, if you were speaking to an audience of scientists, perhaps as a *Python regius.* A specific word or term such as *ball python* refers to an individual member of a class of more general things, such as *serpent* or *snake.*

Specific words are often concrete words, which appeal to one of our five senses, whereas general words are often abstract words, which refer to ideas or qualities. A linguistic theory known as *general semantics* holds that the more concrete your words, the clearer your communication. Semanticists use a "ladder of abstraction" to illustrate how something can be described in either concrete or abstract language. Figure 10.2 shows an example of this: The words are most abstract at the top of the ladder and become more concrete as you move down the ladder.

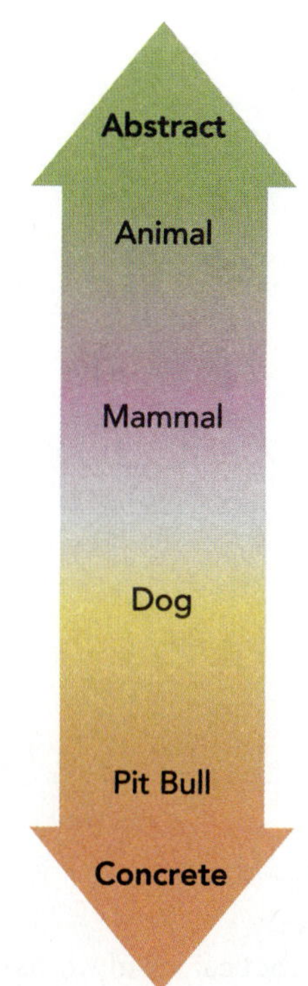


FIGURE 10.2 *A "ladder of abstraction" is used by semanticists to show how a concept, idea, or thing can be described in either concrete or abstract terms.*

Specific, concrete nouns create memorable images, as in this speech delivered by a Wake Forest University student:

> Sometimes when I sleep, I can still hear the voices of my life—night crickets, lions' mating calls, my father's advice, my friend's laughter; I can still hear the voices of Africa.[2]

Specific, concrete verbs can be especially effective. The late Representative Barbara Jordan of Texas, whose language skills one speechwriter describes as "legendary," recognized the power of concrete verbs.[3] For example, the first draft of a passage in her 1992 Democratic National Convention keynote stated:

> The American dream is not dead. It is injured, it is sick, but it is not dead.

Jordan revised the line to read:

> The American dream is not dead. It is gasping for breath, but it is not dead.

The concrete verb phrase "gasping for breath" brings alive the image Jordan intended to create.

At the opposite end of the language spectrum from specific, concrete words is the **cliché**, the overused expression that may make listeners "start tuning out and completely miss the message."[4] In one recent poll, the most annoying cliché was *at the end of the day*, followed by *at this moment in time*. Also on the list were *24/7, absolutely, awesome, ballpark figure*, and *I hear what you're saying*. Like most clichés, these words and phrases were at one time original and interesting, but their overuse has doomed them. Substitute specific, concrete words for clichés.

When searching for a specific, concrete word, you may want to consult a **thesaurus**. But in searching for an alternative word, do not feel that you have to choose the most obscure or unusual term to vary your description. Simple language will often evoke the most vivid image for your listeners.

## Use Simple Words

The best language is often the simplest. Your words should be immediately understandable to your listeners. Don't try to impress them with jargon and pompous language. Instead, as linguist Paul Roberts advises,

> Decide what you want to say and say it as vigorously as possible . . . and in plain words.[5]

In his classic essay "Politics and the English Language," George Orwell lists rules for clear writing, including this prescription for simplicity:

> Never use a long word where a short one will do. If it is possible to cut a word out, always cut it out. Never use a foreign phrase, a scientific word, or a jargon word if you can think of an everyday English equivalent.[6]

Record your practice sessions. As you review the recording, listen for chances to express yourself with simpler and fewer words. Used wisely, simple words communicate with great power and precision.

## Use Words Correctly

> I was listening to the car radio one day when a woman reading the news referred to someone as a suede-o-intellectual. I pondered through three traffic lights until I realized she wasn't talking about shoes, but a pseudointellectual.[7]

A public speech is not the place to demonstrate your lack of familiarity with English vocabulary and grammar. In fact, your effectiveness with your audience depends in part on your ability to use the English language correctly. If you are unsure of the way to apply a grammatical rule, seek assistance from a good English usage handbook. If you are unsure of a word's pronunciation or meaning, use a dictionary.

Language operates on two levels, and perhaps the greatest challenge to using words correctly is remaining aware of connotations as well as denotations.

- **Denotation**. The **denotation** of a word is its literal meaning, the definition you find in a dictionary. For example, the denotation of the word *notorious* is "famous."
- **Connotation**. The **connotation** of a word is not usually found in a dictionary, but it consists of the meaning we associate with the word, based on our experiences. *Notorious* connotes fame for some dire deed. *Notorious* and *famous* are not really interchangeable. It is just as important to consider the connotations of the words you use as it is to consider the denotations.

**cliché**
An overused expression

**thesaurus**
An alphabetical list of words and their synonyms

**denotation**
The literal meaning of a word

**connotation**
The meaning listeners associate with a word, based on their experience

Sometimes connotations are personal. For example, the word *table* is defined denotatively as a piece of furniture consisting of a smooth, flat slab affixed on legs. But when you think of the word *table*, you may think of the old oak *table* your grandparents used to have; *table* may evoke for you an image of playing checkers with your grandmother. This is a personal connotation of the word, a unique meaning based on your own experiences. Personal meanings are difficult to predict, but as a public speaker you should be aware of the possibility of triggering audience members' personal connotations. This awareness is particularly important when you are discussing highly emotional or controversial topics.

And finally, if your audience includes people whose first language is not English, to whom the nuances of connotation may not be readily apparent, it may be necessary to explain your intentions in more detail, rather than rely on word associations.

## Use Words Concisely

Consider these suggestions for getting to the point:

- **Eliminate words and phrases that add no meaning to your message.** Keeping your words concise helps your audience follow your organization and can enhance your credibility. Here are phrases you could always eliminate from your speech:

  In my opinion (just state the opinion)
  And all that (meaningless)
  When all is said and done (just say it)
  As a matter of fact (just state the fact)
  Before I begin, I'd like to say (you've already begun—just say it)

- **Avoid narrating your speaking technique.** There's no need to say, "Here's an interesting story that I think you will like." Just tell the story. Or why say, "I'd like to now offer several facts about this matter"? Just state the facts. Yes, it's useful to provide signposts and internal summaries throughout your message—redundancy is needed in oral messages—but be careful not to provide a cluttering narration about the techniques you're using.
- **Avoid long phrases when a short one will do.** Say things as succinctly as possible:

| **Instead of saying . . .** | **Say . . .** |
|---|---|
| So, for that reason | So |
| But at the same time | But |
| In today's society | Today |
| Due to the fact | Because |
| In the course of | During |
| In the final analysis | Finally |

*Keeping your speech concise can help your listeners to take your message seriously. Many observers criticize Sarah Palin's speaking style for being too wordy.*
[Photo: Eric Engman/Stringer/Getty Images]

### RECAP: Using Words Effectively

To hold your audience's attention, keep your language specific and concrete.
To keep your language simple, avoid a long word when a short one will do.
To use your language correctly, consider connotative as well as denotative meanings.
To speak clearly, be as succinct as possible.

# Adapting Your Language Style to Diverse Listeners

To communicate successfully with the diverse group of listeners who comprise your audience, make sure your language is understandable, appropriate, and unbiased.

## Use Language That Your Audience Can Understand

Even if you and all your public-speaking classmates speak English, you probably speak many varieties of the language. Perhaps some of your classmates speak in an **ethnic vernacular**, such as "Spanglish," the combination of English and Spanish often heard near the United States–Mexico border; Cajun, with its influx of French words, frequently spoken in Louisiana; or African American Vernacular English (AAVE). Some of you may reflect where you grew up by your use of **regionalisms**, words or phrases specific to one part of the country but rarely used in quite the same way in other places. Others of you may frequently use **jargon**, the specialized language of your profession or hobby.

**ethnic vernacular**
A variety of English that includes words and phrases used by a specific ethnic group

**regionalism**
A word or phrase used uniquely by speakers in one part of a country

**jargon**
The specialized language of a profession

**standard U.S. English**
The English taught by schools and used in the media, business, and government in the United States

When you give a speech to those who share your ethnic, regional, or professional background, you can communicate successfully with them using these specialized varieties of English. However, when you give a speech to an audience as diverse as the members of your public-speaking class, where do you find a linguistic common ground?

The answer is to use standard U.S. English. **Standard U.S. English** is the language taught by schools and used in the media, business, and the government in the United States. "Standard" does not imply that standard U.S. English is inherently right and all other forms are wrong, only that it conforms to a standard that most speakers of U.S. English will readily understand—even though they may represent a variety of ethnic, regional, and professional backgrounds.

## Use Appropriate Language

Shortly after the September 11, 2001, terrorist attacks, Vice President Dick Cheney made remarks in which he referred to Pakistanis as "Paks." Although he was speaking admiringly of the Pakistani people, he was chided for his use of the term. The variation *Paki* is considered a slur, and *Pak* is only slightly less offensive. Columnist William Safire remarked that "Cheney probably picked up *Paks* in his Pentagon days, but innocent intent is an excuse only once; now he is sensitized, as are we all."[8]

A speaker whose language defames any group—people of particular ethnic, racial, and religious backgrounds or sexual orientations; women; people with disabilities—or whose language might be otherwise considered offensive or risqué runs a great risk of antagonizing audience members. In fact, one study suggests that derogatory language used to describe people with disabilities adversely affects an audience's perceptions of the speaker's persuasiveness, competence, trustworthiness, and sociability.[9]

*You can use standard English to be understandable to most audiences, but you will always want to adapt your words to your audience to avoid bias and to use appropriate terms. What adaptations would you make for this audience?*

[Photo: George Doyle/Getty Images]

## Use Unbiased Language

Even speakers who would never dream of using overtly offensive language may find it difficult to avoid language that more subtly stereotypes or discriminates. Sexist language falls largely into this second category.

Not many years ago, a singular masculine pronoun (*he, him, his*) was the accepted way to refer to a person of unspecified sex:

Everyone should bring *his* book to class tomorrow.

This usage is now considered sexist and unacceptable. Instead, you may include both a masculine and a feminine pronoun:

Everyone should bring *his* or *her* book to class tomorrow.

Or you may reword the sentence so that it is plural and thus gender neutral:

> All students should bring *their* books to class tomorrow.

Also now considered sexist is the use of a masculine noun to refer generically to all people. The editors of *The American Heritage Dictionary of the English Language*, Fourth Edition, consulted a usage panel of 200 writers and scholars on such questions as whether the word *man* was acceptable as meaning "human" in some instances.[10] Only 58 percent of the women on the panel found such usage appropriate. To put it another way: If you were speaking to an audience of these distinguished women, you would offend 42 percent of them by using a phrase such as *modern man*. Although the word *man* is the primary offender, you should also monitor your use of such masculine nouns as *waiter, chairman, fireman*, and *congressman*. Instead choose such gender-neutral alternatives as *server, chair, firefighter*, and *member of Congress*.

CONSIDER THE AUDIENCE

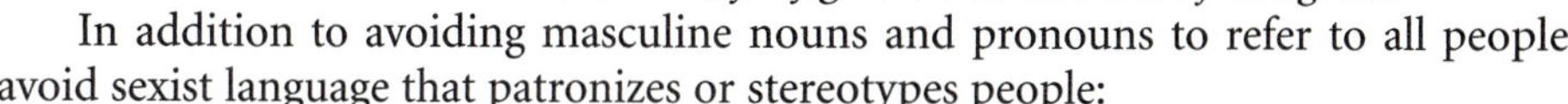

In addition to avoiding masculine nouns and pronouns to refer to all people, avoid sexist language that patronizes or stereotypes people:

| **Sexist** | **Unbiased** |
|---|---|
| President Barack Obama and Michelle enrolled daughters Malia and Sasha in The Sidwell Friends School in Washington, D.C. | President and Mrs. Obama enrolled daughters Malia and Sasha in The Sidwell Friends School in Washington, D.C.<br>*or*<br>Barack and Michelle Obama enrolled daughters Malia and Sasha in The Sidwell Friends School in Washington, D.C. |
| The policeman is an underpaid professional who risks his life daily. | Police are underpaid professionals who risk their lives daily. |
| The male nurse took good care of his patients. (*Note:* The phrase "male nurse" implies that nursing is a typically female profession. The pronoun *his* clarifies the sex of the nurse.) | The nurse took good care of his patients. |

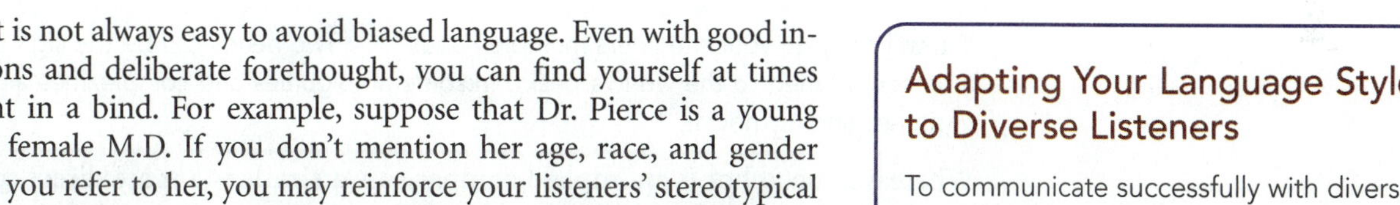

It is not always easy to avoid biased language. Even with good intentions and deliberate forethought, you can find yourself at times caught in a bind. For example, suppose that Dr. Pierce is a young black female M.D. If you don't mention her age, race, and gender when you refer to her, you may reinforce your listeners' stereotypical image of a physician as middle-aged, white, and male. But if you *do* mention these factors, you may be suspected of implying that Dr. Pierce's achievement is unusual. There is no easy answer to this dilemma or others like it. You will have to consider your audience, purpose, and the occasion in deciding how best to identify Dr. Pierce.

As women and members of racial, ethnic, and other minorities have become increasingly visible in such professions as medicine, law, engineering, and politics, the public has grown to expect unbiased, inclusive language from news commentators, teachers, textbooks, and magazines—and from public speakers. Language that does not reflect these changes will disrupt your ability to communicate your message to your audience, which may well include members of the minority group to which you are referring.

**RECAP**

**Adapting Your Language Style to Diverse Listeners**

- To communicate successfully with diverse listeners, use language your audience can understand.
- To avoid offending your audience, use appropriate language.
- To communicate sensitivity to diverse subgroups, use unbiased language.

# Crafting Memorable Word Structures

The president of the United States is scheduled to make an important speech in your hometown. You attend the speech and find his thirty-minute presentation both interesting and informative. In the evening, you turn on the news to see how the networks cover his address. All three major networks excerpt the same ten-second portion of his speech. Why? What makes certain portions of a speech quotable or memorable? Former presidential speechwriter Peggy Noonan has said:

> Great speeches have always had great soundbites. . . . They sum up a point, or make a point in language that is pithy or profound.[11]

In other words, memorable speeches are stylistically distinctive. They create arresting images. And they have what a marketing-communication specialist has termed "ear appeal":

> "Ear appeal" phrases can be like the haunting songs of a musical that the members of the audience find themselves humming on the way home. Even if people want to forget them, they can't.[12]

Earlier in this chapter, we discussed the importance of using words that are concrete, unbiased, vivid, simple, and correct. In this section, we turn our attention to groups of words—phrases and sentences—that create drama, figurative images, and cadences. The memorable word structures summarized in Table 10.1 (page 227) can help you craft a speech that has both "eye and ear appeal."[13]

## Creating Figurative Images

One way to make your message memorable is to use figures of speech to create arresting images. A **figure of speech** deviates from the ordinary, expected meanings of words, to make a description or comparison unique, vivid, and memorable. Common figures of speech include metaphors, similes, and personification.

- **Metaphors and similes** A **metaphor** is an implied comparison of two things that are similar in some vital way. Writer Tim O'Brien used the metaphor of "two heads" to challenge a student audience to remain open-minded throughout their lives:

> You will carry on your shoulders multiple heads. . . . Two heads can be the sign of a person attuned to the world's pesky, irksome ambiguities and complexities and mysteries and unknowns.[14]

Whereas a metaphor is an implied comparison, a **simile** is a more direct comparison that includes the word *like* or *as*. In a March 2007 speech commemorating the Selma, Alabama, voting rights march of 1965, Barack Obama used a simile to compare the marchers to Moses:

> Like Moses, they challenged Pharaoh. . . .[15]

Speakers often turn to metaphor and simile in times that are especially momentous or overwhelming—times when, as one speaker has said, "the ordinary diction of our lives finds itself unequal to a challenge."[16] In the hours and days after the September 11, 2001, terrorist attacks on the United States, various speakers used such metaphorical phrases as "one more circle of Dante's hell"; "nuclear winter"; and "the crater of a volcano" to describe the site of the destroyed World Trade Center buildings in New York.[17] Such language is often categorized as **crisis rhetoric**.

- **Personification** **Personification** is the attribution of human qualities to inanimate things or ideas. Franklin Roosevelt personified nature as a generous living provider in this line from his first inaugural address:

> Nature still offers her bounty and human efforts have multiplied it. Plenty is at our doorstep.[18]

**figure of speech**
Language that deviates from the ordinary, expected meaning of words to make a description or comparison unique, vivid, and memorable

**metaphor**
An implied comparison between two things or concepts

**simile**
A comparison between two things that uses the word *like* or *as*

**crisis rhetoric**
Language used by speakers during momentous or overwhelming times

**personification**
The attribution of human qualities to inanimate things or ideas

## Creating Drama

Another way to make phrases and sentences memorable is to use the potential of such structures to create drama in your speech—to keep the audience in suspense or to catch them slightly off guard by saying something in a way that differs from the way they expected you to say it.

- **Use a short sentence to express a vitally important thought**. We have already talked about the value of using short, simple words. Short, simple sentences can have much the same power. Columnist George F. Will points out that the most eloquent sentence in Lincoln's memorable second inaugural address is just four words long:[19]

> And the war came.

Other strategies for achieving drama in your speech include three stylistic devices: omission, inversion, and suspension.

- **Use omission: Leave out a word or phrase that the audience expects to hear.** When telegrams were a more common means of communication, senders tried to use as few words as possible because they were charged by the word, and the more they could leave out, the cheaper the telegram was. But the words you leave out must be understood by your listeners or readers. For example, a captain of a World War II Navy destroyer used **omission** to inform headquarters of his successful efforts at sighting and sinking an enemy submarine. He spared all details when he cabled back to headquarters: "Sighted sub—sank same." Using as few words as possible, he communicated his message in a memorable way. About 2,000 years earlier, another military commander informed his superiors in Rome of his conquest of Gaul with the economical message: "I came, I saw, I conquered." That commander was Julius Caesar.
- **Use inversion: Reverse the normal word order of a phrase or sentence.** John F. Kennedy used **inversion** when he changed the usual subject-verb-object sentence pattern to object-subject-verb in this brief statement from his inaugural speech:

> This much we pledge. . . .[20]

Similarly, Barack Obama inverted the word order of this statement in his own inaugural address:

> That we are in the midst of crisis is now well understood.[21]

- **Use suspension: Place a key word or phrase at the end of a sentence rather than at the beginning**. When you read a mystery novel, you are held in suspense until you reach the end and learn "who done it." The stylistic technique of verbal **suspension** does something similar. Like inversion, suspension changes the expected word order or sentence pattern, in this case to give a key word or phrase the emphasis afforded by placement at the end of a sentence. Obama employed suspension to emphasize the verb *do* in his inaugural address declaration,

> All this we can do. All this we will do.[22]

Advertisers use the technique of suspension frequently. A few years ago, the Coca-Cola Company used suspension as the cornerstone of its worldwide advertising campaign. Rather than saying "Coke goes better with everything," the copywriter decided to stylize the message by making *Coke* the last word in the sentence. The slogan became "Things go better with Coke." Again, the stylized version was more memorable because it used language in an unexpected way.

## Creating Cadence

Even very small children can memorize nursery rhymes and commercial jingles with relative ease. As we grow older, we may make up rhythms and rhymes to help us

**omission**
Leaving out a word or phrase the listener expects to hear

**inversion**
Reversing the normal word order of a phrase or sentence

**suspension**
Withholding a key word or phrase until the end of a sentence

remember such facts as "Thirty days hath September / April June, and November" and "Red sky at night / A sailor's delight." Why? Rhythms are memorable. The public speaker can take advantage of language rhythms, not by speaking in singsong patterns, but by using such stylistic devices as repetition, parallelism, antithesis, and alliteration.

- **Repetition** **Repetition** of a key word or phrase gives rhythm and power to your message and makes it memorable. Perhaps the best-known modern example of repetition in a speech is Martin Luther King Jr.'s ringing declaration, "I have a dream." Repeated eight times in King's August 28, 1963, speech at the Lincoln Memorial in Washington, D.C., the phrase became the title by which the speech is best known.

- **Parallelism** Whereas *repetition* refers to using identical words, **parallelism** refers to using identical grammatical patterns. When he accepted the Nobel Peace Prize in 2009, Barack Obama used parallel grammatical structures to express optimism:

> We can acknowledge that oppression will always be with us, and still strive for justice. We can admit the intractability of depravation and still strive for dignity. We can understand that there will be war, and still strive for peace.[23]

**repetition**
Use of a key word or phrase more than once for emphasis

**parallelism**
Use of the same grammatical pattern for two or more phrases, clauses, or sentences

**antithesis**
Opposition, such as that used in two-part sentences in which the second part contrasts in meaning with the first

The three sentences that begin with "We can acknowledge," "We can admit," and "We can understand" follow the same grammatical pattern of *pronoun* (*We*) + *two verb phrases.*

- **Antithesis** The word *antithesis* means "opposition." In language style, a sentence that uses **antithesis** has two parts with parallel structures but contrasting meanings. Speakers have long realized the dramatic potential of antithesis. In his first inaugural address, Franklin Roosevelt declared:

> Our true destiny is not to be ministered unto but to minister to ourselves and to our fellow men.[24]

*In her April 2007 convocation address following the shooting deaths at Virginia Tech, poet and Virginia Tech Professor Nikki Giovanni repeated no less than five times the ringing affirmation, "We are Virginia Tech."*[25]

[Photo: AP Wide World Photos/Steve Helber]

Hillary Clinton used antithesis in a speech delivered during her 2008 campaign for the presidential nomination:

> In the end the true test is not the speeches a president delivers, it's whether the president delivers on the speeches.[26]

Antithesis is not restricted to politicians. When William Faulkner accepted the Nobel Prize for literature in 1950, he spoke the now famous antithetical phrase,

> I believe that man will not merely endure: he will prevail.[27]

An antithetical statement is a good way to end a speech. The cadence it creates will make the statement memorable.

- **Alliteration** **Alliteration** is the repetition of a consonant sound (usually an initial consonant) several times in a phrase, clause, or sentence. Alliteration adds cadence to a thought. Consider these examples:

| **Alliterative Phrase** | **Speaker** | **Occasion** |
|---|---|---|
| *discipline and direction* | Franklin Roosevelt | first inaugural address[28] |
| *confidence and courage* | Franklin Roosevelt | first fireside chat[29] |
| *disaster and disappointment* | Winston Churchill | speech urging British resistence[30] |
| *virility, valour, and civic virtue* | Winston Churchill | speech to U.S. Congress [31] |
| *friends and former foes* | Barack Obama | inaugural address[32] |

Used sparingly, alliteration can add cadence to your rhetoric.

**alliteration**
The repetition of a consonant sound (usually the first consonant) several times in a phrase, clause, or sentence

## TABLE 10.1 Crafting Memorable Word Structures

| Word Structures with Figurative Imagery | |
|---|---|
| Metaphor | Makes an implied comparison. |
| Simile | Compares by using the word *like* or *as*. |
| Personification | Attributes human qualities to inanimate things or ideas. |
| **Word Structures with Drama** | |
| Short sentence | Emphasizes an important idea by stating it in a few well-chosen words. |
| Omission | Boils an idea down to its essence by leaving out understood words. |
| Inversion | Reverses the expected order of words and phrases. |
| Suspension | Places a key word at the end of a phrase or sentence. |
| **Word Structures with Cadence** | |
| Repetition | Repeats a key word or phrase several times for emphasis. |
| Parallelism | Uses the same grammatical pattern. |
| Antithesis | Uses parallel structures but opposing meanings in two parts of a sentence. |
| Alliteration | Uses the same consonant sound twice or more in a phrase. |

## LEARNING FROM GREAT SPEAKERS

### John F. Kennedy (1917–1963)

The inaugural address of John F. Kennedy, the 35th president of the United States, is one of the great speeches of history, in large part because of its memorable style. Kennedy had told his speechwriter Ted Sorensen to study Lincoln's Gettysburg Address and discover the secrets of its success.[33] Sorensen found that Lincoln had relied heavily on short words; as a result, 71 percent of Kennedy's speech was composed of monosyllabic words. Kennedy also copied some of the sentence patterns Lincoln had used. The most famous stylistic device of Kennedy's speech, however, the antithetical "Ask not," was Kennedy's own.

You don't need a professional speechwriter to make your speeches memorable. To polish your prose, consider using short sentences or the techniques of omission, inversion, and suspension. Use such devices as repetition, parallelism, antithesis, and alliteration to create a memorable cadence. You need not overdo it. Just one or two well-polished phrases in your talk can be like just the right notes in a song.

[Photo: AP Wide World Photos]

## Analyzing an Example of Memorable Word Structure

We'd like to illustrate all techniques for creating drama and cadence with one final example.[34] If you asked almost anyone for the most quoted line from John F. Kennedy's speeches, that quote would probably be "Ask not what your country can do for you; ask what you can do for your country," from his inaugural address. Besides expressing a noble thought, a prime reason this line is so quotable is that it uses so many stylistic techniques.

"Ask not . . ." is an example of omission. The subject, *you*, is not stated. "Ask not" is also an example of inversion. In casual everyday conversation, we would usually say "do not ask" rather than "ask not." The inversion makes the opening powerful and attention-grabbing.

The sentence also employs the technique of suspension. The key message, "ask what you can do for your country," is suspended, or delayed, until the end of the sentence. If the sentence structure had been reversed, the impact would not have been as dramatic. Consider: "Ask what you can do for your country rather than what your country can do for you."

Kennedy used parallelism and antithesis. The sentence is made up of two clauses with parallel construction, one in opposition to the other.

He also used the technique of repetition. He used a form of the word *you* four times in a sentence of seventeen words. In fact, he used only eight different words in his seventeen-word sentence. Just one word in the entire sentence, *not*, occurs only once.

Finally, Kennedy added alliteration to the sentence with the words *ask*, *can*, and *country*. The alliterative *k* sound is repeated at more or less even intervals.

Although the passage we have analyzed does not include figurative images, the speech from which it comes does contain memorable figurative language, most notably the metaphors "chains of poverty," "beachhead of cooperation," and "jungle of suspicion." Kennedy used figurative imagery, drama, and cadence to give his inaugural address "eye and ear appeal" and make it memorable—not just to those who heard it initially, but also to those of us who hear, read, and study it more than fifty years later.

# Using Memorable Word Structures Effectively

Having explored ways to add style and interest to the language of your speech, we must now consider how best to put those techniques into practice.

- **Use distinctive stylistic devices sparingly.** Even though we have made great claims for the value of style, do not overdo it. Including too much highly stylized language can put the focus on your language rather than on your content.
- **Use stylistic devices at specific points in your speech.** Save your use of stylistic devices for times during your speech when you want your audience to remember your key ideas or when you wish to capture their attention. Some kitchen mixers have a "burst of power" switch to help churn through difficult mixing chores with extra force. Think of the stylistic devices we have reviewed as opportunities to provide a burst of power to your ideas. Use them in your opening sentences, statements of key ideas, and conclusion.
- **Use stylistic devices to economize.** When sentences become too long or complex, see if you can recast them with antithesis or suspension. Also remember the possibility of omission.

## CONFIDENTLY CONNECTING WITH YOUR AUDIENCE

### Use Words to Manage Your Anxiety

Even as you work on polishing your language for your listeners, give yourself an affirming mental pep talk. If you find your anxiety level increasing, remind yourself that you are knowledgeable and prepared to connect with your audience. Think positively, and translate that positive thinking into words of affirmation for yourself.

# STUDY GUIDE

## Differentiating Oral and Written Language Styles

Oral language is more personal and less formal than written style. Speakers must also provide their audiences with more repetition than writers should use.

## Using Words Effectively

Effective speakers use specific, concrete words to evoke clear mental images in their listeners. They also choose the simplest appropriate words. As a speaker, be sure to use words correctly and to keep in mind the connotations of words, as well as their dictionary definitions. And speak concisely, eliminating unnecessary words and phrases.

### Being Audience-Centered

- Your credibility and effectiveness with your audience depends in part on your ability to use the English language correctly.
- Be aware of the possibility that your words may trigger personal connotations for listeners.

### A Question of Ethics

- A high school principal asked a student graduation speaker to avoid using the word *rape* in her graduation speech. The student, who had been raped as a 14-year-old sophomore, argued that she wanted to use the concrete word to help her emphasize to her classmates that they could overcome even the most devastating experiences in life. The principal countered that he was suggesting ways to make the language of the speech more appropriate to the occasion and the audience.[35] What is your opinion on this issue? What would you advise the speaker to do?

### Speaker's Homepage: Using Internet Resources to Polish Your Spoken Prose

Consider the following Web sites when you want help finding the words you need for your speech.

- To find the meaning of a word or choose just the right word, try the dictionary and thesaurus at Merriam-Webster Online: www.merriam-webster.com. You can also use a collection of specialty dictionaries and thesauruses: www.yourdictionary.com.
- The Rhyme Zone at www.rhymezone.com can help you find a rhyming word.
- For grammar and style help, check the style guides offered by Bartleby: www.bartleby.com/usage.

## Adapting Your Language Style to Diverse Listeners

Use language your listeners can understand. Use appropriate language to avoid offending your audience. Use unbiased language to communicate in a sensitive way to members of subgroups in your audience.

### Being Audience-Centered

- People in your audience whose first language is not English may not be familiar with the nuances of figures of speech or the connotations of some words. It may be necessary to explain your intentions in detail, rather than rely on word association.

### A Question of Ethics

- A letter to an advice columnist suggested that the term *maiden name*, used to refer to the surname a married woman had when single, is offensive to married women who do not change their surname to that of their husband.[36] Do you agree that the term *maiden name* is sexist? Why or why not? How does this question affect you as a public speaker?

## Crafting Memorable Word Structures

You can create arresting images through such figures of speech as metaphors, similes, and personification. You can create drama by using short sentences for important ideas, strategically omitting unneeded words, and structuring sentences with key words at the end to create suspense. Use repetition, alliteration, parallelism, and antithesis to create memorable word cadence.

### Using What You've Learned

- The following are memorable metaphors from historical speeches:[37]

  I have but one lamp by which my feet are guided, and that is the lamp of experience.

  an iron curtain

  snake pit of racial hatred

  Speak softly and carry a big stick.

  First, explain what each metaphor means. Then express the same idea in ordinary language and explain what is gained or lost in doing so.

## Using Memorable Word Structures Effectively

Avoid overusing the stylistic devices described in this chapter. Look for ways to streamline your words for more impact. Use stylistic devices that help you make sentences shorter and simpler.

### Being Audience-Centered

- Save your use of stylistic devices for key ideas that you want your audience to remember or points in your speech when you wish to capture listeners' attention.

### Using What You've Learned

- A friend asks for advice on polishing the language in her speech. Offer her at least three general suggestions, based on this chapter, for using language effectively.

# SPEECH WORKSHOP

## Conducting a "Language Style Audit" of Your Speech

To help make your speech interesting and memorable, do a language style audit. Using either your preparation outline or your speaking notes, try to find one or more passages that you can revise by applying specific stylistic techniques to add vividness and interest. Use the following checklist to help you revise your words.

## Use Words Effectively

- What words can you make more **concrete**? (See pages 219–220 for tips on making your words concrete.)

| Abstract Word | Concrete Word |
|---|---|
| | |

- Can you replace any unnecessarily long or complex words with shorter, more **simple** words? (See page 220 for recommendations for making your words simple.)

| Long, Complex Word | Short, Simple Word |
|---|---|
| | |

- Are you using **correct** words? (See pages 220–227 for reminders about using words correctly.) List corrections to your grammar and word usage.

| Incorrect Word | Correct Word |
|---|---|
| | |

## Use Words to Add Interest

- Where can you add an appropriate **metaphor** or **simile**? (See page 224 for tips on using metaphors and similes.) ______

- Which long, complex sentences can you make briefer and more to the point? (See page 225 for examples of short sentences and **omission**.) ______

- Can you find a way to use **inversion** or **suspension**? (See page 225 for examples and tips on using these stylistic techniques.) ______

- Can you **repeat** key words or phrases or cast them as **parallel** grammatical structures? (See page 226.) ______

- Can you find a place in your speech to use **antithesis**? (See pages 226–227.) ______

- Can you find a passage in which you might use **alliteration**? (Remember to use this technique sparingly; see page 227.) ______

SPEAK THE SPEECH, I PRAY YOU, AS I PRONOUNCED IT TO YOU, TRIPPINGLY ON THE TONGUE.

—WILLIAM SHAKESPEARE

Francesco Granacci (1477–1543), *Dispute of St. Apollonia.* Accademia, Florence, Italy. Finsiel/Alinari/Art Resource, N.Y.

OUTLINE

# 11 Delivering Your Speech

OBJECTIVES

**After studying this chapter you should be able to do the following:**

1. Identify three reasons delivery is important to a public speaker.
2. Identify and describe four types of delivery.
3. Identify and illustrate physical characteristics of effective delivery.
4. Describe the steps to follow when you rehearse your speech.
5. List four suggestions for enhancing the final delivery of your speech.

What's more important: what you say or how you say it? Delivery has long been considered an important part of public speaking. But is the delivery of your speech more important than the content of your message? Since ancient Greece, people have argued about the role delivery plays in public speaking.

More than 2,300 years ago, some thinkers held that delivery was not an "elevated" topic of study. In his classic treatise *The Rhetoric,* written in 333 B.C.E., Aristotle claimed that "the battle should be fought out on the facts of the case alone; and therefore everything outside the direct proof is really superfluous." Writing in the first century C.E., Quintilian, Roman rhetorician and author of the first book on speech training, acknowledged the importance of delivery when he said that the beginning speaker should strive for an "extempore," or conversational, delivery style. His countryman, the great orator Cicero, claimed that without effective delivery, "a speaker of the highest mental capacity can be held in no esteem, whereas one of moderate abilities, with this qualification, may surpass even those of the highest talent." Sixteen centuries later, the elocution movement carried the emphasis on delivery to an extreme. For elocutionists, speech training consisted largely of techniques and exercises for improving posture, movement, and vocal quality.[1]

Today, communication teachers believe that both content and delivery contribute to speaking effectiveness. One survey suggested that "developing effective delivery" is a primary goal of most speech teachers.[2] Considerable research supports the claim that delivery plays an important role in influencing how audiences react to a speaker and his or her message. It is your audience who will determine whether you are successful. Delivery counts.

Although courses in public speaking are offered in countries throughout the world, most of the formal instruction about how to deliver a speech is offered in the United States. Since it's not possible for us to provide a comprehensive compendium of each cultural expectation you may face as you give speeches in a variety of cultural settings, our advice about speech delivery will be closely related to the discipline of communication as practiced in the United States. But as we discuss speech delivery throughout this chapter, we will offer suggestions for meeting the expectations and preferences of other cultures.

# The Power of Speech Delivery

The way you hold your notes, your gestures and stance, and your impatient adjustment of your glasses all contribute to the overall effect of your speech. **Nonverbal communication** is communication other than through written or spoken language that creates meaning for someone. Nonverbal factors such as your eye contact, posture, vocal quality, and facial expression play a major role in the communication process. As much as 65 percent of the social meaning of messages is based on nonverbal expression.[3] Why does your delivery hold such power to affect how your audience will receive your message? One reason is that listeners expect a good speaker to provide good delivery. Your unspoken message is also how you express your feelings and emotions to an audience. And ultimately, an audience believes what it *sees* more than what you *say*.

## Listeners Expect Effective Delivery

**nonverbal communication**
Communication other than written or spoken language that creates meaning

**nonverbal expectancy theory**
A communication theory that suggests that if listeners' expectations about how communication should be expressed are violated, listeners will feel less favorable toward the communicator of the message

In a public-speaking situation, nonverbal elements have an important influence on the audience's perceptions about a speaker's effectiveness. Communication researcher Judee Burgoon and her colleagues have developed a theory called **nonverbal expectancy theory**. The essence of the theory is this: People have certain expectations as to how you should communicate.[4] If you don't behave as people think you should, your listeners will feel that you have violated their expectations. The theory predicts that if a listener expects you to have effective delivery, and your delivery is poor, you will lose credibility. There is evidence that although many speakers do not deliver speeches effectively, audiences nevertheless expect a good speech to be well delivered.

Different audiences prefer different styles of delivery; there is no ideal style of delivery or set of prescribed gestures that is appropriate for all audiences. As we have also emphasized, audience members with different cultural backgrounds will hold different assumptions about how a speech should be presented. In our discussion of delivery, we note how the cultural and ethnic background of your audience affects the delivery style your listeners prefer.

More than one hundred years ago, speakers were taught to deliver orations using a more formal style of speaking than most people prefer today. In newsreels of speakers during the early part of the twentieth century, their gestures and movements look stilted and unnatural because they were taught to use dramatic, planned gestures. If you are speaking to an audience of a thousand people, using a microphone to reach the back of the auditorium, your listeners may expect a more formal delivery style. But your public-speaking class members would probably find it odd if you spoke to them using a formal oratorical style that resembled the way a politician would have addressed a political rally in 1910.

What do most people consider effective delivery today? Effective speech delivery for most North American listeners has been described as "platform conversation." Effective delivery today includes having good eye contact with your listeners. It includes using appropriate gestures, just as you do in conversations with your friends (but, of course, avoiding distracting mannerisms such as jingling change in your pockets or unconsciously playing with your hair). Effective delivery also means your voice has a natural, conversational tone, varied inflection (rather than a droning monotone), and an intensity that communicates that you're interested in your listeners.

**emotional contagion theory**
A theory suggesting that people tend to "catch" the emotions of others

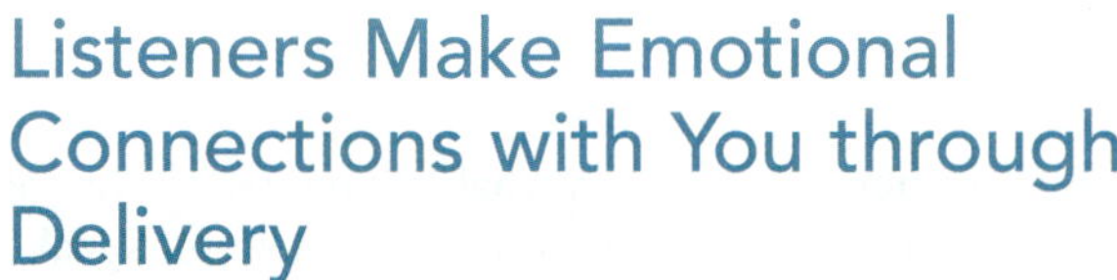

## Listeners Make Emotional Connections with You through Delivery

Nonverbal behavior is particularly important in communicating feelings, emotions, attitudes, likes, and dislikes to an audience. One researcher found that we communicate as little as 7 percent of the emotional impact of a message by the words we use.[5] About 38 percent hinges on such qualities of voice as inflection, intensity, or loudness, and 55 percent hinges on our facial expressions. Generalizing from these findings, we may say that we communicate approximately 93 percent of emotional meaning nonverbally. Although some scholars question whether these findings can be applied to all communication settings, the research does suggest that the manner of delivery provides important information about a speaker's feelings and emotions.[6] Being aware of your audience's expectations can help you determine the amount of emotional expression you exhibit to your listeners.

Another reason to pay attention to how you communicate emotions when delivering a speech is that emotions are contagious. **Emotional contagion theory** suggests that people tend to "catch" the emotions of others.[7] If you want your listeners to feel a certain emotion, then it's important for you to express that emotion yourself. Have you ever noticed that when you watch a movie in a crowded movie theater where others are laughing, you're more likely to laugh too? Producers of TV situation comedies use a laugh track or record the laughter of a live audience to enhance the emotional reactions of home viewers; these producers know that emotions are contagious.

*Audience members respond to a speaker's nonverbal behavior as strongly as they do to the verbal message. A good speaker uses facial expression and body language to connect with the audience emotionally.*

[Photo: SuperStock, Inc.]

RECAP

**The Power of Speech Delivery**

Nonverbal communication:

- creates a majority of the meaning of a speech.
- disappoints audiences when it violates their expectations.
- communicates almost all the emotion in a speech.
- can help listeners "catch" the speaker's feelings.
- is often more believable than words.

Your delivery enhances the overall feelings that listeners have toward you and your speech. One study found that when a speaker's delivery was effective, the audience felt greater pleasure and had a more positive emotional response than when the same speaker had poor delivery.[8] In addition to these stronger emotional responses, listeners seemed to understand speakers better and to believe them more when their delivery was good. Clearly, if you want your audience to respond positively to both you and your message, it pays to polish your delivery.

## Listeners Believe What They See

"I'm very glad to speak with you tonight," drones the speaker in a monotone, eyes glued to his notes. His audience probably does not believe him. When our nonverbal delivery contradicts what we say, people generally believe the nonverbal message. In this case, the speaker is communicating that he's *not* glad to be talking to this audience.

We usually believe nonverbal messages because they are more difficult to fake. Although we can monitor certain parts of our nonverbal behavior, it is difficult to control all of it consciously. Research suggests that a person trying to deceive someone may speak with a higher vocal pitch, at a slower rate, and with more pronunciation mistakes than normal.[9] Blushing, sweating, and changed breathing patterns also often belie our stated meaning. As the saying goes, "What you do speaks so loud, I can't hear what you say."

# Methods of Delivery

The style of delivery you choose will influence your nonverbal behaviors. There are four basic methods of delivery from which a speaker can choose: manuscript speaking, memorized speaking, impromptu speaking, and extemporaneous speaking. They are summarized in Table 11.1 on page 239. Let's consider each in some detail.

## Manuscript Speaking

You have a speech to present and are afraid you will forget what you have prepared to say. So you write your speech and then read it to your audience.

Speech teachers frown on this approach, particularly for public-speaking students. Reading is usually a poor way to deliver a speech. Although it may provide some insurance against forgetting the speech, **manuscript speaking** is rarely done well enough to be interesting. You have probably attended a lecture that was read and wondered, "Why doesn't he just make a copy of the speech for everyone in the audience rather than reading it to us?"

However, some speeches should be read. One advantage of reading from a manuscript is that you can choose your words very carefully when dealing with a sensitive and critical issue. The president of the United States, for example, often finds it useful to have his remarks carefully scripted. There are times, however, when it is impossible to have a manuscript speech at hand.

When possible, during times of crisis, statements to the press by government, education, or business leaders should be carefully crafted rather than tossed off casually. An inaccurate or misspoken statement could have serious consequences.

On those occasions when you do need to use a manuscript, here are several tips to help you deliver your message effectively:[10]

- Indicate in writing on your manuscript where to pause or emphasize certain words.
- Type your speech in short, easy-to scan phrases.

**manuscript speaking**
Reading a speech from a written text

**TABLE 11.1 Methods of Delivery**

| Method | Description | Disadvantages | Advantages |
|---|---|---|---|
| Manuscript speaking | Reading your speech from a prepared text | • Your speech is likely to sound as if it is being read.<br>• It takes considerable skill and practice to make the message sound interesting. | • You can craft the message carefully, which is especially important if it is being presented to the media.<br>• The language can be beautifully refined, polished, and stylized. |
| Memorized speaking | Giving a speech from memory without using notes | • You may forget your speech.<br>• You may sound overrehearsed and mechanical. | • You can have direct eye contact with the audience.<br>• You can move around freely or use gestures while speaking, since you don't need notes. |
| Impromptu speaking | Delivering a speech without preparing in advance | • Your speech is likely to be less well organized and smoothly delivered.<br>• Your lack of advance preparation and research makes it more difficult to cite evidence and supporting material for the message. | • You can more easily adapt to how your audience is reacting to you and your message during the speech.<br>• The audience sees and hears an authentic speech that is spontaneously delivered without notes. |
| Extemporaneous speaking | Knowing the major ideas, which have been outlined, but not memorizing the exact wording | • It takes time to prepare an extemporaneous speech.<br>• It takes skill to deliver the speech well. | • It is well organized and well researched.<br>• Your speech sounds spontaneous and yet appropriately polished. |

- Use only the upper two-thirds of the paper for your manuscript.
- Establish eye contact with listeners; don't look over their heads.
- Make eye contact at the ends of sentences.
- Use your normal, natural speed of delivery.
- If you're afraid you'll lose your place, unobtrusively use your index finger to keep your place in the manuscript.
- Speak with natural vocal variation; vary your pitch, inflection, and rhythm so that you don't sound like you're reading.
- Practice with your manuscript.
- Use appropriate and natural gestures and movement.

## Memorized Speaking

"All right," you think, "since reading a speech is hard to pull off, I'll write my speech out word for word and then memorize it." You're pretty sure that no one will be able to tell because you won't be using notes. **Memorized speaking** also has the advantage of allowing you to have maximum eye contact with the audience. But the key differences between speaking and writing are evident in a memorized speech, just as they can be heard in a manuscript speech. Most memorized speeches *sound* stiff, stilted,

**memorized speaking**
Delivering a speech word for word from memory without using notes

and overrehearsed. You also run the risk of forgetting parts of your speech and awkwardly searching for words in front of your audience. And you won't be able to make on-the-spot adaptations to your listeners if your speech is memorized. For these reasons, speech teachers do not encourage their students to memorize speeches for class presentation.

If you are accepting an award, introducing a speaker, making announcements, or delivering other brief remarks, however, a memorized delivery style is sometimes acceptable. But as with manuscript speaking, you must take care to make your presentation sound lively and interesting.

## Impromptu Speaking

You have undoubtedly already delivered many impromptu presentations. Your response to a question posed by a teacher in class and your unrehearsed rebuttal to a comment made by a colleague during a meeting are examples of impromptu presentations. The impromptu method is often described as "thinking on your feet" or "speaking off the cuff." The advantage of **impromptu speaking** is that you can speak informally, maintaining direct eye contact with the audience. But unless a speaker is extremely talented or has learned and practiced the techniques of impromptu speaking, the speech itself will be unimpressive. An impromptu speech usually lacks logical organization and thorough research. There are times, of course, when you may be called on to speak without advance warning or to improvise when something goes awry in your efforts to deliver your planned message. This was the case when President Bill Clinton was delivering his first State of the Union address in 1993 and the teleprompter scrolled the wrong text of his speech for seven minutes. What did he do as millions of people watched on television? He kept going. Drawing on his years of speaking experience, he continued to speak; no one watching knew about the error until afterward.

If you know you will be giving a speech, prepare and rehearse it. Don't just make mental notes or assume that you will find the words when you need them. It was Mark Twain who said, "A good impromptu speech takes about three weeks to prepare."

The Reverend Jesse Jackson is known for his skill as an impromptu speaker. It's been reported that he got a *D* in his preaching class because he refused to write his sermons out word for word as his professor requested. He was able to deliver impromptu orations that skillfully and powerfully moved listeners to respond to his message. Once, knowing he was to speak after one of Jackson's charismatically delivered speeches, Martin Luther King Jr. allegedly developed a sudden case of laryngitis.[11] The Reverend Jackson certainly has speaking talent, but he also uses principles and skills that you can use to enhance your impromptu speaking ability. When you are called on to deliver an improvised or impromptu speech, the following guidelines can help ease you through it.

- **Consider your audience.** Just as you have learned to do in other speaking situations, when you are called on for impromptu remarks, think first of your audience. Who are the members of your audience? What are their common characteristics and interests? What do they know about your topic? What do they expect you to say? What is the occasion of your speech? A quick mental review of these questions will help ensure that even impromptu remarks are audience-centered.
- **Be brief.** When you are asked to deliver an off-the-cuff speech, your audience knows the circumstances and will not expect or even want a lengthy discourse. One to three minutes is a realistic time frame for most impromptu situations. Some spur-of-the-moment remarks, such as press statements, may be even shorter.
- **Organize!** Even off-the-cuff remarks should not falter or ramble. Effective impromptu speakers still organize their ideas into an introduction, body,

**impromptu speaking**
Delivering a speech without advance preparation

and conclusion. Consider organizing your points using a simple organizational strategy such as chronological order or a topical pattern. A variation on the chronological pattern is the past, present, future model of addressing an issue. This pattern is well known to students who compete in impromptu speaking contests. The speaker organizes the impromptu speech by discussing (1) what has happened in the past, (2) what is happening now, and (3) what may happen in the future.

- **Speak honestly, but with reserve, from personal experience and knowledge.** Because there is no opportunity to conduct any kind of research before delivering an impromptu speech, you will have to speak from your own experience and knowledge. Remember, audiences almost always respond favorably to personal illustrations, so use any appropriate and relevant ones that come to mind. Of course, the more knowledge you have about the subject to be discussed, the easier it will be to speak about it off the cuff. But do not make up information or provide facts or figures you're not certain about. An honest "I don't know" or a very brief statement is more appropriate.
- **Be cautious.** No matter how much knowledge you have, if your subject is at all sensitive or your information is classified, be careful when discussing it during your impromptu speech. If asked about a controversial topic, give an honest but noncommittal answer. You can always elaborate later, but you can never take back something rash you have already said. It is better to be cautious than sorry!

## Extemporaneous Speaking

If you are not reading from a manuscript, reciting from memory, or speaking impromptu, what's left? **Extemporaneous speaking** is the approach most communication teachers recommend for most situations. When delivering a speech extemporaneously, you speak from a written or memorized general outline, but you do not have the exact wording in front of you or in memory. You have rehearsed the speech so that you know key ideas and their organization, but not to the degree that the speech sounds memorized. An extemporaneous style is conversational; it gives your audience the impression that the speech is being created as they listen to it, and to some extent it is. Martin Luther King Jr. was an expert in speaking extemporaneously; he typically did not use a manuscript when he spoke. He had notes, but he often drew on the energy of his audience as well as his own natural speaking talents to make his oratory come alive.[12] As Dr. King noted when delivering his stirring "I Have a Dream" speech, "I started out reading the speech then all of a sudden this thing came out of me that I have used—I'd used it many times before, that thing about 'I have a dream'—and I just felt I wanted to use it here."[13] He made a good decision to improvise. According to a study by the National Endowment for the Humanities, high school seniors were more likely to know the source of "I Have a Dream" (97 percent) than that of the Gettysburg Address or the Declaration of Independence.[14] You can use the same extemporaneous techniques he used to draw on your audience's energy and make your speech a living message rather than a canned presentation.

Audiences prefer to hear something live rather than something canned. Even though you can't tell the difference between a taped or live performance when it is broadcast on TV, you would probably prefer seeing it live. Seeing something happening now provides added interest and excitement. An extemporaneous speech sounds live rather than as though it were prepared yesterday or weeks ago. The extemporaneous method reflects the advantages of a well-organized speech delivered in an interesting and vivid manner.

**extemporaneous speaking**
Speaking from a written or memorized speech outline without having memorized the exact wording of the speech

RECAP

**Methods of Delivery**

- Manuscript—use only when exact wording is crucial
- Memorized—can sound stiff or be forgotten
- Impromptu—use only when preparation is not possible
- Extemporaneous—most recommended for speech class

How do you develop an extemporaneous delivery style? Here are tips for what to do at three stages in your rehearsal:

- Early rehearsal: When you first rehearse your speech, use as many notes as you need to help you remember your ideas; but each time you rehearse, rely less and less on your notes.
- Later rehearsal: When you find yourself starting to use exactly the same words each time you rehearse, you're memorizing your speech; either stop rehearsing or consider other ways of expressing your ideas.
- Final rehearsal: Revise your speaking notes so that you need only brief notes or notes for only lengthy quotations.

## Characteristics of Effective Delivery

You have learned the importance of effective delivery and have identified four methods of delivery. You now know that for most speaking situations, you should strive for a conversational style. But you may still have a number of specific questions about enhancing the effectiveness of your delivery. Typical concerns include "What do I do with my hands?" "Is it all right to move around while I speak?" "How can I make my voice sound interesting?" Although these concerns may seem daunting, being confident about your ability to present a well-prepared and well-rehearsed speech is the best antidote to jitters about delivery. Practice and a focus on communicating your message to your audience are vital for effective communication and great for your confidence.

To help answer specific questions about presenting a speech, we consider seven categories of nonverbal behavior that affect delivery. Specifically, we will help you improve your eye contact, use appropriate gestures, move meaningfully, maintain an appropriate posture, use facial expressions to communicate emotion, use your voice both to be understood and to maintain interest, and ensure that your personal appearance is appropriate. The ancient Roman orator Cicero, author of *De Oratore*, called these behaviors the "language of the body."[15]

### LEARNING FROM GREAT SPEAKERS

**Marcus Tullius Cicero** (106–43 B.C.E)

Although the ancient Greeks contributed much to the study and practice of public speaking, they focused very little on delivery. Marcus Tullius Cicero, a Roman, was one of the first to emphasize the importance of delivery, especially gestures and voice. In addition to writing about effective speaking, most notably in his three-volume *De Oratore*, Cicero himself was a great speaker. He became especially well known for his effective delivery, which he developed by studying the techniques of actors and by rehearsing.

You, too, can benefit from the techniques that Cicero used. To enhance the effectiveness of your delivery, practice good eye contact, appropriate gestures, and vocal variation. In addition, practice speaking while standing and imagine that you are presenting your speech to your audience. Spending time rehearsing your speech will not only help you feel more comfortable presenting your message, it will also enhance your ability to connect with your listeners.

[Photo: Araldo de Luca/CORBIS]

## Eye Contact

Of all the aspects of delivery discussed in this chapter, the most important one in a public-speaking situation for North Americans is eye contact. Eye contact with your audience opens communication, keeps your audience interested, and makes you more believable. Each of these functions contributes to the success of your delivery. Eye contact also provides you with feedback about how your speech is coming across.

Making eye contact with your listeners clearly shows that you are ready to talk to them. Most people start a conversation by looking at the person they are going to talk to. The same process occurs in public speaking.

Once you've started talking, continued eye contact lets you know how your audience is responding to your speech. You don't need to look at your listeners continuously. As the need arises, you should certainly look at your notes, but you should also look at your listeners frequently, just to see what they're doing.

Most listeners will think you are capable and trustworthy if you look them in the eye. Several studies document a relationship between eye contact and increased speaker credibility.[16] Speakers with less than 50 percent eye contact are considered unfriendly, uninformed, inexperienced, and even dishonest by their listeners.

Another study showed that those audience members who had more than 50 percent eye contact with their speaker performed better in postspeech tests than did those who had less than 50 percent eye contact.[17] However, not all people from all cultures prefer the same amount of direct eye contact when listening to someone talk. In interpersonal contexts, people from Asian cultures, for example, expect less direct eye contact when communicating with others than do North Americans.

**Using Eye Contact Effectively** Most audiences in the United States prefer that you establish eye contact with them even before you begin your speech with your attention-catching introduction. When it's time to speak, calmly walk to the lectern or to the front of the audience, pause briefly, and look at your audience before you say anything. Eye contact nonverbally sends the message, "I am interested in you; tune me in; I have something I want to share with you."

Here are other tips for effectively establishing eye contact with your audience:

- Have your opening sentence well enough in mind so that you can deliver it without looking at your notes or away from your listeners.
- Establish eye contact with the entire audience, not just with those in the front row or with only one or two people.
- Look to the back as well as the front, and from one side of your audience to the other. But you need not rhythmically move your head back and forth like a lighthouse beacon; it's best not to establish a predictable pattern for your eye contact.
- Look at individuals, establishing person-to-person contact with them—not so long that it will make a listener feel uncomfortable, but long enough to establish the feeling that you are talking directly to that individual.
- Don't look over your listeners' heads; establish eye-to-eye contact.

## Gestures

The next time you have a conversation with someone, notice how both of you use your hands and bodies to communicate. Important points are emphasized with gestures. You also gesture to indicate places, to enumerate items, and to describe objects. Gestures have the same functions for public speakers. Yet many people who gesture easily and appropriately in the course of everyday conversation aren't sure what to do with their hands when they find themselves in front of an audience.

There is evidence that gestures vary from culture to culture. When he was mayor of New York City during the 1930s and 1940s, Fiorello La Guardia, fluent in Yiddish and Italian as well as in English, would speak the language appropriate for each audience. One researcher studied newsreels of the mayor and discovered that with the sound turned off, viewers could still identify the language the mayor was speaking. How? When speaking English, he used minimal gestures. When speaking Italian, he used broad, sweeping gestures. And when speaking Yiddish, he used short and choppy hand movements.

Cultural expectations can help you make decisions about your approach to using gestures. Listeners from Japan and China, for example, prefer a quieter, less flamboyant use of gestures. One Web site that offers tips for people conducting business in India suggests "When you wish to point, use your chin or your full hand, but never just a single finger, as this gesture is used only with inferiors. The chin is not used to signal to superiors. The best way to point is with the full hand."[18] When one of your authors spoke in England, several listeners noted the use of "typical American gestures and movement." British listeners seem to prefer that the speaker stay behind a lectern and use relatively few gestures. Other Europeans agree they can spot an American speaker because Americans are typically more animated in their use of gestures, movement, and facial expressions than are most European speakers.

Public-speaking teachers often observe several unusual, inappropriate, and unnatural gestures among their students. One common problem is keeping your hands behind your back in a "parade rest" pose. We are not suggesting that you never put your hands behind your back, only that standing at parade rest during an entire speech looks awkward and unnatural and may distract your audience.

Another common position is standing with one hand on the hip in a "broken wing" pose. Worse than the "broken wing" is both hands resting on the hips in a "double broken wing." The speaker looks as though he or she might burst into a rendition of "I'm a Little Teapot." Again, we are not suggesting that you should never place your hands on your hips, only that to hold that one pose throughout a speech looks unnatural and will keep you from using other gestures.

Few poses are more awkward-looking than when a speaker clutches one arm, as if grazed by a bullet. The audience half expects the speaker to call out reassuringly, "Don't worry, Ma; it's only a flesh wound." Similarly, keeping your hands in your pockets can make you look as if you were afraid to let go of your change or your keys.

Some students clasp their hands and let them drop in front of them in a distracting "fig leaf clutch." Gestures can distract your audience in various other ways as well. Grasping the lectern until your knuckles turn white or just letting your hands flop around without purpose or control does little to help you communicate your message.

**Functions of Gestures** If you don't know what to do with your hands, think about the message you want to communicate. As in ordinary conversation, your hands should simply help emphasize or reinforce your verbal message. Specifically, your gestures can lend strength to or detract from what you have to say by (1) repeating, (2) contradicting, (3) substituting, (4) complementing, (5) emphasizing, and (6) regulating.

- **Repeating.** Gestures can help you repeat your verbal message. For example, you can say, "I have three major points to talk about today," while holding up three fingers. Or you can describe an object as 12 inches long while holding your hands about a foot apart. Repeating what you say through nonverbal means can reinforce your message.

- **Contradicting.** Because your audience will believe what you communicate nonverbally sooner than what you communicate verbally, monitor your gestures to make sure that they are not contradicting what you say. It is difficult to convey an image of control and confidence while using flailing gestures and awkward poses.
- **Substituting.** Not only can your behavior reinforce or contradict what you say, but your gestures can also substitute for your message. Without uttering a word, you can hold up the palm of your hand to calm a noisy crowd. Flashing two fingers to form a V for "victory" or raising a clenched fist are common examples of gestures that substitute for a verbal message.
- **Complementing.** Gestures can also add meaning to your verbal message. A politician who declines to comment on a reporter's question while holding up her hands to augment her verbal refusal is relying on the gesture to complement or provide further meaning to her verbal message.
- **Emphasizing.** You can give emphasis to what you say by using an appropriate gesture. A shaking fist or a slicing gesture with one or both hands helps emphasize a message. So does pounding your fist into the palm of your hand. Other gestures can be less dramatic yet still lend emphasis to what you say. You should try to allow your gestures to arise from the content of your speech and your emotions.
- **Regulating.** Gestures can also regulate the exchange between you and your audience. If you want the audience to respond to a question, you can extend both palms to invite a response. During a question-and-answer session, your gestures can signal when you want to talk and when you want to invite others to do so.

*The best gestures are natural, definite, and consistent with your message. Gestures can substitute for words, complement or emphasize them, or regulate the exchange between you and the audience. Which purpose is this speaker's gesture serving?*

[Photo: Masterfile Stock Image Library]

**Using Gestures Effectively** One hundred years ago, elocutionists taught their students how to gesture to communicate specific emotions or messages. Today teachers of speech have a different approach. Rather than prescribe gestures for specific situations, they feel it is more useful to offer suitable criteria (standards) by which to judge effective gestures, regardless of what is being said. Here are guidelines to consider when working on your delivery.

- **Stay natural.** Gestures should be *relaxed*, not tense or rigid. Your gestures should flow with your message. Avoid sawing or slashing through the air with your hands unless you are trying to emphasize a particularly dramatic point.
- **Be definite.** Gestures should appear *definite* rather than as accidental brief jerks of your hands or arms. If you want to gesture, go ahead and gesture. Avoid minor hand movements that will be masked by the lectern.
- **Use gestures that are consistent with your message.** Gestures should be *appropriate* for the verbal content of your speech. If you are excited, gesture more vigorously. But remember that prerehearsed gestures that do not arise naturally from what you are trying to say are likely to appear awkward and stilted.
- **Vary your gestures.** Strive for *variety* and versatility in your use of gesture. Try not to use just one hand or one all-purpose gesture. Gestures can be used for a variety of purposes, such as enumerating, pointing, describing, and symbolizing an idea or concept (such as clasping your hands together to suggest agreement or coming together).
- **Don't overdo it.** Gestures should be *unobtrusive*; your audience should focus not on the beauty or appropriateness of your gestures but on your message.

**TABLE 11.2 Characteristics of Effective Gestures**

| The Most Effective Gestures Are . . . |
|---|
| • Natural: Your gestures should be a natural fit with both your message and your personality. |
| • Definite: Make your gestures look purposeful rather than accidental. |
| • Consistent with your words: Monitor your gestures to make sure they reinforce your verbal message. |
| • Varied: Use different types of gestures rather than only one. |
| • Unobtrusive: Your gestures should not call attention to themselves. |
| • Appropriate: Gestures should be adapted to your audience and the occasion. |

Your purpose is to communicate a message to your audience, not to perform for your listeners to the extent that your delivery receives more attention than your message.

- **Coordinate gestures with what you say.** Gestures should be *well timed* to coincide with your verbal message. When you announce that you have three major points, your gesture of enumeration should occur simultaneously with your utterance of the word *three.* It would be poor timing to announce that you have three points, pause for a second or two, and then hold up three fingers.

- **Make your gestures appropriate to your audience and situation.** Gestures must be adapted to the audience. In more formal speaking situations, particularly when speaking to a large audience, bolder, more sweeping, and more dramatic gestures are appropriate. A small audience in a less formal setting calls for less formal gestures.

These tips are summarized in Table 11.2. You also need to keep one important principle in mind: Use gestures that work best for you. Don't try to be someone you are not. President Barack Obama's style may work for him, but you are not Barack Obama. Your gestures should fit your own personality. It may be better to use no gestures—to just put your hands comfortably at your side—than to use awkward, distracting gestures or to try to counterfeit someone else's gestures. Your nonverbal delivery should flow from *your* message.

## Movement

Should you walk around during your speech, or should you stay in one place? If there is a lectern, should you stand behind it, or would it be acceptable to stand in front of it or to the side? Is it all right to sit down while you speak? Can you move among the audience, as several popular daytime television hosts like to do? You may well find yourself pondering one or more of these questions while preparing for your speeches. The following discussion may help you answer them.

You may want to move purposefully about while delivering your speech, but take care that your movement does not detract from your message. If the audience focuses on your movement rather than on what you are saying, it would be better to stand still. An absence of movement is better than distracting movement. In short, your movement should be consistent with the verbal content of your message. It should make sense rather than appear as aimless wandering.

Robert Frost said, "Good fences make good neighbors." Professional speech coach Brent Filson says, however, "For my money, good fences make lousy speeches."[19] He recommends, as do we, that you eliminate physical barriers between you and the audience. For more formal occasions, you will be expected to stand behind a lectern to deliver your message. But even on those occasions, it can be appropriate to move from behind the lectern to make a point, signal a change in mood, or turn to another idea.

Your movement and other nonverbal cues can help you establish immediacy with your listeners. Psychologist Albert Mehrabian defines **immediacy** as "the degree of physical or psychological closeness between people."[20] **Immediacy behaviors** are those that literally or psychologically make your audience feel closer to you; because they create this perception of closeness, immediacy behaviors enhance the quality of the relationship between you and your audience.[21] Immediacy behaviors include:

- Standing or moving closer to your listeners
- Coming out from behind a lectern
- Using appropriate levels of eye contact
- Smiling while talking and, more specifically, smiling at individual audience members
- Using appropriate gestures
- Having an appropriately relaxed posture
- Moving purposefully

Over three decades of research on the immediacy cues used by teachers in North American classrooms clearly establishes that teachers who are more immediate enhance student learning, increase student motivation to learn, and have higher teacher evaluations.[22] It seems logical to suggest that public speakers who increase immediacy will have similar positive results. One cautionary note: Listeners—not the speaker—determine the appropriate amount of immediacy. Be vigilantly audience-centered as you seek the appropriate level of immediacy between you and your listeners.

In addition to fostering immediacy, movement can signal the beginning of a new idea or major point in your speech. As you make a transition statement or change from a serious subject to a more humorous one, movement can be a good way to signal that your approach to the speaking situation is changing.

Your use of movement during your speech should make sense to your listeners. Avoid random pacing and overly dramatic gestures. Temper our advice about proximity and other delivery variables by adapting to the cultural expectations of your audience.

## Posture

Although there have been few formal studies of posture in relation to public speaking, there is evidence that the way you carry your body communicates significant information. One study even suggests that your stance can reflect on your credibility as a speaker.[23] Slouching over the lectern, for example, does not project an image of vitality and interest in your audience.

Whereas your face and voice play the major role in communicating a specific emotion, your posture communicates the *intensity* of that emotion. If you are happy, your face and voice reflect your happiness; your posture communicates the intensity of your joy.[24]

Since the days of the elocutionists, few speech teachers or public-speaking texts have advocated specific postures for public speakers. Today we believe that the specific stance you adopt should come about naturally, as a result of what you have to say, the environment, and the formality or informality of the occasion. For example, during a very informal presentation, it may be perfectly appropriate as well as comfortable and natural to sit on the edge of a desk. Most speech teachers, however, do not encourage students to sit while delivering classroom speeches. In general, avoid slouched shoulders, shifting from foot to foot, or drooping your head. Your posture

**immediacy**
The degree of perceived physical or psychological closeness between people

**immediacy behaviors**
Behaviors such as making eye contact, making appropriate gestures, and adjusting physical distance that enhance the quality of the relationship between speaker and listeners

should not call attention to itself. Instead, it should reflect your interest in the speaking event and your attention to the task at hand.

To help you stand tall when delivering a speech, here are two tips to keep in mind. First, stand up straight while pulling your shoulder blades back just a bit. Second, imagine that your head is being held up by a string so that you have direct eye contact with your listeners while standing tall. You don't need to stay frozen in this position. But when you find yourself starting to slump or slouch, pulling your shoulders back and tugging on the imaginary string will give your posture an immediate positive boost.

## Facial Expression

Media experts today doubt that Abraham Lincoln would have survived as a politician in our appearance-conscious age of telegenic politicians. His facial expression, according to those who saw him, seemed wooden and unvaried.

Your face plays a key role in expressing your thoughts, and especially your emotions and attitudes.[25] Your audience sees your face before they hear what you are going to say. Thus, you have an opportunity to set the emotional tone for your message before you start speaking. We are not advocating that you adopt a phony smile that looks insincere and plastered on your face, but a pleasant facial expression helps establish a positive emotional climate. Your facial expression should naturally vary to be consistent with your message. Present somber news with a more serious expression. To communicate interest in your listeners, keep your expression alert and friendly.

Although humans are physically capable of producing thousands of different facial expressions, our faces most often express only six primary emotions: happiness, anger, surprise, sadness, disgust, and fear. But when we speak to others, our faces are a blend of expressions rather than communicators of a single emotion. According to cross-cultural studies by social psychologist Paul Ekman, the facial expressions of these emotions are virtually universal, so even a culturally diverse audience will usually be able to read your emotional expressions clearly.[26] When you rehearse your speech, consider standing in front of a mirror—or, better yet, videotape yourself practicing your speech. Are you allowing your face to help communicate the emotional tone of your thoughts?

## Vocal Delivery

Have you ever listened to a radio announcer and imagined what he or she looked like, only later to see a photograph of the announcer that drastically altered your image? Vocal clues play an important part in creating the impression we have of a speaker. Based on vocal clues alone, you make inferences about a person's age, status, occupation, ethnic origin, income, and a variety of other matters. As a public speaker, your voice is one of your most important delivery tools in conveying your ideas to your audience. Your credibility as a speaker and your ability to communicate your ideas clearly to your listeners will in large part depend on your vocal delivery.

Vocal delivery includes pitch, speech rate, volume, pronunciation, articulation, pauses, and general variation of the voice. A speaker has at least two key vocal obligations to an audience: Speak to be understood, and speak with vocal variety to maintain interest.

**Speaking to Be Understood** To be understood, you need to consider four aspects of vocal delivery: volume, articulation, dialect, and pronunciation.

**volume**
The softness or loudness of a speaker's voice

- **Volume.** The fundamental purpose of your vocal delivery is to speak loudly enough that your audience can hear you. The **volume** of your speech is determined by the amount of air you project through your larynx, or voice box. More air equals more volume of sound. In fact, the way you breathe has more impact on the sound of your voice than almost anything else. To the ancient orators, a person's breath was the source of spiritual power. To breathe is to be filled with a positive, powerful source of energy.

In order to breathe properly, you need to understand how to use your breathing muscles. Your diaphragm, a muscle that lies between your lungs and your abdomen, helps control sound volume by increasing air flow from your lungs through your voice box. If you put your hands on the hollow in the center of your rib cage and say "Ho-ho-ho," you will feel your muscles contracting and the air being forced out of your lungs. Breathing from your diaphragm—that is, consciously expanding and contracting your abdomen as you breathe in and out, rather than merely expanding your chest as air flows into your lungs—can increase the volume of sound as well as enhance the quality of your voice.

• **Articulation.** The process of producing speech sounds clearly and distinctly is **articulation**. In addition to speaking loudly enough, you need to say your words so that your audience can understand them. Without distinct enunciation, or articulation of the sounds that make up words, your listeners may not understand you or may fault you for simply not knowing how to speak clearly and fluently. Here are some commonly misarticulated words.[27]

| | |
|---|---|
| *Dint* instead of *didn't* | *Soun* instead of *sound* |
| *Lemme* instead of *let me* | *Wanna* instead of *want to* |
| *Mornin* instead of *morning* | *Wep* instead of *wept* |
| *Seeya* instead of *see you* | *Whadayado* instead of *what do you do* |

Many errors in articulation result from simple laziness. It takes effort to articulate speech sounds clearly. Sometimes we are in a hurry to express our ideas, but more often we simply get into the habit of mumbling, slurring, and abbreviating. Such speech flaws may not keep your audience from understanding you, but poor enunciation does reflect on your credibility as a speaker.

The best way to improve your articulation of sounds is first to identify those words or phrases that you have a tendency to slur or chop. Once you have identified them, practice saying the words correctly. Make sure you can hear the difference between the improper and proper pronunciation. A speech teacher can help you check your articulation.

• **Dialect.** Most newscasters in North America use what is called standard American pronunciation and do not typically have a strong dialect. A **dialect** is a consistent style of pronouncing words that is common to an ethnic group or a geographic region such as the South, New England, or the upper Midwest. In the southern part of the United States, people prolong some vowel sounds when they speak. And in the northern Midwest, the word *about* sometimes sounds a bit like "aboat." It took a bit of adjustment for many Americans to get used to John Kennedy's Bostonian pronunciation of Cuba as "Cuber" and Harvard as "Hahvahd." Lyndon Johnson's Texas twang was a sharp contrast to Kennedy's New England sound. And George W. Bush's Texas lilt also contrasted with the slight southern drawl of his predecessor, Bill Clinton. Although President Obama has less of an identifiable dialect than either Clinton or Bush, he sometimes clips the ends of his words.

Are dialects detrimental to effective communication with an audience? Although a speaker's dialect may pigeonhole that person as being from a certain part of the country, it won't necessarily affect the audience's comprehension of the information unless the dialect is so pronounced that the listeners can't understand the speaker's words. Research does suggest, however, that listeners tend to prefer a dialect similar to their own.[28] Many well-known and effective speakers have distinct dialects; Jesse Jackson, Bill Clinton, George W. Bush, and humorist Garrison

**articulation**
The production of clear and distinct speech sounds

**dialect**
A consistent style of pronouncing words that is common to an ethnic group or geographic region

Keillor all have some degree of regional dialects. We don't recommend that you eliminate your own mild dialect; but if your word pronunciation is significantly distracting to your listeners, you might consider modifying it.

The four elements of a dialect include intonation pattern, vowel production, consonant production, and speaking rate. A typical North American intonation pattern is predominantly a rising and falling pattern. The pattern looks something like this:

"Good morning. How are you?"

Intonation patterns of other languages, such as Hindi, may remain on almost the exact same pitch level; native North American ears find the monotone pitch distracting.

A second element in any dialect is the way vowel sounds are produced. Many people who speak English as a second language often clip, or shorten, the vowel sounds, which can make comprehension more challenging. Stretching or elongating vowels within words can be a useful skill for such speakers to develop. If this is a vocal skill you need to cultivate, consider recording your speech and then comparing it with the standard American pronunciation you hear on TV or radio.

Consonant production, the third element in vocal dialects, varies depending on what language you are speaking. It is sometimes difficult to produce clear consonants that are not overdone. Consonants that are so soft as to be almost unheard may produce a long blur of unintelligible sound rather than a crisply articulated sound.

A fourth and final element in vocal dialect is speaking rate. People whose first language is not English sometimes speak too fast, in the hope this will create the impression that they are very familiar with English. Slowing the rate just a bit often enhances comprehension for native English speakers listening to someone less familiar with English pronunciation. A rate that is too fast also contributes to problems with clipped vowels, soft or absent consonants, and an intonation pattern that is on one pitch level rather than comfortably varied.

- **Pronunciation.** Whereas articulation relates to the clarity of sounds, **pronunciation** concerns the degree to which sounds conform to those assigned to words in standard English. Mispronouncing words can detract from a speaker's credibility.[29] Often, however, we are not aware that we are not using standard pronunciation unless someone points it out.

Some speakers reverse speech sounds, saying "aks" instead of "ask," for example. Some allow an *r* sound to intrude into some words, saying "warsh" instead of "wash," or leave out sounds in the middle of a word by saying "actchally" instead of "actually" or "Febuary" instead of "February." Some speakers also accent syllables in nonstandard ways; they say "po´lice" instead of "po lice´" or "um´brella" rather than "um brel´la."

If English is not your native language, you may have to spend extra time working on your pronunciation and articulation. Here are two useful tips to help you. First, make an effort to prolong vowel sounds. Speeeeak tooooo proooooloooong eeeeeeach voooooowel soooooound yoooooooou maaaaaaaake. Second, to reduce choppy-sounding word pronunciation, blend the end of one word into the beginning of the next. Make your speech flow from one word to the next, instead of separating it into individual chunks of sound.[30]

### Speaking with Variety

To speak with variety is to vary your pitch, rate of speech, and pauses. It is primarily through the quality of our voices, as well as our facial expressions, that we communicate whether we are happy, sad, bored, or excited. If your vocal clues suggest that you are bored with your topic, your audience will probably be bored also. Appropriate variation in vocal pitch and rate as well as appropriate use of pauses can add zest to your speech and help maintain audience attention.

- **Pitch.** Vocal **pitch** is how high or low your voice sounds. You can sing because you can change the pitch of your voice to produce a melody. Lack of variation

**pronunciation**
The use of sounds to form words clearly and accurately

**pitch**
How high or low your voice sounds

in pitch has been consistently identified as one of the most distracting characteristics of ineffective speakers: A monotone is boring.

Everyone has a habitual pitch. This is the range of your voice during normal conversation. Some people have a habitually high pitch, others have a low pitch. The pitch of your voice is determined by how fast the folds in your vocal cords vibrate. The faster the vibration, the higher the pitch. Male vocal folds open and close approximately 100 to 150 times each second; female vocal folds vibrate about 200 times per second, giving them a higher vocal pitch.

Your voice has **inflection** when you raise or lower the pitch as you pronounce words or sounds. Your inflection helps determine the meaning of your utterances. A surprised "ah!" sounds different from a disappointed "ah" or "ah?" Your vocal inflection is thus an important indicator of your emotions and gives clues as to how to interpret your speech.

In some cultures, vocal inflection plays a major role in helping people interpret the meaning of words. For example, Thai, Vietnamese, and Mandarin Chinese languages purposely use such inflections as monotone, low, falling, high, and rising.[31] If you are a native speaker of a language in which pitch influences meaning, be mindful that listeners do not expect this in many Western languages, although all languages rely on inflection to provide nuances of meaning.

The best public speakers appropriately vary their inflection. We're not suggesting that you need to imitate a top-forty radio disk jockey when you speak. But variation in your vocal inflection and overall pitch helps you communicate the subtlety of your ideas.

Record your speech as you rehearse, and evaluate your use of pitch and inflection critically. If you are not satisfied with your inflection, consider practicing your speech with exaggerated variations in vocal pitch. Although you would not deliver your speech this way, it may help you explore the expressive options available to you.

- **Rate.** How fast do you talk? Most speakers average between 120 and 180 words per minute. There is no "best" speaking rate. The skill of great speakers does not depend on a standard rate of speech. Daniel Webster purportedly spoke at about 90 words per minute, Franklin Roosevelt at 110, John F. Kennedy at a quick-paced 180. Martin Luther King Jr. started his "I Have a Dream" speech at 92 words a minute and was speaking at 145 words per minute during his conclusion.[32] The best rate depends on two factors: your speaking style and the content of your message.

A common fault of many beginning speakers is to deliver a speech too quickly. One symptom of speech anxiety is that you tend to rush through your speech to get it over with. Feedback from others can help you determine whether your rate is too rapid. Recording your message and listening critically to your speaking rate can also help you assess whether you are speaking at the proper speed. Fewer speakers have the problem of speaking too slowly, but a turtle-paced speech will almost certainly make it more difficult for your audience to maintain interest. Remember, your listeners can grasp information much faster than you can speak it.

- **Pauses.** It was Mark Twain who said, "The right word may be effective, but no word was ever as effective as a rightly timed pause." An appropriate pause can often do more to accent your message than any other vocal characteristic. President Kennedy's famous line, "Ask not what your country can do for you; ask what you can do for your country," was effective not only because of its language but also because it was delivered with a pause dividing the two thoughts. Try delivering that line without the pause; it just doesn't have the same power.

Effective use of pauses, also known as *effective timing*, can greatly enhance the impact of your message. Whether you are trying to tell a joke, a serious tale, or a dramatic story, your use of a pause can determine the effectiveness of your anecdote. Jon Stewart, Jay Leno, David Letterman, Conan O'Brien, and Ellen Degeneres are masters at timing a punch line.

**inflection**
The variation in the pitch of the voice

*A stationary microphone, like this one, can limit a speaker's movements severely. When you use any microphone, you must also be careful to avoid explosive word pronunciations or annoying microphone noises.*
[Photo: Stephen Coburn/Shutterstock]

Beware, however, of the vocalized pause. Many beginning public speakers are uncomfortable with silence and so, rather than pausing where it seems natural and normal, they vocalize sounds such as "umm," "er," "you know," and "ah." We think you will agree that "Ask not, ah, what your, er, country can do, ah, for you; ask, you know, what you, umm, can do, er, for your, uh, country" just doesn't have the same impact as the unadorned original statement.

One research study counted how frequently certain people use "uhs."[33] Science professors in this study said "uh" about 1.4 times a minute; humanities professors timed in at 4.8 times a minute—almost 3.5 times as often. Another psychologist counted the "ums" per minute of well-known speakers. *Wheel of Fortune* host Pat Sajak won the count with almost 10 "ums" per minute; and, although he sometimes pokes fun at well-known politicians who use vocalized pauses, David Letterman was a close second with 8.1. President Bill Clinton had only .79 vocalized pause per minute. Vice President Dan Quayle had only .1. As a public speaker, you don't want to be the winner of this contest by having the most "uhs" and "ums" when you speak. Vocalized pauses will annoy your audience and detract from your credibility; eliminate them.

Silence can be an effective tool in emphasizing a particular word or sentence. A well-timed pause coupled with eye contact can powerfully accent your thought. Asking a rhetorical question of your audience such as "How many of you would like to improve your communication skills?" will be more effective if you pause after asking the question rather than rushing into the next thought. Silence is a way of saying to your audience, "Think about this for a moment." Pianist Arthur Schnabel said this about silence and music: "The notes I handle no better than many pianists. But the pauses between the notes, ah, that is where the art resides."[34] In speech, too, an effective use of a pause can add emphasis and interest.

**Using a Microphone** "Testing. Testing. One . . . two . . . three. Is this on?" These are not effective opening remarks. Yet countless public speakers have found themselves trying to begin a speech, only to be upstaged by an uncooperative public address system. No matter how polished your gestures or well-intoned your vocal cues, if you are inaudible or you use a microphone awkwardly, your speech will not have the desired effect.

There are three kinds of microphones, only one of which demands much technique. The **lavaliere microphone** is the clip-on type often used by newspeople and interviewees. Worn on the front of a shirt or dress, it requires no particular care other than not to thump it or to accidentally knock it off. The **boom microphone** is used by makers of movies and TV shows. It hangs over the heads of the speakers and is remote-controlled, so the speaker need not be particularly concerned with it. The third kind of microphone, and the most common, is the **stationary microphone**. This is the type that is most often attached to a lectern, sitting on a desk, or standing on the floor. Generally, the stationary microphones used today are multidirectional. You do not have to remain frozen in front of a stationary mike while delivering your speech. However, you do need to take some other precautions when using one.

**lavaliere microphone**
A microphone that can be clipped to an article of clothing or worn on a cord around your neck

**boom microphone**
A microphone that is suspended from a bar and moved to follow the speaker; often used in movies and TV

**stationary microphone**
A microphone attached to a lectern, sitting on a desk, or standing on the floor

First, if you have a fully stationary microphone, rather than one that converts to a hand mike, you will have to remain behind the microphone, with your mouth about the same distance from the mike at all times to avoid distracting fluctuations in the volume of sound. You can turn your head from side to side and use gestures, but you will have to limit other movements.

Second, microphones amplify sloppy habits of pronunciation and enunciation. Therefore, you need to speak clearly and crisply when using a mike. Be especially careful when articulating such "explosive" sounding consonants as *B* and *P*; they can be overamplified by the microphone and produce a slight popping sound. Similarly, a microphone can intensify the sibilance of the *S* sound at the beginning or ending of words (such as in *hiss*, *sometime*, or *specials*). You may have to articulate these sounds with slightly less intensity to avoid creating overamplified, distracting noises.

Third, if you must test a microphone, count or ask the audience whether they can hear you. Blowing on a microphone produces an irritating noise! Do not tap, pound, or shuffle anything near the microphone. These noises, too, will be heard by the audience loudly and clearly. If you are using note cards, quietly slide them aside as you progress through your speech.

Finally, when you are delivering your speech, speak directly into the microphone to make sure that your words are appropriately amplified. Some speakers lower their volume and become inaudible when they have a microphone in front of them.

Under ideal circumstances, you will be able to practice beforehand with the same type of microphone you will use when you speak. If you have the chance, figure out where to stand for the best sound quality and how sensitive the mike is to extraneous noise. Practice will accustom you to any voice distortion or echo that might occur so that these sound qualities do not surprise you during your speech.

## Personal Appearance

Most people have expectations about the way a speaker should look. One of your audience analysis tasks is to identify what those audience expectations are. This can be trickier than it might at first seem. John T. Molloy has written two books, *Dress for Success* and *Dress for Success for Women*, in an effort to identify what the well-dressed businessperson should wear. But as some of his own research points out, appropriate wardrobe varies depending on climate, custom, culture, and audience expectations. For example, most CEOs who speak to their stockholders at the annual stockholders meeting typically wear a suit and tie—but not Steve Jobs, head of Apple. To communicate his casual and contemporary approach to business, he often wears jeans and a sweater.

There is considerable evidence that your personal appearance affects how your audience responds to you and your message, particularly during the opening moments of your presentation. If you violate their expectations about appearance, you will be less successful in achieving your purpose. One study found, for example, that men who have a nose ring are less likely to be hired during a job interview.[35] Yet this research conclusion is based on a specific situation and time; years from now, a nose ring may have no impact, either positive or negative, on a person's credibility. Our point: It's the audience and the cultural expectations of audience members that determine whether a speaker's personal appearance is appropriate or not, not some fashion guru or magazine editor.

RECAP

### Characteristics of Effective Delivery

- High level of eye contact with the entire audience
- Culturally appropriate, natural, non-distracting gestures
- Purposeful, non-distracting, immediacy-cueing movement
- Straight but natural standing posture, matching intensity of message
- Culturally appropriate facial expressions, matching message
- Audible volume, clear articulation, minimized dialect
- Varied vocal pitch and speaking rate
- Competent use of microphone
- Clean grooming and clothing appropriate to audience and situation

# Audience Diversity and Delivery

Most of the suggestions we have offered in this chapter assume that your listeners will be expecting a typical North American approach to delivery. However, these

assumptions are based on research responses from U.S. college students, who are predominantly white and in their late teens or early twenties, so our suggestions are not applicable to every audience. As we have stressed throughout the book, you need to adapt your presentation to the expectations of your listeners, especially those from different cultural backgrounds. Consider the following suggestions to help you develop strategies for adapting both your verbal and your nonverbal messages for a culturally diverse audience.

- **Avoid an ethnocentric mind-set.** As you learned in Chapter 4, *ethnocentrism* is the assumption that your own cultural approaches are superior to those of other cultures. When considering how to adapt your delivery style to your audience, try to view different approaches and preferences not as right or wrong but merely as different from your own.
- **Consider using a less dramatic style for predominantly high-context listeners.** As you recall from Chapter 4, a high-context culture places considerable emphasis on unspoken messages. Therefore, for a high-context audience, you need not be overly expressive. For example, for many Japanese people, a delivery style that included exuberant gestures, overly dramatic facial expressions, and frequent movements might seem overdone. A more subtle, less demonstrative approach would create less "noise" and be more effective.
- **Consult with other speakers who have presented to your audience.** Talk with people you may know who are familiar with the cultural expectations of the audience you will address. Ask specific questions. For example, when speaking in Poland, one of the authors expected the speech to start promptly at 11 A.M., as announced in the program and on posters. By 11:10 it was clear the speech would not begin on time. In Poland, it turns out, all students know about the "academic quarter." This means that most lectures and speeches begin at least 15 minutes—a quarter hour—after the announced starting time. If the author had asked another professor about the audience's expectations, he would have known this custom in advance. As you observe or talk with speakers who have addressed your target audience, ask these questions:

  What are audience expectations about where I should stand while speaking?

  Do listeners like direct eye contact?

  When will the audience expect me to start and end my talk?

  Will listeners find movement and gestures distracting or welcome?
- **Monitor your level of immediacy with your audience.** As we noted earlier, speaker immediacy involves how close you are to your listeners, the amount of eye contact you display, and whether you speak from behind or in front of a lectern. North Americans seem to prefer immediacy behaviors from speakers. Some cultures may expect less immediacy; the key is not to violate what listeners expect.[36] For example, we've been told that Japanese audiences don't expect speakers to move from behind a lectern and stand very close to listeners. Even in small seminars, Japanese speakers and teachers typically stay behind the lectern.
- **Monitor your expression of emotion.** Not all cultures interpret and express emotions the same way. People from the Middle East and the Mediterranean are typically more expressive and animated in their conversation than are Europeans.[37] As we noted in Chapter 4, people from a high-context culture—a culture in which nonverbal messages are exceptionally important (such as Japanese or Chinese)—place greater emphasis on your delivery of a message than do people from a low-context culture (such as North Americans).[38] Remember, however, that even though you may be speaking to an audience from a low-context culture—a culture that places a high value on verbal messages—you do not have license to ignore how you deliver a message. Delivery is always important. But audience members from a high-context culture will rely heavily on your unspoken message to help them interpret what you are saying.

## DON'T GET LOST IN TRANSLATION

When you are invited to address listeners who speak a language different from your own and your message is being translated, consider the following tips to ensure that your message will be understood:

- Learn enough of the language to provide at least an opening greeting in the language of your listeners: "Good morning" (*Buenos dias*) or "Good evening" (*Buenos noches*).
- Speak more slowly than normal, to give your translator time to listen and repeat your message.
- If you'd planned on speaking for 20 minutes, cut your content in half because your translator will be repeating what you say in the language of your audience.
- Use short, simple sentences. Pause frequently to give your translator time to translate your message.
- If possible, give your translator an outline of your message.
- Avoid slang, jargon, and figures of speech such as "pony up," "elephant in the room," "piggyback," "clear as a bell," and "thick as thieves."
- Use jokes and humor with caution: Jokes often do not translate well.
- Consider using PowerPoint™ slides; the slides can help your translator. If possible, have your PowerPoint slides translated into the language of your audience.
- If your audience shows nonverbal clues that something you (or your translator) said is unclear, ask the audience if your message is clear.

Source: "Don't Get Lost in Translation," *Herald,* Vol. 157, 4 (April 2010), p. 32. Reprinted with permission of Community of Christ.

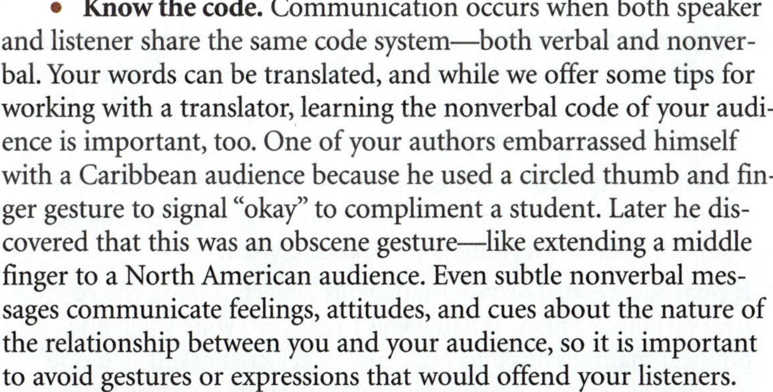

• **Know the code.** Communication occurs when both speaker and listener share the same code system—both verbal and nonverbal. Your words can be translated, and while we offer some tips for working with a translator, learning the nonverbal code of your audience is important, too. One of your authors embarrassed himself with a Caribbean audience because he used a circled thumb and finger gesture to signal "okay" to compliment a student. Later he discovered that this was an obscene gesture—like extending a middle finger to a North American audience. Even subtle nonverbal messages communicate feelings, attitudes, and cues about the nature of the relationship between you and your audience, so it is important to avoid gestures or expressions that would offend your listeners.

Although we cannot provide a comprehensive description of each cultural expectation you may face in every educational and professional setting, we can remind you to keep cultural expectations in mind when you rehearse and deliver a speech. We are not suggesting that you abandon your own cultural expectations about speech delivery. Rather, we urge you to become sensitive and responsive to cultural differences. There is no universal dictionary of nonverbal meaning, so spend some time asking people who are from the same culture as your prospective audience about what gestures and expressions your audience will appreciate.

### RECAP: Audience Diversity and Delivery

- Avoid ethnocentrism.
- Use more subtle nonverbals for high-context listeners.
- Match immediacy behavior and expression of emotion to culture.
- Learn nonverbal gesture codes; avoid embarrassment.
- Seek advice from speakers experienced with the audience.

## Rehearsing Your Speech: Some Final Tips

Just knowing some of the characteristics of effective speech delivery will not make you a better speaker unless you can put those principles into practice. Effective public speaking is a skill that takes practice. Practicing takes the form of rehearsing. As indicated in Figure 11.1, rehearsing your speech helps you prepare to deliver your speech to an audience.

Select and Narrow Topic
Determine Purpose
Develop Central Idea
Generate Main Ideas
Gather Supporting Material
Organize Speech
Rehearse Speech
Deliver Speech
CONSIDER THE AUDIENCE

FIGURE 11.1 *Rehearsing your speech delivery will help you present your speech with confidence.*

Do you want to make a good grade on your next speech? Research suggests that one of the best predictors of the effectiveness of a speech is the amount of time you spend preparing and rehearsing it; instructors gave higher grades to students who spent more time rehearsing their speeches and lower grades to students who spent less time preparing and rehearsing.[39] The following suggestions can help you make the most of your rehearsal time.

- **Finish drafting your speech outline at least two days before your speech performance.** The more time you have to work on putting it all together, the better.
- **Before you prepare the speaking notes to use in front of your audience, rehearse your speech aloud.** This will help you determine where you will need notes to prompt yourself.
- **Time your speech.** Revise your speech as necessary to keep it within the time limits set by your instructor or whoever invited you to speak.
- **Prepare your speaking notes.** Use whatever system works best for you. Some speakers use pictorial symbols to remind themselves of a story or an idea. Others use complete sentences or just words and phrases in an outline pattern to prompt them. Many teachers advocate using note cards for speaking notes.
- **Rehearse your speech standing up.** This will help you get a feel for your use of gestures as well as your vocal delivery. Do not try to memorize your speech or choreograph specific gestures. As you rehearse, you may want to modify your speaking notes to reflect appropriate changes.
- **If you can, present your speech to someone else so that you can practice establishing eye contact.** Seek feedback from your captive audience about both your delivery and your speech content.
- **If possible, record or videotape your speech during the rehearsal stage.** This will allow you to observe your vocal and physical mannerisms and make necessary changes. If you don't have a video camera, you may find it useful to practice before a mirror so that you can observe your body language—it's low-tech, but it still works.
- **Rehearse using all your presentation aids.** As we discuss in the next chapter, don't wait until the last minute to plan, prepare, and rehearse with flipcharts, slides, overhead transparencies, or other aids that you will need to manipulate as you speak.
- **Your final rehearsals should re-create, as much as possible, the speaking situation you will face.** If you will be speaking in a

RECAP

### Rehearsing Your Speech

- Spend more time preparing and rehearsing, to earn a higher grade.
- Finish outline two days before speech.
- Rehearse aloud and time your speech before making speaking notes.
- Make rehearsals as much like the real speech as possible.
- Critique video of your rehearsal.

## DEVELOPING YOUR SPEECH STEP BY STEP

### Rehearse Your Speech

Karen begins to rehearse her speech. From the beginning, she stands and speaks aloud, practicing gestures and movement that seem appropriate to her message.

At first, Karen uses her preparation outline (pp. 208–209) as speaking notes. These early rehearsals go pretty well, but the speech is running slightly long. She needs to edit a bit.

Karen considers her listeners again. What part of her speech might be least effective with them? The reference to NHTSA administrator Jeffrey Runge's 2002 speech is dated and doesn't really add much substance to her argument. So she decides to cut that material before she prepares her speaking notes and continues rehearsing.

large classroom, find a large classroom in which to rehearse your speech. If your audience will be seated informally in a semicircle, then this should be the context in which you rehearse your speech. The more realistic the rehearsal, the more confidence you will gain.

- **Practice good delivery skills while rehearsing.** Remember this maxim: Practice *makes* perfect if practice *is* perfect.

# Delivering Your Speech

The day of your speech arrives, and you are ready. Using information about your audience as an anchor, you have developed a speech on an interesting topic and with a fine-tuned purpose. Your central idea is clearly identified. You have gathered interesting and relevant supporting material and organized it well. Your speech has an appropriate introduction, a logically arranged body, and a clear conclusion that nicely summarizes your key theme. You have rehearsed your speech several times; it is not memorized,

## CONFIDENTLY CONNECTING WITH YOUR AUDIENCE

### Re-create the Speech Environment When You Rehearse

As you rehearse your speech, don't just sit at your desk and mentally review your message. Instead, stand up and imagine that you are in the very room in which you will deliver your speech. Or, if it is possible, rehearse your speech in the room in which you will present your speech. Even just by imagining the exact room and audience you will have when presenting your speech, you are helping to manage your anxiety. When you do give your speech, you will have less anxiety because you've had experience imagining or presenting your speech in the environment in which you will speak.

## DEVELOPING YOUR SPEECH STEP BY STEP

### Deliver Your Speech

The long-awaited day of Karen's speech has come. She slept well last night and ate a light breakfast before arriving at the contest site on the campus of the University of Mississippi.

Waiting her turn to speak, Karen breathes deeply and visualizes herself delivering her speech calmly and confidently. When her name is called, she walks to the front of the room and establishes eye contact with her audience before she begins to speak.

During her speech, Karen focuses on adapting her message to her listeners. She looks at individual members of her audience, uses purposeful and well-timed gestures, and speaks loudly and clearly.

Even before she hears the applause, Karen knows that her speech has been a success.

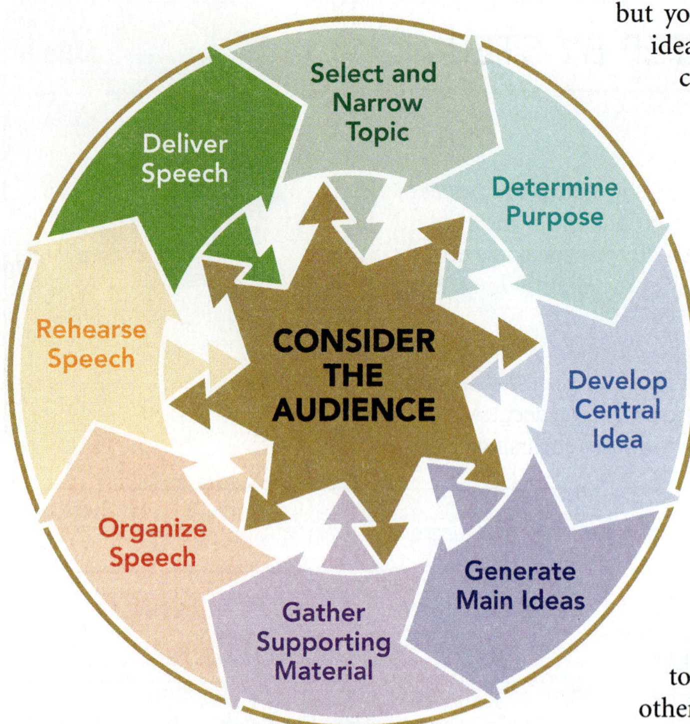


FIGURE 11.2 *Delivering the speech is the culmination of the audience-centered approach to the speechmaking process.*

but you are comfortable with the way you express the major ideas. Your last task is calmly and confidently to communicate with your audience. You are ready to deliver your speech.

As the time for presenting your speech to your audience approaches, consider the following suggestions to help you prepare for a successful performance (see Figure 11.2).

- **Be well rested.** Get plenty of sleep before your speech. Last-minute, late-night final preparations can take the edge off your performance. Many professional public speakers also advocate that you watch what you eat before you speak; a heavy meal or too much caffeine can have a negative effect on your performance.
- **Review the suggestions in Chapter 1 for becoming a confident speaker.** It is normal to have prespeech jitters. But if you have developed a well-organized, audience-centered message on a topic of genuine interest to you, you're doing all the right things to make your speech a success. Remember some of the other tips for developing confidence: Re-create the speech environment when you rehearse. Use deep breathing techniques to help you relax. Make sure you are especially familiar with your introduction and conclusion. Act calm to feel calm.
- **Arrive early for your speaking engagement.** If the room is in an unfamiliar location, give yourself plenty of time to find it. As we suggested in Chapter 5, you may want to rearrange the furniture or make other changes in the speaking environment. If you are using audiovisual equipment, check to see that it is working properly and set up your support material carefully. You might even project a slide or two to make sure they are in the tray right side up. Budget your time so you do not spend your moments before you speak hurriedly looking for a parking place or frantically trying to attend to last-minute details.
- **Visualize success.** Picture yourself delivering your speech in an effective way. Also, remind yourself of the effort you have spent preparing for your speech. A final mental rehearsal can boost your confidence and help ensure success.

RECAP

**Delivering Your Speech**

- Get a good night's rest.
- Eat carefully.
- Arrive early.
- Visualize success.
- Reinforce your confidence with tips from Chapter 1.

Even though we have identified many time-tested methods for enhancing your speech delivery, keep in mind that speech delivery is an art rather than a science. The manner of your delivery should reflect your personality and individual style.

# Responding to Questions

It's possible that a speech you deliver will be followed by a question-and-answer (Q & A) session. These sessions can be especially challenging because although you may not know the questions in advance, you will be expected to deliver your answers thoughtfully and smoothly. During a Q & A session, your delivery method changes to impromptu speaking. In addition to the suggestions for impromptu speaking we offered earlier, here are additional tips to make the Q & A period less challenging.[40]

Preparation can help you manage a question-and-answer session smoothly to bring a successful end to the delivery of your speech.

[Photo: Getty Images Inc. RF]

• **Prepare.** One of the best ways to prepare for a Q & A session is to anticipate the questions you may be asked. How do you anticipate questions? You analyze your audience. Think of possible questions those particular listeners might ask, and then rehearse your answers. Prior to presidential debates, candidates have their staff members pepper them with questions so the candidates can practice responding. Perhaps your friends can ask you questions after you've rehearsed your speech for them.

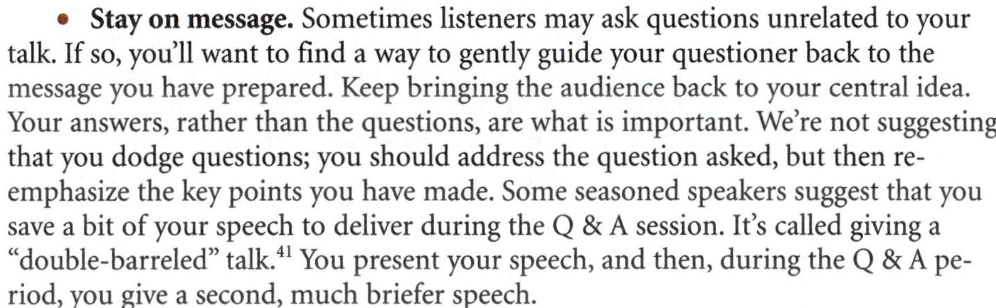

• **Repeat or rephrase the question.** Repeating a question helps in four ways. First, your paraphrase makes sure that everyone can hear the question. Second, paraphrasing ensures that you understand the question before you go charging off with your answer. Third, by paraphrasing, you can succinctly summarize rambling questions. And finally, repeating the question gives you just a bit of time to think about your answer.

• **Stay on message.** Sometimes listeners may ask questions unrelated to your talk. If so, you'll want to find a way to gently guide your questioner back to the message you have prepared. Keep bringing the audience back to your central idea. Your answers, rather than the questions, are what is important. We're not suggesting that you dodge questions; you should address the question asked, but then reemphasize the key points you have made. Some seasoned speakers suggest that you save a bit of your speech to deliver during the Q & A session. It's called giving a "double-barreled" talk.[41] You present your speech, and then, during the Q & A period, you give a second, much briefer speech.

• **Respond to the audience, not just the person who asked the question.** Although you can start your response by having eye contact with the person who asked you a question, make sure that you stay audience-centered. Look at the entire audience and keep in mind that your response should be relevant to them. If the questioner wants specific information that is of interest only to that person, you could speak with the questioner individually after your speech.

• **Ask yourself the first question.** One way to prime the audience for the Q & A session is to ask yourself a challenging question first. For example, you might say, "As we move into Q & A, a number of you may be wondering . . . ." State the question and answer it. Doing this also gives you a comfortable way to make a transition between the speech and the Q & A period. Asking yourself a tough question tells the audience that you're open for serious questions, and it snaps them to attention as well.

• **Listen nonjudgmentally.** Use the effective listening skills that we discussed in Chapter 3. Keep your eyes focused on the person asking the question, lean forward slightly, and give your full attention to the questioner. Audience members expect speakers to be polite and attentive. If you think the question is stupid, don't say so. Just listen and respond courteously. Audience members can judge for themselves whether a question is appropriate or not. Don't wince, grimace, or scowl at the questioner. You'll gain more credibility by keeping your cool than by losing your composure.

• **Neutralize hostile questions.** Every hostile question gives you an opportunity to score points with your listeners. You'll have your listeners' attention; use that attention to your advantage. The following strategies can help.

*Restate the question.* If the question was a lengthy attack, focus on the essence of the issue. If the question is "Your ideas are just wrong! I'm angry that you have no clue as to how to proceed. Your proposal has been a disaster in the past. Why are you still trying to make it work?" a paraphrase could be "You're asking me why I'm still trying to implement a program that hasn't been successful. From your perspective, the program has failed."

*Acknowledge emotions.* For example, you could say, "I can understand why you are angry. I share your anger and frustration. It's because of my frustration that I want to give my proposal more time to work."

*Don't make the issue personal.* Even when a hostile questioner has made you the villain, don't attack the person who asked the question. Keep the conversation focused on issues, not on personalities.

*Get to the heart of the issue.* Respond directly to a hostile question. Consider restating the evidence you presented in your speech. Or provide new insights to support your position.

- **When you don't know, admit it.** If you've been asked a question to which you don't know the answer, just say so. You can promise to find out more information and then get back to the person later. (If you make such a promise, follow through on it. Ask for the person's business card or e-mail address at the end of the Q & A session.)
- **Be brief.** Even if you've anticipated questions and have a "double-barreled" talk, make it short and to the point.
- **Use organizational signposts.** Quickly organize your responses. If you have two responses to a question, let your listeners know it. Then use a verbal signpost (a statement that clues your audience in to how you're organizing your message) by saying, "I have two responses. First . . ." When you get to your second point, say, "My second point is . . . ." These signposts will both help you stay organized and impress your listeners with your clarity.
- **Indicate when the Q & A period is concluding.** Tell your audience, "I have time for two more questions." Let them know that the Q & A session will soon conclude. Even if you have someone helping you moderate the discussion, you should remain in charge of concluding the session.

RECAP

### Responding to Questions

- Prepare; ask the first question yourself.
- Listen nonjudgmentally; repeat or rephrase questions.
- Respond to the whole audience.
- Bring off-topic questions back to your message.
- Acknowledge emotions, keep to the issue, and avoid personal responses to hostile questions.
- Admit it when you don't know the answer.
- Keep answers brief and organized.
- Warn audience when Q & A is ending.

# STUDY GUIDE

## The Power of Speech Delivery

Nonverbal communication conveys the majority of the meaning of your speech and nearly all of your emotions to an audience. Nonverbal expectancy theory suggests that your credibility as a speaker depends on meeting your audience's expectations about nonverbal communication. Audiences will believe what they see in your nonverbal communication more readily than what they hear in your words.

### A Question of Ethics

- What can listeners do to be less distracted by the delivery and emotional elements of a speaker's message and to focus more on the substance or content of the message?

## Methods of Delivery

Of the four methods of delivery—manuscript, memorized, impromptu, and extemporaneous—the extemporaneous method is the most desirable in most situations. Speak from an outline without memorizing the exact words.

### Being Audience-Centered

- Select your delivery method to best connect with your audience, as well as to achieve your speaking goal.

### Using What You've Learned

- Roger was so nervous about his first speech that he practiced it again and again. He could have given the speech in his sleep. He had some great examples, and his instructor had praised his outline. But as he gave his speech, he saw his classmates tuning out. What might he have done wrong, and how could he have rescued his speech?

## Characteristics of Effective Delivery

Eye contact is the single most important delivery variable. Make eye contact with the whole audience before and throughout your speech. Your gestures and movements should appear natural and relaxed, definite, consistent with your message, varied, unobtrusive, and coordinated with what you say, as well as appropriate to your audience and situation. Use your posture, facial expressions, and vocal cues—including pitch, rate of speaking, and use of pauses—to communicate your emotions. Be sure to speak loudly enough and to articulate clearly.

### Being Audience-Centered

- Your use of gestures can provide cues to your audience about whether you wish them to respond or to ask questions about your message; an open-palm gesture, for example, often suggests you are open for questions or audience interaction.
- Use of gestures while speaking varies from culture to culture; for example, listeners from Japan and China usually prefer calm, less flamboyant gestures.
- If English is not your native language, you may have to spend extra time working on your pronunciation and articulation. Two helpful tips to consider: (1) Prolong your vowel sounds and (2) reduce choppy word pronunciation by blending the end of one word into the beginning of the next word.

### Using What You've Learned

- Monique is self-conscious about her hand gestures, and she often just puts her hands behind her back. What advice would you give Monique to help her use gestures more effectively?
- Professor Murray speaks slowly and in a monotone; consequently, many of her students do not like to listen to her music history lectures. What can she do to give her voice variety?

### A Question of Ethics

- Most politicians at the state or national level hire image consultants to help them project the most positive impression of their skills and abilities. Is it ethical to use such consultants, especially when their sole objective is to manipulate constituents into thinking the speaker is more credible than he or she really is?

### Speaker's Homepage: Proper Pronunciation

- The CMU Pronouncing Dictionary

  This Web site, developed at Carnegie Mellon University, uses phonetic markings to show you the proper pronunciations of words: www.speech.cs.cmu.edu/cgi-bin/cmudict/

## Audience Diversity and Delivery

Consult with other speakers familiar with your audience to help you avoid ethnocentrism. Consider using a more subtle delivery style with high-context audiences, and match immediacy and emotional expression to the cultural expectations of the majority of listeners. Learn variations in meanings of nonverbal gestures across cultures to avoid giving offense.

### Being Audience-Centered

- Monitor your expression of emotion; not all cultures interpret and express emotion in the same way. People from high-context cultures will likely place greater emphasis on your delivery of a message than will people from low-context cultures (such as North Americans).

## Rehearsing Your Speech: Some Final Tips

Leave at least two days to focus on your speech delivery and develop your speaking notes. As much as possible, recreate the speech environment when you rehearse.

### Being Audience-Centered

- Rehearse your speech while keeping your audience in mind; imagine that your audience is in front of you as you practice presenting your message.

## Delivering Your Speech

Get a good night's rest before a speech. Visualize success and reinforce your confidence using the suggestions from Chapter 1 of this book. Arrive early so that you have time to prepare the environment and are not stressed by running late.

### Speaker's Homepage: Evaluating Speaker Delivery

It's one thing to read about speech delivery, but it's quite another to see and hear speakers deliver a message. Use what you've learned in this chapter to evaluate the delivery strengths and weaknesses of the speeches at the following sites.

- History Channel Archive of Speeches: Each day a famous speech is presented. There is also a RealAudio archive of famous speeches: www.history.com/media.do.
- MSU Vincent Voice Library: This site will permit you to hear recordings of the voices of U.S. presidents and other historical figures: http:vvl.lib.msu.edu/index.cfm.

## Responding to Questions

Prepare for Q & A and be ready to ask the first question yourself. Listen nonjudgmentally and repeat or rephrase questions. Respond briefly and to the whole audience. Use strategies described in this chapter to neutralize hostile questions and bring off-topic questions back to your message. Admit it when you don't know an answer. Use organizational signposts to clarify answers and to signal the end of Q & A.

# SPEECH WORKSHOP

## Improving Your Speech Delivery

Make a video of your speech as you rehearse it. Watch the video and answer the following questions to evaluate your delivery.

### Delivery Style

Did I use an extemporaneous delivery style? _____ yes _____ no

Ideas for improving my delivery style:

Did I use appropriate notes, but not read or recite my speech? _____ yes _____ no

Ideas for improvement:

### Eye Contact

Did I establish eye contact with my audience before I began my speech? _____ yes _____ no

Did I maintain eye contact during my speech? _____ yes _____ no

Ideas for improving my eye contact:

### Physical Delivery

Did I use gestures in a natural way? _____ yes _____ no

Ideas for improving my gestures:

Did I have an appropriate posture? _____ yes _____ no

Ideas for improving my posture:

### Facial Expression

Did I have appropriate and varied facial expressions? _____ yes _____ no

Ideas for improving my facial expressions:

### Vocal Delivery

Did I speak loudly enough to be heard clearly? _____ yes _____ no

Ideas for improving my volume:

Did I speak with vocal variety? _____ yes _____ no

Ideas for improving my variety of voice:

THE SOUL NEVER THINKS WITHOUT A PICTURE.

—ARISTOTLE

Hieronymus Bosch (c. 1450–1516), *The Conjurer,* 1475–1480. Musée Municipal, Saint-Germain-en-Laye, France. Photo: Scala/White Images/Art Resource, N.Y.

OUTLINE

# 12 Using Presentation Aids

OBJECTIVES

**After studying this chapter you should be able to do the following:**

1. Discuss five ways in which presentation aids help communicate ideas to an audience.
2. Describe the use of three-dimensional presentation aids.
3. Identify ways of producing and using two-dimensional presentation aids including PowerPoint™.
4. Discuss the uses of audiovisual aids.
5. Identify guidelines for developing presentation aids.
6. Identify guidelines for using presentation aids.

Perhaps it has happened to you. A professor flashes one PowerPoint™ slide after another while droning on about British history or some other topic. As you sit there, bored out of your socks, you think, "Why doesn't she just hand out the PowerPoint slides or simply put them online and let us go? I don't need her to read her notes to me." Following such a mind-numbing experience, you can understand the phrase "Death by PowerPoint."

PowerPoint and the multitude of other presentation aids that speakers may use—especially visual aids—are powerful tools: They can help communicate your ideas with greater clarity and impact than can words alone. But they can also overwhelm your speech or be so redundant that your audience tunes you out. This chapter will help you avoid being a PowerPoint "executioner" and ensure that your presentation aids add life to your speech rather than kill your message.

A **presentation aid** is any object that reinforces your point visually or aurally so that your audience can better understand it. Charts, photographs, posters, drawings, graphs, PowerPoint slides, movies, and videos are the types of presentation aids that we will discuss. Some of them, such as movies and videos, call on sound as well as sight to help you make your point.

When you are first required to give a speech using presentation aids, you may wonder, "How can I use presentation aids in an informative or persuasive speech? Those kinds of speeches don't lend themselves to visual images." As it happens, almost any speech can benefit from presentation aids. A speech for which you are expected to use presentation aids is not as different from other types of speeches as you might at first think. Your general objective is still to inform, persuade, or entertain. The key difference is that you will use supporting material that can be seen, rather than only heard, by an audience.

In this chapter, we look at presentation aids as an important communication tool, and we examine several kinds. Toward the end of the chapter, we suggest guidelines for using presentation aids in your speeches.

# The Value of Presentation Aids

Presentation aids are invaluable to an audience-centered speaker. They help your audience *understand* and *remember* your message, and they help you communicate the *organization* of ideas, gain and maintain *attention*, and illustrate a *sequence* of events or procedures.[1]

- **Presentation aids enhance understanding.** Of your five senses, you learn more from sight than from all the others combined. In fact, it has been estimated that more than 80 percent of all information comes to you through sight.[2] To many people, seeing is believing. We are a visually oriented society. For example, most of us learn the news by seeing it presented on TV or the Internet. Because your audience is accustomed to visual reinforcement, it is wise to consider how you can increase their understanding of your speech by using presentation aids.
- **Presentation aids enhance memory.** Your audience will not only have an improved understanding of your speech, but they will also better remember what you say as a result of visual reinforcement.[3] There is evidence that high-tech presentation aids enhance learning.[4] Researchers estimate that you remember 10 percent of what you read, 20 percent of what you hear, 30 percent of what you see, and 50 percent of what you simultaneously hear and see. For example, in your speech about the languages spoken in Africa, your audience is more likely to remember words in Arabic, Swahili, and Hausa if you display the words visually, rather than just speak them.
- **Presentation aids help listeners organize ideas.** Most listeners need help understanding the structure of a speech. Even if you clearly lay out your major points, use effective internal summaries, and make clear transition statements, your listeners will welcome additional help. Briefly listing major ideas on a PowerPoint slide, a chart, or a poster can add clarity to your talk and help your audience grasp your main ideas. Visually presenting your major ideas during your introduction, for example, can help your audience follow them as you bring them into the body of your speech. And you can display key ideas during your conclusion to help summarize your message succinctly.

**presentation aid**
Anything tangible (drawings, charts, graphs, video images, photographs, sounds) that helps communicate an idea to an audience

- **Presentation aids help you gain and maintain attention.** Keshia began her speech about poverty in the United States by showing a photo of the face of an undernourished child. She immediately had the attention of her audience. Chuck began his speech with the flash of his camera to introduce his photography lecture. He certainly alerted his audience at that point. Midway through her speech about the lyrics in rap music, Tomoko not only spoke the words but also displayed a giant poster of the song lyrics so that her audience could read the words and sing along. Presentation aids not only grab the attention of your listeners but also hold their interest when words alone might not.
- **Presentation aids help illustrate a sequence of events or procedures.** If your purpose is to inform an audience about a process—how to do something or how something functions—you can do this best through actual demonstrations or with a series of visuals. Whether your objective is instructing people on how to make a soufflé or how to build a greenhouse, demonstrating the step-by-step procedures helps your audience understand them.[5] If you wish to explain how hydroelectric power is generated, a series of diagrams can help your listeners understand and visualize the process.

When demonstrating how to make something, such as your prize-winning cinnamon rolls, you can prepare each step of the process ahead of time and show your audience each example as you describe the relevant step; for example, you might have the dough already mixed and ready to demonstrate how you sprinkle on the cinnamon. A climax to your speech could be to unveil a finished pan of rolls still warm from the oven. If time does not permit you to demonstrate how to prepare your rolls, you could have on hand a series of diagrams and photographs to illustrate each step of the procedure.

Today's audiences expect visual support. Contemporary audiences are quite different from those of over a century ago when Thomas Edison invented the kinetoscope, a precursor of the movie camera. Edison said, "When we started out it took the average audience a long time to assimilate each image. They weren't trained to visualize more than one thought at a time."[6] Times have changed. The predominance of visual images—on TV, in movies, on the Internet and our iPods and phones—attests to how central images are in the communication of information to modern audiences.

Contemporary communicators understand the power of visual rhetoric in informing and persuading others. **Visual rhetoric** is the use of images as an integrated element in the total communication effort a speaker makes to achieve his or her speaking goal.[7] To be a visual rhetorician is to assume the role of an audience member and consider not only what a listener hears but also what a listener sees. A speech should

**visual rhetoric**
The use of images as an integrated element in the total communication effort a speaker makes to achieve the speaking goal

## LEARNING FROM GREAT SPEAKERS

### Ronald Reagan (1911–2004)

The 40th president of the United States, Ronald Reagan, has often been called "The Great Communicator." His early experience in radio and film served him well as he spoke not only to the audience assembled in front of him, but to those listening and watching via television. Reagan's inaugural address in 1981 was the first to be delivered from a podium on the west side of the U.S. Capitol building. From this site, the television cameras could broadcast sweeping views of the national monuments—fitting presentation aids for Reagan's patriotic address.[8]

Reagan was a master of using visual support to reinforce his rhetorical point. When you present your speeches, consider how well-selected presentation aids could support your verbal message. Listeners believe what they see; appropriate visual aids help you gain and maintain your listeners' attention. Imagine that you are in your audience when you present your message. Consider how the visual rhetoric as well as the words you speak will impact your listeners.

[Photo: Bob Daugherty/AP Wide World Photos]

RECAP

**The Value of Presentation Aids**

They help your audience
- understand your message.
- remember your message.
- understand the organization of your message.
- maintain attention.
- understand a sequence of events or procedures.

be more than just what a speaker says, with a few PowerPoint slides or other visual aids added as an afterthought. Today's listeners are sophisticated and more likely than listeners of even a few years ago to expect a visually satisfying message to help them make sense of what you are saying.

# Types of Presentation Aids

The first question many students ask when they learn they are required to use presentation aids is "What type of presentation aid should I use?" We will discuss three classes of presentation aids: three-dimensional, two-dimensional, and audiovisual.

## Three-Dimensional Presentation Aids

**Objects** You have played the trombone since you were in fifth grade, so you decide to give an informative speech about the history and function of this instrument. Your trombone is the obvious presentation aid that you would show to your audience as you describe how it works. You might even play a few measures to demonstrate its sound and your talent. Or perhaps you are an art major and you have just finished a watercolor painting. Why not bring your picture to class to illustrate your talk about watercolor techniques?

Objects add interest because they are tangible. They can be touched, smelled, heard, and even tasted, as well as seen. Objects are real, and audiences like the real thing.

When you use an object to illustrate an idea, make sure that you can handle the object with ease. If an object is too large, it can be unwieldy and difficult to show to your audience. Tiny objects can only be seen close up. It will be impossible for your listeners to see the detail on your antique thimble, the intricate needlework on your cross-stitch sampler, or the attention to detail in your miniature log cabin. Other objects can be dangerous to handle. One speaker, who attempted a demonstration of how to string an archery bow, made his audience extremely uncomfortable when his almost-strung bow flew over their heads. He certainly got their attention, but he lost his credibility.

**Models** If it is not possible to bring along the object you would like to show your audience, consider showing them a **model** of it. You cannot bring a World War II fighter plane to class, so buy or build a scale model instead. To illustrate her lecture about human anatomy, one student brought a plastic model of a skeleton; an actual human skeleton would have been difficult to get and carry to class. Similarly, colleges and universities do not allow firearms on campus. A drawing that shows the features of a gun is a much safer presentation aid than a real gun or even a toy gun. If you need to show the movable parts of a gun, perhaps a papier-mâché, plastic, or wood model would serve. Make sure, however, that any model you use is large enough to be seen by all members of your audience. When Brad brought his collection of miniature hand-carved guitars to illustrate his talk on rock music, his tiny visuals didn't add to the message; they detracted from it.

**People** At least since Ronald Reagan, U.S. presidents have used people as visual aids during their State of the Union addresses, relating a poignant story and then asking the protagonist of the story, seated in the balcony, to stand and be recognized. One speechwriter noted that presidents have learned to use this strategy to especially good effect, finding it "a way of coming down from the stage, as it were, and mingling with the crowd."[9]

**model**
A small object that represents a larger object

In classroom speeches, too, people can serve as presentation aids. Amelia, a choreographer for the Ballet Folklorico Mexicano, wanted to illustrate an intricate Latin folk dance, so she arranged to have one of the troupe's dancers attend her speech to demonstrate the dance.

Using people to illustrate your message can be tricky, however. It is usually unwise to ask for spur-of-the-moment help from volunteers while you are delivering your speech. Instead, choose a trusted friend or colleague before your presentation so that you can fully inform him or her about what needs to be done. Rehearse your speech using your living presentation aid.

Also, it is distracting to have your support person stand beside you doing nothing. If you don't need the person to demonstrate something during your opening remarks, wait and introduce the person to your audience when needed.

Finally, do not allow your assistants to run away with the show. For example, don't let your dance student perform the *pas de bourré* longer than necessary to illustrate your technique. Nor should you permit your models to prance about provocatively while displaying your dress designs. And don't allow your buddy to throw you when you demonstrate the wrestling hold that made you the district wrestling champ. Remember, your presentation aids are always subordinate to your speech. You must remain in control.

Generally, *you* can serve as your own presentation aid to demonstrate or illustrate major points. If you are talking about tennis, you might use your racquet to illustrate your superb backhand or to show the proper way to hold it. If you are a nurse or an emergency room technician giving a talk about medical procedures, by all means wear your uniform to establish your credibility.

*Three-dimensional models can help you to explain an object, process, or procedure to your audience in situations where it is impractical or impossible to use the actual object.*

[Photo: © Cultura Limited/SuperStock]

## Two-Dimensional Presentation Aids

The most common presentation aids are two-dimensional: drawings, photographs, maps, graphs, charts, flipcharts, and chalkboards. A few presenters continue to use overhead transparencies. Although two-dimensional aids are the most common, you'll more than likely incorporate them into PowerPoint slides to illustrate your message. As we discuss two-dimensional visual aids, we'll offer general suggestions both for using them in the old-fashioned way and for incorporating them into PowerPoint. A little later in the chapter we'll focus exclusively on how to use PowerPoint graphics.

**Drawings** Drawings are popular and often-used presentation aids because they are easy and inexpensive to make. Drawings can be tailored to your specific needs. To illustrate the functions of the human brain, for example, one student traced an outline of the brain and labeled it to indicate where brain functions are located. Another student wanted to show the different sizes and shapes of tree leaves in the area, so she drew enlarged pictures of the leaves, using appropriate shades of green.

You don't have to be a master artist to develop effective drawings. As a rule, large and simple line drawings are more effective for stage presentations than are detailed images. If you have absolutely no faith in your artistic skill, you can probably find a friend or relative who can help you prepare a useful drawing, or you may be able to use computer software to generate simple line drawings.

**Photographs** Photographs can be used to show objects or places that cannot be illustrated with drawings or that an audience cannot view directly. The problem with photos, however, is that they are usually too small to be seen clearly from a distance. If your listeners occupy only two or three rows, it might be possible to hold a photograph close enough for them to see a key feature of the picture. The details will not be visible, however, beyond the first row. Passing a photograph among your listeners is not a good idea either; it creates competition for your audience's attention.

The only way to be sure that a printed photograph will be effective as a presentation aid for a large audience is to enlarge it. You can enlarge your photos at a photo developing store. If you're using non-digital images, you can scan them and have them enlarged. You can easily find photography services online to send your digital photos to enlargement. Or, if you're using PowerPoint, you can import your photos into PowerPoint slides to make them large enough for everyone to see.

**Slides** Twenty years ago, in the era BP (Before PowerPoint), public speakers who wanted to illustrate a talk with photos used 36-millimeter slides. A theater professor might, for example, project slides of his trip to Greece depicting what an ancient Greek theater looked like.

But slides have several disadvantages: The room has to be darkened, and slides require special projectors (with bulbs that often burn out just as the room lights are dimmed). In addition, slides need to be loaded properly or they could be projected upside down. Today a speaker rarely uses slides because of the advantages of PowerPoint: The room not need be as dark, written titles can be added, and images are easily cropped and enlarged. Photo developing stores can convert your slides into digital images that you can use more effectively in PowerPoint presentations.

**Maps** Most maps are designed to be read from a distance of no more than two feet. As with photographs, the details on most maps won't be visible to your audience. You could use a large map, however, to show general features of an area. Or you could use a magnified version of your map. Certain copiers can enlarge images as much as 200 percent. It is possible, using a color copier, to enlarge a standard map of Europe enough for listeners in the last row to see the general features of the continent. Using a dark marker, one speaker highlighted the borders on a map of Europe to indicate the countries she had visited the previous summer (see Figure 12.1). She used a red marker to show the path of her journey.

**graph**
A pictorial representation of statistical data

**Graphs** A **graph** is a pictorial representation of statistical data in an easy-to-understand format. Most graphs used in speeches are prepared using either Excel or Word and then displayed as PowerPoint slides.

FIGURE 12.1 *A map can be an effective visual aid, especially when the speaker personalizes it by highlighting relevant information—such as the route followed in a journey from Edinburgh to Warsaw.*

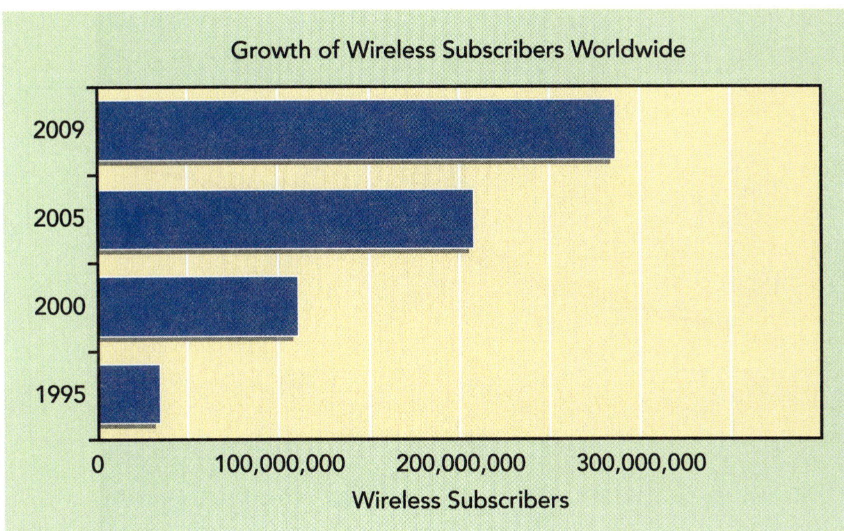


FIGURE 12.2 *Bar graphs can help summarize statistical information clearly so that the information is immediately visible to your audience.*

Source: Data from CTIA The Wireless Association, *2010 CTIA Semi-Annual Wireless Industry Survey* <www.ctia.org/advocacy/research/index.cfm/AID/10316>

Why use a graph? Because statistics are abstract summaries of many examples, most listeners find that graphs help make the data more concrete and easier to understand. Yet research also suggests that in addition to presenting information in a graph, it's important to narrate the information presented.[10] Don't just show it—talk about it. Graphs are particularly effective for showing overall trends and relationships among data. The four most common types of graphs are bar graphs, pie graphs, line graphs, and picture graphs.

- **Bar Graphs.** A **bar graph** consists of flat areas—bars—of various lengths to represent information. The bar graph in Figure 12.2 clearly shows the growth rates of wireless subscribers. This graph makes the information clear and immediately visible. By comparison, words and numbers are more difficult to assimilate, especially in something as ephemeral as a speech.
- **Pie Graphs.** A **pie graph** shows the individual shares of a whole. The pie graph in Figure 12.3 shows the top Internet search providers. Pie graphs are especially useful in helping your listeners to see quickly how data are distributed in a given category or area.
- **Line Graphs. Line graphs** show relationships between two or more variables. Like bar graphs, line graphs organize statistical data to show overall trends

**bar graph**
A graph in which bars of various lengths represent information

**pie graph**
A circular graph divided into wedges that show each part's percentage of the whole.

**line graph**
A graph that uses lines or curves to show relationships between two or more variables

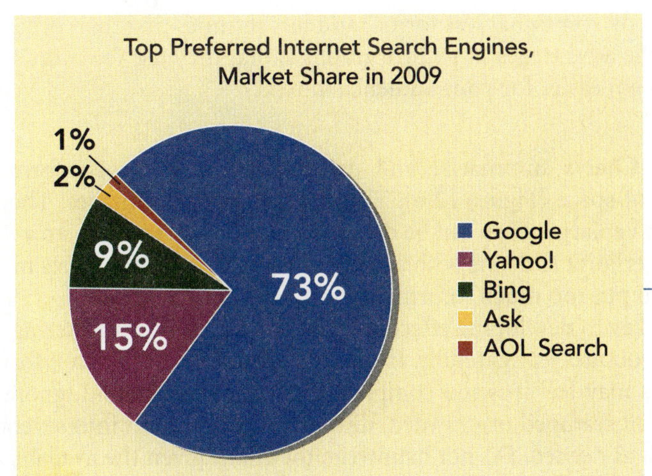


FIGURE 12.3 *A pie graph shows visually the percentage of a whole that belongs to each part of it.*

Source: Data from the SEO Consultants Directory, *2010 Top Ten Search Engines* <www.seoconsultants.com/search-engines>

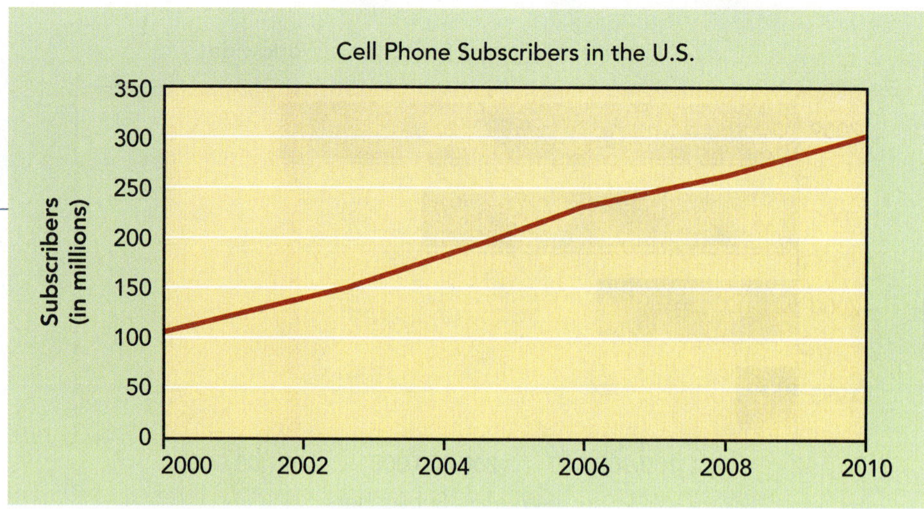


FIGURE 12.4 *Line graphs show relationships between two or more variables.*

Source: Data from Information Please Database, 2010. *Cell Phone Subscribers in the U.S., 1985–2008* <www.infoplease.com/ipa/A0933563.htm>

FIGURE 12.5 *Adding visual symbols, such as those in this picture graph, can help your audience maintain interest and understand complex information.*

Source: From "Prison population rates per 100,000 of the population," *Visual Aid 2*, 2009. Reprinted by permission of Black Dog Publishing and Draught Associates.

(Figure 12.4). A line graph can cover a greater span of time or numbers than a bar graph without looking cluttered or confusing. As with other types of presentation aids, a simple line graph communicates better than a cluttered one.

- **Picture Graphs.** In place of either a line or a bar, you can use pictures, or symbols, to supplement the data you are summarizing (Figure 12.5). **Picture graphs** look somewhat less formal and less intimidating than other kinds of graphs. One of the advantages of picture graphs is that they use few words or labels, which makes them easier for your audience to read.

**Charts** **Charts** summarize and present a great deal of information in a small amount of space (Figure 12.6). They have several advantages: They are easy to use, reuse, and enlarge. They can be displayed in a variety of ways, on a flipchart, a poster, or a PowerPoint slide. As with all other presentation aids, charts must be simple. Do not try to put too much information on one chart.

The key to developing effective charts is to prepare the lettering of the words and phrases you use very carefully. If the chart contains too much information, audience members may feel it is too complicated to understand, and ignore it. If your chart looks at all cramped or crowded, divide the information into several charts and display each as needed. Do not handwrite the chart; given the availability of computers, a hand-lettered chart may seem unprofessional. We suggest using computer software

**picture graph**
A graph that uses images or pictures to symbolize data

**chart**
A display that summarizes information by using words, numbers, or images

| Team | W | L | Percent | GB | Streak |
|---|---|---|---|---|---|
| Toronto | 84 | 59 | .583 | — | Won 2 |
| Baltimore | 78 | 64 | .549 | $5\frac{1}{2}$ | Lost 2 |
| Milwaukee | 77 | 65 | .542 | $6\frac{1}{2}$ | Won 2 |
| New York | 69 | 74 | .483 | 15 | Lost 1 |

FIGURE 12.6 *Charts summarize and present a great deal of information in a small amount of space.*

to prepare large charts or graphs. Make sure your letters are large enough to be seen clearly in the back row. Use simple words or phrases, and eliminate unnecessary words.

**Flipcharts** A flipchart consists of a large pad of paper resting on an easel. Flipcharts are often used in business presentations and training sessions, although the prevalence of computer graphics software has reduced their use in corporate presentations. You can either prepare your visual aids before your speech or draw on the paper while speaking. Flipcharts are easy to use. During your presentation, you need only flip the page to reveal your next visual. Flipcharts are best used when you have brief information to display or when you want to summarize comments from audience members during a presentation.

Most experienced flipchart users recommend that you use lined paper to keep your words and drawings neat and well organized. Another suggestion is to pencil in speaking notes on the chart that only you can see. Brief notes on a flipchart are less cumbersome to use than notes on cards or a clipboard. If you do use notes, however, be sure that they are few and brief; using too many notes will tempt you to read rather than have eye contact with your audience.

**Chalkboards and Whiteboards** A fixture in classrooms for centuries, chalkboards are often used to offer visual support for spoken words. Whiteboards are replacing chalkboards in both education and business settings; these more contemporary boards serve the same function as chalkboards, but instead of writing on a black or green slate with a piece of chalk, the speaker writes on a whiteboard with a marker. Chalkboards and whiteboards have several advantages: They are inexpensive, simple to use, and low-tech, so you don't need to worry about extension cords or special training.

Although you can find a chalkboard or whiteboard in most classrooms and boardrooms, many public-speaking teachers discourage overuse of them. Why? When you write on the board, you have your back to your audience; you do not have eye contact! Some speakers try to avoid that problem by writing on the board before their speech starts. But then listeners often look at the visual rather than listening to the introductory remarks. Moreover, chalkboards and whiteboards are probably the least novel presentation aids, so they are not particularly effective at getting or holding audience attention.

Use a board only for brief phrases or for very simple line diagrams that can be drawn in just a few seconds. It is usually better to prepare a chart, graph, or drawing on a poster or an overhead transparency than to use a chalkboard or whiteboard.

**Overhead Transparencies** Before PowerPoint became common, using an overhead projector was a standard method of displaying words, drawings, and images when teaching or speaking. An overhead projector projects images drawn on clear sheets of plastic, called *transparencies*, onto a screen so that the images can be seen by a large group. Overhead projectors allow you to maintain eye contact with your audience as your write on the transparency. In addition, the overhead doesn't require that you turn off the lights in the room. Although you may want to dim the lights a bit, most images can be seen clearly in normal room light.

Although most teachers and speakers today use PowerPoint slides rather than overhead transparencies to display visual images, we discuss the use of overhead transparencies for three reasons: First, some speakers prepare transparencies as a backup method of projecting their PowerPoint slides—especially when the speaker is delivering an important presentation and the images are vital to the talk. Second, there may be times when, as a speaker, you'd like to summarize information *during* your talk. It is easy to draw a simple diagram, make a brief list of facts or numbers, or summarize comments made by audience members, using overhead transparencies. Finally, transparencies are relatively easy to use.

If you do prepare an overhead transparency, apply the same principles and tips we present when developing PowerPoint slides. Make sure your images can be seen by everyone in the audience. Control the timing of the images you project by turning the projector off when not in use. And just as with any presentation aid, practice using the equipment you'll use during your speech.

## PowerPoint Presentation Aids

Richard had worked hard on his presentation to the finance committee. He had prepared an impressive-looking poster, distributed a handout of his key conclusions, and rehearsed his speech so that he had a well-polished delivery. But as he sat down after concluding his speech, certain he had dazzled his listeners, a colleague poked him and asked, "Why didn't you use PowerPoint slides?"

**Basic Principles of Using PowerPoint** Most audiences, especially those in the corporate world, expect a speaker to use PowerPoint—a popular software program that helps you create and present images, photos, words, charts, and graphs. Although PowerPoint or any other computer-generated graphic can be overused and, like any presentation aid, can distract from your message if used improperly, it nonetheless opens up professional-looking possibilities for illustrating your speech.

One of the biggest problems with PowerPoint presentations is that a speaker may be tempted to shovel large amounts of information at listeners without regard for the listeners' attention span. Research supports our now-familiar admonition that the audience should be foremost in your mind as you develop visual images to support your verbal message.[11]

Since most students learn PowerPoint skills in school, you will no doubt be familiar with the basic elements of developing a PowerPoint slide. And because you've undoubtedly seen many PowerPoint presentations, you also know that you can incorporate video clips as well as digital photo images on a PowerPoint slide. But, as with any presentation aid, the images or clips that you choose to display must help develop your central idea; otherwise, they will distract your audience from it.

You don't have to be a professional artist to develop attractive PowerPoint slides. That's the key advantage of using computer-generated graphics—virtually anyone can use them to craft professional-looking images. In addition to learning the mechanics of the software program, keep the following tips in mind when using PowerPoint.[12] These tips are also summarized in Table 12.1.

TABLE 12.1 Develop Effective PowerPoint Visuals

| | |
|---|---|
| Make visuals simple | • Use no more than seven lines of text on a single slide<br>• Use bullets<br>• Use parallel structure |
| Make visuals unified | • Use a common visual image on each slide<br>• Use a common font<br>• Use a similar background or style for each slide |
| Choose fonts carefully | • Use serif fonts to increase ease of reading<br>• Use *script* and **sans serif** fonts sparingly<br>• Use decorative fonts only for dramatic impact |
| Choose colors carefully | • Use red and orange to communicate warmth<br>• Use green and blue to communicate calm coolness<br>• Be cautious about using red and green together<br>• Use a light background with darker text to catch attention |
| Create your visuals well in advance of your presentation | • Use your time to integrate your verbal message with your visual message<br>• Seek advice and assistance from others to help polish your visuals<br>• Practice using your visuals when you rehearse your speech |

## Tips for Using PowerPoint

**Keep Sights and Sounds Simple** In most aspects of communication, simple is better. Even though you *can* use fancy fonts and add as many images as you like to your visual, we have a suggestion for you: Don't. Keep in mind what we've stressed throughout this chapter: Presentation aids *support* your message; they are not your message. Or, as CEO John W. Roe wisely expressed, "Visual aids should be made to steer, not to row."[13]

What are some techniques for keeping your visual message simple? Consider these principles:

- Use no more than seven lines of text on any single visual.
- Use bullet points to designate individual items or thoughts.
- Use bullets in parallel structure (such as beginning each bulleted phrase with the same word, as we do in this list).
- Use the heading of each slide to summarize the essential point of the visual; if listeners read only the headings of your visuals, they should still be able to follow the key points of the story you're telling.[14]

Most graphics software let you add sound effects to highlight your message. But the sound of a racecar zooming across the computer screen or a typewriter clacking as letters pop in place can detract from your speech. Cute sounds will lose their novelty after the first slide or two and can become irritating. We suggest that *you* be the sound track, not your computer.

**Control PowerPoint Images** When using PowerPoint slides with a computer, there may be times when you want to speak to your audience and not refer to a slide

FIGURE 12.7 *Copyright-free clip art is readily available at many Web sites. It can give a professional look to your visuals and memorably reinforce your verbal messages.*

**Common Meeting Mistakes**

✓ Missed the meeting
✓ Missed part of the meeting
✓ Did other work during the meeting

or image. Use a blank PowerPoint slide or, if it's within easy reach, simply cover the projector lens when you don't want the audience to be looking at a slide.

**Repeat Visual Elements to Unify Your Presentation** Use a common visual element, such as a bullet or other symbol, at the beginning of each word or phrase on a list. Use common color schemes and spacing to give your visuals coherence. Also, avoid mixing different fonts. You get a professional, polished look when you use the same visual style for each of your images.

The most significant advantage of computer graphics is the ease with which they allow you to display visual images. Both color and black-and-white images are available as **clip art**. Clip art consists of pictures and other images that are either in printed form or stored in a computer file. You can incorporate these images into your visuals. Clip art (as shown in Figure 12.7) can give your visuals and graphics a professional touch even if you did not excel in art class.

**Choose a Typeface with Care** You'll be able to choose from among dozens of typefaces and **fonts**. But make an informed choice rather than use a typeface just because it strikes your fancy. Graphic designers divide typefaces into four types: serif, sans serif, script, and decorative. You'll see each of these illustrated in Figure 12.8. Serif fonts, like the one you are reading now, are easier to read for longer passages because the little lines at the tops and bottoms of the letters (called *serifs*) help guide the eye from one letter to the next. Sans serif fonts (*sans* means "without") do not have the extra lines. Script fonts are designed to look like handwriting; although interesting and dramatic, script fonts should be used sparingly because they are harder to read. And you should use decorative fonts only when you want to communicate a special tone or mood. Regardless of which font style or typeface you use, don't use more than one or two typefaces on a single visual; if you do use two, designers suggest they should be from different font categories.

**Make Informed Decisions about Using Color** Color communicates. Red and orange are warm colors that communicate excitement and interest (which is why most fast-food restaurant chains use red, yellow, and orange in their color schemes; they want to make you hungry and catch your attention). Cooler colors such as green and blue have a more calming effect on viewers. Warm colors tend to come forward and jump out at the viewer, whereas cooler colors recede into the background. What are the implications of the power of color to communicate? Consider using warm colors for positive messages (for example, "Profits are up") and cooler colors for more negative messages ("We're losing money").

Designers caution against using certain color combinations. For example, if some audience members are color-blind, they won't be able to distinguish between red and green. And you don't want to get carried away with using color. To unify your

**clip art**
Images or pictures stored in a computer file or in printed form that can be used in a presentation aid

**font**
A particular style of typeface

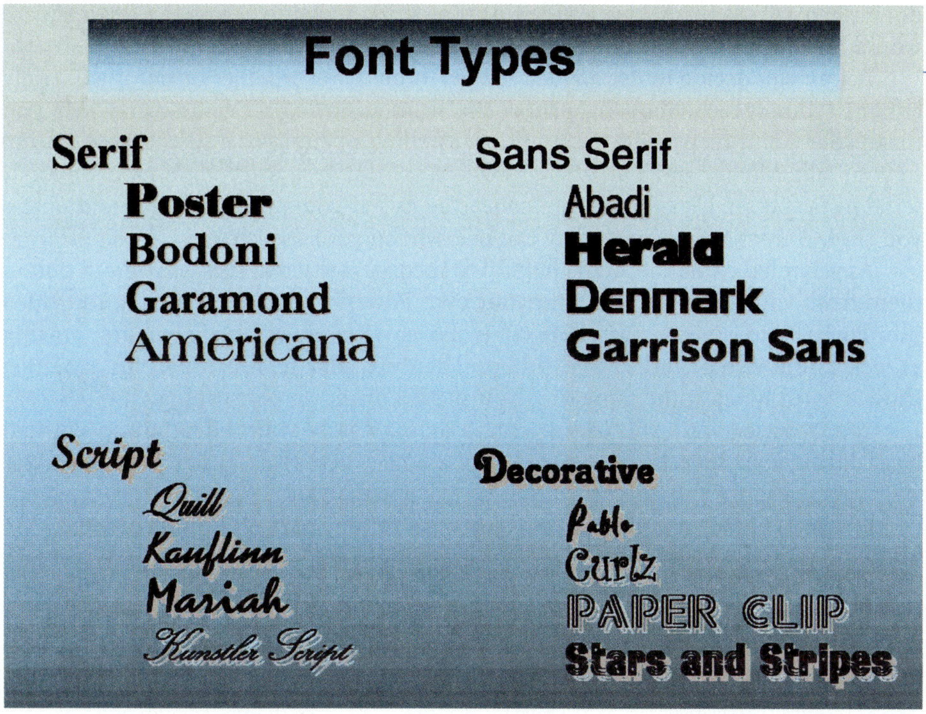

FIGURE 12.8 *Typefaces grouped by font type.*

presentation, use the same background color on all visuals and no more than two colors for words. A light background with darker-colored words can have a pleasing effect and is easy to see.

**Allow Plenty of Time to Prepare Your Presentation Aids** Prepare your presentation aids well in advance of your speaking date so that you can make them as attractive and polished-looking as possible. Avoid late-night, last-minute constructions. A sloppy, amateurish presentation aid will convey the impression that you are not a credible speaker, even if you have spent many hours preparing the speech itself. If you haven't used computer-generated graphics before, don't expect to whip out the software manual and produce professional-looking images the night before your presentation. Focus your final hours on rehearsing, not on learning a computer program.

## Audiovisual Aids

Audiovisual aids combine sound and images to communicate ideas. With audiovisual aids you combine the power of visual rhetoric with a supporting audio track. You are undoubtedly familiar with media that combine images and sound. In addition to using computer software to import sounds and music, you can use DVDs, videotapes, iPods or other MP3 players, as well as more traditional audio aids to help you communicate your ideas.

**Video Aids** If you are using video images to support your talk, you'll likely get the images from prerecorded digital video disks (DVDs), video recordings you make yourself, or from Internet sites such as YouTube or Hulu. It's now easy to record video images and audio clips to support speech ideas; digital video cameras are inexpensive and widely available. If, for example, you want to illustrate the frustration of not being able to park on your campus, a video of full parking lots and harried commuters hunting for parking spots would help you make your point. Or to explain how litter and trash make your

### CONFIDENTLY CONNECTING WITH YOUR AUDIENCE

#### Practice with Your Presentation Aids to Boost Your Confidence

One source of communication apprehension is uncertainty. By rehearsing with your presentation aids, you reduce uncertainty about your presentation. Whether you are using PowerPoint slides or some other technology, be sure you have practiced using the equipment you will use when you present your message. By reducing the chance for errors and technical miscues, you will also be increasing your confidence in your ability to use your presentation aids without a hitch.

downtown area look shabby, a video of the debris blowing across the town square would make your point better than would words alone.

Before you decide to use a video image, think about whether or not it will really enhance your speech. Showing a short clip from a movie or TV show may help you make your point or provide an attention-catching opening or a memorable closing to your talk. Movies and TV shows, however, are not designed to be supporting material for a speech. Usually they are conceived as self-contained packages, and unless you show only short excerpts, they can overwhelm your speech.

As we noted earlier, it can be helpful to incorporate video files (if you can obtain them from your video source) into your own PowerPoint slides. Building the video into PowerPoint can give you more control over precisely what clip you are showing as well as the visual context and timing when you play it. You could, for example, show printed lyrics at the same time you show a musician performing.

You can use a variety of other technologies to store your videos and play them back during your speech:

- **DVD/Videotape player.** You may wish to play part of a prerecorded movie or TV show from a DVD or a videotape. DVD players have several advantages over the older technology of videotape players. Not only does a DVD have excellent picture quality, but it can be started and stopped with precision.
- **Computers and other electronic devices.** You can store and play your own videos or clips from other sources on your computer, your iPad, or your iPod or other MP3 player. Unless the audience is very small, all of these options will require you to hook your device to a monitor or a projection system. A 25-inch screen is generally visible to an audience of 25 or 30 people. For a larger audience, you will need either several TVs or monitors or a large-projection TV system. Make sure monitors are available and compatible with your device, or bring your own.
- **The Internet.** If the room in which you are delivering your speech has Internet access, you could skip storing your video and instead play the video directly from YouTube or another Internet source. Playing video directly from the Internet does, however, carry the risk of losing an Internet connection prior to or during your speech. It will also involve having the technology to access the Internet—either your own equipment or whatever is available in the room.

When using any of these technologies, you'll want to practice using your video and make sure all the equipment you need is available. Unless you're using a wireless system, for example, you might need a cable to connect your storage device to a monitor. We also recommend that, before you give your speech, you do a technical run-through, ensuring that your video image will be ready when you want it.

**Audio Aids** Audio can be used to complement visual displays. As with video, you can either create your own audio content or use prerecorded sources. You also have a number of options for storage and playback. You might play a few measures of Bach's *Toccata and Fugue in D Minor* from a CD or from your iPod—or even live, on a portable electronic keyboard—to illustrate a point.

Used sparingly, sound can effectively establish a mood or support your points. While showing PowerPoint slides of her recent Caribbean vacation, one student used a recording of soft steel drum music as an introductory background for her talk. Another student played excerpts of taped interviews with frustrated students who had difficulty figuring out the most recent changes in how to apply for financial aid.

RECAP

### Types of Presentation Aids

- **3-D Aids:** Objects, Models, People
- **2-D Aids:** Drawings, Photos, Slides, Maps, Graphs, Charts, Flipcharts, Chalkboards and Whiteboards, Overhead Transparencies
- **PowerPoint Aids**
- **Audiovisual Aids:** Video, Audio

As with video, be sure to rehearse with and master any technology involved with audio aids; and don't let your soundtrack overwhelm or distract from your own words.

# Guidelines for Developing Presentation Aids

The following guidelines offer commonsense and research-based strategies that can help you prepare effective presentation aids for your speeches.

## Make Them Easy to See

Without a doubt, the most violated principle of using presentation aids in public speaking is "Make it big!" Countless speeches have been accompanied by a chart or graph with writing too small to read, a PowerPoint image not large enough to be legible, or a graph on a flipchart that simply can't be deciphered from the back row. If the only principle you carry away from this chapter is to make your presentation aid large enough to be seen by all in your audience, you will have gained more skill than a majority of speakers who use presentation aids in speeches. *Write big!*

## Keep Them Simple

Simple presentation aids usually communicate best. Some students think that the visuals accompanying a speech must be as complicated as a Broadway production, complete with lights and costumes. Resist trying to make your visuals complicated. Indeed, *any* complexity is too much complexity. Text should be limited to key words or phrases. Lengthy dissertations on poster board or an overhead usually do more harm than good. Don't cram too much information on one chart or overhead. If you have a great deal of information, it is better to use two or three simple charts or overhead transparencies than to attempt to put all your words on one visual.

Here's an outline of an informative speech that uses simple visual aids (which could be displayed on charts or as computer-generated graphics) to clearly communicate the ideas the speaker wishes to convey.[15]

| | |
|---|---|
| TOPIC: | Standard editorial symbols |
| GENERAL PURPOSE: | To inform |
| SPECIFIC PURPOSE: | At the end of my speech, the audience should be able to use and interpret ten standard symbols for editorial changes in written material. |

I. The following seven editorial symbols are commonly used to change written text.
   A. Use the "pigtail" symbol to delete a letter, a word, or a phrase. 
   B. Use a caret (it looks like a housetop) to insert a space, a letter, new text, or punctuation. 
   C. Use what look like two sideways parentheses to remove unwanted space. 
   D. Use this squiggle line to transpose letters, words, or phrases.  
   E. Draw three lines under letters to capitalize them. 
   F. Draw a slash through letters to change them to lowercase.

G. Write the word *stet* to undo previous editing marks.

II. Three editorial symbols are used to rearrange the format of text.

A. Use brackets to add or remove indents or to correct the alignment of text.

B. Use backward bracket marks around text that you want centered on the page.

C. Use a symbol that looks like a backward *p* to mark the beginning of a new paragraph.

After the speech, the speaker could give each audience member a one-page handout summarizing these editorial markings.

## Select the Right Presentation Aid

Because there are so many choices, you may wonder, "How do I decide which presentation aid to use?" Here are some suggestions.

- **Consider your audience.** Factors such as audience size dictate the size of the visual you select. If you have a large audience, do not choose a presentation aid unless everyone will be able to see it clearly. The age, interests, and attitudes of your audience also affect your selection of audiovisual support.
- **Think of your speech objective.** Don't select a presentation aid until you have decided on the purpose of your speech.
- **Take into account your own skills and experience.** Use only equipment with which you are comfortable or have had practical experience.
- **Know the room in which you will speak.** If the room has large windows with no shades and no way to dim the lights, do not consider using visuals that require a darkened room.

RECAP

### Guidelines for Developing Presentation Aids

- Make them big.
- Keep them simple.
- Match them to your audience, objectives, skills, and setting.
- Keep them safe and legal.

## Do Not Use Dangerous or Illegal Presentation Aids

Earlier we described a speech in which the speaker accidentally caused an archery bow to fly over the heads of his startled audience. Not only did he lose credibility because he was unable to string the bow successfully, he also endangered his audience by turning his presentation aid into a flying missile. Dangerous or illegal presentation aids may either shock your audience or physically endanger them. Such aids will also detract from your message. They are never worth the risk of a ruined speech or an injured audience member. If your speech seems to call for a dangerous or illegal object or substance, substitute a picture, a chart, or some other representational device.

# Guidelines for Using Presentation Aids

Now that we have offered strategies for developing effective presentation aids, here are tips for using them for maximum audience impact.

## Rehearse with Your Presentation Aids

Beware of letting your presentation aids overshadow you as you deliver your speech. It is especially tempting to talk to your PowerPoint slides, as this speaker is doing, rather than maintain eye contact with your audience.
[Photo: © David Young-Wolff/PhotoEdit]

Jane nervously approached her speech teacher ten minutes before class. She wondered whether class could start immediately because her presentation aid was melting. She had planned to explain how to get various stains out of clothing, and her first demonstration would show how to remove chewing gum. But she had forgotten the gum, so she had to ask for a volunteer from the audience to spit out his gum so she could use it in her demonstration. The ice she had brought to rub on the sticky gum had by this time melted. All she could do was dribble lukewarm water on the gummed-up cloth in an unsuccessful effort to demonstrate her cleaning method. It didn't work. To make matters worse, when she tried to set her poster in the chalkboard tray, it kept falling to the floor. She ended up embarrassed and on the edge of tears. It was obvious that she had not rehearsed with her presentation aids.

Unlike Jane, Marti knew she had an important presentation the next day, and she was well prepared. Because she was going to use PowerPoint in her presentation, she carefully developed each visual to coordinate with her talk. She rehearsed her speech in the same room in which she would be speaking; she also practiced her presentation using the same computer that she would use for her speech. She sailed through her presentation without a hitch. Although the unexpected can always happen, Marti's thorough preparation and rehearsal boosted both her confidence and her credibility with her listeners.

Your appearance before your audience should not be the first time you deliver your speech while holding up your chart, turning on the overhead projector, operating the slide projector, or using the flipchart. Practice with your presentation aids until you are at ease with them.

## Make Eye Contact with Your Audience, Not with Your Presentation Aids

You may be tempted to talk to your presentation aid rather than to your audience. Your focus, however, should remain on your audience. You will need to glance at your visual to make sure that it isn't upside down and that it is the proper one. But do not face it while giving your talk. Keep looking your audience in the eye.

## Explain Your Presentation Aids

Some speakers believe that they need not explain a presentation aid; they think it's enough just to show it to their audience. Resist this approach. When you exhibit your chart showing the overall decline in the stock market, tell your audience what point you are trying to make. Visual support performs the same function as verbal support: It helps you communicate an idea. Make sure that your audience knows what that idea is. Don't just unceremoniously announce, "Here are the recent statistics on birth rates in the United States" and hold up your visual without further explanation. Tell the audience how to interpret the data. Always set your visuals in a context.

*Animals are neither predictable nor dependable as presentation aids.*

[Photo: Jason Moore/ZUMA Press/NewCom]

## Do Not Pass Objects among Members of Your Audience

You realize that your marble collection will be too small to see, so you decide to pass some of your most stunning marbles around while you talk. Bad idea. While you are excitedly describing some of your cat's-eye marbles, you have provided a distraction for your audience. People will be more interested in seeing and touching the marbles than in hearing you talk about them.

What can you do when your object is too small to see without passing it around? If no other speaker follows your speech, you can invite audience members to come up and see your object when your speech is over. If your audience is only two or three rows deep, you can even hold up the object and move in close to the audience to show it while you maintain control.

## Use Animals with Caution

Most actors are unwilling to work with animals—and for good reason. At best, they may steal the show. And most often they are unpredictable. You may *think* you have the smartest, best-trained dog in the world, but you really do not know how your dog will react to a strange environment and an unfamiliar audience. The risk of having an animal detract from your speech may be too great to make planning a speech around one worthwhile.

A zealous student at a midwestern university a few years ago decided to give a speech on cattle. What better presentation aid, he thought, than a cow? He brought the cow to campus and led her up several flights of stairs to his classroom. The speech in fact went well. But the student had neglected to consider one significant problem: Cows will go up stairs but not down them. (The cow had to be hoisted out a window.)

Another student had a handsome, well-trained German shepherd guard dog. The class was enjoying his speech and his demonstrations of the dog's prowess until the professor from the next classroom poked his head in the door to ask for some chalk. The dog lunged, snarling and with teeth bared, at the unsuspecting professor. Fortunately, he missed—but the speech was concluded prematurely. These and other examples emphasize our point: Use animals with care, if at all.

## Use Handouts Effectively

Many speech instructors believe that you should not distribute handouts during a speech. Handing out papers in the middle of your presentation will only distract your audience. However, many audiences in businesses and other types of organizations expect a summary of your key ideas in written form. If you do find it necessary to use written material to reinforce your presentation, keep the following suggestions in mind.

- **Don't distribute your handout during the presentation unless your listeners must refer to the material while you're talking about it.** Do not distribute handouts that have only a marginal relevance to your verbal message. They will defeat your purpose.

- **Control listeners' attention.** If you do distribute a handout and you see that your listeners are giving the written material more attention than they are giving you, tell them where in the handout you want them to focus. For example, you could say, "I see that many of you are interested in the second and third pages of the report. I'll discuss those items in just a few moments. I'd like to talk now about a few examples before we get to page 2."
- **After distributing your handouts, tell audience members to keep the material face down until you're ready to talk about the material.** This will help listeners not to be tempted to peek at your handout instead of keeping their focus on you and your message.
- **Make sure you clearly number the pages on your handout material.** This will make it easy for you to direct audience members to specific pages in your handouts.
- **To make sure your listeners know what page of your handout you want them to focus on, prepare images of each page.** You'll be able to display the specific page you're talking about. Even if the words are too small for audience members to read, they will be able to see what page you're on if they miss your announcement. With a PowerPoint slide or transparency, you can also quickly point to the paragraph or chart on the page you want them to focus on. It's not a good idea, however, to economize by only displaying detailed material and not providing handouts. The print will be too small to be seen clearly.
- **If your listeners do not need the information during your presentation, tell them that you will distribute a summary of the key ideas at the end of your talk.** Your handout might refer to the specific action you want your audience to take, as well as summarize the key information you have discussed.

## Time the Use of Visuals to Control Your Audience's Attention

A skillful speaker knows when to show a supporting visual and when to put it away. It's not wise to begin your speech with all your charts, graphs, and drawings in full view unless you are going to refer to them in your opening remarks. Time the display of your visuals to coincide with your discussion of the information contained in them.

Jessica was proud of the huge replica of the human mouth that she had constructed to illustrate her talk on the proper way to brush one's teeth. It stood over two feet tall and was painted pink and white. It was a true work of art. As she began her speech, she set her mouth model in full view of the audience. She opened her speech with a brief history of dentistry in America. But her listeners never heard a word; they were fascinated by the model. Jessica would have done better to cover her presentation with a cloth and then dramatically reveal it when she wanted to illustrate proper tooth brushing.

Here are a few more suggestions for timing your presentation aids:

- **If possible, use a remote control to advance PowerPoint images** so you do not have to stay anchored near the computer to advance each slide.
- **Turn the PowerPoint image off, or, if possible, cover the projector lens** so the audience's focus returns to you if you are making a point or telling a story not related to a PowerPoint image. You don't want an image or bulleted list of words unrelated to your message to compete for your listeners' attention.
- **Consider asking someone to help you hold your presentation aid or turn the pages of your flipchart.** Make sure you rehearse with your assistant beforehand so that all goes smoothly during your presentation.

## Use Technology Effectively

You may be tempted to use some of the newer technologies we have described because of their novelty rather than their value in helping you communicate your message. Some novice speakers will overuse presentation aids simply because they can quickly produce eye-catching visuals. Resist this temptation.

Don't assume that the hardware and software you need will be available in the room where you are speaking. Be sure to ask what kinds of technology exist.

Even if you have asked and you are appropriately prepared based on the information you were given, have a backup plan. You may want to bring your own laptop or a backup flash drive or other device for storing your PowerPoint slides. If your images are vital to presenting your message, consider a backup plan to the PowerPoint slides, such as having your images on transparencies or having hard copies of the images that, although too small to be seen clearly, will be better than nothing.

In spite of the potential problems that using technology may present, innovations such as video and PowerPoint images are destined to play a growing role in public speaking. In this technology- and image-dependent culture, listeners expect technology to support a message. Nonetheless, when using technology, keep the basic principles we've offered in mind: Make it big, integrate the words and images into your talk, and properly time your visuals to coincide with your message content. And don't forget to rehearse using the same technology you will use during your talk.

RECAP

### Guidelines for Using Presentation Aids

- Prepare carefully and practice with aids.
- Maintain eye contact with audience.
- Tell about the aid.
- Don't pass around objects.
- Be careful with animals.
- Use handouts and technology effectively.
- Control audience's attention.
- Remember Murphy's Law.

## Remember Murphy's Law

According to Murphy's Law, if something can go wrong, it will. When you use presentation aids, you increase the chances that problems or snags will develop when you present your speech. The chart may fall off the easel, you may not find the chalk, the bulb in the overhead projector may burn out. We are not saying that you should be a pessimist but that you should have backup supplies and a backup plan in case your plans go awry.

If something doesn't go as you planned, do your best to keep your speech on track. If the chart falls, pick it up and keep talking; don't offer lengthy apologies. If you can't find the chalk, ask a friend to go on a chalk hunt in another room. A thorough rehearsal, a double-check on your equipment, back-up images, and such extra supplies as extension cords and masking tape can help repeal Murphy's Law.

# STUDY GUIDE

## The Value of Presentation Aids

Presentation aids are tools that help you communicate your ideas more dramatically than words alone can. They help improve listeners' understanding and recollection of your ideas. They can also help you communicate the organization of your ideas, gain and maintain the audience's attention, and illustrate a sequence of events or procedures.

### Being Audience-Centered

- Use presentation aids to support your speech if they will help your listeners understand, remember, or attend to your message. Also use presentation aids when they will help you organize your message or illustrate a sequence of events or procedures for your listeners.

## Types of Presentation Aids

Three-dimensional presentation aids include objects, models, and people. Two-dimensional presentation aids include drawings, photographs, slides, maps, graphs, charts, flipcharts, projected transparencies, and chalkboards. Software graphics packages can be used to produce many presentation aids inexpensively and efficiently. Audiovisual aids include DVDs and videotapes. Audio aids such as tapes and compact disks can also help communicate ideas to your listeners.

### Using What You've Learned

- Nikki plans to give a talk to the Rotary Club in an effort to encourage the club members to support a local bond issue for a new library. She wants to make sure they understand how cramped and inadequate the current library is. What type of visual support could she use to make her point?
- Professor Chou uses only the chalkboard to illustrate her anthropology lectures and then only occasionally writes a word or two. What other types of visual or auditory aids could Professor Chou use in teaching?

## Guidelines for Developing Presentation Aids

When you prepare your presentation aids, make sure your visuals are large enough to be seen clearly by all of your listeners. Adapt your presentation aids to your audience, the speaking environment, and the objectives of your speech. Prepare your visuals well in advance, and make sure they are not illegal or dangerous to use.

### Being Audience-Centered

- When using computer-generated graphics (such as PowerPoint slides), don't let the technology overwhelm your audience: Use simple, brief lines of text and images.
- People from high-context cultures are more likely to focus on the pictures and images in your presentation aids. People from low-context cultures may be especially interested in the words and text included on your visuals.
- When you are speaking to an audience whose first language is not the same as your own, consider using images or pictures to help them remember your ideas.

### Speaker's Homepage: Using the Internet as a Source for Visuals for Your Speeches

The Internet brings the resources of the world's art museums, as well as its newspapers and magazines, to your fingertips. Here's a sampling of sites that you can explore as sources of visuals for your speech.

- Art Links: www.artcyclopedia.com
- Time & Life Photo Site: www.timelifepictures.com/
- American Memory Collection, from the Library of Congress: www.memory.loc.gov/
- Yahoo!: http://www.yahoo.com/
- Google Images: www.images.google.com/

## Guidelines for Using Presentation Aids

As you present your speech, remember to look at your audience, not at your presentation aid; talk about your visual, don't just show it; avoid passing objects among your audience; use handouts to reinforce the main points in your speech; time your visuals carefully; and be sure to have backup supplies and a contingency plan.

### Being Audience-Centered

- Revealing one line of text at a time when you are projecting a list of items on an overhead projector helps maintain audience interest.
- Maintain eye contact with your audience, not with your presentation aid.

- As a general rule, don't pass objects among your audience while you speak.
- If you are using an interpreter because of language differences, give a copy of your presentation aids to your interpreter before you speak so that he or she can easily translate your message.

## Using What You've Learned

- Mayor Bryan is going to address the board of directors of a large microchip firm, hoping to lure them to his community. He plans to use handouts, several charts, a short video clip, and an overhead projector to show several transparencies. What advice would you give the mayor to make sure his presentation is effective?

## A Question of Ethics

- Ceally wants to educate his college classmates about the increased use of profanity in contemporary music. He would like to play sound clips of some of the most offensive lyrics to illustrate his point. Would you advise Ceally to play these songs, even though doing so might offend members of the audience?
- Derrick is planning to give a speech about emergency first aid. His brother is a paramedic and a licensed nurse. Is it ethical for Derrick to wear his brother's paramedic uniform without telling his listeners that the outfit belongs to his brother?

# SPEECH WORKSHOP

## A Checklist for Using Effective Presentation Aids

Consult this checklist to ensure that you are using presentation aids appropriately.

### Developing Your Presentation Aids

- ☐ Are my presentation aids easy to see?
- ☐ Are my presentation aids simple and uncluttered?
- ☐ Do my presentation aids suit my audience, speech objectives, and speech environment?
- ☐ Are my presentation aids attractive and professional in appearance?
- ☐ Are my presentation aids legal and nonthreatening to my audience?
- ☐ Did I rehearse using my presentation aids?

### Using Your Presentation Aids

- ☐ Do I look at my listeners rather than at my presentation aids while speaking?
- ☐ Do I explain my presentation aids rather than just show them?
- ☐ If I use handouts, do I carefully time when I distribute the handouts?
- ☐ Do I focus my audience's attention on my presentation aid and then have them focus on what I am saying when appropriate?
- ☐ Can I skillfully operate any computers, video, audio, or other hardware or software I plan to use during my presentation?

NOT ONLY IS THERE AN ART IN KNOWING A THING, BUT ALSO A CERTAIN ART IN TEACHING IT.

—CICERO

*Schoolmaster of the Jullundur Doab Seated with Two Pupils* (1838–1839). Punjab style. British Library, London, Great Britain. Photo: HIP/Art Resource, N.Y.

OUTLINE

# 13 Speaking to Inform

OBJECTIVES

**After studying this chapter you should be able to do the following:**

1. Identify three goals of speaking to inform.
2. Describe five different types of informative speeches.
3. Effectively and appropriately use four strategies to enhance audience understanding.
4. Effectively and appropriately use three strategies to maintain audience interest.
5. Effectively and appropriately use four strategies to enhance audience recall of information presented in an informative speech.

As you participate in your company's management training class, the group facilitator turns to you and asks you to summarize your team's discussion about the importance of leadership.

Your sociology professor requires each student to give an oral report describing the latest findings from the U.S. census.

At the conclusion of your weekly staff meeting, your boss asks you to give a brief report summarizing the new product you and your team are developing.

In each of these situations, your task is to give information to someone. Whether you are having a spontaneous conversation or delivering a rehearsed speech, you will often find that your speaking purpose is to inform or teach someone something you know. One survey of both speech teachers and students who had taken a speech course found that the single most important skill taught in a public-speaking class is how to give an informative speech.[1]

A **speech to inform** shares information with others to enhance their knowledge or understanding of the information, concepts, and ideas you present. When you inform someone, you assume the role of a teacher by defining, illustrating, or elaborating on a topic. You're not trying to persuade listeners by asking them to change their behavior. You are giving them information that is useful or interesting.

When you inform, you're typically attempting to achieve three goals:

- *You speak to enhance understanding.* Understanding occurs when a listener accurately interprets the intended meaning of a message.
- *You speak to maintain interest.* You may have carefully selected words, examples and illustrations that your listeners would understand, but if your listeners become bored and do not focus on your message, you won't achieve your informative-speaking goal.
- *You speak to be remembered.* In Chapter 3 we noted that one day after hearing a presentation, most listeners remember only about half of what they were told. Two days after the presentation, they recall only about 25 percent. Your job as an informative speaker is to improve on those statistics.

Conveying information to others is a useful skill in most walks of life. You may find that informing others will be an important part of your job. As a regional manager of a national corporation, you may have to report sales figures every fiscal quarter; as an accountant, you may have to teach your administrative assistant how to organize your files. Other activities, such as teaching a Chinese cooking class or chairing monthly meetings of the Baker Street Irregulars, can also require you to provide information.

In this chapter, we will suggest ways to build on your experience and enhance your skill in informing others. We will identify different types of informative speeches and provide suggestions for achieving your informative-speaking goals: enhancing understanding, maintaining interest, and improving listener recall. Finally, we'll review the audience-centered model of public speaking to help you plan and present your informative message.

# Types of Informative Speeches

Informative speeches can be classified according to the subject areas they cover. In many informative presentations you will deliver, your topic will be provided for you, or the nature of the specific speaking opportunity will dictate what you talk about. If, for example, you're updating your boss about a project your work team has been developing, you need not wrack your brain for a speech topic. The topic for your speech is prescribed for you. But if you have an invitation (or assignment) to give an informative speech and the topic choice is up to you, you may need help selecting a topic and developing your purpose. Understanding the different types of informative speeches can give you ideas about what to talk about.

**speech to inform**
A speech that teaches others new information, ideas, concepts, principles, or processes in order to enhance their knowledge or understanding about something

Classifying the type of informative speech you give can also help you decide how to organize your message. As you will see in Table 13.1 on page 291 and in the following discussion, the demands of your topic and purpose often dictate a structure for your speech. As you look at these suggestions about structure, however, remember that good organization is only one factor that determines your audience's ability to process your

## LEARNING FROM GREAT SPEAKERS

### Oprah Winfrey (1954– )

One of *Time* magazine's 100 Most Influential People of the late 20th and early 21st centuries, Oprah Winfrey is best known as the host of the television talk show that was broadcast for 25 years. Because of her passion, knowledge, and skill in connecting with her listeners, she continues to have a tremendous influence on what people talk about and read. She uses her power as a communicator to inform her listeners about ideas, authors, and causes about which she feels passionate. Her physical immediacy, listening skill, and humor all helped to stimulate and reinforce communication among the show's participants and make her messages interesting and memorable.

Oprah Winfrey illustrates how an effective communicator is not afraid to share her natural enthusiasm for a topic with her listeners. When sharing information with your listeners, it's important to let yourself reveal your natural interest in and passion for your subject. That can only happen if you are talking about ideas and topics that are important to you and about which you have strong feelings. So when you must select a topic for an informative talk, choose one that genuinely interests you.

[Photo: Charles Rex Arbogast/AP Wide World Photos]

**TABLE 13.1** Types of Informative Speeches

| Subject | Purpose | Typical Organizational Pattern | Sample Topics |
|---|---|---|---|
| Objects | Present information about tangible things | Topical<br>Spatial<br>Chronological | The Rosetta Stone<br>Museums<br>International space station<br>Voting machines |
| Procedures | Review how something works or describe a process | Chronological<br>Topical<br>Complexity | How to . . .<br>Fix a carburetor<br>Operate a nuclear-power plant<br>Buy a quality used car<br>Trap lobsters |
| People | Describe famous people or personal acquaintances | Chronological<br>Topical | Sojourner Truth<br>Nelson Mandela<br>Indira Gandhi<br>Your granddad<br>Your favorite teacher |
| Events | Describe an event that either has happened or will happen | Chronological<br>Topical<br>Spatial | The death of Michael Jackson<br>Inauguration Day<br>Cinco de Mayo |
| Ideas | Present abstract information or discuss principles, concepts, theories, or issues | Topical<br>Complexity | Communism<br>Immigration<br>Buddhism<br>Reincarnation |

message. After discussing types of informative speeches, we will offer specific techniques to help your audience understand, maintain interest in, and remember your message.

## Speeches about Objects

A speech about an object might be about anything tangible—anything you can see or touch. You may or may not show the actual object to your audience while you are talking about it. (Chapter 12 suggests ways to use objects as presentation aids to illustrate your ideas.) Almost any kind of object could form the basis of an interesting speech:

Something from your own collection (rocks, comic books, antiques, baseball cards)
Sports cars
Cellos
Smart phones
Digital video cameras
WWII Memorial
Toys
Antique Fiestaware
Staffordshire dogs

The time limit for your speech will determine the amount of detail you can share with your listeners. Even in a 30- to 45-minute presentation, you cannot talk about every aspect of any of the objects listed above. So you will need to focus on a specific purpose. Here's a sample outline for a speech about an object:

| | |
|---|---|
| TOPIC: | Dead Sea Scrolls |
| GENERAL PURPOSE: | To inform |
| SPECIFIC PURPOSE: | At the end of my speech, my audience should be able to describe how the Dead Sea Scrolls were found, why they are important to society, and the key content of the ancient manuscripts. |

*Informative speeches can be classified according to their topic. The type of speech you are giving can help you decide how to organize it. What might be the main ideas in this speaker's talk?*

[Photo: ©Spencer Grant/Alamy]

I. The Dead Sea Scrolls were found by accident.
   A. The scrolls were found in caves near the Dead Sea.
   B. The scrolls were first discovered by a shepherd in 1947.
   C. In the late 1940s and early 1950s, archeologists and Bedouins found ten caves that contained Dead Sea Scrolls.

II. The Dead Sea Scrolls are important to society.
   A. The Dead Sea Scrolls are the oldest known manuscripts of any books of the Bible.
   B. The Dead Sea Scrolls give us a look at Jewish life in Palestine over 2000 years ago.

III. The content of the Dead Sea Scrolls gives us a glimpse of the past.
   A. The Dead Sea Scrolls include all the books of the Old Testament except the book of Esther.
   B. The Dead Sea Scrolls include fragments of the Septuagint, the earliest Greek translation of the Old Testament.
   C. The Dead Sea Scrolls include a collection of hymns sung by the inhabitants of the Qumran Valley.

Speeches about objects may be organized topically, chronologically, or spatially. The speech about the Dead Sea Scrolls is organized topically. It could, however, be revised and organized chronologically: The first major idea could be Jewish life in Palestine 2000 years ago. The second point could describe how the scrolls were found in the 1940s and 1950s. The final major idea could be the construction in the 1960s of the museum in Jerusalem that houses the famous scrolls. Or the speech could even be organized spatially, describing the physical layout of the caves in which the scrolls were found.

## Speeches about Procedures

A speech about a procedure explains how something works (for example, the human circulatory system) or describes a process that produces a particular outcome (such as how grapes become wine). At the close of such a speech, your audience should be able to describe, understand, or perform the procedure you have described. Here are examples of procedures that could be the topics of effective informative presentations:

How state laws are made
How the U.S. patent system works
How an e-book reader works
How to refinish furniture
How to select an inexpensive stereo system
How to plant an organic garden
How to select a graduate school

Notice that all these examples start with the word *how*. A speech about a procedure usually focuses on how a process is completed or how something can be accomplished. Speeches about procedures are often presented in workshops or other training situations in which people learn skills.

Anita, describing how to develop a new training curriculum in teamwork skills, used an organizational strategy that grouped some of her steps together like this:

I. Conduct a needs assessment of your department.
   A. Identify the method of assessing department needs.
      1. Consider using questionnaires.
      2. Consider using interviews.
      3. Consider using focus groups.
   B. Implement the needs assessment.

II. Identify the topics that should be presented in the training.
   A. Specify topics that all members of the department need.
   B. Specify topics that only some members of the department need.

III. Write training objectives.
   A. Write objectives that are measurable.
   B. Write objectives that are specific.
   C. Write objectives that are attainable.

IV. Develop lesson plans for the training.
   A. Identify the training methods you will use.
   B. Identify the materials you will need.

Anita's audience will remember the four general steps much more easily than if each aspect of the curriculum-development process were presented as a separate step.

Many speeches about procedures include visual aids (see Chapter 12). Whether you are teaching people how to hang wallpaper or how to give a speech, showing them how to do something is almost always more effective than just telling them how to do it.

## Speeches about People

A biographical speech could be about someone famous or about someone you know personally. Most of us enjoy hearing about the lives of real people, famous or not, living or dead, who had some special quality. The key to presenting an effective biographical speech is to be selective: Don't try to cover every detail of your subject's life. Relate the key elements in the person's career, personality, or other significant life features so that you are building to a particular point rather than just reciting facts about an individual. Perhaps your grandfather was known for his generosity, for example. Mention notable examples of his philanthropy. If you are talking about a well-known personality, pick information or a period that is not widely known, such as the person's childhood or private hobby.

One speaker gave a memorable speech about his neighbor:

> To enter Hazel's house is to enter a combination greenhouse and zoo. Plants are everywhere; it looks and feels like a tropical jungle. Her home is always warm and humid. Her dog Peppy, her cat Bones, a bird named Elmer, and a fish called Frank can be seen through the philodendron, ferns, and pansies. While Hazel loves her plants and animals, she loves people even more. Her finest hours are spent serving coffee and homemade chocolate pie to her friends and neighbors, playing Uno with family until late in the evening, and just visiting about the good old days. Hazel is one of a kind.

Note how the speech captures Hazel's personality and charm. Speeches about people should give your listeners the feeling that the person is a unique, authentic individual.

One way to talk about a person's life is in chronological order—birth, school, career, marriage, achievements, death. However, when you want to present a specific theme, such as "Winston Churchill, master of English prose," you may decide to organize key experiences topically. First you would discuss Churchill's achievements as a brilliant orator whose words defied Germany in 1940, and then you would trace the origins of his skill to his work as a cub reporter in South Africa during the Boer War of 1899–1902.

## Speeches about Events

Where were you on September 11, 2001? Even though you may have been in elementary school, chances are that you clearly remember where you were and what you were doing on that and other similarly fateful days. Major events punctuate our lives and mark the passage of time.

A major event can form the basis of a fascinating informative speech. You can choose to talk about either an event that you have witnessed or one you have researched. Your goal is to describe the event in concrete, tangible terms and to bring the experience to life for your audience. Were you living in New Orleans when Hurricane Katrina struck? Have you witnessed the inauguration of a president, governor, or senator? Have you experienced the ravages of a flood or earthquake? Or you may want to re-create an event that your parents or grandparents lived through. What was it like to be in Pearl Harbor on December 7, 1941?

You may have heard a recording of the famous radio broadcast of the explosion and crash of the dirigible *Hindenburg*. The announcer's ability to describe both the scene and the incredible emotion of the moment has made that broadcast a classic. As that broadcaster was able to do, your purpose as an informative speaker describing an event is to make that event come alive for your listeners and to help them visualize the scene.

Most speeches built around an event follow a chronological arrangement. But a speech about an event might also describe the complex issues or causes behind the event and thus be organized topically. For example, if you were to talk about the Civil War, you might choose to focus on the three causes of the war:

I. Political

II. Economic

III. Social

Although these main points are topical, specific subpoints may be organized chronologically. However you choose to organize your speech about an event, your audience should be enthralled by your vivid description.

## Speeches about Ideas

Speeches about ideas are usually more abstract than other types of speeches. The following principles, concepts, and theories might be topics of idea speeches:

Principles of communication
Freedom of speech
Evolution
Theories of aging
Islam
Communal living
Positive psychology

Most speeches about ideas are organized topically (by logical subdivisions of the central idea) or according to complexity (from simple ideas to more complex ones). The following example illustrates how one student organized an idea topic into an informative speech:

| | |
|---|---|
| TOPIC: | Communication theory |
| GENERAL PURPOSE: | To inform |
| SPECIFIC PURPOSE: | At the end of my speech, the audience should be able to identify and describe three functions and three types of communication theory. |

I. Communication theory has three important functions.
   A. Communication theory helps explain how communication works.
   B. Communication theory helps us make predictions about how people will communicate with others.
   C. Communication theory helps us control communication situations because we can explain and predict communication behavior.

II. There are three main types of communication theory.
   A. Communication systems theory helps explain the transactive nature of communication.
   B. Rhetorical communication theory helps us explain and predict how public speakers influence others.
   C. Functional group communication theory identifies the important group-communication behaviors that can enhance group communication.

# Strategies to Enhance Audience Understanding

The skill of teaching and enhancing understanding is obviously important to teachers, but it's also important to virtually any profession. Whether you're a college professor, chief executive officer of a Fortune 500 company, or a parent raising a family, you will be called on to teach and explain. At the heart of creating understanding in someone is the ability to describe both old and new ideas. Just because an idea, term, or concept has been around for centuries doesn't mean that it is easy to understand. A person hearing an old idea for the first time goes through the same process as if he or she were learning about the latest cutting-edge idea. How do you enhance someone's knowledge or understanding? We can suggest several powerful strategies.

## Speak with Clarity

To speak with clarity is to express ideas so that the listener understands the intended message accurately. Speaking clearly is an obvious goal of an informative speaker. What is not so obvious is *how* to speak clearly. As a speaker you may think you're being clear, but only the listener can tell you whether he or she has received your message. One interesting study made the point that because the information is clear to you, you'll likely think it's also clear to your listener.[2] People were asked to tap the rhythm of well-known songs such as "Happy Birthday to You" or "The Star Spangled Banner" so that another person could guess the song just by hearing the rhythm. About half of the people who tapped the song thought that the listener would easily figure out which song was being tapped. However, less than 2 percent of the listeners could identify the song. (Try it—see if you can beat the 2 percent average.) The point: When you know something, you're likely to think it's clear to someone else. Whether it's how to drive a car or how to care for an aardvark, if you are already familiar with a topic, you're likely to think your task of communicating an idea to someone is easier than it is. Give careful thought to how you will help listeners understand your message. The most effective speakers (those whose message is both understood and appropriately acted on) build in success by consciously developing and presenting ideas with their listeners in mind, rather than flinging information at listeners and hoping some of it sticks.

Communication researcher Joseph Chesebro has summarized several research-based strategies you can use to enhance message clarity.[3]

- Preview your main ideas in your introduction.
- Tell your listeners how what you present relates to a previous point.

- Frequently summarize key ideas.
- Provide a visual outline to help listeners follow your ideas.
- Provide a handout prior to your talk with the major points outlined; leave space so that listeners can jot down key ideas.
- Once you announce your topic and outline, stay on message.

Another important suggestion for enhancing message clarity is this: *Don't present too much information too quickly.* Audiences can comprehend only so much information. If you present too much information, your listeners won't understand all of the details. Burying your listeners in an avalanche of details, data, and dates is a surefire way to make them stop listening. If you need to share detailed information, put that information in writing.

## Use Principles and Techniques of Adult Learning

Most public-speaking audiences you face will consist of adults. Perhaps you've heard of **pedagogy**, the art and science of teaching children to learn. The word *pedagogy* is based on the Greek words *paid*, which means "child," and *agogus*, which means "guide." Thus, pedagogy is the art and science of teaching children. Adult learning is called **andragogy**.[4] *Andr* is the Greek word that means "adult." Andragogy is the art and science of teaching adults. Researchers and scholars have found andragogical approaches that are best for adults. (If you're a college student over the age of 18, you are an adult learner.) What are andragogical, or adult-learning, principles? Here are the most important ones.

- **Provide information that can be used immediately.** Most people who work in business have an in-basket on their desk to receive letters that must be read and work that must be done. Each of us also has a kind of mental in-basket, an agenda for what we want or need to accomplish. If you present adult listeners with information that they can apply immediately to their "in-basket," they are more likely to focus on and understand your message.
- **Actively involve listeners in the learning process.** Rather than have your listeners sit passively as you speak, ask questions for them to think about or, in some cases, to respond to on the spot.
- **Connect listeners' life experiences with the new information they learn.** Adult listeners are more likely to understand your message when you help them connect new information with their past experiences. The primary way to do this is to know the kinds of experiences that your listeners have had, and then to refer to those experiences as you present your ideas.
- **Make new information relevant to listeners' needs and their busy lives.** Most adults are busy—probably, if pressed, most will say they are too busy for their own good. So when speaking to an adult audience, realize that any information or ideas you share will more likely be heard and understood if you relate what you say to their chock-full-of-activity lives. People working, going to school, raising families, and being involved in their communities need to be shown how the ideas you share are relevant to them.
- **Help listeners solve their problems.** Most people have problems and are looking for solutions to them. People will be more likely to pay attention to information that helps them better understand and solve their problems.

**pedagogy**
The art and science of teaching children

**andragogy**
The art and science of teaching adults

## Clarify Unfamiliar Ideas or Complex Processes

If you want to tell your listeners about a complex process, you will need more than definitions to explain what you mean. Research suggests that you can demystify a complex process if you first provide a simple overview of the process with an analogy, a vivid description, or a word picture.[5]

**Use Analogies** If a speaker were to say "The Milky Way galaxy is big," you'd have a vague idea that the cluster of stars and space material that make up the Milky Way was large. But if the speaker said "If the Milky Way galaxy were as big as the continent of North America, our solar system would fit inside a coffee cup," you'd have a better idea of just how big the Milky Way is and, by comparison, how small our solar system is.[6] As we discussed in Chapter 6, an analogy is a comparison of two things. It's an especially useful technique for describing complex processes because it can help someone understand something difficult to grasp (the size of the Milky Way) by comparing it to something already understood (the size of a coffee cup).[7]

By helping your listeners compare something new to something they already know or can visualize, you help to make your message clear. Here's an example of this idea based on what professor of business Chip Heath and communication consultant Dan Heath call the principle of "using what's there—using the information you have (what's there) and relating it to something more familiar."[8] Try this short exercise. Take 15 seconds to memorize the letters below; then close the book and write the letters exactly as they appear here.

J FKFB INAT OUP SNA SAI RS

Most people, say these experts, remember about half of the letters. Now, look below to see the same letters organized differently. The letters haven't changed, but we have regrouped them into acronyms that may make more sense to you. We are more likely to make sense out of something that we already have a mental category for. An analogy works in the same way.

JFK FBI NATO UPS NASA IRS

**Use Vivid Description** When you *describe,* you provide more detail than you do when you define something. Using descriptive terms that bring a process to life is especially effective when you want to clarify something that is complex. Descriptions answer questions about the who, what, where, why, and when of the process. Who is involved in the process? What is the process, idea, or event that you want to describe? Where and when does the process take place? Why does it occur, or why is it important to the audience? (Not all of these questions will apply to every description.)

**Use a Word Picture** A **word picture** is a lively description that helps your listeners form a mental image by appealing to their senses of sight, taste, smell, sound, and touch.

To create an effective word picture, begin by forming your own clear mental image of the person, place, or object before you try to describe it. See it with your "mind's eye."

- What would a listener see if he or she were looking at it?
- What would listeners hear?
- If they could touch it, how would it feel to them?
- If your listeners could smell or taste it, what would that be like?

**word picture**
A vivid description that appeals to the senses

To describe these sensations, choose the most specific and vivid words possible. Onomatopoeic words—words that sound like the sounds they name—such as *buzz, snort, hum, crackle,* or *hiss,* are powerful. So are similes and other comparisons. "The rock was rough as sandpaper" and "the pebble was as smooth as a baby's skin" appeal to both the visual and the tactile senses.

Be sure to describe the emotions that a listener might feel if he or she were to experience the situation you relate. Ultimately, your goal is to use just the right words to evoke an emotional response from the listener. If you experienced the situation, describe your own emotions. Use specific adjectives rather than general terms such as *happy* or *sad*. One speaker, talking about receiving her first speech assignment, described her reaction with these words:

> My heart stopped. Panic began to rise up inside. Me? . . . For the next five days I lived in dreaded anticipation of the forthcoming event.[9]

*Like most audiences, the members of this audience of medical students have a variety of learning styles. Can you identify audience members who appear to be auditory learners, visual print learners, visual learners, and kinesthetic learners? As a speaker, you should aim to craft a message that addresses this variety of learning styles.*

[Photo: Doug Menuez/Ironical/Getty Images]

Note how effectively her choice of such words and phrases as "my heart stopped," "panic," and "dreaded anticipation" describe her terror at the prospect of making a speech—much more so than if she had said simply, "I was scared."

The more vividly and accurately you can describe emotion, the more intimately involved in your description the audience will become. The Speech Workshop at the end of the chapter offers step-by-step guidance you can use to create word pictures for your next informative speech.

## Appeal to a Variety of Learning Styles

Would you rather hear a lecture, read the lecture, or see pictures about what the speaker is saying? Your choice reflects your preferred learning style. Not everyone has a single preferred style, but many people do. Four common styles are auditory, visual print, visual, and kinesthetic.

- **Auditory learners.** If you'd rather listen to a recorded audio book than read a book, you may be an auditory learner, a person who learns best by hearing.
- **Visual print learners.** If you learn best by seeing words in print, then you are a visual print learner. Most likely you would much rather read material than hear it presented orally.
- **Visual learners.** Barraged daily with images from TV and the Internet, many people have grown to depend on more than words alone to help them remember ideas and information. They are visual learners, who learn best with words and images.
- **Kinesthetic learners.** Kinesthetic learners learn best by moving while learning. They would rather try something than hear it, watch it, or read about it. These learners like active learning methods such as writing while listening or, better yet, participating in group activities.

As you develop your speech and your supporting materials, consider how you can appeal to a variety of learning styles at the same time. Since you'll be giving a speech, your auditory learners will like that. Visual learners like and expect an informative talk to be illustrated with PowerPoint™ images. They will appreciate seeing pictures or having statistics summarized using bar or line graphs or pie charts. Kinesthetic learners will appreciate movement, even small movements such as raising their hands in response to questions. Visual print learners will appreciate handouts, which you could distribute after your talk.

### Enhancing Audience Understanding

RECAP

- Keep your message clear.
- Apply adult-learning principles.
- Clarify the unfamiliar or complex:
  - Use analogies.
  - Use vivid descriptions.
  - Use word pictures.
- Plan for many different learning styles.

# Strategies to Maintain Audience Interest

Before you can inform someone, you must gain and maintain his or her interest. No matter how carefully crafted your definitions, how skillfully delivered your description, or how visually reinforcing your presentation aid, if your listeners aren't paying attention, you won't achieve your goal of informing them. Strategies for gaining and holding interest are vital in achieving your speaking goal.

In discussing how to develop attention-catching introductions in Chapter 8, we itemized specific techniques for gaining your listeners' attention. The following strategies build on those techniques.

## Motivate Your Audience to Listen to You

Most audiences will probably not be waiting breathlessly for you to talk to them. You will need to motivate them to listen to you.

Some situations have built-in motivations for listeners. A teacher can say, "There will be a test covering my lecture tomorrow. It will count toward 50 percent of your semester grade." Such methods may not make the teacher popular, but they will certainly motivate the class to listen. Similarly, a boss might say, "Your ability to use these sales principles will determine whether you keep your job." Your boss's statement will probably motivate you to learn the company's sales principles. However, because you will rarely have the power to motivate your listeners with such strong-arm tactics, you will need to find more creative ways to get your audience to listen to you.

Never assume that your listeners will be interested in what you have to say. Pique their interest with a rhetorical question. Tell them a story. Tell them how the information you present will be of value to them. As the British writer G. K. Chesterton once said, "There is no such thing as an uninteresting topic; there are only uninterested people."[10]

*When your audience is interested in your speech, they are more likely to learn the information you want to share with them. Strategies you can use to hold an audience's interest include pointing out why the information is important to them, telling stories, relating your information to listeners' lives, and surprising them with something they didn't expect.*

[Photo: Exactostock/SuperStock]

## Tell a Story

Good stories with interesting characters and riveting plots have fascinated listeners for millennia; the words "once upon a time" are usually sure-fire attention-getters. A good story is inherently interesting.

The characteristics of a well-told tale are simple yet powerful. Stories are also a way of connecting your message to people from a variety of cultural backgrounds.[11] Here we elaborate on some of the ideas about storytelling we introduced in Chapter 6. A good story includes conflict, incorporates action, creates suspense, and may also include humor.

- **A good story includes conflict.** Stories that pit one side against another foster attention, as do descriptions of opposing ideas and forces in government, religion, or personal relationships. The Greeks learned long ago that the essential ingredient for a good play, be it comedy or tragedy, is conflict.
- **A good story incorporates action.** An audience is more likely to listen to an action-packed message than to one that listlessly lingers on an idea. Good stories have a beginning that sets the stage, a heart that moves to a conclusion, and then an ending that ties up all the loose ends. The key to interest is a plot that moves along.
- **A good story creates suspense.** TV dramas and soap operas long ago proved that the way to ensure high ratings is to tell a story with the outcome in doubt. Suspense is created when the characters in the story may do one of several things. Keeping people on the edge of their seats because they don't know what will happen next is another element in good storytelling.
- **A good story may incorporate humor.** A fisherman went into a sporting-goods store. The salesperson offered the man a wonderful lure for trout: It had beautiful colors, eight hooks, and looked just like a rare Buckner bug. Finally, the fisherman asked the salesperson, "Do fish really like this thing?"

  "I don't know," admitted the salesperson, "I don't sell to fish."

  We could have simply said, "It's important to be audience-centered." But using a bit of humor makes the point while holding the listener's attention.

  Not all stories have to be funny. Stories may be sad or dramatic without humor. But adding humor at an appropriate time usually helps maintain interest and attention.

## Present Information That Relates to Your Listeners

Throughout this book we have encouraged you to develop an audience-centered approach to public speaking. Being an audience-centered informative speaker means being aware of information that your audience can use. If, for example, you are going to teach your audience about recycling, be sure to talk about specific recycling efforts on your campus or in your own community. Adapt your message to the people who will be in your audience.

## Use the Unexpected

On a flight from Dallas, Texas, to San Diego, California, flight attendant Karen Wood made this announcement:

> If I could have your attention for a few moments, we sure would love to point out these safety features. If you haven't been in an automobile since 1965, the proper way to fasten your seat belt is to slide the flat end into the buckle. To unfasten, lift up on the buckle and it will release.

## SAMPLE INFORMATIVE SPEECH

### CHOOSING A SPEECH TOPIC

*by Roger Fringer*[12]

Today I'd like to talk to you about [pause] tables. Tables are wood . . . usually . . . and they are. . . . How often do we sit in a class and feel the intelligence draining out of us? In a speech class, we are given the opportunity to add to that feeling or to add to the intelligence. Selecting a meaningful speech topic will make our speeches interesting, important, as well as being informative. As students, we've all been in the situation of being more anxious than necessary because we are talking about an unfamiliar or uninteresting speech topic. In our public speaking class, we spend a number of hours giving speeches and listening to them. If we have four days of speeches, at what—seven speech topics [per day]—that equals 28 hours spent listening to speeches. Let's not forget that we are paying to listen to those speeches. If our tuition is say, $15,000 a year, that's $875 that we have spent listening to those 28 hours of speeches. We work hard for our tuition, so we should spend it wisely. Spending it wisely means we don't waste our time. We don't waste our own time on preparing and giving the speeches, and we don't waste our classmates' time who have to listen to our speeches. The solution is simple if we take choosing our topic seriously.

I recommend that we choose topics following *The Three I's* to guide us. The first I is to make speeches *interesting*. By doing so, we can alleviate the boredom that so often permeates the public speaking classroom. If the topic is interesting to us, we will present it in a manner that shows our interest. We will also keep our audience's attention when we know, as students, they can be thinking about a million other things. Choosing

Roger cleverly captures attention by purposefully starting with an unimaginative topic and using halting delivery that makes listeners wonder, "What's this really about?"

Roger establishes a common bond with his listeners by relating to them as fellow students confronted with the same problem: how to select a topic for a speech.

Rather than just say we waste time and money listening to speeches, Roger uses statistics specifically adapted to his audience; this is a good example of being audience-centered.

He clearly previews his major ideas and links them together by using words that all begin with *I*.

> As the song goes, there might be fifty ways to leave your lover, but there are only six ways to leave this aircraft: two forward exit doors, two over-wing removable window exits, and two aft exit doors. The location of each exit is clearly marked with signs overhead, as well as red and white disco lights along the floor of the aisle.
>
> Made ya look![13]

This clever flight attendant took a predictable announcement and added a few surprises and novel interpretations to make a boring but important message interesting. With just a little thought about how to make your message less predictable, you can add zest and interest to your talks. Listeners will focus on the unexpected. The sample informative speech on this page and the next includes a surprise in the introduction.

Advertisers spend a lot of time trying to get your attention: A young couple is traveling in their car, having a normal, natural conversation and then BAM! CRUNCH!—someone who has run a red light slams into their car. The announcer intones, "Life comes at you fast." You look at the crumpled car and are stunned at how quickly an everyday experience changes in an instant. Like an effective ad, a good speaker knows how to surprise an audience with the same impact as this visual commercial—except that a speaker uses words and stories to metaphorically grab a listener by the shoulders and force him or her to focus on the message.

Besides surprising your listeners, you might maintain their attention by creating mystery or suspense. Stories are a great way to add drama and interest to a talk—especially a story that moves audience members to try to solve a riddle or a problem. One technique for creating a "mini mystery" is to ask a rhetorical question. You don't necessarily expect an audible answer from audience members, but you do want them to have a mental response. Here's an example: "Would you know what to do if you were stranded, out of gas, at night, without your cell phone?" By getting listeners to ponder your

RECAP

### Keeping the Audience Interested

- Tell them why they should want to listen.
- Tell them a good story.
    - Describe conflict.
    - Describe action.
    - Create suspense.
    - Use humor when appropriate.
- Tell them how it affects them.
- Tell them something that surprises them.

an interesting topic will also alleviate some of the angst, anxiety we feel while giving the speech topic.

The second I is to make the speech *important*. The speech should not only be interesting but important to us. It should be relevant to our lives now or in the future.

Here he uses a signpost by clearly noting he's moved to his second point.

The third I is to make the speech *informative*. Let's not waste our tuition money by not learning anything new in those 28 hours of class time. This is our opportunity to learn from each other's experiences and expertise.

Again, he uses a verbal signpost to indicate that this is his third point.

Now, just picture yourself putting these ideas into practice. Imagine sitting in a classroom, listening to your classmates talk about issues or ideas that are important to them. They are so excited that you can't help but be excited about the topic with them. You're learning from their life experiences, experiences that you would not have had the opportunity to learn about if it had not been for their speech. Then, imagine being able to talk about the experiences and knowledge that are important to you. Sometimes you only have seven minutes to express what is most important to you. Besides that, it's to a captive audience that has no choice but to listen to you. There are few times in our lives when we can have an impact on someone else's life, and we have only a short amount of time to do it. But in our public speaking class, we can have that chance. Let's all think about how we use our time and energy in our public speaking class. I don't want to waste my time or have any unnecessary stress over [pause] tables. I would like all of us to use our opportunities wisely by choosing topics that are interesting, important, and informative.

Although Roger's primary purpose is to inform, he uses a hypothetical example to tell the audience how the information he has given them will help them solve a problem: how to find a good speech topic.

Roger provides closure to his message by making a reference to the example he used in his introduction.



question, you've gotten them actively engaged in your message rather than passively processing your words.[14]

# Strategies to Enhance Audience Recall

Think of the best teacher you ever had. He or she was probably a good lecturer with a special talent for being not only clear and interesting but also memorable. The very fact that you can remember your teacher is a testament to his or her talent. Like teachers, some speakers are better than others at presenting information in a memorable way. In this section, we review strategies that will help your audiences remember you and your message.

## Build In Redundancy

It is seldom necessary for writers to repeat themselves. If readers don't quite understand a passage, they can go back and read it again. When you speak, however, it is useful to repeat key points. Audience members generally cannot stop you if a point in your speech is unclear or if their minds wander.

How do you make your message redundant without insulting your listeners' intelligence? We've already mentioned several techniques in this book. Permit us some redundancy here to make our point. A clear preview at the beginning of your talk and a summary statement in your conclusion are the most straightforward ways to make sure listeners get your points. Including an internal summary—a short summary after key points during your speech—is another technique to help audiences remember key ideas. Using numeric signposts (numbering key ideas by saying, "My first point is . . . , My second point is . . . , And now here's my third point . . .") is another way of making sure your audience can identify and remember key points. A reinforcing visual aid that displays your key ideas can also enhance recall. If you really want to ensure that listeners come away from your speech with essential information, consider preparing a handout or an outline of key ideas. (But as we noted in the last chapter, when using a handout, make sure the audience remains focused on you, not on your handout.)

## Make Your Key Ideas Short and Simple

When we say make your messages simple, we don't mean you should give 30-second speeches (although we're sure some speakers and listeners would prefer half-minute speeches to longer, more drawn-out versions). Rather, we mean that when you can distill your key ideas down to brief and simple phrases, your audiences will be more likely to remember what you say.[15]

Can you remember more than seven things? One classic research study concluded that people can hold only about seven pieces of information (such as the numbers in a seven-digit phone number) in their short-term memory.[16] If you want your listeners to remember your message, don't bombard them with a lengthy list. With the advent of PowerPoint, some speakers may be tempted to spray listeners with a shower of bulleted information. Resist this temptation.

An important speech-preparation technique that we've suggested is to crystallize the central idea of your message into a one-sentence summary of your speech. To help your audience remember your central idea statement, make it short enough to fit on a car bumper sticker. For example, rather than say "The specific words people use and the way people express themselves are influenced by culture and other socioeconomic forces," say "Language shapes our culture and culture shapes our language." The message is not only shorter, but it uses the technique of antithesis (opposition expressed with a parallel sentence structure) that we discussed in Chapter 10. Perhaps you've heard the same advice expressed as the KISS principle: *Keep It Simple, Sweetheart.* Make your message simple enough for anyone to grasp quickly. Here's the idea phrased as a bumper sticker: Make it short and simple.

## Pace Your Information Flow

Organize your speech so that you present an even flow of information, rather than bunch up many significant details around one point. If you present too much new information too quickly, you may overwhelm your audience. Their ability to understand may falter.[17]

You should be especially sensitive to the flow of information if your topic is new or unfamiliar to your listeners. Make sure that your audience has time to process any new information you present. Use supporting materials both to help clarify new information and to slow down the pace of your presentation.

Again, do not try to see how much detail and content you can cram into a speech. Your job is to present information so that the audience can grasp it, not to show off how much you know.

## Reinforce Key Ideas

This last point is one of the most powerful techniques of all: Reinforce key ideas verbally or nonverbally to make your idea memorable.

**Reinforce Ideas Verbally** You can reinforce an idea verbally by using such phrases as "This is the most important point" and "Be sure to remember this next point; it's the most compelling one." Suppose you have four suggestions for helping your listeners avoid a serious sunburn, and your last suggestion is the most important. How can you make sure your audience knows that? Just tell them. "Of all the suggestions I've given you, this last tip is the most important one. The higher the SPF level on your sunscreen, the better." Be careful not to overuse this technique. If you claim that every other point is a key point, soon your audience will no longer believe you.

RECAP

### Enhancing Audience Recall

- Build in redundancy: Say it again.
- Say it short and simple.
- Say it at steady pace.
- Don't just say it; use visuals and nonverbals.

**Reinforce Key Ideas Nonverbally** How can you draw attention to key ideas nonverbally? Just the way you deliver an idea can give it special emphasis. Gestures serve the purpose of accenting or emphasizing key phrases, as italics do in written messages.

A well-placed pause can provide emphasis and reinforcement to set off a point. Pausing just before or just after making an important point will focus attention on your thought. Raising or lowering your voice can also reinforce a key idea.

Movement can help emphasize major ideas. Moving from behind the lectern to tell a personal anecdote can signal that something special and more intimate is about to be said. As we discussed in Chapter 11, your movement and gestures should be meaningful and natural, rather than seeming arbitrary or forced. Your need to emphasize an idea can provide the motivation for making a meaningful movement.

# Developing an Audience-Centered Informative Speech

In this chapter, we've described types of informative speeches and offered numerous principles to follow in helping your listeners understand, maintain interest in, and remember your message. But, faced with an informative speaking opportunity, you may still wonder how to go about preparing an informative speech. Our advice: Use the audience-centered speaking model, shown in Figure 13.1, to guide you step-by-step through the process.

## Consider Your Audience

As with any type of speech, an informative talk requires that you consider three general questions of audience analysis: To whom are you speaking? What are their interests, attitudes, beliefs, and values? What do they expect from you? When your general purpose is to inform, you should focus on specific aspects of these three general questions. Part of considering who your audience is will include figuring out, as best you can, their preferred learning styles. Determining listeners' interests, attitudes, beliefs, and values can help you balance your use of strategies to enhance understanding and recall with your need for strategies to maintain interest. You won't need to work as hard to maintain the interest of an audience who is already highly interested in your topic, for example. Careful consideration of the audience's expectations can also help you maintain their interest, perhaps by surprising them with something they do not expect.

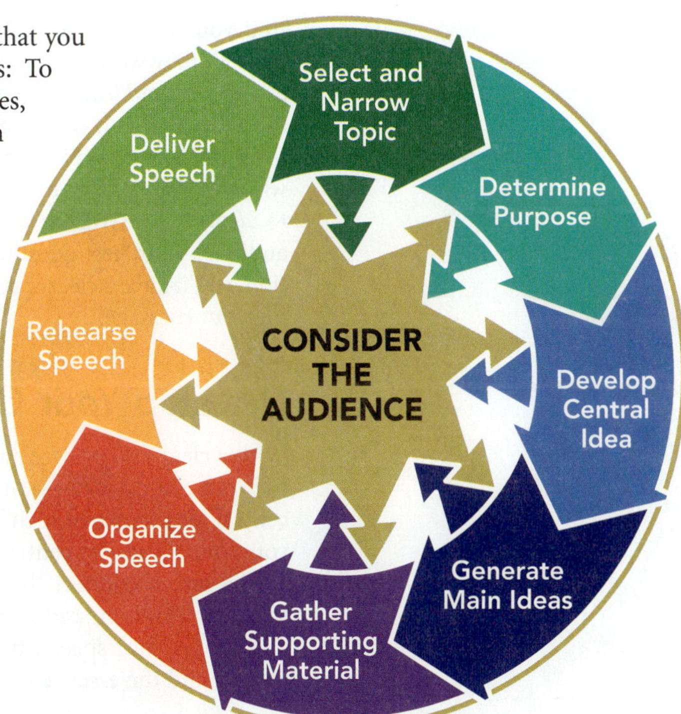


FIGURE 13.1 *You can follow the steps of the audience-centered model of public speaking to craft a successful informative speech.*

## Select and Narrow Your Informational Topic

As you select and narrow your topic for an informative presentation, it's especially important to keep your audience in mind. During the early stages of preparing your message, ask yourself, and answer, the question "What do they already know about my topic?" If you misjudge what an audience already knows about your topic, that misjudgment may hamper your development of an effective and precise specific-purpose statement.

You should also consider the question "How interested are they in my topic?" If your audience is both knowledgeable about and interested in your topic, you can provide greater detail and build on the information they already have. If they are likely to be uninterested or uninformed, then you'll need to establish, early in your message, a clear and engaging reason they should tune you in.

## Determine Your Informative Purpose

You already know that your general purpose is to inform. You also need to develop a specific behavioral purpose. That is, you need to identify what you'd like the audience to be able to *do* when your finish your speech. "Wait a minute," you might think. "Shouldn't an informative speech be about what the audience should *learn,* rather than *do*?" Yes, your purpose is focused on what you want the audience to learn, but we suggest you phrase your learning goal in terms of behavior. Say what you want your audience to *state, describe, identify, list,* or otherwise *do* to demonstrate their learning.

Here's an example of an imprecise specific-purpose sentence: *At the end of my speech, the audience should know some background about C. S. Lewis'* The Chronicles of Narnia. The word *know* isn't very specific, nor is the phrase *some background.* Precisely what do you want your listeners to know? How can they demonstrate that knowledge? Here's a more precise and effective specific informative-purpose statement: *At the end of my speech, the audience should be able to state three reasons C. S. Lewis wrote* The Chronicles of Narnia.

Why is being precise useful to you? A precise specific-purpose sentence will guide you as you develop your central idea and main ideas, and it is especially important when you organize your message. Merely indicating that you want your audience to know or appreciate some general information provides an unclear roadmap for getting your audience where you want them to go. If you don't know where you're headed, they won't either. Using specific verbs like *state, re-state, summarize, describe, enumerate,* and *list,* and avoiding fuzzy words like *know* and *appreciate,* will focus your thoughts and your message. Think of your specific-purpose sentence as a test question that you're writing for your audience. A test question that asks what you *know* about why the Narnia Chronicles were written is less specific than a question that asks you to *identify three reasons* why the stories were written. You may never actually ask your audience your "test question," but by thinking of your specific purpose as a test question, you'll have a clearer goal in mind, one that will help you in other areas of preparing your message.

## Develop Your Central Idea

With a clear and precise specific-purpose sentence, you'll be better prepared to identify your central idea—a one-sentence summary of your message. Rather than a fuzzy central idea sentence such as "C. S. Lewis wrote the Narnia stories for many reasons," your more specific central idea might be, "Three reasons Lewis wrote the Narnia stories are to connect the 'pictures' he visualized in his head, to write an engaging story for children, and to make a larger point about Christianity." Your central idea sentence is your speech in brief. Someone who heard only your central idea would understand the essence of your message.

## Generate Your Main Ideas

If you've developed a specific-purpose sentence and have a well-crafted central idea sentence, it should be easy to generate your main ideas. In our C. S. Lewis example, we identified in our central idea three reasons Lewis wrote the stories.

Those three reasons will become the main ideas of the speech. The type of informative talk you are planning will influence your central and main ideas. A speech about an object may lend itself to certain main ideas such as history, features, and uses of the object, whereas a speech about a person might be more likely to have main ideas related to the person's accomplishments or relationship to you, the speaker.

## Gather Your Supporting Materials

As you read and research, you look for examples, illustrations, stories, statistics, and other materials that help you achieve your specific purpose. The type of informative speech you plan to make will often suggest ideas for supporting materials. Biographical details and stories will most likely support a speech about a person. Stories, examples, or statistics may help you teach your audience about an event or idea. Remember that supporting materials include presentation aids. As we noted earlier in this chapter, visual aids often make "how-to" speeches about procedures more effective. Speeches about objects also often benefit from visual aids, especially when the actual object is appropriate to show. As you gather supporting material, continue to think about your audience, who will ultimately judge whether your supporting material is interesting and helpful.

### CONFIDENTLY CONNECTING WITH YOUR AUDIENCE

#### Focus on Your Information Rather Than on Your Fear

You nurture your fear when you focus on your anxiety. Consciously keep your mind off your fear and focused on the message you will present. When you feel your anxiety level rising, do something related to improving your speech rather than let your anxiety get the best of you. Consider reviewing your introduction, taking another look at your main points, or glancing at your conclusion one more time. By changing your focus from your fear to preparing your talk, you are changing the stimulus that may be triggering additional anxiety.

## Organize Your Speech

In developing a specific purpose and identifying main ideas, you've already been working on the organization of your message. As you keep your audience in mind, you now determine what the best sequence of your main points should be. Your topic and purpose can also help guide you. As we discussed earlier in the chapter, different types of informative speeches lend themselves to different organizational patterns.

## Rehearse Your Presentation

With your well-prepared notes in hand, you're ready to rehearse your speech. As we suggested in Chapter 11, you'll want to rehearse your speech aloud while standing. By recreating the experience of actually delivering your speech, not only are you polishing your delivery, but you will better manage any apprehension you may have. For informative speeches, it is especially helpful to rehearse in front of other people, especially people who are similar to your listeners, if possible. Seek their feedback about whether you are effectively teaching them about your topic. You may even wish to ask your sample audience the test question you developed as your specific-purpose statement, to determine whether your speech is meeting your learning objectives.

### RECAP

#### Audience-Centered Informative Speaking

- Select topic—Consider who the audience is and their interests.
- Narrow topic—Find out what the audience already knows.
- Determine purpose—State specific audience actions that will show learning.
- Formulate central and main ideas—Make them clear and simple.
- Gather supporting material—Decide what will help audience maintain interest and learn.
- Organize—Match topic with audience needs.
- Rehearse—Get sample audience feedback.
- Deliver—Adapt to ensure audience comprehension.

## Deliver Your Speech

Finally, you're ready to deliver your speech to your audience. With good eye contact, a clear voice, and effective gestures, you command your audience's attention with your well-rehearsed speech. As we discussed in Chapter 11, effective speakers continually look for ways to adapt and modify their message as they speak. Such adaptation is especially important in informative speaking. As you speak, watch your audience closely for signs—such as puzzled facial expressions—that indicate they do not understand something. Be alert, too, for signs of wandering attention, such as fidgeting or lack of eye contact. Be prepared to adapt your message, using the strategies discussed earlier in this chapter for enhancing listeners' understanding and maintaining their attention.

# STUDY GUIDE

## Types of Informative Speeches

To inform is to teach someone something you know. Informative speeches have three goals—to enhance understanding, to maintain interest, and to be remembered. To achieve these goals, you can deliver several different types of informative speeches. Speeches about objects discuss tangible things. Speeches about procedures explain a process or describe how something works. Speeches about people can be about either the famous or the little known. Speeches about events describe major occurrences or personal experiences. Speeches about ideas discuss often abstract principles, concepts, or theories.

### A Question of Ethics

- You are a chemistry major considering whether you should give a speech to your public-speaking class about how pipe bombs are made. Is this an appropriate topic for your audience?

## Strategies to Enhance Audience Understanding

To enhance your listeners' understanding of a message: (1) define ideas clearly, (2) use principles and techniques of adult learning, (3) clarify unfamiliar ideas or complex processes, (4) use descriptions effectively, and (5) combine spoken words, visuals, and kinesthetic opportunities to appeal to listeners with a variety of learning styles.

### Being Audience-Centered

- When you are presenting completely new information to listeners, use simple, familiar examples.
- When you're describing a complex process, use analogies and word pictures, in addition to definitions, to explain what you mean. Visual images can also help communicate clearly to people from a variety of cultural backgrounds, especially those who may not clearly understand your words.
- Remember that adult listeners are problem-oriented. They also like to hear information that they can use immediately, to be actively involved in the learning process, to connect their life experience with the new information they learn, and to know how the new information is relevant to their needs and busy lives.

### Using What You've Learned

- Hillary Webster, M.D., will be addressing a medical convention of other physicians to discuss the weight-loss technique she has recently used successfully with her patients. What advice would you give to help her present an effective talk?

### A Question of Ethics

- In order to give your five-minute speech about nuclear energy, you must greatly simplify what is a very complex process. How can you avoid misrepresenting your topic? Should you let your audience know that you are oversimplifying the process?

### Speaker's Homepage: Adult Learning and Learning Styles

Many different Web sites enable you to explore learning styles and the principles of adult learning to get you started. You can apply that information as you plan your informative speeches. Here are two:

- Ageless Learner. This commercial site offers a good summary of adult learning principles as well as several self-quizzes, including one on learning styles. http://agelesslearner.com/
- Learning Styles Online. Gives a very thorough rundown of many possible learning styles and lets you take a free quiz to see which styles you prefer. http://www.learning-styles-online.com/

## Strategies to Maintain Audience Interest

To gain and maintain interest in your informative talk, follow three important principles. First, motivate your audience to listen to you. Second, tell a story; a well-told story almost always works to keep listeners focused on you and your message. Third, present information that relates to your listeners' interests; in essence, be audience-centered. Finally, use the unexpected to surprise your audience.

### Being Audience-Centered

- Most audiences will probably not be waiting breathlessly for you to talk to them. You will need to motivate them to listen to you. Think about what they are interested in and how they can apply the information you will share.

- Many cultural groups, such as those from the Middle East, prefer stories and illustrations rather than detailed definitions and data.

### Using What You've Learned

- Ken's boss has given him the task of presenting a report to a group of potential investors about his company's recent productivity trends. The presentation includes many statistics. What suggestions would you offer to help Ken give an interesting and effective informative presentation?

### A Question of Ethics

- Before giving a speech to your class in which you share a story that includes personal information about one of your friends, should you ask permission from your friend?

## Strategies to Enhance Audience Recall

Help your listeners remember what you tell them by being redundant. Be sure to keep your main ideas short and simple. Pacing the flow of your information helps listeners recall your ideas. Reinforcing important points verbally and nonverbally can also help your audience members remember them.

### Being Audience-Centered

- Redundancy can be especially helpful when you and the audience have language differences. Build redundancy with preview statements, internal summaries, and closing summaries.

## Audience-Centered Informative Speaking

You can apply principles of informative speaking to adapt the audience-centered model of speaking. Choose and narrow your topic by determining what the audience already knows. Use action words in your specific-purpose statement. The needs of your audience and topic will help you organize your speech and gather supporting materials. Seek audience feedback on your teaching effectiveness as you rehearse, and adapt your delivery, if needed, to ensure that the audience understands your message.

### Using What You've Learned

- You have been asked to speak to a kindergarten class about your chosen profession. Identify approaches to this task that would help make your message clear, interesting, and memorable to your audience.

# SPEECH WORKSHOP

## Developing a Vivid Word Picture

A word picture is a lively description of something that helps your listeners form a mental image by appealing to their senses of sight, taste, smell, sound, and touch. Consider the following steps as you develop a vivid word picture for your next speech.

**Step One:** What image do you want your listeners to see or experience in their mind's eye? It could be a specific place you describe, part of a story you tell, or an experience you describe. Indicate what your listeners would see if they were actually in the place or situation you are describing.

They would see . . .

**Step Two:** Describe what your listeners would hear if they were actually in the place you are describing in your word picture.

They would hear . . .

**Step Three:** Describe aromas that listeners might smell.

They would smell . . .

**Step Four:** Describe what listeners might be feeling or touching.

They would touch or feel . . .

**Step Five:** If appropriate, describe what listeners would taste.

They would taste . . .

**Step Six:** Describe the emotion listeners might feel if they were actually experiencing the events depicted in your word picture.

They would feel . . .

. . . THE POWER OF SPEECH, TO STIR MEN'S BLOOD.

—WILLIAM SHAKESPEARE

Hans Grundig (1910–1958). ©ARS, N.Y. *Assembly of the German Communist Party [KPD Versammlung]*. 1932. Oil on canvas, 67 × 122 cm. Inv. A IV 54. Photo: Klaus Goeken. Nationalgalerie, Staatliche Museen, Berlin, Germany. Bildarchiv Preussischer Kulturbesitz/Art Resource, N.Y.

OUTLINE

# 14 Understanding Principles of Persuasive Speaking

OBJECTIVES

**After studying this chapter you should be able to do the following:**

1. Define persuasion.
2. Describe cognitive dissonance.
3. Identify Maslow's five levels of motivational needs.
4. Select and develop an appropriate topic for a persuasive speech.
5. Identify three principles of persuasive speaking.

It probably happens to you more than 600 times each day. It appears as commercials on TV and radio; as advertisements in magazines and newspapers and on billboards; and as fund-raising letters from politicians and charities. It also occurs when you are asked to give money to a worthy cause or to donate blood. "It" is persuasion. Efforts to persuade you occur at an average rate of once every two and a half minutes each day.[1] Because persuasion is such an ever-present part of your life, it is important for you to understand how it works. What are the principles of an activity that can shape your attitudes and behavior? What do car salespeople, advertising copywriters, and politicians know about how to influence your thinking and behavior that you don't know?

In this chapter, we discuss how persuasion works. Such information can sharpen your persuasive skills and can also help you become a more informed receiver of persuasive messages. We will define persuasion and discuss the psychological principles underlying efforts to persuade others. We will also discuss tips for choosing a persuasive speech topic and developing arguments for your speeches. In Chapter 15, we will examine specific strategies for crafting a persuasive speech.

In Chapter 13, we discussed strategies for informative speaking—the oral presentation of new information to listeners so that they will understand and remember what is communicated. The purposes of informing and persuading are closely related. Why inform an audience? Why give new information to others? We often provide information to give listeners new insights that may affect their attitudes and behavior. Information alone has the potential to convince others, but when information is coupled with strategies to persuade, the chances of success increase. Persuasive speakers try to influence their listeners' points of view or behavior. If you want your listeners to respond to your persuasive appeal, you will need to think carefully about the way you structure your message to achieve your specific purpose.

In a persuasive speech, the speaker asks the audience to make a choice, rather than just informing them of the options. As a persuasive speaker, you will do more than teach; you will ask your listeners to respond to the information you share. Audience analysis is crucial to achieving your goal. To advocate a particular view or position successfully, you must understand your listeners' attitudes, beliefs, values, and behavior.

# Persuasion Defined

**Persuasion** is the process of changing or reinforcing attitudes, beliefs, values, or behavior. Note that when trying to persuade someone, you may not necessarily try to change someone's point of view or behavior but, instead, aim to *reinforce* it. Your listeners may already like, believe, or value something or *sometimes* do what you'd like them do do; you are trying to strengthen their current perspective. Suppose, for example, that your persuasive purpose is to get people to use their recycling trash bins. The audience may already think that recycling is a good thing and may even use their recycling bins at least some of the time. Your speaking goal is to reinforce their behavior so that they use the recycling bins every time.

Because the goal of persuasion is to change or reinforce attitudes, beliefs, values, or behavior, it's important to clarify how these elements differ. Having a clear idea of precisely which of these elements you want to change or reinforce can help you develop your persuasive strategy.

**persuasion**
The process of changing or reinforcing a listener's attitudes, beliefs, values, or behavior

**attitude**
A learned predisposition to respond favorably or unfavorably toward something; likes and dislikes

## Changing or Reinforcing Audience Attitudes

Our attitudes represent our likes and dislikes. Stated more technically, an **attitude** is a learned predisposition to respond favorably or unfavorably toward something.[2] In a persuasive speech, you might try to persuade your listeners to favor or oppose a new shopping mall, to like bats because of their ability to eat insects, or to dislike an increase in the sales tax.

## Changing or Reinforcing Audience Beliefs

A persuasive speech could also attempt to change or reinforce a belief. A **belief** is what you understand to be true or false. If you believe in something, you are convinced that it exists or is true. You have structured your sense of what is real and what is unreal to account for the existence of whatever you believe. If you believe in God, you have structured your sense of what is real and unreal to recognize the existence of God. Beliefs are typically based on past experiences. If you believe the sun will rise in the east again tomorrow, or that nuclear power is safe, you base these beliefs either on what you've directly experienced or on the experience of someone you find trustworthy. Beliefs are usually based on evidence, but we hold some beliefs based on faith—we haven't directly experienced something, but we believe anyway.

## Changing or Reinforcing Audience Values

A persuasive speech could also seek to change or reinforce a value. A **value** is an enduring concept of right or wrong, good or bad. If you value something, you classify it as good or desirable, and you tend to think of its opposite or its absence as bad or wrong. If you do not value something, you are indifferent to it. Values form the basis of your life goals and the motivating force behind your behavior. Most Americans value honesty, trustworthiness, freedom, loyalty, marriage, family, and money. Understanding what your listeners value can help you refine your analysis of them and adapt the content of your speech to those values.

Why is it useful to make distinctions among attitudes, beliefs, and values? Since the essence of persuasion is to change or reinforce these three kinds of predispositions, it is very useful to know exactly which one you are targeting. Of the three, audience values are the most stable. Most of us acquired our values when we were very young and have held on to them into adulthood. Our values, therefore, are generally deeply ingrained. It is not impossible to change the values of your listeners, but it is much more difficult than trying to change a belief or an attitude. Political and religious points of view, which are usually based on long-held values, are especially difficult to modify.

A belief is more susceptible to change than a value is, but it is still difficult to alter. Beliefs are changed by evidence. You might have a difficult time, for example, trying to change someone's belief that the world is flat; you would need to show that existing evidence supports a different conclusion. Usually it takes a great deal of evidence to change a belief and alter the way your audience structures reality.

Attitudes (likes and dislikes) are easier to change than either beliefs or values. Today we may approve of the president of the United States; tomorrow we may disapprove of him because of an action he has taken. We may still *believe* that the country is financially stable because of the president's programs, and we may still *value* a democratic form of government, but our *attitude* toward the president has changed because of this policy decision.

As Figure 14.1, on page 316, shows, values are the most deeply ingrained of the three predispositions; they change least frequently. That's why values are at the core of the model. Beliefs change, but not as much as attitudes. Trying to change an audience's attitudes is easier than attempting to change their values. We suggest that you think carefully about your purpose for making a persuasive speech. Know with certainty whether your objective is to change or to reinforce an attitude, a belief, or a value. Then decide what you have to do to achieve your objective.

**belief**
A way we structure reality to accept something as true or false

**value**
An enduring concept of good and bad, right and wrong

Attitudes

Beliefs

Values

FIGURE 14.1 **Audience Attitudes, Beliefs, and Values.** *The target of your speech affects its chances of successfully persuading your audience. Attitudes form the outer ring of this model because they are easier to change than beliefs or core values. Beliefs can be changed, but not as easily as attitudes. Values are at the core of the model because they are the most deeply ingrained and change the least frequently.*

### Changing or Reinforcing Audience Behaviors

Persuasive messages often attempt to do more than change or reinforce attitudes, beliefs, or values—they may attempt to change or strengthen behaviors. Getting listeners to eat less, not to smoke tobacco, not to consume drugs, not to drink and drive, or to exercise more are typical goals of the persuasive messages that we hear. It seems logical that knowing someone's attitudes, beliefs, and values will let us predict precisely how that person will behave. But we are complicated creatures, and human behavior is not always neatly predictable. Sometimes our attitudes, beliefs, and values may not appear consistent with how we act. For example, you may know that if you're on a low-carb diet, you should avoid that second helping of Dad's homemade chocolate cake; but you cut off a slice and gobble it up anyway.

## How Persuasion Works

Now that you know what persuasion is and how attitudes, beliefs, and values influence your behavior, you may still have questions about how persuasion actually works. Knowing how and why listeners change their minds and their behavior can help you construct more effective persuasive messages.

Besides enabling you to persuade others, understanding how persuasion works can help you analyze why *you* are sometimes persuaded to think or behave in certain ways. Being conscious of why you respond to specific persuasive messages can help you be a better, more discriminating listener to persuasive pitches.

Many theories and considerable research describe how persuasion works. We'll discuss two approaches here: first, a classical approach identified by Aristotle, and second, a more contemporary theory that builds on the classical approach.

RECAP

**Defining Persuasion**

Persuasion attempts to change or reinforce:

- Attitudes
- Beliefs
- Values
- Behavior

### Aristotle's Traditional Approach: Using Ethos, Logos, and Pathos to Persuade

Aristotle, a Greek philosopher and rhetorician who lived and wrote in the fourth century B.C.E., was the source of many ideas about communication in general and persuasion in particular. As we noted in Chapter 3, he defined *rhetoric* as the process of discovering in any particular case the available means of persuasion. When the goal is to persuade, the communicator selects symbols (words and nonverbal messages, including images and music) to change attitudes, beliefs, values, or behavior. Aristotle identified three general methods (or, using his language, "available means") to persuade: ethos, logos, and pathos.[3]

**ETHOS** To use **ethos** to persuade, an effective communicator presents information that is credible. Aristotle believed that in order to be credible, a public speaker should be ethical, possess good character, have common sense, and be concerned for the well-being of the audience. The more credible and ethical a speaker is perceived to be, the greater the chances are that a listener will believe in, trust, and positively respond to the persuasive message of the speaker. So one of the means or methods of persuasion is for the communicator to present information that can be trusted and to be believable and trustworthy himself or herself. When a friend wants to convince you to

**ethos**
The term Aristotle used to refer to a speaker's credibility

let him borrow your car, he may say, "Trust me. I promise not to do anything whacky with your car. I'm a responsible guy." He's appealing to his credibility as an ethical, trusted friend. We'll discuss specific strategies to enhance your credibility and thus your persuasiveness, in the next chapter.

**LOGOS** Another means of persuading others is to use **logos**. The word *logos* literally means "the word." Aristotle used this term to refer to the rational, logical arguments that a speaker uses to persuade someone. A skilled persuader not only reaches a logical conclusion but also supports the message with evidence and reasoning. The friend who wants to borrow your car may use a logical, rational argument supported with evidence to get your car keys. He may say, "I borrowed your car last week and I returned it without a scratch. I also borrowed it the week before that and there were no problems—and I filled the tank with gas. So if you loan me your car today, I'll return it just like I did in the past." Your friend is appealing to your rational side by using evidence to support his conclusion that your car will be returned in good shape. In Chapter 15 we'll provide strategies for developing logical, rational arguments and supporting those arguments with solid evidence.

**PATHOS** Aristotle used the term **pathos** to refer to the use of appeals to emotion. We sometimes hold attitudes, beliefs, and values that are not logical but that simply make us feel positive. Likewise, we sometimes do things or buy things to make ourselves feel happy, powerful, or energized. The friend who wants to borrow your wheels may also use pathos—an emotional appeal—to get you to turn over your car keys. He may say, "Look, without transportation I can't get to my doctor's appointment. I'm feeling sick. I need your help. Friends help friends, and I could use a good friend right now." Your buddy is tugging on your emotional heartstrings to motivate you to loan him your car. He's hoping to convince you to behave in a way that makes you feel positive about yourself.

What are effective ways to appeal to listeners' emotions? Use emotion-arousing stories and concrete examples, as well as pictures and music. In the next chapter we'll identify more ethical strategies to appeal to emotions when persuading others.

All three traditional means of persuasion—ethos (ethical credibility), logos (logic), and pathos (emotion)—are ways of motivating a listener to think or behave in certain ways. **Motivation** is the underlying internal force that drives people to achieve their goals. Our motives explain why we do things.[4] Several factors motivate people to respond to persuasive messages: the need to restore balance to their lives and avoid stress, the need to avoid pain, and the desire to increase pleasure have been documented as motives that influence attitudes, beliefs, values, and behavior.

## ELM'S Contemporary Approach: Using a Direct or Indirect Path to Persuade

A newer, research-based framework for understanding how persuasion works is called the **elaboration likelihood model (ELM) of persuasion.**[5] This theory with a long name is actually a simple idea that offers an explanation of how people are persuaded to do something or think about something. Rather than prescribe how to craft a persuasive message from the standpoint of the speaker, as Aristotle does, ELM theory describes how audience members *interpret* persuasive messages. It's an audience-centered theory of how people make sense of persuasive communication.

To **elaborate** means that you *think* about the information, ideas, and issues related to the content of the message you hear. When you elaborate on a message, you are critically evaluating what you hear by paying special attention to the arguments and the evidence the speaker is using. The likelihood of whether or not you elaborate

**logos**
Literally, "the word"; the term Aristotle used to refer to logic—the formal system of using rules to reach a conclusion

**pathos**
The term used by Aristotle to refer to appeals to human emotion

**motivation**
The internal force that drives people to achieve their goals

**elaboration likelihood model (ELM) of persuasion**
The theory that people can be persuaded by logic, evidence, and reasoning, or through a more peripheral route that may depend on the credibility of the speaker, the sheer number of arguments presented, or emotional appeals

**elaborate**
From the standpoint of the elaboration likelihood model (ELM) of persuasion, to think about information, ideas, and issues related to the content of a message

(hence the term *elaboration likelihood model*) on a message varies from person to person and depends on the topic of the message.

The theory suggests that there are two ways you can be persuaded: first, the **direct persuasion route** that you follow when you elaborate, or critically evaluate, a message, and second, the **indirect persuasion route**, in which you don't elaborate and are instead influenced by the more peripheral factors of the message and the messenger.

**direct persuasion route**
Persuasion that occurs when audience members critically examine evidence and arguments

**indirect persuasion route**
Persuasion that occurs as a result of factors peripheral to a speaker's logic and argument, such as the speaker's charisma or emotional appeals

### The Direct Persuasion Route

If you elaborate on a message, you will likely be persuaded by the logic, reasoning, arguments, and evidence presented to you. When you elaborate, you consider what Aristotle would call the underlying logos, or logic, of the message. You carefully consider the facts and then make a thoughtful decision as to whether to believe or do what the persuader wants. For example, you buy a good data package for your smart phone because you are convinced you will benefit from constant access to the Internet; you've read the literature and have made a logical, rational decision. There may be times, however, when you think you are making a decision based on logic, but instead you are being persuaded by less obvious strategies via an indirect path.

### The Indirect Persuasion Route

A second way you can be persuaded, according to ELM theory, is a more indirect or peripheral route. If you don't elaborate (that is, if you don't use critical thinking skills while listening), you simply draw on an overall impression of what the speaker says and how the speaker says it. The indirect route is a more intuitive process. You can be persuaded by such indirect factors as catchy music used in an advertisement or your positive reaction to the salesperson who wants to sell you a product. It's not an evaluation of the logic or content of the advertisement or the salesperson's words that persuades you, it's the overall feeling you have about the product or the salesperson that triggers your purchase. When hearing a speech, you may be persuaded by the appearance of the speaker (he looks nice; I trust him); by the sheer number of research studies in support of the speaker's proposal (there are so many reasons to accept this speaker's proposal; she's convinced me); or by the speaker's use of an emotionally charged story (I can't let that little girl starve; I'll donate 50 cents to save her).

*Advertisers know that people are often persuaded via the indirect route. Many advertisers use scantily clad, attractive models in their print and online advertising, or catchy tunes for broadcast, in hopes that these peripheral elements will persuade viewers to make a purchase.*
[Photo: Kiselev Andrey Valerevic/ Shutterstock]

These two theories, Aristotle's theory and ELM theory, both suggest that persuasion is a complex process. Not all of us are persuaded in the same way. Aristotle's theory emphasizes what a *speaker* should do to influence an audience. If the speaker discovers the proper application of a credible and ethical message (ethos), logic (logos), and emotion (pathos), then persuasion is likely to occur. ELM theory describes how *listeners* process the messages they hear. Listeners can be persuaded when they directly elaborate (or actively think about what they hear) and logically ponder how evidence and reasoning make sense. Or, if they do not elaborate, listeners may be persuaded indirectly, based on peripheral factors that don't require as much thought to process, such as the personal appearance of the speaker or the speaker's delivery.

Both theories give insight as to how you can persuade others and how others persuade you. Because you may not know whether your listeners are directly or indirectly influenced by your message (whether they are elaborating or not), you will want to use a balance of ethos, logos, and pathos as you think about how to persuade your listeners. However, it's your *audience*, not you, that ultimately make sense out of what they hear. So, in addition to the carefully constructed logic and well-reasoned arguments that you present, you need to be attuned to the indirect factors that can influence your listeners, such as your delivery, your appearance, and a general impression of how prepared you seem to be.

These two theories also help explain how *you* are influenced by others. You are influenced by the ethical appeal, logical arguments, and emotions of a speaker. In addition, ELM theory suggests you may be directly affected by the logic and arguments of a speaker; or you may be influenced, even when you're not aware of it, by such peripheral or indirect elements of the message as the speaker's appearance and delivery. Remaining aware of how you are being persuaded can make you a more effective consumer of the multitude of persuasive messages that come your way each day.

**RECAP**

### Models of Persuasion

Aristotle's Classical Approach

- Ethos
- Logos
- Pathos

Elaboration Likelihood Model

- Direct route—via elaboration
- Indirect route—without elaboration

# How to Motivate Listeners

It's late at night and you're watching your favorite talk show. The program is interrupted by a commercial extolling the virtues of a well-known brand of ice cream. Suddenly you remember that you have some of the advertised flavor, Royal Rocky Road. You apparently hadn't realized how hungry you were for ice cream until the ad reminded you of the lip-smacking goodness of the cold, creamy, smooth treat. Before you know it, you are at the freezer, helping yourself to a couple of scoops of ice cream.

If the maker of that commercial knew how effective it had been, he or she would be overjoyed. The ad was persuasive, and it changed your behavior because the message was tailor-made for you. What principles explain why you were motivated to go to the freezer at midnight for a carton of ice cream? At the heart of the persuasion process is the audience-centered process of motivating listeners to respond to a message. Persuasion works when listeners are motivated to respond. An audience is more likely to be persuaded when you help members solve their problems or meet their needs. They can also be motivated when you convince them good things will happen to them if they follow your advice, or bad things will occur if they don't. We next discuss several ways to motivate listeners; these approaches are summarized in Table 14.1, on page 320.

## Use Cognitive Dissonance

Dissonance theory is based on the principle that people strive to solve problems and manage stress and tension in a way that is consistent with their attitudes, beliefs, and values.[6] According to the theory, when you are presented with information inconsistent with your current attitudes, beliefs, values, or behavior, you become aware that you have a problem; you experience a kind of discomfort called **cognitive dissonance**. The word *cognitive* has to do with our thoughts. *Dissonance* means "lack of harmony or agreement." When you think of a dissonant chord in music, you probably think of a collection of sounds that are unpleasant or not in tune with the melody or other chords. Most people seek to avoid problems or feelings of dissonance. Cognitive dissonance, then, means that you are experiencing a way of thinking that is inconsistent and uncomfortable. If, for example, you smoke cigarettes and a speaker reminds you that smoking is unhealthy, this reminder creates dissonance. You can restore balance and solve the problem either by no longer smoking or by rejecting the message that smoking is harmful.

**cognitive dissonance**
The sense of mental discomfort that prompts a person to change when new information conflicts with previously organized thought patterns

Creating dissonance with a persuasive speech can be an effective way to change attitudes and behavior. The first tactic in such a speech is to identify an existing problem or need. For example, a speaker seeking to ban aerosol sprays could begin her

**TABLE 14.1 How to Motivate Listeners to Respond to Your Persuasive Message**

| | Description | Example of Message |
|---|---|---|
| **Use Cognitive Dissonance** | Telling listeners about existing problems or information that is inconsistent with their currently held beliefs or known information creates psychological discomfort. | Would you be able to support your family if you were injured and couldn't work? If you're worried about having enough money for food and rent, consider buying our disability insurance policy. It will provide a steady income if you can't work because of injury or sickness. |
| **Use Listeners' Needs** | People are motivated by unmet needs. The most basic needs are physiological, followed by safety needs, social needs, self-esteem needs, and finally, self-actualization needs. | You could be the envy of people you know if you purchase this sleek new sports car. You will be perceived as a person of high status in your community. |
| **Use Positive Motivation** | People will be more likely to change their thinking or pursue a particular course of action if they are convinced that good things will happen to them if they support what the speaker advocates. | You should take a course in public speaking because it will increase your prospects of getting a good job. Effective communication skills are the most sought-after skills in today's workplace. |
| **Use Negative Motivation** | People seek to avoid pain and discomfort. They will be motivated to support what a speaker advocates if they are convinced that bad things will happen to them unless they do. | If there is a hurricane, tornado, earthquake, or other natural disaster, the electrical power may be out and you will not be able to fill your car with gas. Without the basics of food and water, you could die. You need to be prepared for a worst-case scenario by having an emergency stockpile of water, food, and gas for your car. |

speech by focusing on a need we all share, such as the need to preserve the environment. The speaker could then point out that the use of aerosol sprays depletes the ozone layer that protects us from the sun's harmful rays. The speaker is deliberately creating dissonance. She knows that people in her audience appreciate the convenience of aerosol sprays, so their attitudes about protecting the environment will *conflict with* their feelings about getting housework done easily or styling their hair effectively. Then she would aim at restoring the audience's sense of balance by claiming that her solution—using nonaerosol sprays—can resolve the conflict. With this strategy, the speaker may motivate audience members to change their behavior. That change is the speaker's objective.

Political candidates use a similar strategy. A mayoral candidate usually tries first to make his or her audience aware of problems in the community, then to blame the current mayor for most of the problems. Once dissonance has been created, the candidate then suggests that the problems would be solved, or at least managed better, if he or she were elected mayor. Using the principles of dissonance theory, the mayoral candidate first upsets the audience, then restores their balance and feeling of comfort by offering a solution to the city's problems: his or her selection as mayor.

In using dissonance theory to persuade, speakers have an ethical responsibility not to rely on false claims to create dissonance. Claiming that a problem exists when it does not or creating dissonance about a problem that is unlikely to happen is

Effective public-service messages often use cognitive dissonance to change people's behaviors. This technique is also often effective for public speakers.
[Photo: Sonda Dawes/The Image Works]

unethical. When listening to a persuasive message, pay particular attention to the evidence that a speaker uses to convince you that a problem really does exist.

**How Listeners Cope with Dissonance** Effective persuasion requires more than simply creating dissonance and then suggesting a solution. When your listeners confront dissonant information, a number of options are available to them besides following your suggestions. You need to be aware of the other ways your audience might react before you can reduce their cognitive dissonance.[7]

- **Listeners may discredit the source.** Instead of believing everything you say, your listeners could choose to discredit you. Suppose you drive a Japanese-made car and you hear a speaker whose father owns a Chevrolet dealership advocate that all Americans should drive cars made in the United States. You could agree with him, or you could decide that the speaker is biased because of his father's occupation. Instead of selling your Japanese-made car and buying an American-made car, you could doubt the speaker's credibility and ignore the suggestion to buy American automobiles. As a persuasive speaker, you need to ensure that your audience will perceive you as competent and trustworthy so that they will accept your message.
- **Listeners may reinterpret the message.** A second way your listeners might overcome cognitive dissonance and restore balance is to hear what they want to hear. They may choose to focus on the parts of your message that are consistent with what they already believe and ignore the unfamiliar or controversial parts. Your job as an effective public speaker is to make your message as clear as possible so that your audience will not reinterpret it. If you tell a customer looking at a new kind of computer software that it takes ten steps to get into the word-processing program but that the program is easy to use, the customer might focus on those first ten steps and decide that the software would be too hard to use. Choose your words carefully; use simple, vivid examples to keep listeners focused on what's most important.
- **Listeners may seek new information.** Another way that listeners cope with cognitive dissonance is to seek more information on the subject. Your audience members may look for additional information to negate your position and to refute

your well-created arguments. For example, as the owner of a minivan, you would experience dissonance if you heard a speaker describe the recent rash of safety problems with minivans. You might turn to a friend and whisper, "Is this true? Are minivans really dangerous? I've always thought they were safe." You would want new information to validate your ownership of a minivan.

- **Listeners may stop listening.** Some messages are so much at odds with listeners' attitudes, beliefs, and values that an audience may decide to stop listening. Most of us do not seek opportunities to hear or read messages that oppose our opinions. It is unlikely that a staunch Democrat would attend a fund-raiser for the state Republican party. The principle of selective exposure suggests that we tend to pay attention to messages that are consistent with our points of view and to avoid those that are not. When we do find ourselves trapped in a situation in which we must hear a message that doesn't support our beliefs, we tend to stop listening. Being aware of the existing attitudes, beliefs, and values of your audience can help you ensure that they won't tune you out.

- **Listeners may change their attitudes, beliefs, values, or behavior.** A fifth way an audience may respond to dissonant information is to do as the speaker wants them to. As we have noted, if listeners change their attitudes, they will reduce the dissonance that they experience. You listen to a life-insurance salesperson tell you that when you die, your family will have no financial support. This creates dissonance; you prefer to think of your family as happy and secure. So you take out a $250,000 policy to protect your family. This action restores your sense of balance. The salesperson has persuaded you successfully. The goals of advertising copywriters, salespeople, and political candidates are similar: They want you to experience dissonance so that you will change your attitudes, beliefs, values, or behavior.

RECAP

### Coping with Cognitive Dissonance

When your message gives listeners conflicting thoughts, they might:

- try to discredit you; you need to be competent and trustworthy.
- reinterpret your message; you need to be sure it's clear.
- seek other information; you need to make your information convincing.
- stop listening; you need to make your message interesting.
- be persuaded.

## Use Listeners' Needs

Need is one of the best motivators. The person who is looking at a new car because he or she needs one is more likely to buy than the person who is just thinking about how nice it would be to drive the latest model. The more you understand what your listeners need, the greater the chances are that you can gain and hold their attention and ultimately get them to do what you want. The classic theory that outlines basic human needs was developed by Abraham Maslow.[8] Maslow suggested that there is a hierarchy of needs that motivate everyone's behavior. Basic physiological needs (for food, water, and air) have to be satisfied before we can be motivated to respond to higher-level needs. Figure 14.2 illustrates Maslow's five levels of needs, with the most basic at the bottom. Although the hierarchical nature of Maslow's needs has not been consistently supported by research (we can be motivated by several needs at the same time), Maslow's hierarchy provides a useful checklist of what can potentially motivate a listener. When attempting to persuade an audience, a public speaker tries to stimulate these needs in order to change or reinforce attitudes, beliefs, values, or behavior. Let's examine each of these needs.

**Physiological Needs** The most basic needs for all humans are physiological: We all need air, water, and food. According to Maslow's theory, unless those needs are met, it will be difficult to motivate a listener to satisfy other needs. If your listeners are hot, tired, and thirsty, it will be more difficult to persuade them to vote for your candidate, buy your insurance policy, or sign your petition in support of local pet-leash laws. Be sensitive to the basic physiological needs of your audience so that your appeals to higher-level needs will be heard.

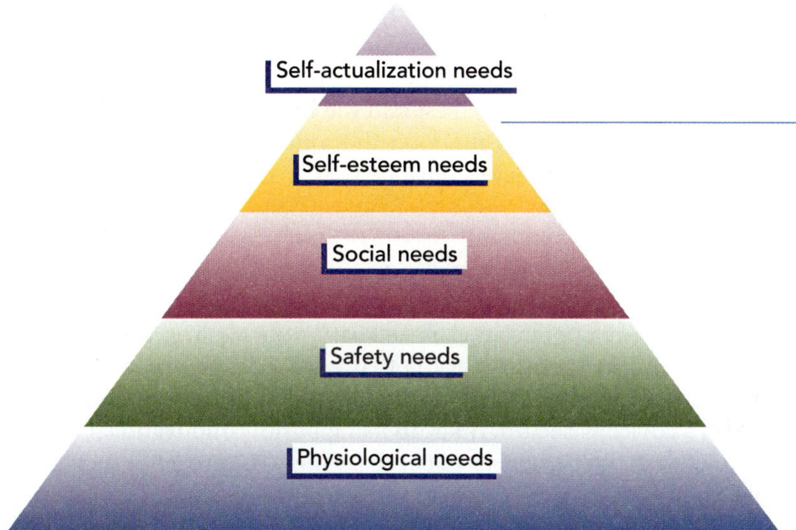


FIGURE 14.2 Maslow's Hierarchy of Needs.

Source: Maslow, Abraham (1954). *Motivation and Personality.* New York: HarperCollins.

**Safety Needs** Listeners are concerned about their safety. We all have a need to feel safe, secure, and protected, and we need to be able to predict that our own and our loved ones' needs for safety will be met. The classic presentation from insurance salespeople includes appeals to our need for safety and security. Many insurance sales efforts include photos of wrecked cars, anecdotes of people who were in ill health and could not pay their bills, or tales of the head of a household who passed away, leaving the basic needs of a family unmet. Appeals to use safety belts, stop smoking, start exercising, and use condoms all play to our need for safety and security.

In a speech titled "Emissions Tampering: Get the Lead Out," John appealed to his listeners' need for safety and security when he began with these observations:

> A major American producer is currently dumping over 8,000 tons of lead into our air each year, which in turn adversely affects human health. The producers of this waste are tampering with pollution control devices in order to cut costs. This tampering escalates the amount of noxious gases you and I inhale by 300 to 800 percent. That producer is the American motorist.[9]

**Social Needs** We all need to feel loved and valued. We need contact with others and reassurance that they care about us. According to Maslow, these social needs translate into our need for a sense of belonging to a group (fraternity, religious organization, friends). Powerful persuasive appeals are based on our need for social contact. We are encouraged to buy a product or support a particular issue because others are buying the product or supporting the issue. The message is that to be liked and respected by others, we must buy the same things they do or support the same causes they support.

**Self-Esteem Needs** The need for self-esteem reflects our desire to think well of ourselves. Civil rights activist Jesse Jackson is known for appealing often to the self-worth of his listeners by inviting them to chant "I am somebody." This is a direct appeal to his listeners' need for self-esteem. Advertisers also appeal to that need when they encourage us to believe that we will be noticed by others or stand out in the crowd if we purchase their product. Commercials promoting luxury cars usually invite you to picture yourself in the driver's seat with a beautiful companion beside you while you receive looks of envy from those you pass on the road.

**Self-Actualization Needs** At the top of Maslow's hierarchy is the need for **self-actualization.** This is the need to fully realize one's highest potential. For many years, the U.S. Army used the slogan "Be all that you can be" to tap into the need for self-actualization. Calls to be the best and the brightest are appeals to self-actualization. According to Maslow's assumption that our needs are organized into a hierarchy, needs at the other four levels must be satisfied before we can be motivated to satisfy the highest-level need.

## Use Positive Motivation

A Depression-era politician claimed that a vote for him would result in a return to prosperity: "A chicken in every pot" was his positive motivational appeal. Positive motivational appeals are statements suggesting that good things will happen if the speaker's advice is heeded. A key to using positive motivational appeals effectively is to know what your listeners value. Knowing what audience members view as desirable, good, and virtuous can help you select the benefits of your persuasive proposal that best appeal to them.

**Emphasize Positive Values** What do most people value? A comfortable, prosperous life; stimulating, exciting activity; a sense of accomplishment; world, community, and personal peace; and happiness are some of the many things people value. How can you use those values in a persuasive speech? When identifying reasons for your audience to think, feel, or behave as you want them to, review those common values to determine what benefits would accrue to your listeners. If, for example, you want your listeners to enroll in a sign-language course, what would the benefits be to the audience? You could stress the sense of accomplishment, contribution to society, or increased opportunities for friendship that would develop if they learned this skill. A speech advocating that recording companies print the lyrics of all songs on the label of the recording could appeal to family values.

**Emphasize Benefits, Not Just Features** A **benefit** is a good result or something that creates a positive feeling for the listener. A **feature** is simply a characteristic of whatever it is that you're talking about. A benefit creates a positive emotional sizzle that appeals to the heart. A feature elicits a rational, cognitive reaction—it appeals to the head. Heart usually trumps head when persuading others.

Most salespeople know that it is not enough just to identify, in general terms, the features of their product. They must translate those features into an obvious benefit that enhances the customer's quality of life. It is not enough for the real-estate salesperson to say, "This floor is the new no-wax vinyl." It is more effective to add, "And this means that you will never have to get down on your hands and knees to scrub another floor." When using positive motivational appeals, be sure your listeners know how the benefits of your proposal can improve their quality of life or the lives of their loved ones.

## Use Negative Motivation

"If you don't stop that, I'm going to tell Mom!" Whether he or she realizes it or not, the sibling who threatens to tell Mom is using a persuasive technique called *fear appeal.* One of the oldest methods of trying to change someone's attitude or behavior, the use of a threat is also one of the most effective. In essence, the appeal to fear takes the form of an "if–then" statement: If you don't do *X*, then awful things will happen to you. A persuader builds an argument on the assertion that a need will not be met unless the desired behavior or attitude change occurs. The principal reason that appeals to fear continue to be made in persuasive messages is that they work. A variety of research studies support the following principles for using fear appeals.[10]

**self-actualization need**
The need to achieve one's highest potential

**benefit**
A good result or something that creates a positive emotional response in the listener.

**feature**
A characteristic of something you are describing.

- **A strong threat to a loved one tends to be more successful than a fear appeal directed at the audience members themselves.** A speaker using this principle might say, "Unless you see that your children wear safety belts, they could easily be injured or killed in an auto accident."
- **The more competent, trustworthy, or respected the speaker, the greater the likelihood that an appeal to fear will be successful.** A speaker with less credibility will be more successful with moderate threats. The U.S. Surgeon General will be more successful in convincing people to get a flu shot than you will.
- **Fear appeals are more successful if you can convince your listeners that the threat is real and will probably occur unless they take the action you are advocating.** For example, you could dramatically announce, "Last year, thousands of smokers developed lung cancer and died. Unless you stop smoking, there is a high probability that you could develop lung cancer, too."
- **In general, increasing the intensity of a fear appeal increases the chances that the fear appeal will be effective.** This is especially true if the listener can take action (the action the persuader is suggesting) to reduce the threat.[11] In the past, some researchers and public-speaking textbooks reported that when a speaker creates an excessive amount of fear and anxiety in listeners, the listeners may find the appeal so strong and annoying that they stop listening. More comprehensive research, however, has concluded that there is a direct link between the intensity or strength of the fear appeal and the likelihood that audience members will be persuaded. Fear appeals work. Strong fear appeals seem to work even better than mild ones, assuming there is evidence to back up the threat made by a credible speaker. The speaker who uses fear appeals has an ethical responsibility to be truthful and not exaggerate when trying to arouse listeners' fear.

- **Fear appeals are more successful when you can convince your listeners that they have the power to make a change that will reduce the fear-causing threat.** As a speaker, your goal is not only to arouse their fear, but also to empower them to act. When providing a solution to the fear-inducing problem, make sure you tell your listeners what they can do to reduce the threat.[12] If, for example, you tell your listeners that unless they lose weight, they will die prematurely, they may want to shed pounds but think it's just too hard to do. You'll be a more effective persuader if you couple your fear-arousing message (lose weight or die early) with a strategy to make weight loss achievable (here's a diet plan that you can follow; it is simple and it works). The audience-centered principle again applies. You may think the solution is evident, but will your listeners think the same thing? View the solution from your listeners' point of view.

The effectiveness of the fear appeal is based on the theories of cognitive dissonance and Maslow's hierarchy of needs. The fear aroused creates dissonance, which can be reduced by following the recommendation of the persuader. Appeals to fear are also based on targeting an unmet need. Fear appeals depend on a convincing insistence that a need will go unmet unless a particular action or attitude change occurs.

Cognitive dissonance, needs, and appeals to the emotions, both positive and negative, can all persuade listeners to change their attitudes, beliefs, values, and behavior. Realize, however, that persuasion is not as simple as these approaches may lead you to believe. There is no precise formula for motivating and convincing an audience; attitude change occurs differently in each individual. Persuasion is an art that draws on science. Cultivating a

RECAP

### Using Fear Appeals Effectively

Fear appeals are more effective when

- the fear appeal is directed toward loved ones
- you have high credibility
- the threat is perceived as real and may actually happen
- the fear appeal is strongly supported by evidence
- the fear appeal empowers listeners to act

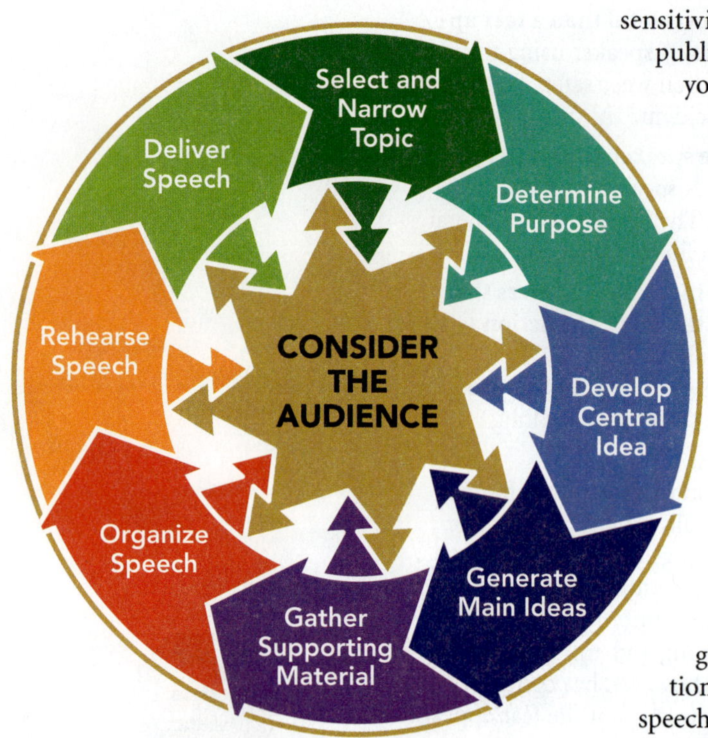


FIGURE 14.3 *Considering the audience is central to all speechmaking, especially persuasive speaking.*

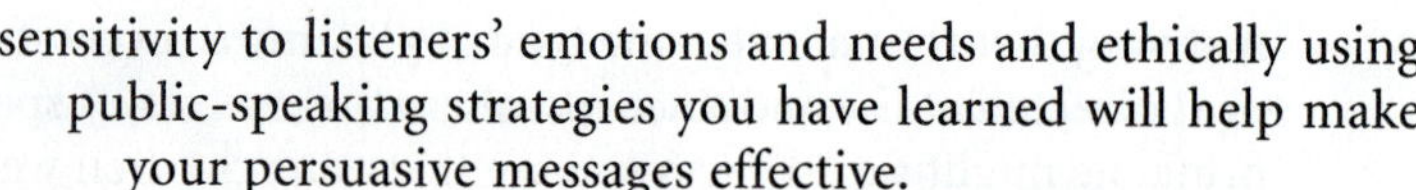
sensitivity to listeners' emotions and needs and ethically using public-speaking strategies you have learned will help make your persuasive messages effective.

# How to Develop Your Persuasive Speech

Now that you understand what persuasion is and how it works, let's turn our attention to the task of preparing a persuasive speech. The process of developing a persuasive speech follows the same audience-centered path you would take to develop any speech.

In the remaining portion of this chapter and in the next, we will amplify our discussion of these essential steps, providing examples and strategies to help you prepare a persuasive message. In this chapter we'll give you tips for getting started with the speech-construction process. As illustrated by our now-familiar model of the speechmaking process in Figure 14.3, you consider your audience at every step when attempting to persuade listeners. In the next chapter, we will provide additional practical strategies to help you enhance your credibility, use emotional persuasive appeals, and use evidence and reasoning as supportive material. We'll also present special strategies for organizing persuasive messages.

## Consider the Audience

Although being audience-centered is important in every speaking situation, it is vital when your objective is to persuade. It would be a challenge to persuade someone without knowing something about his or her interests, attitudes, beliefs, values, and behaviors.

Remember that while you're speaking, audience members have a variety of thoughts running through their heads. Your job as a persuader is to develop a message that anticipates, as best you can, what your audience may be thinking and feeling when they listen to you. You may want to review the elements of audience analysis and adaptation that we presented in Chapter 4 to help you think more concretely about who your listeners are and why they should listen to you.

**Consider Audience Diversity** One essential aspect of being audience-centered is being sensitive to the culturally diverse nature of most contemporary audiences. In our multicultural society, how persuasion works for one cultural group is different from how it works for others. Researchers have discovered no universal, cross-cultural approach to persuasion that is effective in every culture. North Americans, for example, tend to place considerable importance on direct observations and verifiable facts. Our court system places great stock in eyewitness testimony. People in some Chinese cultures, however, consider such evidence unreliable because they believe that what people observe is always influenced by personal motives. In some African cultures, personal testimony is also often suspect; it is reasoned that if you speak up to defend someone, you must have an ulterior motive and therefore your observation is discounted.[13] Although your audience may not include listeners from Africa or China, given the growing diversity of Americans, it is increasingly likely that it may. Or you may have listeners from other cultures with still different perspectives. Our point: Don't design a persuasive message using strategies that would be effective only for those with your cultural background. An effective communicator is especially sensitive to cultural differences between himself or herself and the audience, while at the same time being cautious not to make stereotypical assumptions about an audience based only on cultural factors.

**Remember Your Ethical Responsibilities as a Persuader** As you think about your audience and how to adapt your message to them, we remind you of your ethical responsibilities when persuading others. Fabricating evidence or trying to frighten your listeners with bogus information is unethical. Creating dissonance in the minds of your listeners based on information that you know to be untrue is also unethical. Adapting to your listeners does not mean that you tell people only what they want to hear. It means developing an ethical message that your listeners will listen to thoughtfully.

## Select and Narrow Your Persuasive Topic

Deciding on a persuasive speech topic sometimes stumps beginning speakers. But rather than pick the first idea that pops into your mind, select a topic that is important to you. What are you passionate about? What issues stir your heart and mind? You'll present a better speech if you've selected a topic you can speak about with sincere conviction. In addition to your interests, always reflect on your audience's passions and convictions. The ideal topic speaks to a need, concern, or issue of the audience as well as to your own interests and zeal.

Controversial issues make excellent sources for persuasive topics. A controversial issue is a question about which people disagree: Should the university increase tuition so that faculty members can have a salary increase? Should public schools distribute condoms to students? Should the government provide health insurance to all citizens? In choosing a controversial topic, you need to be audience-centered—to know the local, state, national, or international issues that interest your listeners. In addition, the best persuasive speech topics focus on important rather than frivolous issues.

### LEARNING FROM GREAT SPEAKERS

#### Elizabeth Cady Stanton (1815–1902)

Elizabeth Cady Stanton began her preparation for persuasive speaking by reading most of her father's law library while she was still a young woman. Incensed by the gender discrimination she found entrenched in the law, she embarked on a long career of speaking out for women's rights. Stanton gave perhaps her most famous persuasive speech to the first Women's Convention held in 1848 in Seneca Falls, New York. The success of that speech was evident in the results: One hundred men and women signed a Declaration of Sentiments that called for equal rights for women. Throughout the next half-century, Stanton frequently spoke out passionately and forcefully, not only for women's suffrage, but on such related issues as co-education, equal wages, birth control, property rights for women, and reform of the divorce laws.[14]

Successful persuaders have strong feelings about their messages. They believe in their cause. But in addition to their strong passion, they have researched the issues and are knowledgeable about their messages. So besides having strong convictions about what you are advocating, you need to research your topic and immerse yourself in the issues you will present to your listeners—both the pros and the cons of what you advocate.

[Image: The Granger Collection]

Pay attention to the media and the Internet to stay current on the important issues of the day. Read an online newspaper or magazine, or subscribe to a newspaper or weekly news magazine to keep in touch with issues and topics of interest. Another interesting source of controversial issues is talk radio programs. Both national and local radio call-in programs may give you ideas that are appropriate for a persuasive speech. You might also monitor chat rooms on the Internet or the homepages of print and broadcast media Web sites for ideas. Even when you already have a clear idea of your speech topic, keeping up with the media and the Internet can give you additional ideas to help narrow your topic or find interesting and appropriate supporting material.

## Determine Your Persuasive Purpose

When you want to persuade others, you don't always have to strive for dramatic changes in their attitudes, beliefs, values, and behavior. People rarely make major life changes after hearing just one persuasive message. Your speaking goal may be only to move listeners a bit closer to your ultimate persuasive objective.

**Social judgment theory** suggests that when listeners are confronted with a persuasive message, their responses fall into one of three categories: (1) a latitude of acceptance, in which they generally agree with the speaker; (2) a latitude of rejection, in which they disagree with the speaker; or (3) a latitude of noncommitment, in which they are not yet committed either to agree or to disagree—they are not sure how to respond.[15]

It is important to know which latitude your listeners are in before you begin so that you can choose a realistic persuasive goal. If most of your listeners are in the latitude of rejection, it will be difficult to move them to the latitude of acceptance in a single ten-minute speech. As shown in Figure 14.4, perhaps the best you can do is make them less certain about rejecting your idea by moving them to the latitude of noncommitment.

**social judgment theory**
A theory that categorizes listener responses to a persuasive message according to the latitude of acceptance, the latitude of rejection, or the latitude of noncommitment

**proposition**
A statement that summarizes the ideas with which a speaker wants an audience to agree

## Develop Your Central Idea and Main Ideas

The overall structure of your speech flows from your central idea and the main ideas that support your central idea. Your central idea, as you recall, is a one-sentence summary of your speech. When persuading others, most speakers find it useful to state their central idea in the form of a proposition. A **proposition** is a statement with which you want your audience to agree. In the following list, note how each proposition is actually the central idea of the speech:

All students should be required to take a foreign language.

Organic gardening is better for the environment than gardening with chemicals.

The United States should not provide economic aid to other countries.

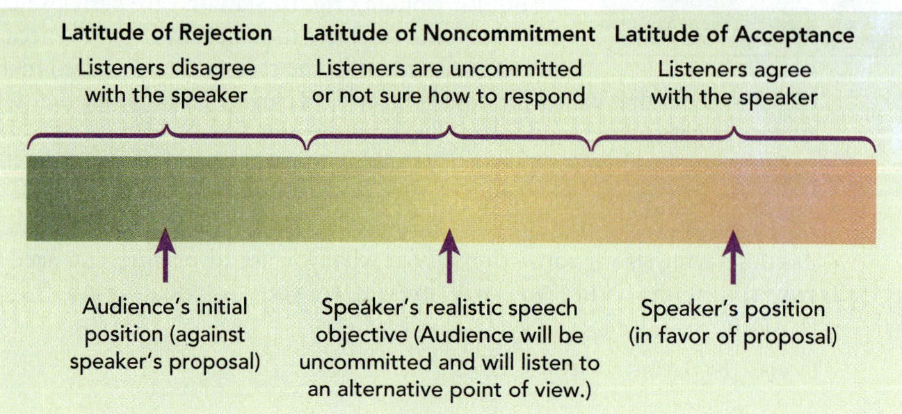


FIGURE 14.4 **A Model of Social Judgment Theory** *When developing your specific persuasive objective for one speech, be realistic. According to social judgment theory, your goal may be to nudge your audience along the continuum of acceptance, toward the latitude of noncommitment, rather than to propel them from one end to the other.*

TABLE 14.2 Persuasive Propositions: Developing Your Central Idea

| Type | Definition | Examples |
|---|---|---|
| Proposition of fact | A statement that focuses on whether something is true or false. Debatable propositions of fact can be good topics for persuasive speeches. | Undebatable: The state legislature has raised tuition 10 percent during the last three years.<br>Debatable: There are more terrorist attacks in the world today than at any previous time in human history. |
| Proposition of value | A statement that either asserts that something is better than something else or presumes what is right and wrong or good and bad. | The electoral college is a better way to elect presidents than a direct popular vote would be.<br>It is better to keep your financial records on a personal computer than to make calculations by hand. |
| Proposition of policy | A statement that advocates a change in policy or procedures. | Our community should adopt a curfew for all citizens under eighteen.<br>All handguns should be abolished. |

The three categories of propositions are: propositions of fact, propositions of value, and propositions of policy. These three types of propositions are summarized in Table 14.2. Determining which category your persuasive proposition fits into not only can help you clarify your central idea, but can also give you an idea of how to select specific persuasive strategies that will help you achieve your specific purpose. Let's examine each type of proposition in more detail.

**Proposition of Fact** A **proposition of fact** focuses on whether something is true or false or on whether it did or did not happen. Some propositions of fact are undebatable: Al Gore received more votes nationwide than George W. Bush in the 2000 presidential election. The San Francisco Giants won the 2010 World Series. Texas is bigger than Poland. Each of these statements is a proposition of fact that can be verified simply by consulting an appropriate source. For that reason, they do not make good topics for persuasive speeches.

Other propositions of fact will take time and skill—perhaps an entire persuasive speech—to prove. Here are examples of debatable propositions of fact that would make good topics:

When women joined the military, the quality of the military improved.

Adults who were abused as children by their parents are more likely to abuse their own children.

U.S. foreign policy has increased the chance that the United States will experience more terrorist attacks.

Global climate change is not occurring in our atmosphere.

To prove each of these propositions, a speaker would need to offer specific supporting evidence. To persuade listeners to agree with a proposition of fact, the speaker must focus on changing or reinforcing their beliefs. Most persuasive speeches that focus on propositions of fact begin by identifying one or more reasons why the proposition is true.

The following persuasive speech outline on the topic of low-carb diets is based on a proposition of fact:

**proposition of fact**
A proposition that focuses on whether something is true or false or whether it did or did not happen

TOPIC: Low-carbohydrate diets
GENERAL PURPOSE: To persuade
PROPOSITION: Low-carbohydrate diets are safe and effective.
SPECIFIC PURPOSE: At the end of my speech, audience members will agree that low-carb diets are safe and effective.
MAIN IDEAS:

I. Carbohydrates are a significant part of our diets.
   A. Many people eat a significant amount of fast food that is laden with carbohydrates.
   B. Lunches provided by the cafeterias in elementary schools include significant amounts of carbohydrates.
   C. Many people eat a significant amount of highly processed, carb-rich foods.
II. Carbohydrates are making people fat and unhealthy.
   A. A diet rich in carbohydrates leads to obesity.
   B. A diet rich in carbohydrates leads to Type II diabetes.
III. Low-carb diets are a safe and effective way to lose weight and maintain your health.
   A. The safety of such low-carb diets as the South Beach diet or the Atkins diet is documented by research.
   B. The effectiveness of such low-carb diets is documented by research.

**Proposition of Value** A **proposition of value** is a statement that calls for the listener to judge the worth or importance of something. Values, as you recall, are enduring concepts of good or bad, right or wrong. Value propositions are statements that something is either good or bad or that one thing or course of action is better than another. Consider these examples:

It is wrong to turn away immigrants who want to come to the United States.

Communication is a better major than home economics.

A private-school education is more valuable than a public-school education.

It is better for citizens to carry concealed weapons than to let criminals rule society.

Each of these propositions either directly states or implies that something is better than something else. Value propositions often directly compare two things and suggest that one option is better than another.

Manny designed his speech to convince an audience that reggae music is better than rock music.

TOPIC: Reggae music
GENERAL PURPOSE: To persuade
PROPOSITION: Reggae music is better than rock music for three reasons.
SPECIFIC PURPOSE: After listening to my speech, the audience should listen to reggae music more often than they listen to rock music.
MAIN IDEAS:

I. Reggae music communicates a message of equality for all people.
II. Reggae music and its rhythms evoke a positive, uplifting mood.
III. Reggae music draws on a variety of cultural and ethnic traditions.

**proposition of value**
A proposition that calls for the listener to judge the worth or importance of something

**Proposition of Policy** The third type of proposition, a **proposition of policy**, advocates a specific action—changing a policy, procedure, or behavior. Note how all the following propositions of policy include the word *should*; this is a tip-off that the speaker is advocating a change in policy or procedure.

The Gifted and Talented Program in our school district should have a full-time coordinator.

Our community should set aside one day each month as "Community Cleanup Day."

Senior citizens should pay for more of their medical costs.

In a speech based on a proposition of policy, Paul aimed to convince his audience that academic tenure for college professors should be abolished. He organized his speech topically, identifying reasons academic tenure is no longer a sound policy for most colleges and universities. To support his proposition of policy, he used several propositions of fact. Note, too, that Paul's specific purpose involved specific action on the part of his audience.

| | |
|---|---|
| TOPIC: | Academic tenure |
| GENERAL PURPOSE: | To persuade |
| PROPOSITION: | Our college, along with other colleges and universities, should abolish academic tenure. |
| SPECIFIC PURPOSE: | After listening to my speech, audience members should sign a petition calling for the abolition of academic tenure. |
| MAIN IDEAS: | I. Academic tenure is outdated.<br>II. Academic tenure is abused.<br>III. Academic tenure contributes to ineffective education. |

Here's another outline for a persuasive speech based on a proposition of policy. Again, note how the main ideas are propositions of fact used to support the proposition of policy.

| | |
|---|---|
| TOPIC: | Computer education |
| GENERAL PURPOSE: | To persuade |
| PROPOSITION: | Every person in our society should know how to use a personal computer. |
| SPECIFIC PURPOSE: | After listening to my speech, all audience members who have not had a computer course should sign up for one. |
| MAIN IDEAS: | I. Most people who own a personal computer do not know how to use most of its features.<br>II. Computer skills will help you with your academic studies.<br>III. Computer skills will help you get a good job, regardless of your major or profession. |

## Gather Supporting Material

When gathering supporting material for your persuasive message, you look for the available means of persuasion to support the main ideas that you have developed to achieve your specific purpose. Recall from earlier in this chapter that Aristotle proposed three primary ways, or available means, of persuading listeners: (1) being a

**proposition of policy**
A proposition that advocates change in a policy, procedure, or behavior

credible and ethical speaker, which includes using credible and ethical supporting material; (2) using effective logic and reasoning to support your main ideas; and (3) using appropriate emotional support. Because the supporting material you develop and use is vital to the effectiveness of your persuasive goal, we devote a major portion of the next chapter to these three means of persuasion.

## CONFIDENTLY CONNECTING WITH YOUR AUDIENCE

### Breathe to Relax

When you feel your body start to tense, take a deep, relaxing breath to help quiet your fears. It's normal to experience a quickened heartbeat and a change in your breathing patterns as physiological responses to increased anxiety. To signal to your brain that *you* are in charge, consciously take several slow breaths. As you breathe, make your breaths unobtrusive; no one need know that you are using a deep breathing technique to manage your fear. Whether you are at your seat in your classroom getting ready to be the next speaker or sitting on a platform in front of an audience, a few slow, calming breaths will help you relax and calm your spirit.

## Organize Your Persuasive Speech

After identifying and gathering ethical, logical, and appropriate emotional support for your message, you'll make final decisions about how to organize your message. As with any speech, you'll have an introduction that should get the audience's attention, give the audience a reason to listen to your message, introduce the subject, establish your credibility, and preview your main ideas. The body of your speech should have clearly identified major points with appropriate transitions, signposts, and internal summaries to make sure your key ideas are understandable to your listeners. And finally, you'll have a conclusion that summarizes the essence of your message and provides closure to your speech. When your goal is to persuade, it is especially important to consider your audience and your specific purpose as you consider how you will begin your message, organize your ideas, and conclude your talk. We'll discuss specific approaches and tips for organizing a persuasive speech in the next chapter.

## Rehearse and Deliver Your Speech

To bring your ideas to life, the last two elements of the speech-making process are to rehearse your message out loud and then, finally, to present your talk to your audience. When your goal is to persuade, you may want to make a special effort to rehearse your speech in front of another person or to run some of your ideas past others to check the overall clarity and structure of your message. It is through your delivery that you communicate your passion and enthusiasm for your ideas, so it would be worthwhile to review the suggestions and prescriptions we offered in Chapter 11 for how to ensure that your speech is well delivered.

Although you may have a well-crafted message, without ample emotional energy, your speech may not achieve its purpose. Your eye contact, gestures, movement, posture, facial expression, vocal delivery and personal appearance are the means by which you'll reinforce your credibility and logic, as well as make an authentic emotional connection with your listeners.

Recall, too, that the elaboration likelihood model predicts that your delivery can, in itself, be persuasive to some of your listeners. No matter how well-reasoned your message, at least some of your listeners are likely to fail to elaborate, or critically consider it. These listeners may instead be persuaded by an indirect route, one based on the emotional connection you make with them in the course of delivering your speech.

## RECAP

### Audience-Centered Persuasive Speaking

- Consider audience attitudes, beliefs, values.
- Consider audience diversity.
- Controversial issues make good topics.
- Use social judgment theory to determine purpose.
- State your central idea as a proposition.
- Find supporting materials that reinforce your credibility, logic, and emotional appeals.
- Keep the organization clear.
- Get feedback as you rehearse.
- Deliver with appropriate emotion.

# STUDY GUIDE

## Persuasion Defined

Persuasion is the process of changing or reinforcing attitudes, beliefs, values, or behavior. Attitudes are learned predispositions to respond favorably or unfavorably toward something. A belief is a person's understanding of what is true and what is false. A value is a conception of right and wrong.

### Being Audience-Centered

- When persuading others, it is important that you understand your listeners' attitudes, beliefs, values, and behavior.

### A Question of Ethics

- Zeta plans to give a persuasive speech to convince her classmates that term limits should be imposed for senators and members of Congress—even though she is personally against term limits. Is it ethical to develop a persuasive message that supports an attitude or belief with which you personally disagree?

### How Persuasion Works

Various theories explain how persuasion works to change or reinforce attitudes, beliefs, and values, which are the determinants of behavior. You can incorporate this theoretical knowledge into your speech preparation in order to deliver a persuasive message.

### Being Audience-Centered

- Researchers have discovered no universal, cross-cultural approach to persuasion that is effective in every culture.

### Using What You've Learned

- If you were attempting to sell a new computer system to the administration of your school, what persuasive principles would you draw on to develop your message?

### Speaker's Homepage: Finding Out about Congressional Legislation for Persuasive Speeches

If you plan to give a persuasive speech regarding an issue about which there is pertinent legislation pending in the U.S. Congress or with your state or local government, these sites can help you find the latest information about the pending legislation.

- U.S. Congress. Access the Congressional Record, which tells what Congress does every day. www.gpoaccess.gov/crecord/index.html
- U.S. Government Information Sources. This is a directory to sources of information about various aspects of the federal government. www2.etown.edu/vl/usgovt.html
- State and Local Governments on the Net. This directory helps you get to the Internet presence of your local or state government. www.statelocalgov.net/index.cfm

## How to Motivate Listeners

There are several ways to motivate listeners. One approach is based on the theory of cognitive dissonance, the human tendency to strive for balance or consistency in our thoughts. When a persuasive message invites us to change our attitudes, beliefs, values, or behavior, we respond by trying to maintain intellectual balance, or cognitive consistency.

A second theory explains why we are motivated to respond to persuasion by proposing that we wish to satisfy certain needs. Abraham Maslow identified a five-level hierarchy of physiological, safety, social, self-esteem, and self-actualization needs.

Third, positive motivational appeals can help you develop a persuasive message by encouraging listeners to respond favorably to your message.

A fourth approach to persuasion is the use of negative motivational appeals—notably, appeals to fear. Fear can motivate us to respond favorably to a persuasive suggestion. To avoid pain or discomfort, we may follow the recommendation of a persuasive speaker.

### Being Audience-Centered

- Persuasion is an art rather than an exact science; your audience's cultural background and expectations play a significant role in determining which persuasive strategies will be effective and appropriate.

### Using What You've Learned

- Your local chamber of commerce has asked for your advice in developing a speakers' bureau that would address public-safety issues in your community. What suggestions would you offer to motivate citizens to behave in ways that would protect them from AIDS, traffic, and severe weather?

### A Question of Ethics

- Tom plans to begin his speech on driver safety using a graphic photo of traffic-accident victims who were maimed or killed because they did not use safety belts. Would such a graphic use of fear appeals be ethical?

## How to Develop Your Persuasive Speech

Speakers can prepare a persuasive speech by applying broad principles of persuasion to the same processes they use to prepare and present any other kind of speech. A key first concern is to consider the audience. The next concern is to choose an appropriate topic. When crafting your central idea for your persuasive speech, develop a proposition of fact, value, or policy that is reasonable based on your audience's background and expectations.

### Being Audience-Centered

- Consider the interests and backgrounds of your listeners when selecting and narrowing your persuasive speech topic.
- If you are speaking to a culturally diverse audience, don't design a persuasive message using strategies that would be effective only for those who share your cultural background.

### Using What You've Learned

- Martha has been asked to speak to the Association for the Preservation of the Environment. What possible persuasive topics and propositions would be appropriate for her audience?

# SPEECH WORKSHOP

## Developing a Persuasive Speech

Answer the following questions to develop a persuasive speech topic, specific purpose, and persuasive strategy.

1. What is my persuasive speech topic? (Note: Use the topic selection workshop on pages 130–131 to help you develop a persuasive speech topic.)

   ______________________________

   ______________________________

2. a. What are the key audience attitudes toward my speech topic? That is, what are their likes and dislikes?

   ______________________________

   ______________________________

   b. What are the audience beliefs (what they perceive as true or false) about your topic and the issues?

   ______________________________

   ______________________________

   c. What are the audience's core values (what they perceive as right or wrong, good or bad)?

   ______________________________

   ______________________________

3. State the specific purpose of your persuasive speech: At the end of my speech, the audience should be able to ______________________________

4. State the central idea of your speech, a one-sentence summary of your message.

   ______________________________

   ______________________________

5. Determine whether your central idea is a proposition of fact, value, or policy.

   _____ It's a statement of fact if you are trying to prove that something is true or false or that something did or did not happen. (Hint: A proposition of fact is supported with evidence that something did or did not occur.)

   _____ It's a statement of value if you want the audience to judge the worth or importance of something. (Hint: A proposition of value seeks to convince a listener that something is good, bad, better, or worse than something else.)

   _____ It's a statement of policy if you are suggesting that the audience should take some action, such as to change a policy, procedure, behavior, attitude, or belief. (Hint: A proposition of policy usually includes the word *should*.)

6. How can you motivate your listeners to change or reinforce their attitudes, beliefs, values, or behavior?

   _____ Can you create dissonance? How?

   _____ What specific audience needs can you address?

   _____ How can you use positive motivation?

   _____ How can you ethically use fear appeals or negative motivation?

SPEECH IS POWER: SPEECH IS TO PERSUADE, TO CONVERT, TO COMPEL.

—RALPH WALDO EMERSON

Felix Joseph Barrias (1822-1907), *Camille Desmoulins (1760–1794) Harangueing the Patriots in the Gardens of the Palais Royal.* Musée Municipal, Chalons-sur-Marne, France. Photo: Scala/White Images/Art Resource, N.Y.

OUTLINE

# 15 Using Persuasive Strategies

OBJECTIVES

**After studying this chapter you should be able to do the following:**

1. Identify strategies to improve your initial, derived, and terminal credibility.
2. Use principles of effective reasoning to develop a persuasive message.
3. Employ effective techniques of using emotional appeal in a persuasive speech.
4. Adapt your persuasive message to receptive, neutral, and unreceptive audiences.
5. Identify strategies for effectively organizing a persuasive speech.

"Persuasion," said rhetoric scholar Donald C. Bryant, "is the process of adjusting ideas to people and people to ideas."[1] To be an audience-centered persuasive speaker is to use ethical and effective strategies to adjust your message so that listeners will thoughtfully respond to your presentation. But precisely what are the strategies that can enhance your credibility, help you develop logical arguments, and use emotional appeals to speak to the hearts of your listeners? In the last chapter, we noted that Aristotle defined rhetoric as the process of discovering the available means of persuasion. In this chapter, we provide more detailed strategies to help you prepare your persuasive speech. Specifically, we will suggest how to gain credibility, develop well-reasoned arguments, and move your audience with emotion. We will also discuss how to adapt your specific message to your audience, and we will end with suggestions for organizing your persuasive message.

# Enhancing Your Credibility

If you were going to buy a new car, to whom would you turn for advice? Perhaps you would ask a trusted family member, or you might seek advice from *Consumer Reports*, a monthly publication that reports studies of various products on the market, among them automobiles. In other words, you would probably turn to a source that you consider knowledgeable, competent, and trustworthy—a source you think is credible.

You'll recall from Chapter 8 that *credibility* is the audience's perception of a speaker's competence, trustworthiness, and dynamism. As a public speaker, especially one who wishes to persuade an audience, you hope that your listeners will have a favorable attitude toward you. Current research points clearly to a relationship between credibility and speech effectiveness: The more believable you are to your listener, the more effective you will be as a persuasive communicator.

As we noted in Chapter 14, Aristotle used the term *ethos* to refer to a speaker's credibility. He thought that to be credible, a public speaker should be ethical, possess good character, have common sense, and be concerned for the well-being of the audience. Quintilian, a Roman teacher of public speaking, also believed that an effective public speaker should be a person of good character. Quintilian's advice was that a speaker should be "a good person speaking well." The importance to a speaker of a positive public image has been recognized for centuries. But don't get the idea that credibility is something that a speaker inherently possesses or lacks. Credibility is based on the listeners' mindset regarding the speaker. Your listeners, not you, determine whether you have credibility or lack it.

## Elements of Your Credibility

Credibility is not just a single factor or single view of you on the part of your audience. Your credibility is made up of several elements. Aristotle's speculations as to the factors that influence a speaker's credibility have been generally supported by modern experimental studies. To be credible, you should be perceived as competent, trustworthy, and dynamic.

**Competence** To be a **competent** speaker is to be considered informed, skilled, or knowledgeable about one's subject. When a used-car salesperson sings the virtues of a car on his lot, you want to know what qualifies him to give believable information about the car.

Do competent speakers always get positive results? Although there are no absolutes, one comprehensive study found that the candidates for U.S. president who emphasized policy proposals more than their own character in their campaign speeches were more likely to win elections.[2] Although audiences are certainly swayed by a variety of issues, they seem to highly value solid ideas that enhance competence.

When you give a speech, you will be more persuasive if you convince your listeners that you are knowledgeable about your topic. If, for example, you say it would be a good idea for everyone to have a medical checkup each year, your listeners might mentally ask, "Why? What are your qualifications to make such a proposal?" But if you support your conclusion with medical statistics showing how having a physical exam each year leads to a dramatically prolonged life, you enhance the credibility of your suggestion. Thus, one way to enhance your competence is to cite credible evidence to support your point.

**Trustworthiness** A second major factor that influences your audience's response to you is **trustworthiness**. You trust people whom you believe to be honest. While delivering your speech, you have to convey honesty and sincerity. Your audience will be looking for evidence that they can trust you, that you are believable.

**competent**
Being informed, skilled, or knowledgeable about one's subject.

**trustworthiness**
An aspect of a speaker's credibility that reflects whether the speaker is perceived as believable and honest

*Your dynamism, or energy level, is one of the factors that contributes to your credibility as a persuasive speaker.*

[Photo: Martin Beraud/Stone/Getty]

Earning an audience's trust is not something that you can do simply by saying "Trust me." You earn trust by demonstrating that you have had experience dealing with the issues you talk about. Your listeners would be more likely to trust your advice about how to tour Europe on $50 a day if you had been there than they would if you took your information from a travel guide. Your trustworthiness may be suspect if you advocate something that will result in a direct benefit to you. That's why salespersons and politicians are often stereotyped as being untrustworthy; if you do what they say, they will clearly benefit from a sales commission if you buy a product, or gain power and position if you give your vote.

**Dynamism** A third factor in credibility is the speaker's **dynamism**, or energy. Dynamism is often projected through delivery. **Charisma** is a form of dynamism. A charismatic person possesses charm, talent, magnetism, and other qualities that make the person attractive and energetic. Many people considered presidents Franklin Roosevelt and Ronald Reagan charismatic speakers.

## Phases of Your Credibility

Your credibility in the minds of your listeners evolves over time. Speakers typically establish their credibility in three phases: (1) initial credibility, (2) derived credibility, and (3) terminal credibility.

**Initial Credibility** The first phase is called **initial credibility**. This is the impression of your credibility your listeners have even before you speak. Giving careful thought to your appearance and establishing eye contact before you begin your talk will enhance both your confidence and your credibility. It is also wise to prepare a brief description of your credentials and accomplishments so that the person who introduces you can use it in his or her introductory remarks. Even if you are not asked for a statement beforehand, be prepared with one.

**Derived Credibility** The second phase in the evolution of your credibility is called **derived credibility**. This is the perception the audience develops about you after they meet you and as they see you present yourself and your message. Most of this book presents principles and skills that help establish your credibility as a speaker. Several specific research-supported skills for enhancing your credibility as

**dynamism**
An aspect of a speaker's credibility that reflects whether the speaker is perceived as energetic

**charisma**
Characteristic of a talented, charming, attractive speaker

**initial credibility**
The impression of a speaker's credibility that listeners have before the speaker starts a speech

**derived credibility**
The perception of a speaker's credibility that is formed during a speech

you speak include establishing common ground with your audience, supporting your key arguments with evidence, and presenting a well-organized and well-delivered message.

You establish common ground by indicating in your opening remarks that you share the values and concerns of your audience. To begin to persuade an audience that she understands why budget cuts upset parents, a politician might speak of her own children. If you are a student persuading classmates to enroll in an economics class, you could stress that understanding economic issues will be useful as they face the process of interviewing for a job. Of course, you have an ethical responsibility to be truthful when outlining the common goals you and your audience share.

Having evidence to support your persuasive conclusions strengthens your credibility.[3] Margo was baffled as to why her plea for donations for the homeless fell flat. No one offered financial support for her cause when she concluded her speech. Why? She had offered no proof that there really were homeless people in the community. If she had provided well-documented evidence that there was a problem and that the organization she supported could effectively solve the problem, she would have been more likely to gain support for her position.

Presenting a well-organized message also enhances your credibility as a competent and rational advocate.[4] Rambling, emotional requests rarely change or reinforce listeners' opinions or behavior. Regardless of the organizational pattern you use, it is crucial to ensure that your message is logically structured and uses appropriate internal summaries, signposts, and the enumeration of key ideas.

Your delivery also affects your derived credibility. For most North Americans, regular eye contact, varied vocal inflection, and appropriate attire have positive influences on your ability to persuade listeners to respond to your message.[5] Why does delivery affect how persuasive you are? Researchers suggest that when your listeners expect you to be a good speaker and you aren't, they are less likely to do what you ask them to do.[6] So don't violate their expectations by presenting a poorly delivered speech. Effective delivery also enhances your ability to persuade because it helps gain and maintain listener attention and affects whether listeners will like you.[7] If you can arouse listeners' attention, and if they like you, you'll be more persuasive than if you don't gain their attention and they don't like you. Do speakers who use humor enhance their credibility? There is some evidence that although using humor may contribute to making listeners like you, humor does not have a major impact on ultimately persuading listeners to support your message.[8]

**RECAP**

**How to Enhance Your Credibility**

**Initial Credibility:**
- Carefully consider your appearance.
- Establish eye contact before speaking.
- Provide a summary of your credentials.

**Derived Credibility:**
- Establish common ground.
- Support arguments with evidence.
- Organize your speech well.
- Deliver your speech well.

**Terminal Credibility:**
- End with eye contact.
- Be prepared for questions.

**Terminal Credibility** The last phase of credibility, called **terminal credibility**, or final credibility, is the perception of your credibility your listeners have when you finish your speech. The lasting impression you make on your audience is influenced by how you were first perceived (initial credibility) and what you did as you presented your message (derived credibility). It is also influenced by your behavior as, and immediately after, you conclude your speech. For example, maintain eye contact with your audience as you deliver your speech conclusion. Also, don't start leaving the lectern or speaking area until you have finished your closing sentence. Even if there is no planned question-and-answer period following your speech, be ready to respond to questions from interested listeners.

## Using Logic and Evidence to Persuade

**terminal credibility**
The final impression listeners have of a speaker's credibility, after a speech concludes

"We need to cut taxes to improve the economy," claimed the politician on a Sunday-morning talk show. "The stock market has lost 300 points this month. People aren't buying things. A tax cut will put money in their pockets and give the economy a boost." In an effort to persuade reluctant members of her political party to support a tax cut, this politician was using a logical argument supported with evidence that stock prices were dropping. As we noted in Chapter 3 when we discussed how to be a critical listener, logic is a formal system of rules for making inferences. Because wise audience members will be listening, persuasive speakers need to give careful attention to the way they use logic to reach a conclusion. Aristotle called logic *logos*, which means "the word." Using words as well as statistical information to develop logical arguments can make your persuasive efforts more convincing. It can also clarify your own thinking and help make your points clear to your listeners. Logic is central to all persuasive speeches. In Chapter 3, we introduced a discussion of logic and evidence to help you become a critical listener or consumer of messages. Here we'll amplify that discussion to help you use logical arguments and evidence to persuade others.

Aristotle said that any persuasive speech has two parts: First, you state your case. Second, you prove your case. In essence, he was saying that you must present evidence and then use appropriate reasoning to lead your listeners to the conclusion you advocate. Reasoning is the process of drawing a conclusion from evidence. The Sunday-morning talk-show politician reached the conclusion that a tax cut was necessary because stock prices had tumbled and people weren't buying things. Evidence consists of the facts, examples, statistics, and expert opinions that you use to support the points you wish to make. When advancing an argument, it is your task to prove your point. Proof consists of the evidence you offer plus the conclusion you draw from it. The evidence in the claim made by the politician was lower stock-market values and fewer people buying things. The conclusion: We need a tax cut to stimulate the economy. Let's consider the two key elements of proof in greater detail. Specifically, we will look more closely at types of reasoning and ways of testing the quality of evidence.

## Understanding Types of Reasoning

Developing well-reasoned arguments for persuasive messages has been important since antiquity. If your arguments are structured in a rational way, you will have a greater chance of persuading your listeners. There are three major ways to structure an argument to reach a logical conclusion: inductively (including reasoning by analogy), deductively, and causally. These three structures are summarized in Table 15.1, on page 342. Let's examine each in detail.

### Inductive Reasoning

Reasoning that arrives at a general conclusion from specific instances or examples is known as **inductive reasoning**. Using this classical approach, you reach a general conclusion based on specific examples, facts, statistics, and opinions. You may not know for a certainty that the specific instances prove that the conclusion is true, but you decide that, in all *probability*, the specific instances support the general conclusion. According to contemporary logicians, you reason inductively when you claim that an outcome is probably true because of specific evidence.

For example, if you were giving a speech attempting to convince your audience that foreign cars are unreliable, you might use inductive reasoning to make your point. You could announce that you recently bought a foreign car that gave you trouble. Your cousin also bought a foreign car that kept stalling on the freeway. Finally, your English professor told you her foreign car has broken down several times in the past few weeks. Based on these specific examples, you ask your audience to agree with your general conclusion: Foreign cars are unreliable.

**inductive reasoning**
Reasoning that uses specific instances or examples to reach a general, probable conclusion

### Testing the Validity of Inductive Reasoning

As a persuasive speaker, your job is to construct a sound argument. That means basing your generalization on evidence. When you listen to a persuasive message, notice how the speaker tries to

## TABLE 15.1 Comparing Types of Reasoning

| | Inductive Reasoning | Deductive Reasoning | Causal Reasoning |
|---|---|---|---|
| Reasoning begins with . . . | Specific examples | A general statement | Something known |
| Reasoning ends with . . . | A specific conclusion | A specific conclusion | A speculation about something unknown occurring, based on what is known |
| Conclusion of reasoning is that something is . . . | Probable or improbable | True or false | Likely or not likely |
| Goal of reasoning is . . . | To reach a general conclusion or discover something new | To reach a specific conclusion by applying what is known | To link something known with something unknown |
| Example | When tougher drug laws went into effect in Kansas City and St. Louis, drug traffic was reduced. The United States should therefore institute tougher drug laws because they will decrease drug use nationwide. | Instituting tough drug laws in medium-sized communities results in diminished drug-related crime. San Marcos, Texas, is a medium-sized community. San Marcos should institute tough drug laws in order to reduce drug-related crimes. | Since the 70-mile-per-hour speed limit was reinstated, traffic deaths have increased. The increased highway speed has caused an increase in highway deaths. |

support his or her conclusion. To judge the validity of a **generalization** arrived at inductively, ask the following questions.

- **Are there enough specific instances to support the conclusion?** Are three examples of problems with foreign cars enough to prove your point that foreign cars are generally unreliable? Of the several million foreign cars manufactured, three cars, especially if they are of different makes, are not a large sample. If those examples were supported by additional statistical evidence that more than 50 percent of foreign-car owners complained of serious engine malfunctions, the evidence would be more convincing.
- **Are the specific instances typical?** Are the three examples you cite representative of all foreign cars manufactured? How do you know? What are the data on the performance of foreign cars? Also, are you, your cousin, and your professor typical of most car owners? The three of you may be careless about routine maintenance of your autos.
- **Are the instances recent?** If the foreign cars you are using as examples of poor reliability are more than three years old, you cannot reasonably conclude that today's foreign cars are unreliable products. Age alone may explain the poor performance of your sample.

The logic in this example of problematic foreign cars, therefore, is not particularly sound. The speaker would need considerably more evidence to prove his or her point.

**generalization**
An all-encompassing statement

**Reasoning by Analogy** Reasoning by analogy is a special type of inductive reasoning. An *analogy* is a comparison. This form of inductive reasoning compares one thing, person, or process with another, to predict how something will perform and respond. In previous chapters we've suggested that using an analogy is an effective way to clarify ideas and enhance message interest. When you observe that two things have a number of characteristics in common and that a certain fact about one is likely to be true of the other, you have drawn an analogy, reasoning from one example to reach a conclusion about the other. If you try to convince an audience that because laws against using a cell phone while driving in a school zone have cut down on injuries to children in Florida and Missouri, those laws should therefore should be instituted in Kansas, you are reasoning by analogy. You would also be reasoning by analogy if you claimed that because capital punishment reduced crime in Brazil, it should therefore should be used in the United States as well. But as with reasoning by generalization, there are questions that you should ask to check the validity of your conclusions.

- **Do the ways in which the two things are alike outweigh the ways they are different?** Can you compare the crime statistics of Brazil to those of the United States and claim to make a valid comparison? Are the data collected in the same way in both countries? Could other factors besides the cell phone laws in Texas and Louisiana account for the lower automobile accident death rate? Maybe differences in speed limits in school zones in those states can account for the difference.
- **Is the assertion true?** Is it really true that capital punishment has deterred crime in Brazil? You will need to give reasons the comparison you are making is valid and evidence that will prove your conclusion true.

### Deductive Reasoning

According to a centuries-old perspective, reasoning from a general statement or principle to reach a specific conclusion is called **deductive reasoning**. This is just the opposite of inductive reasoning. Contemporary logic specialists add that when the conclusion is *certain* rather than probable, you are reasoning deductively. The certainty of your conclusion is based on the validity or truth in the general statement that forms the basis of your argument.

Deductive reasoning can be structured in the form of a syllogism. A **syllogism** is a way of organizing an argument into three elements: a major premise, a minor premise, and a conclusion. To reach a conclusion deductively, you start with a general statement that serves as the **major premise**. In a speech attempting to convince your audience that the communication professor teaching your public-speaking class is a top-notch teacher, you might use a deductive reasoning process. Your major premise is "All communication professors have excellent teaching skills." The certainty of your conclusion hinges on the soundness of your major premise. The **minor premise** is a more specific statement about an example that is linked to the major premise. The minor premise in the argument you are advancing is "John Smith, our teacher, is a communication professor." The **conclusion** is based on the major premise and the more specific minor premise. In reasoning deductively, you need to ensure that both the major premise and the minor premise are true and can be supported with evidence. The conclusion to our syllogism is "John Smith has excellent teaching skills." The persuasive power of deductive reasoning derives from the fact that the conclusion cannot be questioned *if* the premises are accepted as true.

Here's another example you might hear in a speech. Ann was trying to convince the city council to refuse a building permit to Mega-Low-Mart, a large chain discount store that wants to move into her town. She believes the new store would threaten her downtown clothing boutique. Here's the deductive structure of the argument she advanced:

| | |
|---|---|
| **Major premise:** | Every time a large discount store moves into a small community, the merchants in the downtown area lose business and the town loses tax revenue from downtown merchants. |
| **Minor premise:** | Mega-Low-Mart is a large discount store that wants to build a store in our town. |
| **Conclusion:** | If Mega-Low-Mart is permitted to open a store in our town, the merchants in the downtown area will lose business and the city will lose tax revenue. |

**deductive reasoning**
Reasoning that moves from a general statement of principle to a specific, certain conclusion

**syllogism**
A three-part argument that consists of a major premise, a minor premise, and a conclusion

**major premise**
A general statement that is the first element of a syllogism

**minor premise**
A specific statement about an example that is linked to the major premise; the second element of a syllogism

**conclusion**
The logical outcome of a deductive argument, which stems from the major premise and the minor premise

The strength of Ann's argument rests on the validity of her major premise. Her argument is sound if she can prove that the presence of large chain discount stores does, in fact, result in a loss of business and tax revenue for merchants in nearby towns. (Also note Ann's efforts to be audience-centered; addressing the city council, she argues that not only will she lose money, but the city will lose tax revenue as well—something in which city council members are deeply interested.) In constructing arguments for your persuasive messages, assess the soundness of the major premise on which you build your argument. Likewise, when listening to a persuasive pitch from someone using a deductive argument, critically evaluate the accuracy of the major premise.

To test the truth of an argument organized deductively, consider the following questions.

- **Is the major premise (general statement) true?** In our example about communication professors, is it really true that *all* communication professors have excellent teaching skills? What evidence do you have to support this statement? The power of deductive reasoning hinges in part on whether your generalization is true.
- **Is the minor premise (the particular statement) also true?** If your minor premise is false, your syllogism can collapse right there. In our example, it is easy enough to verify that John Smith is a communication professor. But not all minor premises can be verified as easily. For example, it would be difficult to prove the minor premise in this example:

  Major premise: All gods are immortal.

  Minor premise: Zeus is a god.

  Conclusion: Therefore, Zeus is immortal.

  We can accept the major premise as true because immortality is part of the definition of *god*. But proving that Zeus is a god would be very difficult. In this case, the truth of the conclusion hinges on the truth of the minor premise.

**Causal Reasoning** A third type of reasoning is called **causal reasoning.** When you reason by cause, you relate two or more events in such a way as to conclude that one or more of the events caused the others. For example, you might argue that having unprotected sex causes the spread of AIDS.

There are two ways to structure a causal argument. First, you can reason from cause to effect, moving from a known fact to a predicted result. You know, for example, that interest rates have increased in the past week. Therefore, you might argue that *because* the rates are increasing, the Dow Jones Industrial Average will decrease. In this case, you move from something that has occurred (rising interest rates) to something that has not yet occurred (decrease in the Dow). Weather forecasters use the same method of reasoning when they predict the weather. They base a conclusion about tomorrow's weather on what they know about today's meteorological conditions.

A second way to frame a causal argument is to reason backward, from known effect to unknown cause. You know, for example, that a major earthquake has occurred (known effect). To explain this event, you propose that the cause of the earthquake was a shift in a fault line (unknown cause). You cannot be sure of the cause, but you are certain of the effect. A candidate for president of the United States may claim that the cause of current high unemployment (known effect) is mismanagement by the present administration (unknown cause). He then constructs an argument to prove that his assertion is accurate. To prove his case, he needs to have evidence that the present administration mismanaged the economy. The key to developing strong causal arguments is in the use of evidence to link something known with something unknown. An understanding of the appropriate use of evidence can enhance inductive, deductive, and causal reasoning.

**causal reasoning**
Reasoning in which the relationship between two or more events leads you to conclude that one or more of the events caused the others

## Persuading the Culturally Diverse Audience

Effective strategies for developing your persuasive objective will vary depending on the background and cultural expectations of your listeners. If a good portion of your audience has a cultural background different from your own, it's wise not to assume that they will have the same assumptions about what is logical and reasonable that you have. Cultural differences may require that you modify your reasoning and evidence, your appeal to listeners to take a specific action (whether you should make direct or indirect appeals), your overall message structure, and/or your delivery style.

**Reasoning** Most of the logical, rational methods of reasoning discussed in this chapter evolved from classical Greek and Roman traditions of argument. Rhetoricians from the United States typically use a straightforward, factual-inductive method of supporting ideas and reaching conclusions.[9] They identify facts and link them to support a specific proposition or conclusion. For example, in a speech to prove that the government spends more money than it receives, a speaker could cite year-by-year statistics on income and expenditures to document the point. North Americans also like debates involving a direct clash of ideas and opinions. Our low-context culture encourages people to be more direct and forthright in dealing with issues and disagreement than do high-context cultures.

Not all cultures assume a direct, linear, methodical approach to supporting ideas and proving a point.[10] People from high-context cultures, for example, may expect that participants will establish a personal relationship before debating issues. Some cultures use a deductive pattern of reasoning rather than an inductive pattern. They begin with a general premise and then link it to a specific situation when they attempt to persuade listeners. During several recent trips to Russia, your authors noticed that to argue that Communism was ineffective, many Russians started with a general assumption: Communism didn't work. Then they used this assumption to explain specific current problems in areas such as transportation and education.

Middle Eastern cultures usually do not use standard inductive or deductive structures. They are more likely to use narrative methods to persuade an audience. They tell stories that evoke feelings and emotions and use extended analogies, examples, and illustrations, allowing their listeners to draw their own conclusions by inductive association.[11]

Although this book stresses the kind of inductive reasoning that will be persuasive to most North Americans, you may need to use alternative strategies if your audience is from another cultural tradition. Consider the following general principles to help you construct arguments that a culturally diverse audience will find persuasive.

**Use Appropriate Evidence** According to intercultural communication scholars Myron Lustig and Jolene Koester, "There are no universally accepted standards about what constitutes evidence."[12] They suggest that for some Muslim and Christian audiences, parables or stories are a dramatically effective way to make a point. A story is told and a principle is derived from the lesson of the story. For most North Americans and Europeans, a superior form of evidence is an observed fact. A study by two communication scholars reported that both African Americans and Hispanic Americans found statistical evidence more persuasive than stories alone.[13] Statistics, said the respondents, are more believable and verifiable; stories can more easily be modified. In some African cultures, eyewitness testimony is often not perceived as credible; it's believed that if you speak up to report what you saw, you may have a particular slant on the event, and therefore what you have to say may not be believable.[14] What may be convincing evidence to you may not be such an obvious piece of evidence for others. If you are uncertain whether your listeners will perceive your evidence as valid and reliable, you could test your evidence on a small group of people who will be in your audience before you address the entire group.

*The cultures of your audience members should influence the delivery of your persuasive message, as well as the types of reason and evidence, message structure, and appeals to emotion that you include.*

[Photo Hill Street Studios/Blend Images/Getty Images]

**Use Appropriate Appeals to Action** In some high-context cultures, such as in Japan and China, the conclusion to your message can be stated indirectly. Rather than spell out the precise action explicitly, you can imply what you'd like your listeners to do. In a low-context culture such as the United States, listeners may generally expect you to state more directly the action you'd like your audience members to take.

**Use Appropriate Message Structure** Most North Americans tend to like a well-organized message with a clear, explicit link between the evidence used and the conclusion drawn. North Americans are also comfortable with a structure that focuses on a problem and then offers a solution, or a message in which causes are identified and the effects are specified. Audiences in the Middle East, however, would expect less formal structure and greater use of a narrative style of message development. The audience either infers the point or the speaker may conclude by making the point clear. Being indirect or implicit may sometimes be the best persuasive strategy.

Not all audiences expect a speech to sound like the summation of an attorney making a legal case: loaded with evidence. In fact, some lawyers decide, after "reading" the jury, that the best way to conclude their case is to tell a story rather than to present a litany of the facts and evidence.

**Use an Appropriate Delivery Style** We've placed a considerable emphasis on logos by appropriately emphasizing logical structure and the use of evidence. But another cultural factor that influences how receptive listeners are to a message is the presentation style of the speaker. A speaker's overall style includes the use of emotional appeals, delivery style, language choice, and rhythmic quality of the words and gestures used. Some Latin American listeners, for example, expect speakers to express more emotion and passion when speaking than North American listeners are accustomed to. If you focus only on analyzing and adapting to the audience's expectations about logic and reasoning, without also considering the overall impression you make on your audience, you may present compelling arguments but still not achieve your overall goal. The best way to assess the preferred speaking style of an audience with which you're not familiar is to observe other successful speakers addressing the

RECAP

### Adapting to Culturally Diverse Audiences

Ethically adapt your message according to cultural preferences for:

- Method of reasoning
- Acceptable evidence
- Obvious appeals to action
- Linear or narrative organization
- Delivery style

audience you will face. Or talk with audience members before you speak to identify expectations and communication-style preferences.

## Supporting Your Reasoning with Evidence

You cannot persuade by simply stating a conclusion without proving it with evidence. Evidence in persuasive speeches consists of facts, examples, statistics, and expert opinions.

In Chapter 6, we discussed using these types of supporting material in speeches. When attempting to persuade listeners, it is essential to make sure that your evidence logically supports the inductive, deductive, or causal reasoning you are using to reach your conclusion.

**Facts** When using facts to support your conclusion, make sure each fact is really a fact. A ***fact*** is something that has been directly observed to be true or can be proved to be true. The shape of the earth, the number of women university presidents, the winner of the 2011 Super Bowl have all been directly observed or counted. Without direct observation or measurement, we can only make an inference. An ***inference*** is a conclusion based on available evidence, or partial information. It's a fact that sales of foreign-made cars are increasing in the United States; it's an inference that foreign-made cars are the highest-quality cars.

**Examples** **Examples** are illustrations that are used to dramatize or clarify a fact. Only valid, true examples can be used to help prove a point. For example, one speaker, in an effort to document the increased violence in children's television programs, told her audience, "Last Saturday morning as I watched cartoons with my daughter, I was shocked by the countless times we saw examples of beatings and even the death of the cartoon characters in one half-hour program." The conclusion she wanted her audience to reach: Put an end to senseless violence in children's television programs.

A hypothetical example, one that is fabricated to illustrate a point, should not be used to reach a conclusion. It should be used only to clarify. David encouraged his listeners to join him in an effort to clean up the San Marcos River. He wanted to motivate his audience to help by asking them to "imagine bringing your children to the river ten years from now. You see the river bottom littered with cans and bottles." His example, while effective in helping the audience to visualize what might happen in the future, does not prove that the river ecosystem will deteriorate. It only illustrates what might happen if action isn't taken.

**Opinions** *Opinions* can serve as evidence if they are expressed by an expert, someone who can add credibility to your conclusion. The best opinions to use in support of a persuasive argument are those expressed by someone known to be unbiased, fair, and accurate. If the U.S. Surgeon General has expressed an opinion regarding drug testing, his or her opinion would be helpful evidence. Even so, opinions are usually most persuasive when they are combined with other evidence, such as facts or statistics, that support the expert's position.

**Statistics** A *statistic* is a number used to summarize several facts or samples. In an award-winning speech, Jeffrey Jamison used statistics effectively to document the serious problem of alkali batteries polluting the environment. He cited evidence from the *New York Times* documenting that "—each year we are adding 150 tons of mercury, 130 tons of lead, and 170 tons of cadmium to the environment."[15] Without these statistics, Jeffrey's claim that alkali batteries are detrimental to the environment would not have been as potent. Again, you may want to review the discussion on the appropriate use of statistics in Chapter 6.

**fact**
Something that has been directly observed to be true or can be proven to be true by verifiable evidence

**inference**
A conclusion based on available evidence or partial information

**example**
An illustration used to dramatize or clarify a fact

Does the type of evidence you use make a difference in whether your listeners will support your ideas? One research study found that examples and illustrations go a long way in helping to persuade listeners.[16] Additional research documents the clear power of statistical evidence to persuade.[17] And yet another research study concluded that using *both* statistics and specific examples is especially effective in persuading listeners.[18] Poignant examples may touch listeners' hearts, but statistical evidence appeals to their intellect. Because we believe that messages should be audience-centered rather than source-centered, we suggest that you consider your listeners to determine the kind of evidence that will be the most convincing to them.

If you are using an inductive-reasoning strategy (reasoning from specific examples to a general conclusion), you need to make sure you have enough facts, examples, statistics, and credible opinions to support your conclusion. If you reason deductively (from a generalization to a specific conclusion), you need evidence to document the truth of your initial generalization. When developing an argument using causal reasoning, evidence is also vital as you attempt to establish that one or more events caused something to happen.

## Using Evidence Effectively

We've identified what evidence is and why it's important to use evidence to support your conclusions. But what are the strategies for using evidence effectively? Here are a few suggestions.[19]

**Use Credible Evidence** Your listeners are more likely to respond to your arguments when they believe the evidence you use is credible—from a trustworthy, knowledgeable and unbiased source. Remember, it's the listener, not you, who determines whether evidence is credible.

One type of evidence that is especially powerful is reluctant testimony. **Reluctant testimony** is a statement by someone who has reversed his or her position on a given issue, or a statement that is not in the speaker's best interest. For example, at one point the owner of a large construction company, who wanted the contract to build a new dam, was in favor of building the new dam to create a water reservoir. But after further thought, he changed his mind and now is against building the dam. The reluctant testimony of that construction company owner would bolster your argument that the dam is a financial boondoggle. Reluctant testimony is especially effective when presented to a skeptical audience; it demonstrates how another person has changed his or her mind and implicitly suggests that listeners should do the same.[20]

**reluctant testimony**
A statement by someone who has reversed his or her position on a given issue

**RECAP**

**Effective Evidence**

You can use four types of evidence:

- Facts
- Examples
- Opinions
- Statistics

The most effective evidence is:

- Credible
- New
- Specific
- Part of a story

**Use New Evidence** By "new" we don't just mean recent, although contemporary evidence is often perceived to be more credible than out-of-date evidence. But besides seeking up-to-date evidence, try to find evidence to support your point that the listener hasn't heard before—evidence that's new to the listener. You don't want your listener to think, "Oh, I've heard all of that before." Audience members are more likely to keep focusing on your message when they are learning something new.

**Use Specific Evidence** "Many people will be hurt if we don't do something now to stop global warming," said Julia. How many people will be hurt? What precisely will happen? Julia would make her point more effectively if she offered specific evidence that, for example, identified how many homes would be lost as a result of rising ocean levels rather than speaking of "many people" or "a lot of people."

**Use Evidence to Tell a Story** Facts, examples, statistics, and opinions may be credible, new, and specific—yet your evidence will be even more powerful if it fits together to tell a story to make your point. Besides listing the problems that will occur because of global warming, Julia could personalize the evidence by telling a story about how the rising ocean levels will hurt individual families. Using evidence to support a story adds emotional power to your message and makes your evidence seem less abstract.[21]

## Avoiding Faulty Reasoning

We have emphasized the importance of developing sound, logical arguments supported with appropriate evidence. You have an ethical responsibility to use your skill to construct arguments that are well supported with logical reasoning and sound evidence. Not all people who try to persuade you will use sound arguments to get you to vote for them, buy their product, or donate money to their cause. Many persuaders use inappropriate techniques called fallacies. A **fallacy** is false reasoning that occurs when someone attempts to persuade without adequate evidence or with arguments that are irrelevant or inappropriate. You will be both a better and more ethical speaker and a better listener if you are aware of the following fallacies.

**Causal Fallacy** The Latin term for the causal fallacy is *post hoc, ergo propter hoc,* which translates as "after this, therefore, because of this." The **causal fallacy** is making a faulty causal connection. Simply because one event follows another does not mean that the two are related. If you declared that your school's football team won this time because you sang your school song before the game, you would be guilty of a causal fallacy. There are undoubtedly other factors that explain why your team won, such as good preparation or facing a weaker opposing team. For something to be a cause, it has to have the power to bring about a result. "That howling storm last night knocked down the tree in our backyard" is a logical causal explanation.

Here are more examples of causal fallacies:

> The increased earthquake and hurricane activity is caused by the increase in violence and war in our society.
>
> As long as you wear this lucky rabbit's foot, you will never have an automobile accident.

In each instance, there is not enough evidence to support the cause-effect conclusion.

**Bandwagon Fallacy** Someone who argues that "everybody thinks it's a good idea, so you should too" is using the **bandwagon fallacy**. Simply because "everyone" is "jumping on the bandwagon," or supporting a particular point of view, does not make the point of view correct. Sometimes speakers use the bandwagon fallacy in more subtle ways in their efforts to persuade:

> Everybody knows that talk radio is our primary link to a free and democratic society.
>
> Most people agree that we spend too much time worrying about the future of Medicare.

Beware of sweeping statements that include you and others without offering any evidence that the speaker has solicited opinions.

**Either/Or Fallacy** Someone who argues that there are only two approaches to a problem is trying to oversimplify the issue by using the **either/or fallacy**. "It's either vote for higher property taxes or close the library," asserts Daryl at a public hearing on tax increases. Such a statement ignores all other possible solutions to a complex problem. When you hear someone simplifying the available options by saying it's either this or that, you should be on guard for the either/or fallacy. Rarely is any issue

**fallacy**
False reasoning that occurs when someone attempts to persuade without adequate evidence or with arguments that are irrelevant or inappropriate

**causal fallacy**
A faulty cause-and-effect connection between two things or events

**bandwagon fallacy**
Reasoning that suggests that because everyone else believes something or is doing something, then it must be valid or correct

**either/or fallacy**
The oversimplification of an issue into a choice between only two outcomes or possibilities

as simple as a choice between only two alternatives. The following are examples of inappropriate either/or reasoning:

Either television violence is reduced, or we will have an increase in child and spouse abuse.

Either more people start volunteering their time to work for their community, or your taxes will increase.

**Hasty Generalization** A person who reaches a conclusion from too little evidence or nonexistent evidence is making a **hasty generalization**. For example, that one person became ill after eating the meat loaf in the cafeteria does not mean that everyone eating in the cafeteria will develop food poisoning. Here are additional hasty generalizations:

It's clear that our schools can't educate children well—my niece went to school for six years and she still can't read at her grade level.

The city does a terrible job of taking care of the elderly—my grandmother lives in a city-owned nursing home, and the floors there are always filthy.

**Ad Hominem** Also known as attacking the person, an **ad hominem** (Latin for "to the man") approach involves attacking characteristics of the person who is proposing an idea rather than attacking the idea itself. A statement such as "We know Janice's idea won't work because she has never had a good idea" does not really deal with the idea, which may be valid. Don't dismiss an idea solely because you have been turned against the person who presented it. Here are examples of ad hominem attacks:

She was educated in a foreign country and could not possibly have good ideas for improving education in our community.

Tony is an awful musician and is not sensitive enough to chair the parking committee.

**Red Herring** The **red herring** fallacy is used when someone attacks an issue by using irrelevant facts or arguments as distractions. This fallacy gets its name from an old trick of dragging a red herring across a trail to divert the dogs that may be following. Speakers use a red herring when they want to distract an audience from the real issues. For example, a politician who has been accused of taking bribes calls a press conference. During the press conference, he talks about the evils of child pornography rather than addressing the charge against him. He is using the red herring technique to divert attention from the real issue—did he or did he not take the bribe? Consider another example of a fallacious argument using the red herring method, from a speech against gun control: The real problem is not eliminating handguns; the real problem is that pawnshops that sell guns are controlled by the Mafia.

**Appeal to Misplaced Authority** When ads use baseball catchers to endorse automobiles and TV heroes to sell political candidates or an airline or a hotel, we are faced with the fallacious **appeal to misplaced authority**. Although we have great respect for these people in their own fields, they are no more expert than we are in the areas they are promoting. As both a public speaker and a listener, you must recognize what is valid expert testimony and what is not. For example, a physicist who speaks on the laws of nature or the structure of matter could reasonably be accepted as an expert. But when the physicist speaks on politics, his or her opinion is not that of an expert and may be no more significant than your own. The following examples are appeals to misplaced authority:

Former Congressman Smith endorses the new art museum, so every business should get behind it, too.

Katie Couric thinks this cookie recipe is the best, so you will like it too.

**hasty generalization**
A conclusion reached without adequate evidence

**ad hominem**
An attack on irrelevant personal characteristics of the person who is proposing an idea, rather than on the idea itself

**red herring**
Irrelevant facts or information used to distract someone from the issue under discussion

**appeal to misplaced authority**
Use of the testimony of an expert in a given field to endorse an idea or product for which the expert does not have the appropriate credentials or expertise

**Non Sequitur** When you argue that a new parking garage should not be built on campus because the grass has not been mowed on the football field for three weeks, you are guilty of a **non sequitur** (Latin for "it does not follow"). Grass growing on the football field has nothing to do with the parking problem. Your conclusion simply does not follow from your statement. The following are examples of non sequitur conclusions:

We should not give students condoms because TV has such a pervasive influence on our youth today.

You should endorse me for Congress because I have three children.

We need more parking on our campus because we are the national football champions.

RECAP

### Avoid These Fallacies

- Causal Fallacy
- Bandwagon
- Either/Or
- Hasty Generalization
- Ad Hominem
- Red Herring
- Appeal to Misplaced Authority
- Non Sequitur

## Using Emotion to Persuade

Roger Ailes, media executive and former political communication consultant, has nominated several memorable moments as outstanding illustrations of speakers using emotional messages powerfully and effectively.[22]

> Martin Luther King, announcing his vision of brotherhood and equality at the Lincoln Memorial in 1963, extolled, "I have a dream!"
>
> General Douglas MacArthur, in announcing his retirement before a joint session of Congress, April 19, 1951, closed his speech with "Old soldiers never die; they just fade away. And like the old soldier of that ballad, I now close my military career and just fade away."
>
> President Ronald Reagan, in his 1986 speech to help a grieving nation cope with the death of the space shuttle *Challenger* crew, said, "The crew of the space shuttle *Challenger* honored us by the manner in which they lived their lives. We will never forget them, nor the last time we saw them, this morning as they prepared for their journey and waved goodbye and slipped the surly bonds of earth to touch the face of God."

**non sequitur**
Latin for "it does not follow"; an idea or conclusion that does not logically relate to or follow from the previous idea or conclusion

## LEARNING FROM GREAT SPEAKERS

### Franklin Delano Roosevelt (1882–1945)

The 32nd president of the United States, Franklin D. Roosevelt, is remembered as a great speaker, one who rekindled hope in the American people when he took office during the Great Depression. Roosevelt played an active role in crafting his first inaugural address, editing verb tenses to heighten immediacy and substituting strong verbs for weak ones. Roosevelt delivered the speech emphatically and used pauses strategically to ensure applause. He succeeded in persuading the American people that "the only thing we have to fear is fear itself," and he rallied the nation behind his New Deal for economic recovery.[23]

Roosevelt was a master in knowing his audience and skillfully using rhetorical strategies to move his audience with both logic and emotion. When presenting your persuasive messages, it's vital to consider the logical arguments that will resonate with your listener's minds as well as the emotional messages that will speak to their hearts.

[Photo AP Wide World Photos]

Emotion is a powerful way to move an audience and support your persuasive purpose. An appeal to emotion (or what Aristotle called *pathos*) can be an effective way to achieve a desired response from an audience. Whereas logical arguments may appeal to our reason, emotional arguments generally appeal to nonrational sentiments. Often we make decisions based not on logic but on emotion.

**Emotional response theory** suggests that emotional responses can be classified along three dimensions—pleasure, arousal, and dominance.[24] First, you respond with varying degrees of *pleasure* or *displeasure*. Pleasurable stimuli consist of such things as images of smiling, healthy babies or daydreams about winning millions in a sweepstakes. Stimuli causing displeasure may be TV news stories of child abuse or dreadful images of terrorism.

A second dimension of emotional responses exists on a continuum of *arousal–nonarousal*. You become aroused emotionally, for example, by seeing a snake in your driveway, or you may be lulled into a state of nonarousal by a boring lecture.

The third dimension of emotional responses is one's feeling of *dominance* or *powerlessness* when confronted with some stimulus. When thinking about the destructive force of nuclear weapons or the omnipotence of God, you may feel insignificant and powerless. Or perhaps you feel a sense of power when you imagine yourself conducting a symphony or winning an election.

These three dimensions—pleasure, arousal, and dominance—are believed to form the bases of all emotional responses. Theory predicts that if listeners feel pleasure and are also aroused by something, such as a political candidate or a product, they will tend to form a favorable view of the candidate or product. A listener's feeling of being dominant has to do with being in control and having permission to behave as he or she wishes. A listener who feels dominant is more likely to respond to the message.

As a public speaker trying to sway your listeners to your viewpoint, your job is to use emotional appeals to achieve your goal. If you wanted to persuade your listeners that capital punishment should be banned, you would try to arouse feelings of displeasure and turn them against capital punishment. Advertisers selling soft drinks typically strive to arouse feelings of pleasure in those who think of their product. Smiling people, upbeat music, and good times are usually part of the formula for selling soda pop.

## Tips for Using Emotion to Persuade

Although emotional response theory may help you understand how emotions work, as a public speaker your key concern is "How can I ethically use emotional appeals to achieve my persuasive purpose?" Let's consider several methods.

**Use Concrete Examples That Help Your Listeners Visualize What You Describe** This speaker used a vivid description of the devastation caused by a tornado in Saragosa, Texas, to evoke strong emotions and persuade listeners to take proper precautions when a storm warning is sounded.

> The town is no more. No homes in the western Texas town remain standing. The church where twenty-one people perished looks like a heap of twisted metal and mortar. A child's doll can be seen in the street. The owner, four-year-old Maria, will no longer play with her favorite toy; she was killed along with five of her playmates when the twister roared through the elementary school.

**Use Emotion-Arousing Words** Words and phrases can trigger emotional responses in your listeners. *Mother*, *flag*, *freedom*, and *slavery* are among a large number of emotionally loaded words. Patriotic slogans such as "Remember Pearl Harbor" and "Remember 9/11" can produce strong emotional responses.[25]

**emotional response theory**
Human emotional responses can be classified as eliciting feelings of pleasure, arousal, or dominance

### Use Nonverbal Behavior to Communicate Your Emotional Response

The great Roman orator Cicero believed that if you want your listeners to experience a certain emotion, you should first model that emotion for them. If you want an audience to feel anger at a particular law or event, you must display anger and indignation in your voice, movement, and gesture. As we have noted, delivery plays the key role in communicating your emotional responses. When you want your audience to become excited about and interested in your message, you must communicate that excitement and interest through your delivery.

**Use Visual Images to Evoke Emotions** In addition to nonverbal expressions, pictures or images of emotion-arousing scenes can amplify your speech. An image of a lonely homeowner looking out over his waterlogged house following a ravaging flood in Houston, Texas, can communicate his sense of despair. A picture of children in war-torn Macedonia can communicate the devastating effects of violence with greater impact than mere words can. In contrast, a photo of a refugee mother and child reunited after an enforced separation can communicate the true meaning of joy. You can use similar images as visual aids to evoke your audience's emotions, both positive and negative. Remember, however, that when you use visual images, you have the same ethical responsibilities as you have when you use verbal forms of support: Make sure your image is from a credible source and that it has not been altered or taken out of context.

**Use Appropriate Metaphors and Similes** A metaphor is an implied comparison between two things. The person who says, "Our lives are quilts upon which we stitch the patterns of our character. If you don't pay attention to the ethical dimension of the decisions you make, you will be more likely to make a hideous pattern in your life quilt," is using a metaphor. A simile makes a direct comparison between two things using the word *like* or *as*. Here's an example: "Not visiting your academic counselor regularly is like being a gambler in a high-stakes poker game; you're taking a big chance that you're taking the right courses." Several research studies have found that speakers who use appropriate and interesting metaphors and similes are more persuasive than those who don't use such stylistic devices.[26] Using metaphors and similes can create a fresh, emotional perspective on a persuasive point; they can both enhance your credibility and develop an emotional image in a way that nonmetaphorical language cannot.[27]

**Use Appropriate Fear Appeals** The threat that harm will come to your listeners unless they follow your advice is an appeal to fear. As discussed in Chapter 14, listeners can be motivated to change their behavior if appeals to fear are used appropriately. Research suggests that high fear arousal ("You will be killed in an auto accident unless you wear a safety belt") is more effective than moderate or low appeals, if you are a highly credible speaker.[28]

**Consider Using Appeals to Several Emotions** Appealing to the fears and anxieties of your listeners is one of the most common types of emotional appeals used to persuade, but you could also elicit several other emotions to help achieve your persuasive goal.

- **Hope.** Listeners could be motivated to respond to the prospect of a brighter tomorrow. When Franklin Roosevelt said, "The only thing we have to fear is fear itself," he was invoking hope for the future, as was President Obama in his upbeat campaign phrase, "Yes, we can!"
- **Pride.** When a politician says, "It's time to restore our nation's legacy as a beacon of freedom for all people," she is appealing to national pride. To appeal to pride is to invoke feelings of pleasure and satisfaction based on

*President Obama appealed to several emotions during his campaign speeches. He acknowledged voters' fears and anger with problems facing the country, then offered hope, summarized in the audience member's sign, "Change we can believe in!"*

[Photo: Alex Worg/Getty Images Inc. RF]

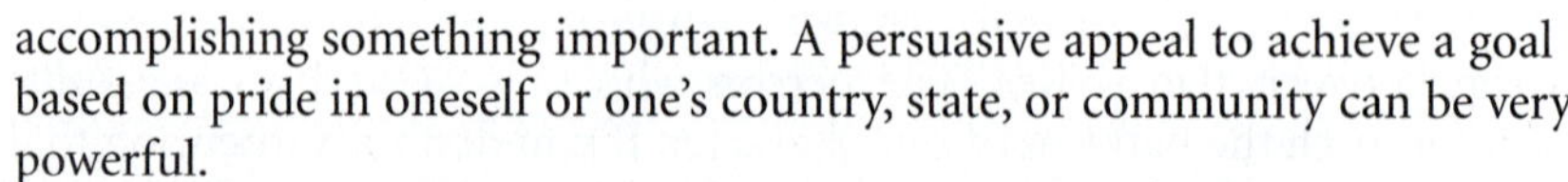

accomplishing something important. A persuasive appeal to achieve a goal based on pride in oneself or one's country, state, or community can be very powerful.

- **Courage.** Challenging your audience to take a bold stand or to step away from the crowd can emotionally charge your listeners to take action. Referring to courageous men and women as role models can help motivate your listeners to take similar actions. Patrick Henry's famous "Give me liberty, or give me death!" speech appealed to his audience to take a courageous stand on the issues before them.
- **Reverence.** The appeal to the sacred and the revered can be an effective way to motivate. Sacred traditions, revered institutions, and cherished and celebrated individuals can inspire your audience to change or reinforce attitudes, beliefs, values, or behavior. The late Mother Teresa, holy writings, and the school your listeners attended are examples of people, things, and institutions that your listeners may perceive as sacred. As an audience-centered speaker, however, you need to remember that what may be sacred to one individual or audience may not be sacred to another.

**Tap Audience Members' Beliefs in Shared Myths** Often people talk about a myth as something that is factually untrue. The Easter Bunny, the Tooth Fairy, and Santa Claus are often labeled myths. But in a rhetorical sense, a **myth** is a belief held in common by a group of people and based on their values, cultural heritage, and faith. A myth may be factual—or it may be based on a partial truth that a group of people believes to be true. Myths are the "big" stories that give meaning and coherence to a group of people or a culture. The myth of the Old West is that the pioneers of yesteryear were strong, adventurous people who sacrificed their lives in search of a better tomorrow. Similarly, our parents, grandparents, and great-grandparents belonged to "the greatest generation" because they overcame a devastating economic depression and were triumphant in two world wars. The myth of the 1950s was that U.S. families were prosperous and lived like Ward and June Cleaver and their sons, Wally and "The Beaver," in the TV program *Leave It to Beaver*. Religious myths are beliefs shared by a group of faithful disciples. So a myth is not necessarily false—it is

**myth**
A shared belief based on the underlying values, cultural heritage, and faith of a group of people

a belief that a group of people share, one that provides emotional support for the way they view the world.

As a public speaker, you can draw on the myths you and your audience members share to provide emotional and motivational support for your message. Referring to a shared myth is a way to identify with your listeners and help them see how your ideas support their ideas; it can help you develop a common bond with audience members. In trying to convince his listeners to vote, Jason argued, "We can't let down those who fought for our freedom. We must vote to honor those who died for the privilege of voting that we enjoy today." He was drawing on the powerful myth that people have died for our freedoms. To gain parent support for a new high school, Cynthia said, "Our grandparents and great-grandparents lived through the Great Depression and the world wars of the past century so that we can send our children to the best public schools in the world. Vote for the new high school." She was appealing to the myth that the previous generation sacrificed, which gave us a responsibility to sacrifice for our children. Again we emphasize that *myth* does not mean "false" or "made up." People *did* die for our freedom, and our grandparents and great-grandparents *did* live through the Depression and two world wars; a myth is powerful because the audience knows that those events occurred. Myth is the powerful underlying story that evokes an emotional response to a message.

Politicians use myth when they show pictures of themselves surrounded by their families. The underlying myth is "I cherish what you cherish—to live in a country that supports and nurtures the family values we hold dear." Appealing directly or indirectly to the commonly held myths of an audience is a powerful way to evoke emotional support for your message. But as with any form of support, especially emotional support, you have an ethical responsibility to use this strategy wisely and not to exploit your listeners.

## Using Emotional Appeals: Ethical Issues

Regardless of which emotions you use to motivate your audience, you have an obligation to be ethical and forthright. Making false claims, misusing evidence to arouse emotions, or relying only on emotions without offering evidence to support a conclusion violates ethical standards of effective public speaking.

A **demagogue** is a speaker who attempts to gain power or control over others by using impassioned emotional pleas and appealing to listeners' prejudices. The word *demagogue* comes from the Greek word *demagogos*, meaning "popular leader." Speakers who become popular by substituting emotion and fallacies in place of well-supported reasoning are guilty of demagoguery. During the early 1950s, Wisconsin Senator Joseph McCarthy sought to convince the nation that Communists had infiltrated government, education, and the entertainment industry. This was at the height of the Cold War, and anything or anyone remotely connected to Communism elicited an immediate negative emotional response. For a time, McCarthy was successful in persuading people that there were Communists among us. His evidence, however, was scanty, and he relied primarily on scaring his listeners about the potential evil of alleged Communists. His failure to produce any real evidence and his unethical use of fear appeals eventually undermined his credibility and earned him a reputation as a demagogue. You have an ethical responsibility not to misuse emotional appeals when persuading others.

**demagogue**
A speaker who gains control over others by using unethical emotional pleas and appeals to listeners' prejudices

Credibility, reasoning, and emotional appeals are the chief means of persuading an audience. Your use of these persuasive strategies depends on the composition of your audience. As we have observed several times before, an early task in the public-speaking process

RECAP

### Tips for Using Emotion to Persuade

- Use concrete examples.
- Use emotion-arousing words.
- Use visual images.
- Use appropriate metaphors and similes.
- Use appropriate fear appeals.
- Appeal to a variety of emotions.
- Communicate emotions nonverbally.
- Tap into shared myths.

is to analyze your audience. This is particularly important in persuasion. Audience members are not just sitting there waiting to respond to every suggestion a speaker makes.

# Strategies for Adapting Ideas to People and People to Ideas

We opened this chapter with Donald C. Bryant's pithy definition of persuasion as "the process of adjusting ideas to people and people to ideas."[29] His description of the rhetorical process gets at the heart of what an effective persuader does—he or she ethically adapts the message and the delivery to create agreement.

Audience members may hold differing views of you and your subject. Your task is to find out whether there is a prevailing viewpoint held by a majority of your listeners. If they are generally friendly toward you and your ideas, you need to design your speech differently from the way you would if your listeners were neutral, apathetic, or hostile. Research studies as well as seasoned public speakers can offer useful suggestions for adapting your approach to your audience. We will discuss three general responses your audience may have to you: receptive, neutral, and unreceptive.

## Persuading the Receptive Audience

It is always a pleasure to face an audience that already supports you and your message. In speaking to a receptive group, you can explore your ideas in greater depth than otherwise. Here are suggestions that may help you make the most of that kind of speaking opportunity.

**Identify with Your Audience** To establish common ground with her audience of fellow students, Rita told them, "Just like most of you, I struggle to pay my way through college. That's why I support expanding the campus work-study program." Like Rita, if you are a college student speaking to other college students with similar backgrounds and pressures, point to your similar backgrounds and struggles. Emphasize the similarities between you and your audience. What other common interests do you have? The introductory portion of your speech is a good place to mention those common interests.

**Clearly State Your Speaking Objective** When speaking to a group of her campaign workers, mayoral candidate Maria Hernandez stated early in her speech, "My reason for coming here today is to ask each of you to volunteer three hours a week to help me become the next mayor of our city." We have stressed several times how important it is to provide an overview of your major point or purpose. This is particularly so when speaking to a group who will support your point of view.[30]

**Tell Your Audience Exactly What You Want Them to Do** Besides telling your listeners what your speaking objective is, you can also tell them how you expect them to respond to your message. Be explicit in directing your listeners' behavior.

**Ask Listeners for an Immediate Show of Support** Asking for an immediate show of support helps to cement the positive response you have developed during your speech. For example, Christian evangelists usually speak to favorable audiences. Evangelist Billy Graham, who spoke to more people in live public-speaking situations than anyone else in the twentieth century, always asked those who support his Christian message to come forward at the end of his sermon.

**Use Emotional Appeals Effectively** You are more likely to move a favorable audience to action with strong emotional appeals while also reminding them of the evidence that supports your conclusion. When the audience already supports your position, you need not spend a great deal of time on lengthy, detailed explanations or factual information. You can usually assume that your listeners already know much of that material.

**Make It Easy for Your Listeners to Act** It is a good idea not only to tell your listeners precisely what you want them to do and ask for an immediate response, but also to make sure that what you're asking them to do is clear and easy. If you're asking them to write or e-mail someone, hand out postcards already addressed to the recipient, or distribute an e-mail address printed on a card for handy reference. If you want listeners to call someone, make sure each person has the phone number—it's even better if you can give a toll-free number.

## Persuading the Neutral Audience

Think how many lectures you go to with an attitude of indifference. Probably quite a few. Many audiences will fall somewhere between wildly enthusiastic and unreceptive; they will simply be neutral or indifferent. They may be neutral because they don't know much about your topic or because they haven't made up their minds whether to support your point of view. They may also be indifferent because they don't see how the topic or issue affects them. Regardless of the reason for your listeners' indifference, your challenge is to interest them in your message. Let's look at some approaches to gaining their attention and keeping their interest.

**Capture Your Listeners' Attention Early in Your Speech** "Bill Farmer died last year, but he's about to fulfill his lifelong dream of going into space."[31] In a speech about the high cost of funerals, Karmen's provocative opening statement effectively captures the attention of her listeners.

**Refer to Beliefs That Many Listeners Share** When speaking to a neutral audience, identify common concerns and values that you plan to address. Martin Luther King's "I Have a Dream" speech (Appendix B) includes references to his listeners' common beliefs.

**Relate Your Topic Not Only to Your Listeners but Also to Their Families, Friends, and Loved Ones** You can capture the interest of your listeners by appealing to the needs of people they care about. Parents will be interested in ideas and policies that affect their children. People are generally interested in matters that may affect their friends, neighbors, and others with whom they identify, such as members of their own religion or economic or social class.

**Be Realistic about What You Can Accomplish** Don't overestimate the response you may receive from a neutral audience. People who start with an attitude of indifference are probably not going to become as enthusiastic as you are after hearing just one speech. Persuasion does not occur all at once or on a first hearing of arguments.

## Persuading the Unreceptive Audience

One of the biggest challenges in public speaking is to persuade audience members who are against you or your message. If they are hostile toward you personally, your job is to seek ways to enhance your credibility and persuade them to listen to you. If they are unreceptive to your point of view, there are several approaches that you can use to encourage them to listen to you.

## CONFIDENTLY CONNECTING WITH YOUR AUDIENCE

### Enhance Your Initial Credibility

Initial credibility is the impression your listeners have of you before you deliver your speech. Strategies for enhancing your initial credibility are likely to enhance your confidence as well.

For example, prepare a brief written statement of your credentials and accomplishments so that the person who introduces you can give accurate and relevant information about you to the audience. Give careful thought to your appearance, and establish eye contact with your listeners before you begin to talk. You will feel more confident when you know that your audience believes you to be credible before you even begin to speak.

**Don't Announce Immediately That You Plan to Change Their Minds** Paul wondered why his opening sales pitch ("Good morning. I plan to convince you to purchase this fine set of knives at a cost to you of only $250") was not greeted enthusiastically. If you immediately and bluntly tell your listeners that you plan to change their opinions, it can make them defensive. It is usually better to take a more subtle approach when announcing your persuasive intent.[32]

**Begin Your Speech by Noting Areas of Agreement before You Discuss Areas of Disagreement** In addressing the school board, one community member began his persuasive effort to convince board members they should not raise taxes by stating, "I think each of us here can agree with one common goal: We want the best education for our children." Once you help your audience understand that there are issues on which you agree (even if only that the topic you will discuss is controversial), your listeners may be more attentive when you explain your position.

**Don't Expect a Major Shift in Attitude from a Hostile Audience** Set a realistic limit on what you can achieve. A realistic goal might be to have your listeners hear you out and at least consider some of your points.

**Acknowledge the Opposing Points of View That Members of Your Audience May Hold** Summarize the reasons individuals may oppose your point of view. Doing this communicates that you at least understand the issues.[33] Your listeners will be more likely to listen to you if they know that you understand their viewpoint. Of course, after you acknowledge the opposing point of view, you will need to cite evidence and use arguments to refute the opposition and support your conclusion. Early in his speech to a neighborhood group about the possibility of building a new airport near their homes, City Manager Anderson acknowledged, "I am aware that a new airport brings unwanted changes to a neighborhood. Noise and increased traffic are not the type of challenges you want near your homes." He went on to identify the actions the city would take to minimize the problems a new airport would cause.

**Establish Your Credibility** Being thought credible is always an important goal of a public speaker, and it is especially important when talking to an unreceptive audience. Let your audience know about the experience, interest, knowledge, and skill that give you special insight into the issues at hand.

**Consider Making Understanding Rather Than Advocacy Your Goal** Sometimes your audience disagrees with you because its members just don't understand your point. Or they may harbor a misconception about you and your message. For example, if your listeners think that AIDS is transferred though kissing or other casual contact rather than through unprotected sexual contact, you'll first have to acknowledge their beliefs and then construct a sound argument to show how inaccurate their assumptions are. To change such a misconception and enhance accurate understanding, experienced speakers use a four-part strategy.[34]

1. **Summarize the common misconceptions about the issue or idea you are discussing.** "Many people think that AIDS can be transmitted through casual contact such as kissing or that it can easily be transmitted by your dentist or physician."

2. **State why these misconceptions may seem reasonable.** Tell your listeners why it is logical for them to hold that view, or identify "facts" they may have heard that would lead them to their current conclusion. "Since AIDS is such a highly contagious disease, it may seem reasonable to think it can be transmitted through such casual contact."
3. **Dismiss the misconceptions and provide evidence to support your point.** Here you need sound and credible data to be persuasive. "In fact, countless medical studies have shown that it is virtually impossible to be infected with the AIDS virus unless you have unprotected sexual contact or use unsterilized hypodermic needles that have also been used by someone who has AIDS." In this instance, you would probably cite specific results from two or three studies to lend credibility to your claim.
4. **State the accurate information that you want your audience to remember.** Reinforce the conclusion you want your listeners to draw from the information you presented with a clear summary statement, such as "According to recent research, the most common factor contributing to the spread of AIDS is unprotected sex. This is true for individuals of both sexes and all sexual orientations."

# Strategies for Organizing Persuasive Messages

Is there one best way to organize a persuasive speech? The answer is no. Specific approaches to organizing speeches depend on audience, message, and desired objective. But how you organize your speech does have a major effect on your listeners' response to your message.

Research suggests that there are some general principles to keep in mind when preparing your persuasive message.[35]

- **If you feel that your audience may be hostile to your point of view, advance your strongest arguments first.** If you save your best argument for last, your audience may have already stopped listening.
- **Do not bury key arguments and evidence in the middle of your message.** Your listeners are more likely to remember information presented first and last.[36] In speaking to his fraternity about the dangers of drunk driving, Frank wisely began his speech with his most powerful evidence: The leading cause of death among college-age males is alcohol-related automobile accidents. He got their attention with his sobering fact.
- **If you want your listeners to take some action, it is best to tell them what you want them to do at the end of your speech.** If you call for action in the middle of your speech, it won't have the power it would have in your conclusion.
- **When you think your listeners are well informed and are familiar with the disadvantages of your proposal, it is usually better to present both sides of an issue, rather than just the advantages of the position you advocate.** If you don't acknowledge arguments your listeners have heard, they will probably think about them anyway.
- **Make reference to the counterarguments, then refute them with evidence and logic.** It may be wise to compare your proposal with an alternative proposal, perhaps one offered by someone else. By comparing and contrasting your solution with another recommendation, you can show how your proposal is better.[37]

TABLE 15.2 Organizational Patterns for Persuasive Messages

| Pattern | Definition | Example |
|---|---|---|
| Problem–solution | Present the problem; then present the solution | I. The national debt is too high.<br>II. We need to raise taxes to lower the debt. |
| Refutation | Anticipate your listeners' key objections to your proposal and then address them. | I. Even though you may think we pay too much tax, we are really undertaxed.<br>II. Even though you may think the national debt will not go down, tax revenue will lower the deficit. |
| Cause and effect | First present the cause of the problem; then note how the problem affects the listeners. Or identify a known effect; then document what causes the effect. | I. The high national debt is caused by too little tax revenue and too much government spending.<br>II. The high national debt will increase both inflation and unemployment. |
| Motivated sequence | A five-step pattern of organizing a speech; its steps are attention, need, satisfaction, visualization, and action. | I. *Attention:* Imagine a pile of $1000 bills 67 miles high. That's our national debt.<br>II. *Need:* The increasing national debt will cause hardships for our children and grandchildren.<br>III. *Satisfaction:* We need higher taxes to reduce our debt.<br>IV. *Visualization:* Imagine our country in the year 2050; it could have low inflation and full employment or be stuck with a debt ten times our debt today.<br>V. *Action:* If you want to lower the debt by increasing tax revenue, sign this petition that I will send to our representatives. |

We discussed ways of organizing speeches in Chapter 7, but there are special ways to organize persuasive speeches. Here we present four organizational patterns: problem–solution, refutation, cause and effect, and the motivated sequence. These four patterns are summarized in Table 15.2, above.

## Problem–Solution

The most basic organizational pattern for a persuasive speech is to make the audience aware of a problem, then present a solution that clearly solves it. Almost any problem can be phrased in terms of something you want more of or less of. The problem–solution pattern works best when a clearly evident problem can be documented and a solution can be proposed to deal with the well-documented problem.

When you are speaking to an apathetic audience, or when listeners are not aware that a problem exists, a problem–solution pattern works nicely. Your challenge will be to provide ample evidence to document that your perception of the problem is accurate. You'll also need to convince your listeners that the solution you advocate is the most appropriate one to resolve the problem.

Many political candidates use a problem–solution approach. *Problem:* The government wastes your tax dollars. *Solution:* Vote for me and I'll see to it that government waste is eliminated. *Problem:* We need more and better jobs. *Solution:* Vote for me and I'll institute a program to put people back to work.

Note in the following outline of Jason's speech, "The Dangers of Electromagnetic Fields," how he plans to first document a clear problem and then recommend strategies for managing the problem.

PROBLEM: Power lines and power stations around the country emit radiation and are now being shown to increase the risk of cancer.

I. Childhood leukemia rates are higher in children who live near large power lines.
II. The International Cancer Research Institute in Lyon, France, published a report linking electromagnetic fields and childhood cancer.

SOLUTION: Steps can be taken to minimize our risk of health hazards caused by electromagnetic energy.

I. The federal government should establish enforceable safety standards for exposure to electromagnetic energy.
II. Contact your local power company to make sure its lines are operated safely.
III. Stop using electric blankets.
IV. Use protective screens for computer-display terminals.

The problem–solution arrangement of ideas applies what you learned about cognitive dissonance in Chapter 14. Identify and document a concern that calls for change, and then suggest specific behaviors that can restore cognitive balance.

## Refutation

Another way to persuade an audience to support your point of view is to prove that the arguments against your position are false—that is, to refute them. To use refutation as a strategy for persuasion, you first identify objections to your position that your listeners might raise and then refute or overcome those objections with arguments and evidence.

Suppose, for example, you plan to speak to a group of real-estate developers to advocate a new zoning ordinance that would reduce the number of building permits granted in your community. Your listeners will undoubtedly have concerns about how the ordinance will affect new housing starts and the overall economic forecast. You could organize your presentation to this group using those two obvious concerns as major issues to refute. Your major points could be as follows:

I. The new zoning ordinance will not cause an overall decrease in the number of new homes built in our community.
II. The new zoning ordinance will have a positive effect on economic growth in our community.

You would be most likely to use refutation as your organizational strategy when your position was being attacked. Or, if you know what your listeners' chief objections are to your persuasive proposal, you could organize your speech around the arguments your listeners hold.

Research suggests that in most cases it is better to present both sides of an issue rather than just the advantages of the position you advocate. Even if you don't acknowledge arguments your listeners have heard, they will probably think about them anyway.

In her speech to promote organ donation, Tasha used the refutation strategy by identifying several myths that, if believed, would keep people from becoming organ donors.* She first identified each myth and then explained why the myth is, in fact, a myth.

I. Myth number 1: *If doctors know I'm an organ donor, they won't work as hard to save me.*
Refutation: Doctors pledge, as part of their Hippocratic oath, that saving your life is paramount. Furthermore, a patient must be declared brain dead before their organs may be taken.

II. Myth number 2: *If I donate my organs, my family will be charged for the surgical costs.*
Refutation: If you donate your organs, there will be no charge to your family.

III. Myth number 3: *I can't have an open casket funeral if I'm an organ donor.*
Refutation: The donor's body is clothed for burial, so there are no visible signs of donation.

IV. Myth number 4: *I can't donate my organs because I am too old.*
Refutation: There is no specific age cut-off for organ donation. The final decision is based on overall organ health, not age.

Tasha could have used the refutation strategy to organize her entire speech, or the refutation technique could be used as a portion of a larger organizational strategy such as problem-solution.

If your persuasive presentation using a refutation strategy will be followed by a question-and-answer forum, you should be prepared to answer questions. Credible evidence, facts, and data will be more effective than emotional arguments alone when you want to persuade an audience that you know is not in favor of your persuasive objective. In your postspeech session, you can use your refutation skills to maintain a favorable audience response to your message in the face of criticism or attacks on the soundness of your logic.

## Cause and Effect

Like the problem–solution pattern to which it is closely related, the cause-and-effect approach was introduced in Chapter 7 as a useful organizational strategy. One way to use the cause-and-effect method is to begin with an effect, or problem, and then identify the causes of the problem in an effort to convince your listeners that the problem is significant. A speech on the growing problem of gangs might focus on poverty, drugs, and a financially crippled school system.

You could also organize a message by noting the problem and then spelling out the effects of the problem. If you identify the problem as too many unsupervised teenagers roaming your community's streets after 11 p.m., you could organize a speech noting the effects this problem is having on your fellow citizens.

The goal of using cause-and-effect organization for a persuasive speech is to convince your listeners that one event caused another. For example, you may try to reason that students in your state have low standardized test scores because they had poor teachers. Of course, you must prove that no other factors are responsible for the low test scores. It may not be the teachers who caused the low test scores; perhaps it was the lack of parent involvement, or one of a number of other factors.

The challenge in using a cause-and-effect organizational strategy is to *prove* that one event *caused* something else to occur. Simply because two events occurred at the same time or in close succession does not prove that there is a cause-and-effect

*Tasha Carlson, "License to Save." From *Winning Orations 2009,* Mankato, MN: Interstate Oratorical Association, 2009. Reprinted with permission.

relationship. Earlier we noted the causal fallacy ("after this, therefore because of this" or *post hoc, ergo propter hoc*). As an example of the challenge in documenting a cause-and-effect relationship, consider a study that found that people who spend several hours daily on the Internet are also psychologically depressed. This finding does not necessarily *prove* that Internet use causes depression—other factors could cause the depression. Perhaps people who are depressed are more likely to use the Internet because they find comfort and security in using technology.

Here's how a persuasive speech could be organized using a cause-and-effect strategy:

I. There is high uncertainty about whether interest rates will increase or decrease. *(cause)*

II. Money markets are unstable in Asia, Eastern Europe, and Latin America. *(cause)*

III. There has been a rise in unemployment. *(cause)*

IV. In the late 1920s in the United States, these three conditions were followed by a stock-market crash. Thus, because of today's similar economic uncertainty, you should decrease the amount of money you have invested in stocks; if you don't, you will lose money. *(effect)*

Another example of a speech using cause and effect is the speech "Prosecution Deferred Is Justice Denied," which appears on pages 366–367. This well-researched speech by Hope Stallings from Berry College won first place in the 2009 Interstate Oratorical Association national competition.

## The Motivated Sequence

The motivated sequence is a five-step organizational plan that has proved successful for several decades. Developed by Alan Monroe, this simple yet effective strategy for organizing speeches incorporates principles that have been confirmed by research and practical experience.[38] Based on the problem–solution pattern, it also uses the cognitive-dissonance approach, which we discussed in Chapter 14: First, disturb your listeners; then point them toward the specific change you want them to adopt. The five steps are attention, need, satisfaction, visualization, and action.

**1. Attention.** Your first goal is to get your listeners' attention. In Chapter 10, we discussed specific attention-catching methods of beginning a speech. Remember the particular benefits of using a personal or hypothetical example, a startling statement, an unusual statistic, a rhetorical question, or a well-worded analogy. The attention step is, in essence, the introduction to your speech.

Heather caught listeners' attention at the start of her award-winning speech "End the Use of Child Soldiers"† with this riveting introduction:

> When 12-year-old Ishmael Beah left his village in Sierra Leone to perform in a talent show in a town just a few miles away, he had no idea that in a matter of only a few days he would lose everything—his family, his friends, and even his childhood. He returned to find that a rebel army had killed his entire family, and decimated his town.

**2. Need.** Having gotten the attention of your audience, you need to establish why your topic, problem, or issue should concern your listeners. Arouse dissonance. Tell your audience why the current program, politician, or whatever you're attempting to change is not working. Convince them there is a need for a change. You must

†Heather Zupanic, "End the Use Child Soldiers." Speech excerpts on pages 363 through 365 from *Winning Orations 2009*, Mankato, MN: Interstate Oratorical Association, 2009. Reprinted with permission.

also convince your listeners that this need for change affects them directly. During the need step, you should develop logical arguments backed by ample evidence to support your position.

To document the significance of the problem of children being used as soldiers and the need to do something to address the problem, Heather provided specific evidence:

> According to the United Nations Web site, last accessed April 2, 2009, at any one time, 300,000 children under the age of 18 are forced to fight in military conflicts. As Peter Warren Singer, director of the 21st Century Defense Initiative at the Brookings Institute, states, child warfare is not only a human rights travesty, but also a great threat to global and national security.

She personalized the problem for her audience this way: "Clearly, this crisis is having an enormous impact on the children themselves, on their nation states, and finally on our own country."

**3. Satisfaction.** After you present the problem or need for concern, you next briefly identify how your plan will satisfy the need. What is your solution to the problem? At this point in the speech, you need not go into great detail. Present enough information so that your listeners have a general understanding of how the problem may be solved.

Heather suggested that a solution to the problem of children serving as soldiers included using the United Nations to take legal action to enforce existing treaties and to bring this issue to the attention of government leaders throughout the world. At this point in her speech, she kept her solution—to involve government leaders—general. She waited until the end of her speech to provide specific action that audience members could take to implement her solution. Heather also reinforced the urgency of the need for the audience to act by stating, "Clearly, the time has come to take a stand against the atrocities that child solders face."

**4. Visualization.** Now you need to give your audience a sense of what it would be like if your solution were or were not adopted. You could take a *positive-visualization* approach: Paint a picture with words to communicate how wonderful the future will be if your solution is adopted. You could take a *negative-visualization* approach: Tell your listeners how awful things will be if your solution is not adopted. If they think things are bad now, just wait; things will get worse. Or you could present both a positive and a negative visualization of the future: The problem will be solved if your solution is adopted, and the world will be a much worse place if your solution is not adopted.

Heather wanted her listeners to visualize the significant negative results likely to occur if the problem of child soldiers went unsolved. She began with a general statement of what would happen to children if no action were taken.

> The first consequence of child warfare is that these children are left with serious emotional and psychological scarring due to the violence and abuse they must endure.

She further painted her negative picture by using a specific emotional example in which she described additional consequences.

> Ten-year-old Jacques from the Congo described how the Mayi-Mayi militia would often starve him and beat him severely. He says, "I would see others die in front of me. I was hungry very often and I was scared."

Heather also pointed out that if the problem is not addressed soon, it will grow, and more children will be negatively affected.

Heather used only a negative visualization approach. She could, however, have made her visualization step even stronger by combining negative and positive visualization. Such an approach would have added to Heather's descriptions of what would happen if no action were taken, a description of the benefits of addressing the problem now. Heather might, for example, have helped her listeners visualize the virtues of taking action, by describing poignant scenes of children being reunited with their families. Using both a positive and a negative visualization approach demonstrates how the solution you present in the satisfaction step directly addresses the problem you described in the need step of your motivated sequence.

Martin Luther King Jr. drew on visualization as a rhetorical strategy in his moving "I Have a Dream" speech (Appendix B). Note how King powerfully and poetically paints a picture with words that continue to provide hope and inspiration today.

> I have a dream that one day this nation will rise up and live out the true meaning of its creed, "We hold these truths to be self-evident, that all men are created equal."
>
> I have a dream that one day on the red hills of Georgia the sons of former slaves and the sons of former slaveowners will be able to sit down together at the table of brotherhood.
>
> I have a dream that one day even the state of Mississippi, a state sweltering with the heat of injustice, sweltering with the heat of oppression, will be transformed into an oasis of freedom and justice.
>
> I have a dream that my four little children will one day live in a nation where they will be judged not by the color of their skin but by the content of their character. I have a dream today.
>
> I have a dream that one day, down in Alabama, with its vicious racists, with its governor having his lips dripping with the words of interposition and nullification, one day right there in Alabama little black boys and black girls will be able to join hands with little white boys and white girls as sisters and brothers. I have a dream today.
>
> I have a dream that one day every valley shall be exalted, every hill and mountain shall be made low, the rough places will be made plain and the crooked places will be made straight, and the glory of the Lord shall be revealed, and all flesh shall see it together.[39]

**5. Action.** This last step forms the basis of your conclusion. You tell your audience the specific action they can take to implement your solution. Identify exactly what you want your listeners to do. Give them simple, clear, easy-to-follow steps to achieve your goal. For example, you could give them a phone number to call for more information, provide an address so that they can write a letter of support, hand them a petition to sign at the end of your speech, or tell them for whom to vote. Outline the specific action you want them to take.

Heather offered specific actions her listeners could take to address the problem of children serving as soldiers: "The first step we can take is to petition the members of the United Nations to enforce the treaties they have signed, and we can do this by joining the Red Hand Campaign." She made her action step simple and easy when she further explained to her audience:

> You can join this campaign by simply signing your name to a pre-written letter and tracing your hand on a red piece of construction paper after this [speech]. I will then cut and paste your handprint to your letter and forward them on to the UN.

The best action step spells out precisely the action your audience should take. Here, Heather tells her listeners what to do and what will happen next.

You can modify the motivated sequence to suit the needs of your topic and your audience. If, for example, you are speaking to a receptive audience, you do not have to spend a great deal of time on the need step. They already agree that the need is serious. They may, however, want to learn about specific actions that they can take to implement a solution to the problem. Therefore, you would be wise to emphasize the satisfaction and action steps.

# SAMPLE PERSUASIVE SPEECH

## PROSECUTION DEFERRED IS JUSTICE DENIED

*Hope Stallings, Berry College*

What do Morgan Stanley, Wachovia, Fannie Mae, Merrill Lynch, and AIG all have in common? You might say that they all contributed to the credit crisis in September, and according to the *Washington Post* of March 25, 2009, the ensuing $787 billion government bailout of big business. And you'd be right—partially. You see, these corporations have something else in common. In the past five years, each has been indicted on criminal charges like fraud. Never heard about the trial or verdict? That's because in spite of their fraudulent behavior, these corporations never went to court. They avoided media spotlight, investor scrutiny, and public outrage by entering into deferred prosecution agreements. The *Record* of July 21, 2008, explains that deferred prosecution agreements allow corporations to avoid criminal convictions by paying a small fine out of court. In other words, these companies paid our government to ensure that we remain ignorant, and we have, right up to the collapse of our economy and our personal financial security.

Hope begins her speech with a rhetorical question to get her listeners' attention.

In their current form deferred prosecution agreements, or DPAs, are unethical, unjust, and flat out wrong. In this new day, we must work together with our new administration and new Congress to reform madness and reclaim justice. To become a part of this reformation of DPAs, we first need to understand the details of deferred prosecution agreements; we'll then consider causes, and finally formulate solutions.

Because her audience is likely supportive of her persuasive goal, she explicitly provides an overview of her message signaling that she will identify causes of the problem and then present solutions.

According to the *Mondaq News Alert* of April 22, 2008, a deferred prosecution agreement occurs when a prosecutor files an indictment for a company that has committed a crime, and that indictment is put on hold in exchange for a commitment by that company to reform and pay a fine. If the company meets the obligations listed in the agreement, the prosecutor, also called a corporate monitor, asks the judge to dismiss the indictment, and the company gets away without a criminal conviction. In a DPA, the government collects fines and then appoints a corporate monitor to impose internal changes with little to no Department of Justice guidelines. *American Banker* of December 12, 2008, reports that DPAs are becoming unfortunately more common, as our now frail banking system means that banks and corporations that formerly might have been a target of criminal charges may now face the lighter load of a DPA. And the numbers agree. The *Corporate Crime Reporter* revealed on January 29, 2009, that between 2003 and 2009, there were 112 reported corporate DPAs, compared to only 11 between 1992 and 2001.

Here, Hope provides statistics to support her argument that the problem has recently gotten worse.

One hundred twelve might not seem like many, but consider the devastating impact that just one of these ineffective DPAs can have on our economy. The *Wall Street Journal* of March 27, 2009, reports that in 2004, insurance giant AIG avoided criminal charges for fraud by entering into a deferred prosecution agreement. AIG paid a $126 million fine and was appointed a corporate monitor, but in 2008, found itself under another federal investigation for the same thing; the *Wall Street Journal* says that this time, AIG's fraud contributed to its downfall in September's credit crisis. And AIG is not alone. Even household names such as American Express, Monster.com, Chevron, AmSouth Bank, KPMG, and Countrywide Financial have all avoided criminal convictions by entering into DPAs. Or consider the case of Powers Fasteners, which entered into a DPA to avoid a manslaughter charge after the Boston Big Dig tunnel collapse. According to the *Washington Post* of December 18, 2008, Powers Fasteners agreed to pay $16 million and recall the faulty epoxy that caused the collapse. But that's cold consolation to the family of Milena DeValle, who was killed after being crushed by 26 tons of ceiling panels as a result of the epoxy. DPAs are allowing corporations to get away with murder. Literally.

Deferred prosecution agreements clearly run counter to our ideals of justice and fairness. We therefore need to understand why they occur, namely corporate corruption, government collusion, and public delusion.

Hope provides a clear transition from her description of the problem to her listing of the causes of the problem.

The first cause of this problem is that corporations have abandoned ethical behavior in search of profit. The *Associated Press* reported on March 10, 2008, that though deferred prosecution agreements were originally designed to allow individuals such as juveniles and first-time drug offenders to reform without the stigma of a conviction, corporations started entering into DPAs about fifteen years ago for the same reasons: to avoid the scandal and revenue decrease associated with criminal charges. And if the corporation's

Source: From *Winning Orations, 2009,* Mankato, MN: Interstate Oratorical Association, 2009. Reprinted by permission.

executives pull the right strings, it will even get to choose its own corporate monitor in the DPA. According to the previously cited *Mondaq News Alert*, the corporate monitor is either appointed by the U.S. Department of Justice or selected by the corporation itself. Because this monitor acts as a prosecutor, judge, and jury for the corporation with few guidelines, choosing a former employee, friend, or political ally for a corporate monitor often results in no internal changes and the indictment still being dropped.

The second cause is that the government is in collusion with Corporate America. The October 2008 issue of the *Metropolitan Corporate Counsel* reported that the post-indictment collapse of Arthur Andersen prompted U.S. Attorney General Larry Thompson to release the Thompson Memorandum, which made it easier for corporations to enter into DPAs. By encouraging corporations to enter into DPAs, the Department of Justice sought to save the economy from the results of another fraud scandal while cleaning out the court docket and staying friendly with big business. *Time* Magazine of March 30, 2009, states that Washington simply looked the other way in regards to corporate crime, allowing corporations to break rules without serious repercussions in order to make friends.

She uses clear signposts to enumerate the number of specific causes of the problem that she is presenting.

The final cause is public delusion. Since the collapse of Enron, we've been deluded into thinking that we've got it all covered. The events of the last few months have made it tragically and abundantly clear that we do not. According to the *Associated Press* of April 7, 2009, deferred prosecution agreements didn't draw any attention until 2008 after it was disclosed that John Ashcroft had been secretly selected as a corporate monitor. With the Ashcroft assignment, DPAs finally made the news. But because it's difficult to explain deferred prosecution agreements without using legal or financial jargon, DPAs have not been widely discussed by the mainstream media that seeks to write on a fourth-grade reading level. Additionally, the U.S. House of Representatives documents revealed on May 22, 2008, that some DPAs are never made public at all, and even Congress and the Department of Justice have difficulties counting just how many have occurred covertly in recent years.

Now that we understand the catastrophic impact of DPAs on our economy and personal economic well-being, we should be sufficiently angry to do something about it. I wish I could say that solutions come on three levels: corporate, governmental, and individual, but I can't. The fact is, we've hoped for too long that corporations could monitor themselves, and we've all felt the results of their failure to do so. Now is the time for the government to step in with the support of the people and change the current state of DPAs.

Here, she uses transition phrases to summarize her analysis and then point her audience toward the solutions she will suggest.

Though banishing corporate deferred prosecution agreements completely is a long-term solution, it is more practical for Congress to pass legislation altering DPAs and mandating that they be made public. Representatives Bill Pascrell and Steve Cohen are attempting to do just that through the Accountability in Deferred Prosecution Act. The *States News Service* of April 2, 2009, reveals that the Accountability in Deferred Prosecution Act of 2009 will regulate corporate deferred prosecution agreements in federal criminal cases. The bill will set guidelines ensuring an open and public process, and will prevent corporations from choosing their own corporate monitor, which brings us to personal solutions.

We must become active in this fight for justice, through political activism and encouraging awareness. Contact your congressional representatives in support of the Accountability in Deferred Prosecution Act of 2009. Without encouragement from us, the bill may not gain enough votes to pass the House and Senate. Second, though it sounds cliché, we must spread awareness of this issue. Because the cause of public delusion can only be solved by awareness, and as long as we're apathetic about awareness of DPAs, the problems will continue. I challenge you to take two minutes—just two minutes—today to talk to someone else at this tournament about DPAs. Mention it to your friends or coworkers back home; contact your local media. I have compiled a fact sheet to help you do just that; please take one after the round. Also visit my Web site www.dangersofdpas.org, on which you can find the latest news about DPAs, examples of real-life DPAs, and links to contact your representatives in support of the Accountability in Deferred Prosecution Act. By taking small steps toward awareness now, we can ignite change.

Hope encourages her listeners to take a specific action step to address the problem she has documented.

So today, by understanding the problems, causes and solutions of corporate deferred prosecution agreements, we've learned how to become a part of the reformation. We cannot let these corporate wrongdoings continue. AIG, Fannie Mae, and Merrill Lynch are institutions that we've trusted with our financial investments, and until the trust between institution and individual can be reestablished, we must invest in reforms that will end this shameful, unethical, and unjust practice of corporate deferred prosecution agreements once and for all.

In her conclusion, Hope provides a brief summary statement of the problem and offers a final motivational message to encourage her listeners to join her in taking action to solve the problem.

Conversely, if you are speaking to a hostile audience, you should spend considerable time on the need step. Convince your audience that the problem is significant and that they should be concerned about the problem. You would probably not propose a lengthy, detailed action.

If your audience is neutral or indifferent, spend time getting their attention and inviting their interest in the problem. The attention and need steps should be emphasized.

The motivated sequence is a guide, not an absolute formula. Use it and the other suggestions about speech organization to help you achieve your specific objective. Be audience-centered; adapt your message to your listeners.

# STUDY GUIDE

## Enhancing Your Credibility

Credibility is a listener's view of a speaker. The three factors contributing to credibility are competence, trustworthiness, and dynamism. Initial credibility is your listeners' idea of your credibility before you start speaking. Derived credibility is the perception they form while you speak. Terminal credibility is the perception that remains after you've finished speaking. Specific strategies can enhance all three types of credibility.

### Being Audience-Centered

- Keep the cultural expectations of your listeners in mind when using strategies to establish or maintain your credibility; credibility is in the mind of the beholder.

### Using What You've Learned

- Imagine that you are delivering your final speech of the semester in your public-speaking class. What specific strategies can you implement to enhance your initial, derived, and final credibility as a public speaker in the minds of your classmates?

## Using Logic and Evidence to Persuade

The effectiveness of logical arguments hinges on the proof you employ. Proof consists of evidence plus the reasoning that you use to draw conclusions from the evidence. Three types of reasoning are inductive reasoning, which moves from specific instances or examples to reach a general, probable conclusion; deductive reasoning, which moves from a general statement to reach a specific, more certain conclusion; and causal reasoning, relating two or more events so as to be able to conclude that one or more of the events caused the others. You can use four types of evidence: facts, examples, opinions, and statistics. Avoid using fallacious arguments.

### Being Audience-Centered

- Refer to counterarguments your audience may already know, and then refute these counterarguments with evidence and logic.
- Middle Eastern cultures usually do not use standard inductive- or deductive-reasoning structures; they are more likely to use narrative (story telling) strategies to evoke feelings and emotions, allowing their listeners to draw their own conclusions by inductive associations. In some high-context cultures such as Japan and China, the conclusion to a message is stated indirectly. In a low-context culture such as the United States, listeners may generally expect you to make a more direct statement of the action you'd like your audience members to take.

### Using What You've Learned

- Josh is speaking to his neighborhood homeowners' association, attempting to persuade his neighbors that a crime-watch program should be organized. What logical arguments and emotional strategies would help him ethically achieve his persuasive objective?

### A Question of Ethics

- Tony was surfing the Internet and found just the statistics he needs for his persuasive speech. Yet he does not know the original source of the statistics—just the Internet address. Is that sufficient documentation for the statistics?

### Speaker's Homepage: Information Triage: Identifying Reasoning Fallacies

The following Web sites amplify our discussion of reasoning fallacies to help you assess the arguments in persuasive messages you encounter:

- www.nizkor.org/features/fallacies/
- www.unc.edu/depts/wcweb/handouts/fallacies.html
- www.fallacyfiles.org/
- http://info-pollution.com/fallacies.htm

## Using Emotion to Persuade

Emotional response theory has identified three dimensions of emotional response to a message: pleasure–displeasure, arousal–nonarousal, and dominance–powerlessness. Specific suggestions for appealing to audience emotions include using examples; emotion-arousing words; nonverbal behavior; selected appeals to fear; and appeals to such emotions as hope, pride, courage, and the revered.

### Being Audience-Centered

- Before debating issues, people from high-context cultures often prefer to establish a personal relationship between speaker and listener.

### A Question of Ethics

- Karl believes strongly that the tragedy of the Holocaust could occur again. He plans to show exceptionally graphic photographs of Holocaust victims during his speech to his public-speaking class. Is it ethical to show graphic, emotion-arousing photos to a captive audience?

## Strategies for Adapting Ideas to People and People to Ideas

You must use different strategies and adapt your message in order to persuade receptive, neutral, and unreceptive audiences.

### Being Audience-Centered

- To persuade the receptive audience, consider the following strategies: Identify with the audience. State your speaking objective. Tell the audience members what you want them to do. Ask for an immediate show of support. Use emotional appeals effectively. Make it easy for your listeners to act.
- To persuade the neutral audience, draw on these persuasive approaches: Capture your listeners' attention early in your speech by referring to beliefs that many listeners share. Relate your topic not only to your listeners but also to their families, friends, and loved ones. Be realistic in what you expect to accomplish.
- For an unreceptive audience, consider these persuasive strategies: Don't immediately announce that you plan to change your listeners' minds. Begin your speech by noting areas of agreement before you discuss areas of disagreement. Establish your credibility early in your message. Acknowledge the opposing points of view that members of your audience may hold. Consider making understanding rather than advocacy your goal. Advance your strongest argument first. Don't expect a major shift in attitude from a hostile audience.

### A Question of Ethics

- Martika wants to convince her classmates, a captive audience, that they should join her in a twenty-four-hour sit-in at the university president's office to protest the recent increase in tuition and fees. The president has made it clear that any attempt to occupy his office after normal office hours will result in arrests. Is it appropriate for Martika to use a classroom speech to encourage her classmates to participate in the sit-in?

## Strategies for Organizing Persuasive Messages

Four patterns for organizing a persuasive speech are problem–solution, refutation, cause-and-effect, and the motivated sequence. The five steps of the motivated sequence are attention, need, satisfaction, visualization, and action. Adapt the motivated sequence to your specific audience and persuasive objective.

### Being Audience-Centered

- If you want your listeners to take some action following your speech, it is best to tell them during the conclusion of your speech what you want them to do.

### Using What You've Learned

- Janice is pondering options for organizing her persuasive speech, which has the following purpose: "The audience should be able to support the establishment of a wellness program for our company." Using this purpose, draft the main ideas for a speech organized according to each of the following organizational patterns: problem–solution, refutation, cause-and-effect, the motivated sequence.

# SPEECH WORKSHOP

## Adapting Ideas to People and People to Ideas

**Step One:** Based on your analysis of your audience, indicate on the following 10-point scale, with 1 representing most receptive, whether they are receptive, neutral, or unreceptive to your persuasive message:

| Generally receptive | | | | Generally neutral | | | Generally unreceptive | | |
|---|---|---|---|---|---|---|---|---|---|
| 1 | 2 | 3 | 4 | 5 | 6 | 7 | 8 | 9 | 10 |

**Step Two:** Based on your rating, how you will adapt your message to your audience.

| Questions to Consider | Your Answers |
|---|---|
| **If my audience is receptive:**<br>• How will I identify with them?<br>• How will I clearly state my objective?<br>• What emotional appeals will be ethical and appropriate?<br>• How will I phrase my request for an immediate show of support?<br>• How will I make it easy for my listeners to respond? | |
| **If my audience is neutral:**<br>• How will I capture and maintain my listeners' attention?<br>• What common beliefs of my audience should I refer to?<br>• How will I relate my topic and the issues to audience members' friends, family, and loved ones?<br>• What can I realistically expect to accomplish in one speech? | |
| **If my audience is unreceptive:**<br>• How will I establish my credibility?<br>• How will I avoid telling listeners I plan to change their minds?<br>• What areas of agreement with my audience will I stress?<br>• How can I acknowledge opposing points of view my audience holds?<br>• How will I try to help my audience better understand my ideas and change any misconceptions they might hold?<br>• What can I realistically expect to accomplish in one speech? | |

HISTORIANS AGREE THAT THE GREATEST BANQUET SPEECH IN HISTORY WAS THE ONE BY THE ANCIENT GREEK PHILOSOPHER SOCRATES MOMENTS AFTER HE DRANK HEMLOCK. "GACK," HE SAID, FALLING FACE-FIRST INTO HIS CHICKEN. THE OTHER GREEKS APPLAUDED LIKE CRAZY.

—DAVE BARRY

Francois-Louis Joseph Watteau (1758–1823), *The Death of Socrates*, (1780). Oil on canvas, 133 × 174 cm. Photo: Phillipp Bernard/Réunion des Musées Nationaux/Art Resource, N.Y.

## OUTLINE

# 16 Speaking for Special Occasions and Purposes

OBJECTIVES

**After studying this chapter you should be able to do the following:**

1. Identify and explain the requirements for two types of speaking situations likely to arise in the workplace.
2. List and describe nine types of ceremonial speeches.
3. Explain the purpose and characteristics of an after-dinner speech.
4. List and explain strategies for creating humor in a speech.

There is money in public speaking. Many of the politicians, athletes, and entertainment personalities who speak professionally earn six- or even seven-figure fees for a single talk.

- Broadcaster Katie Couric earned $110,000 for delivering a commencement speech at the University of Oklahoma.[1]
- Former vice president Al Gore's fee for speaking on global climate change, the subject of his film *An Inconvenient Truth*, is $125,000.[2]
- Former president George W. Bush has charged about $150,000 per speech since leaving the presidency.[3]
- Former British prime minister Tony Blair has made as much as $360,000 for a single speech.[4]

- And former president Bill Clinton made nearly $40 million in speaking fees in the six years after he left the White House.[5]

But the record speaking fee may still be the $2 million for two 20-minute speeches given by former president Ronald Reagan to a Japanese company in 1989.[6]

Although most of us will never be rewarded so lavishly for our public-speaking efforts, it is likely that at some time we will be asked to make a business or professional presentation or to speak on some occasion that calls for celebration, commemoration, inspiration, or entertainment. Special occasions are important enough and frequent enough to merit study, regardless of the likelihood of their resulting in wealth or fame for the speaker.

In this chapter, we discuss the various types of speeches that may be called for on special occasions, and we examine the specific and unique audience expectations for each. First, we will discuss two speaking situations that are likely to occur in the workplace. Then we will turn our attention to several types of ceremonial speeches and the after-dinner speech.

# Public Speaking in the Workplace

Nearly every job requires some public-speaking skills. In many careers and professions, public speaking is a daily part of the job. Workplace audiences may range from a group of three managers to a huge auditorium filled with company employees. Presentations may take the form of routine meeting management, reports to company executives, training seminars within the company, or public-relations speeches to people outside the company. The occasions and opportunities are many, and chances are good that you will be asked or expected to do some on-the-job public speaking in the course of your career.

## Group Presentations

After a group has reached a decision, solved a problem, or uncovered new information, group members often present their findings to others. The audience-centered

*The skills you learn in public speaking class can help you when you are part of a group presentation.*

[Photo: Bob Daemmrich/PhotoEdit Inc.]

principles of preparing an effective speech apply to group members who are designing a group oral presentation just as they do to individual speakers.

As our familiar model in Figure 16.1 suggests, the central and most important step is to analyze the audience who will listen to the presentation. Who are these listeners? What are their interests and backgrounds? And what do they need to know? One business consultant suggests:

> Tune your audience in to radio station WIIFM—What's In It For Me. Tell your listeners where the benefits are for them, and they'll listen to everything you have to say.[7]

As you do when developing an individual speech, make sure you have a clear purpose and a central idea divided into logical main ideas. This is a group effort, so you need to make sure *each* group member can articulate the purpose, the central idea, main ideas, key supporting material, and the overall outline for the presentation.

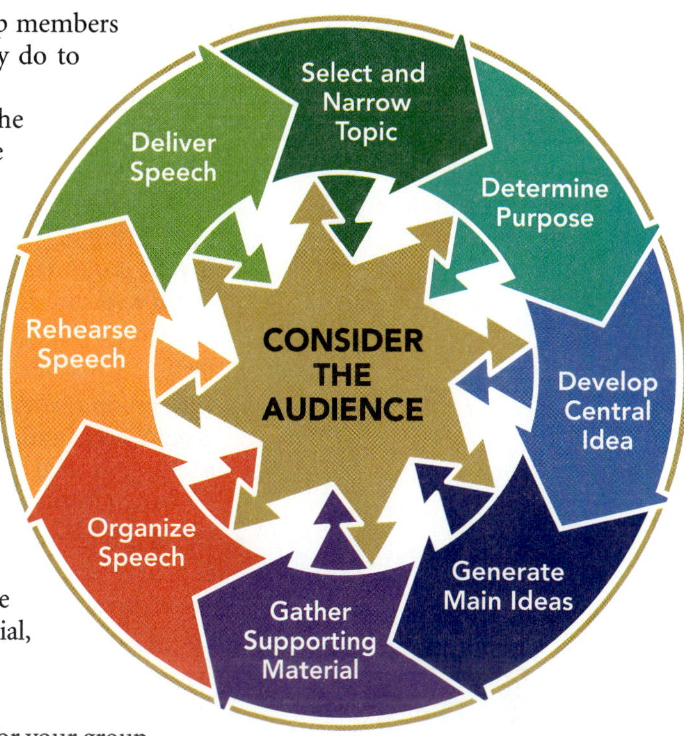


FIGURE 16.1 *Use the audience-centered model of public speaking to help your group plan a group presentation.*

**Selecting a Presentation Format** Unless a format for your group presentation has been specified, your group will need to determine how to deliver the presentation. Three primary formats for sharing reports and recommendations with an audience are the symposium presentation, the forum presentation, and the panel discussion.

- A **symposium** is a public discussion during which the members of a group share responsibility for presenting information to an audience. Usually a moderator and the group members are seated in front of the audience, and each group member is prepared to deliver a brief report. Each speaker should know what the others will present so the same ground is not covered twice. At the end of the speeches, the moderator may summarize the key points. The audience can then participate in a question-and-answer session or a forum presentation.
- In a **forum** presentation, audience members direct questions and comments to a group, and group members respond with short impromptu speeches. In ancient Rome, the *forum* was a marketplace where citizens went to shop and discuss the hot issues of the day. It later became a public meeting place where political speeches were often delivered.

  A forum often follows a more structured presentation, such as a symposium or a prepared speech by one group member. Forum presentations work best when all group members know the issues and are prepared to respond unhesitatingly to questioners.
- A **panel discussion** is an informative group presentation. Individuals on the panel may use notes on key facts or statistics, but they do not present formal speeches. Usually a panel discussion is organized and led by an appointed chairperson or moderator.

  An effective moderator gets all the panelists to participate, summarizes their statements, and serves as a gatekeeper to make sure that no member of the panel dominates the discussion. Panel discussions are often followed by a question-and-answer period, or forum.

**symposium**
A public discussion in which a series of short speeches is presented to an audience

**forum**
A question-and-answer session that usually follows a public discussion or symposium

**panel discussion**
A group discussion designed to inform an audience about issues or a problem or to make recommendations

**Planning a Group Presentation** Working in groups requires a coordinated team effort. If you are used to developing reports and speeches on your own, it may be a challenge to work with others on a group assignment. Consider these suggestions for enhancing teamwork:

- **Make sure group members understand the task or assignment, and work together to identify a topic.** Take a few moments to verbalize the goals and objectives of the assignment. Don't immediately plunge in and try to start dividing up the work just so you can hurry off to your next class or responsibility.
- **If your group assignment is to solve a problem or to inform the audience about a specific issue, try brainstorming to develop a topic or question** (see Chapter 5). Then assess your audience's interests as well as group members' interests and talents to help you choose among your ideas.
- **Give group members individual assignments.** After you decide on your group's presentation topic, divide up the tasks involved in investigating the issues. Also, devise a plan for keeping in touch with one another frequently to share information and ideas.
- **Develop a group outline and decide on an approach.** After group members have researched key issues, begin drafting an outline of your group presentation.
- **Decide on your presentation approach.** Determine whether you will use a symposium, a forum, a panel presentation, or some combination of these approaches. Make decisions about who will present which portions of your outline. Your presentation should have an introduction and a conclusion that reflect your group's work as an integrated problem-solving team.
- **Rehearse the presentation.** Just as you would for an individual speech, rehearse the presentation. If you are using visual aids, be sure to incorporate them in your rehearsal. Also, be sure to time your presentation when you rehearse.
- **Incorporate principles and skills of effective audience-centered public speaking when giving the group presentation.** Adapt to your listeners. Your delivery and comments should be well organized and fluent. Your visual aids should enhance your presentation by being clear and attractive.

**Making A Group Presentation** By now it should be clear that the skills needed for giving a group presentation mirror those we've presented throughout the book. But because a group presentation creates the additional challenge of coordinating your communication efforts with other group or team members, keep the following tips in mind as you offer your conclusions or recommendations.

- **Clarify your purpose.** Just as with an individual speech, it's important for listeners to know what your group's speaking goal is and to understand why you are presenting the information to them; it's also important for each group member to be reminded of the overarching goal of the presentation. It would be useful if the first speaker could ensure that the audience has a good understanding of the group's purpose. If your group is responding to a specific discussion question, it may be useful to write the question or purpose of the presentation on a chalkboard, whiteboard, flipchart, or overhead transparency.
- **Use presentation aids effectively.** You can use presentation aids not only to clarify your purpose, but also to summarize key findings and recommendations. Visual aids can serve the important function of unifying your group presentation. If your group is using PowerPoint™ visuals, consider having each group member use the same template and font style to add to the coordinated look and feel of your presentation.
- **Choose someone to serve as coordinator or moderator.** Groups need a balance between structure and interaction. Without adequate structure, conversation can bounce from person to person and the presentation will lack a clear

focus. A moderator can help provide needed structure to a group presentation by introducing both the topic and the group members. A moderator can also help keep track of time and ensure that no one either dominates the discussion or speaks too little.

- **Be ready to answer questions.** Communication, as we've emphasized, is more than just giving people information; it also includes responding to feedback and questions from listeners. Group presentations often include a question-and-answer session (forum) following the presentation. Besides being informed about your topic, it's a wise idea to have thoroughly read any written report the group has distributed.

In Chapter 11, we presented strategies for responding to questions, including tips for responding to hostile questions. If someone asks a question that has just been asked and answered, or asks an irrelevant or poorly worded question, don't criticize the questioner. Be polite, tactful, and gracious. Rather than self-righteously saying, "That's a dumb question" or "Someone just asked that," calmly provide an answer and move on. If you don't understand a question, ask for more clarification. Also, don't let a questioner start making a speech. If it looks like a questioner is using the question-and-answer period to give an oration, gently ask, "And what is your question?" or "How can we help you?" This approach should elicit a question that you can then address and return the communication process back to the control of the group.

RECAP

### Tips for Successful Group Presentations

Work as a group to:

- Understand the task.
- Brainstorm problem solutions.
- Choose a presentation format.
- Outline and rehearse the presentation.
- Make the presentation and answer questions.

Contribute to the group as an individual:

- Complete your assignment.
- Contribute to meetings and rehearsals.
- Participate in the presentation.

## Public-Relations Speeches

People who work for professional associations, blood banks, utility companies, government agencies, universities, churches, or charitable institutions, as well as those employed by commercial enterprises, are often called on to speak to an audience about what their organization does or about a special project the organization has taken on. These speeches are **public-relations speeches.** They are designed to inform the public and improve relations with them—either in general, or because a particular program or situation has raised questions.

A public-relations speaker begins by discussing the need or problem that has prompted the speech. Then he or she goes on to explain how the company or organization is working to meet the need or solve the problem—or why it believes there is no problem.

It is important in public-relations speaking to anticipate criticism. The speaker may acknowledge and counter potential problems or objections, especially when past presenters have encountered opposition to the policy or program. The speaker should emphasize the positive aspects of the policy or program and take care not to become defensive. He or she wants to leave the impression that the company or organization has carefully worked through the potential pitfalls and drawbacks. It should be noted that not all public-relations speeches make policy recommendations. Many simply summarize information for those who need to know. For example, local developer Jack Brooks is well aware that many of those present at the city council meeting are opposed to his developing an area of land within the popular Smythson Creek greenbelt. Rather than ignore their objections, he deliberately and carefully addresses them:

> Many of you here tonight played in the Smythson Creek greenbelt as children. It was there that you learned to swim and that you hiked with your friends. I, too, share memories of those experiences.

**public-relations speech**
A speech designed to inform the public, to strengthen alliances with them, and in some cases to recommend policy

I want to assure you that my proposed development will actually help to preserve the greenbelt. We will dedicate in perpetuity an acre of unspoiled greenbelt for each acre we develop. Further, we will actively seek to preserve that unspoiled land by hiring an environmental specialist to oversee its protection.

As things stand now, we risk losing the entire greenbelt to pollution and unmanaged use. I can promise a desirable residential development, plus the preservation of at least half the natural environment.

## CONFIDENTLY CONNECTING WITH YOUR AUDIENCE

### Seek a Variety of Speaking Opportunities

The more positive experiences you have when speaking publicly, the more likely you are to grow more confident when you speak.[8] Look at new speaking situations as opportunities to increase your confidence so that communication apprehension becomes less of an obstacle when you speak to others.

# Ceremonial Speaking

**Kairos** is the Greek term rhetoricians use to describe the circumstances surrounding or the occasion for a speech. If the occasion is one that brings people together to celebrate, thank, or praise someone, or to mourn, a speech given on that occasion is known as a **ceremonial**, or **epideictic, speech**. We will explore nine types of ceremonial speeches: introductions, toasts, award presentations, nominations, acceptances, keynote addresses, commencement addresses, commemorative addresses and tributes, and eulogies.

## Introductions

Most of us have heard poor introductions. A nervous speaker making a **speech of introduction** stands up and mispronounces the main speaker's name. Or the introducer speaks for five or ten minutes before yielding to the main speaker. An introductory speech is much like an informative speech: The speaker: delivering the introduction provides information to the audience about the main speaker. The ultimate purpose of an introduction, however, is to arouse interest in the speaker and his or her topic. When you are asked to give a speech of introduction for a featured speaker or an honored guest, your purposes are similar to those of a good opening to a speech: You need to get the attention of the audience, build the speaker's credibility, and introduce the speaker's general subject. You also need to make the speaker feel welcome while revealing some of the speaker's personal qualities so that the audience can feel they know the speaker more intimately. The two cardinal rules for giving introductory speeches are: Be brief and be accurate.

- **Be brief.** The audience has come to hear the main speaker or honor the guest, not to listen to you.
- **Be accurate.** Nothing so disturbs a speaker as having to begin by correcting the introducer. If you are going to introduce someone at a meeting or dinner, ask that person to supply you with biographical data beforehand. If someone else provides you with the speaker's background, make sure the information is accurate. Be certain that you know how to pronounce the speaker's name and any other names or terms you will need to use.

The following short speech of introduction adheres to the two criteria: It's brief and it's accurate.

This evening, friends, we have the opportunity to hear one of the most innovative mayors in the history of our community. Mary Norris's experience in running her own real-estate business gave her an opportunity to pilot a new approach to attracting new businesses to our community, even before she was elected mayor in last year's landslide victory. She was recently recognized as the most successful mayor in our state by the Good Government League. Not only is she a skilled manager and spokesperson for our city, but she is also a warm and caring person. I am pleased to introduce my friend Mary Norris.

**kairos**
The circumstances surrounding or the occasion for a speech

**ceremonial (epideictic) speech**
A speech delivered on a special occasion for celebration, thanksgiving, praise, or mourning

**speech of introduction**
A speech that provides information about another speaker

Finally, keep the needs of your audience in mind at all times. If the person you are introducing truly needs no introduction to the group, do not give one! Just welcome the speaker and step aside. (Note that the President of the United States is always introduced simply: "Ladies and gentlemen, the President of the United States.")

## Toasts

*Wedding receptions are ceremonial occasions at which you may be expected to give a toast or a speech. When called upon to make a ceremonial speech, keep your audience at the forefront of your mind.*

[Photo: Blend Images/Superstock Royalty Free]

Most people are asked at one time or another to provide a **toast** for some momentous occasion—a wedding, a celebration of the birth of a baby, a reunion of friends, a successful business venture. A toast is a brief salute to such an occasion, usually accompanied by a round of drinks and immediately followed by the raising or clinking together of glasses or goblets. The custom is said to have taken its name from the old custom of tossing a bit of bread or a crouton into a beverage for flavoring.[9] "Drinking the toast" was somewhat like enjoying a dunked doughnut.

The modern toast is usually quite short—only a few sentences at most. Some toasts are very personal, as, for example, one given by a wedding guest who is a close friend of both the bride and the groom:

> I would like to say a few words about this couple. You see, I knew Rachel and Ben before they were a couple—when they were friends. I first met Rachel when we were freshmen in high school. Her sarcastic sense of humor has kept me laughing ever since.[10]

In contrast, a toast made by someone who does not know the primary celebrants so well may be more generic. Here is an example of such a generic wedding toast:

> When the roaring flames of your love have burned down to embers, may you find that you've married your best friend.[11]

If you are asked to make an impromptu toast, let your audience and the occasion dictate what you say. Sincerity is more important than wit. At a dinner your authors attended in Moscow a few years ago, all the guests were asked to stand at some point during the meal and offer a toast. Although this Russian custom took us by surprise, one of our friends gave a heartfelt and well-received toast that went something like this:

> We have spent the past week enjoying both the natural beauty and the man-made marvels of your country. We have visited the exquisite palaces of the czars and stood in amazement before some of the world's great art treasures. But we have also discovered that the most important national resource of Russia is the warmth of her people. Here's to new and lasting friendships.

Our Russian hosts were most appreciative. The rest of us were impressed. Mary's toast was a resounding success because she spoke sincerely about her audience and the occasion.

## Award Presentations

Presenting an award is somewhat like introducing a speaker or a guest: Remember that the audience did not come to hear you, but to see and hear the winner of the award. Nevertheless, delivering a **presentation speech** is an important responsibility, one that has several distinct components.

First, when presenting an award, you should refer to the occasion of the presentation. Awards are often given to mark the anniversary of a special event, the

**toast**
A brief salute to a momentous occasion

**presentation speech**
A speech that accompanies the presentation of an award

completion of a long-range task, the accomplishments of a lifetime, or high achievement in some field.

Next, you should talk about the history and significance of the award. This section of the speech may be fairly long if the audience knows little about the award; it will be brief if the audience is already familiar with the history and purpose of the award. Whatever the award, a discussion of its significance will add to its meaning for the person who receives it.

Finally, you will name the person to whom the award has been given. The longest part of this segment is the description of the achievements that elicited the award. That description should be given in glowing terms. Hyperbole is appropriate here. If the name of the person receiving the award has already been made public, you may refer to him or her by name throughout your description. If you are going to announce the individual's name for the first time, you will probably want to recite the achievements first and leave the person's name for last. Even though some members of the audience may recognize the recipient from your description, you should still save the drama of the actual announcement until the last moment.

## Nominations

**Nomination speeches** are similar to award presentations. They too involve noting the occasion and describing the purpose and significance of, in this case, the office to be filled. The person making the nomination should explain clearly why the nominee's skills, talents, and past achievements serve as qualifications for the position. And the actual nomination should come at the end of the speech. When Senate minority leader Everett Dirksen nominated Barry Goldwater for the Republican presidential candidacy in 1964, he emphasized those personal qualities of the admittedly controversial candidate that he thought would appeal to the audience:

> Whether in commerce or finance, in business or industry, in private or public service, there is such a thing as Competence. . . . Barry Goldwater has demonstrated it over and over in his every activity. As Chief of Staff of his state National Guard, he brought about its desegregation shortly after World War II and long before Civil Rights became a burning issue. He brought integration to his own retail enterprises. For his own employees he established the five-day week and a health and life insurance plan. All this was done without fanfare or the marching of bands.[12]

And Dirksen ended his speech with the nomination itself:

> I nominate my friend and colleague Barry Goldwater of Arizona to be the Republican candidate for President of the United States.

## Acceptances

Anyone who receives an award or a nomination usually responds with a brief **acceptance speech**. Acceptance speeches may have something of a bad name because of the lengthy, emotional, rambling, and generally boring speeches delivered annually on prime-time TV by the winners of the film industry's Oscars. The late humorist Erma Bombeck once wryly noted,

> People exchange wedding vows in under thirty seconds. . . . You only get thirty seconds to come up with the final "Jeopardy" answer. My kids can demolish a pizza in thirty seconds.
>
> So how long does it take to say, "Thank you?"[13]

**nomination speech**
A speech that officially names someone as a candidate for an office or a position

**acceptance speech**
A speech of thanks for an award, nomination, or other honor

The same audience who may resent a long oration will readily appreciate a brief, heartfelt expression of thanks. In fact, brief acceptance speeches can be quite insightful, even inspiring, and they can leave the audience feeling no doubt that the right person won the award. Two months before he died in 1979, John Wayne accepted an honorary Oscar with these touching words:

> Thank you, ladies and gentlemen. Your applause is just about the only medicine a fella would ever need. I'm mighty pleased I can amble here tonight. Oscar and I have something in common. Oscar first came on the Hollywood scene in 1928. So did I. We're both a little weatherbeaten, but we're still here and plan to be around a whole lot longer.[14]

If you ever have to give an acceptance speech, it may be an impromptu speech because you may not know that you have won until the award is presented. A fairly simple formula should help you compose a good acceptance speech on the spur of the moment.

First, you should thank the person making the presentation and the organization that he or she represents. It is also gracious to thank a few people who have contributed greatly to your success—but resist thanking everyone you have ever known, down to the family dog.

Next, you should comment on the meaning or significance of the award to you. You may also wish to reflect on the larger significance of the award to the people and the ideals it honors, as did President Barack Obama in his acceptance of the Nobel Peace Prize in 2009:

> I receive this honor with deep gratitude and great humility. It is an award that speaks to our highest aspirations—that for all the cruelty and hardship of our world, we are not mere prisoners of fate. Our actions matter, and can bend history in the direction of justice.[15]

Finally, try to find some meaning the award may have for your audience—people who respect your accomplishments and who may themselves aspire to similar achievements. In what has become one of the most often quoted acceptance speeches ever made, novelist William Faulkner dedicated his 1950 Nobel Prize for Literature to

> the young men and women already dedicated to the same anguish and travail, among whom is already that one who will some day stand here where I am standing.[16]

## Keynote Addresses

A **keynote address** is usually presented at or near the beginning of a meeting or conference. The keynote emphasizes the importance of the topic or the purpose of the meeting, motivates the audience to learn more or work harder, and sets the theme and tone for other speakers and events.

The hardest task the keynote speaker faces is being specific enough to arouse interest and inspire the audience. One way a keynote speaker can interest and inspire is to incorporate examples and illustrations to which the audience can relate. The late Texas congresswoman Barbara Jordan delivered keynote addresses at two Democratic National Conventions, one in 1976 and the other in 1992. Note how she used specific examples in this excerpt from the 1992 address:

> The American dream . . . is slipping away from too many. It is slipping away from too many black and brown mothers and their children; from the homeless of every color and sex; from the immigrants living in communities without water and sewer systems. The American dream is slipping away from the workers whose jobs are no longer there because we are better at building war equipment that sits in warehouses than we are at building decent housing.[17]

**keynote address**
A speech that sets the theme and tone for a meeting or conference

## Commencement Addresses

Cartoonist Garry Trudeau has said that **commencement addresses** "were invented largely in the belief that outgoing college students should never be released into the world until they have been properly sedated."[18] Unfortunately, most commencement speeches deserve Trudeau's assessment. Commencement speakers are often oblivious to their audience on an occasion that demands and deserves audience-centeredness. To be audience centered, a commencement speaker must fulfill two important functions.

First, the commencement speaker should praise the graduating class. Because the audience includes the families and friends of the graduates, the commencement speaker can gain their goodwill (as well as that of the graduates themselves) by pointing out the significance of the graduates' accomplishments. Political commentator Rachel Maddow congratulated the 2010 graduates of Smith College with these words:

> You are graduating from Smith College. You are well-prepared. You are poised. You're well-connected. You are wicked smart. You are already accomplished.[19]

Second, the audience-centered commencement speaker should turn graduates toward the future. A commencement address is not the proper forum in which to bemoan the world's inevitable destruction or the certain gloomy economic future of today's graduates. Rather, commencement speakers should suggest bright new goals and try to inspire the graduates to reach for them, as President Obama told the 2010 graduates of Hampton University:

> And it now falls to you, the Class of 2010, to write the next great chapter in America's story; to meet the tests of your own time; and to take up the ongoing work of fulfilling our founding promise.[20]

Commencement speakers who want to be audience-centered can learn from Hewlett Packard CEO Carly S. Fiorina, who consulted by e-mail with the graduating class of the Massachusetts Institute of Technology, whom she was scheduled to address. She discovered that students wanted a speech based on life experience, not theory, and advice on how to make the decisions they needed to make in life. And, Fiorina adds, "On one point there was complete unanimity: Please don't run over your time."[21]

## Commemorative Addresses and Tributes

**Commemorative addresses**—those delivered during ceremonies held to celebrate some past event—are often combined with tributes to the person or persons involved. For example, a speech given on the Fourth of July both commemorates the signing of the Declaration of Independence and pays tribute to those who signed it. Your town's sesquicentennial celebrates both the founding and the founders of the town. And if you were asked to speak at the reception for your grandparents' fiftieth wedding anniversary, you would probably relate the stories they've told you of their wedding day and then go on to praise their accomplishments during their fifty years together.

The speaker who commemorates or pays tribute is, in part, an informative speaker. He or she needs to present some facts about the event and/or the people being celebrated. Then the speaker builds on those facts, urging the audience to let past accomplishments inspire them to achieve new goals. Speaking at Pointe du Hoc, France, during ceremonies in June 1994 to commemorate the fifty-year anniversary of D-Day, President Bill Clinton paid tribute to the assembled veterans:

> We are the children of your sacrifice. We are the sons and daughters you saved from tyranny's reach. We grew up behind the shield of the strong alliances you forged in blood upon these beaches, on the shores of the Pacific and in the skies above us. We flourished in the nation you came home to build. The most difficult days of your lives bought us fifty years of freedom.[22]

**commencement address**
A speech delivered at a graduation or commencement ceremony

**commemorative address**
A speech delivered during ceremonies held in memory of some past event and/or the person or persons involved

His tribute completed, Clinton added this challenge:

> Let us carry on the work you began here. You completed your mission here, but the mission of freedom goes on; the battle continues.

## Eulogies

A **eulogy**—a speech of tribute delivered when someone has died—can be one of the most significant and memorable and also one of the most challenging forms of commemorative address. As the editor of a recent collection of eulogies notes,

> A good eulogy can be . . . a bridge between the living and the dead, between us and them, memory and eternity. The more specific and real the remembrances spoken, the stronger the bridge.[23]

When you deliver a eulogy, you should mention—indeed, linger on—the unique achievements of the person to whom you are paying tribute and, of course, express a sense of loss. It is also proper in a eulogy to include personal and even humorous recollections of the person who has died. In his eulogy for his beloved Aunt Betty, John T. Masterson, Jr., related this humorous story:

> Whereas other relatives sent books, clothing, or sensible toys for Christmas and birthdays, Aunt Betty tended toward the offbeat. . . . There was the year she (or the mail order house) got the order number wrong and sent me reflective driveway markers for Christmas. The thing about Aunt Betty was that if you received a gift like that, you didn't recognize it as a mistake; instead, my family and I sat around the Christmas tree trying to figure out the joke![24]

Finally, turn to the living, and encourage them to transcend their sorrow and sense of loss and feel instead gratitude that the dead person was once alive among them. In her eulogy for civil rights pioneer Rosa Parks, Oprah Winfrey shared her own gratitude for Parks's actions:

> That day that you refused to give up your seat on the bus, you, Sister Rosa, changed the trajectory of my life and the lives of so many other people in the world. I would not be standing here today nor standing where I stand every day had she not chosen to sit down.[25]

**RECAP**

### Types of Ceremonial Speeches

- Introductions
- Toasts
- Award presentations
- Nominations
- Acceptances
- Keynote addresses
- Commencement addresses
- Commemorative addresses and tributes
- Eulogies

# After-Dinner Speaking: Using Humor Effectively

> If you are a human being or even a reasonably alert shrub, chances are that sooner or later a club or organization will ask you to give a speech. The United States is infested with clubs and organizations, constantly engaging in a variety of worth-while group activities such as (1) eating lunch; (2) eating dinner; (3) eating breakfast; and of course (4) holding banquets. The result is that there is a constant demand for post-meal speakers, because otherwise all you'd hear would be the sounds of digestion.[26]

With typically irreverent wit, columnist Dave Barry thus begins his observations of the activity known as after-dinner speaking. Certainly he is right about one thing: the popularity of mealtime meetings and banquets with business and professional organizations and service clubs. And such a meeting inevitably requires an **after-dinner speech**.

**eulogy**
A speech of tribute delivered when someone has died

**after-dinner speech**
An entertaining speech, usually delivered in conjunction with a mealtime meeting or banquet

## LEARNING FROM GREAT SPEAKERS

### Dave Barry (1947– )

Syndicated columnist and Pulitzer Prize–winning commentator Dave Barry is much in demand as a special-occasion speaker at conferences, corporate meetings, writers' and speakers' groups, and great speakers series. A recent review of a speech Barry presented at the New York State Writer's Institute credits his success as a humorous speaker to his wit, sense of timing, and ability to tell a story well.[27]

Much of Dave Barry's humor comes from seeing everyday events in a new light. As you consider adding humor to your talks, look for the humor in your own life and the lives of your listeners. Poking fun at yourself can especially help you score points with your audience.

[Photo: Getty Images, Inc.]

Interestingly, not only is the after-dinner speech not always after *dinner* (as Barry points out, the meal is just as likely to be breakfast or lunch), but it is also not always *after* anything. The after-dinner speech may be delivered before the meal or even between courses. Former first lady Barbara Bush preferred to schedule speeches first and dinner later during state dinners. In another variation, Librarian of Congress James Billington, at a dinner in honor of philosopher Alexis de Tocqueville, served up one speech between each course, "so that one had to earn the next course by listening to the speech preceding it."[28] Regardless of the variation, the after-dinner speech is something of an institution, one with which a public speaker should be prepared to cope.

After-dinner speeches may present information or persuade, but their primary purpose is to entertain—arguably the most inherently audience-centered of the three general purposes for speaking discussed in Chapter 5. We summarize several strategies for entertaining audiences with humor in Table 16.1 and discuss them in detail next.

## Humorous Topics

Because humor is listener-centered, the central question for the after-dinner speaker seeking a topic must be this: What do audiences find funny?

**TABLE 16.1 Strategies for Achieving Humor in After-Dinner Speeches**

| Strategy | Description |
|---|---|
| Humorous Topics | Inherently funny subjects or humorous treatments of more serious subjects |
| Humorous Stories | Funny anecdotes |
| Humorous Verbal Strategies | |
| Play on words | An intentional error such as puns, spoonerisms, and malapropisms |
| Hyperbole | Exaggeration |
| Understatement | Downplaying a fact or event |
| Verbal irony | Saying just the opposite of what one means |
| Wit | An unexpected turn at the end of a fact or incident |
| Humorous Nonverbal Strategies | Physical or vocal elements such as posture, gesture, pauses, and intonation |

The Comedy Gym in Austin, Texas, a school for aspiring stand-up comedians, advocates that speakers start with "themselves, their lives, what makes them laugh."[29] Audiences almost always enjoy hearing a speaker poke fun at himself or herself. Comedy writer John Macks points out that self-deprecating humor is "an instant way to establish a rapport with an audience."[30]

Even serious subjects can lend themselves to humorous presentations. One speechwriter notes that humor can help a speaker achieve rapport with the audience and can help the audience remember the speaker's message:

> If you can find a way to make a point with humor, you've improved the odds of making your message stick. For example, say you're expecting a tax increase, and you want to let your audience know. You might say, "Well, Congress has finally decided how to divide up the pie; trouble is, *we're* the pie."[31]

Increased taxes, not an inherently humorous topic, can still be treated humorously. So can other serious topics. Earlier in this chapter we discussed the use of humor in eulogies. Gun control and the U.S. health care industry, two subjects tackled by Michael Moore in the films *Bowling for Columbine* and *Sicko*, respectively, are examples of serious topics made more palatable to listeners by the use of humor. For example, in *Sicko*,

> a scrolling text of the pre-existing medical conditions that insurance companies use to reject prospective applicants is set to the *Star Wars* theme against an outer-space backdrop.[32]

Although Moore's medium is film rather than speech, the same principle applies: Many serious subjects can be treated with humor.

Are any subjects *in*appropriate for an after-dinner speech? A few years ago, comedian Robin Williams appeared on *The Tonight Show with Jay Leno* to talk about a new film in which Williams played a Protestant minister. Spinning off from that character, Williams launched into a comic treatment of pedophilia among Catholic priests that provoked outrage from Catholic organizations.

While Williams's comic routines often push the boundaries of propriety and taste, audience-centered public speakers should exercise greater restraint. Because it is the audience that "gives attempts at humor their success or failure,"[33] topics that might create a great deal of emotional noise (such as grief or anger) for particular audiences would not be good topics for humorous speeches to those groups. A humorous treatment of childhood cancer would most likely only distress an audience of parents who had lost children to that disease.

## Humorous Stories

Humorous stories should be simple. Complicated stories and jokes are rarely perceived by audiences as funny. Jay Leno claims that "Jokes work best when they're easy to understand."[34]

Successful after-dinner speakers also need a broad repertoire. One successful after-dinner speaker says that she tries

> to get about 25 to 30 jokes, anecdotes or one-liners before I write the speech. This will be reduced to the best and most appropriate 6 or 7, but one needs as much material as possible to begin with.[35]

Finally, it is important to know your anecdotes very well. Nothing deflates a humorous story more than getting halfway through one and saying, "Oh, and I forgot to tell you. . . ." Rehearse your jokes. Only if you know the material can you hope to deliver it with the intonation and timing that will make it funny.

## Humorous Verbal Strategies

Either a humorous anecdote or a one-liner may rely on any of the following verbal strategies for humorous effect.

**Play on Words** Most of us are familiar with **puns**, which rely on double meanings to create humor. For example, an old joke in which an exasperated speaker tries to explain the meaning of "hide" by shouting, "Hide! Hide! A cow's outside!" provokes the response, "I'm not afraid of cows." The joke relies on two meanings of the word *hide:* to conceal oneself and the skin (*outside*) of an animal.

Another play on words is the **spoonerism**, named for William Spooner, a professor at Oxford University in the 1930s who frequently used it (inadvertently, in his case). A spoonerism occurs when someone switches the initial sounds of words in a single phrase: "sublic peaking" instead of "public speaking," for example. In one joke that relies on a spoonerism, the Chatanooga Choo-choo becomes the "cat who chewed the new shoes." Many parodies and satires employ spoonerisms to avoid charges of libel or copyright infringement; a spoonerism might be employed to name a boy wizard "Perry Hotter."

A third play on words is the **malapropism**, named for the unfortunate Mrs. Malaprop in Richard Brinsley Sheridan's eighteenth-century play *The School for Scandal.* A malapropism is the mistaken use of a word that sounds much like the intended word: "destruction" for "instruction," for example.

**Hyperbole** **Hyperbole**, or exaggeration, is often funny. In an after-dinner speech on "The Alphabet and Simplified Spelling," Mark Twain claimed,

> Simplified spelling brought about sun-spots, the San Francisco earthquake, and the recent business depression, which we would never have had if spelling had been left all alone.[36]

Of course, spelling could not have caused such catastrophes, so by using hyperbole, Twain makes his point in a humorous way.

**Understatement** The opposite of hyperbole, **understatement** involves downplaying a fact or event. Microsoft founder and Harvard dropout Bill Gates downplayed his meteoric success by telling the Harvard class of 2007,

> I did the best of everyone who failed.[37]

**Verbal Irony** A speaker who employs **verbal irony** says just the opposite of what he or she really means. Student Chris O'Keefe opens his speech on reading Shakespeare with this statement:

> At a certain point in my life, I came to the realization that I wanted to spend my life's effort to become a great playwright.[38]

Chris reveals the verbal irony of the statement when he continues,

> It has been about an hour and a half now and the feeling is still going strong.

**Wit** One of the most frequently used verbal strategies for achieving humor is the use of **wit**: relating an incident that takes an unexpected turn at the end. Research suggests that witty humor may enhance a speaker's credibility.[39] Accepting the 2007 Oscar for Best Actress, Helen Mirren paid tribute to the monarch she had portrayed on screen in *The Queen*,

> For 50 years and more, Elizabeth Windsor has maintained her dignity, her sense of duty and her hairstyle.[40]

**pun**
The use of double meanings to create humor

**spoonerism**
A phrase in which the initial sounds of words are switched

**malapropism**
The mistaken use of a word that sounds much like the intended word

**hyperbole**
Exaggeration

**understatement**
Downplaying a fact or event

**verbal irony**
Saying the opposite of what one means

**wit**
Relating an incident that takes an unexpected turn at the end

The wit occurs in the final phrase "her hairstyle," which catches off-guard the audience anticipating another majestic attribute.

## Humorous Nonverbal Strategies

After-dinner speakers often create humor through such nonverbal cues as posture, gesture, and voice. Well-timed pauses are especially crucial delivery cues for after-dinner speakers to master. One experienced after-dinner speaker advocates "a slight pause before the punch line, then pause while the audience is laughing."[41]

It is true that some people seem to be "naturally" funny. If you are not one of them—if, for example, you struggle to get a laugh from even the funniest joke—you may still be able to use the strategies outlined above to prepare and deliver an after-dinner speech that is lighthearted and clever, if not uproariously funny. Such a speech can still be a success.

# STUDY GUIDE

## Public Speaking in the Workplace

Public-speaking skills are used frequently in the workplace when making group presentations or representing your company or profession before the public. Group presentation formats include symposium, forum, and panel discussion events. Group members should work individually and with the group to plan and make group presentations. Public-relations speeches inform the public and improve an organization's relationships with its public.

### Being Audience-Centered

- Workplace audiences may range from a group of three managers to a huge auditorium filled with company employees. Try to find out what size audience you will be speaking to.
- When you make a business presentation, tell the members of your audience what benefits will accrue to them directly as a result of your proposal.
- It is important in public-relations speaking to anticipate criticism.

### Using What You've Learned

- A friend asks your advice about how to prepare for her first speech to her colleagues in a new job. Explain how she can apply some of the principles and skills you have learned in public-speaking class as she presents her report.

## Ceremonial Speaking

Chances are that at some time you will be called on to speak at an occasion that calls for celebration, commemoration, inspiration, or entertainment. These special-occasion speeches require you to use critical thinking to apply your speaking skills to unique situations. This chapter offers advice for making these ceremonial speeches, including introductions, toasts, award presentations, nominations, acceptances, keynote addresses, commencement addresses, commemorative addresses and tributes, and eulogies.

### Being Audience-Centered

- When you introduce a speaker or present an award, remember that the audience did not come to hear you. Be brief.
- A commencement is an occasion that demands and deserves audience-centeredness.
- When called on to deliver a eulogy, encourage your audience to transcend their sorrow and sense of loss and, instead, to feel gratitude that the dead person was once alive among them.

### Using What You've Learned

- You have been asked to introduce at your school a Pulitzer Prize–winning poet who will be reading from her work. What will you do to ensure that you follow the two cardinal rules of introductory speeches?

### A Question of Ethics

- Several Web sites offer eulogy writing services or prewritten generic eulogies, such as a eulogy "for a grandmother," for fees around $30 to $40. If you were asked to deliver a eulogy, would it be ethical to buy such a speech?

### Speaker's Homepage: A Toast to You and Yours: Tips for Making Toasts

These useful and interesting Internet sites can help you find just the words to make a toast memorable and meaningful:

- How to Make a Toast. E-How offers a step-by-step guide. http://www.ehow.com/how_2161714_make-a-toast.html
- The Toast of the Evening offers examples of Mark Twain's classic after-dinner speeches and toasts. http://etext.virginia.edu/railton/onstage/speeches.html
- Wedding Speeches and Toasts. Yahoo! provides a list of sites that offer wedding toasts. http://dir.yahoo.com/Society_and_Culture/Weddings/Speeches_and_Toasts/

## After-Dinner Speaking: Using Humor Effectively

After-dinner speaking is an established institution in which speakers entertain through the use of humorous topics and stories, humorous verbal strategies, and humorous nonverbal strategies.

### A Question of Ethics

- You were a member of the jury during a highly publicized and controversial murder trial. After the verdict is delivered, you find yourself in great demand as a keynote speaker for meetings of local organizations. Several offer to pay you well. Is it ethical to cash in on your experiences in this way?

# SPEECH WORKSHOP

## Introducing a Speaker

Use the following worksheet to help you prepare a brief, accurate introduction of another speaker.

**Person's name:**

**Educational background:**

**Experience related to the topic he/she will discuss:**

**Awards and recognition received:**

**Personal characteristics (e.g., hard working, caring, selfless volunteer):**

# Epilogue

Now that you are about to complete your public-speaking course, you may barely be able to resist the temptation to pat yourself on the back. Before taking this course, you, like the survey population we mentioned in Chapter 1, may have feared public speaking more than death! But you have survived and perhaps even excelled. Now you can file away your notes and will never have to give another speech, right?

Wrong!

There is indeed life after public-speaking class—a life that will demand frequent practice and sharpening of the skills to which you have been introduced in this course. Your classroom experience has taught you how to become a better public speaker. We hope that it has also taught you to become your own best critic—able to say, "I need to make more eye contact," or "I need a statistic to prove this point," or "I need a transition here." But one course cannot make you a polished speaker. Learning to speak in public is an ongoing process rather than a static goal.

In the years to come, both in college and beyond, you will use and continue to develop your public-speaking skills in many areas of your professional and personal life. In Chapter 1, we discussed some of the skills you would learn and practice as a public speaker: organization, audience analysis and adaptation, research, effective presentation, and critical listening. Certainly you will find yourself applying these skills to numerous situations—to speaking opportunities, of course, but also to other situations that require critical listening and analytic thinking. As you take other courses, apply for a job, prepare a report for your company, attend city council meetings, and go about your day-to-day personal business, you will find yourself using the skills you learned in your public-speaking class.

Chances are that you will also find yourself in a number of actual public-speaking situations. Perhaps you will give few "laboratory" speeches like those you have given in your speech class. But you will undoubtedly deliver one or more of the types of special-occasion speeches that we discussed in Chapter 16. You will make a business presentation, introduce a speaker, present or receive an award, deliver a speech to commemorate a person or an occasion, give a book review, make a sales pitch. And you will look back to this course for guidance.

You will not remember every detail of the course or of this book. But we hope that you will remember the bottom line: that to be effective, public speaking must be *audience-centered*. Every step of the public-speaking process, from selecting and narrowing the topic, to preparing the speech, to final delivery, must be approached with the audience in mind. If the audience does not understand your message or does not respond as you had hoped, your speech cannot be a success, regardless of the hours of research or rehearsal you may have dedicated to the task.

One final note about the audience-centered approach: Being audience-centered is not the same as being manipulative. As we discussed in Chapter 1, if you adapt to your audience to the extent that you abandon your own values and sense of truth, you have become an unethical speaker rather than an audience-centered one. An audience-centered speaker does not tell an audience only what its members want to hear.

One type of special-occasion speech discussed in Chapter 16 was the commencement address. Your completion of this course is also the commencement—the beginning—of your continuing development as a public speaker. The traditional theme of the commencement speaker is "Go forth. You have been prepared for the future." We leave you with that thought: Go forth. You have been prepared for the future.

*Your completion of this course is the commencement of your continuing development as a public speaker.*
[Photo: Bill Aron/PhotoEdit Inc.]

# A Speaking in Small Groups

Groups are an integral part of our lives. Work groups, family groups, therapy groups, committees, and class-project groups are just a few of the groups in which we may participate at one time or another. Chances are that you have had considerable experience in communicating in small groups.

Why learn about group communication in a public-speaking class? Aristotle identified the link between public speaking and group discussion over two thousand years ago when he wrote "Rhetoric is the counterpart of dialectic." He meant that our efforts to persuade are closely linked to our group efforts to search for truth.

In Aristotle's time, people gathered to discuss and decide public issues in a democratic manner. Today we still turn to a committee, jury, or task force to get facts and make recommendations. We still "search for truth" in groups. And, as in ancient Athens, once we believe we have found the truth, we present the message to others in speeches and lectures.

In this appendix, you will learn key communication principles and skills to help you work as a productive member of a small group. Specifically, you will discover what small group communication is, learn ways to improve group problem solving, enhance your leadership skills, and become an effective group participant or group leader.[1]

What is **small group communication**? It is interaction among from three to a dozen people who share a common purpose, feel a sense of belonging to the group, and influence one another. Communication in groups larger than twelve people usually resembles public speaking more than small group communication.

**small group communication** Interaction among from three to twelve people who share a common purpose, feel a sense of belonging to the group, and influence one another

Working in groups has several advantages compared to working on projects alone. Groups typically make better-quality decisions than do individuals, for several reasons:[2]

- Groups usually have more information available.
- Groups are often more creative; the very presence of others can spark innovation.
- When you work in groups, you're more likely to remember what you discussed because you were actively involved in processing information.
- Group participation usually results in group members' being more satisfied with their results than if someone had just told them what to do.

Although we've characterized working in groups as a positive experience, you also know that working in groups can be challenging. Here are potential disadvantages of working in groups:[3]

- Group members may use excessive pressure to get others to conform to their point of view.
- One person may dominate the discussion.
- Group members may rely too much on others and may not do their part.
- Group work is more time-consuming (many people consider this the biggest disadvantage).

The goal of this Appendix is to help decrease the disadvantages and increase the advantages of working with others.

Is there a difference between a group and a team? Yes. A **team** is a coordinated small group of people organized to work together, with clearly defined roles and responsibilities, explicitly stated rules for operation, and well-defined goals.[4] A team is a special kind of group that, as our definition suggests, coordinates its efforts through a clearly defined structure of who does what. All teams are groups, but not all groups are teams. Think of a sports team in which members play by rules, have assigned roles, and have a clear objective—to win the game. Work teams too have well-defined procedures for accomplishing tasks. Teams are formed for a variety of reasons, such as to sell products, elect a political candidate, or build an international space station.

# Solving Problems in Groups and Teams

A central purpose of many groups and teams is to solve problems. Problem solving is a means of finding ways of overcoming obstacles to achieve a desired goal: How can we raise money for the new library? What should be done to improve the local economy? How can we make higher education affordable for everyone in our state? Each of these questions implies that there is an obstacle (lack of money) blocking the achievement of a desired goal (new library, stronger local economy, affordable education).

Imagine that you have been asked to suggest ways to make a college education more affordable. The problem: The high cost of higher education keeps many people from attending college. How would you begin to organize a group to solve this problem? In 1910, John Dewey, philosopher and educator, identified a method of problem solving that he called **reflective thinking.**[5] His multistep method has been adapted by many groups as a way to organize the process of solving problems. Here are his suggestions: (1) Identify and define the problem, (2) analyze the problem, (3) generate possible solutions, (4) select the best solution, and (5) test and implement the solution. Although not every problem-solving discussion has to follow these steps, reflective thinking does provide a helpful blueprint that can relieve some of the uncertainty that exists when groups try to solve problems.

## 1. Identify and Define the Problem

Groups work best when they define their problem clearly and early in their problem-solving process. To reach a clear definition, the group should consider the following questions:

- What is the specific problem that concerns us?
- What terms, concepts, or ideas do we need to understand in order to solve the problem?
- Who is harmed by the problem?
- When do the harmful effects occur?

Policy questions can help define a problem and also identify the course of action that should be taken to solve it. As you recall from Chapter 14, policy questions often begin with a phrase such as "What should be done about" or "What could be done to improve." Here are examples:

- What should be done to improve security at U.S. airports?
- What should be done to increase employment in our state?
- What steps could be taken to improve the U.S. trade balance with other countries?

**team**
A coordinated small group of people organized to work together, with clearly defined roles and responsibilities, explicit rules, and well-defined goals

**reflective thinking**
A method of structuring a problem-solving discussion that involves (1) identifying and defining the problem, (2) analyzing the problem, (3) generating possible solutions, (4) selecting the best solution, and (5) testing and implementing the solution

If your group were investigating the high cost of pursuing a college education, for example, after defining such key terms as "higher education" and "college" and gathering statistics about the magnitude of the problem, you could phrase your policy question this way: "What could be done to reduce the high cost of attending college?"

## 2. Analyze the Problem

Ray Kroc, founder of McDonald's, said, "Nothing is particularly hard if you divide it into small jobs." Once the group understands the problem and has a well-worded question, the next step is to analyze the problem. **Analysis** is a process of examining the causes, effects, symptoms, history, and other background information that will help a group reach a solution. When analyzing a problem, a group should consider the following questions:

- What is the history of the problem?
- How extensive is the problem?
- What are the causes, effects, and symptoms of the problem?
- Can the problem be subdivided for further definition and analysis?
- What methods do we already have for solving the problem, and what are their limitations?
- What obstacles might keep us from reaching a solution?

To analyze the problem of the high cost of attending college, your discussion group will have to use a library or the Internet to research the history of the problem and existing methods of solving it (see Chapter 6).

Included in the process of analyzing the problem is identifying criteria. **Criteria** are standards for identifying an acceptable solution. They help you recognize a good solution when you discover one; criteria also help the group stay focused on its goal. Typical criteria for an acceptable solution specify that the solution should be implemented on schedule, should be agreed to by all group members, should be achieved within a given budget, and should remove the obstacles causing the problem.

## 3. Generate Possible Solutions

When your discussion group has identified, defined, and analyzed the problem, you will be ready to generate possible solutions using group brainstorming.

Use the following guidelines:

- **Set aside judgment and criticism.** Criticism and faultfinding stifle creativity. If group members find withholding judgment difficult, have the individual members write suggestions on paper first and then share the ideas with the group.
- **Think of as many possible solutions to the problem as you can.** All ideas are acceptable, even wild and crazy ones. Piggyback off one another's ideas. All members must come up with at least one idea.
- **Have a member of the group record all the ideas that are mentioned.** Use a flipchart or chalkboard, if possible, so that all group members can see and respond to the ideas.
- **After a set time has elapsed, evaluate the ideas, using criteria the group has established.** Approach the solutions positively. Do not be quick to dismiss an idea, but do voice any concerns or questions you might have. The group can brainstorm again later if it needs more creative ideas.

Some groups have found it useful to use technology to help them generate options and solutions.[6] For example, group members can brainstorm solutions to a problem individually, then e-mail their list of ideas to each other. Or the group's

**analysis**
Examination of the causes, effects, and history of a problem in order to understand it better

**criteria**
Standards for identifying an acceptable solution to a problem

leader could collect all of the ideas, eliminate duplicate suggestions, and then share them with the group. Research suggests that groups can generate more ideas if group members first generate ideas individually and then collaborate.[7]

## 4. Select the Best Solution

Next, the group needs to select the solution that best meets the criteria and solves the problem. At this point, the group may need to modify its criteria or even its definition of the problem.

Research suggests that after narrowing the list of possible solutions, the most effective groups carefully consider the pros and the cons of each proposed solution.[8] Groups that don't do this often make poor decisions because they haven't carefully evaluated the implications of their solution; they haven't looked before they leaped.

To help in evaluating the solution, consider the following questions:

- Which of the suggested solutions deals best with the obstacles?
- Does the suggestion solve the problem in both the short term and the long term?
- What are the advantages and disadvantages of the suggested solution?
- Does the solution meet the established criteria?
- Should the group revise its criteria?
- What is required to implement the solution?
- When can the group implement the solution?
- What result will indicate success?

If the group is to reach agreement on a solution, some group members will need to abandon their attachment to their individual ideas for the overall good of the group. Experts who have studied how to achieve **consensus**—support for the final decision by all members—suggest that summarizing frequently and keeping the group oriented toward its goal are helpful. Emphasizing where group members agree, clarifying misunderstandings, writing down known facts for all members to see, and keeping the discussion focused on issues rather than on emotions are also strategies that facilitate group consensus.[9]

## 5. Test and Implement the Solution

The group's work is not finished when it has identified a solution. "How can we put the solution into practice?" and "How can we evaluate the quality of the solution?" have yet to be addressed. The group may want to develop a step-by-step plan that describes the process for implementing the solution, a time frame for implementation, and a list of individuals who will be responsible for carrying out specific tasks.

**RECAP**

**Steps in Problem Solving**

1. Identify and clearly define the problem.
2. Analyze the problem and identify criteria.
3. Generate possible solutions.
4. Select the best solution.
5. Test and implement the solution.

# Participating in Small Groups

To be an effective group participant, you have to understand how to manage the problem-solving process. But knowing the steps is not enough; you also need to prepare for meetings, evaluate evidence, effectively summarize the group's progress, listen courteously, and be sensitive to conflict.

## Come Prepared for Group Discussions

To contribute to group meetings, you need to be informed about the issues. Prepare for group discussions by researching the issues. If the issue before your group is the use of

**consensus**
The support and commitment of all group members to the decision of the group

asbestos in school buildings, for example, research the most recent scientific findings about the risks of this hazardous material. Chapter 6 described how to use library databases and the Internet to gather information for your speeches. Use those research techniques to prepare for group deliberations as well. Bring your research notes to the group; don't just rely on your memory or your personal opinion to carry you through the discussion. Without research, you will not be able to analyze the problem adequately.

## Do Not Suggest Solutions before Analyzing the Problem

Research suggests that you should analyze a problem thoroughly before trying to zero in on a solution.[10] Resist the temptation to settle quickly on one solution until your group has systematically examined the causes, effects, history, and symptoms of a problem.

## Evaluate Evidence

One study found that a key difference between groups that make successful decisions and those that don't is group members' ability to examine and evaluate evidence.[11] Ineffective groups are more likely to reach decisions quickly without considering the validity of evidence (or sometimes without any evidence at all). Such groups usually reach flawed conclusions.

## Help Summarize the Group's Progress

Because it is easy for groups to get off the subject, group members need to summarize frequently what has been achieved and to point the group toward the goal or task at hand. One research study suggests that periodic overviews of the discussion's progress can help the group stay on target.[12] Ask questions about the discussion process rather than about the topic under consideration: "Where are we now?" "Could someone summarize what we have accomplished?" and "Aren't we getting off the subject?"

## Listen and Respond Courteously to Others

Chapter 3's suggestions for improving listening skills are useful when you work in groups, but understanding what others say is not enough. You also need to respect their points of view. Even when you disagree with someone's ideas, keep your emotions in check and respond courteously. Being closed-minded and defensive usually breeds group conflict.

## Help Manage Conflict

In the course of exchanging ideas and opinions about controversial issues, disagreements are bound to occur.[13] You can help prevent conflicts from derailing the problem-solving process by doing the following:

- Keep the discussion focused on issues, not on personalities.
- Rely on facts rather than on personal opinions for evidence.
- Seek ways to compromise; don't assume that there must be a winner and a loser.
- Try to clarify misunderstandings in meaning.
- Be descriptive rather than evaluative and judgmental.
- Keep emotions in check.

If you can apply these basic principles, you can help make your group an effective problem-solving team.

# Leading Small Groups

Rudyard Kipling wrote, "For the strength of the pack is the wolf, and the strength of the wolf is the pack." Group members typically need a leader to help the group collaborate effectively and efficiently, and a leader needs followers in order to lead. In essence, **leadership** is the process of influencing others through communication. Some see a leader as one individual empowered to delegate work and direct the group. In reality, however, group leadership is often shared.

## Leadership Responsibilities

Leaders are needed to help accomplish tasks and to maintain a healthy social climate for the group. Rarely does one person perform all these leadership responsibilities, even if a leader is formally appointed or elected. Most often a number of individual group members assume some specific leadership task, based on their personalities, skills, sensitivity, and the group's needs. If you determine that the group needs a clearer focus on the task or that maintenance roles are needed, be ready to influence the group appropriately to help get the job done in a positive, productive way. Leaders of large or formal groups may use parliamentary procedure to bring structure to meetings, for example. If you find yourself in such a leadership situation, Web sites such as Robert's Rules of Order (www.robertsrules.com) can help you implement parliamentary procedure. Table A.1 lists specific roles for both *task* leaders and *maintenance* leaders.

**leadership**
The process of influencing others through communication

### TABLE A.1 Leadership Roles in Groups and Teams

| | Leadership Role | Description |
|---|---|---|
| **Task Leaders** | Agenda setter | Helps establish the group's agenda |
| Help get tasks accomplished | Secretary | Takes notes during meetings and distributes handouts before and during the meeting |
| | Initiator | Proposes new ideas or approaches to group problem solving |
| | Information seeker | Asks for facts or other information that helps the group deal with the issues and may also ask for clarification of ideas or obscure facts |
| | Opinion seeker | Asks for clarification of the values and opinions expressed by group members |
| | Information giver | Provides facts, examples, statistics, and other evidence that helps the group achieve its task |
| | Opinion giver | Offers opinions about the ideas under discussion |
| | Elaborator | Provides examples to show how ideas or suggestions would work |
| | Evaluator | Makes an effort to judge the evidence and the conclusion the group reaches |
| | Energizer | Tries to spur the group to further action and productivity |
| **Group Maintenance Leaders** | Encourager | Offers praise, understanding, and acceptance of others' ideas |
| Help maintain a healthy social climate | Harmonizer | Mediates disagreements that occur between group members |
| | Compromiser | Attempts to resolve conflicts by trying to find an acceptable middle ground between disagreeing group members |
| | Gatekeeper | Encourages the participation of less talkative group members and tries to limit lengthy contributions of other group members |

*Source:* Adapted from Kenneth D. Benne and Paul Sheats, "Functional Roles of Group Members," *Journal of Social Issues* 4 (Spring 1948): 41–49.

## Leadership Styles

Leaders can be described by the types of behavior, or leadership styles, that they exhibit as they influence the group to help achieve its goal. When you are called on to lead, do you give orders and expect others to follow you? Or do you ask the group to vote on the course of action to follow? Or maybe you don't try to influence the group at all; perhaps you prefer to hang back and let the group work out its own problems.

These strategies describe three general leadership styles: *authoritarian*, *democratic*, and *laissez-faire*.[14] Authoritarian leaders assume positions of superiority, giving orders and assuming control of the group's activity. Although authoritarian leaders can usually organize group activities with a high degree of efficiency and virtually eliminate uncertainty about who should do what, most problem-solving groups prefer democratic leaders.

Having more faith in their groups than do authoritarian leaders, democratic leaders involve group members in the decision-making process rather than dictate what should be done. Democratic leaders focus more on guiding discussion than on issuing commands.

Laissez-faire leaders allow group members complete freedom in all aspects of the decision-making process. They do little to help the group achieve its goal. This style of leadership (or nonleadership) often leaves a group frustrated because the group then lacks guidance and has to struggle with organizing the work. Table A.2 compares the three styles.

What is the most effective leadership style? Research suggests that no single style is effective in every group situation. Sometimes a group needs a strong authoritarian leader to make decisions quickly so that the group can achieve its goal. Although

**TABLE A.2 Leadership Style**

| | Authoritarian Leaders | Democratic Leaders | Laissez-Faire Leaders |
|---|---|---|---|
| **Group Policy Formation** | All determinations of policy are made by the leader. | All policies are a matter of group discussion and decision; leader assigns and encourages group discussion and decision making. | Complete freedom for individual or group decisions; minimal leader participation |
| **Group Activity Development** | Group techniques and activities are dictated by the leader, one at a time; future steps are always largely unknown to group members. | Discussion yields broad perspectives and general steps to the group goal; when technical advice is needed, leader suggests alternative procedures. | Leader supplies various materials, making it clear that he or she can supply information when asked, but takes no other part in the discussion. |
| **Source of Work Assignments** | Leader dictates specific work tasks and teams; leader tends to remain aloof from active group participation except when directing activities. | Members are free to work with anyone; group decides on division of tasks. | Complete non-participation by leader |
| **Praise/Criticism** | Leader tends to be personal in praise or criticism of each member. | Leader is objective and fact-oriented in praise and criticism, trying to be a regular group member in spirit without doing too much of the work. | Leader offers infrequent spontaneous comments on member activities and makes no attempt to appraise or control the course of events. |

most groups prefer a democratic leadership style, leaders sometimes need to assert their authority to get the job done. The best leadership style depends on the nature of the group task, the power of the leader, and the relationship between the leader and his or her followers.

One contemporary approach to leadership is transformational leadership. Transformational leadership is not so much a particular style of leadership as it is a quality or characteristic of relating to others.[15] **Transformational leadership** is the process of influencing others by building a shared vision of the future, inspiring others to achieve, developing high-quality individual relationships with others, and helping people see how what they do is related to a larger framework or system. To be a transformational leader is not just to perform specific tasks or skills, but to have a philosophy of helping others see the big picture and inspiring them to make the vision of the future reality.[16] Transformational leaders are good communicators who support and encourage rather than demean or demand.

**transformational leadership** The process of influencing others by building a shared vision of the future, inspiring others to achieve, developing high-quality individual relationships with others, and helping people see how what they do is related to a larger framework or system

### Leaders of Small Groups

RECAP

1. Contribute to task and maintenance.
2. Adapt their leadership style to group needs.
3. Work toward transformational leadership.

# B Speeches for Analysis and Discussion

## I Have a Dream*

### by Martin Luther King Jr., Washington, D.C., August 28, 1963

I am happy to join with you today in what will go down in history as the greatest demonstration for freedom in the history of our nation.

Five score years ago, a great American, in whose symbolic shadow we stand today, signed the Emancipation Proclamation. This momentous decree came as a great beacon light of hope to millions of Negro slaves, who had been seared in the flames of withering injustice. It came as a joyous daybreak to end the long night of their captivity.

But one hundred years later, the Negro is still not free. One hundred years later, the life of the Negro is still sadly crippled by the manacles of segregation and the chains of discrimination. One hundred years later, the Negro lives on a lonely island of poverty in the midst of a vast ocean of material prosperity. One hundred years later, the Negro is still languished in the corners of American society and finds himself an exile in his own land. And so we've come here today to dramatize a shameful condition.

In a sense we've come to our nation's Capitol to cash a check. When the architects of our republic wrote the magnificent words of the Constitution and the Declaration of Independence, they were signing a promissory note to which every American was to fall heir. This note was a promise that all men—yes, black men as well as white men—would be guaranteed the inalienable rights of life, liberty, and the pursuit of happiness.

It is obvious today that America has defaulted on this promissory note insofar as her citizens of color are concerned. Instead of honoring this sacred obligation, America has given the Negro people a bad check—a check which has come back marked "insufficient funds."

But we refuse to believe that the bank of justice is bankrupt. We refuse to believe that there are insufficient funds in the great vaults of opportunity of this nation. And so we've come to cash this check—a check that will give us upon demand the riches of freedom and the security of justice.

We have also come to this hallowed spot to remind America of the fierce urgency of now. This is no time to engage in the luxury of cooling off or to take the tranquilizing drug of gradualism. Now is the time to make the real promises of democracy. Now is the time to rise from the dark and desolate valley of segregation to the sunlit



NOTE: You can watch and listen to this speech and to President Obama's inaugural address, which follows, on YouTube (www.youtube.com).

path of racial justice. Now is the time to lift our nation from the quicksands of racial injustice to the solid rock of brotherhood. Now is the time to make justice a reality for all of God's children.

It would be fatal for the nation to overlook the urgency of the moment. This sweltering summer of the Negro's legitimate discontent will not pass until there is an invigorating autumn of freedom and equality. Nineteen sixty-three is not an end, but a beginning. Those who hope that the Negro needed to blow off steam and will now be content will have a rude awakening if the nation returns to business as usual. There will be neither rest nor tranquility in America until the Negro is granted his citizenship rights. The whirlwinds of revolt will continue to shake the foundations of our nation until the bright day of justice emerges.

But there is something that I must say to my people, who stand on the warm threshold which leads into the palace of justice. In the process of gaining our rightful place, we must not be guilty of wrongful deeds. Let us not seek to satisfy our thirst for freedom by drinking from the cup of bitterness and hatred.

We must forever conduct our struggle on the high plane of dignity and discipline. We must not allow our creative protest to degenerate into physical violence. Again and again we must rise to the majestic heights of meeting physical force with soul force.

The marvelous new militance which has engulfed the Negro community must not lead us to a distrust of all white people. For many of our white brothers, as evidenced by their presence here today, have come to realize that their destiny is tied up with our destiny. They have come to realize that their freedom is inextricably bound to our freedom. We cannot walk alone.

As we walk, we must make the pledge that we shall always march ahead. We cannot turn back. There are those who are asking the devotees of civil rights, "When will you be satisfied?" We can never be satisfied as long as the Negro is the victim of the unspeakable horrors of police brutality. We can never be satisfied as long as our bodies, heavy with the fatigue of travel, cannot gain lodging in the motels of the highways and hotels of the cities. We cannot be satisfied as long as the Negro's basic mobility is from a smaller ghetto to a larger one. We can never be satisfied as long as our children are stripped of their selfhood and robbed of their dignity by signs stating "For Whites Only." We cannot be satisfied as long as a Negro in Mississippi cannot vote and a Negro in New York believes he has nothing for which to vote. No, no, we are not satisfied, and we will not be satisfied until justice rolls down like waters, and righteousness like a mighty stream.

I am not unmindful that some of you have come here out of great trials and tribulations. Some of you have come fresh from narrow jail cells. Some of you have come from areas where your quest for freedom left you battered by the storms of persecution and staggered by the winds of police brutality. You have been the veterans of creative suffering. Continue to work with the faith that unearned suffering is redemptive.

Go back to Mississippi, go back to Alabama, go back to South Carolina, go back to Georgia, go back to Louisiana, go back to the slums and ghettos of our Northern cities, knowing that somehow this situation can and will be changed. Let us not wallow in the valley of despair.

I say to you today, my friends, so even though we face the difficulties of today and tomorrow, I still have a dream. It is a dream deeply rooted in the American dream.

I have a dream that one day this nation will rise up and live out the true meaning of its creed, "We hold these truths to be self-evident, that all men are created equal."

I have a dream that one day on the red hills of Georgia the sons of former slaves and the sons of former slaveowners will be able to sit down together at the table of brotherhood.

I have a dream that one day even the state of Mississippi, a state sweltering with the heat of injustice, sweltering with the heat of oppression, will be transformed into an oasis of freedom and justice.

I have a dream that my four little children will one day live in a nation where they will not be judged by the color of their skin but by the content of their character. I have a dream today.

I have a dream that one day, down in Alabama, with its vicious racists, with its governor having his lips dripping with the words of interposition and nullification, one day right there in Alabama little black boys and black girls will be able to join hands with little white boys and white girls as sisters and brothers. I have a dream today.

I have a dream that one day every valley shall be exalted, every hill and mountain shall be made low, the rough places will be made plain and the crooked places will be made straight, and the glory of the Lord shall be revealed, and all flesh shall see it together.

This is our hope. This is the faith that I go back to the South with. With this faith we will be able to hew out of the mountain of despair a stone of hope. With this faith we will be able to transform the jangling discords of our nation into a beautiful symphony of brotherhood. With this faith we will be able to work together, to pray together, to struggle together, to go to jail together, to stand up for freedom together knowing that we will be free one day.

This will be the day—this will be the day when all of God's children will be able to sing with new meaning, "My country 'tis of thee, sweet land of liberty, of thee I sing. Land where my fathers died, land of the Pilgrims' pride, from every mountainside, let freedom ring." And if America is to be a great nation, this must become true.

So let freedom ring from the prodigious hilltops of New Hampshire. Let freedom ring from the mighty mountains of New York. Let freedom ring from the heightening Alleghenies of Pennsylvania!

Let freedom ring from the snowcapped Rockies of Colorado! Let freedom ring from the curvaceous slopes of California!

But not only that. Let freedom ring from Stone Mountain of Georgia!

Let freedom ring from Lookout Mountain of Tennessee!

Let freedom ring from every hill and molehill of Mississippi. From every mountainside, let freedom ring.

And when this happens, when we allow freedom to ring—when we let it ring from every village and every hamlet, from every state and every city—we will be able to speed up that day when all of God's children, black men and white men, Jews and Gentiles, Protestants and Catholics, will be able to join hands and sing, in the words of the old Negro spiritual, "Free at last! Free at last! Thank God almighty, we are free at last!"

# Delivering the Gift of Freedom to Future Generations (Inaugural Address)*

## by Barack Obama, January 20, 2009

My fellow citizens:

I stand here today humbled by the task before us, grateful for the trust you have bestowed, mindful of the sacrifices borne by our ancestors. I thank President Bush for his service to our nation, as well as the generosity and cooperation he has shown throughout this transition.

*Barack Obama, "We Will Remake America: Delivering the Gift of Freedom to Future Generations," *Vital Speeches of the Day* (1 February 2009): 50–53.

Forty-four Americans have now taken the presidential oath. The words have been spoken during rising tides of prosperity and the still waters of peace. Yet, every so often, the oath is taken amidst gathering clouds and raging storms. At these moments, America has carried on not simply because of the skill or vision of those in high office, but because We the People have remained faithful to the ideals of our fore bearers, and true to our founding documents.

So it has been. So it must be with this generation of Americans.

That we are in the midst of crisis is now well understood. Our nation is at war, against a far-reaching network of violence and hatred. Our economy is badly weakened, a consequence of greed and irresponsibility on the part of some, but also our collective failure to make hard choices and prepare the nation for a new age. Homes have been lost; jobs shed; businesses shuttered. Our health care is too costly; our schools fail too many; and each day brings further evidence that the ways we use energy strengthen our adversaries and threaten our planet.

These are the indicators of crisis, subject to data and statistics. Less measurable but no less profound is a sapping of confidence across our land—a nagging fear that America's decline is inevitable, and that the next generation must lower its sights.

Today I say to you that the challenges we face are real. They are serious and they are many. They will not be met easily or in a short span of time. But know this, America: they will be met.

On this day, we gather because we have chosen hope over fear, unity of purpose over conflict and discord.

On this day, we come to proclaim an end to the petty grievances and false promises, the recriminations and worn-out dogmas, that for far too long have strangled our politics.

We remain a young nation, but in the words of Scripture, the time has come to set aside childish things. The time has come to reaffirm our enduring spirit; to choose our better history; to carry forward that precious gift, that noble idea, passed on from generation to generation: the God-given promise that all are equal, all are free, and all deserve a chance to pursue their full measure of happiness.

In reaffirming the greatness of our nation, we understand that greatness is never a given. It must be earned. Our journey has never been one of shortcuts or settling for less. It has not been the path for the fainthearted—for those who prefer leisure over work, or seek only the pleasures of riches and fame. Rather, it has been the risk-takers, the doers, the makers of things—some celebrated, but more often men and women obscure in their labor—who have carried us up the long, rugged path toward prosperity and freedom.

For us, they packed up their few worldly possessions and traveled across oceans in search of a new life.

For us, they toiled in sweatshops and settled the West; endured the lash of the whip and plowed the hard earth.

For us, they fought and died, in places like Concord and Gettysburg; Normandy and Khe Sahn.

Time and again, these men and women struggled and sacrificed and worked till their hands were raw so that we might live a better life. They saw America as bigger than the sum of our individual ambitions; greater than all the differences of birth or wealth or faction.

This is the journey we continue today. We remain the most prosperous, powerful nation on Earth. Our workers are no less productive than when this crisis began. Our minds are no less inventive, our goods and services no less needed than they were last week or last month or last year. Our capacity remains undiminished. But our time of standing pat, of protecting narrow interests and putting off unpleasant decisions—that time has surely passed. Starting today, we must pick ourselves up, dust ourselves off, and begin again the work of remaking America.

For everywhere we look, there is work to be done. The state of the economy calls for action, bold and swift, and we will act—not only to create new jobs, but to lay a new foundation for growth. We will build the roads and bridges, the electric grids and digital lines that feed our commerce and bind us together. We will restore science to its rightful place, and wield technology's wonders to raise health care's quality and lower its cost. We will harness the sun and the winds and the soil to fuel our cars and run our factories. And we will transform our schools and colleges and universities to meet the demands of a new age. All this we can do. And all this we will do.

Now, there are some who question the scale of our ambitions—who suggest that our system cannot tolerate too many big plans. Their memories are short. For they have forgotten what this country has already done; what free men and women can achieve when imagination is joined to common purpose, and necessity to courage.

What the cynics fail to understand is that the ground has shifted beneath them—that the stale political arguments that have consumed us for so long no longer apply. The question we ask today is not whether our government is too big or too small, but whether it works—whether it helps families find jobs at a decent wage, care they can afford, a retirement that is dignified. Where the answer is yes, we intend to move forward. Where the answer is no, programs will end. And those of us who manage the public's dollars will be held to account—to spend wisely, reform bad habits, and do our business in the light of day—because only then can we restore the vital trust between a people and their government.

Nor is the question before us whether the market is a force for good or ill. Its power to generate wealth and expand freedom is unmatched, but this crisis has reminded us that without a watchful eye, the market can spin out of control—and that a nation cannot prosper long when it favors only the prosperous. The success of our economy has always depended not just on the size of our gross domestic product, but on the reach of our prosperity; on our ability to extend opportunity to every willing heart—not out of charity, but because it is the surest route to our common good.

As for our common defense, we reject as false the choice between our safety and our ideals. Our Founding Fathers, faced with perils we can scarcely imagine, drafted a charter to assure the rule of law and the rights of man, a charter expanded by the blood of generations. Those ideals still light the world, and we will not give them up for expedience's sake. And so to all other peoples and governments who are watching today, from the grandest capitals to the small village where my father was born: know that America is a friend of each nation and every man, woman and child who seeks a future of peace and dignity, and that we are ready to lead once more.

Recall that earlier generations faced down fascism and communism not just with missiles and tanks, but with sturdy alliances and enduring convictions. They understood that our power alone cannot protect us, nor does it entitle us to do as we please. Instead, they knew that our power grows through its prudent use; our security emanates from the justness of our cause, the force of our example the tempering qualities of humility and restraint.

We are the keepers of this legacy. Guided by these principles once more, we can meet those new threats that demand even greater effort—even greater cooperation and understanding between nations. We will begin to responsibly leave Iraq to its people, and forge a hard-earned peace in Afghanistan. With old friends and former foes, we will work tirelessly to lessen the nuclear threat, and roll back the specter of a warming planet. We will not apologize for our way of life, nor will we waver in its defense, and for those who seek to advance their aims by inducing terror and slaughtering innocents, we say to you now that our spirit is stronger and cannot be broken; you cannot outlast us, and we will defeat you.

For we know that our patchwork heritage is a strength, not a weakness. We are a nation of Christians and Muslims, Jews and Hindus—and nonbelievers. We are shaped by every language and culture, drawn from every end of this Earth; and because we have tasted the bitter swill of civil war and segregation, and emerged from that dark chapter stronger and more united, we cannot help but believe that the old hatreds shall someday pass; that the lines of tribe shall soon dissolve; that as the world grows smaller, our common humanity shall reveal itself; and that America must play its role in ushering in a new era of peace.

To the Muslim world, we seek a new way forward, based on mutual interest and mutual respect. To those leaders around the globe who seek to sow conflict, or blame their society's ills on the West: know that your people will judge you on what you can build, not what you destroy. To those who cling to power through corruption and deceit and the silencing of dissent, know that you are on the wrong side of history; but that we will extend a hand if you are willing to unclench your fist.

To the people of poor nations, we pledge to work alongside you to make your farms flourish and let clean waters flow; to nourish starved bodies and feed hungry minds. And to those nations like ours that enjoy relative plenty, we say we can no longer afford indifference to suffering outside our borders; nor can we consume the world's resources without regard to effect. For the world has changed, and we must change with it.

As we consider the road that unfolds before us, we remember with humble gratitude those brave Americans who, at this very hour, patrol far-off deserts and distant mountains. They have something to tell us today, just as the fallen heroes who lie in Arlington whisper through the ages. We honor them not only because they are guardians of our liberty, but because they embody the spirit of service; a willingness to find meaning in something greater than themselves. And yet, at this moment—a moment that will define a generation—it is precisely this spirit that must inhabit us all.

For as much as government can do and must do, it is ultimately the faith and determination of the American people upon which this nation relies. It is the kindness to take in a stranger when the levees break, the selflessness of workers who would rather cut their hours than see a friend lose their job which sees us through our darkest hours. It is the firefighter's courage to storm a stairway filled with smoke, but also a parent's willingness to nurture a child, that finally decides our fate.

Our challenges may be new. The instruments with which we meet them may be new. But those values upon which our success depends—hard work and honesty, courage and fair play, tolerance and curiosity, loyalty and patriotism—these things are old. These things are true. They have been the quiet force of progress throughout our history. What is demanded then is a return to these truths. What is required of us now is a new era of responsibility—a recognition, on the part of every American, that we have duties to ourselves, our nation and the world; duties that we do not grudgingly accept but rather seize gladly, firm in the knowledge that there is nothing so satisfying to the spirit, so defining of our character, than giving our all to a difficult task.

This is the price and the promise of citizenship.

This is the source of our confidence—the knowledge that God calls on us to shape an uncertain destiny.

This is the meaning of our liberty and our creed—why men and women and children of every race and every faith can join in celebration across this magnificent Mall, and why a man whose father less than 60 years ago might not have been served at a local restaurant can now stand before you to take a most sacred oath.

So let us mark this day with remembrance, of who we are and how far we have traveled. In the year of America's birth, in the coldest of months, a small band of patriots huddled by dying campfires on the shores of an icy river. The capital was abandoned. The enemy was advancing. The snow was stained with blood. At a moment when the outcome of our revolution was most in doubt, the father of our nation ordered these words be read to the people:

> "Let it be told to the future world . . . that in the depth of winter, when nothing but hope and virtue could survive . . . that the city and the country, alarmed at one common danger, came forth to meet [it]."

America. In the face of our common dangers, in this winter of our hardship, let us remember these timeless words. With hope and virtue, let us brave once more the icy currents, and endure what storms may come. Let it be said by our children's children that when we were tested, we refused to let this journey end, that we did not turn back, nor did we falter; and with eyes fixed on the horizon and God's grace upon us, we carried forth that great gift of freedom and delivered it safely to future generations.

## Find Your Passion, and Find a Way to Get Paid to Follow It*

### by Anne Lynam Goddard, May 16, 2009

Thank you for that kind introduction. And my thanks to my wonderful alma mater for the great honor of inviting me to speak on this special day.

It is always a joy to come back here, to the fond memories of a place that played such an important role in my life. But it is really exciting to be here on a day that is so important in the lives of each and every one of you.

I think it's safe to say that have I have a lot in common with just about every one of the faces I see here today.

Parents, not only are you and I pretty much in the same generation, but a year ago I was in the same situation you are in right this moment. I was listening to a commencement speaker at my son's graduation from Virginia Tech.

So I believe I know what you're feeling: joy, of course, at what your son or daughter has achieved (Oh yes, and that those tuition bills won't be arriving every semester any more); relief that you and your child made it through pretty much unscathed.

And maybe just a *little* apprehension, that your mature, responsible young adult might be tempted to tell you some of the things that really went on here, when you weren't around.

I also have a lot in common with you new graduates too, though you may find that a little hard to believe.

After all when I went to school here we were pretty much in the technological Dark Ages. Can you image going a whole day, let alone four years without a single text or Tweet? Well, we didn't even have fax machines. (Your parents can explain to you what those are).

IPods? Forget it. The Walkman hadn't even been invented yet.

I wrote my papers in long hand then typed them out because the personal computer had not moved very far from Steve Jobs' and Steve Wozniak's garage.

I graduated the year *Saturday Night Fever* came out, along with the first *Star Wars* movie, and the first *Rocky* . . . and gas cost 65 cents a gallon.

Yes, it was long, *long* time ago.

But even though the times were very different, I do have a lot in common with the class of 2009 graduates . . . because like many of you, I was profoundly changed by my years here.

If you had asked me when I arrived here in 1973 who among my classmates was the *least* likely to be chosen to be a future commencement speaker, I would have chosen . . . myself without a doubt.

My Irish immigrant parents quit school when they were 13. The nuns had to convince my mom that college was a good idea for her daughters, and I was the first in my family to go out of state to school—travelling all the way from New Jersey to Assumption.

Now I have to admit that, pretty early on, I gave my mom some reasons to have second thoughts about letting me go. In those days, one of the campus traditions was a tug of war across the duck pond. The losing team, of course, wound up in the pond.

*"Find Your Passion, and Find a Way to Get Paid to Follow It," as appeared in *Vital Speeches of the Day* (1 October 2009): 75:10. Reprinted by permission of Anne Lynam Goddard.

Well, the tug of war took place the first month I was here; my team lost; and we got good and soaked. So all of the girls ran to our dorm and threw our jeans in the dryer. Unfortunately, when it came time to sort out the clothes, mine got lost—my favorite pair of blue jeans was nowhere to be found.

So now I had to explain to my conservative Irish Catholic mother how I managed to lose my pants during my first month away at college.

Bless her heart, she let me stay. And before long Assumption was expanding my horizons. First, I was introduced to an exotic life form—the American Protestant. Yes, because I'd grown up in an Irish Catholic community, I had to come all the way to Worcester to meet someone who wasn't from a parish.

And then Assumption exposed me to something even more out of the ordinary, something that had been the object of fascination—and fear—while I was growing up—the public school student.

Of course, there were no public school students in my Catholic schools. Not only that, whenever anything bad happened in my town, the nuns assured us that public school students had done it. Assumption helped me get rid of that stereotype.

And that was just the start. I'm sure that the class of '09 is filled with better writers and thinkers, thanks to Assumption. My time here certainly taught me how to analyze something and write my opinion on it in a convincing manner.

I'll bet that many of you have gained leadership skills from your time here. I'm grateful for the leadership opportunities Assumption provided, though of course some of those were the kinds of lessons you learn from making mistakes.

For example, I learned pretty quickly that I have a problem with acronyms. Dr. David Siddle, a professor of human services and rehabilitation studies, was a major influence on me. He encouraged me to become a leader of the National Rehabilitation Association. Unfortunately, in the first meeting announcements I wrote I abbreviated the organization's name with the initials "NRA." My husband, who is a gun control activist, still gives me a hard time about that today.

I have to admit, that was not the worst example of acronym problems. I was a residence advisor for several years. One of my duties was organizing the welcoming parties for administrators, who would come to live with us on our dorm floor for a semester. One year, our guest was the Assistant to the Dean. So I prepared a big sign inviting our residents to come to a welcome party. I wrote the words "Assistant to the Dean" in huge letters. Unfortunately, I abbreviated "assistant" with the letters "A.S.S"

Fortunately, that administrator had a sense of humor.

I'm sure Assumption has expanded your horizons even more than it expanded mine. And I know something else about you 2009 graduates. Although this is one of the most exciting days in your life, it is also a time of . . . well maybe not fear exactly—but "concern" both for you and your parents.

Part of it is the fear of the unknown that all graduates face—my class as well as yours—after four years of knowing where you'll be and who you'll be with the next year, now all the options are open.

But this year there are other reasons to be worried. You are thinking about entering the job market during the worst economic conditions in your lifetime, and in the lifetimes of your parents, too.

I'm sure you've already gotten a lot of advice from people my age and older on what to do about that—getting unsolicited advice is part of the graduation ritual.

I'm about to add to it, so I thought long and hard about what I might say in the hope it might be useful and maybe a little different.

I decided to say some of the things I wished someone had told me on graduation day that would have helped me relax about the future and make my way forward.

The first thing I want to say is, "keep yourself open to new experiences." Assumption expanded your horizons. Don't let the process stop here.

New experiences open your hearts as well as your minds, so you can find the things in life that are enjoyable and rewarding.

Let me give you an example of the power of new experiences that I learned from my own work. Christian Children's Fund was founded in 1938. At the heart of our early operation was a plan to let individual donors contribute a set amount of money per month to "sponsor" an orphaned child in China. That approach continues today. What began as a modest effort to build and operate orphanages, has evolved into a global force working for children encompassing the globe. Today CCF operates in 31 countries and assists about 15.2 million children and family members worldwide.

I'll say more about our work in a moment. But right now I want to tell you that heading up CCF gives me the opportunity to talk with children in developing countries all over the world. And everywhere I go, I ask them the same question, "What do you want to be when you grow up?"

No matter where I go, 99 percent of the kids give the same answer: they want to be teachers. Not business people, doctors, scientists, lawyers . . . *teachers.*

Now keep in mind that these are kids from countries and from cultures that are as different from each other as Boston is from Timbuktu.

The reason they all give the same answer is that poverty has narrowed their horizons—the only kind of professionals they have experience with are teachers.

The only exception came when I recently visited a group of school kids in Ethiopia. When I asked them my question, a lot of them said, "pilots." I was puzzled until I realized their village was in the flight path of an airport, so every day they watched the planes—and the pilots—fly by overhead.

Now clearly, every one of you here today in caps and gowns already has had a much wider range of experiences than the kids I talk with.

But I guarantee you that—as wide as your horizon may be today—it could be much wider. And if you expand it, you will have a chance to learn lessons you never dreamed of and discover the things in life that truly bring you joy.

When I graduated, I thought I had found exactly what I wanted. I loved Worcester, and I was happy working here as a social worker. But I also had the dream to join the Peace Corps. I thought I'd enjoy the two years away, then come back to live my life here.

For me, that time in the Peace Corps working in Kenya expanded my vision in wonderful ways I had never anticipated. First, it taught me some very practical life lessons I don't think I could have ever learned anywhere else.

For example, shortly after my training, I was assigned to a village, and shortly after that I accompanied a local German doctor as he traveled around from one tiny place to another checking on the local medical dispensaries. I guess because I was still in my "developed world" mindset, I did not bring any food and water along with me, not realizing that might be a problem.

Oh yes, and it was Thanksgiving Day, my first outside the U.S. Well, there weren't any 7-11s, no restaurants, no roadside stands—no food at all and hardly any water as we travelled around during a long, long day. Finally, that evening we reached a larger village, with plenty of water, and very generous hosts who said they would feed us.

So they brought out—not a turkey, but . . . a cow . . . a live cow . . . which they proceeded to slaughter, about two feet in front of me.

After I recovered my appetite, I was still starving, but it took hours to finish slaughtering and roasting the animal. By the time we sat down to eat, it was quite dark. Now in Africa when they cook a cow . . . they really cook a cow—pretty much everything, inside and out gets cooked and served. So here I was on Thanksgiving, sitting in the dark hungry, while people passed me parts of a cow I had never seen or even imagined before.

Finally, the German doctor leaned over to me and said, "Pick out something with a bone on it." I did as I was told.

So Kenya quickly taught me to always be self-reliant—and in particular when travelling in the Third World, even on Thanksgiving, bring your own food and water.

But that time in the Peace Corps did much more than that—it accomplished what expanding your horizons always does—it helped me discover what I am passionate about—fighting poverty and helping children.

That passion has taken me from Kenya to Somalia, where I ran a small non-governmental organization or NGO, serving refugees at a time when a million desperate people had come across the border from Ethiopia.

It took me to Bangladesh, where I headed a women's health and development project and saw how women who are better educated and have fewer babies can help break the cycle of poverty for their children. It took me to Indonesia, where I focused on the care and protection of infants and children under five.

And it took me to Egypt, where I was the first female country director for CARE in its 50-year history in Egypt, and where we took on the barriers that keep girls out of school.

And now it has taken me to Christian Children's Fund.

CCF is a charity that combines humanitarian work and development work. In the midst of an emergency, CCF is there, as part of the relief effort. But after the crisis has passed, and others leave, we stay—fighting the root causes of poverty.

Of the very many development organizations in the world—CCF is most identified for its defining focus on children throughout all their stages of development. While we are committed to the health and education of children, we also believe children have the capacity to improve their own lives, to be leaders of the next generation. They can bring lasting change to their families and communities in a way no adult or outsider ever can.

These views are the distinguishing features of CCF. Today, these views take the practical form of a distinctive three-part approach that follows the birth and growth of a child. First goal: healthy and secure infants. Second goal: educated and confident children. The final goal: skilled and involved youth.

Or, we can put it another way:

- Get healthy.
- Get smart.
- Change the world.

I would love for you to join us in the work we and other organizations do in helping children and fighting poverty around the world. The need has never been greater. Economists estimate that the global economic meltdown is forcing up to 53 million more people—a mind-numbing number—into poverty this year. And far, far too many of them will be children. Those numbers are expected to grow much larger until the economy recovers.

But I'm really not here to recruit you to join me in my passion. Instead, more than anything I want you to find your own. Because once you find your passion, you will be taking a huge step toward achieving the kind of happy life everyone dreams of.

After finding your passion, what's next? Simple: find a way to get paid for following it. Now at this point I can see many of you thinking, "Yeah right. Who's going to pay me for *that?*"

Let me say a couple things to answer that question. I'm smack in the middle of the baby boomer generation, and I can't tell you how many people my age and older I talk to who say they wish they had followed their passion and not settled for something less.

Live all around the world in some of the poorest communities in the world . . . and raise a family . . . and have a rewarding career . . . doesn't sound possible, right? But I did it because I decided to do what I was passionate about.

Your passion will give you the power to find a way to make a living doing what you love.

Now I'm sure some of you are thinking, "Well, people who can earn money doing what they love have incredible luck. That's the kind of luck I don't have."

You know, I've been doing a lot of thinking about luck recently, about luck and fate. In the last year, my son was shot four times by the Virginia Tech shooter . . . and we learned my husband had cancer. Both survived, both recovered and both are doing well.

So I know very well that, of course, fate controls our lives in extreme circumstances. But my personal philosophy is that most of the time luck is like the early version of the Mario video game. You know the one where the little platforms are moving up and down, and you have to make sure you jump when you're on one that is moving up.

You're in trouble if you jump when one is moving down.

Luck is like that—if you pay attention, seize the opportunities at the right moment and make that leap—you'll be lucky. You'll find that job that pays you and feeds your passion.

Let me close with a quote. The words of the quote are powerful in themselves, but they have a special meaning because of the circumstances when I first heard them. When I was a CARE director in Egypt, one of my colleagues was CARE director in Iraq. Unfortunately, she was also one of the first casualties of the Iraq war.

A few weeks before she was killed, we were in a meeting, and she said she had just heard Maya Angelou speak. Maya Angelou said, "[the] mission in life is not merely to survive, but to thrive; and to do so with some passion, some compassion, some humor, and some style."

Assumption has given you the tools you need to thrive. Now it's up to you to make a life filled with passion, compassion, humor, and style.

Thank you.

## Sticky Ideas: Low-Tech Solutions to a High-Tech Problem*

### by Richard L. Weaver II, May 18, 2007

One of the many pleasures I had teaching undergraduates was giving Lecture 13, a lecture I simply labeled "Attention." The reason for the "pleasure" was that the fundamental ideas of the lecture and its structure never changed, but I continually updated it with recent, immediate, powerful examples and stories. From the student feedback I received at the end of each semester, it was one of the 15 lectures that did not just stand out, but it made a significant impact.

What's interesting about this lecture on "Attention" is that I learned the fundamental ideas and structure as a graduate teaching assistant at Indiana University. Each graduate teaching assistant, as an assignment, was asked to prepare and deliver a lecture to the rest of the TAs on a topic relevant to the basic-communication course. This lecture on "Attention" wasn't my lecture, but I took excellent notes, then I fleshed them out with my own anecdotes, stories, and examples.

From that exercise in graduate school, I began delivering the "Attention" lecture to every public-speaking class I taught for the next 30 years. I used it because it held students' attention, because they could understand and remember it, because they could believe the information simply because I demonstrated its effectiveness—that is, credibility by visual demonstration, or internal credibility—and, finally, because the material was so practical, sensible, and down-to-earth students were able to apply it directly to the class speeches they were about to give. This is credibility by application.

In the basic-communication course at Bowling Green State University where I gave the "Attention" lecture to over 80,000 students, sometimes as many 1,500 per semester, I had other elements of credibility working on my behalf. I was both the director and designer of the course; writer of the textbook and student workbook; instructor and facilitator of the graduate teaching assistants who taught the small-group sections, and the large-group lecturer for the course. Since this was Lecture 13,

*"Sticky Ideas: Low-Tech Solutions to a High-Tech Problem," as appeared in *Vital Speeches of the Day* (1 August 2007): 73:8. Reprinted with permission of Richard L. Weaver II.

I had 12 opportunities prior to this one to establish and secure my credibility. I am certain that contributed to establishing the credibility of the "Attention" material before I began speaking.

As the title of this speech implies, all educators have a greater problem today than ever before, and the problem is getting worse. The problem, simply put, is the appeal that technology has for the youth of our nation. Let's clarify it. We live in a fast-paced, instant results, eye-catching and attention-arresting, multimedia flash, short-attention span, world where any idea that isn't current, relevant, and immediate—and delivered on a screen—is discarded as obsolete, out-of-date, old-fashioned, defunct, and dead. Many students today can code and decode complex messages in a variety of media, and many, too, are already prepared to communicate with a level of visual sophistication that will carry them through the multimedia-dependent environment of higher education and the modern work environment. The problem is simply: how do educators compete? How do we give our thoughts high-tech appeal in a technology-driven world? What I want to do is provide low-tech solutions to this high-tech problem.

If you, as an educator, manager, supervisor, cleric, or parent, in any venue whether it be the classroom, workplace, professional office, home, or church, temple, or synagogue want to drive your ideas home—make them stick—you have to compete. Compete with what? You must compete with listener expectations (our technology-driven world), compete with what is going on in listeners' heads at the time (their own thoughts and feelings), and compete with any environmental distractions (external noise such as other classrooms, a lawn mower, a noisy kitchen, or just the background noise that occurs when any group of people is assembled). This is a tough assignment, but it becomes even tougher when you consider the characteristics of "attention" itself.

Why do the characteristics of "attention" contribute to the high-tech problem? The characteristics contribute for three reasons. First, the duration of focus of "attention" is short. Did you know, for example, that your attention on anything only lasts for an average of 3 to 7 seconds? And when you concentrate on something, it is seldom that you can hold your attention on whatever it is for more than 30 seconds? The second characteristic of "attention" is that it constantly shifts. Well, that makes sense if you realize it lasts, on average, for just 3 to 7 seconds. It rapidly flits from thing or idea to another like a house fly trying to locate its next great meal. And, the third characteristic of "attention" is that its span is narrow. It is selective. Like a laser, it continually picks up competing stimuli. It just shows you how easily "attention" is diverted to something else—even a passing thought in the listener's mind can be a diversion, deflection, deviation, or alternate route.

What I want to do now, in the remaining part of the lecture, is show you how you can compete in this high-tech world with low-tech solutions. To be successful in holding listener attention, you have to compete successfully! You have to get your listeners to pay attention, to understand and remember what you say, to agree with you or believe you, to care about what you are saying, and to act on it in some way. You have to have "sticky ideas." My claim is that you can compete, but you have to work at it. Low-tech solutions require careful planning and preparation; often, they do not occur spontaneously—unless you're very lucky.

Before I go on, I want to give credit where credit is due. Some of the information I want to share with you comes from a book called *Made to Stick: Why Some Ideas Survive and Others Die* (Random House, 2007), a book by Chip and Dan Heath. Chip is a professor of organizational behavior in the Graduate School of Business at Stanford University, and Dan is a consultant at Duke Corporate Education and a former researcher at Harvard Business School. In addition to the "sticky" part in the title of my speech, I have borrowed a number of my ideas from their excellent book—a book I highly recommend for anyone in the business of educating, whether formally or informally.

One problem that most educators face—any adult whose interest is communicating with others—is something Heath and Heath call "the curse of knowledge," and unless we are aware of it, it is unlikely we will compensate for it.

The curse of knowledge can best be demonstrated by a simple game—a game studied and explained by Elizabeth Newton, who, in 1990, earned a Ph.D. in psychology at Stanford based on her study. She assigned people to one of two roles: "tappers" or "listeners." Tappers received a list of 25 well-known songs like "Happy Birthday" and "The Star-Spangled Banner." Each tapper was asked to pick a song from the list and tap out the rhythm to a listener by knocking on a table. The listener's job was to guess the song based on the rhythm being tapped.

Now, listen to the results. Over the course of Newton's experiment, 120 songs were tapped out, but listeners guessed only 2.5 percent, or 3 out of 120.

You may wonder what made the result worthy of a dissertation in psychology? Before listeners guessed the name of the song, Newton asked tappers to predict the odds that listeners would guess correctly. This is what is stunning: tappers predicted that the odds were 50 percent. They got their message across 1 time in 40, but tappers thought they were getting it across 1 time in 2.

The problem is that tappers have been given knowledge—the song title—and it makes it impossible for them to imagine what it's like to lack that knowledge. When they're tapping, they can't imagine what it's like for listeners to hear isolated taps rather than a song. This is the curse of knowledge—once we know something, we find it hard to imagine what it was like not to know it. Our knowledge has "cursed" us, and it becomes difficult for us to share our knowledge with others because we can't readily re-create our listeners' state of mind.

Heath and Heath remind us that this tapper/listener experiment is reenacted every day with CEOs and front-line employees, teachers and students, politicians and voters, marketers and customers, writers and readers. The reason for the curse of knowledge is the enormous information imbalance, so the immediate point is that if you want to have your ideas compete in a high-tech world, you must first deal directly with the curse of knowledge by taking your ideas and transforming them—by using one of the low-tech solutions.

There are six low-tech solutions we can use to transform our ideas and avoid the curse of knowledge. The first is simplicity, and it requires that we strip ideas down to their core, which means becoming masters of exclusion. It doesn't mean saying something short, dumbing things down, or speaking in sound bites. What we need are ideas that are both simple and profound. Let me give you a simple, yet profound, idea from my discipline—speech communication. The idea is that meaning is a product of social life. We often believe that meanings lie in things, but any meanings that you possess for things are the result of interacting with others about the objects being defined. That is, objects have no meaning for people apart from interacting with other humans.

Let me give you an example. How many of you have ever heard of a "toilet telephone," and I do not mean a telephone in the bathroom?

The only way you would know what a "toilet telephone" is if you were in prison, you have talked with people who have been in prison, or you have read authors who have written about prison behavior. Out of interest, I Googled "toilet telephone," and I found nothing. Inmates know a "toilet telephone" well because they have learned that they can communicate by listening to voices that travel through the sewer pipes in the prison. A simple idea—meaning is a product of social life—but very profound, and secured with an image: a "toilet telephone."

The second low-tech solution to a high-tech problem is using the unexpected. In my lecture, "Attention," I ask my students, "How many of you eat seaweed every day of your life?" Generally, nobody raises his or her hand. Okay, how many of you eat ice cream? No ice cream? How about yogurt or cottage cheese? Do you drink chocolate milk, eat pudding, low-fat cheese, use ketchup, or do you drink nutritional beverage mixes? Next time you drink chocolate milk, look on the side of the carton where it lists ingredients and notice the name carageenan. You say you can't afford any of these, so you eat pet food? None of these hit home? Do you brush your teeth everyday? It's carageenan, which comes from red seaweed, and it is used as a thickener and an emulsifier (which keeps the oils dispersed and in suspension). All of you eat seaweed every day of your life—but don't think of it as seaweed, think of it as a sea vegetable!

The unexpected occurs in every field; all we need to do is to look for it. And when we find it, we need to use it if it is relevant and appropriate.

The third low-tech solution to a high-tech problem is concreteness. My opening example about Lecture 13 revealed concreteness. Here is another. Drowsiness is a major cause of traffic injuries and fatalities. That is an abstract statement that carries little interest value so let me add some concreteness. Many of you have caught yourself dozing off at the wheel. You bolt awake with the chilling realization that disaster was but a split second away. This period, which sometimes lasts as long as 5 seconds, has been termed "microsleeps." Did you know that a car, moving at 60 miles per hour, travels 88 feet in one second. In less than 4 seconds, you've gone the length of a football field. Now, that's concreteness!

The fourth low-tech solution to a high-tech problem is credibility. I discussed credibility earlier in this speech with reference to Lecture 13. The main question is, "What makes people believe ideas?" We believe because our parents or our friends believe. We believe because we've had experiences that led us to our beliefs. We believe because of our religious faith. All are powerful forces—family, personal experience, and faith. But since we have no control over the way these forces affect people, we are left with just one: We believe because we trust authorities—people, if not ourselves, who have expertise in the particular area we're discussing. That is why our personal experience can be a low-tech solution.

Another way to gain credibility is to use statistics—like my description of how far a car moves going 60 miles per hour, in just four seconds. Here is another example. Trying to get listeners to understand what the word "billion" means is a good example of making statistics meaningful. Politicians use the word billion in a casual manner, and there is no doubt it is a difficult number to comprehend. Did you realize that a billion seconds ago it was 1959? A billion minutes ago, Jesus was alive; a billion hours ago, our ancestors were living in the Stone Age; a billion days ago, no one walked on the earth on two feet; a billion dollars ago was only 8 hours and 20 minutes, at the rate our government is spending it—and that does not include spending for the war.

The fifth low-tech solution to a high-tech problem is using emotion. We need to make listeners feel something. For the length of time I was a large-group lecturer, I shared with students the fear I experienced walking into the lecture hall on the first day of my new job. Now you all know that having to give a public speech ranks among the very top fears that everyone possesses? Because all my students had to give speeches, and because all of them believed their lecturer—a professor of speech!—would be free of such a burden, I played on their emotions and showed the specific methods I used to deal with this fear.

Any emotional connection we can make to the needs, wants, and desires of our listeners helps reduce the curse of knowledge, imprints their brain with our ideas, and aids memory. It's as if we leapfrog the brain and hop right into their hearts.

What we have now are five low-tech solutions to a high-tech problem: (1) simplicity, (2) unexpectedness, (3) concreteness, (4) credibility, and (5) emotions. Consider this brief summary as the conclusion of my speech because what I want to end with is the sixth low-tech solution: stories. Stories are among the most powerful of the low-tech solutions, and they can have a profound effect on people. What are the stories that define us? Are these the stories we want to tell, or have others tell about us?

What I have discovered from years of lecturing is that whenever I tell a story, I have the undivided attention of every one of my listeners. Their eyes become riveted; their ears peeled; and they become open vessels waiting to be filled. Often, as I embark on a story, I can hear a pin drop in the auditorium. Stories have the power to enthrall, to hold listeners spellbound, to mesmerize, entrance, dazzle, charm, captivate, and fascinate. If you have a choice between using a statistic or telling a story, use the story. If you want to drive a point home, use a story. If you want to make certain listeners remember a point, use a story.

To preface my story, you need to know that one of the major fears people have about giving a speech is: "What happens if I forget what I'm going to say?" or "What happens if I lose my place?" or "What happens if I draw a complete blank?" It is the fear of what do I do in case of an emergency—or, I don't want to lose face in front of my listeners, especially if they are a group of my peers.

What you see before you right now is a handicapped person—especially handicapped when it comes to being a public speaker. *(Pointing to my four front teeth)* I have no front teeth. The situation is in the process of being remedied; my son-in-law is an oral surgeon, and he is making implants to support permanent front teeth, but let me get back to the story.

About fifty years ago, when I worked at one of the first McDonald's restaurants—the first one in Ann Arbor, Michigan—a couple of us workers were fooling around in the back room fighting. Suddenly, and without warning, a worker by the name of Sonny, raised up his elbow and broke off my front teeth. That began close to fifty years of difficulty.

What the dentist did was to use the good roots of the teeth to drive pegs into them to support pegged teeth. My two front teeth were pegged together along with my lateral incisors—for those of you into the language of dentists.

Well, one day while lecturing, the pegs came loose, and the teeth would not stay in place, so that when I talked, the teeth would drop down into my mouth. Now, what I have not told you about my lecture situation is that I had to give the exact same lecture five times a week because Bowling Green, at that time, did not have a venue large enough to hold all the students enrolled. There were just over 300 students present on this particular day, and I could not postpone or delay the lecture; I had to proceed forward and finish the remaining 30 minutes of lecture material, because they would be held responsible for it on the next exam.

I had no choice, so I removed the teeth, and I talked for 30 minutes without my front teeth. Since I made light of the situation, so did my students, and with every lisp we all laughed at first until we became accustomed to it—together.

But, what I did at the close of the lecture—something that occurred to me right off the top of my head—I would like to do now with everyone here and everyone who may read this speech in the future. Here is what I told my students: Because this is a unique experience—it has never happened to me before, and I hope it never happens again, to be sure—I think we should have a way to signal each other. That is, you should have a way to tell me if we ever meet again, that you were part of this very special experience. So, using the thumb of your right hand, place it behind your front teeth and curl your index finger over the front of your front teeth. Then, bring them forward as if you were taking them out and uncurl your index finger and point right at me.

For several years after that experience, I would meet students on the sidewalks, in restaurants and stores, even once at Cedar Point, and we would share that special time, and we would simply smile—knowing that we had shared a secret message that both of us understood. Now, you have a way, too, to share this special time.

# Land of the Free Because of the Homeless*

### by Shaunna Miller

Recently, multiple headlines across America have identified 6,500 as the number of past and present American service members who commit suicide each year. Shockingly, this annual figure is significantly greater than the number of those killed in Iraq and Afghanistan over the last 6 years combined. Those who choose *not* to take their lives are at high risk for a different ill fate. Today, we will first examine the homelessness of

*From *Winning Orations 2009,* Mankato, MN: Interstate Oratorical Association, 2009. Reprinted by permission.

veterans in America, second, examine why large numbers of our veterans are homeless, and, finally, advance a much needed solution.

The article "Ending Homelessness," released by the *CQ Press* in 2007, reports the US Census Bureau's estimate of over 470,000 homeless on any given night. Sadly, analysis of the plight of our homeless veterans yields devastating numbers. An April 9, 2008, article, "Homeless Veterans by the Numbers," released by the *End Long-Term Homelessness Organization,* revealed that veterans make up only 11% of the total U.S. Adult population. Yet veterans total over 154,000 of the homeless on any given night, 33%. In other words, one-third of homeless persons are those who have served our great country. Just last year while in the city of Baltimore, members of my speech team and I encountered a homeless individual holding a sign that read "Vietnam Vet, I just wanna' eat," While in Phoenix, Arizona, I encountered not one but two homeless veterans. The first, a Vietnam vet, stated, "I can still hear the screams." The second, from the Gulf War era, held a sign that simply read, "I'm a Vet, why lie, I need a beer." In 2006 alone, over 335,000 veterans were homeless at some point during the year. A 2007 *Central News Network* article says studies have revealed that of these homeless veterans, 44,000–64,000 are classified as chronically homeless. The question I'd now like to answer is why.

The predominant cause of homelessness among veterans, newly in the headlines but hardly a new phenomenon, is Post Traumatic Stress Disorder, PTSD. As of November 2007, the National Center for PTSD identified Post Traumatic Stress Disorder as a psychiatric disorder following life-threatening events. The article "Traumatic Brain Injury: Signature Wound of the War" in the June 2008 *American Legion Magazine* identified PTSD as a "Life changing monster." The article went on to describe once healthy individuals as "suddenly anxious, detached, impulsive, sensitive to light and noise, unable to do simple problem solving and prone to emotional outbursts," all of which alter these individuals' ability to function in social and family life and which creates occupational instability, marital problems, divorces, and parenting difficulties. These PTSD-related ailments inevitably lead to a lack of social support, and with no support from family and friends our veterans are becoming homeless.

According to *CNN's* Web posting, as of April 14, 2009, 4,848 Americans have died as a result of the two wars in Iraq and Afghanistan. This number provides us with proof of troop exposure to traumatic events, and these events are resulting in PTSD among our brothers in arms who survive. An October 15, 2008, *USA Today* article by Pauline Jelinek reports that one in every five troops is returning home with PTSD or depression. A June 2008 *Military Medicine* article about Vietnam vets and PTSD documents that 30.9% of the 8.4 million who served in the Vietnam War suffer from PTSD. That is roughly 2,295,600 people. Moreover, Vietnam vets total over 47% of the current homeless veteran population. Consider also these numbers from the article by Pauline Jelinek: Currently over 1.6 million troops have deployed to the two wars in Iraq and Afghanistan. It is estimated that over 300,000 are currently suffering from PTSD. "Surge seen in Number of Homeless Veterans," a November 2007 *New York Times* article, confirmed that our Iraq and Afghanistan veterans are becoming homeless at rates much faster than did veterans from other war eras, specifically Vietnam. If we do not address this issue, we are destined to open the floodgates and incur another postwar homeless epidemic in our very near future. Phil Landis, a chairman of Veterans Village of San Diego, came to this same conclusion when in 2007 he stated, "We're beginning to see, across the country, the first trickle of this generation of warriors in homeless shelters, but we anticipate that it's going to be a tsunami."

We have a serious problem. Now that we have discussed the fundamental cause of homelessness among veterans, let us turn to the solution. You may think I am going to ask you to ask your congressman to create organizations or increase funding for those that already exist. Or maybe you think I am going to ask you to hand over your money on the street, or make a donation. I assure you the answer is none of these. First, according to the VA there is no shortage in the number of organizations dedicated to our homeless veterans. Additionally, Tim Dyhouse for *VFW Magazine* reports that 1.5 million dollars was donated to the VA for PTSD research in April of 2008. Second, handing over your money is definitely not the answer. This approach avoids building relationships with the individuals and ignores the root cause of their homelessness.

The solution is simple: our time. As mentioned before, there is no shortage in the number of organizations geared toward helping these individuals. There is, however, an undeniable shortage in the number of people who run them. What I am asking you for today is simply your time. Become a volunteer. *VFW Magazine's* July 2008 issue tells us 85,000 volunteers saved the VA 218 million dollars during the 2007 fiscal year. If each of us volunteered, imagine where those funds could be reallocated. They would be used for funding the treatment of PTSD, increasing the ability to cope, and decreasing homelessness. Funds could also be redirected to those shelters and organizations which provide much needed food, shelter and necessities.

I would like now to share with you a true story that moved me. One that I hope will inspire you to realize the value of your time. In the article released by *CQ Press,* Amy Sherman is identified as having been approached by a woman asking for money. The woman and her husband were currently living under a nearby bridge. Mrs. Sherman, rather than giving the woman money, took her to a grocery store, then to a thrift store, buying much needed supplies for the woman and her husband. Mrs. Sherman visited the couple weekly, bringing them information related to job and housing opportunities. She continued to visit the couple until one day the couple was gone. I'd like now to leave you to draw your own conclusions as to what happened when Mrs. Sherman ran into the couple months later in a local grocery store. Rest assured, happy endings do exist. If one woman could have such an immense impact on the lives of two individuals, I'll ask you now to consider what impact *we* could have on the lives of these veterans through simply combining our spare time and turning it into tangible help through volunteering.

Today, we cannot escape the homelessness of our veterans as a problem. We have identified PTSD as the major cause, and we have uncovered a simple solution: our time. The information presented today was not meant to question your values; it was meant to appeal to your sense of duty to the men and women whose blood sweat and tears have preserved our right to be here today. These men and women have responded to the call to duty, representing and defending what this country stands for. Still, they are making their beds out of cardboard boxes. What is wrong with this picture? It is a picture that I find hardly justifiable. Ladies and Gentlemen, as a veteran myself, I stand before you with confidence when I say: veterans are among you with chins high, shoulders square and a humble air of dignity. The National Anthem brings tears to our eyes and "Old Glory" warms our hearts with pride. We are your family, friends, colleagues, fellow speech competitors and judges. Though representing a minority, our tired, dusty boots are hard to fill and we have affected the lives of each of you in some way. However, many of our veterans are physically and emotionally exhausted, hungry and homeless. They are our veterans and they need our help.

# Endnotes

## CHAPTER 1


1. Louis Nizer, *Reflections Without Mirrors*, quoted in Jack Valenti, *Speak Up with Confidence: How to Prepare, Learn, and Deliver Effective Speeches* (New York: Morrow, 1982) 34.
2. Judy C. Pearson, Jeffrey T. Child, and David H. Kahl, Jr., "Preparation Meeting Opportunity: How Do College Students Prepare for Public Speeches?" *Communication Quarterly* 54.3 (Aug. 2006): 351.
3. Pearson, Child, and Kahl, "Preparation Meeting Opportunity," 355.
4. James C. Humes, *The Sir Winston Method: Five Secrets of Speaking the Language of Leadership* (New York: Morrow, 1991) 13–14.
5. Charles Schwab, as quoted in Brent Filson, *Executive Speeches: Tips on How to Write and Deliver Speeches from 51 CEOs* (New York: Wiley, 1994) 45.
6. Jerry L. Winsor, Dan B. Curtis, and Ronald D. Stephens, "National Preferences in Business and Communication Education: A Survey Update," *Journal of the Association for Communication Administration* (3 Sept. 1997): 174.
7. University of Wisconsin–River Falls, Career Services, "What Skills and Attributes Employers Seek When Hiring Students." 4 June 2007, <http://www.uwrf.edu/ccs/skills/htm>.
8. Camille Luckenbaugh and Kevin Gray, "Employers Describe Perfect Job Candidate," National Association of Colleges and Employers Survey. 4 June 2007 <http://www.naceweb.org/press/display.asp?year=2003&prid=169>.
9. Randall S. Hansen and Katharine Handson, "What Do Employers Really Want? Top Skills and Values Employers Seek from Job-Seekers." 4 June 2007 <http://www.quintcareers.com/job_skills_values.html>.
10. Dee-Ann Durbin, "Study: Plenty of Jobs for Graduates in 2000," *Austin American-Statesman* 5 Dec. 1999: A28.
11. Dan B. Curtis, Jerry L. Winsor, and Ronald D. Stephens, "National Preferences in Business and Communication Education," *Communication Education* 38 (Jan. 1989): 6–14. See also Iain Hay, "Justifying and Applying Oral Presentations in Geographical Education," *Journal of Geography in Higher Education* 18.1 (1994): 44–45.
12. L. M. Boyd, syndicated column, *Austin American-Statesman* 8 Aug. 2000: E3.
13. Herman Cohen, *The History of Speech Communication: The Emergence of a Discipline: 1914–1945* (Annandale, VA: Speech Communication Association, 1994) 2.
14. PBS, "The March on Washington." 6 June 2004 <www.pbs.org/greatspeeches/timeline/m_king_b1.html>.
15. George W. Bush, Address to the nation on 11 Sept. 2001, *The New York Times* 22 Sept. 2001: A4.
16. Survey conducted by R. H. Bruskin and Associates, *Spectra* 9 (Dec. 1973): 4; D. Wallechinsky, Irving Wallace, and Amy Wallace, *The People's Almanac Presents the Book of Lists* (New York: Morrow, 1977).
17. Steven Booth Butterfield, "Instructional Interventions for Reducing Situational Anxiety and Avoidance," *Communication Education* 37 (1988): 214–23; also see Michael Motley, *Overcoming Your Fear of Public Speaking: A Proven Method* (New York: McGraw-Hill, 1995).
18. Joe Ayres and Theodore S. Hopf, "The Long-Term Effect of Visualization in the Classroom: A Brief Research Report," *Communication Education* 39 (1990): 75–78.
19. John Burk, "Communication Apprehension among Master's of Business Administration Students: Investigating a Gap in Communication Education," *Communication Education* 50 (Jan. 2001): 51–58; Lynne Kelly and James A. Keaten, "Treating Communication Anxiety: Implications of the Communibiological Paradigm," *Communication Education* 49 (Jan. 2000): 45–57; Amber N. Finn, Chris R. Sawyer, and Ralph R. Behnke, "Audience-Perceived Anxiety Patterns of Public Speakers," *Communication Education* 51 (Fall 2003): 470–81.
20. Judy C. Pearson, Lori DeWitt, Jeffery T. Child, David H. Kahl, and Vijay Dandamudi, "Facing the Fear: An Analysis of Speech-Anxiety Content in Public-Speaking Textbooks," *Communication Research Reports* 24 (2007): 159–68.
21. Kay B. Harris, Chris R. Sawyer, and Ralph R. Behnke, "Predicting Speech State Anxiety from Trait Anxiety, Reactivity, and Situational Influences," *Communication Quarterly* 54 (2006): 213–26.
22. Amy M. Bippus and John A. Daly, "What Do People Think Causes Stage Fright? Naïve Attributions About the Reasons for Public-Speaking Anxiety," *Communication Education* 48 (1999): 63–72.
23. Yang Lin and Andrew S. Rancer, "Sex Differences in Intercultural Communication Apprehension, Ethnocentrism, and Intercultural Willingness to Communicate," *Psychological Reports* 92 (2003): 195–200.
24. Graham D. Bodie, "A Racing Heart, Rattling Knees, and Ruminative Thoughts: Defining, Explaining, and Treating Public Speaking Anxiety," *Communication Education* 59.1 (Jan. 2010): 70–105.
25. Amber N. Finn, Chris R. Sawyer, and Paul Schrodt, "Examining the Effect of Exposure Therapy on Public Speaking State Anxiety," *Communication Education* 58 (2009): 92–109.
26. Michael J. Beatty, James C. McCroskey, and A. D. Heisel, "Communication Apprehension as Temperamental Expression: A

Communibiological Paradigm," *Communication Monographs* 65 (1998): 197–219; Michael J. Beatty and Kristin Marie Valencic, "Context-Based Apprehension Versus Planning Demands: A Communibiological Analysis of Anticipatory Public Speaking Anxiety," *Communication Education* 49 (Jan. 2000): 58–71.

27. Kay B. Harris, Chris R. Sawyer, and Ralph R. Behnke, "Predicting Speech State Anxiety from Trait Anxiety, Reactivity, and Situational Influences," *Communication Quarterly* 54 (May 2006): 213–26.
28. Kelly and Keaten, "Treating Communication Anxiety."
29. Maili Porhola, "Orientation Styles in a Public-Speaking Context," paper presented at the National Communication Association convention, Seattle, Washington, Nov. 2000; Ralph R. Behnke and Michael J. Beatty, "A Cognitive-Physiological Model of Speech Anxiety," *Communication Monographs* 48 (1981): 158–63.
30. Shannon C. McCullough, Shelly G. Russell, Ralph R. Behnke, Chris R. Sawyer, and Paul L. Witt, "Anticipatory Public Speaking State Anxiety as a Function of Body Sensations and State of Mind," *Communication Quarterly* 54 (2006): 101–09.
31. Ralph R. Behnke and Chris R. Sawyer, "Public Speaking Anxiety as a Function of Sensitization and Habituation Processes," *Communication Research Reports* 53 (Apr. 2004): 164–73.
32. Paul L. Witt and Ralph R. Behnke, "Anticipatory Speech Anxiety as a Function of Public Speaking Assignment Type," *Communication Education* 55 (2006): 167–77.
33. Maili Porhola, "Arousal Styles During Public Speaking," *Communication Education* 51 (Oct. 2002): 420–38.
34. Kelly and Keaten, "Treating Communication Anxiety."
35. Leon Fletcher, *How to Design and Deliver Speeches* (New York: Longman, 2001) 3.
36. Research suggests that because public-speaking anxiety is complex (both a trait and a state), with multiple and idiosyncratic causes, using a combination of intervention strategies may be best in attempting to manage communication apprehension. See Bodie, "A Racing Heart, Rattling Knees, and Ruminative Thoughts."
37. Desiree C. Duff, Timothy R. Levine, Michael J. Beatty, Jessica Woolbright, and Hee Sun Park, "Testing Public Anxiety Treatments Against a Credible Placebo Control," *Communication Education* 56 (2007): 72–88.
38. Peter D. MacIntyre and J. Renee MacDonald, "Public-Speaking Anxiety: Perceived Competence and Audience Congeniality," *Communication Education* 47 (Oct. 1998): 359–65.
39. Ralph R. Behnke and Chris R. Sawyer, "Public-Speaking Procrastination as a Correlate of Public-Speaking Communication Apprehension and Self-Perceived Public-Speaking Competence," *Communication Research Reports* 16 (1999): 40–47.
40. Quoted by Petula Dovrak, "Channeling the Grief," *Austin American-Statesman*. 14 Oct., 2009: A9.
41. Dovrak, "Channeling the Grief."
42. Joe Ayres, Terry Schliesman, and Debbie Ayres Sonandre, "Practice Makes Perfect but Does It Help Reduce Communication Apprehension?" *Communication Research Reports* 15 (Spring 1998): 170–79.
43. Melanie Booth-Butterfield, "Stifle or Stimulate? The Effects of Communication Task Structure on Apprehensive and Non-Apprehensive Students," *Communication Education* 35 (1986): 337–48; Charles R. Berger, "Speechlessness: Causal Attributions, Emotional Features, and Social Consequences," *Journal of Language & Social Psychology* 23 (June 2004): 147–79.
44. Joe Ayres, Tim Hopf, and Elizabeth Peterson, "A Test of Communication-Orientation Motivation (COM) Therapy," *Communication Reports* 13 (Winter 2000): 35–44; Joe Ayres and Tanichya K. Wongprasert, "Measuring the Impact of Visualization on Mental Imagery: Comparing Prepared Versus Original Drawings," *Communication Research Reports* 20 (Winter 2003): 45–53.
45. Joe Ayers and Theodore S. Hopf, "Visualization: A Means of Reducing Speech Anxiety," *Communication Education* 34 (1985): 318–23. Although researchers have found evidence that visualization is helpful, some question whether visualization techniques work better than just gaining experience in public speaking. Critics of systematic desensitization argue that there may be a placebo effect: Just thinking that a treatment will reduce apprehension may contribute to reduced apprehension. See Duff, Levine, Beatty, Woolbright, and Park, "Testing Public Anxiety Treatments Against a Credible Placebo Control."
46. Ayres and Wongprasert, "Measuring the Impact of Visualization on Mental Imagery."
47. Ayres and Wongprasert, "Measuring the Impact of Visualization on Mental Imagery."
48. Joe Ayres and Debbie M. Ayres Sonandre, "Performance Visualization: Does the Nature of the Speech Model Matter?" *Communication Research Reports* 20 (Summer 2003): 260–68.
49. Duff, Levine, Beatty, Woolbright, and Park, "Testing Public Anxiety Treatments Against a Credible Placebo Control."
50. Joe Ayres and Brian L. Heuett, "An Examination of the Impact of Performance Visualization," *Communication Research Reports* 16 (1999): 29–39.
51. Penny Addison, Ele Clay, Shuang Xie, Chris R. Sawyer, and Ralph R. Behnke, "Worry as a Function of Public Speaking State Anxiety Type," *Communication Reports* 16 (Summer 2003): 125–31.
52. Chad Edwards and Suzanne Walker, "Using Public Speaking Learning Communities to Reduce Communication Apprehension," *Texas Speech Communication Journal* 32 (2007): 65–71; also see Chia-Fang (Sandy) Hsu, "The Relationship of Trait Anxiety, Audience Nonverbal Feedback, and Attributions to Public Speaking State Anxiety," *Communication Research Reports* 26.3 (August 2009): 237–46.
53. Diane Honour, "Speech Performance Anxiety for Non-Native Speakers," *The Florida Communication Journal* 36 (2007): 57–66.
54. Finn, Sawyer, and Schrodt, "Examining the Effect of Exposure Therapy on Public speaking State Anxiety."
55. Lisa M. Schroeder, "The Effects of Skills Training on Communication Satisfaction and Communication Anxiety in the Basic Speech Course," *Communication Research Reports* 19 (2002): 380–88; Alain Morin, "History of Exposure to Audiences as a Developmental Antecedent of Public Self-Consciousness," *Current Research in Social Psychology* 5 (Mar. 2000): 33–46.
56. MacIntyre and MacDonald, "Public-Speaking Anxiety"; Peter D. MacIntyre and K. A. Thivierge, "The Effects of Audience Pleasantness, Audience Familiarity, and Speaking Contexts on Public-Speaking Anxiety and Willingness to Speak," *Communication Quarterly* 43 (1995): 456–66; Peter D. MacIntyre, K. A. Thivierge,

and J. Renee MacDonald, "The Effects of Audience Interest, Responsiveness, and Evaluation on Public-Speaking Anxiety and Related Variables," *Communication Research Reports* 14 (1997): 157–68.

57. MacIntyre and MacDonald, "Public-Speaking Anxiety"; R. B. Rubin, A. M. Rubin, and F. F. Jordan, "Effects of Instruction on Communication Apprehension and Communication Competence," *Communication Education* 46 (1997): 104–14.
58. Stephen R. Covey, *The 7 Habits of Highly Successful People* (New York: Simon and Schuster, 1989).
59. The late Waldo Braden, longtime professor of speech communication at Louisiana State University, presented a memorable speech at the 1982 meeting of the Florida Speech Communication Association in which he emphasized "The audience writes the speech" to indicate the importance and centrality of being an audience-centered speaker.
60. Adetokunbo F. Knowles-Borishade, "Paradigm for Classical African Orature," Christine Kelly et al., eds., *Diversity in Public Communication: A Reader* (Dubuque, IA: Kendall-Hunt, 1994) 100.
61. Patricia A. Sullivan, "Signification and African-American Rhetoric: A Case Study of Jesse Jackson's 'Common Ground and Common Sense' Speech," *Communication Quarterly* 41.1 (1993): 1–15.
62. J. C. Pearson, J. T. Child, and D. H. Kahl, Jr., "Preparation Meeting Opportunity: How Do College Students Prepare for Public Speeches?" *Communication Quarterly*, 54:3 (Aug. 2006): 351–66.
63. Clifford Stoll, as cited in Kevin A. Miller, "Capture: The Essential Survival Skill for Leaders Buckling Under Information Overload," *Leadership* (Spring 1992): 85.
64. Don Hewitt, interview broadcast on *60 Minutes*, 24 Jan. 2010.
65. Greg Winter, "The Chips Are Down: Frito-Lay Cuts Costs with Smaller Servings," *Austin American-Statesman* 2 Jan. 2001: A6.
66. These statistics are from an Allstate Insurance advertisement, *The New York Times* 17 Feb. 2010: A24.
67. We thank Barbara Patton of Texas State University for sharing her speech outline with us.
68. Pearson, Child, and Kahl, "Preparation Meeting Opportunity."

## CHAPTER 2

1. Juan Castillo, "KLBJ-AM Exec: 'I think they made a very bad error in judgment.'" statesman.com. 20 July 2009. 21 June 2010 <http:// www.statesman.com/news/content/news/stories/local/2009/07/21/0721slur.html>.
2. See Wayne Ham, *Man's Living Religions* (Independence, MO: Herald Publishing House, 1966) 39–40; Huston Smith, *The World's Religions* (San Francisco: HarperSanFrancisco, 1991).
3. National Communication Association, "NCA Credo for Communication Ethics," 1999. 27 June 2001 <http://www.natcom.org/conferences/Ethics/ethicsconfcredo99. htm>.
4. Liz Rhoades, "Author Isaacs Calls on Graduates to Speak Up," *Queens Chronicle* 7 June 2007. 10 June 2007 <http://www.zwire.com/site/news.cfm?newsid= 18450494&BRD=2731&PAG=461&dept_id=574902&rfi=6">.
5. Samuel Walker, *Hate Speech* (Lincoln: U of Nebraska P, 1994) 162.
6. "Libel and Slander," *The Ethical Spectacle.* 1 June 1997 <http://www.spectacle.org/freespch/musm/libel.html>.
7. "Three Decades Later, Free Speech Vets Return to UC Berkeley," *Sacramento Bee* 3 Dec. 1994: A1.
8. James S. Tyre, "Legal Definition of Obscenity, Pornography." 1 June 1997 <http://internet.ggu.edu/university_library/reg/_legal_obscene.html>.
9. "Supreme Court Rules: Cyberspace Will Be Free! ACLU Hails Victory in Internet Censorship Challenge." *American Civil Liberties Union Freedom Network.* 26 June 1997. 1 June 1998 <http://www.aclu.org/news/no62697a.html>.
10. Sue Anne Pressley, "Oprah Winfrey Wins Case Filed by Cattlemen," *Washington Post* 27 Feb. 1998. 1 June 1998 <http://www.washingtonpost.com/wp-srv/WPlate/1998-02/ 27/1001-022798-idx.html>.
11. Associated Press, "Free-Speech, Other Groups File Briefs Opposing Patriot Act." 4 Nov. 2003. 13 June 2004 <http://www.firstamendmentcenter.org/news.aspx?id= 12174>.
12. Brian Schweitzer, "Proclamation of Clemency for Montanans Convicted under the Montana Sedition Act in 1918–1919." 3 May 2006. (Thanks to George Moss, Vaughn College, Flushing, NY, for providing the authors with a copy of this document.)
13. Terry Phillips, "Opinion: In Defense of Free Speech and Helen Thomas." MercuryNews.com. 15 June 2010. 21 June 2010 <http://www.mercurynews.com/ci_15303135>.
14. Bill Carter and Felicity Barringer, "Patriotic Time, Dissent Muted," *The New York Times* 28 Sept. 2001: A1.
15. The History Channel, "Mohandas Gandhi, Indian Independence Leader, Speaks to Press Upon Arrival in London." *Great Speeches* 2004. 7 June 2004 <www.historychannel.com/speeches/archive/speech_107.html>.
16. Walker, *Hate Speech*, 2.
17. Christopher N. Osher, "Churchill Part of Bigger Fight." *denverpost.com.* 30 May 2007. 11 June 2007 <http://www.denverpost.com/ci_6015760?source=rss>.
18. Edwin R. Bayley, *Joe McCarthy and the Press* (Madison: Wisconsin U P, 1981) 29.
19. Chidsey Dickson, "Re: question." Online posting. 27 Oct. 2005. WPA Listserv. 27 Oct. 2005 <http://lists.asu.edu/cgi-bin/wa?A2=ind0510&L=WPA-L&P=R117883&I=-3>.
20. "Spurlock Sorry for Speech," *Austin American-Statesman* 29 Mar. 2006: A2.
21. Kathy Fitzpatrick, "U.S. Public Diplomacy," *Vital Speeches of the Day* (15 Apr. 2004): 412–17.
22. Peg Tyre, "Improving on History," *Newsweek* 2 July 2001: 34.
23. *Publication Manual of the American Psychological Association*, 6th ed. (Washington, DC: American Psychological Association, 2010) 16.
24. Scott Jaschik, "Graduation Shame." Insidehighered.com. 22 Apr. 2010. 21 June 2010 <http://www.insidehighered.com/layout/set/print/news/2010/04/22/conncoll>.
25. *The Fundamental Values of Academic Integrity*, Duke University: Center for Academic Integrity, Oct. 1999: 1–2.
26. *Non-Plagiarized College Term Papers.com.* 1996–2010. 21 June 2010 <http://www.non-plagiarized-termpapers.com>.
27. Todd Holm, "Public Speaking Students' Perceptions of Cheating," *Communication Research Reports* (Winter 2002): 70.
28. Waldo W. Braden, *Abraham Lincoln, Public Speaker* (Baton Rouge: Louisiana State U P, 1988) 90.

# CHAPTER 3

1. Study conducted by Paul Cameron, as cited in Ronald B. Adler and Neil Town, *Looking Out/Looking In: Interpersonal Communications* (New York: Holt, Rinehart and Winston, 1981) 218.
2. L. Boyd, Syndicated column, *Austin American-Statesman* 7 Dec. 1995: E7.
3. John T. Masterson, Steven A. Beebe, and Norman H. Watson, *Invitation to Effective Speech Communication* (Glenview, IL: Scott, Foresman, 1989) 4.
4. Laura Ann Janusik, "Building Listening Theory: The Validation of the Conversational Listening Span," *Communication Studies* 58. 2 (2007): 139–56.
5. Frank E. X. Dance, *Speaking Your Mind: Private Thinking and Public Speaking* (Dubuque, IA: Kendall/Hunt, 1994).
6. Ralph G. Nichols and Leonard A. Stevens, "Six Bad Listening Habits," in *Are You Listening?* (New York: McGraw-Hill, 1957).
7. M. Fitch-Hauser, D. A. Barker, and A. Hughes, "Receiver Apprehension and Listening Comprehension: A Linear or Curvilinear Relationship?" *Southern Communication Journal* (1988): 62–71.
8. Joseph L. Chesebro, "Effects of Teacher Clarity and Nonverbal Immediacy on Student Learning, Receiver Apprehension, and Affect," *Communication Education* 52 (Apr. 2003): 135–47.
9. Fitch-Hauser, Barker, and Hughes, "Receiver Apprehension and Listening Comprehension."
10. Albert Mehrabian, *Nonverbal Communication* (Hawthorne, NY: Aldine, 1972).
11. Paul Ekman and Wallace Friesen, "Head and Body Cues in the Judgement of Emotion: A Reformulation," *Perceptual and Motor Skills* 25 (1967): 711–24.
12. K. K. Halone and L. L. Pecchioni, "Relational Listening: A Grounded Theoretical Model," COMMUNICATION REPORTS 14 (2001): 59–71.
13. K. K. Halone and L. L. Pecchioni, "Relational Listening."
14. California Curriculum Project, "César Chávez Biography." Hispanic Biographies, 1994. 8 June 2004 <http://www.sfsu.edu/~cecipp/cesar_chavez/cesarbio5-12.htm>.
15. Paul Rankin, "Listening Ability: Its Importance, Measurement and Development," *Chicago Schools Journal* 12 (Jan. 1930): 177–79.
16. Nichols and Stevens, "Six Bad Listening Habits."
17. Kitty W. Watson, Larry L. Barker, and James B. Weaver, *The Listener Style Inventory* (New Orleans: LA SPECTRA, 1995).
18. S. L. Sargent and James B. Weaver, "Correlates Between Communication Apprehension and Listening Style Preferences," *Communication Research Reports* 14 (1997): 74–78.
19. See Larry L. Barker and Kitty W. Watson, *Listen Up* (New York: St. Martin's Press, 2000); also see M. Imhof, "Who Are We as We Listen? Individual Listening Profiles in Varying contexts," *International Journal of Listening* 18 (2004): 36–45.
20. Sargent and Weaver, "Correlates Between Communication Apprehension and Listening Style Preference."
21. M. D. Kirtley and J. M. Honeycutt, "Listening Styles and Their Correspondence with Second Guessing," *Communication Research Reports* 13 (1996): 174–82.
22. Harold Barrett, *Rhetoric and Civility: Human Development, Narcissism, and the Good Audience* (Albany: SUNY, 1991) 154.
23. Chad Edwards and Suzanne Walker, "Using Public Speaking Learning Communities to Reduce Communication Apprehension," *Texas Speech Communication Journal* 32 (2007): 65–71.
24. Patricia Sullivan, "Signification and African-American Rhetoric: A Case Study of Jesse Jackson's 'Common Ground and Common Sense' Speech," *Communication Quarterly* 41.1 (1993): 11.
25. Mike Allen, Sandra Berkowitz, Steve Hunt, and Allan Louden, "A Meta-Analysis of the Impact of Forensics and Communication Education on Critical Thinking," *Communication Education* 48 (Jan. 1999): 18–30.
26. For a comprehensive list of definitions of rhetoric, see Patricia Bizzell and Bruce Herzberg, eds., *The Rhetorical Tradition: Readings from Classical Times to the Present* (Boston: Bedford, 1990).
27. Aristotle, *On Rhetoric.* Translated by George A. Kennedy (New York: Oxford University Press, 1991) 14.
28. Isocrates, *Isocrates*, Vol. II. Translated by George Norlin (Cambridge, MA: Harvard University Press, 1929). Also see "Isocrates," in Bizzell and Herzberg, *The Rhetorical Tradition.*
29. Kenneth Burke, *A Rhetoric of Motives* (Berkeley: University of California Press, 1950). Also see Barry Brummett, *Reading Rhetorical Theory* (Fort Worth, TX: Harcourt College Publishers, 2000) 741.
30. Cited in Marie Hochmuth, ed., A *History and Criticism of American Public Address*, Vol. 3 (New York: Longmans, Green, 1955) 4; and in James R. Andrews, *The Practice of Rhetorical Criticism* (New York: Macmillan, 1983) 3–4.
31. Andrews, *The Practice of Rhetorical Criticism.*
32. Masterson, Beebe, and Watson, *Invitation to Effective Speech Communication.*
33. Robert Rowland, *Analyzing Rhetoric: A Handbook for the Informed Citizen in a New Millennium* (Dubuque, IA: Kendall/Hunt, 2002) 17–28.

# CHAPTER 4

1. "The Nobel Prize in Literature, 1953." 16 June 2000. 8 June 2004 <www.nobel.se/literature/laureates/1953/index.html>.
2. Robert H. Farrell, ed., *Off the Record: The Private Papers of Harry S Truman* (New York: Harper & Row, 1980) 310.
3. For background information about this quotation see http://answers.google.com/answers/threadview?id=398104
4. N. Howe and W. Strauss, *Millennials Rising: The Next Great Generation* (New York: Vintage, 2000). Also see Hank Karp, Connie Fuller, and Danilo Sirias, *Bridging the Boomer–Xer Gap: Creating Authentic Teams for High Performance at Work* (Palo Alto, CA: Davies-Black, 2002).
5. For an excellent review of gender and persuasibility research see Daniel J. O'Keefe, *Persuasion: Theory and Research* (Newbury Park, CA: Sage, 1990) 176–77. Also see James B. Stiff, *Persuasive Communication* (New York: Guilford Press, 1994) 133–36.
6. O'Keefe, *Persuasion.*
7. O'Keefe, *Persuasion.*
8. Gregory Herek, "Study Offers 'Snapshot' of Sacramento-Area Lesbian, Gay, and Bisexual Community." 23 July 2001 <http://psyweb.ucdavis.edu/rainbow/html/sacramento_study.html>. For an excellent literature review about sexual orientation and communication, see T. P. Mottet, "The Role of Sexual Orientation in Predicting Outcome Value and Anticipated Communication Behaviors," *Communication Quarterly* 48 (2000): 233–39.

9. See R. Lewontin, "The Apportionment of Human Diversity," *Evolutionary Biology* 6 (1973): 381–97; H. A. Yee, H. H. Fairchild, F. Weizmann, and E. G. Wyatt, "Addressing Psychology's Problems with Race," *American Psychologist* 48 (1994): 1132–40; D. Matsumoto and L. Juang, *Culture and Psychology* (Belmont, CA: Wadsworth/Thompson, 2004) 16.
10. The research summarized here is based on pioneering work by Geert Hofstede, *Culture's Consequences: International Differences in Work-Related Values* (Beverly Hills, CA: Sage, 1984). Also see Edward T. Hall, *Beyond Culture* (New York: Doubleday, 1976).
11. M. E. Ryan, "Another Way to Teach Migrant Students," *Los Angeles Times* March 31, 1991: B20, as cited by M. W. Lustig and J. Koester, *Intercultural Competence: Interpersonal Communication Across Cultures* (Boston: Allyn & Bacon, 2003) 11.
12. G. Chen and W. J. Starosta, "A Review of the Concept of Intercultural Sensitivity," *Human Communication* 1 (1997): 7.
13. Eric Schmitt, "Whites in Minority in Largest Cities, the Census Shows," *New York Times* 30 Apr. 2001: A1.
14. Sam Roberts, "New Demographic Racial Gap Emerges," *New York Times* 17 May 2007: A19.
15. United States Census Bureau. 8 Feb. 2010. http://www.prb.org/AmeristateTemplate.
16. David W. Kale, "Ethics in Intercultural Communication," *Intercultural Communication: A Reader*, 6th ed., eds. Larry A. Samovar and Richard E. Porter (Belmont, CA: Wadsworth, 1991) 423; also see discussion in Lustig and Koester, *Intercultural Competence.*
17. Donald E. Brown, "Human Universals and Their Implications," in N. Roughley, ed., *Being Humans: Anthropological Universality and Particularity in Transdisciplinary Perspectives* (New York: Walter de Gruyter, 2000). For an applied discussion of these universals, see Steven Pinker, *The Blank Slate: The Modern Denial of Human Nature* (London: Penguin Books, 2002).
18. Larry A. Samovar and Richard E. Porter, *Communication Between Cultures.* (Stamford, CT: Wadsworth and Thomson Learning, 2006) 29.
19. Karen Summerson, "There's a Lot Riding on Your Times," *Winning Orations 2009* (Mankato, MN: Interstate Oratorical Association, 2009) 20–21.
20. Henry Sweets, "Mark Twain in India," *The Fence Painter: Bulletin of the Mark Twain Boyhood Home Associates* 26 (Winter 1996): 1.
21. For an excellent discussion of how to adapt to specific audience situations, see Jo Sprague and Douglas Stuart, *The Speaker's Handbook* (Belmont, CA: Wadsworth and Thompson, 2005) 345.
22. For example, see Leonard Spinrad and Thelma Spinrad, *Speaker's Lifetime Library* (West Nyack, NY: Parker, 1979).
23. Devorah Lieberman, *Public Speaking in the Multicultural Environment* (Boston: Allyn & Bacon, 2000). Also see Edward T. Hall, *The Silent Language* (Greenwich, CT: Fawcett, 1959); and Edward T. Hall, *The Hidden Dimension* (Garden City, NY: Doubleday, 1966).

## CHAPTER 5

1. Andrew Mytelka, "This Just In: Tim Russert's Crimson Face." *The Chronicle of Higher Education.* 10 June 2005. 12 June 2007 <http://chronicle.com/prm/daily/2005/06/2005061006n.htm>.
2. Roger Fringer, "Choosing a Speech Topic," in Tasha Van Horn, Lori Charron, and Michael Charron, *Allyn & Bacon Video II User's Guide*, 2002.
3. Bruce Gronbeck, from his presidential address delivered at the annual conference of the Speech Communication Association, Nov. 1994.
4. Henry H. Sweets III, "Mark Twain's Lecturing Career Continuation—Part II," *The Fence Painter* (Winter 2000–2001).
5. Charles W. Chesnutt, *Frederick Douglass.* Electronic edition published by Academic Affairs Library, University of North Carolina at Chapel Hill, 2001. 8 June 2004 <docsouth.unc.edu/neh/chesnutt/chesnutt.html>.
6. Alex F. Osborn, *Applied Imagination* (New York: Scribner's, 1962).
7. Monique Russo, "The 'Starving Disease' or Anorexia Nervosa," student speech, University of Miami, 1984.
8. Brian Sosnowchik, "The Cries of American Ailments," *Winning Orations 2000* (Mankato, MN: Interstate Oratorical Association, 2000) 114.
9. Judith Humphrey, "Taking the Stage: How Women Can Achieve a Leadership Presence," *Vital Speeches of the Day* (1 May 2001): 437.
10. Adapted from Erin Gallagher, "Upholstered Furniture Fires: Sitting in the Uneasy Chair," *Winning Orations 2000* (Mankato, MN: Interstate Oratorical Association, 2000) 99–101.
11. "Shuttle Missions," *NASA*, 26 May 2010. 22 June 2010 <http://www.nasa.gov/mission_pages/shuttle/shuttlemissions/list_main.html>.
12. Adapted from Nicole Tremel, "The New Wasteland: Computers," *Winning Orations 2000* (Mankato, MN: Interstate Oratorical Association, 2000) 37–40.
13. Erin Kane, "Alternative Defense," *Winning Orations 1995* (Mankato, MN: Interstate Oratorical Association, 1995) 82.

## CHAPTER 6

1. "Types of Web Sites," Montgomery College, 2005. 28 June 2010 <http://www.montgomerycollege.edu/~cshaw/myDocuments/courses/RD103/Week 5 Starts Feb. 21/Types_Websites.pdf>.
2. Elizabeth Kirk, "Practical Steps in Evaluating Internet Resources." 7 May 2001. 22 May 201 <http://Milton.mse.jhu.edu:8001/research/education/ractical.html>.
3. Michael Cunningham, quoted in Dinitia Smith, "In the Age of the Overamplified, a Resurgence for the Humble Lecture," *New York Times* 17 Mar. 2006: B1, B5.
4. Sandra Zimmer, quoted in Vickie K. Sullivan, "Public Speaking: The Secret Weapon in Career Development," *USA Today* 24–25 May 2005: 133.
5. Hillary Rodham Clinton, "Women's Progress Is Human Progress," *Vital Speeches of the Day* (1 May 2010): 199–203.
6. Kevin Rudd, "The Apology to the Forgotten Australians," *Vital Speeches of the Day* (1 Jan. 2010): 2–6.
7. Olli-Pekka Kallasvuo, "Connecting the Next Billion: The New Frontier of Upward Mobility," *Vital Speeches of the Day* (1 Mar. 2010): 130–33.
8. Eleanor Roosevelt National Historic Site, Hyde Park, New York, "Eleanor Roosevelt and Civil Rights." 9 June 2004 <www.nps.gov/elro/teach-er-vk/lesson-plans/notes-er-and-civil-rights.htm>.
9. Professor Frazer White, University of Miami.

10. Andrew B. Wilson, "How to Craft a Wining Speech," *Vital Speeches of the Day* (1 Sept. 2005): 685–89.
11. Cossolotto, Matthew, "An Urgent Call to Action for Study Abroad Alumni to Help Reduce Our Global Awareness Deficit," *Vital Speeches of the Day* (1 Dec. 2009): 564–68.
12. Barack Obama, "Four Pillars . . . Fundamental to the Future That We Want for Our Children," *Vital Speeches of the Day* (1 Nov. 2009): 488–93.
13. Cossolotto, "An Urgent Call to Action for Study Abroad Alumni to Help Reduce Our Global Awareness Deficit."
14. Jennie Chin Hansen, "Patient Safety: What Can We Do?" *Vital Speeches of the Day* (1 Apr. 2010): 488–93.
15. Steve Ballmer, "How Windows 7 Came to Be, and What It Represents," *Vital Speeches of the Day* (1 Dec. 2009): 556–57.
16. James Stanfill, "Entomophagy: The Other Other White Meat," *Winning Orations 2009* (Mankato, MN: Interstate Oratorical Association, 2009) 24.
17. Elizabeth Cady Stanton, "Address to the First Women's Rights Convention (1858)," *A Treasury of the World's Great Speeches*, ed. Houston Peterson (New York: Simon & Schuster, 1965) 388–92.
18. Indra Nooyi, "Short-Term Demands Vs. Long-Term Responsibilities," *Vital Speeches of the Day* (1 June 2010): 246–50.
19. Ivan Seidenberg, "How the Government Can Promote a Healthy, Competitive Communications Industry," *Vital Speeches of the Day* (1 Dec. 2009): 540-43.
20. "Sorry, You've Got the Wrong Number," *New York Times* 26 May 2001: A17.
21. Paula A. Kerger, "Encore! Encore! Using Media to Revive the Arts," *Vital Speeches of the Day* (1 Apr. 2010): 150–53.
22. Tasha Carlson, "License to Save," *Winning Orations 2009* (Mankato, MN: Interstate Oratorical Association, 2009) 35.
23. "Hurricane Ike: The Aftermath," *Austin American-Statesman* 3 Oct. 2008: B5.
24. Dena Craig, "Clearing the Air about Cigars," *Winning Orations 1998* (Mankato, MN: Interstate Oratorical Association, 1998) 13.
25. Sergio Marchionne, "Navigating the New Automotive Epoch," *Vital Speeches of the Day* (1 Mar. 2010): 134–37.
26. Ralph R. Behnke and Chris R. Sawyer, "Public-Speaking Procrastination as a Correlate of Public-Speaking Communication Apprehension and Self-Perceived Public-Speaking Competence," *Communication Research Reports* 16 (1999): 40–47; J. C. Pearson, J. T. Child, and D. H. Kahl, Jr., "Preparation Meeting Opportunity: How Do College Students Prepare for Public Speeches?" *Communication Quarterly* 54.3 (Aug. 2006): 351–66.
27. Deanna Beaton, "America's Credit Problem: Negligent Credit Reporting Agencies," *Winning Orations 2009* (Mankato, MN: Interstate Oratorical Association, 2009) 40.
28. Alia Mohsen, "Building a Bridge to the Future," *Winning Orations 2009* (Mankato, MN: Interstate Oratorical Association, 2009) 44.

## CHAPTER 7

1. Joel Ayres, "The Impact of Time, Complexity, and Organization on Self-Reports of Speech Anxiety," *Communication Research Reports* 5.1 (June 1988): 58–63.
2. Information in this example comes from National Institutes of Health, "Stem Cells: A Primer," May 2000. 19 July 2001 <http://www.nih.gov/news/stemcell/primer.htm>.
3. Adapted from John Kuehn, untitled speech, *Winning Orations 1994* (Mankato, MN: Interstate Oratorical Association, 1994) 83–85.
4. Dennis Lloyd, "Instant Expert: A Brief History of iPod," *iLounge* (26 June 2004). 20 June 2007 <www.ilounge.com/index.php/articles/comments/instant-expert-a-brief-history-of-ipod/>; "Apple iPod, History of an Icon," *ipod games* 20 June 2007 <www.ipodgames.com/other/ipod.php>.
5. Fact Sheet. *YouTube.com.* 2007. 20 June 2007 <www.youtube.com/t/fact_sheet>; Glenn Chapman, "YouTube Serving Up Two Billion Videos Daily," *Google News* 16 May 2010. 30 June 2010 <http://www.google.com/hostednews/afp/article/ALeqM5jK4sI9GfUTCKAkVGhDzpJ1ACZm9Q>.
6. Philip Shenon, "A Showcase for Indian Artifacts," *New York Times* 29 Aug. 2004: TR 3.
7. Desmond Tutu, "Nobel Lecture, December 11, 1984." 6 Apr. 2004. 10 June 2004 <http://www.nobel.se/peace/laureates/1984/tutu-lecture.html>.
8. Adapted from Vonda Ramey, "Can You Read This?" *Winning Orations 1985* (Mankato, MN: Interstate Oratorical Association, 1985) 32–35.
9. Andrea Thompson, "Future Fury: Hurricane Effects Will Only Get Worse," *Yahoo! News* 19 Sept. 2008. 19 Sept. 2008 <http://news.yahoo.com/s/livescience/20080919/sc_livescience/future-furyhurricaneeffects>.
10. Adapted from Amy Stewart, untitled speech, *Winning Orations 1994* (Mankato, MN: Interstate Oratorical Association, 1994) 47–49.
11. The following information is adapted from Devorah A. Lieberman, *Public Speaking in the Multicultural Environment* (Englewood Cliffs, NJ: Prentice Hall, 1994).
12. Risa Lavizzo-Mourey, "Childhood Obesity," *Vital Speeches of the Day* 15 Apr. 2004.
13. John Seffrin, "The Worst Pandemic in the History of the World," *Vital Speeches of the Day* 1 Apr. 2004.
14. Kristin Rose Cipolla, "Unnecessary Prescription Drugs: A Real Medical Emergency," *Winning Orations 2003* (Mankato, MN: Interstate Oratorical Association, 2003) 10.
15. Nichole Olson, "Flying the Safer Skies," *Winning Orations 2000* (Mankato, MN: Interstate Oratorical Association, 2000) 122.
16. Adapted from Mike Stobbe, "Beachgoers Often Overlook Sand as Danger," *Corpus Christi Caller-Times* 21 June 2007: 12A.
17. Melody Hopkins, "Collegiate Athletes: A Contradiction in Terms," *Winning Orations 1986* (Mankato, MN: Interstate Oratorical Association, 1986) 111.
18. Linh Thu Q. Do, "Children of the Diet Culture," *Winning Orations 1999* (Mankato, MN: Interstate Oratorical Association, 1999) 122.
19. Arwen Williams, "Organic Farming: Why Our Pesticide Paranoia Is Starving the World," *Winning Orations 2000* (Mankato, MN: Interstate Oratorical Association, 2000) 145.
20. Molly A. Lovell, "Hotel Security: The Hidden Crisis," *Winning Orations 1994* (Mankato, MN: Interstate Oratorical Association, 1994) 18.
21. Neela Latey, "U.S. Customs Procedures: Danger to Americans' Health and Society," *Winning Orations 1986* (Mankato, MN: Interstate Oratorical Association, 1986) 22.
22. Susan Stevens, "Teacher Shortage," *Winning Orations 1986* (Mankato, MN: Interstate Oratorical Association, 1986) 27.
23. Heather Green, "Radon in Our Homes," *Winning Orations 1986* (Mankato, MN: Interstate Oratorical Association, 1986) 5.

24. Ben Crosby, "The New College Disease," *Winning Orations 2000* (Mankato, MN: Interstate Oratorical Association, 2000) 133.
25. Lori Van Overbeke, "NutraSweet," *Winning Orations 1986* (Mankato, MN: Interstate Oratorical Association, 1986) 58.

## CHAPTER 8

1. K. Phillip Taylor, "Speech Teachers' Pet Peeves: Student Behaviors That Public Instructors Find Annoying, Irritating, and Unwanted in Student Speeches," *Florida Communication Journal* 33.2 (2005): 56.
2. Chandra Palubiak, "To Tattoo or Not to Tattoo," *Winning Orations 2002* (Mankato, MN: Interstate Oratorical Association, 2002) 11.
3. Sheena Holliday, "Uninvited Visitor," *Winning Orations 2003* (Mankato, MN: Interstate Oratorical Association, 2003) 84.
4. Edwin Pittock, "America's Crisis in Aging," *Vital Speeches of the Day* 1 Feb. 2004.
5. Darnetta Clinkscale, "The Other Crisis in Our Schools," *Vital Speeches of the Day* 1 Apr. 2004.
6. Jennifer Sweeney, "Racial Profiling," *Winning Orations 2000* (Mankato, MN: Interstate Oratorical Association, 2000) 1.
7. Terrika Scott, "Curing Crisis with Community," *Winning Orations 1995* (Mankato, MN: Interstate Oratorical Association, 1995) 11.
8. Theresa Clinkenbeard, "The Loss of Childhood," *Winning Orations 1984* (Mankato, MN: Interstate Oratorical Association, 1984) 4.
9. Thad Noyes, "Dishonest Death Care," *Winning Orations 1999* (Mankato, MN: Interstate Oratorical Association, 1999) 73.
10. Marvin Olasky, "Responding to Disaster," *Vital Speeches of the Day* 1 Nov. 2006: 744.
11. Joe Griffith, *Speaker's Library of Business Stories, Anecdotes, and Humor* (Englewood Cliffs, NJ: Prentice Hall, 1990) 335.
12. Douglas MacArthur, "Farewell to the Cadets," address delivered at West Point, 12 May 1962. Reprinted in Richard L. Johannesen, R. R. Allen, and Wil A. Linkugel, eds., *Contemporary American Speeches*, 7th ed. (Dubuque, IA: Kendall/Hunt, 1992) 393.
13. "Insert Funny Story Here," *Austin American-Statesman* 7 Apr. 2001: A14.
14. Muhtar Kent, "Are We Ready for Tomorrow, Today?" *Vital Speeches of the Day* 1 Mar. 2010: 117–21.
15. Richard Propes, "Alone in the Dark," *Winning Orations 1985* (Mankato, MN: Interstate Oratorical Association, 1985) 22.
16. Luis Proenza, "Relevance, Connectivity and Productivity." *Vital Speeches of the Day* 1 Feb. 2010: 89–92.
17. Adam Winegarden, "The After-Dinner Speech," in Tasha Van Horn, Lori Charron, and Michael Charron, eds., *Allyn & Bacon Video II User's Guide*, 2002.
18. Larry Cox, "A Vision of a World Made New," *Vital Speeches of the Day* 1 Feb. 2004.
19. Chris Miller, " Remember Both the Art and the Business Involved in Collision Repair." *Vital Speeches of the Day* 1 May 2010: 203–13.
20. Laura Bush, remarks at Harlem Renaissance event. *The White House Web site.* 13 Mar. 2002. 11 Mar. 2004 <www.whitehouse.gov/news/releases/2002/03/20020313-11.html>.
21. Student speech, University of Miami, 1981.
22. MacArthur, "Farewell to the Cadets," 396.
23. Lou Gehrig, "Farewell Speech," *Lou Gehrig: The Official Web Site* 23 June 2007 <www.lougehrig.com/about/speech.htm>.
24. Noelle Stephens, "The WWW.CON of Higher Education," *Winning Orations 1999* (Mankato, MN: Interstate Oratorical Association, 1999) 12.
25. John Ryan, "Emissions Tampering: Get the Lead Out," *Winning Orations 1985* (Mankato, MN: Interstate Oratorical Association, 1985) 63.
26. Melanie Loehwing, untitled speech, *Winning Orations 2003* (Mankato, MN: Interstate Oratorical Association, 2003) 23–24.
27. Richard Kelley, "Ready, Aim, Thrive: Strategies for 2007," *Vital Speeches of the Day* 1 Dec. 2006: 763–67.
28. Bono, "Because We Can, We Must." University of Pennsylvania, *Almanac Between Issues* 19 May 2004. 1 July 2010 <http://www.upenn.edu/almanac/between/2004/commence-b.html>.
29. James W. Robinson, "Create a Fireworks Finale," Executive Speeches (April 1989): 41–44. Web 26 June 2007.
30. Martin Luther King Jr., "I Have a Dream," in Richard L. Johannesen, R. R. Allen, and Wil A. Linkugel, eds., *Contemporary American Speeches,* 7th ed. (Dubuque, IA: Kendall/Hunt, 1992) 369. Dr. King's speech is reprinted in this text by arrangement with The Heirs to the Estate of Martin Luther King Jr., c/o Writers House as agent for the proprietor New York, NY. Copyright 1963. Dr. Martin Luther King Jr., copyright renewed 1991 Coretta Scott King.
31. Jake B. Schrum, Investiture Speech as President of Southwestern University, Georgetown, Texas, 4 Apr. 2001.

## CHAPTER 9

1. Judy C. Pearson, Jeffrey T. Child, and David H. Kahl, Jr., "Preparation Meeting Opportunity: How Do College Students Prepare for Public Speeches?" *Communication Quarterly* 54.3 (Aug. 2006): 351–66.
2. John O'Brien, quoted in Brent Filson, *Executive Speeches* (New York: Wiley, 1994) 144–45.
3. Charles Parnell, "Speechwriting: The Profession and the Practice," *Vital Speeches of the Day* (15 Jan. 1990): 56.
4. The sample outlines in this chapter are adapted from Karen Summerson, "There's a Lot Riding on Your Tires," *Winning Orations 2009* (Mankato, MN: Interstate Oratorical Association, 2009) 20–21.
5. Our discussion of how to edit speeches relies heavily on information in Brent Filson, *Executive Speeches: Tips on How to Write and Deliver Speeches from 51 CEOs* (New York: Wiley, 1994) 150–53.
6. Clive Thompson, "PowerPoint Makes You Dumb," *New York Times Magazine* 14 Dec. 2003: 88.
7. John Burns, "Seventy Years Later, Churchill's 'Finest Hour' Yields Insights," *New York Times* 18 June 2010: A8.

## CHAPTER 10

1. Advertisements and headlines compiled by Jay Leno, *Headlines* (New York: Wing Books, 1992).
2. Nemanja Savic, "Hope—in the Voices of Africa," speech delivered at Wake Forest University, 14 May 2006. *Window on Wake Forest.* 15 May 2006. 25 June 2007 < www.wfu.edu/wowf/2006/2006.05.15/orations.html>.

3. Max Woodfin, "Three among Many Lives Jordan Touched," *Austin American-Statesman* 20 Jan. 1996: A13.
4. John Lister, quoted in "At the End of the Day, It Annoys." Associated Press. 24 Mar. 2004. 24 Mar. 2004 <www.cbsnews.com/stories/2004/03/24/world/printable608391.shtml>.
5. Paul Roberts, "How to Say Nothing in Five Hundred Words," in William H. Roberts and Gregoire Turgeson, eds., *About Language* (Boston: Houghton Mifflin, 1986) 28.
6. George Orwell, "Politics and the English Language," in William H. Roberts and Gregoire Turgeson, eds., *About Language* (Boston: Houghton Mifflin, 1986) 282.
7. Erma Bombeck, "Missing Grammar Genes Is, Like, the Problem," *Austin American-Statesman* 3 Mar. 1992.
8. William Safire, "Words at War," *New York Times Magazine* 30 Sept. 2001.
9. John S. Seiter, Jarrod Larsen, and Jacey Skinner, "'Handicapped' or 'Handicapable?': The Effects of Language about Persons with Disabilities on Perceptions of Source Credibility and Persuasiveness," *Communication Reports* 11:1 (1998): 21–31.
10. Edward Rothstein, "Is a Word's Definition in the Mind of the User?" *New York Times* 25 Nov. 2000: A21.
11. Peggy Noonan, *What I Saw at the Revolution* (New York: Random House, 1990) 71.
12. Michael M. Klepper, *I'd Rather Die Than Give a Speech* (New York: Carol Publishing Group, 1994) 45.
13. We acknowledge the following source for several examples used in our discussion of language style: William Jordan, "Rhetorical Style," *Oral Communication Handbook* (Warrensburg, MO: Central Missouri State U, 1971–1972) 32–34.
14. "107th Whittier College Commencement Ceremony." 28 May 2010. 8 July 2010 <http://www.whittier.edu/News/Articles/WhittierCommencement2010.aspx>.
15. Barack Obama, speech delivered on 4 Mar. 2007 in Selma, Alabama in commemoration of the Selma Voting Rights March. *BarackObama.com* 4 Mar. 2007. 26 June 2007 <www.barackobama.com/2007/03/04/selma_voting_rights_march_comm.php>.
16. Samuel Hazo, "Poetry and Public Speech," *Vital Speeches of the Day* (1 Apr. 2007): 685–89.
17. Michiko Kakutani, "Struggling to Find Words for a Horror Beyond Words," *New York Times* 13 Sept. 2001: E1.
18. Franklin Roosevelt, Inaugural address of 1933 (Washington, DC: National Archives and Records Administration, 1988) 22.
19. George F. Will, "'Let Us . . .'? No, Give It a Rest," *Newsweek* 22 Jan. 2001: 64.
20. John F. Kennedy, Inaugural address, 20 Jan. 1961, in Bower Aly and Lucille F. Aly, eds., *Speeches in English* (New York: Random House, 1968) 272.
21. "Obama's Inaugural Speech," *CNNPolitics.com*. 20 Jan. 2009. 8 July 2010 <http://www.cnn.com/2009/POLITICS/01/20/obama.politics/>.
22. "Obama's Inaugural Speech."
23. Barack Obama, "A Just and Lasting Peace," *Vital Speeches of the Day* (1 Feb. 2010): 50–53.
24. Roosevelt, Inaugural address of 1933.
25. Nikki Giovanni, convocation address at Virginia Tech, 17 Apr. 2007. 25 June 2007 <www.vt.edu/remember/archive/giovanni_transcript.php>.
26. Sasha Johnson, "Clinton Says She's Only Candidate Who Can End War." *CNNPolitics.com*. 17 Mar. 2008. 7 July 2010 <http://www.cnn.com/2008/POLITICS/03/17/clinton.war/index.html>.
27. William Faulkner, speech in acceptance of the Nobel Prize for Literature, delivered 10 Dec. 1950, in Houston Peterson, ed., *A Treasury of the World's Great Speeches* (New York: Simon & Schuster, 1965) 814–15.
28. Roosevelt, Inaugural address of 1933.
29. Franklin D. Roosevelt, first fireside chat, 12 Mar. 1933, in Peterson, *Treasury* 751–54.
30. Winston Churchill, "finest hour" address, delivered 18 June 1940, in Peterson, *Treasury* 754–60.
31. Winston Churchill, address to the Congress of the United States, delivered on 26 Dec. 1941, in Bower Aly and Lucille F. Aly, eds., *Speeches in English* (New York: Random House, 1968) 233.
32. "Obama's Inaugural Speech."
33. "JFK's Trumpet Call." 6 June 2004 <www.pbs.org/greatspeeches/timeline/j_kennedy_b1.html>.
34. Adapted from Jordan, *Oral Communication Handbook,* 34.
35. "Reference to Rape Edited from Graduation Speech," *Kansas City Star* 5 June 1995: B3.
36. "Dear Abby," *San Marcos Daily Record* 5 Jan. 1993: 7.
37. Activity developed by Loren Reid, *Speaking Well* (New York: McGraw-Hill, 1982) 96.


## CHAPTER 11


1. For an excellent discussion of the importance of speaker delivery according to both classical and contemporary rhetoricians, see J. Fredal, "The Language of Delivery and the Presentation of Character: Rhetorical Action in Demosthenes' 'Against Meidias,' " *Rhetoric Review* 20 (2001): 251–67.
2. James W. Gibson, John A. Kline, and Charles R. Gruner, "A Reexamination of the First Course in Speech at U.S. Colleges and Universities," *Speech Teacher* 23 (Sept. 1974): 206–14.
3. Ray Birdwhistle, *Kinesics and Context* (Philadelphia: University of Pennsylvania, 1970).
4. Judee K. Burgoon and Beth A. Le Poire, "Nonverbal Cues and Interpersonal Judgments: Participant and Observer Perceptions of Intimacy, Dominance, Composure, and Formality," *Communication Monographs* 66 (1999): 105–24; Beth A. Le Poire and Stephen M. Yoshimura, "The Effects of Expectancies and Actual Communication on Nonverbal Adaptation and Communication Outcomes: A Test of Interaction Adaptation Theory," *Communication Monographs* 66 (1999): 1–30.
5. Albert Mehrabian, *Nonverbal Communication* (Hawthorne, NY: Aldine, 1972).
6. D. Lapakko, "Three Cheers for Language: A Closer Examination of a Widely Cited Study of Nonverbal Communication," *Communication Education* 46 (1997): 63–67.
7. Elaine Hatfield, J. T. Cacioppo, and R. L. Rapson, *Emotional Contagion* (New York: Cambridge University Press, 1994); also see John T. Cacioppo, Gary G. Berntson, Jeff T. Larsen, Kirsten M. Poehlmann, and Tiffany A. Ito, "The Psychophysiology of Emotion," in Michael Lewis and Jeannette M. Haviland-Jones, eds., *Handbook of Emotions*, 2nd ed. (New York: Guilford Press, 2004), 173–91.
8. Steven A. Beebe and Thompson Biggers, "The Effect of Speaker Delivery upon Listener Emotional Response," paper presented at the International Communication Association meeting, May 1989.
9. Paul Ekman, Wallace V. Friesen, and K. R. Schere, "Body Movement and Voice Pitch in Deception Interaction,"

*Semiotica* 16 (1976): 23–27; Mark Knapp, R. P. Hart, and H. S. Dennis, "An Exploration of Deception as a Communication Construct," *Human Communication Research* 1 (1974): 15–29.

10. Roger Ailes, *You Are the Message* (New York: Doubleday, 1989) 37–38.
11. David Gates, "Prince of the Podium," *Newsweek* 14 June 1996: 82.
12. *Austin-American Statesman*, 15 Jan. 2007: A11.
13. Eric J. Sundquist, *King's Dream* (New Haven: Yale University Press, 2009) 14.
14. Sundquist, *King's Dream,* 2.
15. Cicero, *De Oratore,* vol. 4, translated by E. W. Sutton (Cambridge: Harvard University Press, 1988).
16. Steven A. Beebe, "Eye Contact: A Nonverbal Determinant of Speaker Credibility," *Speech Teacher* 23 (Jan. 1974): 21–25; Steven A. Beebe, "Effects of Eye Contact, Posture and Vocal Inflection upon Credibility and Comprehension," *Australian Scan Journal of Nonverbal Communication* 7–8 (1979–1980): 57–70; Martin Cobin, "Response to Eye Contact," *Quarterly Journal of Speech* 48 (1963): 415–19.
17. Beebe, "Eye Contact," 21–25.
18. Khera Communications, "Business Tips for India," *More Business*, 2001. 8 June 2004 <www.morebusiness.com/running_your_business/management/d930585271.brc?highlightstring=Business+Tips+for+India>.
19. Brent Filson, *Executive Speeches: Tips on How to Write and Deliver Speeches from 51 CEOs* (New York: Wiley, 1994).
20. Albert Mehrabian, *Silent Messages* (Belmont, CA: Wadsworth, 1971).
21. For a comprehensive review of immediacy in an instructional context, see Virginia P. Richmond, Derek R. Lange, and James C. McCroskey, "Teacher Immediacy and the Teacher-Student Relationship," in Timothy P. Mottet, Virginia P. Richmond, and James C. McCroskey, *Handbook of Instructional Communication: Rhetorical and Relational Perspectives* (Boston: Allyn & Bacon, 2006) 167–93.
22. See Virginia P. Richmond, Joan Gorham, and James C. McCroskey, "The Relationship Between Selected Immediacy Behaviors and Cognitive Learning," in M. McLaughlin, ed., *Communication Yearbook* 10 (Beverly Hills, CA: Sage, 1987) 574–90; Joan Gorham, "The Relationship Between Verbal Teacher Immediacy Behaviors and Student Learning," *Communication Education* 37 (1988): 40–53; Diane M. Christophel, "The Relationship Among Teacher Immediacy Behaviors, Student Motivation, and Learning," *Communication Education* 39 (1990): 323–40; James C. McCroskey, Virginia P. Richmond, Aino Sallinen, Joan M. Fayer, and Robert A. Barraclough, "A Cross-Cultural and Multi-Behavioral Analysis of the Relationship Between Nonverbal Immediacy and Teacher Evaluation," *Communication Education* 44 (1995): 281–90; Timothy P. Mottet and Steven A. Beebe, "Relationships Between Teacher Nonverbal Immediacy, Student Emotional Response, and Perceived Student Learning," *Communication Research Reports* 19 (Jan. 2002).
23. Michael J. Beatty, "Some Effects of Posture on Speaker Credibility," library paper, University of Central Missouri, 1973.
24. Albert Mehrabian and M. Williams, "Nonverbal Concomitants of Perceived and Intended Persuasiveness," *Journal of Personality and Social Psychology* 13 (1969): 37–58.
25. Paul Ekman, Wallace V. Friesen, and S. S. Tomkins, "Facial Affect Scoring Technique: A First Validity Study," *Semiotica* 3 (1971).
26. Paul Ekman and Wallace Friesen, *Unmasking the Face* (Englewood Cliffs, NJ: Prentice Hall, 1975); D. Keltner and P. Ekman, "Facial Expression of Emotion," in M. Lewis and J. M. Haviland-Jones, eds., *Handbook of Emotions* (New York: Gilford, 2000) 236–49; D. Keltner, P. Ekman, G. S. Gonzaga, and J. Beer, "Facial Expression of Emotion," in R. J. Davidson, K. R. Scherer, and H. H. Goldsmith, eds., *Handbook of Affective Sciences* (New York: Oxford University Press, 2003) 415–32.
27. Adapted from Lester Schilling, *Voice and Diction for the Speech Arts* (San Marcos: Southwest Texas State University, 1979).
28. Mary M. Gill, "Accent and Stereotypes: Their Effect on Perceptions of Teachers and Lecture Comprehension," *Journal of Applied Communication* 22 (1994): 348–61.
29. Kenneth K. Sereno and G. J. Hawkins, "The Effects of Variations in Speakers' Nonfluency upon Audience Ratings of Attitude Toward the Speech Topic and Speakers' Credibility," *Speech Monographs* 34 (1967): 58–74; Gerald R. Miller and M. A. Hewgill, "The Effect of Variations in Nonfluency on Audience Ratings of Source Credibility," *Quarterly Journal of Speech* 50 (1964): 36–44; Mehrabian and Williams, "Nonverbal Concomitants of Perceived and Intended Persuasiveness."
30. These suggestions were made by Jo Sprague and Douglas Stuart, *The Speaker's Handbook* (Fort Worth, TX: Harcourt Brace Jovanovich, 1992) 331, and were based on research by Patricia A. Porter, Margaret Grant, and Mary Draper, *Communicating Effectively in English: Oral Communication for Non-Native Speakers* (Belmont, CA: Wadsworth, 1985).
31. James W. Neuliep, *Intercultural Communication: A Contextual Approach* (Boston: Houghton Mifflin, 2000) 247.
32. Stephen Lucas, *The Art of Public Speaking* (New York: Random House, 1986) 231.
33. Research cited by Leo Fletcher, *How to Design and Deliver Speeches* (New York: Addison Wesley Longman, 2001) 73.
34. "Comment," *The New Yorker* 1 Mar. 1993.
35. John S. Seiter and Andrea Sandry, "Pierced for Success? The Effects of Ear and Nose Piercing on Perceptions of Job Candidates' Credibility, Attractiveness, and Hirability," *Communication Research Reports* 20.4 (2003): 287–98.
36. For an excellent review of the effects of immediacy in the classroom, see Mehrabian, *Silent Messages*; also see James C. McCroskey, Aino Sallinen, Joan M. Fayer, Virginia P. Richmond, and Robert A. Barraclough, "Nonverbal Immediacy and Cognitive Learning: A Cross-Cultural Investigation," *Communication Education* 45 (1996): 200–11.
37. Larry A. Samovar and Richard E. Porter, *Communication Between Cultures* (Stamford, CT: Thomson Learning, 2001) 166.
38. William B. Gudykunst, *Bridging Differences: Effective Intergroup Communication* (Thousand Oaks, CA: Sage, 1998) 12.
39. Kent E. Menzel and Lori J. Carrell, "The Relationship Between Preparation and Performance in Public Speaking," *Communication Education* 43 (1994): 17–26; Tony E. Smith and Ann Bainbridge Frymier, "Get 'Real': Does Practicing Speeches Before an Audience Improve Performance?" *Communication Quarterly* 54.1 (Feb. 2006): 111–25; Judy C. Pearson, Jeffrey T. Child, and David H. Kahl, Jr., "Preparation Meeting Opportunity: How Do College Students Prepare for Pubic Speeches?" *Communication Quarterly* 54.3 (Aug. 2006): 351–66.
40. Filson, *Executive Speeches.*
41. Filson, *Executive Speeches.*

## CHAPTER 12


1. Emil Bohn and David Jabusch, "The Effect of Four Methods of Instruction on the Use of Visual Aids in Speeches," *Western Journal of Speech Communication* 46 (Summer 1982): 253–65.
2. J. S. Wilentz, *The Senses of Man* (New York: Crowell, 1968).
3. Michael E. Patterson, Donald F. Dansereau, and Dianna Newbern, "Effects of Communication Aids and Strategies on Cooperative Teaching," *Journal of Educational Psychology* 84 (1992): 453–61.
4. Louise Rehling, "Teaching in a High-Tech Conference Room: Academic Adaptations and Workplace Simulations," *Journal of Business and Technical Communication* 19.1 (Jan. 2005): 98–113.
5. Richard E. Mayer and Valerie K. Sims, "For Whom Is a Picture Worth a Thousand Words? Extensions of a Dual-Coding Theory of Multimedia Learning," *Journal of Educational Psychology* 86 (1994): 389–401.
6. Brent Filson, *Executive Speeches: Tips on How to Write and Deliver Speeches from 51 CEOs* (New York: Wiley, 1994) 212.
7. Dale Cyphert, "The Problem of PowerPoint: Visual Aid or Visual Rhetoric?" *Business Communication Quarterly* (Mar. 2004): 80–84.
8. PBS, "Ethos." 6 June 2004 <www.pbs.org/greatspeeches/timeline/r_Reagan_b2.html>.
9. Andrew Wilson, "In Defense of Rhetoric," *Toastmaster* 70.2 (Feb. 2004): 8–11.
10. Roxanne Parrott, Kami Sikl, Kelly Dorgan, Celeste Condit, and Tina Harris, "Risk Comprehension and Judgments of Statistical Evidentiary Appeals: When a Picture Is Not Worth a Thousand Words," *Human Communication Research* 31 (July 2005): 423–52.
11. Rebecca B. Worley and Marilyn A. Dyrud, "Presentations and the PowerPoint Problem," *Business Communication Quarterly* 67 (Mar. 2004): 78–80.
12. We acknowledge Dan Cavanaugh's excellent supplement *Preparing Visual Aids for Presentation* (Boston: Allyn & Bacon/Longman, 2001) as a source for many of our tips and suggestions.
13. Filson, *Executive Speeches.*
14. For a good discussion of how to develop and use PowerPoint visuals, see Jerry Weissman, *Presenting to Win: The Art of Telling Your Story* (Upper Saddle River, NJ: Financial Times/Prentice Hall, 2003).
15. We thank Stan Crowley, a student at Texas State University, for his permission to use his speech outline.


## CHAPTER 13


1. John R. Johnson and Nancy Szczupakiewicz, "The Public Speaking Course: Is It Preparing Students with Work-Related Public Speaking Skills?" *Communication Education* 36 (Apr. 1987): 131–37.
2. Pamela J. Hinds, "The Curse of Expertise: The Effects of Expertise and Debiasing Methods on Predicting Novice Performance," *Journal of Experimental Psychology: Applied* 5 (1999): 205–21. Research summarized in Chip Heath and Dan Heath, *Made to Stick: Why Some Ideas Survive and Others Die* (New York: Random House, 2007) 19–21.
3. Joseph L. Chesebro, "Effects of Teacher Clarity and Nonverbal Immediacy on Student Learning, Receiver Apprehension, and Affect," *Communication Education* 52 (Apr. 2003): 135–47.
4. Malcolm Knowles, *The Adult Learner: A Neglected Species*, 3rd ed. (Houston: Gulf Publishing, 1990).
5. Katherine E. Rowan, "A New Pedagogy for Explanatory Public Speaking: Why Arrangement Should Not Substitute for Invention," *Communication Education* 44 (1995): 236–50.
6. Philip Yancy, *Prayer: Does It Make Any Difference?* (Grand Rapids, MI: Zondervan, 2006) 20.
7. Michael A. Boerger and Tracy B. Henley, "The Use of Analogy in Giving Instructions," *Psychological Record* 49 (1999): 193–209.
8. Heath and Heath, *Made to Stick,* 63–64.
9. Marcie Groover, "Learning to Communicate: The Importance of Speech Education in Public Schools," *Winning Orations 1984* (Mankato, MN: Interstate Oratorical Association, 1984) 7.
10. As cited by Eleanor Doan, *The New Speaker's Sourcebook* (Grand Rapids, MI: Zondervan, 1968).
11. C. S. Lewis, "On Stories," *Essays Presented to Charles Williams,* C. S. Lewis, ed. (Oxford: Oxford University Press, 1947); also see Walter R. Fisher, *Communication as Narration: Toward a Philosophy of Reason, Value, and Action* (Columbia: University of South Carolina Press, 1987).
12. Roger Fringer, "Choosing a Speech Topic," *Student Speeches Video* (Allyn & Bacon, 2003).
13. Heath and Heath, *Made to Stick.*
14. See Bruce W. A. Whittlesea and Lisa D. Williams, "The Discrepancy-Attribution Hypothesis II: Expectation, Uncertainty, Surprise, and Feelings of Familiarity," *Journal of Experimental Psychology: Learning, Memory, and Cognition* 2 (2001): 14–33; also see Suzanne Hidi, "Interest and Its Contribution as a Mental Resource for Learning," *Review of Educational Research* 60 (1990): 549–71; Mark Sadoski, Ernest T. Goetz, and Maximo Rodriguez, "Engaging Texts: Effects of Concreteness of Comprehensibility, Interest, and Recall in Four Text Types," *Journal of Educational Psychology* 92 (2000): 85–95.
15. Heath and Heath, *Made to Stick,* 51–52.
16. George Miller, "The Magical Number Seven, Plus or Minus Two," *Psychological Review* 63 (1956): 81–97.
17. D. K. Cruickshank and J. J. Kennedy, "Teacher Clarity," *Teaching &Teacher Education* 2 (1986): 43–67.


## CHAPTER 14


1. Alvin Toffler, *Future Shock* (New York: Bantam, 1970) 3.
2. Martin Fishbein and I. Ajzen, *Belief, Attitude, Intention, and Behavior: An Introduction to Theory and Research* (Reading, MA: Addison-Wesley, 1975).
3. Aristotle, *On Rhetoric,* translated by George A. Kennedy (New York: Oxford University Press, 1991) 14.
4. For a discussion of motivation in social settings, see Douglas T. Kenrick, Steven L. Neuberg, and Robert B. Cialdini, *Social Psychology: Unraveling the Mystery* (Boston: Allyn & Bacon, 2002).
5. For a discussion of the elaboration likelihood model, see R. Petty and D. Wegener, "The Elaboration Likelihood Model: Current Status and Controversies," in S. Chaiken and Y. Trope, eds., *Dual Process Theories in Social Psychology* (New York: Guilford, 1999) 41–72; also see R. Petty and J. T. Cacioppo, *Communication and Persuasion: Central and Peripheral Routes to Attitude Change* (New York: Springer-Verlag, 1986).
6. Leon Festinger, *A Theory of Cognitive Dissonance* (Evanston, IL: Row, Peterson, 1957).

7. For additional discussion, see Wayne C. Minnick, *The Art of Persuasion* (Boston: Houghton Mifflin, 1967).
8. Abraham H. Maslow, "A Theory of Human Motivation," in *Motivation and Personality* (New York: Harper & Row, 1954), chapter 5.
9. John Ryan, "Emissions Tampering: Get the Lead Out," *Winning Orations 1985* (Mankato, MN: Interstate Oratorical Association, 1985) 50.
10. For a discussion of fear appeal research, see Irving L. Janis and Seymour Feshback, "Effects of Fear Arousing Communications," *Journal of Abnormal and Social Psychology* 48 (Jan. 1953): 78–92; Frederick A. Powell and Gerald R. Miller, "Social Approval and Disapproval Cues in Anxiety-Arousing Situations," *Speech Monographs* 34 (June 1967): 152–59; Kenneth L. Higbee, "Fifteen Years of Fear Arousal: Research on Threat Appeals, 1953–68," *Psychological Bulletin* 72 (Dec. 1969): 426–44.
11. Paul A. Mongeau, "Another Look at Fear-Arousing Persuasive Appeals," in Mike Allen and Raymond W. Preiss, eds., *Persuasion: Advances Through Meta-Analysis* (Cresskill, NJ: Hampton Press, 1998) 65.
12. K. Witte, "Putting the Fear Back into Fear Appeals: The Extended Parallel Process Model," *Communication Monographs* 59 (1992): 329–47.
13. See discussions in Myron W. Lustig and Jolene Koester, *Intercultural Competence: Interpersonal Communication Across Cultures* (Boston: Allyn & Bacon, 2009) 347; Larry A. Samovar and Richard E. Porter, *Communication Between Cultures* (Stamford, CT: Wadsworth and Thomson Learning, 2010) 29.
14. Diane Boerner, "Elizabeth Cady Stanton of Johnstown, New York," speech presented at the dedication of the plaque to Elizabeth Cady Stanton in the City Park of Johnstown, New York, on October 21, 1989. 11 June 2004 <www.rootsweb.com/~nyfulton/ecadystan.html>.
15. C. W. Sherif, M. Sherif, and R. E. Nebergall, *Attitudes and Attitude Change: The Social Judgment-Involvement Approach* (Philadelphia: Saunders, 1965).

## CHAPTER 15

1. Donald C. Bryant, "Rhetoric: Its Functions and Its Scope," *Quarterly Journal of Speech* 39 (Dec. 1953): 26.
2. William L. Benoit, "Topic of Presidential Campaign Discourse and Election Outcome," *Western Journal of Communication* 67 (Winter 2003): 97–112.
3. J. C. Reinard, "The Empirical Study of the Persuasive Effects of Evidence: The Status after Fifty Years of Research," *Human Communication Research* 15 (1988): 3–59.
4. James C. McCroskey and R. S. Rehrley, "The Effects of Disorganization and Nonfluency on Attitude Change and Source Credibility," *Speech Monographs* 36 (1969): 13–21.
5. For an excellent meta-analysis of forty-nine studies examining the influence of delivery variables and persuasion, see Chris Segrin, "The Effects of Nonverbal Behavior on Outcomes of Compliance Gaining Attempts," *Communication Studies* 44 (1993): 169–87.
6. Judee K. Burgoon, T. Birk, and M. Pfau, "Nonverbal Behaviors, Persuasion, and Credibility," *Human Communication Research* 17 (1990): 140–69.
7. Segrin, "The Effects of Nonverbal Behavior on Outcomes of Compliance Gaining Attempts."
8. Robin L. Nabi, Emily Moyer-Guse, and Sahara Byrne, "All Joking Aside: A Serious Investigation into the Persuasive Effect of Funny Social Issue Messages," *Communication Monographs* 74 (Mar. 2007): 29–54.
9. For an excellent discussion of the influence of culture on public speaking, see Devorah A. Lieberman, *Public Speaking in the Multicultural Environment* (Englewood Cliffs, NJ: Prentice Hall, 1994) 10.
10. Devorah Lieberman and G. Fisher, "International Negotiation," in Larry A. Samovar and Richard E. Porter, eds., *Intercultural Communication: A Reader* (Belmont, CA: Wadsworth, 1991) 193–200.
11. Lieberman and Fisher, "International Negotiation."
12. Myron W. Lustig and Jolene Koester, *Intercultural Competence: Interpersonal Communication Across Cultures* (Boston: Allyn & Bacon, 2009).
13. K. Ah Yun and L. L. Massi, "The Differential Impact of Race on the Effectiveness of Narrative versus Statistical Appeals to Persuade Individuals to Sign an Organ Donor Card," paper presented at the meeting of the Western States Communication Association, Sacramento, CA; cited by Lisa L. Massi-Lindsey and Kimo Ah Yun, "Examining the Persuasive Effect of Statistical Messages: A Test of Mediating Relationships," *Communication Studies* 54 (Fall 2003): 306–21.
14. Lustig and Koester, *Intercultural Competence,* 241.
15. Jeffrey E. Jamison, "Alkali Batteries: Powering Electronics and Polluting the Environment," *Winning Orations 1991* (Mankato, MN: Interstate Oratorical Association, 1991) 43.
16. H. B. Brosius and A. Bathelt, "The Utility of Exemplars in Persuasive Communications," *Communication Research* 21 (1994): 48–78.
17. Massi-Lindsey and Ah Yun, "Examining the Persuasive Effect of Statistical Messages"; D. C. Kazoleas, "A Comparison of the Persuasive Effectiveness of Qualitative versus Quantitative Evidence: A Test of Explanatory Hypotheses," *Communication Quarterly* 41 (1993): 40–50; also see M. Allen and R. W. Preiss, "Comparing the Persuasiveness of Narrative and Statistical Evidence Using Meta-Analysis," *Communication Research Reports* (1997): 125–31.
18. Franklin J. Boster, Kenzie A. Cameron, Shelly Campo, Wen-Ying Liu, Janet K. Lillie, Esther M. Baker, and Kimo Ah Yun, "The Persuasive Effects of Statistical Evidence in the Presence of Exemplars," *Communication Studies* 51 (Fall 2000): 296–306; also see E. J. Baesler and Judee K. Burgoon, "The Temporal Effects of Story and Statistical Evidence on Belief Change," *Communication Research* 21 (1994): 582–602.
19. Reinard, "The Empirical Study of the Persuasive Effects of Evidence," 37–38.
20. William L. Benoit and I. A. Kennedy, "On Reluctant Testimony," *Communication Quarterly* 47 (1999): 376–87. Although this study raises questions about whether reluctant testimony is persuasive, reluctant testimony as well as neutral testimony is better than testimony perceived to be obviously biased.
21. E. J. Baesler, "Persuasive Effects of Story and Statistical Evidence," *Argumentation and Advocacy* 33 (1997): 170–75.
22. Roger Ailes, *You Are the Message* (New York: Doubleday, 1989).
23. "Franklin Delano Roosevelt: The Great Depression." 6 June 2004 <www.pbs.org/greatspeeches/timeline/f_roosevelt_b.html>.
24. Albert Mehrabian and J. A. Russell, *An Approach to Environmental Psychology* (Cambridge: MIT Press, 1974); T. Biggers

and B. Pryor, "Attitude Change as a Function of Emotion-Eliciting Qualities," *Personality and Social Psychology Bulletin* 8 (1982): 94–99; Steven A. Beebe and T. Biggers, "Emotion-Eliciting Qualities of Speech Delivery and Their Effect on Credibility and Comprehension," paper presented at the annual meeting of the International Communication Association, New Orleans, May 1989.

25. Donald Dean Morely and Kim B. Walker, "The Role of Importance, Novelty, and Plausibility in Producing Belief Change," *Communication Monographs* 54 (1987): 436–42; also see Chip Heath and Dan Heath, *Made to Stick: Why Some Ideas Survive and Others Die* (New York: Random House, 2007) 63–97.
26. John W. Bowers and Michael M. Osborn, "Attitudinal Effects of Selected Types of Concluding Metaphors in Persuasive Speeches," *Speech Monographs* 33 (1966): 147–55; James C. McCroskey and W. H. Combs, "The Effects of the Use of Analogy on Attitude Change and Source Credibility," *Journal of Communication* 19 (1969): 333–39; N. L. Reinsch, "An Investigation of the Effects of the Metaphor and Simile in Persuasive Discourse," *Speech Monographs* 38 (1971): 142–45.
27. Pradeep Sopory and James Price Dillard, "The Persuasive Effects of Metaphor: A Meta-Analysis," *Human Communication Research* 28 (July 2002): 382–419.
28. See Irving Janis and S. Feshback, "Effects of Fear-Arousing Communication," *Journal of Abnormal and Social Psychology* 48 (1953): 78–92; Fredric A. Powell, "The Effects of Anxiety-Arousing Message When Related to Personal, Familial, and Impersonal Referents," *Speech Monographs* 32 (1965): 102–6.
29. Donald C. Bryant, "Rhetoric: Its Functions and Its Scope," *Quarterly Journal of Speech* 39 (Dec. 1953): 26.
30. William L. Benoit, "Forewarning and Persuasion," in Mike Allen and Raymond W. Preiss, eds., *Persuasion: Advances Through Meta-Analysis* (Cresskill, NJ: Hampton Press, 1998) 139–54.
31. Karmen Kirtley, "Grave Matter: The High Cost of Living," *Winning Orations* 1997 (Mankato, MN: Interstate Oratorial Association, 1997).
32. Benoit, "Forewarning and Persuasion."
33. Mike Allen, "Comparing the Persuasive Effectiveness of One- and Two-Sided Messages," in Mike Allen and Raymond W. Preiss, eds., *Persuasion: Advances Through Meta-Analysis* (Cresskill, NJ: Hampton Press, 1998) 87–98.
34. Katherine E. Rowan, "A New Pedagogy for Explanatory Public Speaking: Why Arrangement Should Not Substitute for Invention," *Communication Education* 44 (1995): 236–50.
35. Carl I. Hovland, Arthur A. Lunsdaine, and Fred D. Sheffield, "The Effects of Presenting 'One Side' versus 'Both Sides' in Changing Opinions on a Controversial Subject," in *Experiments on Mass Communication* (Princeton: Princeton University, 1949). Also see Arthur Lunsdaine and Irving Janis, "Resistance to 'Counter-Propaganda' Produced by a One-Sided versus a Two-Sided 'Propaganda' Presentation," *Public Opinion Quarterly* (1953): 311–18.
36. N. Miller and Donald T. Campbell, "Recency and Primacy in Persuasion as a Function of the Timing of Speeches and Measurements," *Journal of Abnormal and Social Psychology* 59 (1959): 1–9; Adrian Furnham, "The Robustness of the Recency Effect: Studies Using Legal Evidence," *Journal of General Psychology* 113 (1986): 351–57; R. Rosnow, "Whatever Happened to the 'Law of Primacy'?" *Journal of Communication* 16 (1966): 10–31.
37. Robert B. Ricco, "Analyzing the Roles of Challenge and Defense in Argumentation," *Argumentation and Advocacy* 39 (Summer 2002): 1–22.
38. Douglas Ehninger, Bruce E. Gronbeck, Ray E. McKerrow, and Alan H. Monroe, *Principles and Types of Speech Communication* (Glenview, IL: Scott, Foresman, 1986) 15.
39. Martin Luther King Jr., "I Have a Dream" (28 Aug. 1963), in Houston Peterson, ed., *A Treasury of the World's Great Speeches* (New York: Simon & Schuster, 1965) 835–39. Dr. King's speech is reprinted in this text by arrangement with The Heirs to the Estate of Martin Luther King Jr., c/o Writers House as agent for the proprietor New York, NY. Copyright 1963. Dr. Martin Luther King Jr., copyright renewed 1991 Coretta Scott King.

## CHAPTER 16

1. Amy Tennery, "The Big Money: Graduation-Speech Racket," *MSNBC.com.* 10 June 2009. 10 June 2009 <http://www.msnbc.msn.com/id/31192270/print/1/displaymode/1098/>.
2. "Al Gore Coming to Saskatchewan," *CBC News* 5 Apr. 2007. 27 June 2007 <www.cbc.ca/canada/saskatchewan/story>.
3. Robert Watts and Michael Sheridan, "Blair Is World's Best Paid Speaker," *London Times* 5 Apr. 2009.
4. Watts and Sheridan, "Blair Is World's Best Paid Speaker."
5. "Clinton's Speaking Fees Nearly Total $40 Million," *Huffington Post* 23 Feb. 2007. 27 June 2007 <www.huffingtonpost.com>.
6. Leslie Wayne, "In World Where Talk Doesn't Come Cheap, Former Officials Are Finding Lucrative Careers," *New York Times* 10 Mar. 2004: A14.
7. Roger E. Flax, "A Manner of Speaking," *Ambassador* (May–June 1991): 37.
8. Peter D. MacIntyre and K. A. Thivierge, "The Effects of Audience Pleasantness, Audience Familiarity, and Speaking Contexts on Public-Speaking Anxiety and Willingness to Speak," *Communication Quarterly* 43 (1995): 456–66.
9. *Slainte! Toasts, Blessings, and Sayings*. Mar. 1998. 28 June 1998 <http://zinnia.umfacad.maine.edu/~donaghue/toasts.html>.
10. Sarah Husberg, "A Wedding Toast," in Tasha Van Horn, Lori Charron, and Michael Charron, eds., *Allyn & Bacon Video II User's Guide*, 2002.
11. Jeff Brooks, *Wedding Toasts*. Mar. 1998. 29 June 1998 <http://zinnia.umfacad.maine.edu/~donaghue/toasts07.html>.
12. Everett M. Dirksen, "Nominating Speech for Barry Goldwater" (15 July 1964), in James R. Andrews and David Zarefsky, eds., *Contemporary American Voices* (New York: Simon & Schuster, 1965) 815.
13. Erma Bombeck, "Abbreviated Thank-you's Allow Us More Time to Study Danson's Head," *Austin American-Statesman* 22 June 1993: F3.
14. Cindy Pearlman, "Oscar Speeches: Statues in Their Hands, Feet in Their Mouths," *Austin American-Statesman* 24 Mar. 1997: E8.
15. Barack Obama, "A Just and Lasting Peace," *Vital Speeches of the Day* (1 Feb. 2010): 50–53.
16. William Faulkner, acceptance of the Nobel prize for literature (10 Dec. 1950), in Houston Peterson, ed., *A Treasury of the World's Great Speeches* (New York: Simon & Schuster, 1965) 815.
17. Barbara Jordan, "Change: From What to What?" *Vital Speeches of the Day* (15 Aug. 1992): 651.

18. David Abel, "Commencement Addresses Leave Audiences Lost," *Boston Globe* 5 June 2000: B4.
19. Rachel Maddow, commencement address. Smith College. 16 May 2010. 14 July 2010 <http://www.smith.edu/collegerelations/com2010.php>.
20. Barack Obama, commencement address. Hampton University. May 2010. 10 May 2010 <http://hamptonroads.com/2010/05/obama-hampton-u-be-role-models-be-mentors>.
21. Abel, "Commencement Addresses Leave Audiences Lost," B4.
22. Bill Clinton, speech at Pointe du Hoc, France (June 1994), as quoted in David Shribman, "President, a Child of World War II, Thanks a Generation," *Boston Globe* 7 June 1994: 1.
23. Cyrus Copeland, "Death, Be Not Ponderous," *New York Times* 31 Oct. 2004.
24. John T. Masterson, Jr., eulogy for Betty Stalvey, New Braunfels, TX, 26 Mar. 2005.
25. Oprah Winfrey, eulogy for Rosa Parks. 2005. 14 July 2010 <http://www.eulogyspeech.net/famous-eulogies/Oprah-Winfrdy-Eulogy-for-Rosa-Parks.shtml>.
26. Dave Barry, "Speak! Speak!" *Austin American-Statesman* 2 June 1991: C4.
27. Michael Eck, "Barry Keeps the Crowd Laughing." *Times Union* (Albany, New York) 5 May 2004. 11 June 2004 <www.albany.edu/writers-inst/tu_barry_dave_page-hall.html>.
28. Sarah Booth Conroy, "State Dinners Offer Speech as First Course," *Austin American-Statesman* 10 Nov. 1989.
29. Debi Martin, "Laugh Lines," *Austin American-Statesman* 20 May 1988: D1.
30. Jon Macks, *How to Be Funny* (New York: Simon & Schuster, 2003).
31. Matt Hughes, "Tricks of the Speechwriter's Trade," *Management Review* 79 (Nov. 1990): 56–58. ABI/INFORM Global, Texas State U–San Marcos Lib., San Marcos, TX. 27 June 2007 <ABI/INFORMGlobal>.
32. Michael Koresky, "Prognosis: Dire, Michael Moore's 'Sicko,'" *indieWIRE* 22 June 2007. 27 June 2007 <www.indiewire.com/movies>.
33. John C. Meyer, "Humor as a Double-Edged Sword: Four Functions of Humor in Communication," *Communication Theory* 10 (Aug. 2000): 311.
34. Joe Queenan, "How to Tell a Joke," *Reader's Digest* Sept. 2003: 73.
35. Alison White, "Writing a Humorous Speech," 3 June 2004 <www.bizinternet.com.au/StGeorges/humour.html>.
36. Mark Twain, "The Alphabet and Simplified Spelling," address at the dedication of the New York Engineers' Club, 9 Dec. 1907. *Mark Twain's Speeches; with an Introduction by William Dean Howells*, Electronic Text Center, University of Virginia Library. 4 June 2004 <etext.lib.Virginia.edu>.
37. Bill Gates, 2007 Harvard commencement address, *Harvard University Gazette Online* 7 June 2007. 27 June 2007 <www.news.harvard.edu/gazette>.
38. Chris O'Keefe, untitled speech, in John K. Boaz and James Brey, eds., *1987 Championship Debates and Speeches* (Speech Communication Association and American Forensic Association, 1987) 99.
39. Owen H. Lynch, "Humorous Communication: Finding a Place for Humor in Communication Research," *Communication Theory* 12.4 (Nov. 2002): 423–45.
40. "Mirren 'Too Busy' to Meet Queen," *BBC News* 10 May 2007. 13 June 2007 <newsvote.bbc.co.uk>.
41. Susan Wallace, "Seriously, How Do I Write a Humorous Speech?" as reported by Mike Dicerbo, Leadership in Action 1 Nov. 2000. 2 June 2004 <www.angelfire.com/az2/D3tmLeadership3/NewsNovSusanWallace.html>.

## APPENDIX A

1. Group communication principles presented in this chapter are adapted from Steven A. Beebe and John T. Masterson, *Communicating in Small Groups: Principles and Practices*, 10th ed. (Boston: Allyn & Bacon, 2012).
2. For discussions of the advantages and disadvantages of working in small groups, see Norman R. F. Maier, "Assets and Liabilities in Group Problem Solving: The Need for an Integrative Function," *Psychological Review* 74 (1967): 239–49; Michael Argyle, *Cooperation: The Basis of Sociability* (London: Routledge, 1991); J. Surowiecki, *The Wisdom of Crowds* (New York: Anchor, 2005); P. R. Laughlin, E. C. Hatch, J. Silver, and L. Boh, "Groups Perform Better Than the Best Individuals on Letters-to-Numbers Problems: Effects on Group Size," *Journal of Personality and Social Psychology* 90 (2006): 644–51.
3. Maier, "Assets and Liabilities in Group Problem Solving"; Argyle, *Cooperation*.
4. Our definition of team is based on a discussion in Beebe and Masterson, *Communicating in Small Groups*; and in Steven A. Beebe, Susan J. Beebe, and Diana K. Ivy, *Communication Principles for a Lifetime* (Boston: Allyn & Bacon, 2010): 240–41; J. R. Katzenback and D. K. Smith, *The Wisdom of Teams: Creating the High-Performance Organization* (New York: Harper Business, 1993); M. Schrage, *No More Teams! Mastering the Dynamics of Creative Collaboration* (New York: Currency Doubleday, 1995); D. D. Chrislip and C. E. Larson, *Collaborative Leadership* (San Francisco, CA: Jossey-Bass, 1994); D. C. Sturbler and K. M. York, "An Exploratory Study of the Team Characteristics Model Using Organizational Teams," *Small Group Research* 38 (2007); 670–95.
5. John Dewey, *How We Think* (Boston: Heath, 1910).
6. H. Barki, "Small Group Brainstorming and Idea Quality: Is Electronic Brainstorming the Most Effective Approach?" *Small Group Research* 32 (2001): 158–205; B. A. Nijstad, W. Stroebe, and H. F. M. Lodewijkx, "Cognitive Stimulation and Interference in Groups: Exposure Effects in an Idea Generation Task," *Journal of Experimental Social Psychology* 38 (2002): 535–44; E. F. Rietzchel, B. A. Jijstad, and W. Stroebe, "Productivity Is Not Enough: A Comparison of Interactive and Nominal Brainstorming Groups on Idea Generation and Selection," *Journal of Experimental Social Psychology* 42 (2006): 244–51; also see P. B. Paulus, M. T. Dzindolet, H. Coskun, and V. K. Putman, "Social and Cognitive Influences in Group Brainstorming: Predicting Production Gains and Losses," *European Review of Social Psychology* 12 (2002): 299–326.
7. K. L. Dugosh, P. B. Paulus, E. J. Roand, and H. C. Yang, "Cognitive Stimulation in Brainstorming," *Journal of Personality and Social Psychology* 79 (2000): 722–35.
8. R. Y. Hirokawa and A. J. Salazar, "Task-Group Communication and Decision-Making Performance," in L. Frey, ed., *The Handbook of Group Communication Theory and Research* (Thousand Oaks, CA: Sage, 1999) 167–91; D. Gouran and R. Y. Hirokawa, "Functional Theory and Communication in

Decision-Making and Problem-Solving Groups: An Expanded View," in R. Y. Hirokawa and M. S. Poole, eds., *Communication and Group Decision Making* (Thousand Oaks, CA: Sage, 1996) 55–80.

9. C. A. VanLear and E. A. Mabry, "Testing Contrasting Interaction Models for Discriminating Between Consensual and Dissentient Decision-Making Groups," *Small Group Research* 30 (1999): 29–58; also see T. J. Saine and D. G. Bock, "A Comparison of the Distributional and Sequential Structures of Interaction in High and Low Consensus Groups," *Central States Speech Journal* 24 (1973): 125–39.
10. Randy Y. Hirokawa and Roger Pace, "A Descriptive Investigation of the Possible Communication-Based Reasons for Effective and Ineffective Group Decision Making," *Communication Monographs* 50 (Dec. 1983): 363–79.
11. Randy Y. Hirokawa, "Group Communication and Problem-Solving Effectiveness: An Investigation of Group Phases," *Human Communication Research* 9 (Summer 1983): 291–305.
12. Dennis S. Gouran, "Variables Related to Consensus in Group Discussion of Question of Policy," *Speech Monographs* 36 (Aug. 1969): 385–91.
13. For a summary of research about conflict management in small groups, see S. M. Farmer and J. Roth, "Conflict-Handling Behavior in Work Groups: Effects of Group Structure, Decision Processes, and Time," *Small Group Research* 29 (1998): 669–713; also see Beebe and Masterson, *Communicating in Small Groups*; J. Sell, M. J. Lovaglia, E. A. Mannix, C. D. Samuelson, and R. K. Wilson, "Investigating Conflict, Power, and Status Within and Among Groups," *Small Group Research* 30 (1999): 44–72.
14. Ralph White and Ronald Lippitt, "Leader Behavior and Member Reaction in Three 'Social Climates,'" in Darwin Cartwright and Alvin Zander, eds., *Group Dynamics*, 3rd ed. (New York: Harper & Row, 1968) 319.
15. Peter M. Senge, "Leading Learning Organizations," in Richard Beckhard et al., eds., *The Leader of the Future* (San Francisco: Jossey-Bass, 1996); Bernard M. Bass and M. J. Avolio, "Transformational Leadership and Organizational Culture," *International Journal of Public Administration* 17 (1994): 541–54; Lynn Little, "Transformational Leadership," *Academic Leadership* 15 (Nov. 1999): 4–5.
16. Francis Y. Yammarino and Alan J. Dubinsky, "Transformational Leadership Theory: Using Levels of Analysis to Determine Boundary Conditions," *Personnel Psychology* 47 (1994): 787–809; L. Little, "Transformational Leadership," *Academic Leadership* 15 (Nov. 1999): 4–9.

# Index